MW00782610

PRESIDENT	POLITICAL	TECHNOLO	
ZACHARY TAYLOR **1849-1850 (W)**	The Great Debate (1850)	Bunsen Burner (	
MILLARD FILLMORE **1850-1853 (W)**	Compromise of 1850 Slave Trade Abolished in D.C. (1850) Know-Nothing Party formed (1853)	Elevator (1852)	Herman Melville "Moby Dick" (1851) H.B. Stowe "Uncle Tom's Cabin" (1852) Hawthorne "The Scarlet Letter" (1852)
FRANKLIN PIERCE **1853-1857 (D)**	Kansas-Nebraska Act (1854) Republican Party formed (1854) Perry opens trade w/Japan (1853)	Florence Nightingale introduces hygiene into hospitals (1855)	Thoreau "Walden" (1854) Whitman "Leaves of Grass" (1855) "Jingle Bells" (1857)
JAMES BUCHANAN **1857-1861 (D)**	Dred Scott v. Sanford (1857) John Brown's Raid (1859) Confederate States formed (1861)	Trans-Atlantic Telegraph (1858) First Am. oil well (1859) Darwin's Theory of Evolution (1859)	J.S. Mill "Essay on Liberty" (1859)
ABRAHAM LINCOLN **1861-1865 (R)**	American Civil War (1861-65) Emancipation Proclamation (1863) Battle of Gettysburg (1863) Pres. Lincoln assassinated (1865)	First legal paper money (1862) Gatling Gun (1862) Red Cross est. (1865)	"Battle Hymn of the Republic" (1862) "When Johnny Comes Marching Home" (1863) Roller Skating (1863)
ANDREW JOHNSON **1865-1869 (R)**	13th Amendment abolishes slavery (1865) Reconstruction Act (1867) Pres. Johnson impeached (1868)	Winchester Rifle (1866) Dynamite (1867) Transcontinental Railroad (1869)	Christian Science (1866) Ku Klux Klan (1866) Alcott "Little Women" (1868)
ULYSSES GRANT **1869-1877 (R)**	15th Amendment (1870) First Blacks in Congress (1870) Battle of Little Big Horn (1876)	Electric Chair (1870) Telephone (1876)	"Whistler's Mother" (1871) Twain "Tom Sawyer" (1876) First Fraternity House (1876)
RUTHERFORD HAYES **1877-1881 (R)**	Reconstruction Ends (1877) Bland-Allison Act (1878)	Phonograph (1878) Electric Light (1879) Iron Suspension Bridge (1880)	First U.S. bicycles (1878) Coney Island (1881) Boston Symphony Orchestra (1881)
JAMES GARFIELD **1881 (R)**	Pres. Garfield assassinated 4 months into office (1881)		Tuskegee Institute
CHESTER ARTHUR **1881-1885 (R)**	Pendleton Act (1883)	Standard Time Zones (1883) Brooklyn Bridge (1883)	Statue of Liberty (1883) Washington Monument (1884) Twain "Huckleberry Finn" (1885)
GROVER CLEVELAND **1885-1889 (D)**	American Federation of Labor (AFL) organized (1886) Apache-Indian War (1886)	Rabies Innoculation (1885) Eastman Camera (1888)	Motion Picture (1889-1927) (silent)

American Government

American Government

SECOND EDITION

Ross K. Baker
Gerald M. Pomper
Wilson C. McWilliams

RUTGERS UNIVERSITY

Macmillan Publishing Company
NEW YORK

Copyright © 1987, Macmillan Publishing Company, a division of Macmillan, Inc.

Printed in the United States of America

All rights reserved. No part of this book may be reproduced or transmitted in any form or by any means, electronic or mechanical, including photocopying, recording, or any information storage and retrieval system, without permission in writing from the publisher.

Earlier edition copyright © 1983 by Macmillan Publishing Company.

Macmillan Publishing Company
866 Third Avenue, New York, New York 10022

Collier Macmillan Canada, Inc.

Library of Congress Cataloging-in-Publication Data

Baker, Ross K.
American government.

Includes bibliographies and index.
1. United States—Politics and government.
I. Pomper, Gerald M. II. McWilliams, Wilson C.
III. Title.
JK274.B294 1987 320.973 86-12464
ISBN 0-02-305480-8

Printing: 1 2 3 4 5 6 7 8 Year: 7 8 9 0 1 2 3 4 5

Acknowledgments for Part-Opening Photos: Part 1, The first cabinet *(Library of Congress);* **Part 2,** Republican National Convention, August 1984 *(Photo by Art Stein; Photo Researchers Inc.);* **Part 3,** The Capitol *(Illustrators' Stock Photos/PSI);* **Part 4,** March on Washington, August 1963 *(© Bruce Davidson/Magnum Photos, Inc.);* **Part 5,** President Reagan with his National Security Advisors *(Illustrators' Stock Photos/PSI).*

ISBN 0-02-305480-8

To our families

Carole, Susannah, and Sally Baker

Marlene, Marc, David, and Miles Pomper

Nancy, Susan, and Helen McWilliams

About the Authors

Colleagues at Rutgers University for nearly two decades, the authors of *American Government* have also collaborated on a series of books analyzing the presidential elections of 1976, 1980, and 1984.

Ross K. Baker is professor of political science at Rutgers University. He received his B.A., M.A., and Ph.D. from the University of Pennsylvania and also attended the University of California, Berkeley. His professional experience includes, in addition to teaching and research, service as a research associate for the Foreign Policy Research Institute of the University of Pennsylvania and research associate at the Brookings Institute in Washington, D.C.

His deep and enduring interest in practical politics has led Professor Baker to work as special assistant to Senators Walter F. Mondale and Birch Bayh and as speech writer for Senator Frank Church during the 1976 Democratic presidential primary elections. In 1982 and 1983, he was a consultant for the House Democratic Caucus.

A frequent contributor to scholarly journals, Professor Baker does not confine his interest solely to the academic discipline of political science. He has written for diverse publications such as *Smithsonian, Money Magazine, The New York Times, The Washington Post,* and *The Nation* and contributes a monthly column to *American Demographics.* The work of which he is most proud is *Friend and Foe in the U.S. Senate,* a study of personal and political relations among senators, that was published in 1980.

Professor Baker lives with his wife Carole, an urban planner, and their children Susannah and Sally.

Gerald M. Pomper is a professor on the political science faculty of Rutgers University and Director of the Center on Political Parties at Rutgers' Eagleton Institute of Politics. He received his B.A. from Columbia University and his Ph.D. from Princeton.

During his academic career, Professor Pomper has written or edited twelve books on American politics, political parties, and elections. Among these works are *Nominating the President* (1963), *Elections in America* (1968 and 1980), *Voter's Choice* (1975 and 1983), and, his latest undertaking, *The Political State of New Jersey,* a collaborative exploration of politics and public policy in that state. Professor Pomper's contribution to the literature of political science also includes numerous scholarly and popular articles.

In the classroom, Professor Pomper has taught courses in American government, political parties and voting, ethnic groups, and political theory. Beyond the academy his activities include serving as president of the local school board, as cochairman of the national Committee on Party Renewal, and as member of the Free Speech Association Committee of the American Civil Liberties Union.

Abroad, Professor Pomper has taught at Tel-Aviv University and Oxford, as well as being European lecturer for the United States Information Agency. At home, he is husband to Dr. Marlene Michels Pomper, a professor of English, and father of three public-spirited sons: Marc, David, and Miles.

Wilson Carey McWilliams received his Ph.D. from the University of California, Berkeley, and taught at Oberlin College and Brooklyn College before joining the political science faculty of Rutgers University, where he teaches American political thought. His particular scholarly interests include international politics, civil rights, and the Constitution.

In 1974, his book *The Idea of Fraternity in America* won the National Historical Society prize. He is a frequent contributor to *Commonweal* and *The Nation*. Pursuing an extension of his interests into religion and politics, Professor McWilliams was an editor and regular columnist for *Worldview,* a journal of religion and international affairs, from 1972 to 1985. He believes his involvement in politics and journalism is partly hereditary; his father, Carey McWilliams, was for many years editor of *The Nation.*

Professor McWilliams lives with his wife, Nancy Riley McWilliams, who is a practicing psychoanalyst, and their two daughters, Susan and Helen.

Preface

Americans live in a nation and a world in which government inevitably affects each inhabitant. Nationally subsidized medical research prolongs life, government regulation helps to clean the air and water, and government spending undergirds the economy. Globally, American weapons and American diplomacy sometimes protect and sometimes threaten existence.

Americans cannot avoid the effects of government; but they can understand its workings better and can use this knowledge of the democracy of the United States to protect their interests and achieve their goals more fully. This book is our contribution to help students gain a more complete understanding of how government works.

Theme Knowledge requires facts, but facts in themselves are meaningless. In this introduction to American government, the many important facts are placed within the contexts of theory. By theory, we mean the collected theories of democratic philosophy, as well as theories of political science. Centrally, the theme of our book is "fragmentation," which we see as the predominant characteristic of the government of the United States. This theme is developed in the Introduction and reappears insistently throughout the book.

Organization The book has five major divisions. We begin with the foundations of American government: democratic philosophy, the Constitution, and Federalism. We then examine the political processes of the nation, including public opinion, the mass media, political parties, voting and elections, and interest groups. In the third part, we focus on the formal institutions of government: Congress, the President, the bureaucracy. Then we turn to the unique institution of the judiciary and to the legal doctrines of civil liberties and civil rights. In the last part, we examine the results of national government, with chapters devoted to foreign and defense policy, the environment, and the economy.

What's New about the Second Edition In the first edition of this book, we provided a theoretical framework, incorporated the latest research in political science, and focused on vital questions of democratic theory and practice. In this second edition, we have tried to maintain these characteristics while extensively revising the text.

The revisions include three new chapters, dealing with the mass media, civil rights, and macroeconomic policy. All of the material is fully up-to-date, including a full analysis of the 1984 presidential election, recent decisions of the Supreme Court, and new actions of the Congress and the President. Following the helpful suggestions of faculty and student readers, we have changed the order of chapters to fit the most common sequence of college courses.

Because undergraduate students are our principal audience, we have been especially concerned in this revision to ease their use of the text. We have added introductions to each part that carry through our theme of "fragmentation." Furthermore, we have made each chapter more readable by using opening vignettes, more lower-level headings, many more charts and other visual aids, extended summaries, and glossary definitions that will add to students' understanding of the boldface terms in the text. Boxed inserts provide case studies and supplementary materials that will reduce the need for outside readings. The appendixes include both the Constitution of the United States and the Declaration of Independence, and separate author and subject indexes complete the text.

Democracy is based ultimately on an act of faith, which is that more informed citizens will achieve more enlightened government. This book is our testament to that faith.

SUPPLEMENTS To aid both students and instructors, *American Government,* Second edition, is accompanied by a student study guide, an instructor's manual, and a test-item file in both booklet and computerized forms. We would like to thank the following people for preparing these ancillaries: Lois Vietri, University of Maryland (study guide); Richard Johnson, Glassboro State University (test bank and instructor's manual); and Lisa Schneider, University of Maryland (data resource manual).

Acknowledgments

We wish to thank the many people at the College Division of Macmillan Publishing Company who provided the initiative for this second edition of *American Government.* Gene Panhorst was a great source of early inspiration. Kate Moran Aker had worked closely with us on the first edition and was instrumental in the decision to produce a second. Tony English and Eben Ludlow played important roles in the conception and execution of the project. The person in the Macmillan operation with whom we had the most continuous contact was our development editor, Anne Pietropinto. Anne's patient persistence was a source of encouragement throughout the writing and editing.

We are similarly grateful to those people who supplied scholarly and practical commentary on the various chapter drafts. Professor Patrick Pierce of St. Mary's College, South Bend, Indiana, rendered great service by his research for Chapters 3 through 8. Professor Charles Jacob of Rutgers University kindly and constructively provided comments on Chapter

10. Professor Michael Hayes of Colgate University was most helpful with his comments on Chapter 15. Among other supportive readers of our chapters were our professional colleagues Scott Keeter of Virginia Commonwealth University, Henry Plotkin of the New Jersey Division of Community Affairs, and Cliff Zukin, director of the New Jersey Poll at the Eagleton Institute of Politics. We would also like to acknowledge the help of Maureen Moakley, Vernon Bogdanor, Frank Smallwood, Patricia Sykes, and the late Phillip Williams.

To ensure that this book describes government as it actually works, we needed the reality test provided by some very able and helpful people who not only understand government but actually partake in it. We are especially grateful to Mary Jane Checci, Esq., former staff director of the Democratic Policy Committee in the United States Senate and Howard Paster of Timmons and Co. for their insights into Congress. Bert Carp, who was deputy director of the Domestic Policy Staff in the White House during the Carter administration and who is now executive vice-president of the National Cable Association, gave us the benefit of his encyclopedic and creative mind. The economic policy chapter was reviewed by Allan I. Mendelowitz, associate director of the International Division of the General Accounting Office.

Edith Saks of the Eagleton Institute of Politics deserves much more than the brief acknowledgment that we can provide. She typed much of the manuscript, cast her own trained eye over the text, and did the extensive photocopying required in a manuscript of this size. But, more important, she was a source of wisdom, inspiration, and solace. She is a rare and wonderful person.

Finally, we would like to acknowledge the general support given by the leadership of the Eagleton Institute of Politics. Alan Rosenthal, the director of the Eagleton Institute, is a colleague to whom we are always grateful. When he went for a year to study at close hand the workings of the Florida legislature, we had the good fortune to benefit from the help of acting director Carl Van Horn.

Reviewers We are also thankful for the thoughtful criticism provided by many colleagues throughout the country.

In the first edition: Professors Lawrence Baum, Ohio State University; Susan Carroll, George Washington University; John E. Chubb, Stanford University; Robert DiClerico, West Virginia University; George Edwards, Texas A&M University; Judith Gillespie, University of Indiana; Benjamin Ginsberg, Cornell University; Alex Gottfried, University of Washington; G. Calvin Mackenzie, Colby College; Donald McCrone, University of Washington; Kenneth R. Mladenka, Texas A&M University; Stuart S. Nagel, University of Illinois, Urbana-Champaign; David Paletz, Duke University; Robert Sahr, Purdue University; L. Earl Shaw, University of Minnesota; and James Young, State University of New York, Binghamton.

In the second edition: Professors David Atkinson, University of Missouri; Harry Basehart, Salisbury State College; Christopher Bosso, Northeastern University; Bonnie Brown, Texas A&M University; Anne Costaine, University of Colorado; Larry Elowitz, Georgia College; Susan Fino, Wayne State University; Diane Fowlkes, Georgia State University; Donald Gross,

University of Kentucky; Steve Kenney, Northeastern University; Henry Kenski, University of Arizona; Forest Lin, Tulsa Junior College; Ben Martin, University of Missouri-Kansas City; Fred Mabbutt, Santa Ana College; William McClenaghan, Oregon State University; Milan Reban, North Texas State University; Louis Reichman, Fullerton College; Dennis Reilly, University of Wisconsin; Carl Schwarz, Fullerton College; Lawson Veasey, University of Central Arkansas; Lois Vietri, University of Maryland; Thomas Wells, Old Dominion University; Clifford Wirth, University of New Hampshire; and James Young, State University of New York, Binghamton.

R. K. B.
G. M. P.
W. C. M.

Contents

Introduction

Throughout this book, you will encounter the term "fragmentation." The concept of fragmentation is the thread that unites the chapters. We carry this theme over from the first edition, published in 1983, but the manner in which fragmentation expresses itself in American society and government constantly changes.

As we shall see in the early chapters of the book, the framers of the Constitution pursued a deliberate strategy of fragmentation in order to maximize the value they prized most highly: freedom. They fragmented the powers of the national government among three branches to reduce the likelihood of tyranny and then further fragmented power between the national government and the states, in the system we call Federalism.

What we mean by fragmentation now, however, is entirely different. Nowadays, this term is associated with the disintegration in authority of many major American institutions, the erosion of areas of public consensus and agreement that once prevailed, and the growth in power of groups with narrow or specialized interests. Fragmentation as a useful tool of government has clearly evolved too far. How did this happen?

When we wrote the first edition of *American Government,* our country was at the crest of a period of individualism so intense that essayist Tom Wolfe dubbed it the "me generation." It was a period in which people searched for private solutions to both individual and social problems. Such behavior was a natural reaction to the disillusionment that had set in when many of the brave hopes of the 1960s came crashing down. Victory over domestic poverty—a goal proclaimed in the 1960s—proved impossible to attain, and experts debated whether the massive social welfare programs of the 1960s and 1970s actually worked. Likewise, the search for a secure world based on our role as the dominant superpower was elusive, as we failed to achieve our political and military objectives in Southeast Asia and were, for more than a year, defied and humiliated by Iran. In terms of public attitudes, then, the two great areas of consensus—the modern welfare state and an anti-Communist foreign policy—had come undone.

Fragmentation also afflicted institutions of government. In less than a decade, the presidency went from being "imperial" under Nixon to "imperiled" under Carter. Far from being the one institution in which special interests were forced to give way to the national interest, the presidency appeared to be a victim of a particularly insidious kind of internal fragmentation. Various interest groups had established beachheads within the presidency itself by successfully placing their representatives or allies on the White House staff.

Congress, an institution by its nature much more parochial in outlook because its members must look out for the interests of the voters they represent in addition to making laws for the entire nation, offered little grounds for hope. Instead, Congress experienced a kind of "hyperfragmentation," in which a House and Senate traditionally divided into committees were further divided into subcommittees in the interest of democratization.

Nor did political parties offer grounds for optimism. While they continued to serve as a bridge between the various branches and levels of government and as the basis for organizing the two houses of Congress, the hold of party on voter and officeholder alike was weakened. More voters declared themselves to be "independent," and more elected officials acted as if they were independent of the party under whose name they were elected. "The Party's Over" was the title of David Broder's view of the organizations that had given form and coherence to American politics for 100 years. The decline of the parties was mirrored in the rise of special interest groups whose activities fragmented public issues into a myriad of narrower issues.

Informal and voluntary institutions suffered no less from fragmentation than the formal institutions of government. The authority of the large, well-established churches declined as more and more people were attracted to sects and fringe religious movements. The curricular unity of colleges and universities gave way to courses of study that were sometimes intellectual smorgasbords. The electronic and print media, which for a time had served as a unifying national cultural force, were fragmented into narrower and more specialized forms: cable television brought fundamentalist religious programming or Spanish language programming, or sports-only programming. Viewers did not ever need to encounter a media source that challenged their beliefs or encouraged them to broaden their interests beyond what already interested them. People spoke of "narrowcasting" to distinguish it from broadcasting: the former having narrow and specialized appeal, the latter appealing to more general tastes and interests.

In the four years since the first edition of this book, the fragmentation picture has somewhat brightened. Ronald Reagan did much to reinvigorate the office of the presidency. The Republican party was rebuilt through the leadership of William Brock and serves as a valuable and efficient resource for GOP candidates. The fragmentation of Congress shows few signs of improving, however, and the Democratic party has, if anything, become even more fragmented. This has come about, paradoxically, as the result of efforts to stem fragmentation.

Americans also think better of themselves and their country. The economic prosperity of the early 1980s was a tonic for the national mood, but as the recovery from the economic doldrums of the 1970s was uneven so was the rekindled sense of national optimism. The jobs of many Americans disappeared in the 1982–83 recession, never to return. There was also an increasing stridency in the national debate over social issues such as abortion and school prayer, and one could even detect a hint of fatigue toward the plight of the poorest Americans on the part of more prosperous citizens.

As the campaign of 1984 faded into history, it was noted that an important subsidiary theme of that campaign was the very question of the extent of our obligations to others and the nature of our ties to something beyond ourselves and our families.

Reflecting on this problem, the distinguished journalist Bill Moyers spoke in these terms in a Thanksgiving editorial:

> We modern, worldly Americans, creatures of high speed, high-tech and self-centered obsessions, might find something to think about in those old notions of covenant and compact, of mutual obligation and the civic self. It was not just a colony that was planted in America but the idea of a commonwealth, of our debt to each other and to the future.

American Government

PART 1

The Structure of American Government

Structure, whether we are talking about buildings or governments, refers to the way in which something is constructed or organized. Structure is concerned with the *design* or *basic framework* that orders the relationship between parts and pulls together even very different parts into a recognizable whole.

In relation to government and politics, this design or basic framework has two elements. First, just as the shape of a building is fundamentally influenced by what the building is meant to do, political structure consists of the *goals, purposes,* and *values* that characterize a political society and that guide people in political life. Even if a political society doesn't agree about goals and values, the kind of disagreements it has will shape the kind of politics it has. For example, if a government pursues a set of goals that are sharply at odds with those of its people, it can only rule by force and repression. By contrast, almost all Americans agree about a number of political values, including their conviction that democracy is the best form of government. But Americans do not always agree about the *meaning* of democracy.

The term *democracy* means "rule by the people" or "rule by the many." Given this fact, do we insist that in order to win an election or to become law, a candidate or a policy must get a *majority* of the vote, 50% plus one? That, after all, is the literal meaning of "majority rule." Or are we satisfied with a simple *plurality,* allowing a candidate or policy to win by getting more votes than any other even if—when there are more than two candidates or policies in competition—no candidate or policy gets more than half the vote? In the United States, we appear to be of mixed mind about this question: we decide most of our elections by a plurality, but we insist that our laws receive at least a majority (and sometimes a two-thirds majority) of legislators.

Similarly, what does it mean to be a *citizen* of a democracy? Aliens as well as citizens are subject to and protected by the laws. Citizens, of course, also have a right to be protected by the United States even when they are in foreign countries, but citizenship means more than that. A citizen, unlike an alien, has rights to *participate in government.* But what rights? We have the right to vote, but not until we are eighteen and not unless we register. Are those limits "democratic"? Arguments about the proper limits of the right to vote have played a vital role in American politics. Until recently, we had to be twenty-one to vote in most states and very few black citizens could vote in the South; until the Nineteenth Amendment, states were free to deny women the right to vote, and so on. Voting, however, is only one of the possible rights of citizens.

In what we sometimes call "pure" democracy, citizens participate *directly* in making laws or in holding public office, as they did in ancient city-state democracies like those of classical Greece. By contrast, the American Constitution provides for *representative government,* in which citizens participate in making laws and ruling through "representatives" and other officials who are responsible to the people. Representative government, in turn, emphasizes the role of leaders and representatives in *setting the agenda,* deciding what issues are politically important and what alternatives people have for dealing with them.

In Chapter 1, we will explore these questions in greater depth, especially by examining some of the ideas about the meaning of democracy that have exerted a profound influence on Americans and in American politics. And we will consider the implications of democratic theory for the practice of American politics today and in the immediate future.

Chapters 2 and 3 turn to a second aspect of political structure: the *methods, institutions,* and *working principles* by which we set about to achieve our goals and values. If Chapter 1 asks the "Why?" questions about American political structure, Chapters 2 and 3 ask the question, "How?" Necessarily, any such discussion must begin—as it does in Chapter 2—with the Constitution, the supreme law of the land.

American government is relatively unique because so much of its structure is the result of conscious design, the vision and planning which, two hundred years ago, resulted in the Constitution of the United States. Alexander Hamilton hoped, in fact, that the American Constitution would prove that human beings are capable of "establishing good government from reflection and choice." But not everything in the structure of American government results from things the framers of the Constitution intended. Ideas different from those conceived by the framers have shaped the Constitution: the Bill of Rights, for example, is the result of the arguments and pressure of the anti-Federalists who opposed the Constitution. A century later, political parties became a basic element in American government, although this would have been disapproved by the Constitution's framers, who regarded political parties or factions with distaste. Political events like the Civil War had shaken and changed the Constitution and the structure of American politics. Chapter 2 will examine these changing aspects of American constitutional government, but it will also make clear that the Constitution still sets the basic framework for American politics.

Federalism, which we discuss in Chapter 3, is a vital part of the contemporary legacy of the Constitution. In its own special way, the Constitution is very clearly a federal document. It refers to persons, citizens, and the people; the only political groups it acknowledges—apart from foreign governments and Indian tribes—are the states. The Constitution forbids any constitutional status for churches; it has been amended three times (the Thirteenth, Fourteenth, and Fifteenth Amendments) to rule out race as a category in law and once (the Nineteenth Amendment) to exclude gender; and it makes no mention of social classes, ethnic communities, or political parties. All of these groups have been important in the practice of American politics, but they are not recognized by the Constitution. The one political group the Constitution emphatically does recognize is the states.

Americans are citizens of both the nation and the states where they live. Political power is divided between national and state governments—only the national government, for example, can conduct foreign policy—but political power is often *shared* by both governments. The boundaries between national and state power overlap and are always coming into conflict. Chapter 3 discusses the ways in which Americans have thought about federalism, the way in which federalism works today, and the relation between federalism and the problem of political fragmentation.

Any country has both material and human resources. Human resources consist of human skills and human commitments—the willingness of people to support particular goals, groups, or leaders. When all the resources in a country are drawn together for common purposes, we refer to them as *aggregated.* When they are scattered, so that the human and material resources of a country are being devoted to differing, conflicting, or incompatible goals, we speak of them as *fragmented.* This book argues that political power in the United States is fragmented to an extent that makes it difficult for Americans to pursue their common goals or to solve their national problems. As Chapters 1, 2, and 3 indicate, political fragmentation is embedded in American ideas of democracy, in the Constitution, and in the design of American federalism. We also hope and believe that American democracy can overcome the problem of fragmentation, and the first three chapters also point to elements of the structure and tradition of American politics that work to counteract fragmentation. The continuing challenge of American democracy is summed up by the motto, E PLURIBUS UNUM, which expresses both a hope and a question: Is it possible, in a diverse republic devoted to liberty, to make "one out of many"?

CHAPTER

1

The Theory of Democracy

Democracy and America, Abraham Lincoln asserted, are bound together so that one cannot survive without the other. American political life tests whether "government of the people, by the people and for the people" will or will not "perish from the earth." Americans have often taken pride in the idea that the United States is a model of democratic politics with a special responsibility to "make the world safe for democracy." Lincoln, however, meant something different by his words at Gettysburg. The relationship between America and democracy puts *us,* not others, on trial.[1] Democracy, as Lincoln understood it, is an awesome commitment, a dedication to "the proposition that all men are created equal."

Nevertheless, "democracy" does not mean the same thing to all people. Lincoln's challenge, for example, ought to make Americans uneasy with the glaring inequalities of political life, the many discriminations and indignities suffered by Americans who are poor, dark-skinned, or female. So it does, for many Americans. Others, however, are not particularly bothered by inequality. They regard it as the price of liberty, and most Americans, apparently, are confident that our institutions, for all their faults, are the best that can be had in an imperfect world.

Outside the United States, there is even more disagreement. Legitimate government and democracy have come to mean the same thing, and no regime dares to admit that it is undemocratic. Everyone seems to agree that democracy is a good thing, but there is little agreement on what the term means. The word *democracy* is subject to a tug-of-war between conflicting definitions that pull the term out of shape. No one doubts that democracy means "rule by the people." That definition, however, only raises new questions. It forces us to ask, What do we mean by "ruling"? Who are "the people"?

Ruling and the Political Process

When Americans speak of "rule by the people," they are likely to be thinking of voters going to the polls to cast their ballots. But voting is only one aspect of political rule and not necessarily the most important one. Ruling includes talking as well as acting, defining and deliberating as well as deciding. Ruling is involved in (1) setting the political agenda and (2) shaping political alternatives as well as (3) deciding among those alternatives. And all of these judgments depend on (4) the definition of basic principles. The people rule only to the extent that they are decisive in *all* these stages of the political process.

Ruling as Setting the Agenda

Ruling begins with **setting the agenda**—that is, identifying certain problems as matters that demand and deserve political attention. The questions we think are important may determine the answers we give: when inflation is an important question for most Americans, they are likely to elect Republicans, as they did in 1980; if more voters are worried about unemployment, as they were in 1982, they are apt to shift to the Democrats.

But the political agenda doesn't just happen. It is the result of persuasion and pressure, public reflection and political events. Before 1973, the question of abortion—so important in the presidential campaign of 1984—was largely confined to *state* politics. When the Supreme Court ruled that abortion is included in the "right to privacy" protected by the federal Constitution, it moved abortion onto the *national* agenda.[2] Defenders of the "Right to Life" were compelled to seek changes in federal law and policy; supporters of "Free Choice" also had to focus their attention on Washington; and candidates for national office were compelled to take some sort of position on the issue.

The Supreme Court moved the question of abortion onto the national political agenda by ruling, in 1973, that abortion is included in the right to privacy. By the early 1980s, the ruling had become extremely controversial. *(Paul Conklin)*

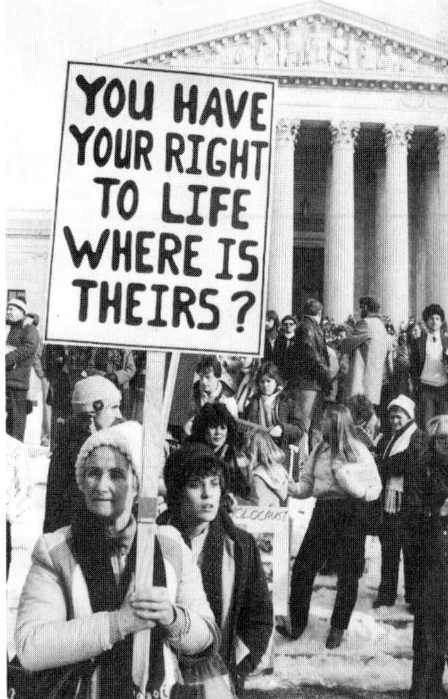

YOU HAVE
YOUR RIGHT
TO LIFE
WHERE IS
THEIRS?

Similarly, the feminist movement made women's rights a crucial issue in public debate, especially by leading Americans to see a *political* dimension in many areas of family and personal life. Until recently, almost everyone thought that if an employer flirted with his or her secretary, it was a private matter and none of our business. Feminists, however, persuaded millions of us to see many such flirtations as "sexual harassment," an illegitimate use of power that is the public's business to prevent. The question of what is and is not permissible in such relationships has become an item on the political agenda.

In practice, of course, the political agenda is influenced by the media, interest groups, and government itself. Democratic theory reminds us, however, that the people rule only to the extent that they set their own agenda.[3]

Ruling as Defining Alternatives

Second, ruling involves framing alternatives. Politics is full of possibilities: there are always a number of different ways of approaching a political problem, just as there are always a good many potential candidates for office. If the government needs more revenue, should it raise the income tax? Should it raise the taxes of the rich more than those of the poor? Should we scrap the graduated income tax and substitute a "flat rate," taxing the same percentage of all income and eliminating all deductions? Or should we have a flat rate with *some* deductions? Or a rate that is not *entirely* flat? Or would it be better to pass a new tax, such as a national sales tax, and leave income taxes alone?

If we state our first responses to such questions, our preferences will probably be scattered, just as votes tend to be in the early presidential primaries when all the candidates are in the race. If we decide by **plurality**—that is, the most number of votes in an election—in favor of the tax or the candidate with the most votes, a relatively small percentage of the people may determine the winner. The other possibility is to narrow the choice by some sort of deliberation—talking, comparing alternatives, rethinking, amending, and refining—dropping off the less persuasive, less desirable, or less popular alternatives until we are left with two and are assured that the winner will have some sort of support from a **majority.** (A majority is at least one more than 50% of the votes in an election.) Ruling is obvious in this process, since it includes some choices and excludes others and also decides what it will take to win.

In fact, defining the terms of choice shapes, and may determine, the choice itself. Every election reminds us of this. In 1980, millions of Americans who did not admire Ronald Reagan voted for him because he represented the only real alternative to Jimmy Carter. In 1984, voters who were reluctant to vote for Reagan did so because they found Walter Mondale even less attractive. In the same way, citizens who dislike busing may favor it if there is no other alternative to segregated schools, and citizens who favor integration in principle may dislike busing so much that they prefer de facto segregation.

Again, whatever may be true of political practice, democratic theory observes that the people rule only to the extent that they shape and define the terms of public choice.

Ruling as Deciding: Policy and Administration

In the most familiar sense of the term, ruling is deciding, choosing between alternatives or determining who wins and who loses. Political decisions at the highest level involve *making* rules—passing laws, laying down goals and standards for policy, or electing representatives to perform those tasks. But rule making is only half the story: a law or a policy is a general rule that must be *applied* to particular cases. Applying and interpreting laws and policies requires judgments and decisions; administration is an essential dimension of rule.

We agree that the lives and properties of American citizens should be protected against attack. That general policy, however, leaves it to someone—usually the president—to decide when Americans are in danger and what to do about it. Ronald Reagan acted on this policy when he judged that Americans in Grenada were endangered by that country's revolutionary government and that the use of military force offered the best hope of protecting them.

Similarly, when Congress passes a law, we do not know what it will mean in practice until we know how it will be carried out. Will officials interpret the law in a broad or narrow way? Will they be "hard" or "soft" in enforcing it? Federal law, for example, provides that schools or colleges may not receive money if they practice discrimination on the basis of sex. Under President Carter, the Justice Department reasoned that if *any* school program discriminated, the school as a *whole* should be denied federal support. The Reagan administration, however, interpreted the law to mean that only those programs that discriminate should be denied money; the federal government should be able to fund other, nondiscriminatory activities. This position obviously reduces the pressure on schools to eliminate discriminatory practices, since they can go on receiving federal money for the rest of their programs. The Reagan administration's interpretation, in other words, was a ruling that virtually created a new law.[4]

Democracy must be concerned with the way in which policies are administered, as well as the way in which they are made. Both are dimensions that set the limits of rule by the people.

Ruling as Defining Basic Principles

Setting the agenda, framing alternatives and making decisions, however, all turn on fundamental principles. We have allowed rulers, like judges, to decide conflicts because (1) we believe that there are *common principles or standards* by which the controversy can be resolved justly, (2) we believe that the ruler *knows* those principles, and (3) we rely on the ruler's ability to *apply* those standards to the case at hand. These three considerations define *authority* as that term is used in political science. A ruler has authority because he or she knows, or at least is thought to know, how to rule rightly.

Defenders of democracy contend that the people understand the principles of ruling at least as well as any ruler and are reasonably able to apply those principles to political practice. Our confidence in the people need not be the same on both these points. We can be convinced that the people are the best judges of the desirability of peace and war without thinking that the people would have known what to do when the Soviet Union invaded Afghanistan in 1979. In an unfamiliar situation like the Afghan crisis, the people themselves will almost certainly seek advice from experts. But in a democracy, the people will have to decide *whom to ask* and *what advice to take.* Citizens need, at least, to be wise in their choice of experts. To that extent, democracy requires the people to decide both questions of principle and practice.

Most of the time, we do not trust the people to make this sort of judgment. We ask physicists about physics, drama critics about plays, and accountants about taxes. Even the strongest supporters of democracy follow this pattern. It appears then that in a democracy you find yourself going to the people for expert judgment on *political* problems—something you would not dream of doing with any other kind of problem.

Politics is different because, at the most basic level, ruling consists of establishing or discovering the scale of justice and injustice, or the measure of political right and political wrong. Our idea of justice reflects our convictions about (1) the *nature* of human beings, in general, and of our own people, in particular, and (2) the *ends* we hope to achieve, our idea of human excellence and the good life. Democracy has confidence in the *capacity of the people to decide what is politically just and unjust,* thus to define the first principles of politics. To put it another way, democracy argues that the people are the best available judges of who we *are* and what we *deserve.*

Democracy and Equality

Although democracy assumes that the people are roughly equal in their understanding of justice, this belief in *political* equality is different from the doctrine that "all men are created equal." The idea of human equality, especially as expressed in Judaism and Christianity, played a vital role in the origin of modern democracies, but it speaks to a different set of questions.

Human equality asserts that human beings are equal in *worth* or *dignity.* If this is so, then we all deserve to be valued equally, but we do not necessarily deserve to rule. We can have a much more favorable opinion of a baseball player than we do about a member of Congress, but we might not want our favorite shortstop to serve in the national legislature. Many adults would sacrifice their own lives to save a child. This seems to suggest that they think the child's life is worth even more than their own. But the same adults would not let children vote or hold high office. The idea that all human beings are equally worthy may *encourage* democracy, but it does not *require* it.

The Declaration of Independence proclaims that we are "created equal," but this equality, according to the Declaration, does not make democracy the only just or legitimate regime. Governments are created by the "consent of the governed," but the governed may consent to regimes other than democracy. The people are free to choose whatever form of government seems "most likely to effect their safety and happiness."*

Who Are the People?

But who among the so-called "people" are entitled to make the decision on what is just? All the people in the world? All the people who happen to be living in the country at a particular time? Obviously, it does not mean all people everywhere. Every democracy must define the people who are to be rulers. In other words, *the character of any democratic regime depends on its definition of citizens and citizenship.*

Citizens and Aliens

First, democracies, like all countries, must distinguish between "our people" and "foreigners," citizens and aliens. A **citizen** is one who is considered a member of a nation or a state. Other countries determine citizenship by *jus sanguinis*—"law of blood"—which confers citizenship on the basis of your

*The Declaration of Independence denounces George III as a tyrant because simply declaring that he was a king would not have been enough to justify the American Revolution.

ancestry. America has been less willing (and less able) than most states to define citizenship in national or ethnic terms. In American law, the dominant principle (following English practice) is *jus soli.* This Latin phrase meaning "law of the soil" means that you are a citizen if you are born here.

The exceptions to that general rule have been unfortunately numerous. Slavery excluded blacks from equal citizenship. Justice Roger B. Taney of the U.S. Supreme Court said as much in the Dred Scott case in 1857.[5] Even after the ratification of the Thirteenth, Fourteenth, and Fifteenth Amendments, racism denied blacks equal citizenship in practice. In the late nineteenth century, the United States excluded immigrants from China and Japan, and in 1921, the National Origins Quota limited immigration in a way that favored immigrants from Northern Europe and the British Isles. During the Second World War, the government put American citizens in concentration camps simply because their ancestry was Japanese.[6] And these are only the most obvious examples.

With all these glaring exceptions, however, the United States has been generally willing to admit people of very diverse origins into citizenship. By European standards, G. K. Chesterton wrote, the United States seemed to be trying to make a nation "out of any old nation that comes along."[7] Even when Japanese were denied the right to become naturalized, any children they had while in this country were declared to be citizens.[8]

But if Americans have generally not made ethnicity a test of citizenship, they have demanded that everyone accept a political creed.[9] Thus, we rejected the idea that race or ethnic group was a qualification for citizenship, but we required citizens to embrace "the American way." But who defines what this means? For many years the House of Representatives had a Committee on Un-American Activities. This usually amused Frenchmen who could not conceive of a "Committee on Un-French Activities." A child born in France, however, must have at least one French parent to be legally considered a citizen.

Democracy, then, does presume common principles and standards, and where people with different cultures and customs come together, as they do

Although U.S. citizenship has historically been accepted as a birthright of those born on American soil, full equality under the law was not a national standard until quite recently. *(Dorothea Lange/ Library of Congress)*

in America, it is hard to escape the conclusion that belief in a public creed, a "civil religion" like the Declaration of Independence, ought to be one requirement of citizenship.[10] Nevertheless, in recent years, the Supreme Court has been inclined to narrow the grounds on which citizenship can be denied or taken away.* In international or domestic society today, people without citizenship have second-class status at best, and being deprived of one's citizenship is almost to lose one's "right to have rights."[11] Certainly, in a democracy, there can be no political equality unless one is a citizen.

Economic and Social Equality

Once citizens are separated from aliens, democracies tend to insist that in order to qualify for political rights, citizens must be capable of independent, reasoned judgment. Ideas about what that sort of judgment requires vary greatly, but democratic regimes can usually agree on some minimum standard. In the most obvious case, we exclude the insane from voting or holding office.

It is more important that we insist on a measure of *social and economic equality* because we think it necessary to political equality. If some citizens are hopelessly dependent on others, they will not be free to follow their own ideas of justice and injustice, and only a part of the people will actually rule. "In the general course of human nature," Alexander Hamilton wrote, "a power over a man's subsistence amounts to a power over his will."[12]

At the time of the Revolution, it was argued that citizenship required the ownership of property. Democracy was possible, in this view, only when almost all citizens held a reasonable amount of property, and property qualifications for voting were normal practice. If democracy excluded those without property from political equality, it also excluded slaves because not only did they not own property, but they were actually the property of someone else. Women were excluded because they were felt to be dependent on men, and children because they were dependent on parents and unable to reason about public questions.

In the nineteenth century, with the rise of industrialism, the majority of Americans gradually became wage earners. Following the example of the ancient city-states, Americans came to argue that government should *guarantee* or *create* some degree of economic and social equality in order to *enable* people to judge freely and play a role in public life. Workers, for example, insisted on public schools and demanded shorter working hours, claiming that they needed education and free time in order to perform their duties as citizens. Movements of today, which demand that the government promote and protect the economic and social equality of racial minorities, women, and the poor, can also seem to be suggesting that true political equality cannot be achieved without economic and social equality.

Some people, of course, want the government to carry equality much farther.† What matters for our purposes, however, is that both the older view, which sought to limit the public to those with property, and the newer

*For example, Congress now cannot deprive a person of citizenship for voting in a foreign election, something it had previously been able to do. *Afroyim* v. *Rusk*, 387 U.S. 253 (1967).

†For example, Herbert Gans, *More Equality* (New York: Random House, 1974).

idea, which brings property to the public, agree that some minimal social and economic equality is needed if political equality is to have any meaning.

The Rule of the Majority

If the people are relatively equal in their understanding of justice, their judgments are all of one kind; then majority rule follows logically from the principles of democracy. If people disagree, the greater number are more likely to be right. Democracy, for practical purposes, has always been the "rule of the many."

But if, according to democratic principles, the majority is more likely to be right, it can easily be wrong. Suppose that we disagree with the majority. Why should we accept its rulings?

Sometimes we go along with the majority because it is stronger than we are. But often, the majority is *not* stronger than the minority. A majority made up of older people, for example, may be weaker than a young and vigorous minority. A minority of soldiers may be stronger than a civilian majority, as we saw in 1982 when the Polish Army imposed martial law on a defiant people. Well-to-do minorities find it easier to organize than majorities, and a disorganized many is no match for a unified few. The newspaper is full of stories about military coups, and Communist regimes, despite their claim of being democratic, rest on the ability of the Communist Party, an elite composed of committed members, to dominate the unorganized.

Since the few are often stronger than the many, a democratic regime relies on the willingness of any stronger minority to abide by the rule of the majority. Why is such a minority willing to be ruled? In the first place, such a minority must feel that its vital interests, the things it would fight to preserve, will be respected by the majority. The majority must not rule in ways the minority finds intolerable. But a government that does not do intolerable things often ends up doing a great many unpleasant ones. For example, a majority that respects the property of the rich may ask them to pay very high taxes. Why should the wealthy minority accept this if it can get its way by force? Any democratic regime, obviously, must have an answer to that question. At the same time, a democracy must look at the other side of the coin. The majority has democratic principle on its side. If it is strong, why should the majority listen to the complaints and obstructions of the minority? Why not follow the rule of "democratic centralism" that the majority decision must always be obeyed? Many democracies fail because they cannot find a satisfactory answer to these questions. Unsuccessful democracies are more common than successful ones. Those that are able to make democracy work find that they need to combine majority rule and minority rights in different ways, and the ways they choose help distinguish one democratic regime from another.

Basic Elements of Democratic Theory

Let us sum up the argument so far. A democracy is defined (1) by its *basic principles,* its ideas of human nature and the good life, and its understanding of justice and injustice, (2) by its definition of *citizenship,* and (3) by its solution to the problems of *majority rule*. Democracies and democratic theories vary with how they define and emphasize these three elements of democratic life.

Three major ideas of democracy have had a major impact on American political life and thought: (1) the ancient idea of democracy that comes from classical Greece, (2) the theory of James Madison and the other authors of *The Federalist,* which was a series of articles written in 1787 to justify the ratification of the Constitution, and (3) the ideas developed by Alexis de Tocqueville in response to mass democracy. Each of these theories deserves careful attention.

Ancient Democracy and the Ideal of the Citizen

Ancient Greece and Modern America

Our idea of democracy, like the word *democracy* itself, originated in ancient Greece. Basically, **democracy** is government in which the people hold the ruling power, either directly or through elected representatives. When the Founders of the American Republic referred to democracy, they had in mind the example of ancient city-states, and the theories of the ancient Greeks continued to exert a powerful influence on American political leaders.

Americans were so attracted by classical ideals that they gave themselves a Senate and a Capitol in imitation of ancient Rome and even renamed Goose Creek, which once flowed in the District of Columbia, the Tiber, after Rome's river.[13] Ancient political science and political practice helped shape our institutions and our hopes.

The Ancient Ideal of Citizenship

To ancient political science, democracy meant citizenship. To be a citizen meant much more than it does today. Today, a citizen of the United States is anyone who is subject to the laws and entitled to the protection of the United States at home or abroad. By contrast, according to Aristotle, a citizen is someone who *participates in ruling,* "ruling and being ruled in turn."[14] We praise "equality before the law," but Greek citizens claimed equality in *making* law. A citizen was expected to share in the responsibilities of ruling as well as in the duty to obey. Similarly, it was assumed that the citizen would have a say in defining the public's alternatives, not merely a chance to choose between alternatives put forward by someone else. When Americans complain about the choices offered to them in an election, they are, in part, regretting that citizenship in America falls short of the Greek ideal.

The equality of all citizens, in the ancient view, meant equal participation and shared rule. Democracy is valuable, in these terms, because it lets all citizens share in public life. Aristotle wrote that we are "political animals," by which he meant that to be fully human, to achieve our greatest excellence or virtue, we need political society.[15] Politics helps us to know ourselves. Deliberating about our political matters forces us to think about our

POLITICAL PERSPECTIVE

DEMOCRACY: TWO MODERN VIEWS

Note the differences in attitude toward democracy of two modern-day thinkers.

Democracy: A Conservative View

[T]he vast majority of men . . . cannot take in new ideas, and they cannot get rid of old fears. They lack the logical sense; they are unable to reason from a set of facts before them, free from emotional distractions. . . . Their minds cannot grasp even the simplest abstractions; all their thinking is done on the level of a few primitive appetites and emotions. . . .

The truth is that the difference between representative democracy and direct democracy is a great deal less marked than political sentimentalists assume. Under both forms, the sovereign mob must employ agents to execute its will, and in either case the agents may have ideas of their own, based upon interests of their own, and the means at hand to do and get what they will. Moreover, their very position gives them a power of influencing the electors that is far above that of any ordinary citizen. . . . Worse, both forms of democracy encounter the difficulty that the generality of citizens, no matter how assiduously they may be instructed, remain congenitally unable to comprehend many of the problems before them, or to consider all of those they do comprehend in an unbiased and intelligent manner.

Source: H. L. Mencken, *Notes on Democracy* (New York: Knopf, 1926), pp. 21–22, 75–76.

Democracy: A Progressive View

Democracy is much broader than . . . a method of conducting government. . . . It is . . . a way of life, social and individual. The keynote of democracy as a way of life may be expressed . . . as the necessity for participation of every mature human being in formation of the values that regulate the living of men together: which is necessary from the standpoint of both the general social welfare and the full development of human beings as individuals. . . .

The foundation of democracy is faith in the capacities of human nature; faith in human intelligence and in the power of pooled and cooperative experience. It is not belief that these things are complete but that if given a show, they will grow and be able to generate progressively the knowledge and wisdom needed to guide collective action. Every autocratic and authoritarian scheme of social action rests on a belief that the needed intelligence is confined to a superior few. . . . The democratic faith has emerged very, very recently in the history of mankind. . . . After democratic political institutions were nominally established, beliefs and ways of looking at life . . . that originated when men and women were externally controlled and subjected to arbitrary power, persisted in the family, the church, business and the school; and experience shows that as long as they persist there, political democracy is not secure.

Source: John Dewey, "Democracy and Educational Administration," *School and Society,* April 3, 1937.

relations with our fellow citizens, to other regimes and other human beings, and to nature as a whole. It forces us to see ourselves as parts of the whole, neither independent nor isolated but, though limited, far from powerless.

Citizenship and Majority Rule

Democracy decides by majority rule, Aristotle observed, but its first principle, which comes even before majority rule, is that *all citizens should share in public life.* In healthy democracies, even a strong minority accepts majority rule because it believes in the principle, the equality of all citizens, from which that rule derives. If that minority believes in the standard that everyone accepts, it will be willing to put up with many painful decisions so long

Socrates warned ancient Greeks that democracy can degenerate into tyranny unless citizens are restrained by an ideal of justice. *(Library of Congress)*

as the majority shows reasonable self-restraint. In fact, the same principle forces the majority to be self-restrained. When equality means that all citizens have an equal right to participate, the majority cannot ignore the minority. If the people as a whole are the best judge, then the many cannot refuse to listen to the few. Majorities may have to decide, but people rule.[16]

If, by contrast, the majority believes that majority rule, and not equal citizenship, is the highest principle, it may silence the minority. But then it will face the argument that a majority of the majority has the right to silence its opponents. In that way lies dictatorship. In fact, the argument that a majority of the majority ought to rule is the fundamental notion in democratic centralism as practiced in the Soviet Union. Greek theorists like Aristotle were aware of these dangers in majority rule. This awareness caused them to insist that citizenship had to dominate a person's attachment to a party and that the good of the public as a whole had to come before one's private interests.

Democracy and Individual Liberty

Since citizens, in the ancient Greek view, had to be free to participate in public life, they had to have political liberty. Aristotle observed, however, that political freedom tends to suggest *individual* freedom, "living as one likes." This second sort of liberty is a danger to democracy.[17] Public-spirited citizens like to live law-abiding lives, and they choose to respect the rights and dignities of their neighbors. If, however, children are taught that freedom is "doing as you like," they will come to the conclusion that any control on them at all amounts to slavery. Gradually, the notion that freedom is "doing as you like" tends to produce individualists who always prefer their private good. The individualist is no democrat. Democratic citizens reject any rule about which they have had no *say,* but the individualist rejects any rule he does not *like*. Individualists would prefer not to be ruled at all, and democracy can never be more than a second choice.

The idea of private, individual freedom encourages people to put their own interests first and to limit them only where they must. Democracy can survive a few citizens who think that way, but not many. As such citizens grow numerous, they no longer feel they have to obey public standards and limit their own ambitions. They tend, in other words, to create tyrannical majorities or strong minorities that will not respect majority rule.

The Common Good and Civic Virtue

In the ancient understanding, then, democracy must attempt to teach its citizens that political liberty is better than individual liberty. Democratic theory makes the case that a person cannot be humanly free except as part of a political society, and that any person's individual good, the good of a part, depends on the good of the whole.

People never wholeheartedly accept that teaching. Our bodies are separate and our senses are private. Our feelings sometimes cause us to sacrifice, but only for things we take to be our own, like family, country, or property. It might be reasonable to support the common good, but our bodies and our senses urge us to "take care of number one." Public-spirited citizens need to control some of their strongest urges. They must try not to prefer their families and friends, their economic interests, or their local communities. They must try not to confuse those private interests with the public good. This "keeping yourself honest" is difficult and it requires self-denial, since we want to side with those we love, whether they are right or wrong. As Aristotle argued, before democratic citizens can rule others, they must first learn how to rule themselves.[18]

The Small State

Ancient political science believed that the small city-state, or *polis,* was desirable because it helped citizens by reducing the tension between private feelings and interests, on the one hand, and the public good, on the other. In a small community, if I pay taxes to build a bridge, I also get to walk on the bridge. I can see a school built by my taxes even if I have no children. Thus I see and experience the benefit of doing my civic duty.

By contrast, in a big country only a few public projects benefit me directly. Most of the things the government asks of me go to benefit people far away and give them things I will never see. If I live in an industrial city, I will not get any *direct* benefit from a National Forest in Montana. In order to see the relationship between my good and the public good, I have to reason that preserving our forests helps assure me enough paper and wood products, restricts flood damage, soil erosion, and the like. But these benefits are indirect, and I discover them only by thinking hard about them, not by experiencing them on a daily basis. If paper is cheap when I go to buy some, my first reaction is not likely to be, "I'm glad my taxes supported the Forest Service." Similarly, many Americans opposed federal guarantees of

When President Carter helped "bail out" New York City in 1978 with $1.65 billion in loan guarantees, many Americans reacted in anger because they failed to see that New York's financial troubles could affect their personal well-being. *(UPI)*

loans to New York City, wondering why they should "bail out" New York. Such guarantees, however, were not proposed only to help New York. They were urged because it was feared that if the nation's financial capital went bankrupt, a financial collapse would follow, injuring every state and city. There were arguments against guaranteeing loans to New York, but the argument had to be made in terms of the complex, invisible relationships between New York and the rest of the country, not in terms of the things we feel in our immediate lives.

To put the case for the small state another way, almost all of us are willing, even happy, to make sacrifices for our friends.* In a small state my friends and the community are more or less the same thing, so a sacrifice for the community is, in effect, a sacrifice for my friends. Of course, in a small state, my enemies may also make up a sizable percentage of the citizenry, but at worst, that will cause me to become involved in the community if for no other reason than to keep my enemies out of power or to take power away from them if they have it. Small political societies inspire strong feelings in us, especially if they are stable and we expect to spend our lives there.

In large states, my friends and enemies will be a tiny fraction of the population. An American would be lucky to have a thousand friends, but among our more than 200 million fellow citizens, even that army of friends is a drop in the bucket. When we think about helping our friends or hurting our enemies, most of us do not think about politics or the government. We think about private acts, loaning our friends money or keeping our enemies from getting promoted. In the large state it is our private affairs about which we feel most strongly.

*Mark Twain makes this argument in his story, "Two Little Tales," in *The Complete Short Stories of Mark Twain,* Charles Neider, ed. (Garden City, N.Y.: Hanover, 1957), pp. 399–408.

The Small State and Political Participation Democracy is easier in a small state in an even more important way. In a small state, citizens can participate more fully and more often in political life. In the first place, it is easier to be heard. In modern America, only a few people have a chance to speak to any considerable number of their fellow citizens. There are too many of us. If we spent twenty-four hours a day listening to political speeches, and each person was allowed to talk for only five minutes, less than 50,000 of us—about two-tenths of 1 percent of the American people as a whole—could speak in any year. In a city of 5,000 or 10,000 adults, however, we would have a reasonable chance to be heard even if people took time out for eating and sleeping. In a town meeting, such as those held in New England towns each spring, almost everyone who wants to speak on an issue can have a say.

Similarly, where there are fewer citizens, I have a much better chance of holding an important office. Large states have more officials, but the number of top-level positions does not change very much. Even very small countries have a chief executive, a foreign minister, a chief justice, and so on. If there are fewer citizens, there will be fewer rivals for such jobs, and I will be more likely to be chosen, just as in a small school I am more likely to win a varsity letter than I am in a large one.[19]

As this suggests, in the small state, citizens can participate in defining political issues as well as in deciding them. It is relatively easy to form groups; we do not need much in the way of money, time, or organization to be effective, and putting those resources together is fairly simple. In small states, we can choose to speak or to listen; in large states, most of us have to listen, whatever we might choose. And in large states, we are less likely to hold office. At most, in large states, we can decide issues as they are defined by others. Citizenship in large states is incomplete in some ways, and individual citizens matter less or at least feel as if they do. Democracy is less comfortable in a large state than in a small one.

Economic Equality and Equal Dignity

In economic terms, the ancient Greeks thought that democracy could not tolerate extremes of wealth and poverty. Too much money makes wealthy people feel they can get by without their fellow citizens. It makes them arrogant, the ancient Greeks argued, just as too little money makes the poor feel desperate, irresponsible, and not apt to care about the good of the country as a whole. If some people grow rich while others grow poor, both the rich and the poor are likely to doubt whether there really is a common good; they cease to have much in common. "It is the duty of a genuine democracy," Aristotle wrote, "to see that the many are not excessively poor. . . . [M]easures should be taken to ensure a permanent level of prosperity." And Aristotle went on to advocate a form of welfare.[20]

For a democracy, the ancient Greeks thought, it would even be better for everyone to be poor if that helped them feel they shared a common good. Democracy does not demand economic equality, but it does require a sense of community and equal dignity. To secure the sense of belonging together, democracy must be willing to choose between allowing wealth to be concentrated in a few hands and achieving the good of society as a whole.[21]

In the ancient view, democracy depends on, and hopes to produce, good citizens who participate in public life. It gives us political liberty, but it depends on the self-control of individuals. We must restrain our private desires in order to promote the common good. We must accept limits to wealth in the interest of the community and restrict the size of the state to achieve greater participation by citizens. Democracy is not an easy form of government, but a stern and demanding one. The French philosopher Rousseau, a friend of popular government, suspected that democracy was suited only to a "nation of gods," not one composed of "mere men."[22]

Madison and the Strategy of Fragmentation

The Framers and Individual Liberty

The framers of the American Constitution rejected the ancient theory of democracy in almost every detail. Alexander Hamilton noticed at the Constitutional Convention that those delegates who favored the greatest role for the people in the new government were as aware as any of the shortcomings of democracy.[23]

For the ancients, human beings were political animals and the chief value of democracy was the chance it gave citizens to participate in public life. The framers of the Constitution saw human beings as "naturally free"—as separate from one another as their bodies. The framers *aimed to protect individual liberty,* not to produce civic virtue. "The first object of government," Madison declared, is protecting the "diversity in the faculties of men."[24]

Alexander Hamilton, a framer of the Constitution, favored a strong central government. *(Library of Congress)*

The ancient Greeks certainly recognized the need for a state to have many different kinds of people because a variety of skills was needed for the good life. But Plato and Aristotle worried that if people were too specialized in their interests, the political society might become fragmented and leave individuals without a sense of the common good, like parts that are unaware of the whole.[25] It is worth repeating that the ancients saw individual freedom as a dangerous idea that had to be restrained in the interests of political freedom, equal citizenship, and rule by all. The framers turned this idea upside-down and elevated individual liberty to first place in political society. Rather than try to limit fragmentation, Madison hoped to make it work to the advantage of a political system dedicated to preserving and fostering private freedom.

All human beings, as the framers understood them, seek to do as they like. By nature, the framers argued, we follow our desires. Most important in their view was the desire for self-preservation. But nature frustrates us. It will not let us do what we want, certainly not without work, and sometimes not at all. In the end, nature kills us. Human beings, in the framers' "new science of politics," are involved in a struggle with nature, and the mastery of nature is the natural aim of all human beings.

Our neighbors frustrate us only a little less than nature does. They will not give us what we want or do what we command. In fact, they make demands on us. They threaten our lives and our property, and they obstruct our aims. We either begin in a "state of war" with others or we very quickly get to that point.

James Madison and the other framers modified the ancients' theory of democracy to suit eighteenth-century ideas of the "science of politics." *(Library of Congress)*

The Social Contract and "Consent of the Governed"

English philosophers like Thomas Hobbes and John Locke, whose writings influenced Madison and the other framers of the Constitution, argued that people come to recognize that this "war of all against all" gets people nowhere. If people are always in danger, they lack the time and the energy to get the better of nature. Logically, individuals are better off joining with others, giving up a portion of their natural liberty to a government in order to better enjoy that portion of their liberties that they do not surrender to government. This social contract theory tells us that government is a device that we invent to protect or enhance *private* interests and rights.

Governments are based on the "consent of the governed," but that does not mean they must be democratic. We can consent to any regime that we think will protect our rights. Political participation is not necessary if we believe that our rights are secure without it. For example, we can choose representatives to protect our interests, leaving us free to pursue our private interest, which is what concerns us the most. Representatives are probably more knowledgeable than we are, and they are more likely to see the "big picture." Representative government is a definite improvement on ancient democracy in the framers' view. Even representative government, however, presents certain problems.

All governments restrict our liberty, and we set them up only when we have to. "What is government itself," Madison asked, "but the greatest of all reflections on human nature?"[26] By this he meant that we always have to be on guard in case government tries to restrict our private rights and interests. Even elected representatives might "betray the interests of the people."[27] The framers' theory does not necessarily lead to democracy, and it certainly discourages the sort of public-spirited citizenship that the ancient Greeks emphasized.

English philosopher John Locke (1632–1704) argued the need for each individual to sacrifice a small portion of freedom so that all might enjoy the benefits of an orderly society. *(Library of Congress)*

Majority Rule and Majority Faction

The framers did think, however, that certain democratic institutions were desirable. Majority rule, which Madison called "the republican principle," protects us against the tyranny of minorities and helps give the government the support necessary to "control the governed." Madison saw the control of the governed as a priority in designing a government.[28] Since people change their minds, we also need elections on a regular basis to ensure that government has the support of the majority.

However, the majority can be tyrannical toward the minority. In fact, if we accept the framers' theory of human nature, we would be surprised if the majority did not become selfish and seek to ride roughshod over the minority. How can the majority, and the government that represents it, be forced to control itself?

George Washington addresses the Constitutional Convention in 1787. The Convention lasted just over three months, and only fifty-five delegates actually attended. *(Library of Congress)*

The Large States and Political Pluralism

Madison and Hamilton argued that the majority can be controlled without a loss of individual freedom, in a large and diverse republic. Small states are undesirable, in the framers' view, because they are weak, unable to preserve themselves, and lack the ability to get the better of nature. Small democracies are especially dangerous. In a **pure democracy**—that is, a democracy in which people rule through direct vote—Madison argued, the majority will probably be tempted to oppress minorities and to silence people whose opinions they oppose; and they will use government to achieve this, since government will be a tool of the majority. In pure democracies, then, people and their property are not safe; violence results, and the government is doomed.

Even **representative government**—in which people rule through elected representatives—in a small state will not help very much because the smaller the state the fewer will be the parties and interests. In Madison's mind this meant that it would be easier to form an oppressive majority because fewer people and interests are needed to put a majority together.

In a large state, Madison argues, the case is different:

> Extend the sphere, and you take in a greater variety of parties and interests; you make it less probable that a majority of the whole will have a common motive to invade the rights of other citizens; or if such a common motive exists, it will be more difficult for all who feel it to discover their own strength, and to act in unison. . . .[29]

Madison, in short, makes two arguments in favor of a large, diverse state. First, in such a state, any majority must be composed of many factions and interests and is not likely to agree about much or for very long. In 1976,

Jimmy Carter won most of the Northeastern states, which were concerned about their loss of industry to the South and Southwest. But Carter's majority also included some of the Sunbelt states, most notably Texas and Florida. Neither group alone could have given Carter a majority. In 1980, Ronald Reagan sought to build a majority including blue-collar trade unionists and antiunion conservatives. This sort of majority, Madison observed, is limited by the conflicts and divisions within it. Add size and complexity, then, and you make it harder to assemble an oppressive majority.

In 1980, Ronald Reagan attracted support from both pro- and antiunion forces—groups normally at odds with each other. Such coalitions have occurred many times in American history, but rarely last until the next election. *(Wide World Photos)*

Privatization

Second, Madison argued, groups find it hard to communicate and organize in a large state. It is difficult enough for us, spread out over a vast country, to find out that many other Americans share some idea or interest of ours. Even if we can locate those who agree with us, we must get them to make a commitment to us and to the cause we favor. Such commitment involves, for example, paying dues, volunteering time, and following the strategies of the organization's leaders. We will learn more about this problem in Chapter 7 when we discuss interest groups.

The stronger our commitments, the stronger our organization will be. But how much time and money will we give up to people who are, after all, strangers to us? An organization finds it easier to win strong loyalties and intense commitments if it is small, the kind of group in which we know the other members, where we can be heard and where we feel we matter. But a small, committed group is likely to be too weak to matter much in a large state. The other side of the coin is that groups large enough to matter will not get much loyalty or allegiance from individuals.

The partial exception to this rule was clear in 1787. Gouverneur Morris told the Constitutional Convention that a large state favors the rich, since the people are scattered and disorganized and the rich have better information and are more likely to be in contact with each other.[30] The rich, in other words, are one kind of small group with enough resources to matter, at least potentially. Madison was willing for the rich to have this advantage in protecting their private liberty, since he expected that the majority, composed of those who were not rich, would be hostile to them. Moreover, Madison thought that there were enough differences of opinion and interest among the rich so that they would not trust each other enough to cooperate for very long.

In the overwhelming majority of cases, Madison argued, if individuals support large parties and interests, their support will not be very intense; they will reserve their strongest loyalties and concerns for themselves and those closest to them. The framers saw Americans as private people divided into many families and small groups, each of them too weak to affect the republic as a whole. They would be law-abiding, or at least orderly, without being forced to be so. As Madison wrote, "The reason of man, like man himself, is timid and cautious when left alone. . . ."[31] Powerlessness in political life would not greatly trouble most citizens, as the framers saw them, because people were really concerned with private life, which they would be free to pursue and in which they would be reasonably secure.

The Division of Powers

Of course, the framers recognized that America would not be quite that simple. The states and local communities gave individuals the chance to form associations with those they knew, in small groups and communities in which each individual was relatively important. The framers felt that they could weaken or overcome such groups, at least with the passing of time. They insisted on the "division of powers" between states and the central or federal government. They wanted the federal government, in its sphere of power, to be able to speak directly to individual citizens rather than have to speak through the state governments. This direct access would make individuals aware of the federal government and, by showing them the limits of the state's power, make them less willing to rely on the state. The citizens' loyalties would thus be divided, and the federal government would have a chance to appeal to "those passions which have the strongest influence upon the human heart."[32]

THE STRATEGY OF FRAGMENTATION In any case, the framers' design was clear. They followed a strategy of **fragmentation**—that is, dividing the loyalties of citizens and limiting their commitment to any one group or association. Politics would be calm and impartial, and the republic would be composed of fundamentally private individuals. In one sense, America would be a democracy. "Rule by the people" could be trusted as a means for *deciding conflicts* because the majority would not be too extreme in its views. The framers did not value or desire, however, the kind of democracy in which citizens, acting in common, *define* the just and unjust. That sort of democracy requires the kind of public-spirited citizen that the ancient Greeks wanted—the kind of citizen for whom the common life is more important than merely private interests. The framers rejected that sort of democracy because they believed it was impractical, since human beings could not be trusted to be just or enlightened. They also thought it undesirable, since human beings were naturally selfish and should be left as free as possible to pursue their own interests. The framers preferred to leave individuals alone rather than to elevate them.

Tocqueville and the Strategy of Aggregation

The Critics of the Framers

The framers had many opponents and critics in America. When the Constitution was submitted to the states, the anti-Federalists battled against it, often borrowing arguments from the ancient Greek philosophers—insisting on a democracy based on small and stable communities where citizens could know one another and their leaders.[33] Anti-Federalist spokespersons argued for institutions that would make it easy for citizens to seek and win office. Political participation, in this view, builds character and is "one of the principal securities of a free people."[34] Thomas Jefferson favored the Constitution, but he shared many of the anti-Federalists' doubts and concerns.

Despite the strength of this opposition, the Constitution was a decisive defeat for the ancient science of politics. Under the Constitution, the larger society would gradually replace the smaller, through the growth of commerce and industry if not through formal political institutions. Americans would, more and more, think in national terms rather than in terms of small, intimate communities.

Thomas Jefferson saw the practical need for the Constitution, though he preferred a government with more popular involvement in political life. *(Library of Congress)*

Jacksonian Democracy

Less than fifty years after the Constitution was adopted, however, the presidency of Andrew Jackson signaled the beginning of an era during which American political institutions became more fully democratic. Laws in the states that required a person to own property in order to vote virtually disappeared, and "universal suffrage" (for white males) became the rule. Mass political parties organized the voters, and ordinary citizens found it easier to run for public office. The "spoils system" made its appearance, and government employees who were not loyal to the party in power were fired and replaced with those who supported the victorious party. Increasing numbers of offices were made elective, often on an annual basis.

Jacksonian democracy has been explained in many ways,* but Alexis de Tocqueville, the great French observer, recognized two crucial aspects of the Jacksonian era. First, it reflected a passionate, almost desperate, desire on the part of large numbers of the people for political participation and democratic citizenship. Without politics, Tocqueville wrote, the American would feel "robbed of one half of his existence." Second, Tocqueville saw that this enthusiasm for political life differed from ancient ideas of citizenship because it was a response to *mass* politics, politics in a large state with a numerous people. America was a new kind of democracy and could only be understood by a "new science of politics," different from both the political science of the ancient Greeks and that of the framers of the Constitution.[35]

The Tyranny of the Majority

In large states, Tocqueville argued, democracy can be vulnerable to the "tyranny of the majority." The framers, of course, had worried about majority factions and set about to make it impossible for such majorities to oppress their opponents. Tocqueville, however, was less concerned about a majority of the people actually organizing to oppress others than he was about "an affair of the mind." He feared psychological oppression by the majority, which would intimidate people.[36]

The idea of equality, Tocqueville observed, denies the authority of one individual over another. When someone tries to tell me what to do, the idea of equality gives me the power to ask, "Who do you think you are?" It allows me to say, "I am just as good as you are and I have a right to my opinion." In the relations of one person with another, equality is a liberating idea that encourages independence.

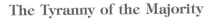

*For two conflicting views, see Arthur Schlesinger, Jr., *The Age of Jackson* (Boston: Little, Brown, 1945), and Lee Benson, *The Concept of Jacksonian Democracy* (Princeton, N.J.: Princeton U.P., 1961).

But when one person faces a group, the effect of equality is different. Equality seems to imply that if one person is as good as another, then many people are better than one. If I oppose the opinion of the group or if I tell it to do something it dislikes, I am likely to be asked, "Who do you think you are? What gives you the right to stand in our way? Do you imagine that you are better than we are?" Equality liberates us in our relations with individuals, but it tends to make it harder for us to oppose a group.

Equality in Small Societies

In the small society, as Tocqueville knew, we can see the majority as no more than so many individuals grouped together. Instead of seeing "the majority," I see Tom, Dick, and Sarah—people with names and faults, each of whom is no better than I. Equality permits me to ignore the opinion of each of these individuals. As a result, it lets me ignore the collective opinion of "the majority." Small communities, Tocqueville commented, "have therefore ever been the cradle of political liberty." Individual citizens in small communities know they matter, and they are likely to have concern for the common good. In small communities, Tocqueville admitted, people are often nosy and pry into one another's private lives, interfering with and trying to control "minute details" and the "arrangements of domestic life." Nevertheless, Tocqueville argued, local tyrannies are limited in their power to oppress us. They are easy to overthrow and easier to escape.[37]

In other words, Tocqueville reverses the framers' argument. The weakness of small states is an advantage, since it limits tyrants and the ambition of individuals. Small states are unstable and disorderly, and according to Tocqueville, this suggests that they allow a good deal of freedom. He is speaking of *political* freedom—the citizens' freedom to speak, act, and share in ruling. This kind of freedom promotes the kind of civic virtue of which the ancient Greeks approved. In the interest of political liberty and freedom, Tocqueville is willing to accept a good deal of limitation on, and interference with, *private* liberty.

It is far easier, as Tocqueville knew, to achieve private liberty in large states where people don't meddle with my private life. In the first place, I do not matter enough, in a large state, to be worth much attention on the part of others, and in any case, their time is taken up with "great projects" that would be impossible in a small state. In a large state, ambition takes our attention away from relations between people. In America, as we know, a "career" tempts people to neglect their families. In small communities, that kind of ambition cannot take us far away from home, and a business is rarely big enough to demand all of our time. Since the framers were concerned about promoting private liberty, it was certainly reasonable of them to prefer a large state.

Large States and Majority Tyranny

A large democracy, however, has its own problems. With so many people, it is far more difficult to oppose the majority. In a small community, I may hope to change enough votes by my own efforts to transform a minority into a majority. If I lived in a place with only 100 voters and the vote was 60 to 40, I would only need to change the minds of 11 voters to win. In a large state, however, it is almost impossible for me to reverse a majority by myself. In a country where 70 million people vote, a narrow majority of 51 percent would mean that I would have to win over 700,000 people to affect the result, a goal well beyond the resources of most of us. People who favor the use of referenda and other forms of "direct democracy" that allow voters to approve or reject laws in the voting booth rather than have the laws enacted in the legislature sometimes forget that this kind of system gives a great advantage to those with the money and organization to influence large numbers of people.

When we face a majority that is very large and well organized, we feel that we must accept what it wants and adjust to it.[38] In mass democracies, this sort of conformity goes beyond simply going along with the majority. Equality tends to make it hard for me to think differently. If few people share my views and so many hold the opposite position, I may begin to doubt that my contrary ideas have any value at all. Experiments in social psychology have demonstrated that individuals put in the position of disagreeing with a strong, consistent majority tend even to doubt the evidence of their senses.[39]

Can the "rule of the people" under such circumstances really produce a valid judgment on what is just or unjust? Under tyranny of the majority, people cannot really deliberate; they are too busy trying to guess what their neighbors think, "one leaning on another and all together on nothing," as Henry David Thoreau put it.[40] Public debate can decide controversies according to prevailing ideas, but it cannot seriously question those ideas.

Individualism and Tyranny of the Majority

Individualism, Tocqueville observed, is no answer to tyranny of the majority. In fact, individualism simply mirrors the tyranny of the majority and even makes it stronger. In the first place, mass democracy makes individuals feel weak and unimportant. In the smaller, private circle of our friends and families, individuals do matter, and they find a dignity that public life does not give them. People in mass democracies are inclined to be individualistic and devoted to private life because political groups and public life make them feel unimportant. To that extent, *individualism is a compensation for the pain of mass society*.

Second, the only way in which we can resist the tyranny of the majority is to combine with others, pooling our resources until we feel strong enough to make a difference. But the "art of association," as Tocqueville called it, means that we must trust people, and political organizing is hard work. Individualism tells us to reject dependence on others, to distrust organization, and to "go it alone." In mass democracy, however, "going it alone" means that we are isolated and vulnerable so that we tend to "go along." In this sense, *individualism adds to the power of majority tyranny*.

As America grew larger and more complicated, Tocqueville predicted, both individualism and the tyranny of the majority were likely to grow stronger. As society grows bigger, we tend to feel smaller, and we are more eager to retreat into private life. This will be especially true because political organizing will grow more difficult. In a bigger society, we have to organize more people and more resources in order to make a difference. The art of association demands more trust and more skill, and we are not likely to have either.

In the end, Tocqueville feared that isolated individuals would come to feel no real bonds of trust or love for anyone. They would, then, be free from all dependence, but imprisoned in the solitudes of their own hearts, hopelessly unable to resist the tyranny of the majority.[41]

Limits to Majority Tyranny

Combining individual freedom and private weakness is precisely the strategy of fragmentation that Madison urged in the hope of uniting private freedom and public order. As Tocqueville saw it, however, Madison had overrated the extent to which human beings are "free" and underrated the extent to which they are political, in need of the encouragement and support of others. Madison tended to assume that human beings are free if they are left alone; Tocqueville argued that those who are alone in a large state are not free at all. Madison wanted to free us from physical restraints, but Tocqueville contended that the really important restraints on liberty are psychological, the limits imposed by our insecurities and fears. As Tocqueville saw it, in protecting us against the tyranny of a visible majority, the framers left us vulnerable to the oppressions of an invisible one, liberating the bodies of Americans only to risk enslaving their spirits.

However, Tocqueville saw several aspects of American life that limited tyranny of the majority. American "manners"—the customs and culture of the people—made American institutions less harmful. Democracy in America was improved, Tocqueville thought, by *religion* and *local community*.[42]

Religion Religion, Tocqueville observed, limited the power of the tyranny of the majority to trespass on "the moral world" of America. Religion represented a law beyond human power or legislation. When the law of the country "permits the Americans to do what they please," Tocqueville wrote, "religion prevents them from conceiving and forbids them to commit what is rash or unjust."[43]

Religion gave even the loneliest Americans a sense that they were not alone, that they mattered in the Divine scheme of things, and that they had an immortal dignity that public opinion could not destroy. Americans who might otherwise have gone along with the majority might oppose it where God commanded: "Dare to be a Daniel," one hymn goes, "dare to stand alone."

Tocqueville argued against an official religion because, in his experience, state support for the church weakened religious commitment. Tocqueville, however, found it almost impossible to imagine democracy existing without religion.

Local Community Local communities were a second vital limit to tyranny of the majority because they permitted political participation. Tocqueville

Americans may not be as influenced by religion today as during Tocqueville's time; nevertheless, religion continues to play an important role in both our history and our private lives. *(Tony Korody/Sygma)*

looked upon the argument of the ancient Greeks in favor of small political states as an attractive ideal, but he doubted that such places were really possible in the modern world.[44] Self-governing localities within a large country would preserve as much of the ancient ideal of citizenship as is possible in modern times, in Tocqueville's view.

In local government, each individual citizen matters more. Active participation—talking or holding office—is much easier. Locally, in fact, we are sometimes forced to participate as jurors, a fact which impressed Tocqueville.[45] In their own towns, citizens could learn at first hand the benefits of political life—fellowship and a sense of shaping one's destiny. Locally, public life can be a source of dignity rather than something that takes it away from us. In all their community organizations, whether public (like the jury or local government) or private (like church organizations, charities, or civic groups), Tocqueville saw participation leading Americans to feel the connection between their own interests and those of a larger group.

Of course, local politics—even when local communities mattered a good deal more than they do today—was rarely a life or death matter, and local patriotism might well be selfish. But the relative unimportance of local politics made local communities suited to be places for learning the art of association. Locally, people could make mistakes (which are always a part of learning), without endangering America as a whole. Even a few bad states and localities, and there have always been some, would probably not fatally harm the country. The localities taught Americans at least a modest civic virtue, "self-interest rightly understood" in contrast to the individualism they were likely to learn elsewhere in American society. He saw the source

Many local communities still provide important political arenas for those Americans who choose to be involved. Here at a public hearing in Pennsylvania the Delaware Water Project is debated between the commission members *(right)* and concerned citizens. *(Tom Kelly)*

of Americans' devotion to the republican form of government in the town and provincial governments of colonial days and believed that the public spirit of the country as a whole was nothing more than the sum of the local pride and patriotism of the many towns and villages.[46]

Political Parties Tocqueville did not admire American political parties, but they did serve to limit majority tyranny and to teach citizenship. Before Tocqueville came to America, Jefferson had reached similar conclusions about the value of local communities. He worried, as Madison had, that local groups might be exclusive and narrow-minded, but Jefferson felt that this could be moderated if not overcome. In small groups, citizens would know and would be likely to choose the best leaders, the "natural aristocracy" of the community. Citizens were likely to trust leaders they knew personally, and those leaders, in turn, could be united to other leaders. This group of leaders could select their "natural aristocracy" as delegates to a still higher body until a chain of personal relationships connected the federal government to the local ward.[47] The ability of the federal government to see things in larger perspective would be communicated to the towns and cities by a chain of personal friendships. This would serve to explain to the local communities their stake in the national issues and problems and encourage them to support the common good.

Traditional political parties in America were built along the lines of this vision of Jefferson's (although Jefferson himself had little fondness for political parties). The chain of personal relationships did create a bond between leaders and followers and made citizens feel, when "our people" were in power, that they had some share in ruling. Both Jefferson's relatively elitist party and Jackson's mass party began as coalitions of "outsiders," suspicious of government and eager to restrict its authority, but once "their people" were in power, they too took a more positive view of federal power.

Voters were less fearful of governmental power when they were assured that those in power shared their feelings and would use that power in ways they approved. At the same time, loyalty to a party often gave the individual the strength needed to resist the tyranny of the majority. It helps Republicans to resist majority views if they can see them as nothing more than Democratic doctrine, and the same holds true for Democrats in Republican communities. Traditional political parties in America did not teach great philosophies, but they trained people in some ordinary political virtues vital to mass democracies.

Tocqueville saw some implications in mass politics that the framers seemed not to have noticed. He followed his argument to its pessimistic conclusion; in so doing, he told Americans that their customs, churches, and communities were very important to them. Tocqueville reminded us that a political society is not just a collection of formal laws and institutions alone. At the heart of a political society is the character of its citizens.

Contemporary Democracy in America

All three versions of democracy—the ancient Greek ideal, Madison's scheme for fragmentation, and Tocqueville's critique of mass democracy—have influenced political thought and institutions in America. All these conflicting ideas can be heard in contemporary politics, often from the same speaker. There is little doubt, however, that contemporary America resembles Madison's design more than either of the other theories. There is not much room for the citizen in modern America.

The Inequality of Wealth

To a great many critics, economic inequality makes American democracy a fraud. Certainly, the inequality of wealth in modern America is enormous. The framers could not imagine the distinctions between rich and poor that exist today. In the years since World War II, we have reduced the amount of poverty in America, but chiefly by government programs that transfer money to poor people. These government programs, in other words, reduced the effect of economic inequality but not inequality itself. Ronald Reagan's policies, moreover, have once again increased the numbers of the poor and accentuated economic inequality. (See Table 1.1.) Clearly, the inequality of wealth has important consequences for American politics. Socialists and others on the political left, for example, have had no trouble in showing that although the rich are not numerous, their influence on policy is much greater than that of the many who are less well-off, that they find it easier to be heard, and that they have an advantage in seeking office that most of us do not enjoy.

This gives rise to two questions. First, inequality of wealth is great but is it excessive? The answers we give to that question will depend on our basic theories of democracy. A Madisonian, who regards government as a device to defend individual diversity, will tend to regard a great deal of inequality as acceptable or even desirable. To someone who regards government as intended to advance the common good, as the ancients and Tocqueville

TABLE 1.1 Shifts in the Income and Social Security Tax Burden, 1980–1984 (Factoring In the Effects of Inflation)

Income Class	Tax Increases from Social Security and Inflation	Net Tax Reduction from Tax Bills of 1981–1982	Net (+) Gain or (−) Loss
Below $10,000	$ 153	$ 58	$ −95
$10,000–20,000	573	387	−186
$20,000–30,000	1,020	882	−138
$30,000–40,000	1,587	1,465	−122
$40,000–50,000	2,346	2,210	−136
$50,000–75,000	3,407	3,305	−102
$75,000–100,000	4,855	5,258	+403
$100,000–200,000	5,979	8,248	+2,269
Above $200,000	7,579	24,982	+17,403

Source: Thomas Byrne Edsall, *The New Politics of Inequality*. New York: Norton, 1984, p. 205. (With thanks to Dr. Lois Vietri, University of Maryland.)

both did in different ways, inequality can be dangerous, especially since inequality between rich and poor may lead citizens to doubt whether the common good really exists.

If we decide that the gap between rich and poor is too great, how should we correct it? If we see citizens as fundamentally private beings, as Madisonian theory does, it will make sense to give them whatever money they need to live an adequate private life. This, evidently, is the theory behind many welfare measures. Supporters of the more political view held by Tocqueville and the ancients, by contrast, are likely to ask for the kind of programs that will make equal participation in civic life easier. Aristotle, for example, argued that grants to the poor should be large enough to enable them to make a start in farming or business because no citizen should be the permanent dependent of the state.[48] Tocqueville or Aristotle would also stress the need to make the poor feel that their conduct and contribution matter, probably by demanding that they give in good citizenship a fair return for what they get in money. Madisonians would be less inclined to meddle and would be more content with people who lived law-abiding, quiet lives.

During Ronald Reagan's first term, there was an increase in the number of Americans living in poverty. *(Jean-Louis Atlan/Sygma)*

The Inequality of Power

The inequality of wealth is a challenging problem, but it is really only the simplest part of a much more difficult problem, the inequality of power. In the first place, America is a vast state with hundreds of millions of people. Our national economy and politics are complicated and confusing, and involved in the lives and destinies of other nations. To understand or influence a society so large, we need organizations that are equally large, bringing together members and resources on a grand scale. The great organizations—the media, the trade unions, the private corporations, and the public agencies—that dominate our national scene create a gigantic inequality of power between ordinary citizens and the leaders and managers of these "private governments." To control, compete with, or regulate such mass organizations, we need still other large organizations, which become problems in their turn.[49]

When power is concentrated like this, it troubles all democratic theorists. Today's followers of Madison, however, are concerned with the number of such "power structures" and the relationships between them. So long as there are enough competing organizations to enable us to say that they "check and balance" or "countervail" one another, Madison's modern followers are happy.* The competition of interest groups becomes the new "self-regulating mechanism" that will guarantee that no group can rule and no majority coalition can be too cohesive.[50]

Many political scientists doubt whether, in practice, the great organizations do check and balance one another. In their view, the leaders of these organizations agree in broad terms about the way in which society should operate, and they differ and compete only on minor issues. As a result, elites can be said to dominate American politics. There is a great deal of difference between elite theorists, but they all deny that the pluralistic vision of contemporary Madisonianism is very realistic in the context of our modern political life.[51]

Even if the Madisonian view is accurate, the relationship of great organizations with one another is only part of the picture. A *world of mass organization and radically unequal power tends to demoralize and causes citizens to withdraw into their private lives*. Organizations large enough to have an impact on policy make their members feel unimportant as individuals in shaping the organization's policies. At best, a small fraction of the members of a mass organization can participate or share in its rule. Most people believe that they cannot change such "private governments," and they certainly cannot create alternatives to them. We either accept these mass organizations as they are or we do without.

We need the mass media, for example, but ordinary citizens are not in a position to construct a new network rivaling ABC, NBC, and CBS or a major newspaper to compete with big city papers. Yet the leaders of the media make decisions that are crucial to our political life. (See Chapter 5.) They act like chairpersons who decide whether or not to recognize speakers. In 1980, the League of Women Voters decided that Congressman John Anderson's 15 percent support in some presidential polls entitled him to participate in the presidential debates the League intended to sponsor. The League also decided that reporters would not be allowed follow-up questions if they thought that the candidates answered wrongly or evasively. When two major networks decided to accept these terms, they became the rules of the game for any such debates. Similar decisions wrote the rules for debate in 1984. Citizens could decide to listen or not to listen; they could not argue for different terms.

*For one example, see John Kenneth Galbraith, *American Capitalism: The Concept of Countervailing Power* (Boston: Houghton, 1952).

Network leaders and decision makers in the mass media do pay attention to public opinion, but this opinion consists of individual, private decisions to view or not to view. We are making choices, but the alternatives are decided by others. For most of us, the media—like the trade unions, the great corporations, and other mass organizations—are useful, but they make us feel small, vulnerable, and dependent. We turn to smaller, private circles, as Tocqueville predicted. There are, for example, more and more small magazines and radio stations appealing to highly specialized audiences, and the new cable and satellite networks seem to be imitating this "narrowcasting." As Benjamin Barber writes,

> There are sports networks, black networks, Christian and Hispanic and business and game show and movie and porn networks—all aimed at audiences who will never again be required to share a common channel or talk to one another.[52]

Our personal interests and our private tastes get a good deal of attention, but our public interests and our common culture get short shrift, and political life, to a growing number of Americans, seems overwhelming.

The Decline of Local Community

The inequality of power, in other words, contributes to feelings of unequal dignity. To make matters worse, we can no longer rely on the protections against tyranny of the majority that Tocqueville saw in nineteenth-century America. Religion has less influence than it did when Tocqueville wrote. Local communities are less important in economic and political life, and we have grown less attached to them. (Americans move much more often than they did in the past, and increasing numbers of Americans take up residence in a home and community expecting to leave them in the not-so-distant future.) Attachments to political parties appear to be weakening along with loyalties to the local communities. These tendencies, and others like them, will be addressed in greater detail later in this book.

Tocqueville would doubtless urge us to limit the growth of mass organizations, where we can, and to strengthen local communities as much as possible. We might hope, thereby, to rebuild some of the foundations of democratic manners and mutual respect.[53] It seems clear, however, that as things stand today we live much more private lives, and even the family seems in danger. We are freer as private individuals, but we often feel lonely and often wonder if our lives have meaning.

The Challenge of Democracy

How democratic is America today? And how well can American institutions and politics deal with the problems of our times?

Contemporary followers of Madison urge us to be content with private liberty. As they remind us, individual freedoms are no small blessing in a world where dictatorship and totalitarian regimes sometimes seem to be the rule. Moreover, Madisonian theorists observe, in America the people still decide. Liberal democracy has its shortcomings, they admit, but in our world it may be the best that we can do.

We think that America can and must do better than that; the Madisonian version of democracy is not enough. Political fragmentation and private liberty are hollow or cruel to all too many Americans. Factions that seek to block change, most notably the wealthy and the corporate elite, find the Madisonian system to their liking. For the disadvantaged, American government is frustrating at best, disillusioning at worst. Individualism is little comfort to those, like women and racial minorities, who need the help of government to overcome the injustices of the past.

Many Americans want an active government capable of pursuing coherent policies to contend with new, grinding economic problems and the threat of thermonuclear war. Millions of Americans, moreover, are not content to choose between alternatives: the choices are too narrow, and the alternatives themselves too exclusive. Many questions never reach the public agenda. Others, like Vietnam or energy conservation, get there late, so that our only choices are painful, needlessly costly in money and human agony. Deciding, on this basis, does not feel at all like ruling. That so many Americans are cynical and bitter toward their own government testifies to the need for some ability to define public questions and choices based on our ideas of what is just and what is unjust. American democracy must ask how far, in our times, it can be brought into line with the ancient ideal of citizenship.

We began this chapter with Lincoln's challenge to the United States, because it seems to us that he speaks to our times as truly as he did to his own. In our examination of American politics and institutions, we will be arguing that the United States was indeed "conceived in liberty," but the well-being of the country and of democracy require us to go beyond the individualism and fragmentation that were Madison's key terms in the definition of freedom. Americans need to find ways to make the liberty of each of us compatible with the dignity of all of us. We need to emphasize the "arts of association" drawing citizens together for public purposes and for the common life.

SUMMARY

Democracy is "rule by the people," which suggests that citizens have the opportunity to define alternatives as well as to decide between them. In a democracy citizens are believed to be capable of understanding the first principles of ruling as well as any ruler and of applying those principles to practice.

The nature of any democracy depends on its definition of citizenship. Our law grants citizenship to those born on American soil. Ethnicity is not generally a test of citizenship; a willingness to accept America's political creed is. Thus, democracy rests on a set of common principles.

A democracy is also characterized by the way in which majority rule and minority rights are combined. It depends on the willingness of a strong minority to accept the rule of the majority.

A review of the ancient Greek brand of democracy indicates how far the framers of our Constitution digressed from it. To the ancients, democracy was tantamount to citizenship, which meant a willingness both to rule and be ruled. Civic virtue was superior to individual freedom; the pursuit of private good could only disrupt society. Small communities offered a climate conducive to democracy by giving citizens the opportunity to participate more fully in public life. Extremes of wealth and poverty could not be tolerated in a democracy without destroying the belief that a common good exists.

The difference between the ancients' notion of democracy and the framers' has to do with their theories of the human condition. Madison and the other framers saw humans as naturally free and sought to protect their individual liberties. According to the social contract theory, people must render up to government only that portion of their liberty necessary to protect the rest of their freedom. Political participation is not necessary—we can choose representatives to defend our interests.

Madison considered majority rule desirable because it protected against the tyranny of minorities and gave government the power to control the governed. The tyranny of the majority would be prevented in a republic composed of diverse interests, which would act as checks upon one another.

The framers' design was to divide the loyalties of citizens and limit their commitments to any one group. The majority would decide conflicts through the compromise achieved between a large number of interest groups, but the majority would not be entrusted with the power to define the just and the unjust.

The Frenchman Alexis de Tocqueville saw that private liberty was easier to protect in large states, where no individual is worth much attention, but he also believed that in a large state it was more difficult to oppose the majority. Individualism was a compensation for the alienation brought about by mass society. Tocqueville predicted that as America grew, so would individualism and the tyranny of the majority. In a bigger society, political organizing was more difficult. Those with money would have the resources to organize and would therefore have the loudest voice.

America's contemporary government resembles Madison's model more than that of the ancient Greeks or Tocqueville. A political regime set up to defend individual liberty will tolerate the sort of economic inequality that typifies our system far more easily than a government intended primarily to advance the common good.

The uneven distribution of wealth is only part of a larger problem, that of the inequality of power. In a world of mass organizations—the media, corporations, trade unions, and public agencies—citizens are allowed to make choices, but the alternatives are decided by others. The tide of cynicism that characterizes American feeling toward government has steadily increased, and if we are to stem it, we must be able to redefine public questions and choices based on our ideas of what is just and what is unjust.

NOTES

1. Gunnar Myrdal, *An American Dilemma* (New York: Harper, 1944), vol. I, p. xliii.
2. *Roe* v. *Wade,* 410 U.S. 113 (1973).
3. Benjamin Barber, *Strong Democracy* (Berkeley: U. of California, 1984), p. 182.
4. *Grove City College* v. *Bell,* 52 LW 4283, Feb. 28, 1984.
5. *Scott* v. *Sandford,* 19 How. 393 (1857).
6. *Korematsu* v. *U.S.,* 323 U.S. 214 (1945).
7. G. K. Chesterton, *What I Saw in America* (New York: Dodd, 1922), p. 14.
8. *U.S.* v. *Wong Kim Ark.,* 169 U.S. 649 (1898).
9. Chesterton, p. 7.
10. Robert Bellah, *The Broken Covenant* (New York: Seabury, 1975).
11. *Trop* v. *Dulles,* 356 U.S. 86 (1958).
12. Alexander Hamilton, James Madison, and John Jay, *The Federalist,* no. 79.
13. James S. Young, *The Washington Community, 1800–1828* (New York: Columbia U. P., 1966), p. 19.
14. Aristotle, *Politics.* Ernest Barker, trans. (Oxford: Clarendon, 1952), p. 93.
15. Ibid., pp. 5, 11.
16. Ibid., p. 258; see also Delba Winthrop, "Aristotle on Participatory Democracy," *Polity,* 11 (1978), pp. 151–71.
17. Aristotle, p. 258.
18. Ibid., p. 105.
19. Ibid., p. 192; see also Bertrand de Jouvenel, "The Chairman's Problem," *American Political Science Review,* 55 (1961), pp. 368–72.
20. Aristotle, pp. 268–69.
21. Ibid., pp. 63–68, 209, 232.
22. J. J. Rousseau, *The Social Contract,* Book III, chap. 4.
23. James Madison, *Notes on Debates in the Federal Convention* (Athens: Ohio U. P., 1966), p. 134.
24. *The Federalist,* no. 10; see also no. 39.
25. Aristotle, pp. 118–20.
26. *The Federalist,* no. 51.
27. Ibid., no. 10.
28. Ibid., no. 10, no. 51.
29. All three quotations are from *The Federalist,* no. 10.
30. Madison, *Notes on Debates,* p. 235; see also p. 194.
31. *The Federalist,* no. 49.

32. Ibid., no. 16.
33. Cecilia Kenyon, ed., *The Anti-Federalists* (Indianapolis: Bobbs, 1966), pp. xcii, 154, 208, 210, 263, 309.
34. Ibid., pp. 148, 310, 312.
35. Alexis de Tocqueville, *Democracy in America* (New York: Schocken, 1961), vol. 1, pp. lxxiii, 293.
36. Ibid., vol. 1, pp. 309–11.
37. Ibid., vol. 1, pp. 176–77.
38. James Bryce, *The American Commonwealth* (New York: Commonwealth, 1908), vol. 2, pp. 358–77.
39. Solomon E. Asch, *Social Psychology* (Englewood Cliffs, N.J.: Prentice-Hall, 1952), chap. 16.
40. Henry David Thoreau, "Life without Principle," *Atlantic Monthly*, 12 (1863), pp. 484–95.
41. Tocqueville, vol. 2, pp. 118–20.
42. Ibid., vol. 1, pp. 354–55, 383.
43. Ibid., vol. 1, pp. 362, 499; see also pp. 355–73.
44. Ibid., vol. 1, p. 179.
45. Ibid., vol. 1, pp. 331–39.
46. Ibid., vol. 1, p. 181.
47. Adrienne Koch and William Peden, eds., *The Life and Selected Writings of Thomas Jefferson* (New York: Modern Library, 1944), pp. 660–62, 676.
48. Aristotle, p. 269.
49. Grant McConnell, *Private Power and American Democracy* (New York: Knopf, 1966).
50. Theodore J. Lowi, *The End of Liberalism* (New York: Norton, 1969).
51. Peter Bachrach, *The Theory of Democratic Elitism: A Critique* (Boston: Little, Brown, 1967).
52. Benjamin R. Barber, "The Tide in New Channels," *The New York Times* (April 21, 1982). This is especially true since the Supreme Court ruled, in 1979, that the Federal Communications Commission may *not* require cable companies to provide equal access.
53. David Price, "Community, 'Mediating Structures' and Public Policy," *Soundings*, 62 (1979), pp. 369–94.

CHAPTER 2

Constitutionalism and the Constitution

Now two centuries old, the American Constitution is a wonder of the political world. In his inaugural address in 1981, Ronald Reagan referred to the orderly change of government under the Constitution as a miracle. So it is, when compared to most countries. Yet Americans, though they often congratulate themselves on the Constitution, usually take it for granted. In part, they do so because the Constitution has worked so well, but it is also true that the framers of the Constitution helped to convince Americans that it can take care of itself. The Constitution reflects the framers' strategy of fragmentation and their conviction that a constitution ought to be, as far as possible, a machine in which political forces are automatically corrected and kept in place by **checks and balances.** The system of checks and balances results from the framers' division of power among three branches of government: the executive, the legislative, and the judicial.

In this chapter, however, we will be arguing that the Constitution is more than formal institutions and mechanisms. It rests, to a very great extent, on the political culture and civic character of the people—their beliefs and values about how politics and government should be carried out, their customs, and their ways of living. The success of American constitutionalism results from the interaction between the formal Constitution (and the theory of the framers on which it is based) and other, quite different institutions and beliefs that are deeply rooted in our political life and culture. Sometimes, these two aspects of American constitutionalism reinforce one another, but often they are in conflict, sometimes mildly and sometimes bitterly. In either case, both the formal and informal sides of American constitutionalism are needed to explain constitutional government in the United States.

After examining the bases of our constitutional government, we will finish the chapter by looking at challenges to constitutional government in contemporary America. Our times do not make it easy for constitutional rule to succeed, and constitutionalism in the

The long history of orderly political change under the American Constitution is almost miraculous when compared with the rest of the world. This attempted coup in 1985 was the sixteenth that Thailand has experienced in the last fifty years. *(Richard Lucas/Gamma)*

United States feels the strains that this kind of government elsewhere in the world experiences. We will also argue, however, that some of the dangers we face today have been produced by a change in the political balance between the formal and informal features of American constitutionalism. We believe that many of today's problems result from the shortcomings of the framers' theory of constitutional government. Now, more than ever, self-regulating mechanisms are not enough. The American Constitution is rare and exceptional and, like priceless things, requires attention and care.

This is especially true because the Constitution is old, one of the few survivors of a bygone political world. The USS *Constitution,* "Old Ironsides," is still afloat only because it has been tended and maintained by skilled and dedicated craftsmen. The Constitution, our ship of state, depends on the care and maintenance provided by citizens who are equally skilled and dedicated. To make this argument, we need to examine (1) the nature of constitutional government, (2) the specific character of American constitutionalism, and (3) those aspects of life today that challenge and threaten constitutional government in the United States.

What Is a Constitution?

Limited Government

The first principle of constitutionalism is that political power must be limited. "All constitutional government," C. H. McIlwain observed, "is limited government."[1]

Constitutions limit the *goals* or ends a government may pursue as well as the *means* it may use. A **constitution**—usually a written document containing the basic ruling principles of a society—ordains legitimate means to the public purposes of a political society. In this sense, a constitution is not "above" politics: it sets forth a particular kind of politics, a political regime or a system of rule.

Constitutional Ends A constitution, in both its specific words and its broader meaning, defines the ends or essential values of a political society.* It is not difficult to discover such fundamental political values in our Constitution. It says that government gets its authority from the people, guarantees every state a "republican form of government," and prohibits Congress from granting titles of nobility. Put these three together and they show that one of our values is political equality. The Constitution also assumes that it is a good thing to promote commerce, especially by rules of trade that apply to all parts of the country.[2] In addition, the framers required that laws be made only after discussion and deliberation. Congress is a deliberative institution that requires also the president to present messages giving reasons for his policies. And though the framers valued political participation much less than did theorists like Aristotle or Tocqueville, the Bill of Rights grants the rights necessary for broad discussion, free speech, petition, and public assembly. Political goals like these are based on a more fundamental idea, the framers' theory that people are "naturally free." They possess individual liberties that cannot be taken from them and that are essential to the pursuit of happiness.

Critics of our Constitution make the argument that the liberty the Constitution affords is merely a negative liberty; although the people are free

*In fact, as Aristotle observed, every time human beings join in some kind of association, they have in mind the achievement of some good. (*Politics*, Ernest Barker trans., Oxford: Clarendon Press, 1952, p. 1)

POLITICAL PERSPECTIVE

CHIEF JUSTICE JOHN MARSHALL ON THE NATURE OF CONSTITUTIONAL GOVERNMENT

That the people have an original right to establish, for their future government, such principles as, in their opinion, shall most conduce to their own happiness is the basis on which the whole American fabric has been erected. The exercise of this original right is a very great exertion; nor can it, nor ought it, to be frequently repeated. The principles, therefore, so established, are deemed fundamental. And as the authority from which they proceed is supreme, and can seldom act, they are designed to be permanent.

This original and supreme will organizes the government and assigns to different departments their respective powers. It may either stop here, or establish certain limits not to be transcended by those departments.

The government of the United States is of the latter description. . . . To what purpose are powers limited, and to what purpose is that limitation committed to writing, if these limits may, at any time, be passed by those intended to be restrained? . . .

The Constitution is either a superior paramount law, unchangeable by ordinary means, or it is on a level with ordinary legislative acts . . . alterable when the legislature shall please to alter it.

If the former part of the alternative be true, then a legislative act contrary to the Constitution is not law; if the latter part be true, then written constitutions are absurd attempts on the part of the people to limit a power in its own nature illimitable.

Source: *Marbury* v. *Madison,* 1 Cranch 137 (1803).

Representative Framers of the United States Constitution

Following the Declaration of Independence, the thirteen states united politically under the Articles of Confederation, a credo that defined cooperation but declared "each state retains its Sovereignty, freedom, and independence." The problems of effectively governing a nation in accordance with such nonrestrictive principles became more and more apparent after 1777, and in 1786 Virginia invited the other states to a conference in Annapolis, Maryland, where a resolution was adopted to hold a convention in May 1787 to "render the Constitution of the Federal Government adequate to the exigencies of the Union." Of the delegates who participated in the convention, nine were particularly representative of the views that ultimately shaped the Constitution.

Signing of the Constitution by Thomas Prichard Rossiter (c. 1872). *(Courtesy Independence National Historical Park.)*

Benjamin Franklin, 1706–1790, Writer and Statesman, Pennsylvania. The oldest delegate attending the Convention, Franklin encouraged the spirit of compromise that made the Constitution possible.

***Benjamin Franklin* by Charles Willson Peale.**
(Courtesy the Historical Society of Pennsylvania.)

Alexander Hamilton, 1755–1804, Lawyer, New York. An advocate of a strong central government, Hamilton proposed a constitution on the British parliamentary model. He initiated the resolution at Annapolis in 1786 that produced the Constitutional Convention a year later.

***Alexander Hamilton* by John Trumbull.**
(Courtesy the National Portrait Gallery, Smithsonian Institution, Washington, D.C. Gift of Henry Cabot Lodge.)

***James Madison* by Chester Harding.**
(Courtesy the National Portrait Gallery, Smithsonian Institution, Washington, D.C.)

James Madison, 1751–1836, Planter, Virginia. Madison's study of political philosophy enabled him to take a leading role in the constitutional debates. His arguments for a strong central government to protect individual liberties won him the title "Father of the Constitution." After the Convention, he joined Alexander Hamilton in contributing to *The Federalist*, a collection of essays encouraging ratification of the Constitution by expounding the principles on which the Constitution was founded.

George Mason, 1725–1792, Planter, Virginia. An opponent of centralization of power and of any compromise on tariff and slave trade issues, Mason helped draft the Constitution but refused to sign it, primarily because the Convention document failed to provide a bill of rights.

George Mason **by D. W. Boudet.**
(Courtesy the Virginia Museum of Fine Arts.)

Gouverneur Morris, 1752–1816, Lawyer, Pennsylvania. A believer in the virtues of aristocracy and the perils of democratic rule, Morris argued for a strong central government and against concessions to slave trade. He was largely responsible for the final literary form of the Constitution.

Gouverneur Morris **by Sharples.**
(Courtesy the National Portrait Gallery, Smithsonian Institution, Washington, D.C.)

Edmund Randolph**, artist unknown.**
(Courtesy the Virginia State Library, Richmond, Virginia.)

Edmund Randolph, 1753–1816, Lawyer, Virginia. Although the version of the Constitution finally adopted was closer to his plan to protect individual rights than to any other proposal offered, Randolph refused to sign the document. Later he became a vigorous promoter of it and worked for its ratification in Virginia.

William Patterson, artist unknown.
(Courtesy the Supreme Court of the United States, Washington, D.C.)

George Washington by Robert Edge Pine.
(Courtesy the National Portrait Gallery, Smithsonian Institution, Washington, D.C.)

William Patterson, 1745–1806, Lawyer, New Jersey. Champion of states' rights, Patterson proposed the New Jersey, or Small States, Plan by which the existing Articles of Confederation would have been merely amended rather than replaced with the Constitution.

James Wilson, 1742–1798, Lawyer, Pennsylvania. Wilson was chiefly responsible for incorporating into the Constitution the principle that sovereignty resides in the people.

James Wilson, artist unknown.
(Courtesy Independence National Historic Park.)

George Washington, 1732–1799, Planter and Commander-in-Chief of the Continental Army during the War of Independence, Virginia. Washington was chosen to preside over the Constitutional Convention and was highly influential as the country's preeminent public figure in getting the Constitution adopted.

Women fought an uphill battle for full political equality—a battle made more difficult because the Constitution specifically limited citizenship to men. *(Library of Congress)*

from control, they are given no positive rights to things like a job or an adequate education. If a citizen can be fired whenever he or she disagrees with an employer, they say, his or her speech is certainly not "free." Under Chief Justice Earl Warren, the Supreme Court interpreted the "equal protection of the laws" in ways that seemed to suggest that people ought to have the right to a minimal standard of living and to an equal education, but it did not come right out and say so. That this sympathetic Court did not proclaim that Americans should enjoy such positive freedoms tells us something about the relationship between the Constitution and the framers' theories of human nature.[3]

The framers were shrewd observers of human nature, but they did not believe in the political equality of women, who were ignored in the Constitution until the Nineteenth Amendment. That blind spot is one evident weakness in their idea of human nature.

By contrast, the framers had no doubt that slaves were entitled to equal rights. They permitted slavery to continue (which we will discuss later) in order to persuade the Southern slaveholding states to enter the union.[4]

Constitutional Means and the Art of Mistrust The framers' compromise with slavery indicates that constitutions must make a judgment on what is possible as well as what is desirable. Whatever we think about human nature, a constitution must be suited to the particular people it is to govern. Few of us, for example, would write the same laws for people who have never known freedom as we would for people accustomed to liberty.[5] The framers knew that they were drafting a constitution for a free people who were willing to try new institutions.[6]

At the same time, the framers were not naive. They expected treason, crime, and domestic violence, and they thought that firm penalties would encourage people to obey the law. But the Constitution also forbids "cruel and unusual punishments" or excessive bail. It rejects the penalty of "corruption of blood," which had been used in Europe to punish treason by holding traitors' children responsible for their parents' crime. The framers believed we should be responsible only for our own crimes. Moreover, the Constitution shows enough faith in the orderliness of the people that in a "well-regulated militia" it allows them to keep and bear arms. The framers viewed human nature as imperfect, but they did not think that the American people were totally irrational or that they would need to be forced to obey the law through the use of terror.

In this balanced view of human nature, the framers were in agreement with constitutional principles. All constitutions presume that human beings are not perfect and, to some extent, all constitutions distrust human reasons and judgment. A constitution is meant to be frustrating; constitutions are truly effective only when governments or majorities are stopped from doing something that they very much want to do and would be able to do if the constitution did not forbid them from doing it.

For example, Alexander Hamilton—like most of the framers—thought that people usually intend to do what is best for the political system as a whole, but he felt that it was foolish to believe that they would always find the best way of achieving it.[7] At a particular time, human beings may be inadequately informed or their perceptions distorted by passions and fears. They may exaggerate the importance of that particular moment and limit their concern to matters that affect them personally. Consequently, our Constitution tries to restrain the momentary will of the people, forcing them to pause and deliberate, in the hope that their real will, or something closer to it, will emerge.

More recently, in the 1950s and 1960s, for example, most American political scientists were impatient with the ability of interest groups and their friends in Congress to block the policies of the president. The president, elected by the whole nation, was regarded as the "representative of the national interest" as opposed to the narrower interests that dominate Congress.[8] Liberals, especially, tended to agree that the powers of the president were much broader than the simple words of the Constitution and that he had wider "implied powers." In the 1970s, Vietnam and Watergate, however, raised alarms about the growth of an "imperial presidency," and former critics of the Constitution were likely to feel new respect for the constitutional limits on presidential power.[9]

In the belief that popular majorities must sometimes be controlled, constitutionalism is obviously undemocratic, but constitutionalism is even more opposed to one-person rule or the rule of a few people. It distrusts all simple forms of government because it distrusts human nature and seeks to limit the public and the government by the rule of law.

The rule of law is valuable in educating citizens for democratic life. Stable institutions help make public life understandable and predictable. Of course, as Hamilton said, the people do not benefit if the laws change so often "that no man who knows what the law is today can guess what it will be tomorrow."[10] Stable laws let citizens see that their actions lead to predictable results. Knowing those results helps make citizens feel responsible for what happens to them, and this encourages them to be responsible. Moreover, constitutional rule lets people have reasonable expectations about the ways in which government will act. If it fails to live up to those expectations, citizens are likely to be shocked or outraged, demanding explanations and launching protests. The security provided by stable laws helps train good citizens and strengthens resistance to tyranny. This stability limits a republic, but it may also strengthen it.

Political Culture and the Rule of Law

Although a constitution may promote good citizenship, it depends even more on the character of the people and the beliefs of the people regarding good government. This is known as **political culture.** The law rules only through human beings who respect what it says and are willing to carry out its commands. A constitution, Woodrow Wilson remarked, draws its "breath and vigor" from the customs, habits, hopes, and desires of a nation.[11] What Wilson was suggesting was that constitutional government requires a constitutional people and a common political culture.

In the first place, constitutionalism requires that the great majority of the people agree about fundamental political values. Constitutional law could not resolve the crisis leading to our Civil War. Differences about the nature of the Union, the meaning of equality, and the rightness of slavery were so great that they dwarfed the things that united North and South. A majority of Northerners refused to turn over escaped slaves to their masters, and they also rejected the Supreme Court's attempt, in the Dred Scott case, to

Our experiment with Prohibition risked undermining respect for all laws because it did not fit the real values of the people. *(Library of Congress)*

Abraham Lincoln strayed from the boundaries of the Constitution, but Americans of his time approved his actions as "necessary" wartime measures. *(Library of Congress)*

decide the place of slavery within the nation. And Southerners, of course, refused to accept the election of Lincoln because they feared his policies more than they respected our institutions or the democratic process.

Even where there is basic agreement within a country, the laws must fit the real values of the people, as opposed to those they merely express. The Eighteenth Amendment, which banned liquor, met all the tests of a constitutional amendment, but it simply did not work. A great many Americans, especially in the cities, rejected the idea of forbidding the sale of liquor and were not prepared to obey it at all. Among the rest of the people, many Americans spoke up in favor of the amendment because to do so was "respectable." The great majority proved unwilling to support the enforcement of the amendment. The law was broken so often as to endanger respect for the law as a whole, and repeal—the Twenty-first Amendment—became necessary in the interests of constitutional government.

The public is the political court of last resort. Abraham Lincoln's suspension of the **writ of *habeas corpus*,** which prevents long detention without trial, was a more serious departure from constitutional tradition than anything Richard Nixon did, but the public agreed that the Civil War made it necessary. Had most people believed that Nixon acted to protect "national security," as he claimed, he would probably have completed his term. The political process, in other words, found favor in what Lincoln did, and did not in Nixon's case. Courts and other institutions have a good deal of authority, and they can influence—sometimes in important ways—how we use and understand words. Nevertheless, they cannot invent or defend for very long meanings that the public will not support. That is the basis for Finley Peter Dunne's saying that "the Supreme Court follows the election returns."[12] In the end, a constitutional government relies on its people and the things they believe; democratic citizens are the last stronghold of constitutional government in a democracy.

Constitutionalism and Change

A constitutional government, however, also seeks to protect the political identity of its people against the force of change. Obviously, a political society must be able to respond to new circumstances. A constitutional system that is not flexible is doomed to shatter. Justice John Marshall once noted that no constitution could possibly provide for every emergency that might come up in later years, and for constitution writers to try to anticipate all future changes in society would be unwise on their part.[13]

At the same time, constitutionalism insists that there are some things that must not change, even in an emergency situation.* To most governments in the world, for example, it has seemed unwise to hold national elections in

*Justice David Davis's rhetoric in *Ex Parte Milligan,* 4 Wall, 2, 120–21 (1866), though extreme, speaks to the general point:

> The Constitution of the United States is a law for rulers and people, equally in war and peace, and covers with the shield of its protection all classes of men, at all times and under all circumstances. No doctrine, involving more pernicious consequences, was ever invented by the wit of man than that any of its provisions can be suspended during any of the great exigencies of government.

wartime because they might divide a nation at a time when unity is important. Despite this sensible argument, Americans, obeying the Constitution, held congressional elections in 1918 and 1942 and a presidential election in 1944. The constitution does not allow elections to be postponed because it regards the consent of the governed as too basic a principle to permit exceptions. Constitutions distinguish institutions—fundamental practices that are, at least, very difficult to change—from policies, laws, and activities that the government can vary as it thinks desirable.

We speak of a constitution as living, growing with the times; but like all living things, a constitution can decay. A constitution has an essential nature that it cannot change without perishing. Rome survived the rise of the Caesars; the Roman Republic did not, even though many of the old forms remained. A world of rapid and massive change is an uncomfortable place for a constitutional regime.[14] For that reason, it is appropriate to turn to the past and to the origins of constitutional government in the United States

The Origins of American Constitutionalism

Organic Constitutionalism in the American Tradition

Constitutionalism was part of the earliest political heritage of America. The colonists brought constitutionalist ideas with them. Britain prided herself on her law and the liberties it protected, and all the colonists, whatever their country of origin, respected the principles that are at the foundation of constitutionalist thought.

Religion taught Americans that there was a *moral law* above and beyond the reach of human will. Religious teaching also confirmed what Americans learned from their experience: human knowledge is incomplete, and human beings are often irrational and sometimes evil. In that view, law is a safe haven and a wise guide, the great bulwark against human error and self-delusion.[15]

Similarly, a great tradition of philosophy, dating back to the ancient Greeks, maintained that reason could discover a *natural law,* principles that mark out the right order of human affairs based on an understanding of who we are and what is our place in nature. In that tradition, human beings are by their very nature social and political. They need society and the political order for the development of their personalities. The individual then owes a great deal to political society, but social and political institutions have the duty to develop the individual's natural aptitude for excellence. Natural law stresses the point that people are dependent on each other. It speaks of things that are right according to nature, rather than of "natural rights" to do as we choose.[16]

Of course, most Americans at the time of the founding were not philosophers, but they were influenced by a similar tradition. According to the **organic theory of constitutionalism,** a people does not "create" a constitution. Since human beings are political animals, it would be more accurate to say that political institutions create a people. "The constitution of a republic," Cicero wrote, "is the work of no single time and no single man."[17]

In this view, a constitution consists of the underlying principles that are found in the actual institutions, habits, and practices of a political society.[18]

Fundamental laws are *discovered* and not made. People played baseball, for example, long before there were official rules. Similarly, Americans had held a great many meetings before General Henry Robert published his Rules of Order. In both cases, the "rule makers" merely made official what people were already doing. Law could not be out of keeping with practice: people would have laughed at a rule that commanded that a batter be given six strikes or counted a foul into the stands as a home run. The rules of baseball or Robert's Rules were followed because readers said, "That's right. That's how we do it," or "That makes sense out of things. That is what we have been trying to do."

In organic theories, the past is the most important factor in the constitution—the political identity—of a people. **Precedent,** or using past cases to interpret current and future ones, is then the most important principle in discovering or interpreting the law. Rules and principles, once discovered and set down, influence what will be done in the future, just as Robert's Rules have guided later political meetings and the Official Rules have come to define baseball. Organic constitutionalism, however, is concerned with shaping the future in order to preserve its links with the past and the present.

The Framers and Mechanistic Constitutionalism

The framers of the American Constitution relied on and sought to use the traditional constitutionalist beliefs of Americans, but they shared only a few of them. Indeed, they considered existing constitutions as the work of "accident and force," so they rejected the authority of the past. They believed in the modern idea that there is a great gap between the way in which human beings live and the way in which they ought to live. The Constitution, as a result, was oriented to the future and sought to be a document worthy of humankind in general and the American people in particular.[19]

The framers aimed to establish a regime based on the "new science of politics," derived from the more modern European political theorists like John Locke and Charles de Montesquieu and from the laws of physics set forth by scientists like Sir Isaac Newton. Hamilton proclaimed that this new science of politics was based on principles that the ancient Greeks had never known and took into account the progress made in science in the years since Aristotle wrote.[20]

A constitution, in this new understanding, should be a rational order in which laws and institutions are like floodgates and dams designed to channel human impulses and passions toward desired ends. This idea is often called a **mechanistic theory of constitutionalism** because (1) it sees constitutions operating like machines and (2) the constitution is designed to produce good results even if its "workmen" are unskilled and take little pride in their work. A mechanistic constitution is designed to be self-regulating, limiting government even when its citizens and leaders are at their worst, just as a self-regulating clock does not depend on the virtue of the person who maintains it.[21]

Traditionally, political theory had argued that a republican or democratic constitution depended on public-spirited citizens—that the clock

The Constitution offers much leeway in interpreting how the United States will provide for its defense—from state militias to standing armies of volunteers to the "draft," which prevailed from World War II through Vietnam. *(Jason Lauré)*

tender had to be virtuous. Since it is hard to train citizens in civic virtue, the framers chose not to depend on it in the Constitution. They turned instead to mechanistic political science rather than hope that statesmen and citizens would have much civic virtue. They had no illusions that human conduct could be made to operate with the same precision as the laws of physics or mechanics but felt that a constitution based on these principles was better than one that was based on the virtue of ordinary mortals.[22]

In the framers' mechanistic theory, a people is essentially a collection of private individuals pursuing private motives. This idea corresponds to the framers' assumption that human beings are, and ought to be, "naturally free,"[23] and that government should try only to control people's behavior, not their souls.

The Articles of Confederation

America's first constitution was the Articles of Confederation, adopted in 1781. The Articles established a union of states. For practical purposes, there was no federal citizenship; only state governments were represented and the federal government spoke to citizens only through the states.

Under the Articles, the national government was entrusted to Congress, a single-house legislature in which each state had one vote. Lawmaking required the support of nine of the thirteen states. Since nine votes were needed no matter how few votes were cast against a measure, any state that was absent or abstained from voting was actually voting against a proposal. Any amendments to the Articles required unanimous consent of all states.

Congress could not tax people directly. It could only issue "requisitions" to the states, which the states had a moral obligation to pay. Even during the first two years of the Articles, when the War of Independence helped unify Americans, the states paid only 15 percent of the amount Congress requested, and Congress was chronically unable to pay the Continental Army or those who had lent money to the national government.

Similarly, Congress lacked real authority to control interstate commerce, although it had the right to negotiate commercial treaties with foreign governments. The states could impose high import taxes or tariffs on the products of any country that discriminated against the exported products of the states.

The Articles, in other words, intended the central government to move slowly, after considerable deliberation, only when a high degree of agreement was reached and even then only by persuasion not force. It was a regime that reflected, and was intended to preserve, the superior position of the states and local communities in American political life and the loyalties of the people. The central government was really dependent on the public spirit of the state regimes.

Despite the framers' criticism of the Articles, the Confederation had a good deal of success. Its forces defeated the British armies when England was a major world power. It made a satisfactory peace. The Confederation also persuaded the states to yield their claims to the Northwest Territories (Ohio, Indiana, Illinois, Michigan, and Wisconsin) to the national government, and it banned slavery from those territories forever.[24]

The framers, however, came to the conclusion that the vices of the Confederation were greater than its virtues. The Articles of Confederation, Madison declared, was "nothing more than a treaty of amity, of concert and alliance between independent and sovereign states." Congress was too often unable to act at all, and when it did act, it was unable to enforce its decisions. Moreover, Madison went on, the central government needed more authority to limit the states and to intervene in their affairs. There were too many different laws, and even these were too often changed. State laws were too frequently unjust, violating the rights of their own citizens, those of other states, and those of the nation as a whole. Finally, like so many of the framers, Madison was alarmed by Shays' Rebellion (an uprising in Western Massachusetts by farmers in debt), and worried that the Articles did not protect the states against domestic violence.[25]

Madison, in other words, urged a central government that could act quickly, by force, against opposition within states or by states themselves. He emphasized decision rather than discussion and the ability to respond to change rather than the desire to preserve continuity at all costs. He was arguing for a new sort of Union in which the central government would be the focus of the loyalty of citizens, directing the Union and limiting and shaping the life of the states.

A great many Americans who were not prepared to go so far were persuaded of the need for a stronger central government and recognized that the rule requiring unanimous consent of all states made it impractical to amend the Articles. An otherwise ineffective meeting in Annapolis, in 1786, called on the state legislatures to send delegates to a convention to examine the Articles of Confederation. All the states but Rhode Island agreed, setting the stage for the Constitutional Convention.

Drafting the Constitution

The Constitution of the United States was the work of a small group of men working for only a short time. To us, the Constitutional Convention looks like a major event in history. At the time, there were delegates to the Convention who thought it was not very important. Of the seventy four delegates chosen by the states, only fifty-five ever attended; New Hampshire's delegates came two months late, and only forty-two delegates stayed on to sign the document. This small group met for a little more than three and a half months during the summer of 1787. That they could accomplish so much in so little time suggests how much they did have in common and how much agreement underlay the Convention's debates.

There were disagreements, of course, which is the reason we have been taught to regard the Constitution as a "bundle of compromises."[26] In fact, as we shall see, there were very few genuine compromises during the convention. Delegates who spoke on behalf of agriculture clashed with those who promoted commerce and manufacturing. Slavery had bitter antagonists and unyielding defenders. Classical republicans, believers in small states and ideals of civic virtue, disagreed with liberal republicans who advocated a large state and individual liberty. The differences between small and large states were only a part of the story. The Virginia delegation included the strongest advocate of the new Constitution, Madison, and its shrewdest critic, George Mason. Hamilton represented New York, but his two colleagues were so opposed to any radical change in the Articles that they left the convention in July and never came back.

Conflict began with the **Virginia Plan,** introduced by Edmund Randolph but really the work of Madison. The Virginia Plan proposed (1) a new constitution that would (2) derive directly from the people rather than the states, and (3) permit the national government to speak directly to the people without going through the state governments. It was (4) an extremely nationalistic document. Congress would be allowed to veto or cancel all state laws that in the opinion of Congress violated the Constitution. The Plan also included (5) a separate executive and judiciary. Finally, it was (6) a relatively democratic document in that a state would have members in the Senate in proportion to its population. Seats in the House of Representatives would also be given to states according to their population, and the House would elect the Senate.

The smaller states, and all those delegates who were devoted to the rights of local communities, were alarmed by this proposal. At first, they responded with the **New Jersey Plan,** which proposed to strengthen the Articles but keep its basic structure intact. Only three states supported this plan, but they did so very forcefully and were able to convince Madison and Randolph to change their original proposal.

Very early, it was decided that state legislatures, not the House, should elect Senators, but as late as June 29 the Convention voted in favor of a Senate based on population. The decision hinged on a few states, and on July 16, the Convention voted 5 states to 4 in favor of a Senate in which states would be equally represented no matter what their population. It was not a "compromise," however: Madison and other partisans of a Senate

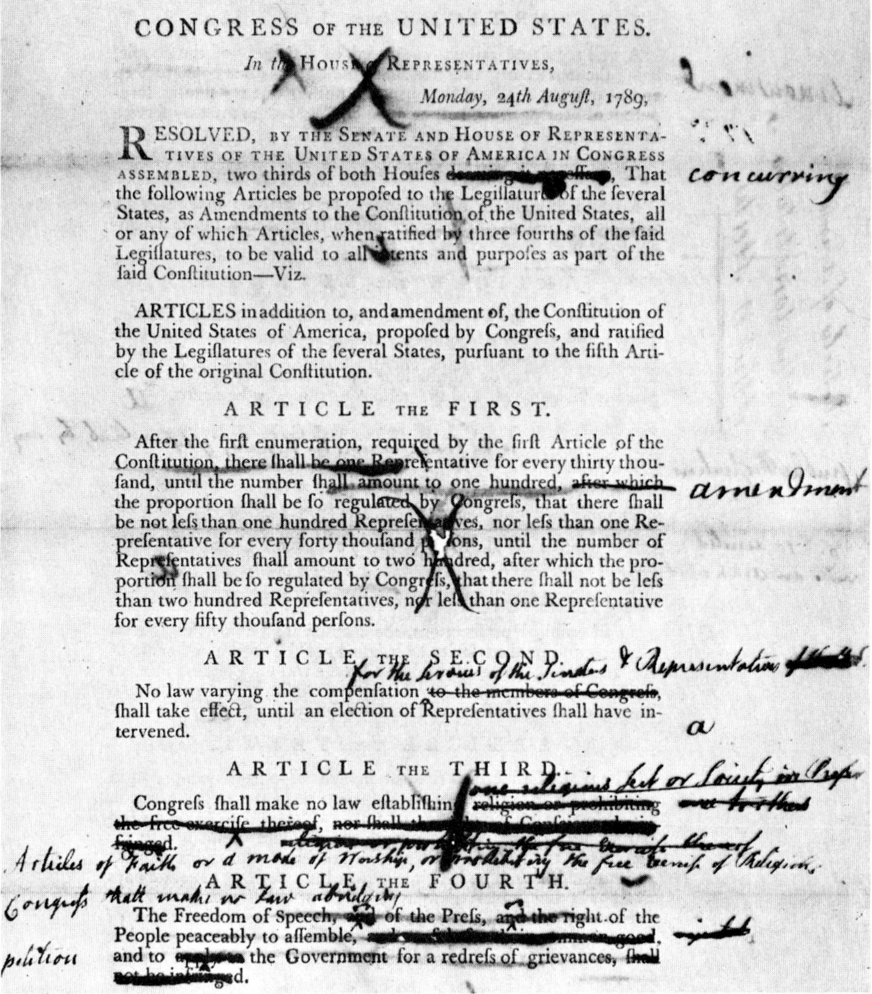

CONGRESS OF THE UNITED STATES.

In the House of Representatives,

Monday, 24th Auguſt, 1789.

RESOLVED, BY THE SENATE AND HOUSE OF REPRESENTATIVES OF THE UNITED STATES OF AMERICA IN CONGRESS ASSEMBLED, two thirds of both Houſes ~~deeming it neceſſary~~, That the following Articles be propoſed to the Legiſlatures of the ſeveral States, as Amendments to the Conſtitution of the United States, all or any of which Articles, when ratified by three fourths of the ſaid Legiſlatures, to be valid to all intents and purpoſes as part of the ſaid Conſtitution—Viz.

ARTICLES in addition to, and amendment of, the Conſtitution of the United States of America, propoſed by Congreſs, and ratified by the Legiſlatures of the ſeveral States, purſuant to the fifth Article of the original Conſtitution.

ARTICLE THE FIRST.

After the firſt enumeration, required by the firſt Article of the Conſtitution, there ſhall be one Repreſentative for every thirty thouſand, until the number ſhall amount to one hundred, ~~after which~~ the proportion ſhall be ſo regulated by Congreſs, that there ſhall be not leſs than one hundred Repreſentatives, nor leſs than one Repreſentative for every forty thouſand perſons, until the number of Repreſentatives ſhall amount to two hundred, after which the proportion ſhall be ſo regulated by Congreſs, that there ſhall not be leſs than two hundred Repreſentatives, nor leſs than one Repreſentative for every fifty thouſand perſons.

ARTICLE THE SECOND.

No law varying the compenſation ~~to the members of Congreſs~~, ſhall take effect, until an election of Repreſentatives ſhall have intervened.

ARTICLE THE THIRD.

Congreſs ſhall make no law eſtabliſhing ~~religion or prohibiting the free exerciſe thereof, nor ſhall the rights of Conſcience be infringed.~~

ARTICLE THE FOURTH.

The Freedom of Speech, ~~and~~ of the Preſs, ~~and the~~ right of the People peaceably to aſſemble, ~~and conſult for their common good~~, and to ~~apply to~~ the Government for a redreſs of grievances, ~~ſhall not be infringed~~.

The framers saw the Constitution as the embodiment of a "revolution which has no parallel in the annals of human history." *(National Archives)*

based on population were violently opposed and continued their efforts to reverse the decision almost until the end of the Convention.

Madison suffered another setback on July 17, when the Convention struck out the proposed veto on state laws. Gouverneur Morris of Pennsylvania, who sympathized with Madison's aim, argued that the veto was impractical because it would "disgust" the states. Madison was still unhappy, and thought, for a time, that this change "doomed" the Constitution.[27]

Similarly, Madison wanted a broad grant of power to the central government, allowing it to act wherever the states were "incompetent" or wherever the "harmony" of the Union was involved. Such terms would give Congress great flexibility in interpreting its authority. Madison favored such "loose construction"; under the Articles, he argued for an "implied right" to use force to make the states behave.[28] It is not surprising that Madison's critics argued that such general terms did not really limit the government. They insisted on listing or "enumerating" the specific powers of Congress, and toward the end of the Convention they won out, although the "necessary and proper" clause (see Art. I, sec. 8, in the Appendix) remained as a crucial concession to Madison's ideas.

Madison was happier with the provisions dealing with the president. The Virginia Plan had proposed a three-person executive, an approach that the Convention rejected quickly in favor of a single president. Originally, however, the president was to be elected by Congress. On July 19, the Convention reversed itself, voting in favor of a scheme very much like the eventual Electoral College. On this vote, Madison changed sides, having been persuaded that an electoral college, chosen by the people, would be a more democratic way of selecting the president than election by Congress, which Madison thought would be controlled by the rich and powerful.[29] The Convention hemmed and hawed, and did not adopt the final Electoral College until September 6, but in the end it did decide in favor of a strong, unified, and relatively democratic presidency.

The most troubling disputes in the Convention, however, concerned slavery. The framers knew that slavery violated their ideas of natural rights. Madison, who had suggested arming and freeing those slaves who were willing to fight in the War of Independence, maintained that it would be

POLITICAL PERSPECTIVE

ECONOMIC INTERESTS: A MAJOR MOTIVE OF THE FRAMERS?

What common ground did the framers share that enabled them to agree? According to one major school of thought, the framers were united by similar economic interests. This does not mean that the framers were necessarily concerned to make profits for themselves; it does imply that they aimed to establish a system of rule by or for the upper class.[31] The most famous book in this tradition, Charles Beard's *An Economic Interpretation of the Constitution* (1913), contended that the framers aimed (1) to defend private property in general, (2) to protect investors who were owed money by the Confederation and the states, and (3) to prevent a rebellion of debtors like Shays' Rebellion.

Thus, the argument goes on, the framers created a government designed to safeguard certain economic interests, especially those of banks and other creditors, through a strong central government able to establish sound money, keep order in the states, and prevent state laws from tampering with contracts.

How sound is this interpretation? It is certainly true that the framers wanted to protect property and see that debts were repaid. They argued specifically in support of that position. A major defect of this economic interpretation, in fact, is that it ignores or minimizes what the framers said, since it sees such arguments as only public excuses for more private interests.

In the last analysis, the framers were motivated by an ambition much more powerful than economic interest. They hoped to win political immortality, founding a large republic that would last—a Rome based on the new science of politics, which would not decline and fall. The framers were completely overwhelmed by the importance and the novelty of what they had done. Madison, for example, spoke of a "revolution which has no parallel in the annals of human society," and of governments which "have no model on the face of the globe." They were creating a new departure in human history: the Great Seal of the United States identifies the Constitution with a new order of the ages (*Novus Ordo Seclorum*). When James Wilson thought of the impact he hoped the Constitution would have on the future of humanity as a whole, he was "lost in the magnitude of the object." The framers did not forget more ordinary details, but it was their vision, not the mechanics, that impressed them most.[32]

wrong to admit to accepting the idea that people could be property. At the same time, slavery had to be acknowledged if the Southern states were to be brought into the Union. Hence, the Convention reached perhaps the only "compromise" accepted by both sides: it agreed to follow the precedent of the Confederation in counting each slave as three-fifths of a person for the purposes of determining how many seats in the House a state was entitled to.[30]

The Convention was, nevertheless, unhappy with that compromise. It reversed an earlier concession to the slave trade and authorized Congress to forbid that trade after twenty years. Even so, the Convention was ashamed of the necessity that forced any concession to slavery. It kept the word "slave" out of the Constitution because the delegates were unwilling to admit they had recognized slavery, let alone having given it official status in the distribution of House seats.

Debate in the Convention was often sharp; feelings were strong; losers were sometimes bitter. In the course of the discussions, delegates often changed positions, but just as often they stuck by their guns. No delegate had it all his own way. The real "great compromise" of the Constitution was that, ultimately, so many delegates agreed that the final document was acceptable despite their objections to certain features. They concluded that it was a "good-enough" regime and an experiment worth trying.

Principles of the American Constitution

The Separation of Public and Private Spheres

The Constitution is a product of the framers' new science of politics and as such is a mechanistic document founded on the theory that human beings are, by nature, concerned with self-preservation and caught up with the mastery of nature. The Constitution assumes that we are naturally private, not political, animals, and that government is a device we invent to further our private ends. In so doing, we "give up" to the government as little authority over our lives as we can and "reserve" everything else for our private affairs. Government, then, is limited to those powers we "delegate" to it, and it is forbidden to interfere in other areas of life. Political society, then, is divided into a "public" and a "private" sphere.

At the same time, the Constitution is concerned with both spheres. Madison expressed it thus:

> In framing a government which is to be administered by men over men, the great difficulty lies in this: You must first enable the government to control the governed, and in the next place, oblige it to control itself.[33]

Political order comes first. Government control of the governed is the primary concern of *all* regimes: only constitutional, and especially republican, government takes the next step in the effort to allow that control to coexist with liberty. And the problem of political order is simple. Naturally private and selfish, human beings always find the law an obstacle to their private goals.

Under ideal circumstances, the framers thought that reason could teach men that it was in their *interest* to join with others in a political order, but humans did not always know what was in their best interest. Interest required work and sacrifice on behalf of the long-term goal of mastery over nature. Personal feelings or *affections,* however, demanded comfort, ease, and immediate satisfaction. Always likely to mislead the individual, the affections were strongest in groups like the family and the local community, where the individual found warmth and the satisfaction of his basic needs. The affections encouraged the individual to identify with these narrow groups and to prefer their interests to those of the larger society, even though large groups, which could accumulate power more easily, served the real interest of the individual much more effectively.

This tendency toward "faction" in private life, the framers believed, could be controlled by the political fragmentation imposed by a large state with numerous factions. Majorities would be scattered and temporary, making only a small appeal to the individual's affection. Groups that could hope to be effective in promoting the private interests of the individual would, in general, be separated from groups that could make claims on a person's feelings. The private sphere could thus operate without the sacrifice of individual liberty.

Woodrow Wilson believed that our Constitution drew its authority from the people's values and character. *(Library of Congress)*

Federalism and the Division of Power

The **division of powers** (see Chapter 3, Federalism) between state and national governments, we should remember, was designed to strengthen this tendency toward fragmentation. Classical political theory, following the same principles that led it to favor the small state, saw federations as associations of states. That is, it presumed that the central government should, like Congress under the Articles, be composed of the delegates from the state governments.

The framers insisted, by contrast, that the central government, in addition to promoting the interests of the people, needed to be able to appeal to their affections, and this required direct contact between citizens and the central government. Hamilton felt strongly that the national government had as much right to appeal directly for the loyalties and support of the citizens as did the states.[34]

Giving some powers to the central or federal government exclusively, the Constitution provides that in these areas the federal government, and it alone, may speak to and for the citizens. Some powers remain in the hands of the states, but an even greater number are shared with the federal government. In the area of shared powers, conflicts of jurisdiction cannot be avoided, but even the exclusive powers of federal and state regimes are often at odds. In time of war, for example, the powers of state governments are seriously affected. When such conflicts occur, citizens' loyalties are divided. Classical federalism told them that they need only obey their individual states, but in American federalism, their loyalties are split.

When such conflicts arise, citizens can leave the issue to the courts. However, the Constitution says that such cases are to be tried by the federal courts, and the framers were sure that federal judges would support federal

TABLE 2.1 The Division of Powers between the National and the State Governments

Central, or Federal Government Alone	Both Federal Government and States	States Alone
Regulation of foreign trade Regulation of interstate commerce Conduct of foreign relations Declaration of war Raising and governing of armies and navies in time of peace Uniform rule of naturalization Coinage of money Uniform rule for bankruptcy Standardization of weights and measures Patents and copyrights	Power to tax Power to borrow Right to spend for general welfare Authority over militia	Direct taxes (except for taxes in proportion to number, Art. I, sec. 2.9). This became a *shared* power with the adoption of the 16th Amendment Qualifications and rules for voting (modified by the 15th, 19th, 24th, and 26th Amendments) Internal government Police power (legislation for the "health, morals, and safety" of the public) Veto over merger of old states or creation of new ones out of the territory of one's own state (Art. IV, sec. 3)
	Limitations	
Bill of Rights	Denial of due process Ex post facto laws Bills of attainder	Laws impairing obligation of contracts Titles of nobility (Art. I, sec. 10)

power. If individual citizens decided to choose where their loyalties lay, the framers assumed that although the people were more emotionally attached to their states than to the federal government, the latter had more important powers, more ability to appeal to ambition, and probably greater efficiency. Since it was in the interest of individuals to line up with the more powerful and efficient unit of government rather than the one to which they were emotionally attached, the framers expected the authority of the federal government to grow with the passing of time. Table 2.1 shows the division of powers in the Constitution of 1787.

The Bill of Rights

Aiming to fragment and weaken the power of factions and localities, the framers were deeply concerned about protecting the private rights of individuals. But they did not believe, originally, that the Constitution required a Bill of Rights.

A Bill of Rights is unnecessary, Madison contended. Since the power of the majority is really checked by the size of the United States and the provisions of the Constitution that fragment power there is no danger to individual rights. Hamilton, on the other hand, claimed that a Bill of Rights is dangerous. It suggests that if natural rights are granted by a constitution, then, by implication, they could be taken away. (The provision for amendments does indeed make it possible to repeal the Bill of Rights.)[35]

Supporters of a Bill of Rights, like Jefferson, answered that listing in detail our rights was important in teaching future generations their rights and liberties. Madison was convinced by Jefferson's argument that a Bill of Rights would shape American culture, helping to create a public opinion devoted to the Constitution and ready to protect its rights.[36] Jefferson and his allies argued, in other words, for a concern for civic virtue, which is absent or neglected in the mechanistic constitutionalism of the framers.

We will discuss the specific provisions of the Bill of Rights and what they mean today in Chapter 12. For the moment, we will just make the point that the Bill of Rights, as Jefferson expected, has played an important role in making Americans aware of their rights.

The Separation of Powers

Madison and the framers, however, were not prepared to rely on citizens or leaders to limit what governments could do. Even government established by consent of the governed tends to go its own way, sidestepping or ignoring public opinion to add to its power. As far as possible, the framers insisted, government must be self-regulating, obliged to control itself. In a famous passage, Madison wrote:

> Ambition must be made to counteract ambition. The interest of the man must be connected to the constitutional rights of the place. It may be a reflection on human nature that such devices should be needed to control the abuses of government. But what is government itself but the greatest of all reflections on human nature.[37]

The **separation of powers** (see Table 2.2), then, does not just divide the federal government into legislative, executive, and judicial sections. It makes those sections overlap and encourages each branch of the government to pursue its own ambition, to collide with and interfere with the other branches. The Senate must advise and consent when the president appoints someone to an important post, and, by two-thirds vote, ratify the treaties the president signs. The House has the power to impeach the president, and if he or she is impeached, the trial takes place in the Senate. The president has the power to veto laws passed by the Congress and to appoint members of the Supreme Court. He or she may address Congress and may call it into special sessions. And these are only the most obvious forms of shared power. The framers designed a complicated government, each part limited by every other, in the hope of limiting that government to those measures necessary for the nation as a whole—measures that also respect individual liberties.

Modern critics of the constitution often point out that the fragmentation inherent in the framers' scheme makes it difficult for the weak and disadvantaged to combine in order to change things as they are. James MacGregor Burns, for example, maintains that since the framers were right

From *Herblock Through the Looking Glass* (W.W. Norton, 1984)

in thinking that many factions effectively prevent tyranny, the "checks and balances" system only adds an unnecessary obstacle that blocks measures for the common good.[38] The framers believed, however, that what the common people really want is to be left alone. It was the wealthy and powerful who wanted an "active government" in the eighteenth century, and people thought at the time that political institutions in a republic had to be small and simple. That argument is strange to our ears, and it indicates some of the changes in the United States since the time of the founding.

Public Purpose

The framers believed that good government liberated human beings from the control of smaller communities, respected their individual rights, and refereed conflicts between competing private interests. Progress and direction were best left to the lawful pursuit of self-interest by private individuals.

Nevertheless, since political society was created to "preserve" individuals and to help in their mastery of nature, it aimed to add to human power. Thus, the Constitution encourages Congress "to promote the Progress of Science and useful Arts." This search for power seems to suggest conflict with other countries. Since men are "ambitious, vindictive, and rapacious," Hamilton argued, war between nations is a common occurrence.[39] As a result, government must have all the power it needs to deal with such conflicts as they occur.

TABLE 2.2 "Checks and Balances" and the Separation of Powers among the Three Branches of the National Government

	Legislative Powers	Executive Powers	Judicial Powers
Congress	Pass all legislation (Art. I, sec. 1)	May compel members to attend, punish disorderly behavior or, by 2/3 vote, expel members (Art. I, sec. 5) May vest the power of appointment to "inferior offices" in the president, the courts, or heads of departments (Art. II, sec. 2)	May establish inferior federal courts (Art. I, sec. 8) May limit the appellate jurisdiction of the Supreme Court (Art. III, sec. 2)
House of Representatives	Must initiate all revenue bills (Art. I, sec. 7)	Chooses president in event no candidate receives a majority in the Electoral College (12th Amendment, modifying Art. II, sec. I)	Judges, in case of disagreement, the president's fitness to serve (25th Amendment) Judges election and qualifications of its own members (Art. I, sec. 5)
Senate		Must advise and consent to appointments (Art. II, sec. 2) Must advise and consent (by a 2/3 vote) to treaties (Art. II, sec. 2) Chooses vice-president in event no candidate receives a majority in the Electoral College (12th Amendment, modifying Art. II, sec. 1)	Power of impeachment (Art. I, sec. 2) Judges election and qualifications of its own members (Art. I, sec. 5) Power to try impeachments (Art. I, sec. 3)
President	Power to veto legislation (Art. I, sec. 7) Power to send messages to Congress, convene special sessions, and to adjourn Congress in case of disagreement between the Houses (Art. II, sec. 3)	Holds "the executive power," power as commander-in-chief, etc. (Art. II, secs. 1, 2)	Appoints judges (Art. II, sec. 2) Power to grant reprieves and pardons, except in cases of impeachment (Art. II, sec. 2)
Supreme Court	Judicial review, derived from the Constitution as "supreme law of the land" (Art. VI)	Judicial review	Judicial power, shared with inferior federal courts (Art. III, sec. 1, 11th Amendment) Original jurisdiction (Art. III, sec. 2) Appellate jurisdiction, except as Congress provides (Art. III, sec. 2)

In the world outside political society, in foreign affairs and in relation to nature, there are common interests growing out of the search for power. In conflicts with other countries, the Constitution makes it easy for the government to speak with one voice. It sets few limits on the conduct of our relations with other countries, and there are no restrictions of any kind on growth, expansion, and material progress. All Americans see the result of that design in the world around them and feel its effects in themselves.

Constitutional Amendments, Formal and Unwritten

Many sections of the Constitution, obviously, have been changed or eliminated by amendments. The procedure for choosing the vice-president was changed early. In the period after the Civil War, the Thirteenth, Fourteenth, and Fifteenth Amendments were added. They were designed to end slavery, restrict racial discrimination, and give equality a higher place among the ends of the Constitution. During the Progressive Era in the early 1900s, the Constitution was amended to allow the people, not the state legislatures, to elect Senators. The income tax was authorized; women were given the vote; and—briefly—the sale of liquor was banned.

Yet, to say this is to call attention to the fact that the political process, our practice, our "ways of living and doing," have all changed the meaning of many passages of the Constitution. For a hundred years, Southern opposition and Northern indifference made the Fourteenth and Fifteenth Amendments useless as protections for the rights of blacks, and even transformed them, through the doctrine that a corporation is a "legal person," into protections for wealth, business, and inequality.[40] The American Constitution, in practice, includes a good deal that is not written in the document itself. Among the unwritten elements of our Constitution are judicial review, political parties, and the order of private life.

JUDICIAL REVIEW The Constitution does not mention **judicial review,** the Supreme Court's right to rule a law unconstitutional. The framers, however, almost certainly intended some such role for the Court. Hamilton felt strongly that the Constitution was far more basic than any law passed by Congress. He also reasoned that if an act of Congress was in conflict with the Constitution, it was the job of the judges to decide in favor of the more basic of the two: the Constitution, since the Constitution came from the people, whereas acts of Congress came only from their representatives.[41]

But Hamilton's view was controversial at the time of the Convention. The Court established its power of judicial review only after considerable controversy, beginning with Justice Marshall's decision in *Marbury* v. *Madison.*[42] Despite controversy over the years, however, judicial review now seems firmly established as a convention of the Constitution.

Judicial review allows the Court to change the balance of the Constitution. For example, in *Myers* v. *U.S.*,[43] the Court ruled that the president could fire a postmaster without the consent of the Senate, even though the postmaster had originally been confirmed by the Senate and had been appointed for a term that had some years to run. Chief Justice Taft argued—correctly—that the framers had intended not to limit the president in removing subordinates he no longer trusts. But in *Humphrey's Executor* v. *U.S.*,[44] the Court held that in the Federal Trade Commission (see Chapter 10), Congress had created a Commission that had both legislative and judicial powers and was intended to carry policies into effect "independent of executive control." The president could not, then, remove a member of the Commission. What is implied here is that Congress can whittle away at the president's power of appointment and his control of executive personnel by creating other agencies like the FTC.[45] This, at least, modifies the separation of powers in important ways.

Moreover, the Supreme Court sometimes takes on tasks originally intended for others. By its own interpretation of the Fourteenth Amendment, the Court has acquired great powers to control how House and state legislative district boundaries are drawn, a matter originally left to Congress and the state legislatures.[46]

Judicial review allows and requires the Court to determine what is essential in the Constitution and what can be changed in order to adapt to new times and opinions. In that sense, the Supreme Court "continues the work of the Convention of 1787" as a permanent body charged with patching and maintaining the Constitution under the stress of change. This task is certainly "political in the highest sense of the word," making the Court's authority only slightly less high than that of the framers.[47] Yet all of this is merely hinted at by the words of the Constitution.

The Organic Constitution: Political Parties Even institutions not mentioned in the Constitution, such as the political parties, have become effective parts of the American Constitution. The framers regarded parties as dangerous factions, but parties proved valuable to citizens in influencing the government and to leaders in organizing public support.

Very early, parties brought about a change in the Constitution. Not expecting disciplined national parties, the framers had expected that the indirect method of electing the president by the people voting for "electors" rather than the candidate would result in votes being scattered among several candidates. In 1800, following the discipline of their party, all of the Democratic-Republican electors cast their votes for Thomas Jefferson and Aaron Burr, assuming that Burr would be vice-president. But the two received the same number of votes, and under Article II, sec. 3, the House of Representatives had to choose between them. The defeated Federalists briefly considered supporting Burr. Jefferson was elected despite such schemes, but the upshot was the Twelfth Amendment, providing that electors should vote for the president and vice-president in separate ballots that clearly set forth the presidential and vice-presidential candidates.

Similarly, parties have transformed the Electoral College into a relic. With very few exceptions, the entire electoral vote of a state goes to the candidate who receives the largest number of votes in that state. The system of awarding states electoral votes based on the number of representatives they have in Congress is still significant, however. It makes "carrying" states the critical factor in presidential elections, which tends to dictate that political parties be organized on a state-by-state basis. It can also result, and has on thirteen occasions since 1828, in a candidate with a minority of the total national vote (popular vote) being elected president. On two occasions

(1876 and 1888) the candidate with a smaller popular vote than his opponent won because his votes were concentrated in states with larger numbers of electoral votes.

Today, by controlling the alternatives available to voters, parties determine the terms and much of the meaning of elections. Except in rare cases, voters hate to waste their votes on minority party candidates, and in many localities, nomination by the dominant party in a primary virtually guarantees that person's election, since the other party is so weak it does not even bother to run a candidate in the general election. By the "white primary," Southern Democratic parties barred blacks from participation in primary elections until quite recently. Since the South was a solidly Democratic region, this kept blacks from having any real role in elections; the real decision was made in the Democratic primary. In 1935, the Court ruled that if political parties adopted the white primary on their own, without authority from the state legislatures, it was constitutional because political parties were like clubs or fraternities. In 1944, however, the Court reversed itself, declaring that primaries were an "integral part" of the election and that parties could not exclude blacks. In 1953, the Court ruled that a private club, which held straw votes whose winners habitually won the Democratic primary, was also a "public" institution within the meaning of the Fourteenth Amendment. These decisions effectively brought the political parties into the Constitution.[48] With the adoption of the Twenty-fourth Amendment forbidding the poll tax (a charge for casting a ballot, which many poor people in the South could not afford), the Constitution was put in the odd position of regulating primaries, while still not having any mention of parties for which primaries exist. Words are not needed: practice has, in effect, written the parties into the Constitution.

The Private Order Most important, the Constitution says very little about the organization of the people's life in the "private sphere." This is not surprising, since the framers believed that people's private lives should be free wherever possible from regulation by the "state." The framers never doubted that society was important in the constitutional design, however, and to some extent they relied on certain vital social institutions. "Our constitution," John Adams remarked, "was made only for a moral and religious people. It is wholly inadequate to the government of any other."[49]

At the same time, the framers feared the control that such institutions exerted over the individual. The family, the church, and local community (as well as such modern "private governments" as corporations and the mass media) cannot legally force citizens to obey them. As the framers knew, however, they may have important influence over local government and have many informal techniques for using their influence. The economic power of corporations can strike at an individual's livelihood; community opinion can threaten his or her reputation and status; smaller groups grant or refuse friendship and love. Most important, family, church, and community dominate early education, shaping the citizen's fundamental beliefs and building invisible forms of control into the personality itself.

The framers sought to preserve such institutions to retain them as moral educators and sources of comfort, but also to fragment them so that they would be relatively unable to oppress the individual or harm the republic. The First Amendment's provisions protecting the free exercise of religion but prohibiting any official state church are an indication of this general policy.

Nevertheless, over the years, the great institutions of the private sphere—family, church, and community—became a vital part of the American constitutional system, limiting American government in their own way. They taught and passed along the traditional culture and values that the framers had rejected. They emphasized the moral affections—love, mercy, and compassion—and the social virtues—sharing, sacrifice, and loyalty to one's friends—even at the cost of personal well-being. In their teaching, human beings are social animals, limited by nature and assigned a place in the natural order of things.

These institutions of the private sphere shared in the creed of the framers and were more influenced by it with time. Nevertheless, the private associations tended to see constitutional government in terms of community and the natural law. In times, when there were economic problems or in the great political crises that the framers could not have anticipated, the private sphere provided its own line of defense for constitutional government. In the rootless, antitraditional, and industrial conditions of modern life, family, church, and community have lost power to, or come under the influence of, national forces like the media, the corporations, and the federal government. Their decline is both a cause and a symptom of the contemporary crisis of constitutional government.

The Challenge to Constitutionalism

The Decline of the Division of Powers between States and the National Government

Today, we often seem to be overwhelmed by technological change. Great powers vanish and old cultures disappear; weapons of mass destruction grow more numerous and hideous. In political life, this change has weakened the mechanisms of the Constitution at almost every point.

The framers, as we have seen, believed in progress and wanted a government that welcomed change. They were impatient with older traditions and local loyalties and were irritated by the foot-dragging of states and communities jealous of their customs, and they shaped the Constitution with that in mind. As the framers intended, the division of powers has become ever more one-sided.

The growth of a national and international economy has deprived state and local governments of any real ability to regulate economic life. Great corporations, which can threaten to take jobs and investments elsewhere, are often able to dictate to state and local governments. Even the federal government has difficulty in controlling the great multinational corporations whose operations and assets are spread throughout the world. Even a great power like the United States has become strikingly vulnerable to international economic change.

For many years, the Supreme Court made a distinction between "manufactures," a local activity under the jurisdiction of the states, and "interstate

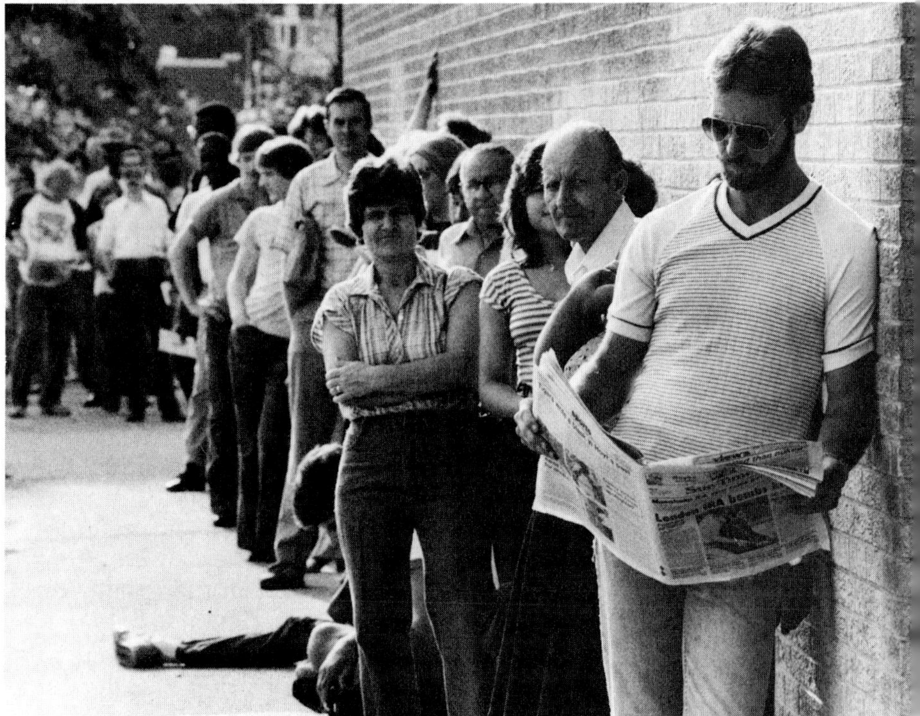

Unemployment and plant closings are fundamentally the result of national economic conditions and they can do terrible damage to localities. As a result, local governments have turned to Washington for assistance. *(©1983 Mark Pokempner/Black Star)*

commerce," subject to federal authority.[50] It soon admitted, however, that as a practical matter, commerce was becoming a single process in which the producers of raw materials, manufacturers, and consumers all logically came under federal authority.[51] Nevertheless, the Supreme Court was unwilling to scrap the old distinction altogether. Strikes, Justice George Sutherland wrote in 1936, are "local controversies . . . affecting local work undertaken to accomplish a local result." Their effect on interstate commerce was "indirect" by nature, Sutherland argued, even if this indirect effect was very great.[52] But the Court reversed itself the following year. Major strikes, which resulted from decisions by national corporations and unions, could not seriously be regarded as "local" conflicts. During the Great Depression of the 1930s, it was all too clear that working conditions were essentially national, not local.[53] Within a few years, the Court effectively opened the whole economy to federal regulation. "In present day industry," the Court declared in *U.S.* v. *Darby,* even "a small part may affect the whole."[54]

It is part of the same process that although welfare has traditionally been a job of local government, states and cities look to the federal government to pay the costs of welfare. Rich and liberal states have often felt exploited by the poor from other states who move there to get more generous welfare benefits. But states cannot prevent migration, and since the Court has ruled that there is a fundamental "right to travel" that must not be inhibited, a state cannot insist that people live in the state for some fixed period before becoming eligible for welfare.[55] Poverty and welfare are really national concerns, outside the control of the cities and states. Despite the Reagan administration's verbal support of a stronger role for state and local governments, Reagan's budgetary proposals—particularly his attack on revenue-sharing (see Chapter 3)—by decreasing the resources available to states and localities, would make their job even more difficult.

Mobility has also weakened the attachment of Americans to home and place. For increasing numbers of Americans, a state or a city is only a place where one happens to be living at the moment. Mobility means that the states and localities have little ability to command the loyalty of the people. The rise of loyalty to the federal government would please the framers, but they would probably be astonished at the size of the change, and they would certainly recognize the difference it makes in the constitutional design.

The Decline of the Separation of Powers between Congress and the Executive

The power of Congress has declined while that of the president has risen, radically changing the separation of powers. As America became an industrial society, it became clear very early that the pace of Congress was too slow to keep up with the rapid changes of the modern political world. Modern institutions have become so complicated that members of Congress are now no more than intelligent amateurs who depend on experts for information. Also the great crises of our time—war, depression, and social disorder—have created overwhelming needs and demands for action.[56]

DELEGATION OF POWER In domestic affairs, for example, Congress has been apt to limit itself to general goals and guidelines, leaving it to the president and his executive branch bureaucracy to work out the details of administration. In fact, this **delegation of legislative power** (see Table 2.2) tends to give great discretion and power to the bureaucrats: the Interstate Commerce Commission is told, for example, to fix "just and reasonable" rates.[57]

Sometimes, Congress passes laws that let administrators *suspend* the law or *bring it into effect* depending on what conditions they encounter. For instance, the president is allowed to make agreements with other countries, lowering the tariff on imported items or raising such tariffs and other trade penalties.[58] The tariff, once the most hotly debated issue in any Congress, has for the most part become a presidential matter exclusively.

In emergencies, Congress usually delegates even more power to the president. During the crisis of the Depression, important laws were passed hastily, delegating very broad authority to the president. The Supreme Court became alarmed, finding that the Congress often "left the matter to the President without standard or rule, to be dealt with as he pleased."[59] It made matters worse that the president sometimes turned this authority over to groups of private persons representing a particular industry. The Court found such delegation unconstitutional, insisting on more precise standards and procedures.

Nevertheless, the Supreme Court eventually admitted that the demands for speed, flexibility, and expertise made delegation a practical necessity, agreeing that rather vague standards were sufficient to permit Congress to delegate its authority.[60] Congress has developed a number of "tools of oversight" (see Chapter 9) designed to enable it to watch and influence the ways in which the president uses delegated power. Yet one of the most important of these, the "legislative veto" (see Chapter 9), was recently held unconstitutional by the Supreme Court. The Court's decision does not make it harder for Congress to delegate power; it only makes it more difficult to *control* that power once it has been delegated.*

In practice, almost every kind of delegation is likely to be upheld by the Supreme Court. Even those who hope that Congress can reverse this trend urge Congress to provide clear policy aims and are willing to leave the executive great freedom to determine the means of carrying out policy.[61]

Foreign Policy In foreign affairs, the weakness of Congress is most obvious. In the first place, speedy, decisive action is crucial. In the past, war was declared only after an attack had taken place, such as our declaration against Japan after the Japanese bombed Pearl Harbor in 1941. If an American president were today presented with satellite pictures showing that Soviet missiles were headed this way, he or she would order our own missiles to be fired without waiting to present evidence of the destruction to Congress and waiting for it to debate a declaration of war.

**INS* v. *Chadha* 103 S.Ct.2764 (1983). Since Congress will find it more difficult to control delegated power, it may become more reluctant to grant such power, but any such result is iffy at best.

Although the Constitution gives Congress the power to declare war, the president may use his power as commander-in-chief to send troops when speedy, decisive action is necessary. Here U.S. troops roll into Grenada to rescue American citizens from a revolutionary Marxist government. *(Jean-Louis Atlan/Sygma)*

Moreover, the president has virtually all the initiative in foreign affairs. The president can, for example, conclude executive agreements with foreign leaders that, although they do not bind his successors, are the "law of the land" without any action by Congress and override the laws of any state.[62]

Congress, by contrast, has only negative powers. It can refuse to appropriate money, and the Senate can veto appointments of ambassadors or fail to ratify treaties, but it cannot really offer alternative policies. In any specific situation, the use of its legislative powers is likely to make Congress seem obstructive, irresponsible, or unpatriotic. This was not the kind of institution the framers had in mind, and we will see in Chapters 8 and 9 more evidence of the growth of presidential power at the expense of Congressional authority.

The Decline of the Private Sphere

The Constitution, however, faces an even more fundamental problem, the decline of the private sphere, the source—in the framers' eyes—of liberty and governmental legitimacy.

Private life is characterized by two elements: private consequences and private responsibility. A private matter is "my business," an area that is simply "no concern of yours," because what I do or do not do has virtually no effect on you, now or in the foreseeable future. Public matters are those which, immediately or in their consequences, are of concern to all or at least to other citizens. Ordinarily, for example, what you wear is "your business." You and your employer may agree that on the job you will wear a uniform, and it is still none of "our business." If, on the other hand, you decide to wear a police uniform without being a member of the force (especially if you try to pass yourself off as a policeman), it becomes "our business" because it misleads the public.[63]

In the early days of the republic, the great majority of human relationships were private ones. Markets were local and businesses were small. Organizations came about by voluntary agreements between more or less equal individuals, and government did not get involved. It was a distant shadow on the life of society, keeping up a small army to deal with the Indians, regulating foreign trade, and watching—rather passively—the currents of commerce. That sense of the *predominance of the private* lasted into the industrial era and was found in the idea of "freedom and contract" as set forth by the Supreme Court:

> the right of the citizen to be free in the enjoyment of all his faculties; to be free to use them in all lawful ways; to live and work where he will; to earn his livelihood by any lawful calling; to pursue any livelihood or avocation and for that purpose to enter into all contracts which may be proper, necessary and essential to his carrying out to a successful conclusion the purposes above mentioned.[64]

An industrial economy, however, makes a hash of such ideas. In a complex national economy, what I agree to is much more likely to affect (and be affected by) others. In a dissenting opinion written in 1936, Justice Stone put the case that the Court would soon make into constitutional law:

> We have had the opportunity to learn that a wage is not always resultant of free bargaining between employers and employees, that it may be forced upon employees by their economic necessities and upon employers by the most ruthless of their competitors. We have had opportunity to perceive more clearly that a wage insufficient to support the worker does not visit its consequences on him alone; that it may profoundly affect the entire economic structure of society and, in any case, that it casts on every taxpayer and on government itself the burden of solving the problems of poverty, subsistence, health, and morals of large numbers in the community. . . . [T]hese public problems a generation ago were for the individual to solve; today, they are the burden of the entire nation.[65]

Of course, government also increasingly trespasses on the private sphere. When the Federal Reserve Board decided to fight inflation by raising interest rates, it made home mortgages much less affordable. But the fact that mortgage interest is a deduction for tax purposes encourages home ownership. These effects are immediate and clear, not distant and indirect. In crucial ways, politics shapes private life.

The decline of the distinction between public and private things is illustrated by the case of *Wickard* v. *Filburn.* In 1942, the Supreme Court ruled that a farmer who raised twenty-three acres of wheat and fed it to his livestock had engaged in "interstate commerce" because, in so doing, he had exerted some effect on the supply and price of wheat. It did not matter that this effect was small, the Court asserted, because "his contribution, taken together with that of many others similarly situated, is far from trivial."[66]

In the Court's argument, the public-private distinction has vanished, at least in economic life. Small-scale family farming is surely the most private of economic activities, but in *Wickard* v. *Filburn* the Court argued that we are so closely tied together that even this sort of farming is of public concern. Individual farmers, from an economic point of view, exist only as parts of the whole. They have identity only insofar as they are part of a larger group of other farmers, a smaller mass within mass industrial society.

The Crisis of the Private Order

The private individual, on whom the framers' theory was based, is increasingly vulnerable in modern America. As Edward Bloustein points out, we are required to give information about ourselves to get credit, qualify for benefits, or pay our taxes; we are open to communication through the telephones and the TV sets in our homes; and new technologies of control, from electronic bugs to computer memories, make it easier to pry into our private dealings.[67]

Wanting to protect the delicate basis of private life, the Supreme Court under Chief Justice Warren subjected police searchers to strict new limitations and struck at electronic bugging by saying that private conversation is a right protected by the Fourth Amendment.[68] Most important, the Court recognized that ignorance, confusion, and psychological pressure can confuse our reasoning ability. In *Miranda* v. *Arizona,* the Court insisted that any person accused of a crime be informed of his or her right to be silent, to consult a lawyer, and to have a lawyer appointed if he or she cannot afford one. What the Court did in the Miranda case was to cast doubt on the framers' theory, for it had declared that isolated human beings are neither rational nor free.[69] Under Chief Justice Warren Burger, the Court has changed its position somewhat, but it has left the basic principles of such decisions intact.

Former Chief Justice Earl Warren spearheaded the Supreme Court's efforts to protect the rights of individuals in modern society. (*Karsh, Ottawa*)

Yet, though the Court has found it relatively easy to protect *individuals* against interference by *government,* the Constitution makes it harder to deal with two other threats to private liberty. In the first place, it is not always possible to protect us against violations of our private space by private persons. The Court has held that Congress can grant individuals the right to have their names removed from mailing lists for materials they consider obscene, and cities can ban noisy sound tracks.[70] But in *Time Inc.* v. *Hill,* the Supreme Court heard a case involving a family which had been terrorized by bandits. Although the Hills wanted to avoid publicity about the incident, the story had been blown up by the media. The Court ruled that the Hills were "public figures," and subject to this kind of publicity, simply because the public had taken an interest in their case. At least in this instance, there was no right to privacy against the media.[71]

Second, it is even more difficult to safeguard the groups and communities on which we depend for nurturance, counsel, and support. Although the Court recognizes that isolated individuals are very far from free in a society that depends on the "art of association," the Constitution encourages us to see problems in terms of individual rights. In *Griswold* v. *Connecticut,* the Court struck down a state law forbidding the distribution of birth control materials to married couples because marriage is entitled to a right of privacy not extended to less intimate associations.[72] But in *Eisenstadt* v. *Baird,* a few years later, the Court asserted that marriage has no special status; the right of privacy is a right of the individual.[73] Similarly, the Court has expanded the private sphere in moral, spiritual, and intellectual life at the expense of groups and communities. For example, though the definition and punishment of murder was perhaps the first question ever brought to public authority, the Court has ruled that states may not define abortion as a prohibited homicide because it is included in the sphere of private rights.[74]

Decisions like these have come at a time when change and mobility, weakening the older institutions of the private order, also have lessened our willingness to make strong commitments to one another. This crisis of the private order has led many groups to look to government for support. The demands for government policies to support or strengthen the family, for the Equal Rights Amendment, for tax credits for tuition paid to church-related schools, for policies to strengthen and stabilize neighborhoods, and for community control, grow out of very different and conflicting political aims and ideas. Nevertheless, these demands also reflect a turning to public life in the hope of preserving or rebuilding the private order.

Such movements challenge the teaching of the framers. They assert in the manner of the ancient Greeks that human beings are political and social animals who need the support of others, and that those limits on government that must be preserved at all costs are those that come from the character of the people. More and more Americans, apparently, are listening to the ancient teaching that the structure of a society is flesh and blood humans, not the constitutional equivalent of cogs, balance wheels, and springs of some self-regulating clock.

SUMMARY

The guiding force of constitutionalism is limited government. As a rule of law, it aims to restrain political power and to establish legitimate means to the ends of political society.

The constitutions of republics presume that humans, although they are imperfect, want good for the political system as a whole. In order to achieve that good, the momentary will of a people must be kept from usurping their real will. Our Constitution attempts to keep the momentary will at bay by making provisions for deliberation over public issues.

The Articles of Confederation, adopted in 1781, was America's first constitution. It guaranteed the superior position of the states in relation to the central government, an imbalance that did not last for long. In 1787, the groundwork for a shift of power and loyalty from state to union was laid by the delegates to the Constitutional Convention.

Although this role of government as the champion of individual freedom was an integral part of American political consciousness, the framers did not initially consider a Bill of Rights necessary to protect the private rights of citizens. They were eventually persuaded by men like Jefferson that such a bill would remind Americans of the scope of their freedom and would draw strong public support for the Constitution.

American government was set up to be self-regulating, since it was assumed that what the common person wants is to be left alone. The framers of the Constitution divided the central government into the legislative, executive, and judicial branches and gave these branches overlapping jurisdiction in the hopes that no section would wield more power than another.

The framers believed one goal of humanity was to master nature through the acquisition of power and the achievement of material well-being. Consequently, the Constitution gives us free rein in our relations with foreign countries and in our search for material betterment.

Many government roles and institutions were established, not because they were written into the Constitution but because they were implied in it. The power of judicial review, by which the Supreme Court interprets what is essential in the Constitution and what can be changed in order for society to adapt to new circumstances, was not mentioned in the Constitution, nor was the political party, an institution that has played a vital part in American political life.

The Constitution barely refers to the private institutions of American life. The framers intended to preserve the family, church, and local community and yet keep them from oppressing the individual. In modern times the decline of these one-time bastions of American society, along with the rise of such influential forces as the media, presents to constitutional government one of its greatest challenges yet.

The growth of mobility and an international economy has loosened the hold states once had over economic life, a phenomenon that upsets the traditional balance of power between state and federal government. This constitutional crisis is compounded by the fact that the separation of powers between Congress and the president is no longer equal. The demand for fast action in the hectic arena of today's political world has forced Congress to delegate details of administration to the executive branch. The power of the president is particularly obvious in the conduct of foreign affairs, a sphere that Congress influences only through negative powers such as the veto.

Constitutional government in America faces an even more serious threat with the decline of the private sphere. More and more, our jobs and spending power are tied to the impersonal workings of an industrial economy, and many decisions made by forces like corporations prevent us from exercising complete control over our lives. The separation between the public and the private, of such utmost importance in our Constitution, has become endangered. When values that form the foundation of American democracy begin to crumble or grow obsolete, the durability of the Constitution must be seriously examined.

NOTES

1. C. H. McIlwain, *Constitutionalism: Ancient and Modern* (Ithaca: Cornell U. P., 1940), p. 23.
2. Walter Berns, "Religion and the Founding Principle," in *The Moral Foundations of the American Republic,* Robert Horwitz, ed. (Charlottesville: U. of Virginia, 1977), p. 177.
3. *Schneider* v. *Smith,* 390 U.S. 17,25 (1968) makes something of a case for positive rights. On the Warren Court and positive rights, see Martin Shapiro and Rocco J. Tresolini, *American Constitutional Law* (New York: Macmillan, 1975), pp. 584–85.
4. Alexander Hamilton, James Madison, and John Jay, *The Federalist,* Max Beloff, ed. (Oxford: Blackwell, 1948), pp. 278–80.
5. Alexis De Tocqueville, *Democracy in America* (New York: Schocken, 1961), vol. 1, pp. 379–80.
6. *The Federalist,* p. 66.
7. Ibid., p. 290.
8. William Leuchtenberg, *Franklin Roosevelt and the New Deal* (New York: Harper, 1963), p. 327.
9. Thomas Cronin, *The State of the Presidency* (Boston: Little, Brown, 1975), pp. 123–52, 289–324.
10. *The Federalist,* p. 320.
11. Finley Peter Dunne, *Mister Dooley's Opinions* (New York: Harper, 1969).
12. *The Federalist.* pp. 122–23; *McCulloch* v. *Maryland,* 4 Wh. 316, 415 (1819).
13. John Dykstra Eusden, *Puritans, Lawyers and Politics* (New Haven: Yale U. P., 1958).
14. Ewart K. Lewis, "The Contribution of Medieval Thought to the American Political Tradition," *American Political Science Review,* 1 (1956), pp. 462–74.
15. Cicero attributes this view to Cato in *De Re Publica.* II, xxi (37).
16. McIlwain, p. 14; see also J. W. Gough, "Fundamental Law in the Seventeenth Century," *Political Studies,* 1 (1953), p. 168, and J. G. A. Pocock, *The Ancient Constitution and the Feudal Law* (New York: Cambridge U. P., 1957).
17. *The Federalist,* pp. 1, 5, 53.
18. Ibid., p. 37.
19. Ibid., p. 62.
20. Ibid., p. 148.
21. Thomas Paine, *The Rights of Man,* in *Political Writings of Thomas Paine* (Chicago: Donohue, 1904), p. 278.
22. Merrill Jensen, *The Articles of Confederation* (Madison: U. of Wisconsin, 1940).
23. James Madison, "Vices of the Political System of the United States," in *The Writings of James Madison,* Gaillard Hunt, ed. (New York: Putnam, 1900–1910), vol. 2, pp. 361–69.
24. This view was popularized by Max Farrand, *The Framing of the Constitution of the United States* (New Haven: Yale U. P., 1913).
25. James Madison, *Notes of Debates in the Federal Convention of 1787.* A. Koch, ed. (Athens: Ohio U. P., 1966), pp. 304–305; Gordon Wood, "Democracy and the Constitution," in Robert Goldwin and William Schambra, eds., *How Democratic Is the Constitution?* (Washington, D.C.: American Enterprise Institute, 1980), p. 10.
26. Irving Brant, *James Madison: The Nationalist, 1780–1787* (Indianapolis: Bobbs, 1948), pp. 108–109.
27. Ann S. Diamond, "Decent Even Though Democratic," in Goldwin and Schambra, pp. 33–34.
28. C. C. Tansill, *Documents Illustrative of the Formation of the Union of American States* (Washington: Government Printing Office, 1927), pp. 588, 618; Brant, pp. 48, 241. On slavery in the Convention, see Staughton Lynd, *Class, Conflict, and Slavery in the Constitution of the United States* (Indianapolis: Bobbs, 1967).
29. In addition to Beard's *An Economic Interpretation of the Constitution* (New York: Macmillan, 1913), important works in this school include Lynd, and Merrill Jensen, *The New Nation*(New York: Random, 1950). Gordon Wood, *The Creation of the American Republic* (New York: Norton, 1972), is a good criticism of these ideas.
30. Madison's views may be found in his Address to the States, *Journal of the Continental Congress,* April 26, 1978; on the "monied interest," see *Writings of James Madison,*vol. 6, pp. 87–94, 104–105, 113–18, 120–23.
31. John Agresto, "Liberty, Virtue, and Republicanism, 1776–1787," *Review of Politics,* 39 (1977), pp. 473–504.
32. Hannah Arendt, *On Revolution* (New York: Viking, 1963), p. 214; *The Federalist,* p. 66; Tansill, p. 274.
33. *The Federalist,* p. 265.
34. Ibid., pp. 76–77.
35. Ibid., p. 441; *Writings of James Madison,*vol. 5, p. 272.
36. *Writings of James Madison,* vol. 6, pp. 70, 85–86, vol. 9, p. 101; *The Papers of James Madison,* W. T. Hutchinson, et al., eds. (Chicago: U. of Chicago, 1962–1977), (Charlottesville: U. of Virginia, 1977–), vol. 11, pp. 298–99; vol. 12, pp. 198–205, 373.
37. *The Federalist,* p. 265; see also *Writings of James Madison,* vol. 6, pp. 67–85; *Papers of James Madison,* vol. 11, p. 299.
38. James MacGregor Burns, *The Deadlock of Democracy* (Englewood Cliffs, N.J.: Prentice-Hall, 1963).
39. *The Federalist,* p. 20.
40. *Santa Clara County* v. *Southern Pacific Railroad,* 118 U.S. 394 (1886); *San Mateo County* v. *Southern Pacific Railroad,* 116 U.S. 138 (1885).
41. *The Federalist,* p. 398.
42. 1 Cr. 137 (1803).
43. 272 U.S. 52 (1926).
44. 295 U.S. 602 (1935).
45. *Wiener* v. *U.S.,* 357 U.S. 349 (1958).
46. *Reynolds* v. *Sims,* 377 U.S. 533 (1964).
47. James Beck, *The Constitution of the United States* (New York: Doran, 1924), p. 221.
48. *Grovey* v. *Townsend,* 295 U.S. 45 (1935); *Smith* v. *Allwright,* 321 U.S. 649 (1944); *Terry* v. *Adams,* 345 U.S. 506 (1953).
49. Cited in John Howe, *The Changing Political Thought of John Adams* (Princeton: Princeton U. P., 1966), p. 185.
50. *U.S.* v. *E. C. Knight,* 156 U.S. 1 (1895).
51. *Swift and Co.* v. *U.S.,* 196 U.S. 375 (1905).
52. *Carter* v. *Carter Coal,* 298 U.S. 238, 308 (1936).
53. *National Labor Relations Board* v. *Jones & Laughlin,* 301 U.S. 1 (1937).
54. *U.S.* v. *Darby,* 312 U.S. 100 (1941).
55. *Shapiro* v. *Thompson,* 394 U.S. 618 (1969).
56. Herman Belz, "Changing Conceptions of Constitutionalism

in the Era of World War II and the Cold War," *Journal of American History,* 59 (1972), p. 645.
57. *I.C.C.* v. *Illinois Central Railroad,* 215 U.S. 452 (1910).
58. *Hampton & Co.* v. *U.S.,* 276 U.S. 394 (1928).
59. *Panama Refining* v. *Ryan,* 293 U.S. 388 (1935).
60. *Opp Cotton Mills* v. *Administrator,* 312 U.S. 126 (1941).
61. Theodore Lowi, *The End of Liberalism* (New York: Norton, 1969.)
62. *U.S.* v. *Curtiss Wright,* 299 U.S. 304 (1936); *U.S.* v. *Belmont,* 301 U.S. 324 (1937).
63. John Dewey, *The Public and Its Problems* (New York: Holt, 1927), p. 12; *Munn* v. *Illinois,* 94 U.S. 113 (1877).
64. *Allgeyer* v. *Louisiana,* 165 U.S. 578 (1897).
65. *Morehead* v. *Tipaldo,* 298 U.S. 587 (1936).
66. *Wickard* v. *Filburn,* 317 U.S. 111, 127–28 (1942).
67. Edward J. Bloustein, "Group Privacy: The Right to Huddle," *Rutgers-Camden Law Journal,* 8, (1977), pp. 220–83.
68. *Mapp* v. *Ohio,* 367 U.S. 643 (1961); *Berger* v. *N.Y.,* 388 U.S. 41 (1967).
69. *Miranda* v. *Arizona,* 384 U.S. 436 (1964).
70. *Rowan* v. *Post Office Department,* 397 U.S. 728 (1970); *Kovacs* v. *Cooper,* 336 U.S. 77 (1949).
71. *Time Inc.* v. *Hill,* 385 U.S. 374 (1967).
72. *Griswold* v. *Connecticut,* 381 U.S. 479 (1965).
73. *Eisenstadt* v. *Baird,* 405 U.S. 438 (1972).
74. *Roe* v. *Wade,* 410 U.S. 113 (1973).

CHAPTER 3

Federalism

Marlene Gold, a college student, is a fictional example of American federalism. She was born in a local hospital, delivered by doctors whose training was subsidized by national funds and whose qualifications were certified by a state examination board. With the aid of a U.S. government loan guarantee, she attends a university that was built according to local building codes and follows the educational directives of the state department of education. On weekends, she drives home, keeping an eye out for local and county police, on an interstate highway, built by the state highway department, and paid for by the national Department of Transportation. Although largely unaware of federalism, Marlene is affected by it daily.

Federalism is one of the major components of the structure of American politics. It is the most obvious legal expression of the general fragmentation of power in the United States. But the real significance of federalism is political. From the Constitutional Convention to the Reagan years, many controversies have centered on the powers of national, state, and local government. Dividing power among different governments benefits some people but can hurt others.

All Americans are citizens of both the nation and the states where they live. Each of these governments—as well as cities, counties, school districts, and other authorities—make laws or regulations, deliver services, levy taxes, and impose obligations. Most decisions involve a sharing of power among these governments. Their cooperation helps to keep Americans alive. The water we drink often comes through dams built by the national government, is then inspected by state authorities, and finally is delivered to our taps by local agencies. Local schoolchildren from poor families eat subsidized lunches, consisting of surplus food accumulated nationally and distributed through the states.

In sharing power, the different levels of government usually cooperate, but they also check and balance each other. If the national armed forces attempt to place a dangerous facility, such as a missile site, near a populated area, they may find it difficult to get construction permits from state and local officials. If school boards discriminate against girls or blacks, they may arouse opposition and incur financial penalties from national officials.

The essence of the American federal relationship is vagueness. Power is fragmented and therefore subject to continuing political controversy. Although the Constitution made the statutes and treaties of the United States "the supreme law of the land," this ringing endorsement of national supremacy did not settle, but rather initiated, an unending debate. Indeed, the relationship between our national and state governments mirrors the varying demands of American society, so there can be no final settlement.

In this chapter, we will deal with four topics. We first examine the historical development of American federalism in legal and political doctrines. Next, we look at the contemporary practice of federalism, and then we match this practice against some of its theoretical values and effects. Finally, to bring the subject up to date, we deal with some contemporary policy issues involving both state and national governments. We will keep returning to these themes:

- Change in the meanings of federalism.
- The political nature of federalism.
- The effect of federalism on American fragmentation.

The Development of Federalism

Federalism in the Constitution

The ambiguity of American **federalism,** the division of power between the states and the national government, is evident from the beginnings of our government. As we have seen in Chapter 2, the Constitutional Convention was itself divided on the allocation of power between the states and the emerging national government. A few delegates favored a modified form of the Articles of Confederation. Although the states were not fully independent under the Articles—only the confederal Congress conducted diplomatic negotiations—they certainly were the principal governing units. The New Jersey Plan retained much of that autonomy. Other delegates wished virtually to abolish the states as meaningful political entities. Although these delegates were ready to keep the states in existence, their original Virginia Plan would have reduced them to clearly inferior status.

The Constitution, as adopted, both formed a strong national government and preserved some autonomy for the states. (The division of powers is summarized in the previous chapter, in Table 2.1.) Instead of establishing one government, the framers kept the existing state governments and created the new national government. Both would rule the same territory and people. They thereby ensured, in part deliberately, that there would be continuing clashes, adjustments and required cooperation. Realists as much

Federalism combines the diversity of states with the unity of central government, symbolized by these cars from many states in front of the Washington Monument. *(John Schultz/ PAR-NYC)*

as philosophers, they were willing to accept ambiguity and to admit that their product was a mixture of principles.

In shaping these governments, the Constitution did establish boundaries, but these limits were not marked by barbed wire but by scratches in the dust of governmental power. The currents of history often have shifted, and sometimes erased, these demarcations. Because it is a document about the national government, the Constitution is largely devoted to this new authority. Its powers are phrased in positive terms—Congress, the president, and the U.S. courts are told what they can do. The restrictions on them, what they cannot do, are explicit only in a few instances. Other limitations, if they exist, must be inferred from the Constitution's language. Therefore, further restrictions require the winning of a political or legal debate.

National and State Powers The national government in Washington (sometimes called the federal government) is provided a series of specific powers. These include the major functions of any sovereign political system—conducting foreign relations, raising armies, borrowing money, and directing other economic matters, such as providing a system of money. Restrictions on the national government essentially deal with the protection of individual rights. The original Constitution, for example, prohibited any religious test for office. Many more protections were added in the Bill of Rights. Otherwise, the national government was relatively uninhibited in the explicit language of the Constitution. In taxation, for example, the only limits were bans on export or "direct" taxes.

States are given less attention in the Constitution. They are generally forbidden to engage in any diplomatic relations with foreign nations, and their military activities, such as creation of a state militia, are subject to national control. They may not interfere with foreign or interstate com-

POLITICAL PERSPECTIVE

THE VARIETY OF AMERICAN STATES

The social foundation of federalism in the United States is the great variety among the American states. This is shown by a few facts.

In population, the states range from California's 23.7 million people (in 1980) and New York's 17.6 million to Alaska's 402,000 and Wyoming's 470,000. The fastest growing state is Nevada, while New York has actually lost people from 1970 to 1980. The center of population in 1980 was in Missouri, the first time this center was located west of the Mississippi river.

When it comes to geographical size, Alaska leads, followed by Texas, whereas Rhode Island is the smallest. The nation stretches from Maine in the East to Washington state and Hawaii in the West, and from Alaska and Minnesota in the North to Florida and Hawaii in the South. The geographical center of the United States is in Kansas.

Americans are greatly affected by their state governments. Their taxes range from $6,316 per person in Alaska and $1,622 in Wyoming, down to $353 in New Hampshire. The highest spending is in California, $42 billion. Government does less in Vermont, which has the lowest budget of any state, $832 million.

Life itself is different across the country. Alaska has the lowest death rate, and Florida the highest. When it comes to cars, however, there is the greatest chance of death in auto accidents in West Virginia and the lowest chance in Rhode Island. The temperature is also different. In Alaska, it was once 80 degrees below zero, but California saw a high of 134. It rains most in Alabama, 67 inches a year, but only 7 inches annually in Arizona.

Every state has some unique attribute. Texas was an independent country for five years. North Carolina, although one of the original colonies, did not join the Union until two years after the Constitutional Convention. The state song of Oklahoma was originally the title song of a Broadway musical. Delaware was the first state to ratify the Constitution, and Hawaii the last to join.

merce (though, as we shall see, the meaning of these terms is not clear). Some protection of individual liberties against state action is also included, but the Bill of Rights as originally written did not restrict the states. Only in the last fifty years has the Supreme Court made these civil liberties generally applicable. This is one example of the changing character of federalism in the United States.

In terms of positive authority, the Constitution does not grant many specific legal powers to the states. Instead, the implicit assumption of our system—made explicit by the Tenth Amendment—is that the states may engage in any activities that are not specifically denied to them or granted exclusively to the federal government. It is for the states to decide whether they want to operate schools and universities, regulate drugs or driving or both, build highways, or tear down slums.

One important state power involves the establishment and control of local governments, since cities and towns are not even mentioned in the Constitution, and must be legally created through state action. Perhaps the most important power of the states is the so-called "police power" (see Chapter 13), a general authority to pass laws necessary to ensure the health, safety, and morals of the community. This is the legal basis for variation in the criminal statutes of the states, and for their controls on motor vehicles, alcohol and drugs, gambling, and public morals.

POLITICAL PERSPECTIVE

HAVE A DRINK?

Federalism has affected matters as personal as drinking alcohol.

For the first hundred years of the Constitution, regulation of drinking was essentially left to the states, with the national government only collecting some taxes on alcohol. Even this limited involvement brought resentment. George Washington had to interrupt his presidency to lead troops to put down a small tax protest called the Whiskey Rebellion.

This *Almanac for the Temperance Crusade*, published in 1875, is an example of the propaganda literature distributed by members of the Prohibitionist Movement. Efforts to bring about national prohibition finally succeeded in 1919. *(The Bettmann Archive)*

In the late nineteenth century, the prohibitionist movement tried to get states to ban all liquor. They ran into the opposition of the Supreme Court, which ruled that only the national government could control the distribution of liquor across state lines, as long as the liquor stayed in its original packages.

Opponents of drinking were able to get Congress to pass legislation that gave the states the right to prohibit drinking. But the antiliquor, temperance groups organized a campaign to abolish drinking throughout the United States. Distributing 165 million pieces of literature and organizing in elections, they were able by 1919 to get the Eighteenth Amendment to the Constitution passed, outlawing the manufacture, distribution and sale of liquor.

Prohibition never really worked. In 1933, in the record time of nine months, the Twenty-first Amendment was added to the Constitution, repealing the ban on alcohol. However, in a kind of cooperative federalism, the amendment also outlawed the transportation of liquor into any state that wanted to keep prohibition.

Today, alcohol is regulated both by the states and the national government. You can buy liquor only by the glass in some states, while elsewhere you can't get a drink in a restaurant. Sometimes liquor is sold in state-owned package stores, and sometimes the law varies from county to county.

The national government makes money from alcohol, since it is the third largest source of its revenue. At the same time, Washington sponsors school programs to warn about alcohol abuse, conducts research into alcoholism, and is considering a ban on television commercials for beer; liquor manufacturers voluntarily keep ads for hard liquor off the air.

Does it make a difference? The best estimates are that the average adult American in 1790 consumed six gallons of alcohol each year. By 1920, when national prohibition began, drinking was down to two gallons. Today, it is less than three a year.

Sources: Peter Odegard, *Pressure Politics* (New York: Columbia U. P., 1928); Mark E. Lender and James K. Martin, *Drinking in America: A History* (New York: Free Press, 1982).

The fact that the states possess reserved powers, however, does not mean that the states alone exercise these powers. A very large share of domestic government activity involves concurrent or shared powers, where both the state and national authorities are involved. There is no specific language in the Constitution that provides for the national government to participate in such state activities as education, law enforcement, highways, or housing—but, in fact, billions of dollars are raised annually in Washington for such programs. The indefinite boundaries of the Constitution have permitted historical shifts in the relative powers and jurisdiction of the different governmental bodies.

Throughout these shifts, there has been one permanent doctrine. As expressed by the Supreme Court, the federalist premise has been that the Constitution "looks to an indestructible Union composed of indestructible States."[1] Defining the relative strength of these two elements has added an important jurisdictional dimension to American politics. It has meant that policy issues must be debated both on the substantive issue—should child labor be abolished?, for example—and in regard to which government should act—is child labor a proper subject for national rather than state legislation? The Supreme Court has been the arbiter to decide these issues.

Increasing National Power In setting the boundaries of federalism, the Supreme Court has generally approved a long-term increase in the authority of the national government. In its decisions, the Court has relied on four clauses in the Constitution. One is the power of Congress to *tax and spend* "for the common Defence and general Welfare of the United States." This phrase has been interpreted to mean not only that the federal government in Washington can tax but that it can use taxes for purposes that, it believes, contribute to defense and welfare. Thus, there is no specific constitutional authority to create a social security system, but it is permissible because old-age insurance is financed through designated taxes.[2]

Another source of national authority is a collective **war power** in the Constitution, which derives from the government's right to raise armies, conduct diplomacy, and engage in war. Under these mandates, the government has been able to impose rationing in wartime, for example, or—in settling the Iranian hostage crisis in 1981—to cancel all private claims against the Teheran government.[3]

There are two other statements in the Constitution that have been critical in defining the federal balance. Congress is given power "*to regulate Commerce* with foreign Nations, and among the several states." It is also granted a vague authority, listed last in this section of the Constitution, "To make all Laws which shall be *necessary and proper* for carrying into Execution the foregoing Powers." We will see the importance of these terse phrases in the following pages.

Federalism in History

Three different kinds of federalism might have developed from the original Constitution. (They are shown in Figure 3.1.) The possibilities are (1) a hierarchy, in which the national government dominates the states and the states in turn dominate the local governments, (2) a complete separation

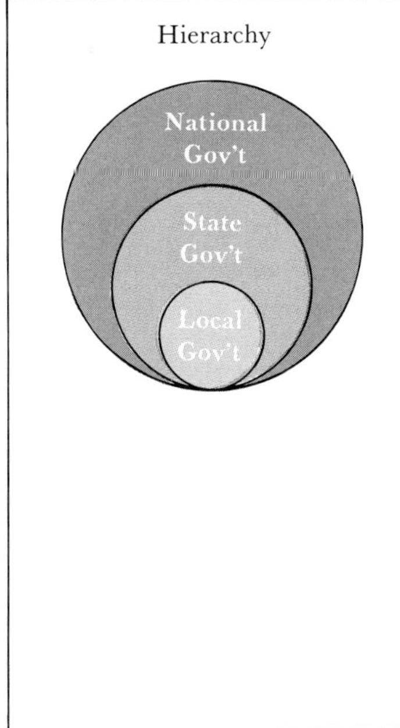

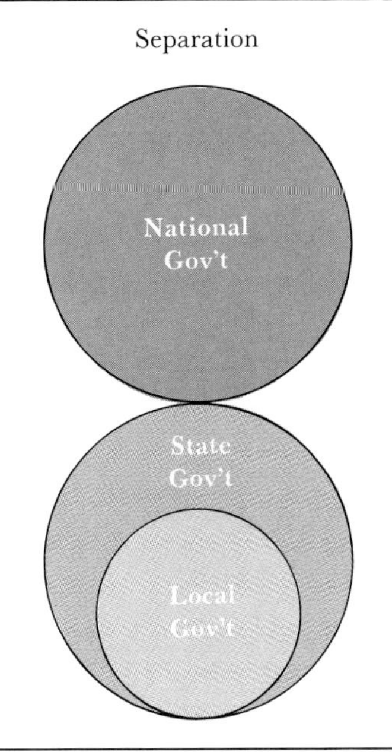

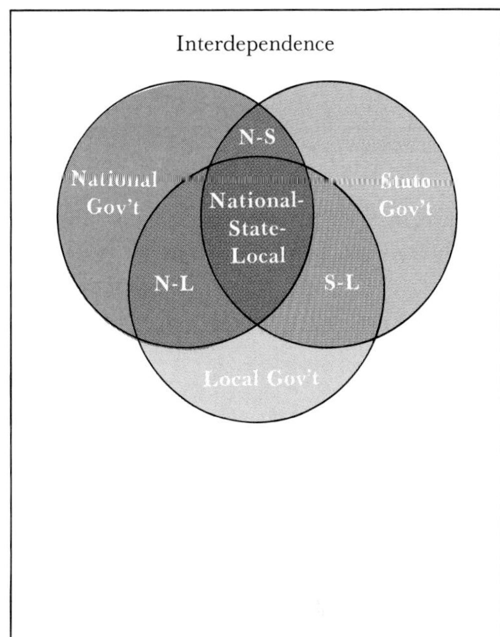

FIGURE 3.1
Models of Federalism
(From Understanding Intergovernmental Relations, *2nd ed., by Deil Wright. Copyright © 1978, 1982 by Wadsworth, Inc. Reprinted by permission of Brooks/Cole Publishing Company, Monterey, California 93940.)*

between the national and state governments, with local units within and under the authority of their states, and (3) overlapping and interdependence among the powers of the three levels.[4]

These differences are like different kinds of families. In a hierarchy, one partner, the wife or husband, takes charge and makes the major decisions while the other passes on these directives to the children who have little say in family matters. With complete separation, the husband might have charge of the cooking, and the wife would be responsible for the car, and one of them would supervise the kids. In an interdependent family, all members would share responsibilities. Like families, government changes over time. Each of these three models has been evident in American history.

Hierarchy National dominance, following the first, hierarchical model, was promoted by John Marshall, Chief Justice of the Supreme Court at the beginning of the nineteenth century. In a number of decisions, he established the continuing Constitutional precedents for a broad interpretation of the national government's power. In 1819, a major case concerned the Bank of the United States, which had been set up by Congress. The Constitution had clearly given Congress the power to regulate the currency, but there was no specific authority to create a bank. In *McCulloch* v. *Maryland,* Marshall filled in the silences of the written Constitution. Interpreting the vague congressional power to make "necessary and proper" laws, the Chief Justice read this "elastic clause" as allowing the national government to use virtually any means to promote its designated goals. He wrote:

> Let the end be legitimate, let it be within the scope of the Constitution, and all means which are appropriate, which are plainly adapted to that end, which are not prohibited, but consistent with the letter and spirit of the Constitution, are constitutional.[5]

Despite claims of "states' rights," the national government has intervened to protect the civil rights of black Americans. Following the climactic 1965 march from Selma to Montgomery, Alabama—shown here—President Lyndon Johnson won passage of the Voting Rights Act later the same year. *(UPI/Bettmann Newsphotos)*

Marshall went on to assert national supremacy. Not only was the Bank legitimate, but the state of Maryland could not tax this agency. In any clash of national and state governments, the general government must be dominant, he declared. In other decisions, the Court he led established a broad national power to regulate interstate commerce. It said that the authorities in Washington could pass laws dealing with virtually any kind of economic activity that affected more than one state.

The power of the national government is now sufficient to affect all aspects of the national economy and its social structure. Whether Congress and the president take action on such questions as energy conservation, employment, farming, or labor is no longer a constitutional question but a political issue. The broad reach of government under the commerce power was dramatically demonstrated during the civil rights movement. Blacks were for decades segregated in the Southern states and not permitted to sleep in motels or to eat in restaurants reserved for whites. When Congress finally moved against segregation under the 1964 Civil Rights Act, it based its actions on its power to regulate interstate commerce not on other provisions (such as the Fourteenth Amendment) that deal specifically with equality under the law. The Supreme Court unanimously upheld this legislation.[6]

Separation At other times, the federal model has been closer to that of the second diagram, a separation between the national and state governments. Particularly in the period from the Civil War to the New Deal, an effort was made to draw a distinct line between the powers of the two governments and to maintain a system of "dual federalism." The Supreme Court saw its role as an arbiter between two sovereign powers and tried to keep them distinct and independent.

Child labor illustrated this approach. At the beginning of this century, children as young as nine years old worked in factories, usually in unsanitary and unsafe conditions. To combat this exploitation, Congress banned any products made by child labor from interstate commerce. But the Court took the side of manufacturers. It declared the national action an invasion of the states' constitutional authority. When the political winds changed, decades later, another Court permitted similar legislation.[7]

INTERDEPENDENCE Since the 1930s, there has been a major expansion of state-national relationships, and some sharing of federal tax revenues with the states, creating the modern model of **cooperative federalism** where the national and state governments cooperate with each other.

In education, for example, all levels of government are involved. The national government runs some schools directly, provides billions of dollars of aid to the states and local areas for almost all school districts, and enforces some regulations (such as nondiscrimination). State governments provide a major share of school spending and establish most regulations on curriculum, teacher certification, and attendance. Local municipalities or school districts actually administer the schools, hire teachers, and enroll pupils.

Federalism in Political Debate

Setting the boundaries of the federal system is a political decision. Federalism has changed—not simply because judges have changed their minds but because the system reflects the political realities and ideological doctrines of the nation. For two hundred years, the division of power between the states and the nation has been debated not only in polite court briefs but in vigorous political conflicts.

HAMILTON AND JEFFERSON Alexander Hamilton, upon the initiation of the new Constitution in 1789, made major efforts to enhance the power of the national government. By a vigorous program of national economic development, he hoped to make the new national government the dominant force in the economy and in the nation. His efforts were opposed by Thomas Jefferson, who became the first prominent defender of "states' rights." Arguing for a limited national role, Jefferson sought to reduce federal activities and expenditures. In his first inaugural address, he argued for "the support of the State governments in all their rights, as the most competent administrations for our domestic concerns and the surest bulwarks against anti-republican tendencies." At the same time, Jefferson endorsed "the preservation of the General Government in its whole constitutional vigor, as the sheet anchor of our peace at home and our safety abroad."[8]

THE CIVIL WAR The Civil War turned the debate from words to blood. Claiming the right to secede from the Union, eleven Southern states established the Confederacy. Abraham Lincoln, while at first willing to accept the continued but restricted existence of slavery, insisted that the national ties must be preserved:

> No state upon its own mere motion can lawfully get out of the Union; that resolves and ordinances to that effect are legally void; and that acts of violence, within any State or States, against the authority of the United States, are insurrectionary or revolutionary.[9]

After four years and 600,000 war deaths, the basic issue was settled. The national government had not only established the principle of perpetual union; it had also assumed broad new powers to direct the society and economy of the United States. The war brought a national currency, a national system of railroad transportation, and the first program of national aid to education through the land-grant colleges.

The New Deal The issues of federalism continued to be disputed, more peacefully, for the next hundred years, centering on such questions as the level of tariffs on imports and control of the currency. (See Chapter 16 on economic policy.) The New Deal of Franklin Roosevelt raised the debate to a higher temperature. To meet the crisis of 25 percent unemployment, widespread bank failures, home foreclosures, and ruined farms, the national government assumed many new functions. Programs were established to provide welfare, work, and housing, to insure bank deposits, conserve soil, and even to aid the arts. Many of these programs were channeled through the states, but the federal balance had clearly tipped toward Washington, as the national government's budget and paid employment doubled from 1933 to 1940.*

Modern Times Federalism remains an issue in contemporary politics. President Ronald Reagan used the occasion of his 1981 inauguration to express his intention to reduce the activity of the federal government, symbolized by moving the ceremony to the west front of the Capitol, facing toward the newer regions of the country. Arguing that "the Federal Government did not create the states; the states created the Federal Government," the new president foretold his program to transfer some functions to the states, while reducing national nonmilitary spending. Four years later, he claimed that his administration had "already started returning to the people and to state and local governments responsibilities better handled by them."[10]

The president's opponents, however, would not agree. Some thought he had done too little, only slowing but not stopping the expansion of national power. Others thought he had done too much, involving the government in such personal matters as religion, or harming the poor and needy by changes in necessary programs. One conclusion is clear, as we mark the Constitution's bicentennial anniversary. Federalism continues to be a major framework for the fragmented political conflicts of the United States.

*By today's standards, the resulting figures would seem small. In 1940, the federal budget was still only $9 billion, the national debt but $43 billion, and total civilian employment little more than a million. See U.S. Bureau of the Census, *Historical Statistics of the United States, Colonial Times to 1957* (Washington, 1960), pp. 710–11.

The Practice of Federalism

Much of the justification and historical description of federalism is phrased in terms of states' rights and the "clashing sovereignties" of the state and national governments. The reality of contemporary federalism is quite different. There are few clear separations between these "levels" of government. In most programs, "cooperative federalism" is the rule. Furthermore, the system does not involve a single national unit and fifty state commonwealths. In addition, there are interstate relationships (the Appalachian Regional Commission), interlocal ties (metropolitan government in Dade County, Florida), public corporations handling governmental functions (the Port of New York Authority), and independent federal agencies (the Tennessee Valley Authority).

These relationships are so varied and complex that the term "federalism," suggesting a simple two-tier division of authority, is deceptive and inaccurate. Specialists in the field now refer to **intergovernmental relationships,** which means "not only national-state and interstate relations but also national-local, state-local, national-state-local, and interlocal relations.[11] The relations among governments are a web, or mesh, with the strings of the web running in all directions—not just up-and-down between the state and federal governments but in all directions. Using a different analogy, Morton Grodzins argued against the traditional idea that American government was a "layer cake," with the three levels of national, state, and locality distinctly separated. Instead, he argued, "A far more accurate image is the rainbow or marble cake, characterized by an inseparable mingle of differently colored ingredients, the colors appearing in vertical and diagonal strands and unexpected whirls. As colors are mixed in the marble cake, so functions are mixed in the American federal system."[12]

Simply because the different governmental bodies are closely related, there is no inevitable conflict between them. Thus, when the national government becomes involved in a particular program, it does not mean that the states and local areas lose their power in that area. Indeed, the opposite is the case most often. Federal activities are usually conducted through

Highway construction is a power shared by national, state, and local governments. *(Chuck Fishman and Contact Press Images, Inc.)*

these other authorities and permit them to do more, not less. We have seen how the legal power of the national government has grown. At the same time, the states have taken on more jobs and have spent more money. Even though there are frequent complaints about the dominance of the national government, the facts are that state spending has increased faster and that state and local governments together now account for the largest proportion of domestic spending.

Overall, the national government certainly spends the most money. But the largest shares of its budget go to the military and veterans, foreign relations, the debt, and Medicare and pensions for the aged. On all other domestic programs, Washington in 1986 spent about $200 billion. By contrast, the states and localities spent more than twice as much, close to $500 billion.[13]

National Grant Programs

National involvement with the states is most significant in the form of *grants,* money sent from the U.S. Treasury to state and local governments. There are four basic varieties: categorical grants, project grants, block grants, and revenue sharing. Differences between them are summarized in Table 3.1. Trends are seen in Figure 3.2.

TABLE 3.1 Four Ways to Spend Money

The system of national grants to the states varies with different kinds of grants. These are some of the basic questions and general answers about the four types.

Categorical	Project	Block	Revenue Sharing
How is the money allocated?			
Congressional formula	Administrator decision	Formula & administrators	Congressional formula
What is the money used for?			
Specific program	Specific program	Broad program	Any program
Must the states and cities also provide money?			
Yes	Usually	Sometimes	No
How much discretion do state and local officials have in spending?			
Limited	Very limited	Broad	Almost full
Which government usually receives the money from Washington?			
State	Local	Local	State, local

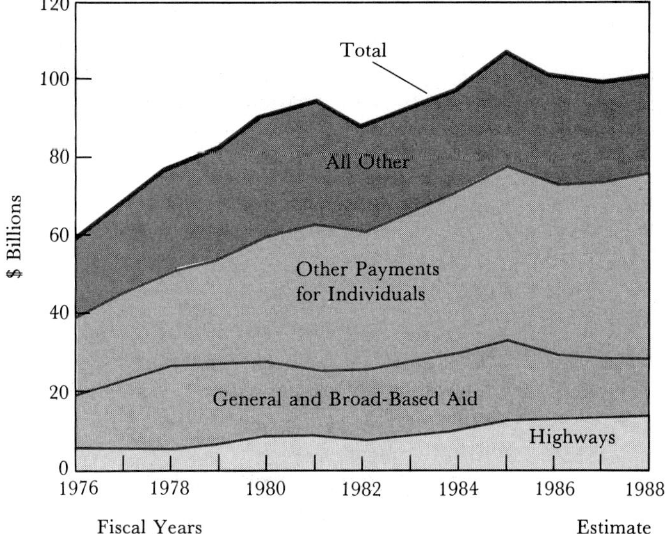

FIGURE 3.2
Federal Grants to State and Local Governments
(U.S. Office of Management and Budget, Special Analyses, Budget of the United States Government, Fiscal Year 1986 *[Washington, 1985], p. H-3.)*

CATEGORICAL GRANTS The original and still most significant form is the **categorical formula grant.** The national government, through Congress, decides that it should support a particular activity, such as highway construction. The total funds provided for this purpose are then divided among the states according to some formula, such as the relative population of each state or its total area, or a combination of factors. In almost every case, there is a requirement for matching funds, perhaps only one state dollar for every nine federal dollars as in the case of interstate highways, perhaps as much as equal state and national contributions.

Each of these elements in a grant involves a political decision with great financial effects on the states. If a program is largely financed by the national government, this means that the state is relatively free of its cost, which is now shared by taxpayers throughout the country. Therefore, each state will argue that its greatest needs require national action and urge a low matching ratio. For example, states with growing populations want grants to build water supply systems. States with declining populations want funds to rehabilitate aged housing.

PROJECT GRANTS After 1960, many programs were of a different variety—**project grants.** Congress still specified the purpose of grants—such as compensatory education for children of low-income families or elimination of rats in urban buildings—but it did not establish a formula for distributing the grants. These decisions were left to national administrators, who allocated funds to different projects submitted by state and local officials. Especially prominent in this "grants explosion" were increased attention to urban areas and to disadvantaged persons—those of low education, low income, and in racial minorities. Moreover, many federal programs circumvented the states, with money going directly to local or regional authorities.

Standing "under the shower of federal grants," state and local officials sought to compete to catch the flow. Since project grants allowed administrative discretion, each state and local agency could hope to get a larger share for itself. "Grantsmanship" became a new professional activity. "Playing the federal grant 'game' became a well-known but time-consuming activity for mayors, city managers, county administrators, school officials, governors, and, of course, program professionals."[14] One small, poor town—Blades, Delaware—was able to garner grants amounting to $3,700 per person.[15]

Block Grants A third variant of fiscal federalism attempts to deal with these problems. This is the system of **block grants,** under which the national government provides funds for a broad policy area, rather than a specific program. As initiated in the Johnson and Nixon administrations, these grants provide support for a function such as law enforcement. The specific actions to be taken under the grant—whether to buy new equipment for police or to use the money for civilian patrols, for example—is left up to the individual state or city. The reputed advantage of block grants is that they allow more variety to meet local conditions, instead of having these decisions made under detailed regulations from Washington. However, an interest group favoring a particular program—such as manufacturers of police revolvers—might prefer that the national government control that expenditure. The concept of block grants is widely applauded. When it comes to practice, however, many ask the old political question, "Whose ox is being gored?"—or shot.

Revenue Sharing The most generous national program is **revenue sharing.** Originated in the Kennedy administration and finally enacted in 1972, this program simply passes federal tax revenues back to the states or localities for whatever programs they wish. There are few federal controls, other than auditing and requirements of nondiscrimination. With virtually "no strings attached," the program is obviously popular with these other governments. Of the original funding of $7 billion, two-thirds went to local governments and one-third to the states.

The revenue-sharing program is justified as a means of allowing diverse states and cities to make their own policy choices. It is an attempt to combine the greater ability of the national government to raise money with the assumed greater ability of the more localized governments to respond to citizen needs. Some groups, of course, do not like the way these latter governments respond and want to maintain federal controls. Many state administrators also prefer to maintain their own financial ties to "their" federal agency, rather than compete for funds from the state governor and legislature. Congress, too, is not eager to give up its power to decide on policy objectives while providing substantial amounts for unknown purposes. Consequently, despite its benefits to all states and localities, the revenue-sharing program is politically vulnerable. When the federal government sought to cut its own spending in 1980, one of the first targets was the state share of these revenues. Then, to help meet the large national government deficits, the local share was also eliminated in the 1986 budget. For the immediate future, it is likely that grants will either be through the popular categorical programs or through block grants.

Trends in Grants A major expansion of national programs occurred over the past quarter of a century. In 1960, the degree of national involvement was relatively limited, with a total of 150 programs, providing $7 billion annually. As the nation turned to new concerns, spending on the environment, health, education, airport construction and job training grew. By 1981, total grants were $95 billion, in over 500 programs.

The Reagan administration was committed to reducing the impact of the national government, aside from the military. It attempted major changes, and did succeed in merging or eliminating some programs, and in reducing the total expenditures to $88 billion. By the second Reagan term, grant spending was over the previous highmark in total dollars, but Washington's relative role had certainly been reduced. The total number of programs had been reduced to 400, and more of them were in block grant form. These trends are illustrated in Figure 3.3.[16]

Whenever money is available, there is also competition for Washington's dollars. Competing areas emphasize different programs, different formulas, and different levels of support. States in the Northeast and Midwest feel that their constituents provide the taxes to pay for benefits to the South and West. To get more of the federal largesse, their representatives have formed a "Frostbelt" caucus in the House, inevitably leading to countermobilization by "Sunbelt" legislators. Each year, these contending groups strive to "get theirs." This interstate competition is another side of the federal structure.

Complaints by the Frostbelt states have been accented by the policy changes of the Reagan administration. By shifting the focus of national efforts from social needs, such as poverty programs, to physical development, such as highways, more funds have gone to the Western states. At the same time, the national government has increased its military spending, which tends to be concentrated in the Sunbelt. The combination of these factors means that some states benefit, while others unwillingly learn that "it is more blessed to give than receive." For example, New Jersey gets only 68 cents from the national government for every dollar its residents pay to

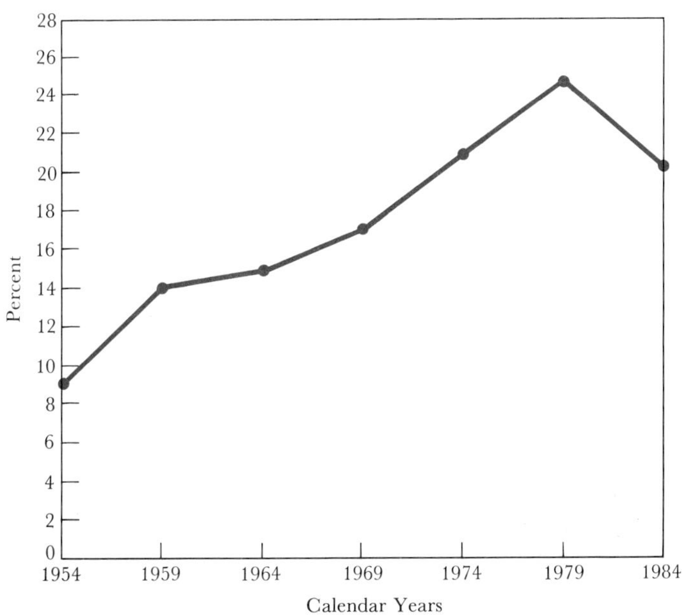

FIGURE 3.3
The Rise and Decline of Federal Aid
Federal aid as a percentage of state-local expenditures after transfers. *(ACIR staff compilation based on* Survey of Current Business *reports.)*

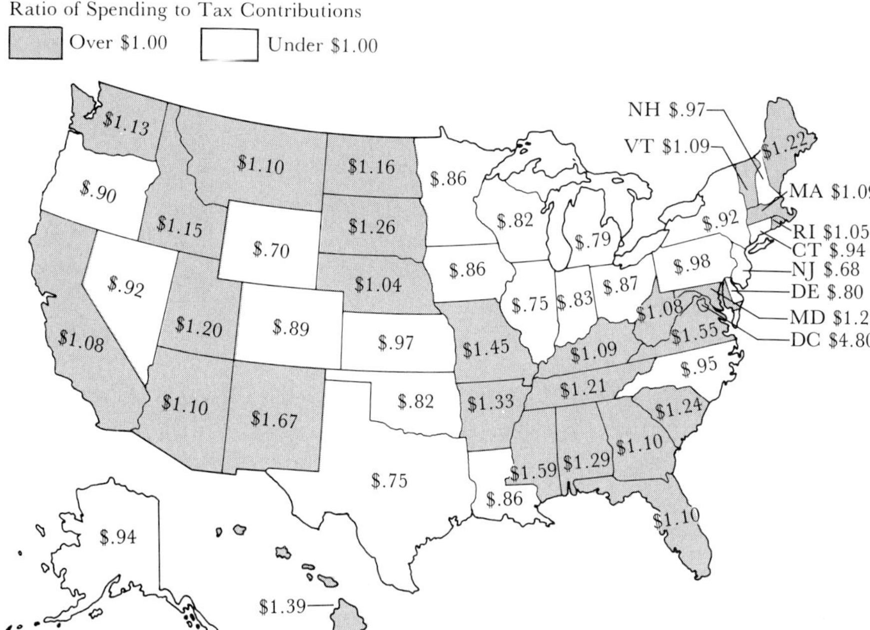

FIGURE 3.4
Federal Spending and State Taxes
The figure shows the federal spending in each state, for both grants and military purposes, for each dollar of tax revenue. *(U.S. Department of Commerce, Bureau of the Census,* Federal Expenditures by State for Fiscal Year 1983 *[Washington, 1984].)*

Washington. In contrast, New Mexico gets $1.67 back for every dollar. The relative gains and losses for each state are shown in Figure 3.4.

Federal Regulation

In the past two decades, intergovernmental relations have taken a new form. The financial relationships of grants, in their different forms, have been supplemented by legal and administrative regulation. Now states and cities are not only given money for such purposes as installing water systems or building public schools, they are also directed to meet certain standards in order to qualify for the money. Maintaining certain water quality levels or providing bilingual education for foreign-born students are examples of such standards.

Regulations are imposed by all branches of the national government. The courts have acted directly in some instances, such as protecting constitutional rights. Congress and the president have approved many laws imposing mandates on state and local governments. By one count, there are thirty-six general regulatory statutes now in effect, as well as many lesser requirements. The major laws are listed in Table 3.2. Most were enacted in the 1970s, and during relatively conservative, Republican administrations. The bureaucracy has actively supplemented these laws with detailed rules of implementation.

National regulations are far less welcome than grant programs. Instead of opening up opportunities, they impose obligations, causing one Democratic governor to protest "the heavy hand of Federal regulation in local programs of every kind: school lunches, libraries, fire protection, street maintenance, the local symphony."[17] These regulations impose a national standard, often disregarding local differences in needs and traditions. Sometimes they are backed up financially with a threat to withhold grant funds. Moreover, the cost can be significant, adding up to as much as a fifth of all aid received locally.[18]

Despite these criticisms, **regulatory federalism**—as this system of conditional grants is called—is likely to persist. Its objectives are often idealistic, promoting such decent goals as a purer environment or more attention to the handicapped. Beyond idealism, the economic unity of the nation makes such matters as clean air and water matters of general, not only local, concern. Politically, the use of regulatory techniques is attractive. Just as "liberals" want to use the power of the national government to provide aid to the poor, "conservatives" want to use that power to foster school prayer. Accomplishing these goals through uniform and rapid federal action is pleasing; seeking the same goals through scattered state action is difficult and likely to be futile.

TABLE 3.2 Major Statutes of Intergovernmental Regulation, 1960–1980

Year	Statute
1964	Civil Rights Act (Title VI)
1965	Highway Beautification Act
	Water Quality Act
1966	National Historic Preservation Act
1967	Wholesome Meat Act
1968	Civil Rights Act (Title VIII)
	Architectural Barriers Act
	Wholesome Poultry Products Act
1969	National Environmental Policy Act
1970	Occupational Safety and Health Act
	Clean Air Act Amendments
	Uniform Relocation Assistance and Real Property Acquisition Policies Act
1972	Federal Water Pollution Control Act Amendments
	Equal Employment Opportunity Act
	Education Act Amendments (Title IX)
	Coastal Zone Management Act
	Federal Insecticide, Fungicide, and Rodenticide Act
1973	Flood Disaster Protection Act
	Rehabilitation Act (Section 504)
	Endangered Species Act
1974	Age Discrimination Employment Act
	Safe Drinking Water Act
	National Health Planning and Resources Development Act
	Emergency Highway Energy Conservation Act
	Family Educational Rights and Privacy Act
	Fair Labor Standards Act Amendments
1975	Education for All Handicapped Children Act
	Age Discrimination Act
1976	Resource Conservation and Recovery Act
1977	Surface Mining Control and Reclamation Act
	Marine Protection Research and Sanctuaries Act Amendments
1978	National Energy Conservation Policy Act
	Public Utility Regulatory Policy Act
	Natural Gas Policy Act

Source: Advisory Commission on Intergovernmental Relations, *Regulatory Federalism: Policy, Process, Impact and Reform* (Washington, 1984), p. 6.

Regulation by the Courts The involvement of the courts in federal regulation is illustrated by the way representatives are chosen in state legislatures. Until 1962, the Supreme Court had taken the position that the states could determine for themselves the composition of state legislatures and other governmental bodies. However, inequality often resulted. Where legislators were chosen from geographical units such as counties, a thinly populated rural area might have the same number of representatives as a dense area with five or ten times the number of people. This meant that urban and suburban residents had far fewer representatives to defend their interests.

POLITICAL PERSPECTIVE

REGULATION AND THE HANDICAPPED

National government policy opposes discrimination against handicapped persons. In practice, there are many difficulties and political conflicts in establishing regulations to achieve this goal.

The law now requires that handicapped persons have access to all facilities constructed with the aid of national funds. Although a worthy objective, this mandate has required alterations in public buildings, such as wheelchair ramps, even if there are no handicapped persons in a community. In setting rules for federal aid to urban transit systems, the Department of Transportation interpreted the law as requiring cities to provide access for wheelchairs by providing lifts on all buses, elevators for subway and elevated rail stations, and modifications of railcars.

How to provide access for handicapped persons to New York City's subways? *(David Margolin/Black Star)*

Meeting these requirements would require total costs—largely borne by the local communities, not the national government—of $6.8 billion to assist a relatively small number of persons. Under court challenge, the Department backtracked. Following the Reagan administration's philosophy of limiting national regulation, its new rules required only that "special efforts" be made to aid the disabled. Advocates for the handicapped found the program totally inadequate and an abandonment of the declared goal of bringing disabled persons into the mainstream of society.

In the most extreme case, New York City estimated that federally mandated changes in its subway system would cost it $3 million for each handicapped rider. Resisting federal, as well as state mandates, the City at first turned down funds it desperately needed. Eventually, a compromise was reached, with local authorities promising to provide lifts on most buses and to spend $50 million, to alter the principal subway stations and to provide alternative van transport.[20]

This case also illustrates some of the politics of federalism. When groups are widely diffused throughout the nation, such as the handicapped, they may be unable to win attention in any one state. When their demands are costly, they are even less likely to succeed. However, by concentrating their efforts in Washington, they may gain some action. They may also be able to use the influence of sympathetic legislators. Senator Robert Dole, himself a disabled war veteran, is the former chair of the Finance Committee and now majority leader. He has consistently used his power to promote improved treatment of the handicapped.

In the case of *Baker* v. *Carr,* the Supreme Court brought the issue under judicial supervision. A series of decisions established the principle of "one person, one vote." Representation in virtually all elections had to be based only on population, and no consideration could be given to such factors as territorial units or community boundaries. The courts have insisted on exact arithmetic equality in the number of persons in each electoral area, even throwing out apportionments where there was less than a 1 percent variation in population among districts.[19]

Sanctions in Regulation Another means of national regulation is through the establishment of requirements, by law or administrative ruling. The most significant example is Title VI of the Civil Rights Act, passed in 1964, and extended in later years. To bar ethnic inequality, it provided that "no person in the United States shall, on the grounds of race, color, or national origin, be excluded from participation in, be denied the benefits of, or be subject to discrimination under any program receiving federal financial assistance."

To enforce this policy of nondiscrimination, the law provided that states would lose their national funds for any program in which they were discriminating. The threat proved effective in advancing school integration. In later years, additional requirements were established, barring discrimination on the basis of sex, age, or physical handicaps. Homosexual groups would like to add a further prohibition against discrimination on the basis of sexual orientation. These later bans have been more difficult to enforce and have caused considerable controversy.

Reagan and Regulation On coming to power, the Reagan administration attempted to reduce the impact of the new regulatory federalism by placing more emphasis on block grants and by simplifying national rules. State and local officials were given more discretion, particularly in health and education programs. Critics charged, however, that the burden of deregulation fell largely on the poor and disadvantaged, such as the handicapped (see the box), who now received less financial and moral support from Washington. In some instances, the Reagan administration also increased regulation. For example, it attempted to control closely the way in which hospitals treated newborn infants with severe birth defects.

The Theory of Federalism

Although we take the federal system for granted, it is not self-evident that federalism is either desirable or inevitable in the United States. We need to look at the theoretical reasons given in defense of the system and to examine its real political benefits.

Theoretical Bases of Federalism

Size and Diversity Geographical size, and its accompanying social diversity, provides one argument for a division of powers between the national and state governments. When the United States was founded, it already stretched down the Atlantic seaboard and contained close to 4 million in-

POLITICAL PERSPECTIVE

POLITICAL CULTURE IN TWO STATES

Above all, Iowans and their politicians are moralistic about their politics. Iowa politics is blatantly characterized by honesty, fair play, honorable intentions, and good government. Iowans' expectations about how government and politics should be conducted are based on such high standards, and generally speaking they are fulfilled so well, that Iowa politics is often not very interesting. There is very little corruption in Iowa politics and, thus, very few of those fascinating politicians who, in less pristine locales, make politics interesting for their chicanery. Peccadillos in politicking or administration bring down the wrath of the state's major newspaper, the *Des Moines Register.* Iowa is rather unusual in that a single newspaper blankets the state.

. . . With its great social-cultural diversity, New York's political style is surprisingly consistent, although certainly not smooth or uniform. The City or downstate style is decidedly aggressive, enterprising, and articulate (even loud). Upstate, the style is more soft-spoken, less "pushy," but equally calculating. Brought together in statewide competition for office and policy, downstate politicians lose some of their abrasive edge while their upstate colleagues become more articulate and enterprising. The result is a political process filled with competition, maneuvering for advantage, and active communication between leaders and followers. The development of television as a vehicle of communication has lessened the dependence of both on stable political organizations, and given politicians much more direct access to voters. Nevertheless, organizations and behind-the-scenes arrangements continue to be a vital part of the political process in New York. Organizing is still in style.

Source: Samuel C. Patterson and Paul A. Smith, in *The Political Life of the American States,* Alan Rosenthal and Maureen Moakley, eds. (New York: Praeger, 1984).

habitants. Each of the original states had a different political history; their economies varied greatly; ethnic and religious backgrounds were widely different; and communication was difficult. It was a rare person who thought of him or herself as an American, rather than a Virginian or New Yorker or, at best, a New Englander or Southerner. With this continental area and social mélange, a single government was not considered possible.

Today, although we do have a strong central government, a national identity, and instant communication, great diversity still remains within the United States. The economic system is integrated, and political institutions are similar from coast to coast, but differences continue. Life—social, religious, and intellectual—is different from one state or region to another. These cultural differences among the states are reflected not only in life styles but in their political character.

Daniel Elazar has delineated three different political cultures evident among the fifty states. Some, particularly in the South, are traditional, where participation is limited to a recognized elite and government is mostly concerned with preserving the existing social order. Others, such as in Upper New England and the upper Midwest, reflect a moralistic culture, where all citizens are expected to work toward achieving a "good community." In other places, such as the Middle Atlantic region and industrial Midwest, an individualistic emphasis is evident, with political professionals brokering the private demands of interest groups.[21]

These cultural differences are not always clear, and no state evidences only a single pattern. Still, states are different in important ways, as shown by the contrasting portraits of Iowa and New York politics in the box. Federalism allows these differences to flourish.

Diversity and size alone, however, are not enough of an explanation of either the origin or the continuation of federalism. At the time of independence, the population of Great Britain was twice that of America, but the mother country was still able to rule centrally. Other nations, as large and varied as ours, once had unitary governments, such as the Chinese and Russian empires. A federal system was never inevitable.

States' rights do not always promote individual freedom. Huey Long—fictionalized in the movie *All the King's Men*—established an authoritarian state government in Louisiana. He was assassinated in 1935. *(Movie Still Archives)*

Federalism and Freedom Federalism has also been said to be essential to freedom, but this argument goes in two contradictory directions. Although the framers agreed that the most important value in society was freedom, they differed on whether the states would actually defend personal liberty. Some framers, such as Madison, worried that the states would restrict liberty. Opponents of the new Constitution (whom history has scorned as "anti-Federalists") believed that freedom could only flourish in small, self-governing communities. To them, local and state government provided an opportunity for full, knowledgeable, and democratic participation, but equality would be lost in a national government.

These opposing views indicate that there is no simple theoretical relationship of federalism to freedom. In practice as well, freedom has sometimes been promoted, and sometimes restricted, by the existence of autonomous states. The division of authority may promote some kinds of freedom, such as effective participation in local affairs. At the same time, it may curb other liberties—as white Southerners' defense of "states rights" long meant suppression of black freedoms. A strong national government may also restrict some liberty, as Washington today regulates many state activities and controls land use in most of the West. At the same time, the national government may promote freedom, as when it enforces the voting rights of ethnic minorities.

Close to the People A different, and common, defense of federalism is that the states are "closer to the people." More than geographical proximity, this argument emphasizes the ease of citizen participation in smaller units. A person can write to the area's legislators, or, more rarely, visit the national representative, but that single citizen would be only one of more than half a million constituents. When dealing with state government, on the other hand, the same person can easily personally meet his or her state legislator, who is likely to live in the same neighborhood or county throughout the year. With many fewer constituents (only 2,500 in New Hampshire), the legislator is able and willing to listen to each individual.

Today, it is uncertain that the state governments are consistently "closer to the people." Theoretically, individual involvement is more likely at local levels, but this activity is not always evident in practice. We would expect a higher turnout in state than in national elections if it were really the case that citizens are more concerned about politics "at home." In fact, participation at the polls is greatest in the choice of the president, lower for governors, and higher in congressional than in state legislative elections. (It is even lower for local or school board elections, even though these officials theoretically should be the most familiar to the voters.)

Furthermore, citizens do not know very much about state government. The names of senators are usually recognizable by the voters, but few know the identity of their state legislator. Both adolescents and their parents have the greatest faith in the national, not state, government. Opinion surveys also have found that less than a third of the informed public pays a "great deal of attention" to state politics, and that fewer citizens follow state affairs than those at national, local, or even international levels.[22]

State government has not always enjoyed public confidence, but its esteem is rising. Back in 1972, most people (39 percent) thought they "got the most for their money" from the national government, followed by the local government (26 percent), and state government trailed behind in public confidence (18 percent). By 1984, the national government was at the bottom (24 percent), with both the states (27 percent) and local governments (35 percent) more esteemed.[23]

At the same time, the voters are of two minds about state government. As seen in Table 3.3, the state legislatures are regarded as more competent than Congress in some matters, such as taxation.[24] On the other hand, the public rejects the traditional argument that state officials are more "in touch" with the people. These data indicate that the states are not universally "closer to" the population and that they seem warm only to some voters, at some times, for some reasons.

TABLE 3.3 Public Assessment of State Legislatures and Congress on Selected Criteria

Response	Is better at overseeing the day-to-day business of government	Is more wasteful	Is more out of touch with what people think	Can be trusted more	Does a better job dealing with inflation	Is closer to the people	Gives taxpayers less value for tax dollars	Does a better job of dealing with the energy crisis
	%	%	%	%	%	%	%	%
State legislature	40	22	77	36	46	17	11	57
Federal Congress	33	56	13	28	19	68	71	23
No difference	15	5	4	21	22	6	9	5
Not sure	12	16	6	15	13	8	9	14
Total	100	99	100	100	100	99	100	99

Source: Louis Harris poll of 1979, reported in Glen Newkirk, "State Legislatures through the People's Eyes," *State Legislatures*, vol. 5 (August/Sept. 1979). p. 8.

Experiment Stations Another advantage claimed for federalism is that it provides opportunities for policy experimentation and innovation. As fifty autonomous governments, the states sometimes do operate as "experiment stations," where a new policy can be tested on a small scale and then imitated by other states or adopted by the federal government for application throughout the nation. Historically, the states have realized this potential in many instances. Illinois and North Dakota took early action to curb railroad and grain storage monopolies considerably before the onset of federal regulation. Wisconsin developed the income tax and Mississippi the sales tax. California has pioneered in the control of air pollution, Oregon in energy conservation, and New Jersey in land-use planning. As Florida developed **"sunshine" laws,** requiring government meetings to be open to the public, Colorado initiated **"sunset" laws,** which require periodic re-examination of programs.

The average state legislature passes nearly as many laws in a two-year period as Congress does. Although much state legislation is concerned only with local or individual matters, important policy initiatives are also evident. Over the years, certain states have become recognized by their sister commonwealths as policy leaders. Innovations adopted by California, New York, and Wisconsin are likely to be imitated generally, whereas Illinois, Michigan, Minnesota, and Texas are looked to for leadership in particular areas.[25]

The state laboratories, however, do not function on their own, nor automatically. Many states are not experiment stations but closer to backwaters. Policy change in these areas is more likely to come from the national government's stimulation than from local initiatives. Quite often, the process is one in which a policy innovation is tried in one or a few states but is not available to most of the nation until the federal government sponsors the program and wins state cooperation by offering financial inducements. Medical care to the poor, for example, was minimal in most states until the federal government adopted the Medicaid program in the 1960s. In general, federal endorsement has been a significant spur to state adoption of innovative policies. A policy supported by the national government is adopted ten years sooner by the average state than a policy without this support.[26] States have served as policy laboratories, but their equipment and experimental manuals have often been supplied by the national government.

Political Benefits of Federalism

In itself, federalism does not protect diversity, insure freedom, guarantee responsiveness to citizens, or induce experimentation. What federalism does promote is politics itself.

Competition The division of governmental authority stimulates continuous and diverse competition among citizens, groups, and officials. It allows a group defeated at one level to try elsewhere and thereby encourages continuing political activity. Citizens have many opportunities to influence public policy, and the division of power results in extended bargaining among different sets of officials. This results in a system of "the multiple crack," where "the normal process of policy-making is one in which individuals and groups take their crack at influencing governmental policy at literally uncountable points in the legislative-administrative process. The process produces, among other things, the characteristic collaborative chaos of the American system."[27]

Laws about labor unions illustrate the process. In most respects, national legislation on unions is dominant over state laws. One part of the U.S. law allows a "union shop," where workers join the union after they are hired. However, states have been allowed to override this national rule and to pass "right-to-work" laws, which outlaw any compulsory union membership. The result is that unions and employers continually clash on a number of battlegrounds. They try to keep or change the national law allowing "right-to-work," and they also fight to pass or repeal these laws in particular states.

Local Majorities An important effect of federalism is to allow local majorities to have their way and a political home, even if they are only a minority nationally. Mormons and ranchers are only small fractions of the national population and could not be expected to have much influence on a single national government. With states operating as separate governments, however, they can use their power to achieve their will in the particular states of Utah and Wyoming. Federalism thereby provides an independent base for different interests and in this way promotes more political competition. In party politics, for example, federalism assures that both Republicans and Democrats will have some positions of power in the states, no matter how badly they are defeated nationally. The existence of autonomous states helps to sustain national political competition.

The independent power accorded local majorities is not necessarily desirable in larger social terms. White majorities in the South long used the doctrine and power of "states rights" to suppress blacks. Those who are dominant economically are more likely to exercise political power as well in a small area, whereas they are subject to greater challenge in larger areas. With decentralization often come "policies generally adhering to maintenance of the status quo and favoring the concrete interests of existing elites."[28] For example, a steel company's air polluting can be controlled by the national government, but state or local governments will be far less likely to regulate a large employer and taxpayer. Federalism sometimes thus contributes to privilege and inequality.

Socialization of Conflict Federalism allows disputes that start in one area to become more general. This means that the system permits the **socialization of conflict**—that is, bringing more people into a political dispute. In the United States, "the most important strategy of politics is concerned with the scope of conflict."[29] As conflict becomes larger or more socialized, not only are more people involved, but the outcome is likely to be different. Civil rights issues, for example, were settled very differently when the scope of conflict was restricted to the states than when it was enlarged to include the entire nation. Realizing the importance of this factor, segregationists attempted to limit the scope, while civil rights groups employed dramatic protests to add more participants to the conflict. Federalism provides this opportunity to socialize state conflicts.

Diffusion of Conflict The opposite process, also inherent in federalism, is the **diffusion of conflict**—that is, spreading out political disputes into smaller areas. One way of settling disputes that are highly contentious in the nation is to define the issue as a matter for state, not national, decision. The result will probably be that one side will be stronger in some areas, but its opponents will be victorious in other areas. This method of handling conflict has been particularly important in dealing with highly emotional issues involving public order and morals. Since the reserved powers of the states most obviously concern these matters, the diffusion of power often has permitted these issues to be fought in several smaller arenas, rather than bring a single nationwide clash. Each state or city applies its own community standards in determining whether to allow massage parlors, pornography, or the sale of marijuana. On such matters, it is difficult to think of national statutes that would satisfy conservative Kansans and jaded New Yorkers. The federalist diffusion of power makes it unnecessary. Decentralizing decisions in this way is a possible means to reduce conflict over contemporary moral issues.

POLITICAL PERSPECTIVE

ABORTION AND FEDERALISM

Abortion is one of the most controversial current public issues. The strong views on "right-to-life" and "right-to-choice" are based on deep moral differences that are almost impossible to compromise. The issue also points out the political character of federalism.

The modern legalization of abortion first occurred in a few states, including California, Colorado, and New York, showing the influence of local majorities. Then, in 1973, the Supreme Court declared abortion a constitutional right of women. This action led to competition among the contending groups. Opponents tried to get the states to initiate a constitutional amendment. They also persuaded Congress to limit the use of national funds for abortions for poor women, and the Reagan administration tried to regulate the advice given to teenagers about birth control. Supporters of legalized abortion had to fight their battles on both state and national levels.

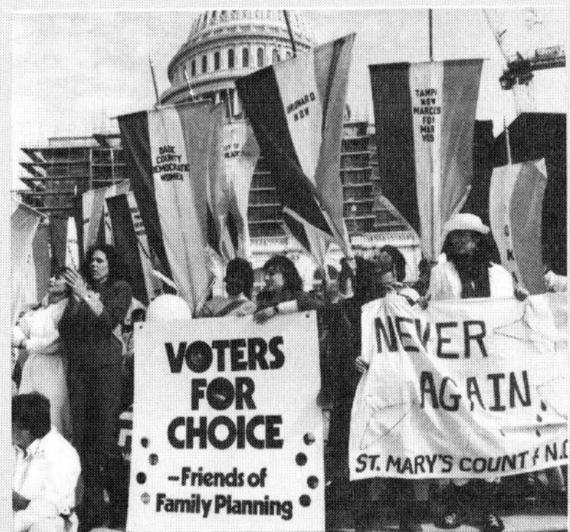

Pro-choice demonstrators holding a rally in front of the Capitol. For controversial issues such as abortion, citizens seek their goals through both state and national action. *(Paul Conklin)*

When the Supreme Court established a national rule about abortion, it meant a "socialization of conflict" on this issue. A constitutional amendment on the subject would have the same effect. If the issue were left entirely to the states, this would mean a "diffusion of conflict," and the single national conflict would then be changed into fifty battles in the fifty states.

Whatever the outcome, the contending groups will seek either national or state action to accomplish their goals. They are most interested in these political objectives. The arguments about federalism are only means to their policy ends.

Contemporary Federalism under Reagan

Conflicting theories and competing practices have characterized American federalism from the time of the Constitutional convention, and these characteristics are equally evident in our own time. In this section, we will examine some contemporary policy issues of federalism. We will pay particular attention to the current efforts of the Reagan administration to redefine the boundaries between the national and state governments.

Three Current Issues

Both national and state governments have responded to demands to control alcohol drinking. A wrecked car is exhibited here as part of a campaign by Mothers Against Drunk Driving (MADD). *(Paul Conklin/ Monkmeyer Press Photo Service)*

TEEN-AGE DRIVING "Drinking and driving don't mix," warns a television ad. Alcohol-related automobile accidents kill 25,000 Americans annually, and the deaths of 5,000 teen-agers each year are particularly poignant, ending lives as they emerge into adulthood. To meet the problem, a uniform minimum drinking age of twenty-one has long been urged. Such a law would reduce drinking among the most accident-prone age group and would prevent teen-agers from driving to states which have lower age requirements.

Regulating drinking is part of the states' basic "police power," their authority to deal with issues of health, safety and morals. Some states have rejected the twenty-one-year rule, sometimes seeing it as discriminating against one age group, sometimes emphasizing other safety measures such as mandatory seat belts. Yet, in establishing a relatively low drinking age, a state would also be affecting persons in neighboring areas, and the country as a whole. In terms of federalism, the issue is whether the national interest in reducing automobile deaths should override state authority.

In 1984, Congress responded to emotional and electoral pressures to "save lives." It disregarded traditional states' rights arguments, such as that of New Hampshire Senator Gordon Humphrey, who asked: "Who are we, the national legislature, which has done a perfectly abysmal job in managing our own business, to tell the states how to manage their business?". Using the powerful instrument of the federal highway program, Congress raised a severe threat. After three years, states refusing to enact a twenty-one-year minimum drinking age would lose 15 percent of their highway funds. President Reagan, who had earlier objected to the bill as an invasion of "states' rights," now embraced the proposal "to protect all of our people." By 1986, virtually all states had complied with the new mandate.[30]

HIGHWAY TRAILERS Highways are the locale of another example of contemporary federalism. In this case, however, there is no moral issue involved, only an illustration of the impact of political pressures in the resolution of federalist disputes.

By 1982, it had become evident that the nation's roads needed considerable work. The interstate highway system, after twenty-five years, had started to deteriorate, and older highways were in considerable disrepair. Moreover, in a time of severe unemployment, a public works program could help to provide jobs and to add new money to the economy. Congress and the president agreed on a major road and public transit program, to be financed by an additional gas tax of 5 cents per gallon.

A considerable part of gas taxes are paid by trucks, and the industry objected to this new cost of doing business. To win its consent, the administration agreed to change existing rules and to permit large double-trailers on the national highway system. New Jersey and Connecticut, seeing the huge vans as threats to safety, banned them from their own roads. However, the national Department of Transportation, invoking the national government's power over interstate commerce, had the authority to overrule these state actions.

What happened nicely illustrates the political nature of federalism. In New Jersey, which had a Republican governor friendly to the Reagan administration, the federal authorities went along with the state ban, and kept double-trailers off the most crowded roads. Connecticut is the same size as New Jersey, and its highways are also heavily used, but it had a Democratic governor. There, despite its ideological commitment to states' rights, the national government used its power to overrule the state and open the highways to heavier traffic.[31]

Aid to Education Committed to democracy, the United States has always valued education. Federal involvement began even before the Constitution was written. In organizing the territories, Congress set aside a square mile in each township for schools, declaring: "Religion, morality and knowledge being necessary to good government and the happiness of mankind, schools and the means of education shall forever be encouraged.[32]

Aid to education exemplifies the basic choices raised in a federal system. Schools are potent emotional symbols of local democracy and often the focus of community life. American education varies greatly among the states, responding to their different goals and traditions, and this variety seems to demonstrate the basic virtues of federalism—local participation, diversity, and experimentation. At the same time, there is a general interest in quality education. Good schools are essential to a good national life and a productive economy, as bad schools create national problems of ignorance and incompetence.

The federal government has been involved in education continually, though only marginally, through most of the nation's two centuries. Usually, its activity was directed toward limited objectives, such as promoting agricultural or vocational training, easing the impact of military families on local schools, or improving science education. In 1965, the Elementary and Secondary Education Act provided considerable federal funds for teaching the children of needy families, books and other teaching resources for both private and public schools, educational research and training, and grants to state departments of education. Later, separate grants were provided for forty-four different programs, including efforts to improve the teaching of art, science, law, consumer life, ethnic groups, women, and even the metric system.

The Reagan administration has sought to change—and reduce—the federal role in two ways, first by reducing total spending in the area by 25 percent or more, and second by consolidating programs into block grants for general purposes. The first purpose was largely achieved, as direct grants for education were cut about 20 percent and reduced below $5 billion. Little change was made, however, in dividing up this smaller amount of money. While twenty-nine relatively minor programs were consolidated into one block grant (and reduced by 15 percent), most interests were successful in protecting their turf. The existing major programs were provided with their own funds, including aid to the disadvantaged and handicapped and to adult, refugee, and vocational education.[33]

The issue is now high on the national agenda. Beginning with a national commission appointed by President Reagan, many groups have seen the threat of a "rising tide of mediocrity" in the public schools. How can the threat be met? Should it be left to the individual states to upgrade their curricula, improve teacher salaries, and improve student performance? Or is there a need for federal action, perhaps by providing grants and national standards toward these objectives? These questions will surely be debated vigorously in the coming years.[34]

Restructuring the Federal System

As he took the presidential oath, Ronald Reagan declared his principal domestic goal: "to curb the size and influence of the Federal establishment and to demand recognition of the distinction between the powers granted to the Federal Government and those reserved to the states or to the people." His echo of a recurring motif in American history became the theme of the new administration.

Limiting Government The Reagan program had a number of goals. One purpose, discussed previously, was to decrease Washington's control over the states, by shifting funds to block grants and reducing administrative regulation. A second purpose was to reduce the total amount of national government spending on domestic programs, especially on social programs. In his first year, Reagan did achieve the first reduction in these programs in a quarter of a century, but later they increased to new highs. Spending was successfully redirected. Programs for job training, social services, and education were particularly affected. Although these programs

A critical view of the effects of President Reagan's budget on Federalism.

(Illustration by AUTH. © 1985, Philadelphia Inquirer/ Washington Post Writers Group; reprinted with permission.)

received almost a fourth of all grants in 1980, they were reduced to a sixth by 1986.

This effort to reduce social spending was also, indirectly, promoted by the president's second-term plan for tax reform. As proposed, the plan would eliminate taxpayers' right to deduct their state and local taxes from the income taxed by Washington. Critics, like Governor Mario Cuomo of New York, argued that this change would make voters resist state taxes. The result, they feared, would be that states would be less able to provide services for their disadvantaged residents.

New Federalism The final, and most ambitious, purpose of the administration was to distinguish clearly between state and federal functions. In his 1982 State of the Union address Reagan proposed a **new federalism.** By this, he meant a federal-state "swap" of major programs. The national government would assume the costly Medicaid program of health care for the poor, while the states would assume full responsibility for social welfare and food stamps. In addition, forty federal programs would be transferred to the states and cities. To help pay for the programs, federal excise taxes would be given to the lower governments, and a transitional "grass roots trust fund" would be established. At the end of four years, the states would have to decide whether to continue these programs with their own resources.[35]

Whatever its theoretical merits, the "new federalism" program had little appeal to the very governors who had been protesting federal involvement. Financially, it seemed a poor bargain to take on new programs with uncertain tax revenues. The proposed swap also seemed to shortchange the states, and it remained unattractive even when the administration agreed to leave the food stamp program in national hands. Rather than rush to accept new responsibilities, the governors suggested national-state conferences to "sort out" governmental functions, or urged the national government to assume the expensive welfare program. Within a year, the proposal was obviously dead, and the president omitted the idea from his later addresses.[36]

Overall, the Republican administration has had a definite impact on the balance of federalism, although less than it wanted. Although Washington still regulates the states in old and new ways—as the adoption of a minimum drinking age shows—more variety is permitted. Federal spending on grants is now above the pre-Reagan levels, but the trend has been slowed, particularly for social programs. The states have accepted some new responsibilities, even replacing most of the money cut from federal grants. An important result of these changes, however, has been to increase the power of the states in regard to their local areas. Water for the "grass roots" is now more likely to come from Tallahassee, Albany, or Helena than from the District of Columbia, but there is still a hand on the faucet.[37]

Political conflicts will not disappear in a new federalism, for states will still need to decide whether to adopt or drop these same programs. Even if they are willing to accept more responsibilities, they will differ on what is appropriately their task. Within each state, the large cities defend the direct ties they have developed with federal agencies and distrust state officials to show the same concern for their problems. Reshuffling functions does not resolve intergovernmental conflicts—it simply may substitute local versus state conflicts for national versus state disputes. The likelihood is for the continuation of the most prominent feature of the federalist system—multiple, persistent, and successive political conflicts.

Conclusion

Like America itself, federalism in the United States is always incomplete and changing. As the society and economy develop, new issues arise, and old doctrines are rephrased. Arguments over the virtues of state rights and the advantages of national uniformity continue. Governments of the different levels are tied together by grants, regulations, and overlapping jurisdictions. Parties and presidents appeal to principle and enlist interests. Programs begin, grow, alter, and occasionally disappear. Legal tenets evolve, with the precedents of the Supreme Court repeated, overruled, and revived. Federalism fragments power, and politics fuses these fragments. It is a disorderly process, now conflictual, now cooperative—but often creative and always compelling.

SUMMARY

In theory, American federalism means the division of power between the national and state governments. In practice, much of their authority overlaps; decisions on domestic matters are made jointly through the interplay of pressure and accommodation. This fragmentation of power generates political controversy over how much jurisdiction should be allotted to the states and how much to the national government on any given issue. The Constitution's vague delineation of the workings of the federal relationship leaves us free continually to redefine the role of each government body, giving our system the leeway it needs to adapt to the changing demands of American society.

Historically, the federal relationship has shown three different patterns. The first is a hierarchical arrangement, in which the national government predominates. Chief Justice John Marshall established early precedents for a liberal interpretation of the national government's power. The second pattern, evident in the period between the Civil War and the New Deal, entailed a clearer separation of national and state authority. The third pattern, that of interdependence, has arisen since the 1930s. In this setup, many governmental operations become the concern of national, state, and local authorities simultaneously; power is shared by the various governmental bodies; and decisions are made through bargaining.

National government involvement with the states comes through grants and through regulation. There are four basic kinds of grants. The *categorical grant* is given for a particular project, and the funds are divided up among the states according to some formula. The *project grant* is distributed by national administrators for use in a particular program. With a *block grant* the government can provide money for a broad policy area. *Revenue sharing* gives national tax revenues to states and localities to use for any program they wish. More recently, the federal relationship has been affected by *regulation.* Laws and administrative rules direct the states to meet certain standards or to perform specific activities.

In theory, federalism has the virtues of maintaining different cultures in a diverse country, keeping government "close to the people," promoting freedom, and facilitating experiments in public policy. In reality, the benefits of federalism are found in its political effects. The system allows different groups to be heard, and permits interests defeated at one level of government to seek their goals in another place. It also allows local majorities, even if they are only a national minority, to maintain a political home. Yet, federalism also contributes to the general fragmentation of American government.

Federalism provides a flexible means to deal with problems that arise from the combination of our integrated economy and diverse population. This flexibility can be seen in two opposing ways of resolving political conflicts. A dispute originating in one area may gradually get a larger audience, as happened with the issue of civil rights. On the other hand, issues that are highly divisive, such as matters of personal morality, can be placed in the hands of the states.

Efforts are made continuously to change American federalism. The Reagan administration has been particularly active in this area. It reduced the growth of national grants to the states, reduced the proportion of spending on social programs, won legislation to consolidate some specific programs into block grants, and eliminated some national regulation. Various proposals have also been made to reallocate programs, shifting some to the national government while transferring the responsibility and cost of many others to the states. These ideas may mark the advent of yet another period in the history of a constantly changing federal system.

NOTES

1. *Texas* v. *White,* 7 Wall 700 (1869).
2. *Helvering* v. *Davis,* 301 U.S. 619 (1937).
3. *Dames and Moore* v. *Regan,* 453 U.S. 654 (1981).
4. Deil S. Wright, *Understanding Intergovernmental Relations* (North Scituate, Mass.: Duxbury, 1978), chap. 2 and p. 20.
5. 4 Wheat, 316 (1819).
6. *Heart of Atlanta Motel* v. *U.S.,* 379 U.S. 421 (1964).
7. *Hammer* v. *Dagenhart,* 247 U.S. 251 (1918).
8. Richard Hofstadter, ed., *Great Issues in American History* (New York: Vintage, 1959), vol. 1, p. 189.
9. Ibid., p. 295.
10. Ronald Reagan, First Inaugural Address, *The New York Times* (Jan. 21, 1981); Second Inaugural Address, *The New York Times,* (Jan. 22, 1985).
11. Wright, p. 8.
12. "The Federal System," in U.S. President's Commission on National Goals, *Goals for Americans* (Englewood Cliffs, N.J.: Prentice-Hall Spectrum, 1960), p. 265.
13. Advisory Commission on Intergovernmental Relations, *Significant Features of Fiscal Federalism* (1982–83), pp. 6, 8, 10; U.S. Department of Commerce, Bureau of the Census, *Governmental Finances in 1982–83.* Series GF83, No. 5 (Washington, 1984), Table 9, p. 17.
14. Wright, p. 56.
15. George E. Hale and Marian Lief Palley, *The Politics of Federal Grants* (Washington: Congressional Quarterly Press, 1981), p. 80.
16. Richard P. Nathan and Fred C. Doolittle, *Effects of the Reagan Program on States and Localities* (Princeton: Urban and Regional Research Center, 1984).
17. Bruce Babbitt, Governor of Arizona, "On States' Rights," *The New York Times* (Sept. 9, 1980), p. A19.
18. Thomas Muller and Michael Fix, "Federal Solicitude, Local Costs: The Impact of Federal Regulation on Municipal Finances," *Regulation* (July/Aug. 1980), pp. 29–36.
19. *Baker* v. *Carr,* 369 U.S. 186 (1962); *Wesbery* v. *Saunders,* 377 U.S. 1 (1963); *Reynolds* v. *Sims,* 377 U.S. 533 (1964); *Karcher* v. *Daggett,* No. 81-2057 (June 22, 1983).
20. *The New York Times* (Sept. 20, 1980); *The New York Times,* (June 29, 1984); *ACIR, Regulatory Federalism,* p. 13; *National Journal,* 16 (Aug. 4, 1984), 1464–69.
21. Daniel J. Elazar, *American Federalism: A View from the States,* 2nd ed. (New York: Crowell, 1972). A newer, and more elaborate, analysis is drawn by Alan Rosenthal, "On Analyzing States," in *The Political Life of the American States,* Rosenthal and Maureen W. Moakley, eds. (New York: Praeger, 1984), chap. 1, and applied in the contributed chapters in this book.
22. M. Kent Jennings and Richard C. Niemi, *The Political Character of Adolescence* (Princeton: Princeton U. P., 1974), p. 277; Kent Jennings and Harmon Zeigler, "The Salience of American State Politics," *American Political Science Review,* 64 (June 1970), pp. 525–26.
23. Advisory Commission on Intergovernmental Relations, *Changing Public Attitudes on Government and Taxes* (Washington, 1982, 1983, 1984).
24. Advisory Commission on Intergovernmental Relations, *The Federal Role in the Federal System: The Dynamics of Growth,* vol. 1, *A Crisis of Confidence and Competence* (Washington, 1980), p. 14.
25. Alan Rosenthal, *Legislative Life* (New York: Harper, 1981), p. 115; Jack L. Walker, "The Diffusion of Innovations among the American States," *American Political Science Review,* 63 (Sept. 1969), pp. 880–99.
26. Susan Welch and Kay Thompson, "The Impact of Federal Incentives on State Policy Innovation," *American Journal of Political Science,* 24 (Nov. 1980), p. 723.
27. Morton Grodzins, *The American System,* Daniel J. Elazar, ed. (Chicago: Rand McNally, 1966), p. 15.
28. Grant McConnell, *Private Power and American Democracy* (New York: Knopf, 1966), p. 114.
29. E. E. Schattschneider, *The Semi-Sovereign People* (New York: Holt, 1960), p. 3.
30. *The New York Times* (June 8, 14, 27, 1984).
31. *The New York Times* (Feb. 22, 1984).
32. This section, on aid to education, was originally written by Patrick A. Pierce. The quotation is from the Northwest Ordinance of 1787, *U.S., Statutes at Large,* I, 52.
33. *Congressional Quarterly Weekly Report,* 40 (Feb. 13, 1982), pp. 265ff.; (Dec. 25, 1982), pp. 3129–3130.
34. See National Commission on Excellence in Education, *A Nation at Risk* (Washington, 1983). The many reports and proposals are summarized in *National Journal,* 15 (July 8, 1983).
35. *Congressional Quarterly Weekly Report,* 40 (Jan. 30, 1982; Feb. 13, 1982), pp. 147ff., 237.
36. *National Journal,* 14 (July 10 and Aug. 14, 1982), pp. 1226, 1432; *Congressional Quarterly Weekly Report,* 41 (Feb. 26, 1983), p. 422.
37. See the state reports summarized in Nathan and Doolittle, pp. 40–48.

PART 2

The Political Process

American government is basically shaped by theories of politics, the Constitution, and federalism—the influences we have considered in the previous three chapters. The reality of that government comes in the political process, which is the subject of the second section of this book, comprising the next five chapters.

The first two sections of the book deal separately with the structure and process of American government, but they are actually closely connected. To see the connection, we can use a long-established image, which pictures a political society as an enlarged human being. People are affected by both their genes and the general characteristics of our species. We have to live as creatures with two arms and two legs, for example. Yet, we also can adapt our biological inheritance to contemporary conditions. We can use our two arms and legs to drive automobiles, to turn a television dial, or to maneuver through space.

Similarly, American government is inevitably affected by its inheritance of ideas and fundamental institutions. Our theory of democracy, our Constitution, and our federal system provide boundaries and channels for what we do as a political society and how we do it. Yet, we also can adapt this societal inheritance to the present day. We can interpret theories, apply the Constitution in varying ways, and alter federalism.

The political process is the means for this adaptation. In Part 2, we will consider five aspects of contemporary politics in the United States: public opinion, the mass media, political parties, voting and elections, and interest groups.

These factors modify the basic elements of American government we discussed in Part 1. Public opinion and elections, for example, make democracy in the United States something different from the theories of the great philosophers. Political parties, never mentioned in the Constitution, have changed the meaning of that document. Mass media and interest groups provide new ways of looking at American society that are quite distinct from the federalist division of a centralized nation and autonomous states.

In each of these chapters, we will return to our theme, the fragmentation of power in American government. The political process in the United States provides some ways to overcome fragmentation, but in other ways it also reinforces the separatist characteristics of our politics. This two-sided aspect of American politics will underlie the specific analyses of Chapters 4 through 8.

We begin, in Chapter 4, with public opinion. In a nation committed to democracy, a unified public with unified opinions would be able to get what it wants; fragmentation would not matter. The theme of this chapter, however, is that such unity does not exist. Instead, we find that there are various publics, that they have varying opinions, and that government responds in a variety of ways.

In Chapter 5, we focus on the mass media, the most recent and possibly most significant influence on modern democratic government. The media do promote unity in American life, as they define a common culture and provide a common interpretation of political events. However, we also argue that the media undermine the community life of the United States. This theme is evident in our discussion of the characteristics of the press and television, of their relations with government, and of their coverage of election campaigns.

Chapter 6 deals with the political parties. We examine theories about the parties, their organizations, the way they nominate candidates, and their effects on public policy. Parties help, we believe, to overcome the general fragmentation of power in the nation. But, at the same time, they are often decentralized, incohesive, and unclear in their policies. Current trends, as we see them, may make it even more difficult for the parties to promote cohesion in our national political life.

Voting and elections are the subject of Chapter 7. We examine who votes, how and why people vote, and the meaning of elections. Voting is the most common political act of individual Americans, and elections are the most important means by which the American people choose leaders and influence policy. Yet, even in these major collective acts of the nation, we will continue to observe a fragmented process.

In Chapter 8, we observe fragmentation even more directly. Interest groups, the subject of this chapter, express the social and ideological divisions of American life. They thereby reinforce the fragmentation already present in the basic structure of the government. We will look at the characteristics of interest groups, their activities, evaluations of their power, and proposed means of control.

This analysis of the political process leads naturally to the following sections of this book, dealing with the formal institutions and policies of American government. Politics translates the ideals of theory and structure into the actualities of government. In the next five chapters, the skeleton of American government will take on the blood and muscle of living humans, as they think, feel, and act.

CHAPTER 4

The Public and Public Opinion

In the late eighteenth century, a small group of revolutionaries decided to overthrow the power of the strongest nation in the world. Without an organized army, without money, and without assured support at home or across the seas, they based their rebellion on public opinion. They could not rely on the theory of the "divine right of kings," because they were themselves renouncing the rule of a hereditary monarch. Nor could they invoke the authority of "historic inevitability" that allowed a political movement to "guide the masses," for Karl Marx was yet to be born.

Instead, the revolutionaries wrote a Declaration, believing that "a decent respect to the opinions of mankind requires that they should declare the causes which impel them," and presented their arguments, to "let facts be submitted to a candid world." In conclusion, they legitimized the independence of the United States "in the name and by the authority of the good people of these colonies."

In our contemporary world, Americans revere public opinion even more, as if professing that "the voice of the people is the voice of God." As presidents seek support, they argue that they have an election "mandate" for their programs. When representatives answer rollcalls, they claim to be following their constituents' wishes. Hidden behind the judicial robes of the Supreme Court is a responsiveness to the latest election returns. Newspapers, interest groups, and individuals call on government to heed popular demands. Even auto manufacturers and television producers claim their products "only give the people what they want."

But American democracy is not a simple system like a water pipe, in which public opinion is poured in one end and public policy comes out, unchanged, at the other. In the previous chapters, we have reviewed the basic institutions of the Constitution and the federal system. American public opinion must operate within these institutional boundaries. Sometimes the force of public opinion is so strong and directed that it flows unimpeded. At other times, opinion is diverted into side channels, or held back by political dams. On other occasions, there is no mighty stream issuing forth from the entire public, but only trickles emitted by particular interests.

Many people assume that there is a single "public" that holds a specific "opinion." That assumption is evident in polls that report, for example, that "the people" favor educational programs or oppose military intervention abroad. The closer we look, however, the more complicated the subject becomes. There are many publics, with varied opinions.

Variety is the theme of this chapter. We will emphasize these points:

- There are many "publics" within the general American public.
- Public opinion varies from time to time, from issue to issue, and from situation to situation.
- Government responds in different ways to these different expressions of public opinion.
- Like the other elements of American politics, public opinion is fragmented, requiring effort and leadership to achieve political action.

We will now deal with four questions: (1) Who is the American public? (2) What are the characteristics of public opinion? (3) What are the opinions of the American public? (4) How does public opinion affect government policy?

Who Is the American Public?

Political Participation

Instead of thinking about a single **public**—that is, the people as a whole—it is more accurate to picture the American citizenry as divided into different segments. Politicians usually pay attention to these particular groups, rather than seek a vague general opinion. The people who are the relevant "public" for agricultural issues, for example, are substantially different from the group concerned with educational reform.

The public is also segmented—divided into different groups—in terms of political participation. While a bare majority of Americans do vote in presidential elections, most adult citizens engage in very few additional political activities. One analysis divided the citizenry into three groups: the politically apathetic (a third of the nation), spectators who watch and cheer but stay out of the battle (60 percent), and a small number of actual "gladiators."[1] The most thorough study found greater, but not universal, involvement: two-thirds of the public engaged in politics beyond voting. However, only a minority did even one "difficult" political act, such as contacting a public official, attending a rally, contributing money to politics, or joining a political organization. Overall, the authors found quite different patterns of

POLITICAL PERSPECTIVE

POLITICAL PARTICIPATION

The major study of American political participation found six different kinds of activity. The extremes are persons who are totally uninvolved and those who engage in almost every kind of activity. Other people specialize. Some vote but do nothing more. Another group are "communalists," who go beyond voting to active involvement in their local areas but shun campaign activities. In contrast are "campaigners" who do just the opposite—work in campaigns but stay out of communal activities. Finally, a small group of "parochial participants" only contact government officials to deal with their personal problems.

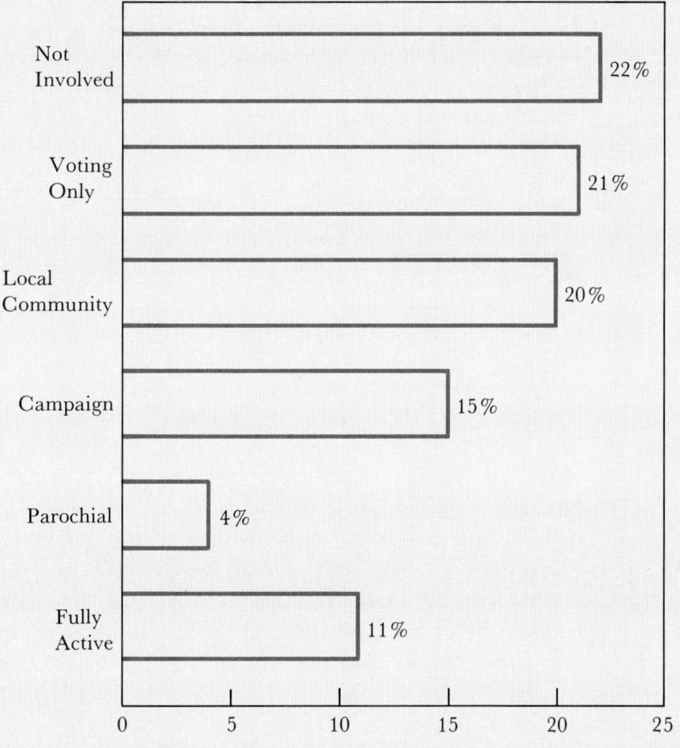

participation among Americans, which are detailed in the box entitled Political Participation.[2]*

The data in Table 4.1 indicate recent levels of political participation in the United States. You can see that although some people totally ignore politics, most adults do engage in relatively simple political acts, such as voting, talking, or watching television. As more costs in effort and time are required, participation decreases, so only about a third of the nation always watches television news or does more in campaigns than simply wear a

*A warning. Much of the data used in this chapter is based on what people tell interviewers. Since people like to appear more civic-minded or more informed than they really are, they sometimes exaggerate.

TABLE 4.1 Political Participation of Americans

Activities	Done by Percentage of Adults
Often watch TV news	77%
Read newspaper daily	57
Talk about politics	55
Vote for president (1980)	53
Watch entire presidential debate	41
Vote for Congress (1982)	38
Watch TV news every evening	37
Attempt to persuade someone how to vote	36
Check off $1.00 on tax return for election financing	32
Vote in presidential primaries (1984)	23
Contact representatives	14
Attend political meetings	8
Wear a campaign button	7
Contribute money to candidate	6
Belong to political club	3

Source: U.S. Bureau of the Census, *Statistical Indicators III* (Washington, 1980); C. Anthony Broh and Charles L. Prysby, *Voting Behavior: The 1980 Election* (Washington: American Political Science Association, 1981); the 1980 *National Election Study*; and *Congressional Quarterly Weekly Report*, 42 (July 7, 1984), pp. 1619–20.

button or display a bumper sticker. Only about a tenth show deeper involvement, such as membership in political clubs or personal financial contributions to candidates. These figures still mean, however, that millions of people are highly active, and most Americans have real but partial personal knowledge of the political world. The United States is not a fully "participatory democracy," but it is more than a closed aristocracy.[3]

Influencing the Public: Political Socialization

Americans' ideas about politics do not arise spontaneously. Just as they learn how to dress and behave, people learn about politics. This process is called **political socialization.** Among the most important influences are the family, religion, and the schools. The mass media are also significant and will be considered in the next chapter.

FAMILY Although politics is not a major concern of most Americans, families still influence political beliefs, as evidenced in the high degree of agreement in the attitudes of parents and their children on many—but not all—issues. One reason for this agreement is that the two generations often share the same social situation; they are members of the same religion and social class and live in the same communities. Living in the same environment, they come to adopt similar ideas. Probably less common is direct political teaching. Some parents and children discuss politics over the dinner table, but such talk is more likely to be about private matters.

Other influences tend to create a generation gap, in which different age groups have different opinions. Each age group inevitably is different and is shaped by different experiences. For today's older voters, attitudes toward American foreign-military policy were greatly affected by the moral and patriotic fervor of the Second World War. For those approaching middle age, these opinions are more likely to be affected by what they considered our immoral and divisive intervention in Vietnam. Today's youth might be more affected by the assertive nationalism of the Reagan administration.

The most complete transmission of attitudes from one generation to the next comes in party loyalties. Leading studies have found that a majority of children express a loyalty to the Democratic or Republican parties as early as the fourth grade and that a majority of adolescents adopt the same party loyalty as their mothers and fathers. Recently, however, more young people are adopting the stance of Independents.[4] When the parents disagree, interestingly, the children are more likely to follow their mothers. The maternal influence is evident among both boys and girls but is particularly strong among daughters of college-educated and politically active women.[5]

Consensus between the generations is much less on other matters. Although agreement on attitudes about race seems to be fairly high, adolescents have tended to take a more liberal attitude than their parents on civil liberties issues such as prayers in the public schools, and freedom of speech for atheists and communists.* Some generational differences diminish over the years, with the younger generation becoming more like its elders, for example, in voting and attitudes toward government. Issue differences, however, tend to persist, particularly those dealing with social, rather than economic, policy.[6]

Schools More formal learning about politics takes place in the classroom, where the study of civics and American history and government is a regular

*Jennings and Neimi, p. 78. These authors also find a low correlation across generations on race issues. However, using a new technique, Russell Dalton finds substantial agreement on these matters between parents and children—see "Reassessing Parental Socialization," *American Political Science Review*, 74 (June 1980), p. 425.

Schools are an important influence in shaping Americans' basic political attitudes. *(Tom Kelly/The Mercury)*

part of the curriculum. Beginning in the earliest grades, there is instruction that combines the transmission of factual material with the building of support for the political system. The third grade worksheet reproduced in the box entitled *America* illustrates this combination.

The schools present a beneficent, positive description of government. Young children believe that "the policeman is my friend," and they transfer this attitude to political figures such as the president, whom they feel "is inherently likable and benevolent, since he would help and protect them more often than not."[7] This idealization diminishes considerably in later years, but attitudes still remain basically positive. Adolescents remain essentially compliant, and most would not defy the law, even in serious cases, such as the arbitrary revocation of drivers' licenses or the refusal of the government to take action against industrial polluters.[8]

Because of their importance in transmitting political values, the schools are subject to considerable pressure from interest groups. Textbooks are analyzed for the direct and indirect messages they provide. Feminist groups want primers to include stories of working women, and civil rights groups have insisted that "Dick and Jane" be both black and white. Seeking to promote its conservative economic values, the National Association of Manufacturers has conducted a program to screen textbooks "to encourage educators to understand the private enterprise system," and has provided its own literature to schools. These efforts, along with "Business Education Days" conducted by the U.S. Chamber of Commerce, have been termed "the most elaborate and costly public relations project in American history."[9]

POLITICAL PERSPECTIVE

AMERICA

We live in the United States of America. The United States of America is our country. We are called Americans.

Our country is divided into 50 states. You live in one of the states right now. Do you know the name of your state?

In America we are free. This means we can move anywhere we want. It means we can do any kind of work we want to do. We can choose the church we want to attend.

America is a rich country. There are many beautiful trees, lakes and rivers. There are many wild animals. The ground is good for growing crops. America has enough food for everyone.

We love America. We are happy and proud to be Americans.

Draw a ring around the right answer.

1. The United States of America is a (city, state, country).
2. There are (48, 50, 13) states in America.
3. People who live here are called (Americans, United States, Alaskans).
4. We should feel (sad, proud, angry) to live in America.
5. America is a (free, bad, new) country.
6. We (lost, live, love) America.

Source: Marc Pomper, Third Grade Workbook, Highland Park, N.J.

The black church has been an important source of leadership and action. *(©Ernesto Bazan/ Magnum Photos, Inc.)*

Despite these activities, the direct effect of schools on political education is not obvious. Civic courses, for example, have been shown to have no substantial impact on the learning of facts about government of high school students.[10] Furthermore, some say the very structure of the school setting, with its emphasis on order and established truth, may discourage the learning of democratic values, such as equality and participation. In any case, schooling cannot explain the attitudes people profess throughout their adult, postgraduate lives.*

Religion Like other peoples, Americans are influenced by their religion, and they attend church services more often than persons in most western nations. At times, religion's impacts are direct: the black churches were the center of voting rights drives; Evangelical preachers attempt to provide prayers in the public schools; and the Catholic hierarchy opposes candidates (such as Geraldine Ferraro in 1984) who accept legalized abortion. The American tradition of the separation of church and state, however, limits these direct effects.

Probably more important are the ways in which religion influences our basic philosophies and ethical beliefs, and therefore influences specific political opinions. Thus, the Protestant emphasis on individual salvation is often reflected in support of individual economic enterprise. Catholic theology focuses more on a community of believers, which is paralleled by the Church's advocacy of social welfare programs. Judaism is based on the concept of an ethical community, and this belief helps to explain why Jews generally support government aid to the disadvantaged.[11]

Influencing Opinions

Family, schools, and religion are long-term influences. They may shape public opinion on specific issues, but they cannot determine it. The party loyalties learned in childhood or the benevolent view of the president ac-

*See the discussions of Richard Merelman and Jennings on "Democratic Politics and the Culture of American Education," *American Political Science Review*, 74 (June 1980), pp. 319–41.

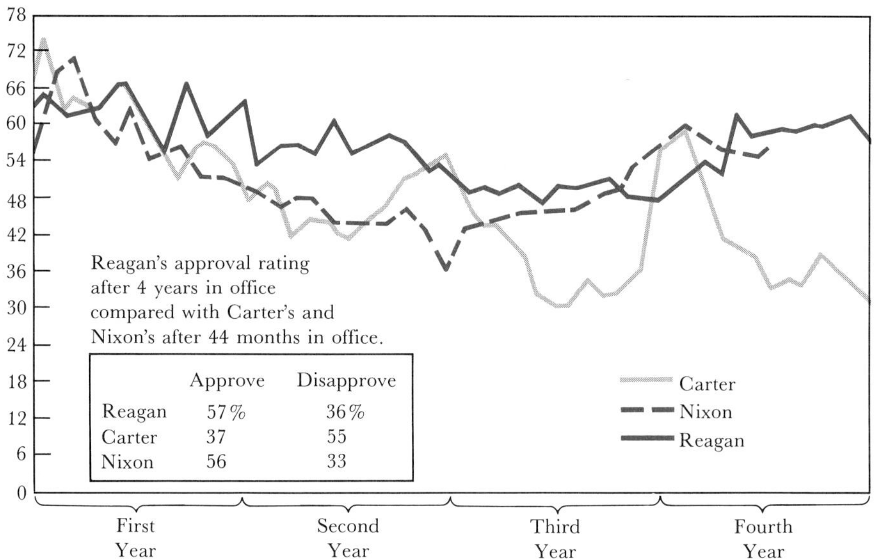

FIGURE 4.1 Popularity of Recent Presidents
(Data from Gallup Organization, Inc.)

quired in school are remembered, but they cannot explain defections from this loyalty in a specific election or the harsh judgment the public renders of a corrupt or incompetent president. Public opinion responds to specific stimuli, such as time trends, the political events of each period, and the actions of political leaders.

Time Trends Presidential popularity illustrates these effects on public opinion. Figure 4.1 shows the degree of support and criticism received by three recent presidents during their full four-year terms, as measured by the simple question, "Do you approve or disapprove of the way Ronald Reagan (or Jimmy Carter or Richard Nixon) is handling his job as President?"[12] When Reagan's policies were unsuccessful, such as during the severe recession of his first two years, the president's standing fell to historic lows. In times of success, such as the 1983 Grenada invasion or the later economic boom, his popularity rose.

Usually, as seen in the chart, there is a long-term trend toward decline in the president's popularity. However popular at first, he cannot fulfill all of his promises or all of the hopes placed in him by the electorate. As some are disappointed, they change their views, leading to a fall in the president's standing. On the other hand, as President Reagan showed, polls can be favorably affected by military action, economic recovery, and personal persuasion. Presidents are not helpless beachcombers, watching an inevitable ebb tide.

While some voters will be disappointed with a president's foreign policy, others may be pleased with economic improvement.* As V. O. Key put it, "the popular majority does not hold together like a ball of sticky popcorn. Rather, no sooner has a popular majority been constructed than it begins to

*See Samuel Kernell, "Explaining Presidential Popularity," *American Political Science Review*, 72 (June 1978), pp. 506–22.

crumble. The maintenance of a supportive majority requires . . . a complex process of interaction between government and populace in which old friends are sustained, old enemies are converted into new friends, old friends become even bitter opponents, and new voters are attracted to the cause."[13]

EVENTS Events raise issues and can change opinion on issues. **Latent opinion**—beliefs that exist but are not active—on an issue such as water pollution can become overt when an oil spill dramatizes the question. Public support for American intervention in Vietnam rose shortly after an apparent attack on a U.S. naval ship in the area in 1965, but that support declined considerably as casualty lists grew. Abstract arguments about the decline in America's oil supplies have been made for decades but were not heard. The events of the Arab oil embargo of 1973 and the reduction of supplies after the 1979 Iranian revolution, however, brought dramatic changes in public attitudes and behavior, including a drastic shift toward small, fuel-efficient cars.

LEADERSHIP The actions of political leaders are events in themselves, and they can strongly influence opinion by their words and deeds. As the British writer Walter Bagehot wrote, "The leading statesmen in a free country have great momentary power. They settle the conversation of mankind. . . . It is they who by a great speech or two, determine what shall be said and what shall be written for long after. . . . In excited states of the public mind they have scarcely any discretion at all. The tendency of the public perturbation determines what shall and what shall not be dealt with. But, upon the other hand, in quiet times statesmen have great powers; where there is no fire lighted they can settle what fire shall be lit."[14]

Religion in the U.S. supports the nation's institutions. Here Jerry Falwell speaks at the Republican Convention in Dallas in 1984. *(Consolidated News Pictures)*

Government officials, and most particularly the president, are usually able to determine the agenda of issues with which the public will be concerned. Sometimes this ability is used frivolously, as when President Kennedy began a brief national craze for 50-mile hikes. In more serious circumstances, the president and others can focus national concern on new problems. Thus, President Truman was able to commit the United States to rebuild Western Europe after the destruction of the Second World War, Senator Hubert Humphrey created the concept of the Peace Corps, and Congressman Jack Kemp initiated public discussion of a new theory of tax cuts and supply side economics.

For the most part, it is political leaders who determine the issues on which electoral campaigns and legislative battles will be fought. Citizens take their cues from leaders who they trust, so a popular president can shift opinion on an issue simply by his endorsement of one side or the other. American attitudes toward Communist China show these influences. For a long time after the Chinese revolution in 1949, a national majority opposed recognition of the Communist government. After Presidents Nixon, Ford, and Carter took successive actions toward normal relations, two-thirds of the public came to favor closer ties with this government.*

*See Connie de Boer, "The Polls: China," *Public Opinion Quarterly*, 44 (Summer 1980), p. 271.

Characteristics of Public Opinion

Politicians and the media—and even textbooks—often refer to the opinion of the public, but what do we mean? If the government is considering a revision in the income tax, how can we discover public opinion on the subject? Can we say it is favorable if there is a supportive majority among the people answering the Gallup poll? Does public opinion include the people who say only "don't know" or "no answer" when interviewed? Is it more correct to define public opinion as the views of a vocal minority, or should we pay more attention to a possibly silent majority? Public opinion is a many-sided concept. Six characteristics, or dimensions, are particularly important.

Dimensions of Public Opinion

DIRECTION One major aspect of public opinion is **direction,** the way people line up on an issue. By examining this characteristic, we learn whether the voters support Walter Mondale or Reagan, or whether they favor lower taxes or a balanced government budget. This information is certainly relevant in a political system that claims legitimacy on the basis of its adherence to majority rule, but it is incomplete information. A policymaker reading the polls, or a student analyzing them, would also want to know other basic characteristics of opinion. A weather vane does not fully explain the weather. Similarly, the direction of public opinion tells us something but does not tell the whole story.

DISTRIBUTION Another vital attribute of opinion is its **distribution** or the form and degree of agreement. Public attitudes may show a large measure of *consensus,* as in support of the principle of free speech, or considerable *conflict*, as in the issue of allowing radicals to teach in public schools. Where there is disagreement, conflict may take different forms. There may be a simple two-sided choice, as in most presidential elections, or there may be multiple options, each with significant public support.

The distribution of opinion takes different forms, as illustrated in Figure 4.2, leading to different political results. Often, opinion is bunched toward the middle, in what is called a "normal distribution." Thus, as seen in the first part of the figure, Americans tend to consider themselves ideological moderates, and this concentration at the center tends to cushion conflicts between liberals on the one side and conservatives on the other. By contrast, opinion may be sharply divided, as in the case of abortion. On other issues, such as school busing, opinion is strongly concentrated at one position. In these instances, the small minority must resort to the courts to win its argument.

As in most aspects of public opinion, the degree of consensus or conflict is not fixed but is likely to vary over time. Racial attitudes are a particularly dramatic example. In 1937, a majority of the country admitted that it would not vote for a "qualified Negro" for president; by 1978, only 18 percent held this opinion. In 1956, two years after the Supreme Court declared school segregation unconstitutional, only a small national majority favored the principle of integration, including only 14 percent of white Southern-

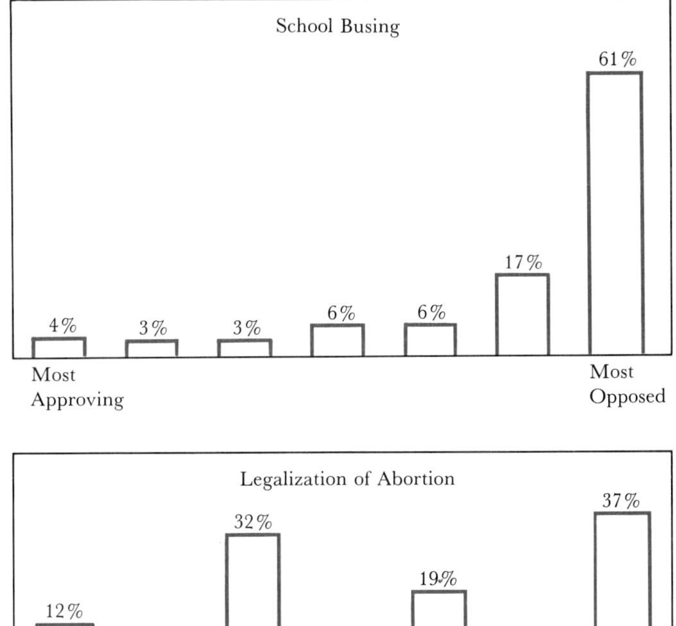

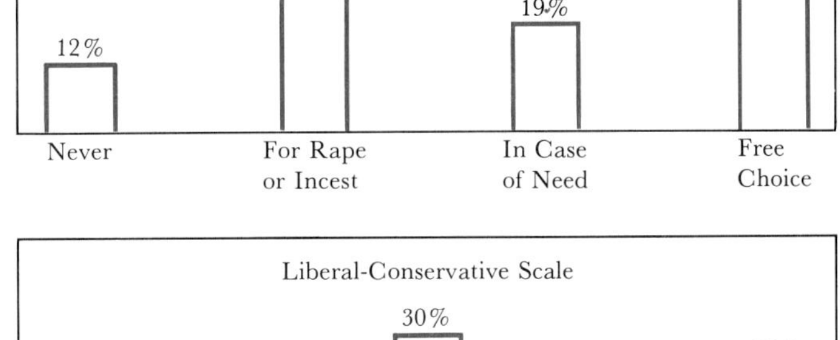

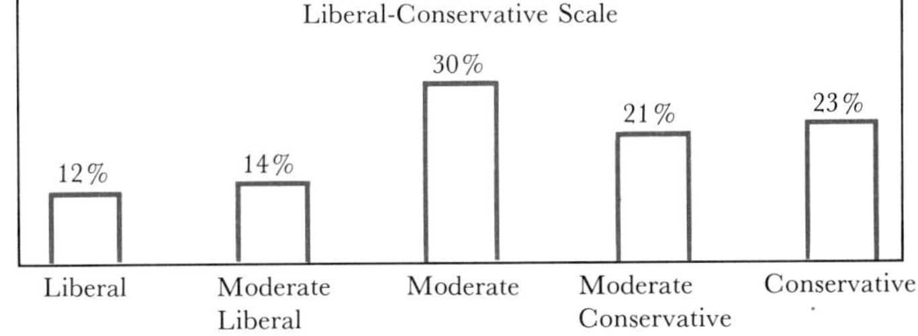

FIGURE 4.2
Distributions of Public Opinions
(Data from National Election Survey, 1980.)

ers. By 1977, 86 percent of the entire white population and nearly three-fourths of white Southerners agreed that black and white children should go to the same schools.[15] On these issues, consensus has replaced conflict.

STABILITY As the previous examples show, public opinion can change considerably over time, and these changes sometimes come quite rapidly. The degree of change over time is the dimension of **stability.** Many candidates have been surprised by their defeat on election day because they assumed that an early lead in opinion polls was an accurate prediction. Polls, at their best, however, tell only what opinion is at the time they are taken. With new influences, particularly new events, opinions can alter. "If all the public phenomena to which people react remained constant through time, presumably attitudes and opinions would remain unchanged. Obviously the stimuli do not remain the same."[16] Furthermore, polls only measure opinion, they do not always forecast future behavior—such as casting a ballot.

The Japanese bombing of Pearl Harbor in 1941 galvanized public opinion and brought us into World War II. *(Library of Congress)*

Opinions change least when they are part of a deeply held system of beliefs that is regularly reinforced by friends, family, and associates. Religious commitment is usually of this sort, but few political beliefs are held as deeply. Opinions on political issues sometimes change rapidly in response to an international or economic crisis. Thus, the hundred and fifty year-old policy of American isolationism ended minutes after the 1941 Japanese attack on Pearl Harbor. American participation in World War II, and in world affairs afterward, became inevitable.

Overall, public opinion shows considerable stability. A comprehensive study of the nation's responses to all poll questions from 1935 to 1979 showed no significant change in opinion on more than half of the policy issues examined over this long period. When the public did alter its opinion, it usually changed gradually. Over the years, Americans became more tolerant of dissent, more supportive of civil rights actions, more permissive toward sexual freedoms, more supportive of international involvement by the United States, and more concerned with the threat of Soviet armaments.[17]

Salience A major reason for instability in opinion is that most issues are not of concern to most people. Although they may respond to a poll interviewer, the topic is not of great **salience** or concern to them. When presented with new stimuli, such as events or the arguments of political leaders, they are readily persuadable.

Issues differ greatly in their salience among different individuals and groups. A topic such as social security is highly relevant to the elderly, who constitute the chief **issue public** (those concerned with a particular issue) on this question. On another matter, such as children's day-care centers, they are less likely to be involved or informed, but others, such as working mothers, will constitute the relevant group. When considering any particular topic, only a relatively small minority is likely to find it salient, and therefore to attempt to influence the government. It is only the most general policy questions that are clearly linked to everyone's life, such as war or a tax reduction, that may concern anything like a majority of the voters. People are more likely to know their personal astrological sign than isolated political facts.[18]

LATENCY We must remember, however, that public opinion is not fixed. Issues that are not salient at one time can become relevant, sometimes very quickly. The concept of latency (see *latent opinion*) refers to unexpressed but potential opinion. Much of the dynamics of politics comes in the arousal of these latent opinions. The victories of the civil rights movement, for example, can be explained by its success in arousing latent American support of equality and bringing this support to bear on the specific questions of school integration and nondiscrimination in public accommodations. The women's movement, similarly, has articulated, and made into a political program, the grievances long but silently held by many women.

Latent opinion helps to set the boundaries of government policy. Support for the public school system is usually a latent opinion but would be aroused if an official appeared to threaten its continuation. Latent opinion can also provide support for new political directions. Barry Goldwater ran for president in 1964 to arouse an allegedly hidden conservative vote, and some radicals have attempted to mobilize the repressed class consciousness of the working class. These efforts do not always succeed, as these examples show, but latent opinions cannot be ignored. Politicians who do so may suffer the fate of Richard Nixon, who believed he could stonewall the Watergate investigation even as public opposition grew.

Since attaining suffrage in 1920, women have continued their struggle for equal rights in other areas. Here members of NOW are shown chained to the White House fence in protest of President Reagan's stand on the Equal Rights Amendment. *(© Ricardo Watson/Illustrators' Stock Photos)*

POLITICAL PERSPECTIVE

ABORTION IN PUBLIC OPINION

The difficult abortion issue also shows the varied characteristics of public opinion and the difficulties in analyzing the mind of the nation.

Generally, the *direction* of U.S. opinion on this issue favors a legalized right to abortion—at least, in certain specific circumstances. The *distribution* of opinion is very sharply divided, as seen in Figure 4.2. Seven of ten persons hold strong views, making this an issue of unusual *intensity*. Because sexual activity is so personal, it is also an issue of great *salience* to the public. As the issue developed, the *latency* of opinion was shown. Following the Supreme Court's legalization of abortion in 1973, public support for the procedure rose above a majority. Since then, opinion has shown great *stability*: the absolute "right-to-life" position is consistently supported by about a small minority of the nation, the absolute "right-to-choice" by a larger group, but still a minority. The majority would permit abortions in some circumstances, and not in others.

Responses can also be affected by the questions asked in a poll. In 1980, by 2 to 1 the public opposed a Constitutional ban on abortions; yet, by a 5 to 4 margin, it also favored the vague idea of a Constitutional amendment "protecting the life of the unborn child." Overwhelmingly, the country believes the decision on abortion should be "left to a woman and her physician," but a slim majority also agrees that abortion " is the equivalent of murder, because a fetus's life has been eliminated."

Sources: Based on Connie de Boer, "The Polls: Abortion," *Public Opinion Quarterly*, 41 (Winter 1977–78), pp. 553–64; CBS News/ The New York Times Poll, August 2–7, 1980; *Public Opinion*, 8 (April/May 1985), pp. 25–28.

INTENSITY In a democracy, all votes count equally and, in a poll, all opinions are equally weighted. In reality, individuals hold these opinions with very different degrees of **intensity,** that is, with more or less deep feeling. Some people have little concern over any issue. To others, the topic is the most important in their political lives, and they will vote, give money to candidates, and lobby representatives to press their point of view. The second group is much more likely to succeed.

Differences of intensity explain many political outcomes. Revolutions are rarely, if ever, majority movements. They succeed because of the intense activity of zealots, who act amid the relative unconcern of the total population. On specific issues, intense activity is most likely when a question involves some broader, or moral, concern. Feminist issues are a notable contemporary example of such concerns and of the effect of intensity. A majority of the country favors legalized abortions and a woman's freedom of choice, but most recent legislative action in Congress and the states has been to restrict access to abortions. A large majority had favored the Equal Rights Amendment, but it failed to be adopted by any state after 1976. The majority opinion on these issues, however, is less intense than the minority opinion. A third of those opposing abortion have "extremely strong" opinions on the issue, making it likely to affect their vote and other political activity, while only one in twenty proponents has the same degree of commitment.[19] We again see that holding an opinion and acting on it are different matters. Because elections, as well as other political decisions, often turn on small margins, the behavioral commitment of these intense groups can be decisive, even in the face of contrary majority opinions.

Measuring Public Opinion

In this chapter, we have been discussing the opinions of the entire American public, as if we had some direct evidence about the beliefs of 175 million adults. Actually, aside from elections, most statements about public opinions are based on conclusions drawn from the statements of a much smaller number of people. The method of obtaining these statements is a specialized skill, involving a number of techniques. Errors in any one of these steps can result in serious misinterpretations.

Sampling To estimate the views of the entire public, those who conduct public opinion surveys choose a sample of people whose attitudes will probably be similar to that of the whole nation. The process is similar to finding out the temperature of a pot of soup. You don't have to eat the whole pot to find out how hot it is; if you stir the pot and take a sample on a spoon, that single spoonful will give you a very close approximation of the temperature throughout the pot.

Pollsters use statistical methods to obtain an accurate sample of the population. The method is called **random (or probability) sampling,** which means choosing respondents so that everybody in the country has a theoretically equal (or statistically known) chance of being contacted. The ideal way to do this might be to put everyone's name in a gigantic hat, shake the hat, and then pick names blindfolded. In practice, what is actually done is to choose households, when interviewing is done face-to-face, or to select telephone numbers when an opinion survey is done over the phone. This method introduces a small distortion in the sample because some households have more people than others and a very few people do not have phones, but these errors can be corrected in the analysis.

If the sampling is done correctly, the eventual results of the survey will probably be very close to the opinions of the entire nation. The closeness follows known statistical laws. For example, if a poll of 1,200 people shows that 60 percent favor gun control laws, the true figure in the entire country is very probably somewhere between 57 percent and 63 percent. For most polling purposes, a 3 percent margin of error is no problem.

In forecasting elections, however, there are two special problems. The persons chosen closely resemble the entire potential electorate, but there is

Copyright © 1984 United Feature Syndicate, Inc. Reprinted with permission.

no certain way to know which of these people will actually vote. Although 60 percent of everybody may favor the Republican candidate, his or her support among the people who actually cast ballots may be quite different. Exit polls, taken at the voting places, avoid this problem. Second, most elections are decided by very small margins. If the pollster says 51 percent favor one side of an issue, while the true figure is 49 percent, this makes

FIGURE 4.3
Exit Poll
Television networks conduct polls throughout the year. On the day of the election, they do brief "exit polls," questioning about 10,000 voters as they leave voting places in a sample of areas across the country. These polls then become the bases for analyses of the election. Below is the questionnaire used by CBS and *The New York Times* in 1984. *(Copyright © 1984 by The New York Times/CBS News Poll. Reprinted by permission.)*

CBS NEWS/NEW YORK TIMES ELECTION DAY POLL

[A] Your Sex:
1. ☐ Male 2.☐ Female

[B] Are You:
1. ☐ White 3.☐ Hispanic
2. ☐ Black 4.☐ Other

[C] In The Presidential Election, Who Did You Just Vote For?
1. ☐ Walter Mondale/Geraldine Ferraro (DEM)
2. ☐ Ronald Reagan/George Bush (REP)
3. ☐ Someone Else 4.☐ Didn't Vote

[D] Which Issues Mattered Most in Deciding How You Voted? (Check up to 2 boxes)
1. ☐ Arms Control/Threat of War
2. ☐ Reducing The Federal Deficit
3. ☐ Policy Toward Central America
4. ☐ Fairness Toward the Poor
5. ☐ Strong U.S. Defense7.☐ Abortion
6. ☐ The Economy 8.☐ None of These

[E]And Which of These Factors Mattered Most? (Check up to 2 boxes)
1. ☐ Experience 8.☐ The Debates
2. ☐ Traditional Values 9.☐ Strong Leadership
3. ☐ My Party's Candidate
4. ☐ His Vision For The Future
5. ☐ The Vice-Presidential Candidates
6. ☐ He's A Real Conservative
7. ☐ Dislike Other Party's Candidate

[F] Do You Think In Order To Reduce the Federal Budget Deficit Substantially, It Will Be Necessary To Raise Taxes?
1. ☐ Yes 2.☐ No

[G] To Which Age Group Do You Belong?
1. ☐ 18-24 3. ☐ 30-44 5. ☐ 60 or over
2. ☐ 25-29 4. ☐ 45-59

[H] When Did You Decide Who To Vote For?
1. ☐ Knew All Along 3.☐ Since The Debates
2. ☐ In September 4.☐ In Last Few Days

[I] Should Abortion Be Legal?
1. ☐ Yes, As It Is Now 3.☐ No
2. ☐ Legal Only In Extreme Circumstances

[J] What Should The U.S. Do First?
1. ☐ Negotiate a Nuclear Freeze With The U.S.S.R.
2. ☐ Strengthen Our Defenses Before Negotiating

[K] Should Federal Spending On The Poor Be:
1. ☐ Increased 3.☐ Decreased
2. ☐ Kept Where It Is Now

[X] Is The Communist Threat In Central America Serious Enough To Justify Having U.S. Military Forces There?
1. ☐ Yes 2.☐ No

[Y] Compared To Four Years Ago, Is The U.S. Economy:
1. ☐ Better Today 3.☐ About The Same
2. ☐ Worse Today

[Z] In The Election For U.S. House of Representatives In This District, Who Did You Just Vote For?
1. ☐ The Democrat 3.☐ Someone Else
2. ☐ The Republican 4.☐ Didn't Vote

[L] Are You, Or Is Any Person Living in Your Household, A Member Of A Labor Union?
1. ☐ Yes, I Am 3.☐ No
2. ☐ Yes, Other Family Member

[M] Who Did You Vote For In The 1980 Presidential Election?
1. ☐ Carter 3.☐ Anderson
2. ☐ Reagan 4.☐ Didn't Vote

[O] On Most Political Matters Do You Consider Yourself:
1. ☐ Liberal 3.☐ Conservative
2. ☐ Moderate

[P] Your Current Occupation:
1. ☐ Professional/Manager
2. ☐ Other White Collar
3. ☐ Blue Collar Worker 6.☐ Agriculture
4. ☐ Looking For Work 7.☐ Homemaker
5. ☐ Full-Time Student 8.☐ Retired

[Q] Has Unemployment in Your Household Been a Serious Problem At Any Time During The Last Four Years?
1. ☐ Yes 2.☐ No

[R] Who Did You Want The Democrats To Nominate in 1984?
1. ☐ Mondale 4.☐ Someone Else
2. ☐ Hart 5.☐ Didn't Care
3. ☐ Jackson

[S] Did You Hear Any National Election Returns On Radio Or Television Today?
1. ☐ Yes 2.☐ No

What Time Did You Hear the Returns?
TIME________

[T] Do You Usually Think Of Yourself As A:
1. ☐ Democrat 3.☐ Republican
2. ☐ Independent

[U] When Did You Most Recently Register To Vote?
1. ☐ 1984: For First Time
2. ☐ 1984: But Not For First Time
3. ☐ 1983 or Earlier

[V] What Was The Last Grade In School You Completed?
1. ☐ Did Not Graduate From High School
2. ☐ High School Graduate
3. ☐ Some College But Not 4 Years
4. ☐ 4 Years Of College Or More

[W] Your Religion:
1. ☐ Protestant 4.☐ Jewish
2. ☐ Catholic 5.☐ Something Else
3. ☐ Other Christian 6.☐ None

[X] Did Your Clergyman Encourage You To Vote For Either Reagan or Mondale?
1. ☐ Yes, Reagan 3.☐ No
2. ☐ Yes, Mondale

[Y] 1983 Total Family Income:
1. ☐ Under $12,500 4.☐ $35-$50,000
2. ☐ $12,500-$24,999 5.☐ Over $50,000
3. ☐ $25,000-$34,999

[Z] Are You Any Of The Following: (Check As Many As Apply)
1. ☐ Married
2. ☐ Born-Again Christian
3. ☐ Of Italian Descent
4. ☐ Military Veteran
5. ☐ School Teacher
6. ☐ Gov't Employee—City, State or Federal
7. ☐ Use Computer at Home or Job

little difference. In an election, however, this error would mean an incorrect prediction.

Question Wording Much care needs to be taken on the way a question is worded. A good question will be neutral and deal with only a single topic, such as, "Whom do you intend to vote for in the presidential election?" A biased question suggests the "right" answer to the person responding, such as "Are you in favor of protecting the rights of unborn children?", or "Do you believe in a woman's rights to make her own decisions?" When questions become complex, and involve more than one issue, it is difficult to know the meaning of an answer. For example, a surveyer might ask, "Do you favor increased military spending and a balanced budget?" Whether the answer is "yes" or "no," we would not be able to tell what combination of public policies the citizens wanted. A better way to ask this question would be to pose alternatives, "Which do you think is more important, to increase military spending, or to balance the budget?"

Question Order A related, and more subtle, problem is the order in which questions are asked. Answers to initial questions may be unthinking, whereas later responses may be affected by fatigue. This technical matter became important politically in 1984, when pollsters using different orderings got very different answers on the public's intended vote for president. Surveys that began by asking about the election found higher support for Reagan than those that deferred the question until later in the interview.

Some pollsters argue that "it is better to warm up people before asking them whom they prefer for president, especially if they have not been thinking about politics"; and others say that "it is better to ask the question before they are biased by other political questions. Professor Seymour Lipset, explaining the variation in poll results, linked this to mixed feelings about the president, theorizing that many turned against him after being questioned about his policies.[20]

Interviewing Even after the most accurate sample is selected and the most neutral questions written, a survey may be mishandled. Everyone in the sample may not be contacted. If those omitted have a common characteristic, such as comprising a disproportionate number of working women, the results will be unrepresentative. Therefore, interviews must be scheduled at a variety of times, to reach all kinds of voters. Another problem may arise in the way an interviewer conducts his or her work. Poll results will be inaccurate if this person will not go into certain neighborhoods, or is not persistent in contacting respondents who are not home at the first attempt, or suggests answers to them.

Polling organizations attempt to control these sources of error in a number of ways. Interviewers are usually not given any discretion in choosing their respondents. Instead, they are given a list of addresses or phone numbers and told exactly whom to speak to—a particular person or kind of person, such as the oldest male or the youngest female adult. The interviewer is instructed how to ask questions neutrally and to avoid having other people in the household suggest answers. Yet, because humans are conducting the interviews, they are always subject to human error.

POLITICAL PERSPECTIVE
POLLING BLOOPERS

Surveying public opinion is a complicated enterprise, requiring care and technical knowledge. Even the experts can get it wrong, as has happened in some notorious election polls. In 1936, a national magazine, the *Literary Digest*, conducted a straw poll among ten million persons owning automobiles and telephones. The editors confidently predicted that Republican Alfred Landon would defeat Franklin Roosevelt for president, but in fact Roosevelt won a landslide victory, carrying all but two states. The *Digest* was humiliated and it soon went out of business. Its mistake was in its sampling. Only the wealthy had cars and phones in the midst of the Depression. With the vote strongly affected by social class, Roosevelt's overwhelming support among the poor and middle-income voters was not represented in the survey.

By 1948, the polling industry was far more sophisticated. Still, virtually every expert incorrectly predicted that Republican Thomas Dewey would defeat Democratic President Harry Truman. This time there were problems of timing and interpretation. Dewey was far ahead at the beginning of the campaign, and some pollsters stopped taking surveys and missed Truman's late comeback. Others didn't believe their own figures, which showed a Democratic surge, and corrected their data to be more "realistic."

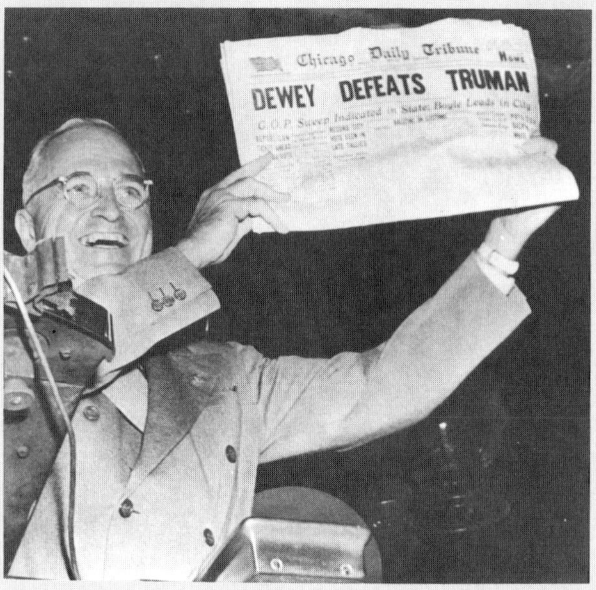

St. Louis Globe Democrat

In 1980 and 1984, pollsters were spared the embarrassment of making the wrong prediction, as they correctly forecast Ronald Reagan's two victories. However, the polls still evidenced the inherent problems of election surveys. In the first year, the polls predicted a close Reagan success, but he actually beat Jimmy Carter by nearly ten percentage points, as the result of a surge of last-week support. In 1984, the polls did get the final result right, but during the year they predicted every possible outcome, from a clear Mondale victory to a Reagan landslide. The changing polls thus reflected the volatility of the electorate.

INTERPRETATION Obtaining the simple numbers on each side of an issue is only the first step in analyzing public opinion. A good analyst will be looking at the other characteristics we have mentioned—distribution, stability, salience, latency, and intensity. A major technique of analysis is comparison. This can take the form of comparing subgroups within the total sample, such as the separate opinions of whites and blacks on questions of civil rights. Another kind of comparison is across time—how popular is a candidate now as against two weeks ago? Even at their best, polls only tell opinion at the time they are administered. They are subject to considerable change as new events affect the public mood. A keen observer, therefore, will look at the trend of opinion, not only its current state, thereby judging the possibilities of further change. Comparisons also can be made between answers. The public may be in favor of tax cuts in responding to one question, for example, but in another question may indicate support for a government program of jobs for the unemployed. An insightful political leader may then be able to change opinion on taxes by stressing the importance of the jobs program. He or she will also remember the distinction between opinion and behavior: voters may not do what they say. That's why candidates are nervous on election day, regardless of their pre-election polls.

Opinions of the American Public

The diverse American publics usually evidence a diversity of opinion. Although there is general acceptance of some basic values, this consensus does not always extend to specific applications of these values. Even less is there agreement on particular issues of public policy.

Unity in Public Opinion

Americans are overwhelmingly and deeply committed to such general beliefs as individual liberty, individualism, equality, the rule of law, civic duty, and patriotism.[21] Note, however, the abstract and unspecific character of these concepts. Does a commitment to liberty mean that all Americans favor free speech for Communists? Does the endorsement of equality mean they want racially integrated schools? Does patriotism mean support for a military draft?

Liberty The American concept of liberty, as we have analyzed it in the first chapter, is essentially negative, emphasizing the absence of restraint on individuals imposed by government. Overwhelmingly, the public believes in the concepts of the Bill of Rights, that government may neither interfere

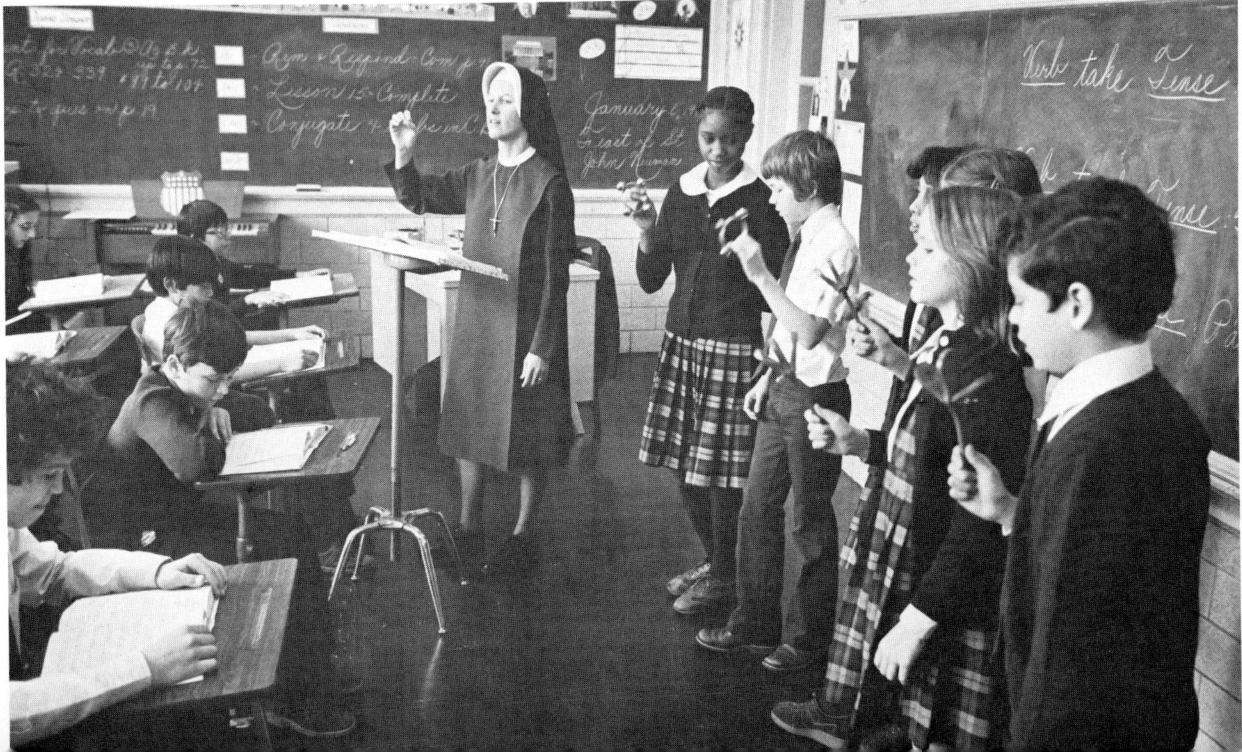

America's private schools, unlike those of many other democracies, receive virtually no financial support from state, local, or federal government. *(Paul Conklin/Monkmeyer Press Photo Service)*

with free speech nor promote religious beliefs. In some respects, the United States carries these principles further than other democracies. In Britain, for example, the press can be restricted in advance from publishing "official secrets," whereas here neither censorship nor penalties before newspaper publication is permitted. In regard to religion, virtually every other nation provides some kind of aid to church-related schools, whereas Americans are wary of such minimal practices as providing free textbooks for religious schools or allowing nondenominational prayers in classrooms.

Individualism By individualism, Americans usually mean that rewards in life should be the result of personal effort, rather than inherited privilege or government aid. The Horatio Alger myth is still widespread, the belief that persons who work hard and behave correctly will achieve success. (In the actual Horatio Alger stories of the nineteenth century, however, the hero succeeded not because of hard work but through luck and the generosity of a wealthy benefactor.) The public generally believes in coping with its own problems, not in government action to deal with such needs as health or economic security. Moreover, "how poorly off a person is has little to do with whether he feels the government should come to his assistance. Those who are jobless or relatively less educated, or black, are not appreciably more likely to believe that the government should help them with their personal problems than those who are employed, well educated, or white."[22] This element of the American Dream is believed even by the unemployed, those who objectively have the least reason to support individualism. Although clearly they are not benefiting from individual effort, the unemployed are just as likely as others to show an overwhelming trust in the possibilities of future social mobility. They do not support such programs as heavy taxation of the wealthy or government ownership of industry.[23]

Equality Equality is another basic American value. It was the first premise of the Declaration of Independence, the most striking aspect of the nation to Tocqueville when he studied the United States sixty years later, and the theme of Martin Luther King's stirring speech, "I Have a Dream." The principle of equality has often been denied in practice, most obviously in racial discrimination. The belief itself remains and provides the moral

The U.S. working class has generally accepted the capitalist system and has focused on increasing work benefits, as well as higher pay and job security. *(Paul Conklin)*

During the 1960s, civil rights leader Martin Luther King struck a chord with millions of Americans when he declared, "I have a dream"—a dream of equality for Americans of all colors. *(UPI)*

basis for efforts, such as the civil rights movement, to resolve the American Dilemma, the conflict between principle and practice. In this struggle blacks, "like the whites, are under the spell of the great national suggestion. With one part of themselves they actually believe, as do the whites, that the Creed is ruling America.[24]

Americans tend to make a distinction, however, between *equality of opportunity*, which they favor, and *equality of condition*, which arouses suspicion. Thus, many people will support antidiscrimination laws, even though they oppose affirmative action programs.

Diversity in Public Opinion

Such basic ideas as liberty, individualism, and equality are widely acknowledged as core American beliefs. They receive support from large proportions of the public, national leaders, and the mass media, and show persistence over decades.* In practice, however, these principles are not always supported. A number of studies reveal this disparity, as Table 4.2 shows. Americans believe in individual liberty, but majorities will also sometimes oppose allowing an atheist or a homosexual to teach in the public schools. Americans believe in equality but also are opposed to the busing of school children to promote integrated schools. Americans believe in individual

*See Theodore Caplow and Howard Bahr, "Half a Century of Change in Adolescent Attitudes," *Public Opinion Quarterly*, 43 (Spring 1979), pp. 1–17.

TABLE 4.2 American Beliefs: General and Specific

General Beliefs	Percent Agreeing
No matter what a person's political beliefs are, he is entitled to the same legal rights and protections as anyone else.	96.4
You can't really be sure whether an opinion is true or not unless people are free to argue against it.	90.8
I believe in free speech for all no matter what their views might be.	88.9
Specific Beliefs	
Freedom does not give anyone the right to teach foreign ideas in our schools.	56.7
A book that contains wrong political views cannot be a good book and does not deserve to be published.	50.3
Any person who hides behind the laws when he is questioned about his activities doesn't deserve much consideration.	75.7

Source: Herbert McClosky, "Consensus and Ideology in American Politics," *American Political Science Review*, vol. 58 (June 1964), pp. 366–67. See also McClosky and Alida Brill, *Dimensions of Tolerance* (New York: Russell Sage, 1983).

Today the vast majority of Americans would consider the Ku Klux Klan an extremist group, but only a few decades ago the KKK enjoyed considerable prestige and support in certain areas of the country. *(James Holland/Stock, Boston)*

effort but also support a large variety of government programs both to aid deprived groups such as the sick, elderly, and poor and to benefit wealthier interests such as homeowners, businesses, and farmers.

Principles and Practices There are similar disparities between principle and practice in regard to other presumably basic American values. A noted study of five nations showed that citizens in the United States had the highest regard for their political institutions, with 85 percent expressing pride, but a majority of the nation thinks we cannot "trust the government in Washington to do what is right most of the time."* The nation believes in the rule of law, but crime rates are among the highest in the world. Tolerance of different viewpoints is an important element in the American democratic creed. Some studies have found that acceptance of unpopular groups is increasing. However, less tolerance is evident when the public is given a hard choice, permitting or prohibiting activity by the specific groups it most dislikes. Only 16 percent would permit a member of their least favorite group—such as Communists or the Ku Klux Klan—to be elected president, and only 34 percent would even allow the least liked group to hold a public rally.[25]

*Gabriel Almond and Sidney Verba, *The Civic Culture* (Princeton: Princeton U.P., 1963), p. 102. By the end of the 1970s, 80 percent of Americans still expressed general pride in their governmental institutions, but less than a third expressed "a great deal of confidence" in any specific branch of the government. Positive feelings did rise in the later years of the Reagan administration, but still fell short of a majority. See Seymour Lipset and William Schneider, *The Confidence Gap* (New York: Free Press, 1983), p. 68, and Lipset, "Feeling Better: Measuring the Nation's Confidence," *Public Opinion*, 8 (April/May 1985), p. 8.

These disparities may be due to hypocrisy—because people don't practice what they preach. They may also be due, according to an alternative explanation, to an intellectual failing because people may not see the logical connection between such general principles as tolerance of free speech, and their specific application to the rights of unpopular groups. According to this explanation, people with more education will better understand these logical connections, and they will be more permissive. In fact, there does tend to be more tolerance among those who are better educated, but similar attitudes are also found among people with less schooling. Tolerance comes as much from political and personal experience as from formal education.

Different Situations Most important, these contradictions can result from the complexities of the political world. Often, more than one principle is involved in a real-life situation. Opposition to the election of a Communist as president need not be simply a denial of political freedom but may be based on a reasonable fear that a Communist president would not respect the principle of free elections. Opposition to school busing may be due to racist attitudes, but it may also be based on a preference for small communities and the environment they provide for fuller individual participation.

In different situations, there are different publics, made up of different people with different views. As Lance Bennett explains, the relevant public is "the collection of individuals who actually form and express opinion on a specific opinion at a particular time. From this perspective, the general public is simply the overall population of individuals or groups from which public opinion emerges in respect to various issues and situations."[26]

Varieties of Public Opinions

The variety of public opinion is apparent when we examine specific instances. One example is the subjects the American public thinks about and what it considers the most important national problem.

Major Concerns In responding to Gallup polls over the period since World War II, Americans often have shifted their focus of attention. Economic matters drew the most interest until 1950. Then, as the cold war, Korea, and other international crises came to the fore, the voters were predominantly concerned with foreign affairs. The civil rights movement and the Vietnam War altered public consciousness and moved these matters to the head of the national agenda. In the 1970s and 1980s, with the onset of the energy crisis and the recurrent price increases, the public again turned its attention primarily to economic concerns.[27]

These trends show the responsiveness of the public to the events of the real world. Opinion is not fixed but varies with these external stimuli. If we look at smaller groups within the nation, we also find that concern depends on the relevance of an issue for these groups. Although the importance of civil rights has varied for the entire nation, it was significant for the South even in the 1950s, and it remains a high priority item for blacks today.

There is also considerable variety in popular attitudes on particular topics. The size of the "issue public" is different from one topic to another: more people care and know about inflation than about nuclear waste disposal. The divisions of opinion also vary from one issue to another. Attitudes on economic policy tend to split people along lines of social class and income, while opinions of matters of life style such as sexual behavior tend to divide along lines of age.

Effect of Education Opinions differ, then, by issue, by group, and by situation. These variations are evident when we look at the data summarized in Table 4.3. It shows the opinions of people with different levels of education on a number of issues. On some issues, the degree of education makes a difference in the direction of opinion; on others it does not. With more education, persons appear to be more favorable toward women's equality, more concerned with minorities, and more permissive in regard to personal behavior. On economic matters, education apparently influences people to be less supportive of government guarantees of employment and the provision of government services. On other issues, such as protection of the environment, grade school or college graduates are not very different.[28]

Other Social Groups Just as we cannot simply categorize people's opinions on the basis of their education, we also must be cautious in looking at other demographic groups. In reality, opinions are normally not very different between age groups, social classes, religious communities, men and women, or blacks and whites. In Figure 4.4, we show one issue that does divide the population on each of these lines. The point to keep in mind, however, is that these are not the typical cases. Even where self-interest might be involved, social divisions are limited. Both men and women, for example, support the principle of sexual equality, and both blacks and whites oppose school busing.

TABLE 4.3 Public Opinion: The Effects of Education

	Less than High School		High School Graduates		Some College		College Graduates	
	For	Against	For	Against	For	Against	For	Against
Increased defense spending	83%	14%	89%	11%	89%	11%	81%	19%
Cut federal services	27	73	43	57	49	51	51	49
More conciliatory (toward Soviet Union)	47	53	49	51	59	41	57	43
Women's equality	55	45	73	27	86	14	90	10
Government job guarantee	52	48	37	63	35	65	30	70
Government help to minorities	31	69	24	76	33	67	39	61
School busing	11	89	8	92	11	89	14	86
Abortion (except rape or incest)	36	64	56	44	64	36	75	25
School prayer	86	14	87	13	85	15	83	17
Maintain environment controls	56	44	48	52	54	46	58	42

Source: 1980 National Election Study.

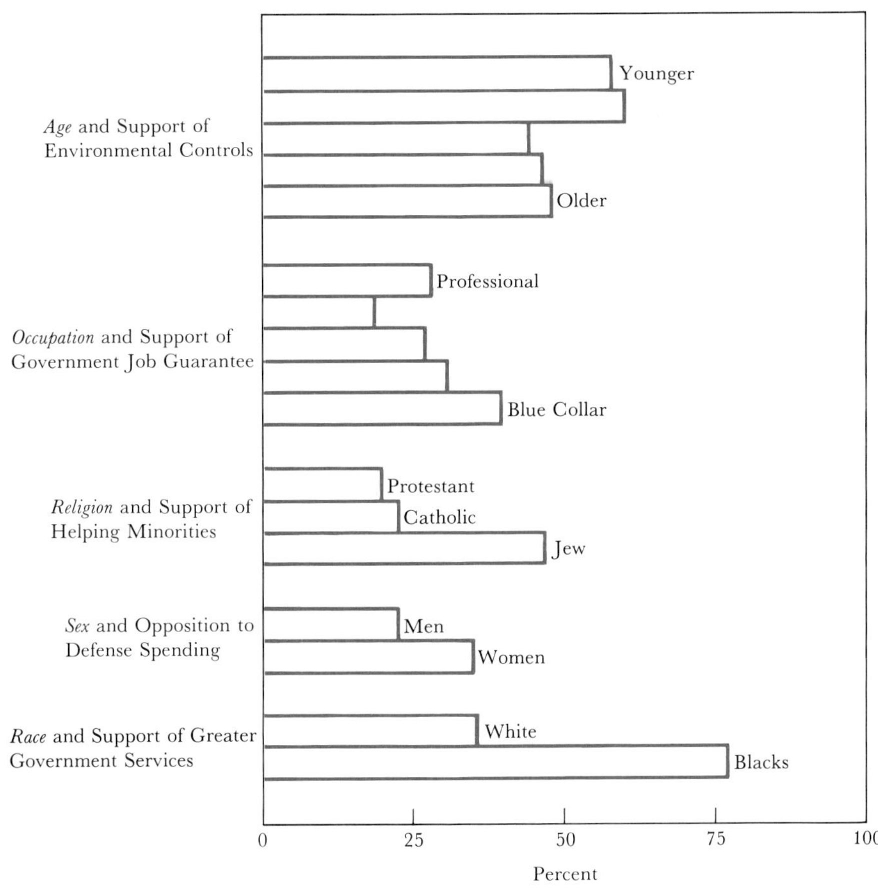

FIGURE 4.4
Opinions of Social Groups on Selected Issues
(Data from National Election Survey, 1980.)

CONSERVATIVES AND LIBERALS The complex meanings of public opinion must be especially kept in mind when considering the general ideology or philosophy of Americans. In everyday conversation and comment, we often hear statements about the liberal attitudes of the young or the conservative nature of the South. Because these terms are usually not clearly defined, their importance for political decisions is not known. Persons with a college education, we have seen, may be considered more liberal than others on personal matters, more conservative on economic questions, and no different on racial policy.

More careful studies, however, have shown that ideology varies in its direction and significance. Three points are important. First, to many citizens, ideology has no significance at all. When asked to place themselves on a scale from extreme liberal to extreme conservative, about a third of the nation has no answer. When asked to define the difference between these two groups, about half of the nation is unable to give a clear response, while those who do answer are as likely to refer to matters of personal behavior as to public policy questions.[29]

To the extent that people do have an ideology, Americans tend to classify themselves toward the right of the political spectrum. About twice as many respondents will describe themselves as very conservative or moderately conservative, compared to those who consider themselves very liberal or

Public opinion in the U.S. has strongly opposed school busing, although different groups oppose it for different reasons. *(UPI/Bettmann Newsphotos)*

moderately liberal. In regard to their abstract philosophy, Americans have shown this attitude consistently, as evidenced in polls from the turbulent period of the 1960s to the present.*

In regard to specific issues, however, Americans often think quite differently. On such matters as providing medical care, or ensuring job safety, both self-styled liberals and conservatives are in support of government action, whereas both ideological groups are opposed to job quotas for racial minorities and in favor of legalized abortion.[30] Overall, in regard to specifics, Americans tend to be liberal, even as they call themselves conservative. Public opinion, in summary, is "mildly schizoid, with people believing in one set of principles, abstractly, while acting according to another set of principles in their political behavior."[31]

IDEOLOGY Given these findings, the usefulness of terms such as conservative or liberal, which define a person's general ideology, may seem questionable. Yet there is some structure to public opinion. By **conservatism** and **liberalism,** the public means some combination of the following ideas:

- Conservatives want to reduce government spending as well as the role of government; liberals want to spend money and increase government activity on behalf of programs aiding various groups.
- Conservatives prefer to slow the pace of change; liberals support action to promote change.
- Conservatives advocate more traditional morality on such questions as religion, sexual relations, and law enforcement; liberals are more permissive.[32]

Sometimes these ideological outlooks clash. For example, many young Reagan voters in 1984 endorsed both the president's conservative economic policies and tax reduction program but opposed his conservative social policies and antiabortion program. However, people usually show more consistency when dealing with issues that are related to each other. Individuals

*Lloyd Free and Hadley Cantril, *The Political Beliefs of Americans* (New York: Simon & Schuster, 1968), chap. 2. This finding is corroborated in the 1978 CBS News/*New York Times* Poll.

who favor government action to provide medical care, for example, also tend to support other social welfare activities, and in this sense can be considered liberals. Other individuals who oppose the Equal Rights Amendment also are likely to oppose the legalization of marijuana, and in this sense they can be considered conservatives.[33]

How great are these connections between opinions on different issues? A number of studies have examined the quality of *constraint*, or the underlying structure in the public's belief system. A well-organized system of beliefs is characterized by high constraint so that issue positions are logically related to one another. When constraint exists, we would expect that someone who takes a position on behalf of racial integration, for example, might also take a position in favor of international cooperation. Some analysts have found little evidence of this philosophical coherence in the mass public. However, there does seem to be a consistency in popular thinking about the government's role in providing services. People who believe that government should help to guarantee jobs also are likely to support its involvement in education and health care. Those who oppose one activity are also likely to oppose the others.[34]

There are some indications that the degree of ideological constraint increased greatly in the turbulent period of the 1960s. A major study of the subject concluded that the proportion of the public thinking of politics in ideological terms had grown from 18 percent in the quiet times of the 1950s to 49 percent by the time of the 1972 election. Furthermore, the public of the 1970s showed a level of constraint in its thinking that was even higher than that of congressional candidates in the earlier period of the 1950s, a group very sophisticated in its political ideology.

This apparent increase in awareness could not be explained by population changes, such as more widespread education or the political maturation of sophisticated young people. Rather, the cause was found in the increasing importance of politics to all groups, stimulated by events such as the Vietnam War and racial conflict, with the result that "political issues now penetrate into the personal hopes and fears of the citizens."[35] However, the development of greater constraint in public opinion is not acknowledged by all analysts.* The controversy should alert us to the unstable character and changing meaning of public opinion.

Public Opinion and Democracy

The ideal of democracy is popular rule. This ideal is sometimes questioned by theorists and is certainly difficult to achieve in practice.

Evaluations of Public Opinion

In the Greek city-state where our theories of politics originated, the entire political community could be gathered in a single place. It made some sense, then, to think of a single public. The Athenian leader, Pericles,

*See W. Lance Bennett, *Public Opinion in American Politics* (New York: Harcourt, 1980), pp. 48–56, for a good discussion of the subject.

praised democracy "because power is in the hands not of a minority but of the whole people. When it is a question of settling private disputes, everyone is equal before the law; when it is a question of putting one person before another in positions of public responsibility, what counts is not membership of a particular class, but the actual ability which the man possesses."[36]

Others feared the force of public opinion. To the great philosopher Plato, democracy was not the glory of Athens but the cause of its decline. Rule by public opinion was as wrong as navigating a ship on which "the sailors are quarrelling over the control of the helm; each thinks he ought to be steering the vessel, though he has never learnt navigation and cannot point to any teacher under whom he has served his apprenticeship; what is more, they assert that navigation is a thing that cannot be taught at all, and are ready to tear to pieces anyone who says it can."[37]

Debate over the quality of public opinion has continued in America. James Madison expressed the ambiguity of the framers of the Constitution. On the one hand, he feared "the superior force of an interested and overbearing majority." On the other hand, he thought it "particularly essential" that representatives "should have an immediate dependence on, and intimate sympathy with, the people." To achieve these ends, as we have already seen, the national government was designed both to allow the expression of public opinion and to fragment this opinion through the competition of factions, the separation of institutions, and the divisions of federalism.[38]

Madison's resolution has incurred conflicting criticisms over the past two hundred years. The Progressive movement, at the beginning of this century, found the restrictions on popular majorities unacceptable. It demanded greater popular power, through three institutional changes: the **initiative,** by which citizens could introduce legislation and constitutional revisions; the **referendum,** which provides for direct vote on such proposals; and the **recall,** which allows removal of public officials before the expiration of their elected terms. Although none of these ideas have been adopted nationally, they do exist in many states, particularly in the West.[39]

Other critics feared that public opinion was already too strong in America. Tocqueville best expressed this concern:

> When an individual or a party is wronged in the United States, to whom can he apply for redress? If to public opinion, public opinion constitutes the majority; if to the legislature, it represents the majority and implicitly obeys it; if to the executive power, it is appointed by the majority and serves as a passive tool in its hands. The public force consists of the majority under arms; the jury is the majority invested with the right of hearing judicial cases; and in certain states even the judges are elected by the majority. However iniquitous or absurd the measure of which you complain, you must submit to it as you can.[40]

Linkages of Opinion to Policy

Even if we accept the ideals of democracy, we obviously cannot expect direct decision making by the entire populace in a nation of continental size. Popular rule, to the extent it exists, must come from linkages between the

TABLE 4.4 Models of Opinion-Policy Linkage

	Public Opinion	
Leaders	**Active**	**Inactive**
Take independent positions	Representatives promote election mandates	Representatives and public share opinions
Follow popular preferences	Representatives interpret mandates	Representatives act as uninstructed trustees

*This typology is adapted from Norman R. Luttbeg, *Public Opinion and Public Policy.* (Homewood, Ill.: Dorsey Press, 1968), chaps. 4–8.

opinions of the public and the actions of its elected representatives. The nature of these linkages depends on the dimension of public opinion we have already examined—its direction, distribution, salience, intensity, latency, and stability.

Linkages between the public and governmental policies depend on two factors—whether the public actively holds and expresses its opinions, and whether representatives independently take positions of their own or seek to follow the wishes of the citizenry. Combining these criteria yields four kinds of linkages, which are diagrammed in Table 4.4.

Mandates The most complete linkage theoretically possible would exist if the public took an outright position on an issue and chose representatives who had pledged themselves to the same position. Public opinion in this case would have a definite direction, and its distribution would reveal a clear majority at one position. The relationship between the governed and the governors would constitute an **electoral mandate.** The conditions necessary for such mandates rarely exist. An election is almost never dominated by a single issue, and candidates do not always take opposing positions on whatever issues are raised. Even in 1968, when the Vietnam War was intensely discussed, less than a majority considered it the most important problem facing the nation. Moreover, the positions of the candidates were not clear or distinct. Richard Nixon's election that year, therefore, was not a clear guide to future action.[41] Specific mandates sometimes occur in smaller contests—a school board election may be fought over increases or decreases in the budget, or congressional candidates may present clear differences on a vital constituency interest such as race relations. More often, election results are clear choices of leaders but murky directives by the public to those leaders.

Typically the public provides a verdict on past conduct and points vaguely toward future directions. Lyndon Johnson's landslide victory in 1964, for example, was an endorsement of his liberal social welfare philosophy but not necessarily a ratification of such specific measures as the war on poverty. A close election, such as 1976, on the other hand, is not a mandate, and even a landslide such as Nixon's victory in 1972 or Reagan's in 1980 may lack a clear issue content.*A more frequent form of mandate probably is the silent mandate. When there is consensus in the public and agreement among competing candidates, some policies are ratified without open debate. The existence of the social security system, for example, is not argued in election campaigns, but its continuation is ensured because it is taken for granted by all candidates.

In most elections, many issues are debated, each of them of concern to a minority of voters. The outcome may turn on the support of one or more of these minorities, and the successful candidate will be particularly responsive to those who provided the critical margin of victory. Questions of taxation and government spending are illustrative. Even though all voters are affected by these policies, it is usually the case that only a minority of votes will be cast on the basis of this issue alone. Still, as in 1984, those who have campaigned for an income tax, or against increased spending, will probably get some critical votes on the basis of this issue alone. If elected, they will then seek to put the promised program into effect and claim an electoral mandate on its behalf.†

Delegation A second form of linkage exists when representatives act as delegates of the public, rather than as advocates of their own positions. Their actions are governed not by the explicit results of an election but by their interpretations of what the public intended. Since mandates are difficult to locate, the representatives must discover the intentions of the public. In this process of discovery, however, they follow the principle that they should defer to the opinion of their constituents and should not impose their own judgment. Representatives would defer to public opinion which was salient and intense on particular issues.

This form of linkage also requires that there be an active public opinion but differs from the first form in making the representative more passive. On many issues, of course, there is no such public opinion. Even a representative who is ready to follow his or her constituents' preferences without question would find it difficult to discover their views on such issues as the importation of Zimbabwe's chrome. On issues of race, by contrast, a lively public opinion is likely to exist in most areas. On these matters, the actions of representative have been found to be closely related to the way they perceive their constituents' preferences. In voting on civil rights bills, representatives are highly likely to follow the voters' wishes, even when they conflict with their own views. Thus, the same representative who supported school segregation when only whites voted in the district, now, with the growth of a black electorate, votes for civil rights bills.[42]

Shared Opinions Public opinion can still influence policy, even if the public is not active in expressing its preferences. This third form of linkage

*See Stanley Kelley, *Interpreting Elections* (Princeton: Princeton U. P., 1983).

†See Leon Epstein, "Electoral Decision and Policy Mandate," *Public Opinion Quarterly*, 28 (Winter 1964), pp. 564–72, and Gerald M. Pomper and Susan Lederman, *Elections in America*, 2nd ed. (New York: Longman, 1980), chap. 6.

would be particularly evident when public opinion showed considerable stability. It would exist when political leaders shared the same kind of opinions as the general citizenry. Because they come from the same area and may be of the same social class or religion or ethnic group, representatives are likely to have what Madison called an inherent sympathy with the problems of their constituents. Emphasizing this sympathy is one of the major techniques used in a congressperson's campaigns:

> Contextually and verbally, he gives them the impression that "I am one of you; I am like you; I think the way you do and I care about the same things you do." Habits of speech—"we in northern Illinois"—convey that impression. So does contextually appropriate humor. . . . From these expressions flow the sense of identification, from which flows, in turn, a measure of trust. The message is, "You can trust me because we are like one another."[43]

Trusteeship Finally, linkage is possible even if there is no active public opinion. Representatives, then, see latency as a major characteristic of popular sentiment and feel less need to consult their constituents. In this situation, officials consider themselves trustees for the public, required to use their own best judgment while acting on behalf of the inarticulate public. On some occasions, officials may even act contrary to the apparent short-term wishes of the public because they feel that with their greater knowledge, they are more aware of the public's long-term interests. A politician may feel compelled to present a profile in courage and hope that later events, or at least history, will justify their conduct. Lincoln's early steps to repress Southern secession and Franklin Roosevelt's aid to Britain are illustrative.

More frequently, officials act as trustees simply because there is no meaningful public opinion on an issue. Few constituents are likely to be interested in such matters as chrome imports or to be knowledgeable about the highly technical questions that are involved in such issues as synthetic fuel production. Most matters of foreign policy, aside from the general preferences on the draft or intervention abroad, are of this nature. Public opinion must still be considered in some way, for no foreign policy can succeed unless it is in accord with the basic beliefs of the public and its willingness to pay its human and financial costs. The linkage between opinion and policy ultimately must exist here as well, but it is long term and indirect. On these matters, representatives almost inevitably must repeat the credo of Edmund Burke, who defined the role of trustee two hundred years ago (see box, page 136).[44]

Conclusion: Policy and Opinion In the United States, we can conclude that government does follow the general preferences of the public, but there is not an automatic or necessarily precise adherence. Monroe, in a study of a fifteen-year period, found that governmental policy followed mass preferences nearly two-thirds of the time. However, he concluded that officials were more likely to conform to popular wishes when the majority favored the status quo than when it wanted change.[45]

Majorities are most likely to get their way on matters of high salience and intensity, such as civil rights. On these issues, another study finds that pub-

POLITICAL PERSPECTIVE

A REPRESENTATIVE'S DUTY TO CONSTITUTENTS

A basic issue about public opinion is whether elected representatives owe their first obligations to their consciences or to their constituents. A classic statement on this problem was made by Edmund Burke.

> Certainly, gentlemen, it ought to be the happiness and glory of a representative to live in the strictest union with his constituents. Their wishes ought to have great weight with him; their opinion high respect; their business unremitted attention. It is his duty to sacrifice his repose, his pleasures, his satisfactions, to theirs; and in all cases, to prefer their interest to his own. But his unbiased opinion, his mature judgment, his enlightened conscience, he ought not to sacrifice to you; to any man, or to any set of men living. These he does not derive from your pleasure; no, nor from the law and the constitution. They are a trust from Providence, for the abuse of which he is deeply answerable. Your representative owes you, not his industry only, but his judgment; and he betrays, instead of serving you, if he sacrifices it to your opinion.
>
> If government were a matter of will upon any side, yours, without question, ought to be superior. But government and legislation are matters of reason and judgment, and not of inclination; and what sort of reason is that in which the determination precedes the discussion; in which one set of men deliberate, and another decide; and where those who form the conclusion are perhaps 300 miles distant from those who hear the arguments?
>
> Parliament is not a CONGRESS of ambassadors from different and hostile interests; which interests each must maintain; as an agent and advocate, against other agents and advocates; but parliament is a DELIBERATIVE assembly of ONE nation, and ONE interest, that of the whole; where, not local purposes, not local prejudges ought to guide, but the general good, resulting from the general reason of the whole. You chose a member indeed; but when you have chosen him, he is not a member of Bristol, but he is a member of PARLIAMENT.
>
> If the local constituent should have an interest, or should form an hasty opinion, evidently opposite to the real good of the rest of the community, the member for that place ought to be as far, as any other, from any endeavor to give it effect.
>
> Your faithful friend, your devoted servant, I shall be to the end of my life; a flatterer you do not wish for. On this point of instructions, however, I think it scarcely possible we ever can have any sort of difference. Perhaps I may give you too much, rather than too little trouble.

Source: Edmund Burke, Speech to the Electors of Bristol (1774).

lic opinion in support of antidiscrimination legislation does eventually get translated into congressional legislation. Such success, however, often does not come until after demonstrations have made the issue visible and until the level of support is quite high. The conservative nature of American institutions slows the implement of public preferences until they are clear and persistent.[46]

A major new study draws an optimistic conclusion on the viability of American democracy. Looking at changes in mass opinion and public policy over forty-five years, its authors find that "public opinion, whatever its sources and quality, is a factor that genuinely affects governmental policies in the United States." Examining 357 changes in what the government was doing from 1935 to 1979, they concluded that at least two-thirds of the time, policy either changed to conform to changes in public opinion or already matched popular wishes. This popular impact was evident on all kinds of issues and in all the institutions of government.[47]

Leadership remains vital. Whatever the influence of public opinion, creative politicians are still needed—to promote electoral decisions, to interpret mandates, to effectuate shared opinions, or to serve as public trustees. There is rarely a single public with a single opinion. The relevant publics and their opinions are shaped by circumstances, events, and the interests of multiple groups. The political world does not exist as an unchanging reality; it must be formed and made coherent by political master builders. The fragmentation of public opinion, like much of American government, requires creative builders to form workable structure from scattered bricks.

SUMMARY

Public opinion is a complex phenomenon. There are a variety of publics, so that the American population evidences different degrees of participation in political acts such as voting or joining party organizations. The influences on these publics and their opinions include both long-term and short-term factors. The long-term influences, known as *political socialization*, include the family, schools, and religion. Opinions also are affected by short-term factors and change over time, depending on events in the world and the actions and words of political leaders.

To understand the significance of the public's attitude on an issue, we must consider a number of factors. These include the direction of opinion; its distribution, or the form and degree of agreement; its stability and potential for change; the intensity of the opinion; and the issue's relevance to people's lives.

Polls are often used to gauge public opinion. If properly conducted, poll results should inform us of the nation's opinions at a given time with reasonable accuracy. This requires obtaining a random sample of the population, framing neutral questions in the right order, and scheduling interviews to obtain a good cross section of respondents. Analysts should look at more than numbers in interpreting results and should always remember that behavior is not the same as opinion—people don't always do what they say.

On some issues, opinion in this country is unified. Americans are deeply committed to such abstract principles as liberty, individualism, and equality. Ideals and practice, however, sometimes clash: Americans believe generally in tolerance but don't always permit expression of unpopular views.

Public opinion also shows great variation, depending on the issue involved, the group holding an opinion, and the specific situation. The complex meanings of public opinion are especially evident in regard to the overall philosophy of Americans: While a plurality of the nation calls itself "conservative," people also tend to favor such specific "liberal" programs as equal rights or government aid to the unemployed.

In the theory of democracy, public opinion is given a major role, even though some writers have questioned the ability of the people. To be effective, democracy needs linkages between the opinions of the public and the actions of elected representatives. There are four kinds of linkages: *Mandates* exist if the public takes a definite position on an issue and chooses representatives pledged to the same position. *Delegation* occurs when representatives interpret, and accept, the opinions of the public. When representatives are similar in background to the electorate, linkage may come through *shared opinion*. Finally, representatives may evidence *trusteeship*, using their own best judgment on behalf of a silent public. Overall, in the United States, the government does follow the general wishes of the public, but there is no automatic connection.

NOTES

1. Lester Milbrath, *Political Participation* (Chicago: Rand McNally, 1965), p. 21.
2. Sidney Verba and Norman Nie, *Participation in America* (New York: Harper & Row, 1972), pp. 33–36, 79–80.
3. The data are drawn from a number of sources, especially: U.S. Bureau of the Census, *Statistical Indicators III* (Washington, 1980); C. Anthony Broh and Charles L. Prysby, *Voting Behavior: The 1980 Election* (Washington: American Political Science Association, 1981); the *1980 National Election Study*; and *Congressional Quarterly Weekly Report*, 42 (July 7, 1984), pp. 1619–20.
4. Fred Greenstein, *Children and Politics* (New Haven: Yale U.P.,

1965), p. 71; M. Kent Jennings and Richard G. Niemi, *The Political Character of Adolescence* (Princeton: Princeton U.P., 1974), p. 39.
5. M. Kent Jennings and Kenneth P. Langton, "Mothers versus Fathers: The Foundations of Political Orientations among Young Americans," *Journal of Politics*, 31 (May 1969), pp. 329–58.
6. Jennings and Niemi, "Continuity and Change in Political Orientations," *American Political Science Review*, 69 (Dec. 1975), pp. 1316–25.
7. David Easton and Jack Dennis, *Children in the Political System* (New York: McGraw-Hill, 1969), p. 189.
8. Roberta S. Sigel and Marilyn B. Hoskin, *The Political Involvement of Adolescents* (New Brunswick: Rutgers U.P., 1981), chap. 6.
9. S. Alexander Rippa, *Education in a Free Society*, 2nd ed. (New York: McKay, 1971), pp. 272–78.
10. Kenneth Langton and M. Kent Jennings, "Political Socialization and the High School Civics Curriculum in the U.S.," *American Political Science Review*, 62 (Sept. 1968), pp. 852–67.
11. The recent effect of religion on attitudes and voting is analyzed by Paul Lopatto, *Religion and the Presidential Election* (New York: Praeger, 1985). On Jewish attitudes, see Lawrence Fuchs, *The Political Behavior of American Jews* (New York: Free Press, 1956).
12. *National Journal,* 16 (Sept. 22, 1984), summarizing data from the Gallup poll.
13. *The Responsible Electorate* (Cambridge: Harvard U.P., 1966), p. 30.
14. *The English Constitution* (Ithaca: Cornell U.P., 1966), pp. 18ff.
15. "Prejudice in Politics," *The Gallup Poll* (Wilmington, Del.: Scholarly Resources, 1979), pp. 214–22; Andrew M. Greeley and Paul B. Sheatsley, "Attitudes Toward Racial Integration," *Scientific American*, 225 (Dec. 1971), pp. 13–19; John G. Condran, "Changes in White Attitudes Toward Blacks: 1963–1977," *Political Opinion Quarterly*, 43 (Winter 1979), pp. 463–76.
16. V. O. Key, Jr., *Public Opinion and American Democracy* (New York: Knopf, 1961), p. 235.
17. Benjamin I. Page and Robert Y. Shapiro, "Changes in Americans' Policy Preferences, 1935–1979," *Public Opinion Quarterly*, 46 (Spring 1982), pp. 24–42.
18. *The Gallup Poll* (Wilmington, Del.: Scholarly Resources, 1979), p. 96; *Current Opinion*, 4 (Oct. 1976), p. 110.
19. Howard Schuman and Stanley Presser, "Heads or Tails, He Wins," *The New York Times* (July 17, 1980).
20. Robert Reinhold, "Polls' Divergence Puzzles Experts," *The New York Times* (Aug. 15, 1984).
21. Donald J. Devine, *The Political Culture of the United States* (Boston: Little, Brown, 1972).
22. Paul Sniderman and Richard Brody, "Coping: The Ethic of Self-Reliance," *American Journal of Political Science*, 21 (Aug. 1977), p. 508.
23. Kay Schlozman and Sidney Verba, *Injury to Insult* (Cambridge: Harvard U.P., 1979), p. 202.
24. Gunnar Myrdal, *An American Dilemma*, Vol. 1 (New York: Harper & Row, 1944), p. 4.
25. John L. Sullivan, James Pierson, and George E. Marcus, *Political Tolerance and American Democracy* (Chicago: U. of Chicago, 1982), p. 67.
26. W. Lance Bennett, *Public Opinion in American Politics* (New York: Harcourt, 1980), p. 13.
27. Tom Smith, "America's Most Important Problem—A Trend Analysis, 1946–1976," *Public Opinion Quarterly*, 44 (Summer 1980), pp. 164–80; *Gallup Reports* (Jan./Feb. 1984), p. 28.
28. *1980 National Election Study.*
29. CBS News/*New York Times* Poll, reported in *The New York Times* (Jan. 22, 1978).
30. Warren E. Miller et al., *American National Election Studies Data Sourcebook, 1952–1978* (Cambridge: Harvard U.P., 1980), Table 3.50.
31. Free and Cantril, p. 180.
32. Kathleen Knight, "Ideological Identification and the Content of the Ideological Agenda: 1960–1980," Paper at the American Political Science Association (Washington, 1984); Norman R. Luttbeg and Michael M. Gant, "The Failure of Liberal/Conservative Ideology as a Cognitive Structure," *Public Opinion Quarterly*, 49 (Spring 1985), pp. 80–93.
33. Alden Raine, *Change in the Political Agenda* (Beverly Hills: Sage, 1977), p. 14.
34. John Jackson, "The Systematic Beliefs of the Mass Public," *Journal of Politics*, 45 (Nov. 1983), pp. 840–65.
35. Norman Nie et al., *The Changing American Voter* (Cambridge: Harvard U.P., 1976), p. 152 and chaps. 8–9.
36. Thucydides, *The Peloponnesian War* (London: Penguin, 1954), p. 145.
37. Plato, *The Republic*, Book 6, 488.
38. James Madison, *The Federalist*, Nos. 10, 52 (New York: Modern Library, 1941), pp. 58, 343.
39. Austin Ranney, "United States of America," in *Referendums*, David Butler and Ranney, eds. (Washington: American Enterprise Association, 1978), chap. 4; David Magleby, *Direct Legislation* (Baltimore: Johns Hopkins U.P., 1983).
40. Alexis de Tocqueville, *Democracy in America*, Vol. 1 (New York: Vintage, 1954), chap. 15, p. 271.
41. Benjamin Page and Richard Brody, "Policy Voting and the Electoral Process: The Vietnam War Issue," *American Political Science Review*, 66 (Sept. 1972), pp. 979–95.
42. Warren E. Miller and Donald E. Stokes, "Constituency Influence in Congress," *American Political Science Review*, 57 (Mar. 1963), pp. 45–56.
43. Richard Fenno, *Home Style* (Boston: Little, Brown, 1978), pp. 58–59.
44. "Speech to the Electors of Bristol," *Works, II* (Boston: Little, Brown, 1866), pp. 89–98.
45. Alan Monroe, "Consistency between Public Preferences and National Policy Decisions," *American Politics Quarterly*, 7 (Jan. 1979), pp. 3–20.
46. Paul Burstein, "Public Opinion, Demonstrations and the Passage of Anti-Discrimination Legislation," *Public Opinion Quarterly*, 43 (Summer 1979), pp. 157–72.
47. Benjamin I. Page and Robert Y. Shapiro, "Effects of Public Opinion on Policy," *American Political Science Review*, 77 (Mar. 1983), pp. 175–90.

CHAPTER 5

The Mass Media

In the last century, two close presidential elections stand out. In the first, the Republican candidate stayed near home, receiving delegations who came to visit his home in Canton, Ohio. His managers distributed campaign propaganda by the millions, including warnings to factory workers that they should report to work after the election only if the Republican candidate won. The Democratic candidate took a different approach; he traveled thousands of miles by railroad. Invoking religious imagery of the martyrdom of Jesus, he urged his fervent audiences to prevent the crucifixion of the "laboring classes" by the financiers of Wall Street. This 1896 contest between William McKinley, the winner, and William Jennings Bryan was waged by personal contacts between the candidates, their party supporters, and the voting public.

Generations later, in 1976, the two major party candidates stood side by side on a television stage in Philadelphia. Superficially, Gerald Ford and Jimmy Carter, who eventually won the election, were conducting a debate before a small audience, and television cameras were there only to report on a "news event." Then, the equipment failed, and no sound could be transmitted. Rather than continue their discussion, the candidates stood mute for almost half an hour, awaiting repairs. The real audience was not gathered in the Philadelphia hall, but was scattered among tens of millions of darkened living rooms. Political communication had become indirect, impersonal, and fragmented.

Today, the mass media dominate American politics, just as they significantly affect all aspects of our national life. The theme of this chapter is how the media simultaneously unify and fragment American society and politics. In one sense, the media unify the country, defining a common culture and providing a common interpretation of the political world. In another sense, however, their effect has been to undermine the community life of the United States. Even if we see the same programs on television, we do not usually engage in

"16 to 1-Free Silver"
Means that a Silver Dollar is worth only 53 Cents.
"Boys_
Popocrats and Silverites have forced me to make a dollar that is worth only 53 cents;
I am Ashamed of such a policy."
"I'm not to blame. I can't sell you a dollars worth for 53 cents I have been obliged to raise the price of my goods."

Today election campaigning is conducted mostly over television, but in the 1896 election emphasis was on personal campaigning and leaflets. The McKinley leaflet here shows opposition to Bryan's free-silver platform. *(Chicago Historical Society)*

face-to-face discussion about these programs. We retain our individual roles as democratic citizens but participate less in a democratic dialogue.

Pursuing this theme, we will consider five aspects of the mass media in this chapter:

1. Their importance in American life.
2. Their basic organizational and operational characteristics.
3. Their relationships with government.
4. Their general effects on American society.
5. Their specific effects on election campaigns.

The Media in American Life

Media Dominance

The unifying aspects of the mass media are quite apparent. The mass media define what the United States means, for our reliance on them is inescapable. We can only learn of a presidential speech, an environmental hazard, or threat of war from the press, not by personal experience. Given the complexity of political events, we can make sense of this reality with the guidance of the media alone. Every day, to learn about the world, Americans buy 63 million newspapers, and 100 million watch television. The importance of the media is indicated by the data in Table 5.1.

The media also help to unify American life-styles. The folk heroes of the society are more likely to be television performers, such as Larry Hagman, or even their fictional counterparts, such as J. R. Ewing, rather than politi-

TABLE 5.1 Media Usage in the United States

Year	TV Evening News Audience	Number of TV Sets	Number of Daily Newspapers	Daily Newspapers Readership
1960	15,140,000	53,300,000	1,763	58,882,000
1965	18,440,000	67,210,000	1,751	60,358,000
1970	20,700,000	88,300,000	1,748	62,108,000
1975	24,460,000	121,100,000	1,768	60,655,000
1979	29,030,000	155,800,000	1,763	62,233,000
1984	45,640,000	191,200,000	1,688	63,340,000

Sources: Television and Cable Factbook (Washington: Television Digest, 1985); *Editor & Publisher Yearbook* (New York, 1985). *'85 Nielsen Report on Television* (Northbrook, Ill.: Nielsen, 1985).

cal statesmen. Although there is still marked diversity in the United States in such characteristics as customs and language, these differences have been eroded by the presentation of unified life-styles to all Americans spoken in a similar dialect through the media. The "tube," in fact, has become the dominant element in our national life. Americans watch it from their first days as infants to their final days in hospitals. Television is universal, and sets are more common in American households than indoor toilets.[1] The average household watches seven hours a day,[2] and schoolchildren spend more time with television than attending school, praying in church, or sharing family dinners.

Concentration The media's influence is also a concentrated impact. Virtually all significant newspaper stories come from the major wire services, Associated Press and United Press International, and they affect the character of news published throughout the nation. Television is the most frequently used and the most trusted news service for public affairs. In fact, there is little competition among the media. Almost 95 percent of Americans live in communities where there are only one newspaper or where "competing" publications are under the same ownership.[3] In television, the field is dominated by the three networks, CBS, NBC, and ABC. Most local stations are affiliates of one of the networks and rely almost entirely on them for their nonlocal news programming. Competition among the three networks is centered on the speed with which they report events or on the form of presentation. As we shall discuss further on, they rarely present different points of view; and their competition, consequently, promotes uniformity not diversity or debate.

Criticisms of the Media

Media Power The pervasiveness and concentration of the media promotes fears that they exercise excessive and undesirable power. These concerns lead to government regulation in some cases, such as the requirement that television and radio provide equal time for major candidates. Furthermore, officials often complain about the media. Every recent president has criticized the press—Kennedy for its disclosure of the Bay of Pigs invasion of Cuba, Johnson for its attacks on his Vietnam policy, Nixon for its investigations of Watergate, Ford for its mocking of his agility, Carter for its treatment of the Iran hostage crisis, and Reagan for its inattention to his economic program. More significant than these personal complaints are the potential effects of the media on the general public's thinking. The press has been seen as dominated by liberals and critics of the government, or as former Vice-President Spiro Agnew phrased it, "nattering nabobs of negativism."[4] Others have found the press conservative in its effects, providing a modern "opiate of the people," diverting the public from a concern for social causes.[5]

Parent groups have lobbied to set guidelines for the TV networks on issues related to children's programming. *(UPI)*

Violence on TV The media are also seen as adversely affecting social behavior. Parent groups, for example, have been critical of the great amount of violence on television, in both entertainment and news programs, and have sought government action to reduce the incidence of murder and mayhem. After congressional hearings and a special investigation by the Surgeon General,[6] the Federal Communications Commission sought voluntary action by the networks to limit such fare in children's programs and in the evening before 9:00 p.m., presumably the universal juvenile bedtime in the nation. Their concern over televised violence has been spurred by incidents such as the following:

> A college athlete was arrested in Grand Junction, Colorado, after he had mailed letters threatening to kill the wife of a bank president unless he was paid $5,000. At the time of his arrest, he stated he got his idea from television shows.
>
> In Los Angeles, a housemaid caught a seven-year-old boy in the act of sprinkling ground glass into the family's lamb stew. There was no malice behind the act. It was purely experimental, having been inspired by curiosity to learn whether it would really work as well as it did on television.[7]

Despite the protests and the networks' response, violence continues on the airwaves. Ten years after the first government report, the Surgeon General issued a new report. It reiterated the earlier findings that violence on television was linked to aggressive behavior by viewers, especially children. Moreover, over time, "the percentage of programs containing violence has remained about the same," and "the number of violent acts per program has increased," so that a typical week of television shows over a hundred acts of violence.[8]

Social Stereotypes Other groups have protested the depiction of sexual abuse, senility among older persons, and stereotyped behavior by women, racial minorities, and homosexuals. The common premise in these protests is that the media are effective in presenting models for behavior and thought. If television shows women as docile and domestic, it is assumed viewers will regard all women as unliberated, just as depictions of religious bigotry will promote anti-Semitism.

Although concern over the effects of the media on public opinion is widespread, these effects are more often asserted than demonstrated. On the most vital public questions, in fact, the media's influence is often limited, sometimes contradictory, and almost always ambiguous. The media are not a monolithic influence. To understand their true impact, we need first to examine basic characteristics of the press and their relationship to government. We can, then, review the evidence of their impact on public opinion.

Characteristics of the Media

The media have the potential to unify American society. However, this potential is not fully achieved, because of basic characteristics. These effects are the result of the structure of the press and of the manner in which it conducts its trade.

Influences on the Media

The Media Are Businesses An important shaping influence is that the press is, in many respects, part of the business community. Newspapers are no longer solely the voices of individual editors promoting their vision of the public good but are largely parts of conglomerate corporations such as the Gannett or Hearst chains. Television and radio are dominated by the networks, which are among the largest and most profitable enterprises in the nation. All of the media depend heavily on advertisers for their revenues.

This dependence does not mean that the press is a capitalist tool. The canons of journalism, and prestige within the profession, emphasize the independent and critical role of the press, and it honors those who detect official corruption and errors. Newspapers will frequently resist an advertiser's threat to withdraw support if an unfavorable story is printed, as television continued to cover the civil rights revolution in the 1960s despite the qualms of corporate sponsors with major interests in the South. Ultimately, both the press and its advertisers need a large audience. If a controversial program will add to that audience, the press will run the story, and advertisers will necessarily go along. More generally, however, the press—as a business—does support the fundamental economic and political institutions of the nation. It is less likely to attempt change in public opinion than to support existing beliefs. It will investigate individual cases of air pollution, for example, but it is unlikely to suggest government ownership of polluting industries. Similarly the press will support motherhood, but it is not likely to advocate abortion.

Independence of the Media The tradition of independence is another major influence on the mass media. Freedom of the press, founded in the Constitution's first amendment, frees newspapers from most regulation and from any prepublication censorship of its material, whereas radio and television are subject to more, but still limited, controls. Thus, the press maintains a posture that is separate from government. It is also formally independent of other groups, such as corporations or political parties. In other nations, newspapers are often the organs of the parties. This practice was followed by the early press in America, with political controversy sparked by such papers as the Federalist *Gazette* and the Jacksonian *Washington Globe*. But the spread of literacy, the invention of the telegraph, and the founding of the Associated Press and of newspapers such as Horace Greeley's New York *Tribune*, enabled the press to become an autonomous influence in politics. Government direction of electronic journalism is the common pattern in other countries. In the United States, the federal government is involved only in regulation and indirect subsidy of public broadcasting.

The autonomous character of the press affects the way in which it presents the news. The press defines itself as a critic or watchdog of government. Its stance is that of suspicion toward public officials, its mode that of investigation into their errors and misbehavior. In democratic theory, the purpose of press freedom is to allow it to be critical, and the press enjoys this role—sometimes even going beyond criticism on issues to the position of personal gadfly. It takes delight, for example, in exchanges such as presidential press conferences. (See box below.)

Media Routines The news media are also affected by the routine procedures developed within their organizations. The selection of items for publication, therefore, does not depend simply on their intrinsic value but depends also on satisfying the internal needs of the newspaper or broadcasting staff. Thus, the relative amount of space given to local, national, and international news is relatively constant in a newspaper because the editors must satisfy the demands of these separate groups of reporters.[9] Reporters are assigned to particular beats, or news sources, and these sub-

POLITICAL PERSPECTIVE

MEDIA DIALOGUE ON PRESIDENT REAGAN'S ABILITIES

Q. What's your response to the people . . . who ask whether you are, in fact, really running things?

A. I've read a little of the fiction that's been going around about that, also. . . . That's a lack of understanding of how our system has been working here, and I will admit I don't think any administration, to my knowledge, has ever exactly worked with the Cabinet and the staff the way we have. . . .

Q. Sir, what's your response to those who suggest that you don't spend enough time at the job of being President?

A. My answer to them is they don't know what they're talking about. And I almost made that a little more blunt right then, but decided—

Q. Go ahead. (laughter)

A. No, it would be unseemly if I did. But they don't know what they're talking about. I have never gone upstairs from that office once that I have not carried an entire evening full of homework with me.

Source: Presidential press conference of February 22, 1984.

jects are more likely to be reported than events where no regular reporter is present. The economic necessities of the press also have consequences for day-to-day coverage, which results in more coverage of planned than breaking news.

In another characteristic routine of the press, reporters imitate one another. No reporters want to seem behind on a story, but they also want to avoid being out of step. This leads to *pack journalism,* where reporters "all fe[e]d off the same pool report, the same daily handout, the same speech by the candidate; the whole pack . . . [is] isolated in the same mobile village. After a while, they beg[i]n to believe the same rumors, subscribe to the same theories, and write the same stories."[10] The press corps does not act as a collection of individual investigators, but rather resembles fashion-conscious women. There are fashion leaders in journalism as well. The topics selected by national political reporters and prestige papers such as *The New York Times* often set the agenda for the rest of the media, whereas the content of stories is typically the homogeneous wire service copy. The result is a seminationalized press, under private ownership, that is similar in its content, style, and interpretations from coast to coast. The effect on public opinion is to limit the individual contribution of any single press element.

Operation of the Media

Media Emphasis of Events The media see themselves as primarily concerned with reporting, rather than interpretation. Therefore, they focus on presenting "real" events. Reporters are uncomfortable with speculation or with investigation of long-term factors. The emphasis is on observable, discrete, and novel events. They seek to report a happening, rather than predicting what may happen, or explaining what did happen. A traffic accident is called "news," but the design of automobiles is not—even though poor design will probably lead to accidents. These emphases are detailed in Table 5.2.

The emphasis on objective events is particularly evident in press coverage of election campaigns. The media focus on discrete and observable happenings, such as a primary victory, a changed issue position, or the winning of a presidential debate, while giving less attention to the meaning of these events. The travels of a candidate can be reported, with a different dateline on each day's story. His continuing philosophical commitments require interpretation and depth, but these qualities are not emphasized in the media.

The press defines news as that which is literally new. As an old maxim has it, "dog bites man" is a true but dull report, while "man bites dog" is more newsworthy, precisely because it is uncommon. More generally, newsmen will not pursue a topic from one day to the next, unless there is additional information forthcoming, and forthcoming close to deadline. Most matters of social importance, by contrast, are long-standing and incremental in their impact, such as the slow depletion of American oil reserves or changes in the age distribution of the population. Politicians use this operating characteristic of the press for their own advantage. The government

TABLE 5.2 What's in the Media: Proportion of Coverage by Newspapers and Television Devoted to Various Subjects

	Chicago Tribune	CBS Local	CBS National
Government/politics			
National institutions	7.1	5.9	13.1
Foreign affairs	9.8	4.6	17.1
Domestic policy	12.6	5.6	7.6
Elections	7.6	6.8	15.2
State and city governments, misc.	4.3	7.9	2.0
Crime and justice			
Police/security/judiciary	10.4	7.9	5.0
Corruption	4.0	4.0	3.3
Individual crime	7.5	7.8	4.0
Economic/social issues			
Economy/business/labor	8.3	7.7	8.5
Minorities/women	2.7	2.1	2.9
Environment/transportation	3.2	9.1	4.0
Accident/health/medicine	4.7	7.1	5.6
Education/media/religion	4.4	4.0	3.0
Leadership style, misc.	2.9	1.5	2.1
Human interest			
Human interest/celebrities/ political gossip	8.1	9.6	4.4
Sports/entertainment	2.6	8.3	2.1

Source: Doris A. Graber, *Mass Media and American Politics*, 2nd ed. (Washington: Congressional Quarterly Press, 1984), pp. 82–83. (Data are from an analysis of Chicago media in 1976).

will release unfavorable news over the weekend so that it is more likely to be unreported "dead news" by Monday. Candidates time their announcements close to the deadlines for the evening telecasts and morning newspapers so that they can appear fresh and be distributed before there is an opportunity for rebuttal by the opposition.

SELECTIVITY OF THE MEDIA Published items show distinct emphases. Preferred items have a high emotional impact: they deal with violence, conflict, disaster, or scandal; concern familiar situations and well-known persons; are close to home; and are timely and novel.[11] Seeking conflict situations, the media pay attention to governmental disagreement, to inconsistencies in candidate statements, and to physical violence. Since harmony—which is probably more evident in reality—does not make for "good news," the media will even search out disagreement where it does not exist.

Television news can be characterized, according to one interpretation, as a series of melodramas, using real world settings to present political "soap

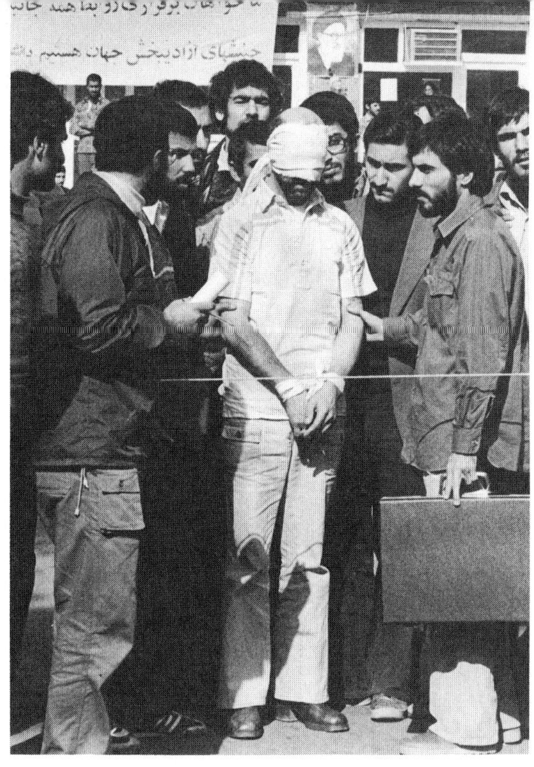

Television's intense coverage of the 1980 Iranian hostage crisis made this a major issue for the public. *(Philippe Ledru/Sygma)*

operas." "The resulting real fiction is at the same time an entertaining, larger-than-life drama that sparks people's interests, yet one that permits them to relate the larger than life to their everyday lives."

The 1980 hostage crisis in Iran is a specific example. Television coverage varied considerably over the extended period of the crisis. For the first six weeks, this story took up two-thirds of the network news. Although the American diplomats remained in captivity, they were then forgotten by reporters except when renewed drama resulted from secret negotiations, the abortive rescue mission, or the eventual release. In casting the Iranian melodrama, "TV news had no trouble labeling heroes, villains, and fools," identifying for each role the American diplomats, the Iranian militants, and the Shah.[12]

The media's focus on conflict and possible scandal created problems for vice-presidential candidate Geraldine Ferraro in 1984. *(Allan Tannenbaum/Sygma)*

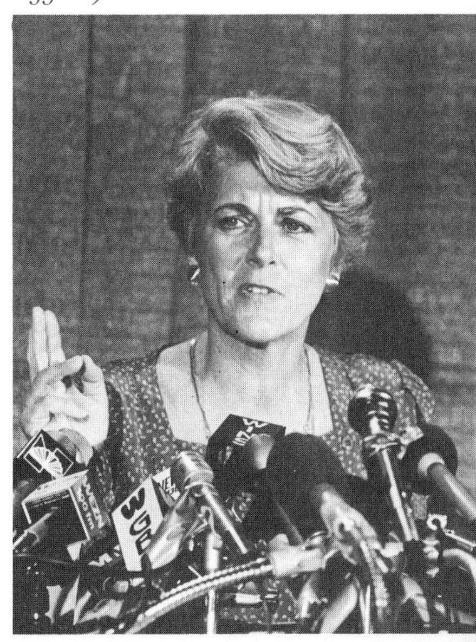

News as Conflict The media often look for news items showing conflict and novelty, even scandal. A good example is found in the treatment of Geraldine Ferraro, the first woman nominated by a major party for national office. When the Congresswoman was selected by the Democrats in July 1984, she was lauded by the press. A month later, seeking a new story, the media burrowed into her family's personal finances, down to the minutiae of complaints by tenants in one building owned by her husband, a real estate broker. In a dramatic press conference, Ms. Ferraro satisfied all critics and was again the darling of the press.

The next month, her opponent, Vice-President George Bush released his own tax returns, which could have raised similar questions about financial probity. By this time, however, the press was bored with the subject, and never pursued it. The different coverage of Ferraro and Bush may also have shown an implicit sexism in the press, holding a woman candidate to a different standard than a man. Another example of the media's search for conflict is provided by Art Buchwald, in his reprinted parody of press coverage of the boring party nominating conventions of 1980. (See box on page 148.)

POLITICAL PERSPECTIVE

TV NEWS: MUCH ADO ABOUT NOTHING

NEW YORK—As a member of the print media, no one stands in as much awe as I do of the electronic media. It is not when they have a good story that they're at their best—it's when they have no story at all and have to stick with it that they really shine.

All three networks excelled last week at the Democratic convention.

I guess the highlight was Wednesday evening. I was watching one of the major channels and there was absolutely nothing going on. The network team rose to the occasion.

"Let's go now to Tammy Dumbarton. Tammy, you had an earlier report that nothing was going to happen in the next hour. Can you confirm that for us?"

"Yes, Lester. I've been talking to the Rhode Island delegation and they have told me they don't plan to do anything."

"That's very interesting, Tammy, stay with it. Let's go to Carlton Finks who is talking to a lady delegate from Delaware."

"Lester, as you know, nothing has taken place here for the last two hours and with me now is Mrs. Cynthia Grogan, a Carter delegate from Delaware who says she has nothing to say. Mrs. Grogan, is this true?"

"That's correct. On behalf of the entire delegation from Delaware I have no news to report."

"I'm sorry, Carlton, I have to switch to the Waldorf where Temple Star has the latest news on what is going on at Kennedy headquarters."

"Lester, I'm standing in the empty lobby of the Waldorf Astoria and over to my right, out of camera range, is the cashier's window. Sen. Kennedy checked out of here sometime today. He came down the elevators and walked out the Park Avenue exit with his family and got into a car."

"What do you think it all means, Temp?"

"Lester, it's too early to say, but I've talked to one of the senator's campaign aides who was closeted in the suite and he said none of it means anything. I'm trying to get confirmation on this now."

"You do that, Temp, and we'll get back to you. Now let's go to Eldon Lloyd who has been standing out on Eighth Avenue and can give us an up-to-date report on the situation there."

"Lester, the traffic on Eighth Avenue is moving very well. Three buses have passed by in the last half-hour going north, and about six minutes ago I saw a 1961 Buick. You don't see many of those around any more. There is something going on in Pennsylvania Station. I believe an Amtrak train is running late, but none of the Amtrak people will talk about it."

"Eldon, will you hold off on that Amtrak report? We've had a bulletin that they've run out of coffee in the Garden concession stand just below us. Ron Peterson is trying to get over there now. Ron, can you get to the stand and check it out?"

"I'm working my way over now, Lester. As you can see, the floor is jammed with people. Okay, here I am. Sir, is it true your concession has run out of coffee?"

"Yes, we have. Hi, Mom and Dad and Danny and Eddie and Sue and the guys at Feagan's Bar."

"What do you plan to do about it?"

"Nothing."

"I guess that clinches it, Lester. It could be the biggest nothing story we've had so far."

"It certainly could be. Well, as you have seen and heard, there is nothing going on here, and we'll stay with the story until its conclusion. In a moment we'll be back with latest coverage of the Democratic convention on our 72nd hour in captivity."

Source: Reprinted with permission of the author, Art Buchwald.

Point-Counterpoint Journalism To present conflict most simply and dramatically, the media engage in **point-counterpoint journalism,** where all issues are seen as having two—and only two—sides. Political debates are simplified into "liberals" versus "conservatives," and foreign policy is boiled down to "us versus them." As part of the laudable attempt to be objective, the press—especially television—tries to present "the other side," and this effort usually means that two relatively extreme positions are presented together. Analysis of the abortion issue, for example, will usually include interviews with dedicated advocates of unlimited abortion versus advocates of total abolition of abortion. Persons taking intermediate positions—as do most Americans—will rarely get a hearing.[13]

Government and the Media

Although formally independent of one another, the media and the government are closely related and interdependent. Both of them contribute to the unity of the United States. At the same time, each of them is fragmented in some ways. The interplay of media and government thus reflects the general patterns of American society.

Government Relations with the Media

Most of the news reported by the press deals with the activities of government, and it obtains its information chiefly from government sources. For its part, the government must rely on the media to disseminate its messages, whether they are information about income taxes or patriotic appeals to join the armed forces. Interdependence has made the press a "fourth branch of government." This semiofficial position continues a tradition dating from the eighteenth century in Europe, when the press was called a "fourth estate," supplementing the power of the feudal classes of king, nobles, and commoners.

Adversarial Relations Versus Cooperation Although the press and government need each other, they do not always like each other. The relationship is inevitably partially adversarial, and incompletely cooperative. Government would like the press to bring only good news and to accept its statements at face value. As we have noted earlier, every president has found some reason to see the media as "irresponsible" or "carping" or "destructive." Conversely, the press, being autonomous, defines its role as a critic and overseer of government. It needs government as the fundamental

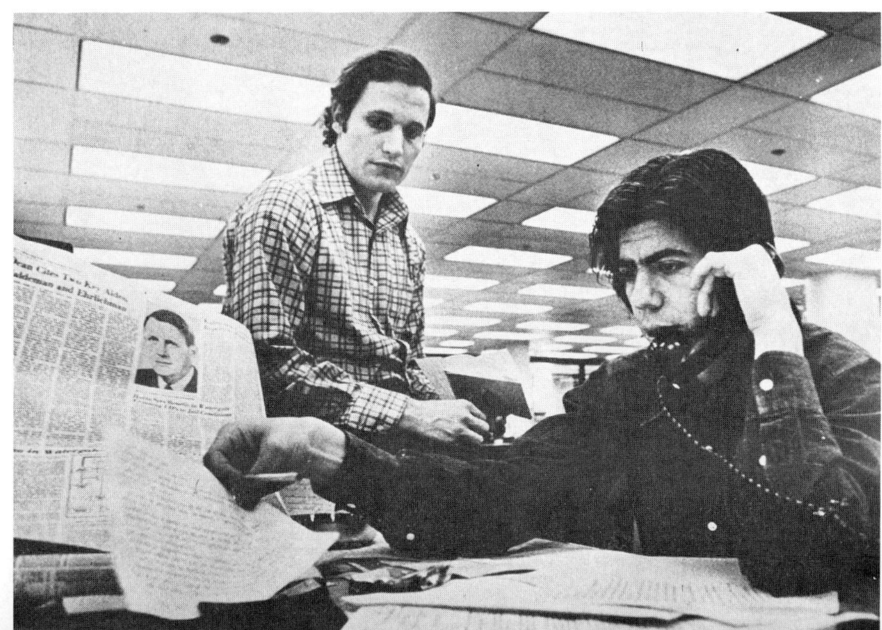

Few journalists can hope for the fame, prestige, and fortune that came to Bob Woodward and Carl Bernstein when they uncovered the Watergate scandal while at *The Washington Post*. *(UPI)*

source of information, but it is rightly suspicious that officials may be using the media for their own purposes.

The adversarial aspect of the government-media relationship is the more dramatic. The press is ever on the lookout for instances of mismanagement, incompetence, and corruption. Each reporter has a secret dream that he or she will uncover the next Watergate scandal and receive the fame, prestige, and fortune that came to Woodward and Bernstein. Public officials are acutely aware of the press, beginning their days with a reading of the major national newspapers and concluding them with viewings of the national television newscasts—sometimes, as was the practice of Lyndon Johnson, watching all three networks simultaneously. Whereas the general public gives only limited attention to government, officials live in more of a closed world, where political matters are predominant, even consuming. They are often more concerned with their "professional reputation" than with their "public prestige."[14] For example, the general public gives little attention to officials other than the president, and the cabinet members are virtually unknown.

The relationship is not simply antagonistic. Because of their mutual dependence and their frequent contacts, government and media also cooperate greatly. The press not only helps to determine professional reputation, it is a major element of the Washington establishment, as well. Although critical of some officials and some policies, it also shares their values. Furthermore, the press is often dependent on government. The largest proportion of news comes not from independent investigations by reporters but from government releases, which are usually disseminated by the media without significant alteration or analysis.[15] Information is itself a source of power, and officials have more information available to them than does the press. Therefore they are likely to hold the upper hand.

This dependence is furthered by an organizational characteristic of the media. Reporters are assigned to particular beats, such as the White House or the Pentagon. They are eager to have their articles accepted for publication or broadcasting, but the availability of these stories usually requires the

POLITICAL PERSPECTIVE

SHAKESPEARE AND THE MEDIA

The press and the rest of the Washington community is like a royal court in which there is constant conversation and gossip about individuals. In this dialogue they fit Shakespeare's description of those who

> Pray and sing, and tell old tales and laugh
> At gilded butterflies, and hear poor rogues
> Talk of court news; and we'll talk with them too,
> Who loses and who wins, who's in, who's out;
> And take upon us the mystery of things,
> As if we were God's spies; and we'll wear out,
> In a wall'd prison, packs and sects of great ones
> That ebb and flow by the moon.

Source: *King Lear,* V:iii, 2–19.

POLITICAL PERSPECTIVE

GOVERNMENT AND THE PRESS: ABRAHAM LINCOLN

Efforts by political leaders to "manage" the press are not new in the twentieth century. In his historical novel *Lincoln,* Gore Vidal relates some of the opinion-forming efforts of the civil war president, of his secretaries, John Hay and John Nicolay, and of Secretary of State William Seward. He also reports on the president's techniques in gaining support for his reelection in 1864 from an influential editor, Horace Greeley of the New York *Tribune.*

> Hay often wrote Washington stories, anonymously, for the New York newspapers. Hay's speciality was inside information about the Administration, which seemed, at first, to be scandalous but then proved to be subtly favorable to the President. He often published in the *World,* a newspaper noted for its virulent hatred of Lincoln. It gave Hay a good deal of pleasure to know that the editor never suspected that he was being manipulated by the President's own secretary. Meanwhile, Hay and Nicolay had seen to it that journalists of every sort had been given military and civilian posts in different parts of the country so that they could then write stories favorable to the Administration for their old newspapers. . . .
>
> Greeley had come around to Lincoln. The *Tribune* was now entirely pro-Lincoln; and had been so even before Atlanta—or B.A., as Nico now termed the dark ages of the Administration, while A.A. designated the new victorious era. It also had not hurt that Greeley had, somehow, got the impression that if Blair should leave the Cabinet, he would be the next Postmaster-General. In fact, when the Tycoon [Lincoln] had been asked recently by a number of New Yorkers if he would consider Greeley, they had been told that, after all, another editor by the name of Benjamin Franklin had been pretty successful in the job. Greeley, who lusted for public office, had taken the bait; and his editorials now oozed honey. . . .

Source: Gore Vidal, *Lincoln* (New York: Random House, Inc., 1984), pp. 390, 580–81.

cooperation of officials. In order to have some story, they often must accept the story provided.

Press Conferences and News Leaks The presidential press conference illustrates these limitations on the press. In form, it is an inquisition of the president by the press, where reporters can ask questions on any topic and be as probing and irreverent as courtesy will allow. In reality, however, presidents have considerable control over these conferences—they determine their frequency and timing, choose the reporters to be recognized, establish the focus by their opening statement, suggest other questions to be asked, and leave after thirty minutes.[16]

Presidents can use various techniques to control news conferences. John Kennedy combined command of facts with spontaneous humor to win over the Washington press corps. Jimmy Carter displayed a detailed involvement in even small points of government policy, while Ronald Reagan developed the ability to provide convincing analogies in support of his arguments. Richard Nixon was prone to defend his personal interests by reference to alleged Constitutional principles. For example, when the Watergate scandal, which would ultimately drive him from office, was developing, Nixon refused to let Congress question John Dean, who had been at the hub of the illegal activities. He invoked the constitutional principle of separation of powers to avoid Congress' investigation of Dean's actions.

News leaks are another kind of interaction between government and the media. For the reporter, a leak is a way to gain an exclusive story, get behind the government's official line, and thereby deepen public awareness and improve his or her own reputation. For the government, however, leaks are undesirable. They result in premature publicity, complicate the confidentiality needed in policymaking, and disrupt personal and bureaucratic relationships. Yet leaks are widely used by individual government officials for various ends. A subordinate unhappy with an emerging policy may leak information in order to arouse relevant interest groups. In other circumstances, officials may feel that their conscience requires them to blow the whistle on their superiors—as in revelations of corruption or the leak of the **Pentagon Papers,** internal documents of the Defense Department that narrated the increasing involvement of the United States in Vietnam in the 1960s. On occasion, leaks are also used for diplomatic purposes, as means of letting a foreign nation know of American intentions without creating a formal controversy.

The political use of leaks was pointedly illustrated in the midst of the 1984 presidential election. President Reagan had been under attack by Democrat Walter Mondale for his failure to meet personally with Soviet leaders in an effort to ease international tensions. On the same day that Mondale released his long-awaited plan to reduce the federal budget deficit, a story was leaked, upstaging the opposition, that the president was planning a meeting with Soviet Foreign Minister Andrei Gromyko. The leak was followed by a formal announcement of the meeting by Reagan, providing him with a second media opportunity to present himself as a peacemaker.

Government Regulation of Media

Government and the media also have more formal relationships, involving restrictions placed on the press. In the case of newspapers, these pertain to judicial restraints on libel and the use of information gathered by reporters that is relevant to criminal trials. There are more restrictions placed on radio and television. Unlike print media, there are technical limits in broadcasting so that if anyone who wanted (and could afford) a station began broadcasting, the result would not be more information for the public but a babble of static on the airwaves. The Federal Communications Commission (FCC) was established to deal with these problems.

Promoting Diversity One goal sought by the FCC has been diversity in ownership. No single corporation can own more than twelve AM or FM radio stations, or more than twelve television stations (and only one in a single media market). Newspaper publishers are not allowed to purchase radio or television outlets in their own communities. However, by 1990, all limitations on ownership will be ended, following the deregulatory goals of the Reagan administration. Yet FCC rules, in themselves, do not promote diversity in television broadcasting because most of the nation's 1,200 stations are affiliated with the three national networks. Radio does evidence greater diversity, probably greater than that in newspapers. The cause of this variety is not government's regulation but the marketplace. It is more difficult to finance a local newspaper than a local radio station. The result is that, although few cities have more than one daily paper, there are 9,000 radio outlets in the country.[17]

The FCC has also sought to promote diversity of programming in a number of ways. Limitations have been placed on the use of network programs, with local stations required to provide a minimum amount of local material in evening prime time. In some instances, these rules have stimulated stations to examine community problems. More often, it has simply meant that the stations use this time for reruns of former network entertainment or for game shows. Other regulations have required a minimum amount of attention to public affairs, restricted such advertisements as cigarettes, and discouraged violence and other offensive material. In 1981, these restrictions were removed from radio broadcasters. Because the number of radio stations has grown enormously, the FCC decided that competition in the marketplace was a sufficient check on abuses of this medium.

FAIRNESS DOCTRINE AND EQUAL TIME Political diversity has been the goal of other regulations. Persons who have been attacked individually have a right of rebuttal on free time. Under a general **fairness doctrine,** broadcasters are obliged to present divergent points of view when they present a program, or to provide time for reply to station editorials. The selection of persons to provide replies is left to the media, and the rule does not apply to material broadcast in regular news programs. Under this principle, for example, stations will sometimes provide time for the opposition party to answer statements in the president's State of the Union address (but not in news conferences). They are unlikely to give access to those who object to public-service advertisements extolling the oil industry. For the most part, the broadcasting industry has been restrictive in promoting controversy on the airwaves.

The most direct regulation of political coverage is the **equal-time provision** of the communications law, which applies only to election campaigns. It requires stations, if they give or sell time to one election candidate, to provide the same opportunity for all opponents, not only those of the minor parties. Because there always are a multitude of minor candidates for an office, including the presidency, broadcasters have been unwilling to give all of the candidates unpaid time to present their programs. Some suggestions have been made that radio and television be required to provide this time.

Debates among political candidates are more complicated. Until 1960, the equal-time rule meant that all candidates, not just the Republicans and Democrats, had to be included in any forum. Reluctant to provide free time for Vegetarians or Socialists, the networks provided little free time for any candidate, whether from a major or minor party. In 1960, however, Congress simply suspended this provision of the law during the campaign, leading to the famous Kennedy-Nixon confrontations. Afterward, beginning in 1976, the debates were held under the legal fiction that they were news events, which could be covered by radio and television without regard to the equal-time mandate. The League of Women Voters has sponsored all of the debates during the general election campaign. In 1984, new groups also began to sponsor debates during the nominating primaries, including the media themselves, and the national parties began to take a more active role in setting the rules.

The characteristics of the media and their relationship to government tend to restrict their impact on public opinion. The press is apt to take safe positions, to criticize individual public officials but not institutions, to restrict itself to objective reporting while de-emphasizing analysis, and to follow established routines. Concentration of ownership and control reduces the diversity of voices in the public dialogue. Dependent on government for much of its information and wary of regulation, the press tends to limit its criticism and to play it safe. To be sure, the public must rely on the media for its information, and government officials are made somewhat more responsive because of press attention. Overall, however, the press does not make the fullest possible contribution to an active democracy.

The Media and Society

Logically, the widespread media should have broad influence, unifying the country. Despite the logic, it is difficult to prove that the media do have any direct effects. For example, there obviously are a great many sexual stimuli in the media, from suggestive television movies to pornographic magazines, and much sexual aberration in the United States (such as rape and child molestation). The coexistence of these two factors does not in itself prove that one causes the other. In fact, a presidential commission that thoroughly researched the question concluded that exposure to pornography actually might decrease such deviant sexual behavior.[18] A second commission, in 1986, did claim a link, but its conclusions were severely criticized.

Certainly, the media do affect American society, but their effects are probably more general. They establish a certain mood in the nation. They also considerably influence the priorities, the agenda, for the society. In these ways, they foster uniformity in the United States.

Setting the Mood

Providing Information The media provide information quickly and identically to all areas of the nation. When the new American republic won its independence, it took three months for any of its new citizens to learn that a peace treaty had been signed with Great Britain, and additional time for the news to penetrate to the Western frontier. Today, news flashes instantaneously around the world, making the entire nation participants in a foreign policy crisis or its resolution. Regional differences in politics have been obscured. Basing their views on the same information, Americans tend to give priority to the same questions. Civil rights or unemployment become national issues as a result, not only problems for the South or the Midwest.[19]

People also learn from the media, sometimes without realizing it. Political learning takes place even among those who are not particularly interested in the news programs they are watching, although there does tend to be more learning among the more interested. And the more people read or watch, the more they learn, regardless of their levels of education or previous knowledge.[20]

The media probably pay more attention to public affairs than their audience prefers. Partially because of their own values and partially because of government requirements in the case of radio and television, the press provides a forum for splinter parties, discussions on issues, and documentaries that is greater than that wished by most of the public, although many of these programs are relegated to obscure time spots. After all, the media do not compel Americans to prefer entertainment to news, yet the ratings and readership surveys repeatedly demonstrate this preference. To some, "what this suggests, therefore, is that the media are, at least in the short run, as much a product of public demands as a force that imposes these lighter interests upon the public at the expense of more serious political matters."[21] Yet, by simply following these public demands, the media also reinforce them. An innovative press might expand the public's consciousness, but American media do not usually see this as their responsibility.

VIDEOMALAISE The media may also affect the emotional attitudes that are vital in political life. One possible effect is **videomalaise,** the negative impact of the media, especially television, on public confidence in government institutions and trust of government leaders. A laboratory test of this theory examined viewers' responses to a CBS documentary critical of the Pentagon's involvement in politics and found that the audience became less supportive of the government after watching the program. More generally, those who were frequent television viewers felt less politically effective and more cynical toward government. Michael Robinson argues that television has a "negativistic, contentious, or anti-institutional bias. . . . These biases, frequently dramatized by film portrayals of violence and aggression, evoke images of American politics and social life which are inordinately sinister and despairing . . . essentially evil and indicative of sociopolitical decay."[22]

Videomalaise is stimulated by television newscasts, according to this theory. These programs tend to take a critical attitude toward governmental officials and to emphasize situations of dramatic conflict. This emphasis does not come from television reporters being radicals but from their being journalists looking for a good story. Scandals, conflicts, and violence make for better pictures and more dramatic accounts.

A critical attitude toward politicians is also evident in news broadcasts. A thorough study of campaign coverage in 1980 found the media were not biased toward one party or the other but that they were critical toward politicians. This attitude was particularly evident on television. While half of the evening news broadcasts on CBS, the largest network, was neutral in character, there was a distinct tilt to the remaining items, two out of three being negative. Critical views were expressed toward almost every candidate, with the most severe treatment reserved for frontrunners in the primaries, and for the incumbent president, Jimmy Carter.[23]

Negative treatment continued in 1984. Of all television news broadcasts, almost three-fourths were neutral in tone. Of the remainder, Democratic candidates Mondale and Ferraro received slightly more positive than negative coverage. The Republicans, however, got a "bad press." President Reagan received ten times more negative than positive coverage, and Vice-President Bush had only negative coverage. The reason for this pattern is not a liberal or Democratic bias by television. Rather, it reflects the media's generally critical attitude toward officeholders and prominent politicians. Just as Carter and Mondale bore the brunt of video attacks in 1980, Reagan and Bush were the victims in 1984.[24]

Continued negative treatment of politicians, Austin Ranney suggests, may weaken the government operated by these politicians. By its intense examination, the media may confirm voters' beliefs "that politics is confusing and boring, and that politicians are liars, blowhards, and hypocrites." The fragmented governmental system of the United States requires negotiation among policymakers, necessitates personal sacrifices by officeholders, and results in incomplete compromises. Television, however, "has raised ordinary people's expectations of what government can and should do, but has made it more difficult for those who govern to meet these expectations."[25]

Confidence in Institutions These negative effects of the news may be exaggerated. Television does emphasize drama, but there can be drama and good pictures in material supportive of government. The nation's Bicentennial in 1976, the ordeal of the Iranian hostages in 1980, the triumph of American athletes in 1984—all promoted patriotism, positive feeling, and support of the governmental system. Ronald Reagan won great personal acclaim, and reelection, by using television to strike upbeat notes, some played to military marches, some in country and western rhythms.

We need to distinguish media criticism of particular government officials from more general attacks on political institutions. A careful study of newspapers reveals that at least in their printed form, the media are not very penetrating in their criticism. Only a tenth of the statements about the nation generally were negative, while then-President Ford received either favorable or neutral comments 62 percent of the time. As illustrated in Figure 5.1, among all institutions only political parties were primarily reported in unfavorable terms. Media criticism did have a significant effect, since readers of such adverse comments, particularly frequent readers, were more distrustful of the government. However, their distrust was "primarily directed at governmental performance rather than at the legitimacy

FIGURE 5.1
Degree of Criticism in Articles about Selected Political Objects
(Arthur Miller et al., "Type-Set Politics: Impact of Newspapers on Public Confidence," American Political Science Review, *73 [March 1979], 71.)*

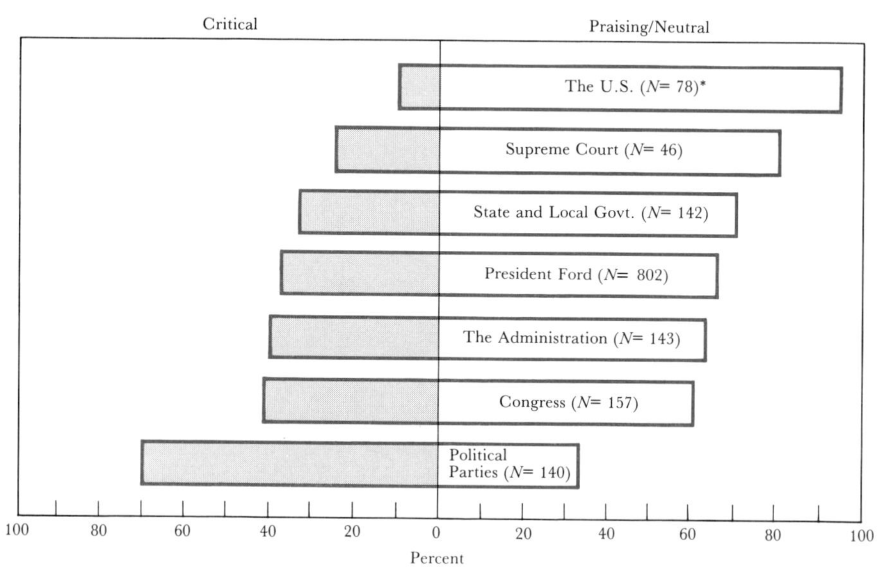

*N = The number of articles about a political object that were available for computing the percentages.

of institutions." Negative newspapers' stories, then, promote dissatisfaction with a particular president or a specific policy but do not in themselves undermine general loyalty to American institutions of government or threaten political stability.

The Conservative Media Rather than promote discontent, the media may reinforce support for existing institutions. An extensive study of four major news sources—CBS, NBC, *Time,* and *Newsweek*—emphasizes this inherently conservative quality of the press. Herbert Gans finds that these sources consistently favor the status quo and the values of the middle class, including political stability, while they persistently portray social change and social disorder in negative terms. The media promotes values such as "responsible capitalism . . . an optimistic faith that in the good society, businessmen and businesswomen will compete with each other in order to create increased prosperity for all; but that they will refrain from unreasonable profits and gross exploitation of workers or customers." That is, journalists basically support the existing system, with some reforms. They look askance at protest activities, showing a "deeper concern for social cohesion, which reflects fears that not only the official rules of the political order, but also the informal rules of the social order are in danger of being destroyed."[26]

Television Entertainment The media may be conservative in a more general sense. This effect could come from their diversionary quality, with the press providing fantasy and escape for the public in place of political discussion. Most material in newspapers and broadcasts is not concerned with public affairs, according to this argument. Television diffuses potential discontent through situation comedies, musical entertainment, and staged violence that invariably ends with the triumph of the good guys. The reality of racial discrimination is displaced by the wealthy setting of "The Jeffersons" and economic discrimination against the aged or women is supplanted by the happy adventures of "The Golden Girls."*

Since 100 million Americans watch television every night, it would seem almost certain that this heavy and continual exposure would have some effect. The character and duration of the effects, however, is uncertain and largely speculative. The values held by Americans are derived from many influences, and television alone cannot be the source of these beliefs.

Moreover, the entertainment programs on the tube are not all of the same kind. The threat of nuclear war, for example, was vividly portrayed on a feature drama, "The Day After," which, in 1983, drew the largest single audience in television history. Such popular programs as "The Bill Cosby Show" or "The Mary Tyler Moore Show" have probably helped to change national stereotypes about the universal misery of the black family or the necessity of marriage for women.

These programs are examples of the veiled messages about politics that are transmitted through programs that are ostensibly presented only as

*This argument was presented early by Bernard Berelson in "Communications and Public Opinion," in *Communications in Modern Society,* Wilbur Schramm, ed. (Urbana: U. of Illinois, 1948), p. 182.

Entertainment programs sometimes carry veiled messages—as does *Cagney and Lacey*, regarding the equality of women. *(Movie Still Archives)*

entertainment. When policewomen "Cagney" and "Lacey" are denied good assignments, the program is making an implicit case for antidiscrimination action by government. When the police working for "Barney Miller" are unable to convict a drug peddler, the audience is being told that judicial procedures are too lenient. Yet, it is unproved that these messages are accepted by the audience, who is mostly concerned with the plot, not the ideology, of the program.

Protest and Violence Press treatment of protest is a vivid illustration of the most important indirect effect of the media. They do not simply transmit information; they define it. Reality is too detailed and too complex to be fully presented. The facts do not speak for themselves: reporters select certain facts and inevitably—reflecting the characteristics of the press previously discussed—prefer some types of facts to others. The political world is not an objective reality simply reflected by reporters—it is created by them. The audience receives a reality that is biased, not politically but journalistically.

A principal bias in the media is toward violence. The real-world chance of being a victim of violence is less than one in a hundred, but in television's world from 30 to 64 percent of people are victims of crime. Consequently, "heavy viewers, exposed to large doses of crime in television drama, believe that the dangers of becoming a crime victim are far greater than they actually are. They fear crime more and are more mistrustful than light television viewers."*

The media's ability to define the world as violent is not new, nor dependent on electronic communication. Newspaper reporter Lincoln Steffens, in the excerpt reprinted here, "The Making of a Crime Wave," did the same a hundred years ago. The concern of the public with violence arises from real-world conditions, as well as from the staple local news coverage of murders, rapes, and muggings. This concern can express itself in various ways, however—from panic over a crime wave to zeal about prison reform. The media are likely to be decisive in this determination.

Setting the Agenda

Besides establishing a mood, the media might unify the nation in a different way—by *agenda setting,* that is, by determining the topics, rather than the content, of public opinion. Some observers argue that the press "may not be successful much of the time in telling people what to think, but it is stunningly successful in telling its readers what to think about."[27] Our attention then becomes focused on one topic or another, not because of the subject's inherent impact but because the media choose to make it important. Modernizing an old philosophical problem, a tree may fall in the forest, but there is no sound until it is reported.

*Graber, p. 138; this finding is disputed by Michael Hughes, "The Fruits of Cultivation Analysis: A Reexamination of Some Effects of Television Watching," *Public Opinion Quarterly*, 44 (Fall 1980), pp. 287–302. See also George Gerbner and Larry Gross, "Living with Television; The Violence Profile," *Journal of Communications*, 26 (Spring 1976), pp. 173–99.

POLITICAL PERSPECTIVE

THE MAKING OF A CRIME WAVE

Every now and then there occurs the phenomenon called a crime wave. New York has such waves periodically; other cities have them and they sweep over the public and nearly drown the lawyers, judges, preachers, and other leading citizens who feel that they must explain and cure these extraordinary outbreaks of lawlessness. Their diagnosis and their remedies are always the same: the disease is lawlessness; the cure is more law, more arrests, swifter trials, and harsher penalties. The sociologists and other scientists go deeper into the wave; the trouble with them is they do not come up.

I enjoy crime waves. I made one once; Jack Riis helped; many reporters joined in the uplift of the rising tide of crime. . . . I called on my assistant, Robert, and told him we must get some crimes. We spent the day buttonholing detectives; I sat an hour asleep in the [police station] basement in vain. Nothing but old stories. Robert saved the day. He learned, and I wrote, of the robbery of a Fifth Avenue club. That was a beat, but Riis had two robberies that were beats on me. By that time the other evening papers were having some thefts of their own. The poker club reporters were loafers only by choice. They could get the news when they had to, and being awakened by the scrap between Riis and me, they broke up their game and went to work, a combine, and they were soon beating me, as Riis was. I was sorry I had started it. Robert and I had to sleep in turns in the basement, and we picked up some crimes, but Riis had two or three a day, and the combine had at least one a day. The morning newspapers not only rewrote ours; they had crimes of their own, which they grouped to show that there was a crime wave. . . .

The police records of crimes and arrests . . . showed no increase at all; on the contrary, the totals of crimes showed a diminution and the arrests an increase. It was only the newspaper reports of crimes that had increased; there was a wave of publicity only. . . . When Riis and I ceased reporting robberies the poker combine resumed their game, and the morning newspapers discovered that the fickle public were "sick of crime" and wanted something else. The monthly magazines and the scientific quarterlies had some belated, heavy, incorrect analysis of the periodicity of lawlessness; they had no way to account for it then. The criminals could work o'nights, honest citizens could sleep, and judges could afford to be more just.

Source: *The Autobiography of Lincoln Steffens* (New York: Harcourt, 1931), pp. 285–91.

Individual Issues There are many individual examples of the media's ability to place topics on the public agenda. Social ills such as malnutrition and environmental deterioration have existed in the United States for decades, but they did not raise widespread concern until NBC produced a documentary on hunger in America and until the press gave extensive coverage to the first Earth Day in 1970. Other stories can become greatly inflated because of their dramatic appeal to the press, such as antiabortion demonstrations during the 1984 election campaign. On the other hand, potentially critical issues may not be debated at all because the media neglect them. The use of ocean resources and the problems of Polish-Americans, one of the largest ethnic groups, are possible examples.

On some topics, the media serve only as communications links, as common carriers of news that they must report. It is certainly true that we learn about the outbreak of war, the results of an election, or an epidemic through the media, but these events inevitably force themselves on the media and the public consciousness. The press determines the place of these items on the public agenda as little as an ocean wave controls the debris that it brings to the shore.

The media, however, do critically affect the *manner* of reports on such

Through dramatic programs such as *The Day After,* TV can focus public attention on the world problem of nuclear weapons. *(Movie Still Archives)*

major events. Wars, elections, and epidemics can be depicted as grave threats or simple problems, just as waves can break harshly or softly. The press can also affect the timing of news, by either anticipating events or simply waiting for them to come to public attention. Some investigative reporters may be able to break a story on political corruption, whereas others will ignore it until the evidence is overwhelming. A notable example of both reactions was the Watergate scandal that eventually led to Richard Nixon's resignation from the presidency. Although two then-obscure reporters for *The Washington Post* did pursue the story, they faced considerable obstacles to their efforts even within their own newspaper, while most of the press originally ignored the issue and public attention was focused on the scandal only after many months. In this climactic case, conclude the most authoritative researchers, the agenda was set by official agencies—the Senate and House investigators, and the press only followed their lead.[28] Media coverage on other issues, such as Vietnam and the civil disturbances of the 1960s, has been found to be poorly related to the objective circumstances. Press attention was highest only after the number of war casualties and urban riots had begun to decline.[29]

Vietnam The Vietnam War is a major historical example of media influence. The press's attention to the war was inevitable, given the rising tide of national commitment and casualties. The principal contribution of the press was providing the means to interpret the conflict. At first, media coverage tended to be supportive of the American involvement, with the press relying on official military sources for its information and accepting their optimistic forecasts of an early victory by the United States. Later, individual reporters began using other sources of information, including personal accounts of political disarray, suppression, battlefield deaths, and civilian horrors. ABC, for example, in 1969 shifted its focus from "fighting the war" to "winding down the war."

The turning point of the war for the United States came in January 1968, at the time of Tet, the Chinese New Year. A major offensive was launched by the North Vietnamese and Viet Cong forces against American strong points. The military result was the ultimate defeat of all of these

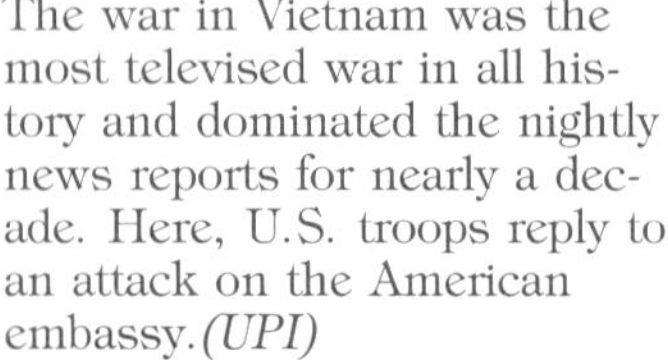

The war in Vietnam was the most televised war in all history and dominated the nightly news reports for nearly a decade. Here, U.S. troops reply to an attack on the American embassy. *(UPI)*

attacks. The press emphasis, however, was on the strength of the attacks and, particularly, on a brief Communist charge into the American embassy in Saigon. This symbolic thrust led the major networks to declare that the war was unwinnable, leading in turn to a shift in public sentiment against the war and to the eventual American withdrawal.[30]

New Issues The effect of the media on the public agenda is greatest when it is dealing with an entirely new issue, on which there is little previous public knowledge or specific commitment. That is why they can strongly influence opinion on such matters as hunger or the environment. The media look for such issues, particularly if they can be portrayed in simple, dramatic, personal, and conflictual terms. Advocates of various causes, in turn, seek the attention. Even a long-standing problem can receive rapid attention when its advocates learn how to use the media for their purposes. Thus, women's inequality has been a latent issue for centuries but received extensive media attention only when its advocates began staging protest marches and other actions easily portrayed on television. Three hundred years of discrimination against blacks became a national issue only when the press was drawn to the drama of sit-ins, voting demonstrations, and the violence of segregationists.

There is an inertial element in public opinion—the greater its mass of previous experience and beliefs, the more difficult it is to move. By contrast, in new situations, where the public has little knowledge, the media can have direct and immediate impact. A classic demonstration of this principle came in the 1930s when space travel was unknown. A radio play, "The War of the Worlds," convinced millions that invaders from another world had landed in New Jersey, and this caused panic throughout the nation.[31] Today, with the experience of moon landings behind them, most Americans know that "Star Wars" is only fiction.

Media Events This influence of the press allows politicians and groups to use **media events,** staged actions to gain the attention of television and newspapers. To get a minute's time on the evening news, candidates walk across an entire state or spend hours listening to health complaints in an old age home.

Public protests, such as the civil rights marches, gain nationwide attention through live television coverage. This photo was taken at the original March on Washington in 1963. *(Bruce Davidson/Magnum Photos, Inc.)*

Violence is sometimes employed to gain media attention. In the 1968 Democratic convention, television gave more attention to the street demonstrations of the radical young people's group, the Yippies, and to the police's violent reaction, than to the nomination proceedings. This confrontation was excellent drama for television and was intended to serve this purpose. As a presidential report concluded, "This theatrical concept was a primary ingredient of their [the Yippies] approach. The audience would be the American public, the means of communication would be the mass media, manipulated to create a distorted image of themselves. The stage would be the streets and the message would be a demonstration of disrespect, irreverence, and ridicule."[32]

The General Agenda The independent ability of the media to shape the public agenda generally—aside from specific issues—is less evident. Some research has found a correspondence between the issues regarded as important by voters and the issues stressed in newspapers and on television.* However, the relationship is not consistent, and even a similarity in the topics emphasized by the public and the press does not show causality. The press might just as well be following the public as the opposite, and both are likely to be reacting to external events.

The most thorough studies of agenda setting show that there is no automatic relationship between the topics emphasized by the media and the subjects uppermost in the public's mind.[33] The similarity depends greatly on the real-world experiences of the audience. Persons who are directly threatened by unemployment or who live in communities with higher rates of violence are more likely to follow the media's emphasis on economics or crime, whereas those who are prosperous or safe are likely to bypass these concerns, regardless of the media's emphasis.

The independent impact of the media is greatest on issues that are remote from people's individual experience—such as the complicated policy question of energy supplies, or a particular, but distant, scandal such as Watergate. The press is particularly likely to affect persons who do not have other sources of information—those who talk less about politics to their friends or have less education. In summary, the media do not fully set the public agenda, they establish some issues on the agenda for some people some of the time.

The Media in Election Campaigns

The news media are critical in political campaigns, where much of the candidates' energy is devoted to winning the attention and favor of newspapers, radio, and television. Since the candidates can meet only a fraction of the voters personally, most of the contest is conducted through the media. Rallies, speeches, and other direct contacts with the voters are not important for their own sake but for the coverage they will produce. Thus candidates create media events to gain publicity—with particular attention to the

*Donald Shaw and Maxwell McCombs have conducted much of this research, most notably in *The Emergence of American Political Issues: The Agenda-Setting Function of the Press* (St. Paul, Minn.: West, 1977).

dramatic pose or the striking phrase that can fit into a headline or a one-minute evening newscast. They schedule events to meet the deadlines of reporters, and they take care that the press has briefings, speech texts, and appropriate "leaks."

Horserace Journalism

Because of their dominant place in American life, the media have the opportunity to unify the electorate, by providing a coherent and full portrait of candidates and issues. Yet, much of this opportunity is lost because of the distinct manner in which the press, particularly television, covers elections.

The Election Game The emphasis is on the election game itself—who is winning and losing—rather than the substance of the contest. This "horse-race" aspect of an election is given twice the coverage by the media as are issues, and even this limited coverage of policy questions is further distorted by the media's emphasis on the relatively few issues on which the candidates take clearly opposed stands.[34] Furthermore, in calling the race, the press puts heavy, undue emphasis on early and isolated events. In the 1976 contest for president, for example, network newscasts provided almost forty times as much coverage of the New Hampshire primary, first in the nation, as of the New York primary, where far more delegates were to be selected.*

One aspect of the election game stressed by the media is the candidate's "expected" performance. Like racehorse touts, reporters establish an early "line" on the candidates. Then, if they fail to meet this standard—and even if they win—they are reported as "falling behind expectations." In 1984, for example, Walter Mondale won a majority in the first nominating contest, the Iowa caucuses—but the press instead focused on Gary Hart.

With emphasis on elections as games, policy issues get only limited attention. Instead, matters of campaign strategy, the use of issues to gain votes, get more attention. Illustratively, in 1984, these matters took up almost two-fifths of television's coverage. Television covered matters such as Reagan's age, Ferraro's finances, or the candidates' off-camera comments. It devoted relatively little time to the policy questions of the federal budget or the nuclear arms race.[35]

Although candidates devote most of their efforts to a discussion of issues, reporters give little attention to these presentations because candidates typically maintain the same positions throughout a campaign. A policy statement is likely to be covered only "if it represents a change in the candidate's position or if the statement is inconsistent with other positions the candidate holds at the same time."[36] The search for novelty also accounts for the media's typical neglect of the considerable amount of issue content in candidate debates. Instead, the focus is on the competitive aspects of the debate, making them measures of success not discussions of policies. The press thereby converts "debates into pseudoprimaries that could be 'won' or 'lost' by the contenders."[37]

*Calculated as stories per elected delegate by Donald R. Matthews, "Winnowing: The New Media and the 1976 Presidential Nominations," in *Race for the Presidency*, James David Barber, ed. (Englewood Cliffs, N.J.: Prentice-Hall, 1978), p. 65.

Presidential Debates Victory in presidential debates has become a major focus of press coverage. Immediately after the candidates have concluded their arguments, commentators will assess their presentations, emphasizing not logic and accuracy but style and success. Media analysis has become so important that candidates immediately send out their "spinmasters," trying to influence the "spin" that reporters will give to their stories.

The public is receptive to these media interpretations. In a 1976 debate, Gerald Ford defended his record on foreign policy by stating that Poland was "not under Soviet domination." Although few viewers noted this inaccuracy, the media considered it a major "gaffe," and their interpretation was eventually accepted by the public. Persons interviewed immediately after the debate tended to believe (by a 44–35 margin) that Ford had done better in the confrontation. Only a day later, after hearing telecasts and reading the papers, the public had been convinced (by 61–19) that he had been decisively defeated.[38]

The same media-induced shift was evident in 1984. The first public response to the Reagan-Mondale debates was that Mondale did somewhat better in the first meeting, and that there was a statistically insignificant Reagan edge in the second. After a few days of media interpretations, the new consensus was that Mondale had first humiliated the president, and then had been clearly bested by a revived opponent. Selective editing and rebroadcasting of the debate (as detailed in the box on page 165) help to explain these shifts.

Election Coverage A media emphasis on victory is also evident at the end of election campaigns, on election night. Using "exit polls," taken as people leave the voting areas, television reporters are able to predict the winners of elections even before all ballots are counted, or even cast. When NBC declared Reagan the victor in 1980 by 8:15 p.m. Eastern time, and Jimmy Carter then conceded defeat, critics feared these statements would discourage Western voters from even participating in an election that was already "decided." Academic research has since validated that fear, showing that there was a significant drop in turnout in these areas.[39]

Nevertheless, the networks have resisted changes in their procedures,

By Bob Gorrell, *The Richmond News Leader*. Reprinted by permission of News America Syndicate.

POLITICAL PERSPECTIVE

NEWS EDITING: REAGAN V. MONDALE

The following news feature illustrates the media's emphasis on conflict and its selectivity. It describes the reporting of the first television debate in 1984 between President Reagan and former Vice-President Mondale.

Television and print reporters reached a unanimous verdict Monday that Walter Mondale beat President Reagan in their first debate.

Deliberations lasted just over eight hours. The crucial evidence, at least for TV, consisted of 21 seconds out of the 100-minute debate. . . .

On Sunday night, all three networks came up with different snippets. By Monday morning all had found—or actually manufactured—the same 21 seconds. It was great for Mondale, devastating to Reagan.

The snippet appears to be a fast-paced exchange in which Reagan, recycling a famous and successful line from his 1980 debate with former President Carter, scores first on Sunday night:

"You know, I wasn't going to say this at all, but I can't help it," Reagan says, in response to a Mondale charge that he would threaten Social Security benefits. "There you go again."

Applause and laughter say his punch has landed. Reagan is seen chuckling. But watch it, sports fans: Mondale is chuckling, too.

First he sets up Reagan: "Remember the last time you said that?"

"Um-hum," Reagan replies.

"You said it when President Carter said that you were going to cut Medicare," Mondale continues. "And what did you do right after the election? You went out and tried to cut $20 billion out of Medicare! And so, when you say, 'There you go again,' people remember this, you know."

Mondale hits the cadences just right this time, as though offering a junior congressman a bit of friendly advice about the perils of baldfaced lying. . . .

Finally the camera lingered on Reagan's wilting face as he took a rare, heavy political punch, on camera, his eyes narrowing, mouth tightening—the Great Communicator at a loss.

Of course, it's not a real moment. Actually, several hundred wordy words and a reporter's windy question separated Reagan's first punch from Mondale's haymaker, which was really the second footnote of rebuttal.

No matter. Any future analyst arguing that Reagan won will have to contend not so much with the real debate as with this artful editing.

Source: Frank Greve, Knight-Ridder Newspapers (Oct. 10, 1984).

Judy Sloan/Gamma Liaison

claiming the protection of freedom of the press and spurred by the desire to outdo their competition. They have agreed not to project results in any state where voting is still in progress. To deal with the general problem, they have suggested that voting take place during a standardized twenty-four-hour period, so that all ballots would be completed, for example, by 8 p.m. in New York, 5 p.m. in Los Angeles, and 1 p.m. in Honolulu. The plan would substantially increase the costs of election administration and might even affect the turnout of some groups. The state of Washington tried a different approach, prohibiting exit polls near voting places. By reducing the ease and accuracy of these surveys, the state legislators expected to discourage their use in media predictions. The courts, however, ruled that this law was an unacceptable restriction of press freedom.

Personality Contests Just as horseraces are about horses, so horserace journalism focuses on the contending candidates. Just as horseraces are more exciting when a dark horse comes up the stretch, so horserace journalism is constantly on the outlook for new candidates coming up from the pack who will make the race more exciting to report.

In 1984, the media's search for new personalities almost effected the nomination of Gary Hart. In their typical search for a dramatic contest, the media first portrayed the Democratic race as a two-person battle between Walter Mondale and Senator John Glenn. When Glenn faded, a new hero was needed. In the first caucus of the year, in Iowa, Mondale won overwhelmingly, but the media emphasis was on the "surprising" 15 percent showing of Hart. In the following weeks, Hart received virtually as much coverage as Mondale, the 3–1 winner in Iowa. When Hart subsequently won primaries in New Hampshire and Vermont—small, unrepresentative, and Republican states—he was officially designated as the "frontrunner." He became the cover feature of five national newsweeklies and briefly jumped into the lead in public opinion polls.[40]

Once he was ahead, Hart himself became the victim of the media. His personality, consistency on issues, and even his age became the subject of searching investigation. Combined with changes in Mondale's strategy and unfavorable rules, he soon lost his chance for the presidential nomination. His rise and fall illustrates the common tendency of the media, particularly television, to be more negative toward frontrunners. Thus, in 1980, negative comments were made four times more often about the leaders than about challengers. This posture results partially from reporters' desire for the exciting copy that comes from a close race and partially from their professional belief that they must give closer scrutiny to a likely president. Together, these motives mean that "a candidate's press was more easily predicted by his position in the polls than by his party or philosophy."[41]

This kind of coverage is related to the basic press characteristics we discussed earlier. By emphasizing the horserace aspect of elections, the media appear to take a more objective position, while an examination of issues or an evaluation of the candidates could be seen as subjective and partisan. In the search for novelty in the news, the press neglects long-standing issue positions, and coverage of campaign debates often dismisses the candidates' statements as "nothing new." Looking for dramatic incidents, the media focus on the images, the personal characteristics and emotional actions of candidates, and give less attention to their ideas and programs.

Media Contributions Despite these limitations, there are many positive contributions of the media to campaigns. In historical perspective, the press, both print and electronic, provides a much more objective comparison among candidates than was true a century ago. Even if the relative attention to issues is limited, the major study of the subject concludes that there is more total time devoted to policy questions than in past decades. Moreover, for all its faults, the press probably gives issues more coverage than their audience really wants. "Complaining about the issuelessness of the media, without considering the issuelessness of the audience is to beat a dead horse, if not a dead 'horse race.'"[42]

Effects in Elections

Media Structure Choices Aside from the manner in which they cover campaign news, the media affect elections generally. Most pervasively, they help to structure the choices available to voters long before the ballots are cast. By the time of an election, the issues have been defined over a long period, the candidates have devoted years to creating their images, and the voter has spent a lifetime in exposure to the media. Repeated assertions of conservative values in the press surely affect voting, as does television's concentration on a new personality. These are long-term effects, which cannot be captured in research confined to the campaign period alone. To attempt to isolate the media's impact by observations taken only at that time is similar to—and as foolish as—judging the effect of water on human life by measuring rainfall one day a year.

Television Candidates Different kinds of candidates are favored in the age of video, for "the TV-room situation calls for a pleasant and friendly presence, a moderate tone of voice, small and natural gestures, and a general conversational manner." Politicians of the future will surely try to emulate Ronald Reagan's mastery of the medium.[43]

As a visual medium, television focuses on personalities, rather than on issues and political parties. Significantly, as the means of political communication have changed, the public has come to disregard parties, expressing less emotion toward them, and giving them less weight in their voting decisions. Instead, they are focusing, along with the media, more on the individual candidates and the issue positions of a Reagan or a Mondale, than on historic loyalties or the programs of the Republicans and Democrats.[44] This change raises serious issues about the survival of the political parties, a question we discuss in Chapter 6.

Television can be of particular help to previously unknown politicians. In minutes, they can reach more people than they could hope to meet personally in a lifetime of handshaking. Andy Warhol, the modern artist, once remarked that, in America, there is a new celebrity every fifteen minutes because the media are constantly searching for new personalities. Jimmy Carter provides a very prominent example of this rule. The future president was once so obscure that he could appear unrecognized on the television panel show "What's My Line?" Unrestricted by previous public perceptions, he could define his own image and rise to prominence by emphasizing personal qualities such as trust and love.

Limited Effects on Voting Much research has been devoted to the effect of the media on voting, in the expectation that greater media exposure would result in greater changes in voting preferences. The surprising finding was quite different—those who pay the most attention to elections often are less likely to change their vote, or else show no difference in their behavior.[45] Other electoral studies have examined the presidential debates. Very few people were found to have changed their candidate preferences after their exposure to the candidates. Rather, the main effects were to reinforce the viewers' previous commitments.[46]

When watching debates, people tend to see what they want to see. In 1984, for example, Reagan supporters were more likely to believe the president had done better in the final election debate, whereas Mondale backers were convinced that the Democrat had the better of the confrontation. (See Figure 5.2.)

But debates do more than just reinforce previous expectations. For example, in the first of the 1984 debates, President Reagan was hesitant and confused in his answers, and his deficiencies were acknowledged by both Republicans and Democrats. Furthermore, debates promote citizen learning. A study of the 1976 programs found, illustratively, that 10 to 20 percent of viewers improved their knowledge of the candidates' positions on the issues. Although few viewers changed their votes as a result, many were persuaded to modify their own beliefs.[47]

Given these findings, which have been corroborated in many contexts, the influence of the media has sometimes been thoroughly dismissed. This judgment has even led to the formulation of a "law of minimal effects," postulating that the effects of the media would be limited by psychological factors:[48] selective exposure, selective attention, selective perception, and selective retention. Thus, partisan Democrats would not watch a Republican candidate as often or as avidly as their own party's nominee; they would give the Republican less attention; they would perceive better qualities in their preferred candidate; and they would remember his points and arguments better than his opponent's.

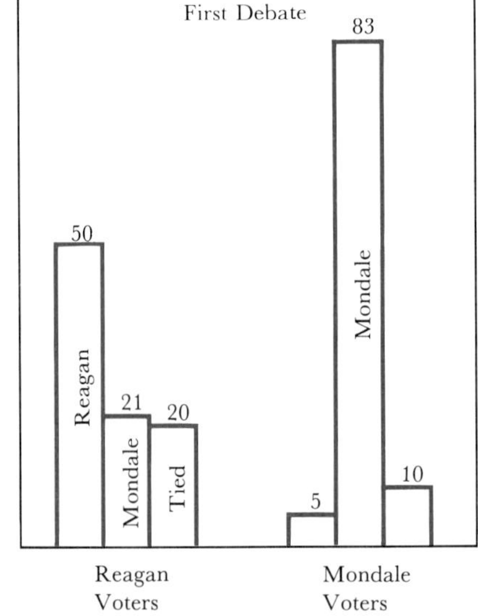

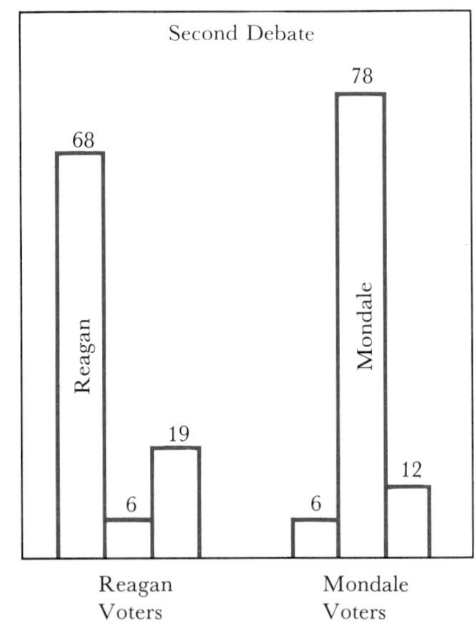

FIGURE 5.2
Who Won the 1984 Debates? The bars show the percentage of each group of voters who saw the debate as won by Reagan, won by Mondale, or tied. Those giving no answer are not included in the chart. *(Based on CBS News/*New York Times *poll, Oct. 7 and Oct. 27, 1984.)*

Media Saturation These limited effects of the media are rather surprising, given their universal and persistent involvement in American lives. One explanation of their restricted impact is this same universality and persistence. This leads to a **saturation effect:** people are so saturated with media that they cannot absorb any more messages. Precisely because the media are everywhere, it is difficult to locate their influence at any specific place. For example, in research to isolate the effect of television on voting, the best method would be to compare persons who use video to those who never watch television. The poor research alternative is to compare persons who watch a great deal with those who watch less. This method is like researching the relationship between sexual intercourse and pregnancy by comparing those who have sex four times a week and those who restrict themselves to once a week. Finding that pregnancy occurs often in both groups does not prove that there is no connection between intercourse and conception. Like sex, television affects everyone, even those who use it little.

The limited direct effects of the mass media also can be attributed to the limited attention that Americans pay to politics and to public affairs in the media. Although the nation is blanketed by newspapers and television, those greatly interested in political reporting are a distinct minority. Newspapers are read and TV watched for many reasons—for sports and weather and local gossip certainly more than for economic indicators and the texts of speeches. Television audiences generally prefer entertainment to information, although "60 Minutes," frequently the leading network program, can gain popularity by combining the two elements. There is a vast audience for the evening network newscasts, but it is a distinct minority of the audience that will later tune in to situation comedies and police dramas. This audience also contains many who are inadvertent watchers waiting inattentively for the later shows. One experiment found that people tuned to a news program were watching only slightly over half the time while the news was broadcast.[49] In summary, the media audience is saturated, carries its own perceptions and experience, and limits its attention. Given these factors, the impact of any particular media event must be limited.

Other Elections The inertial resistance of public opinion to the media is particularly evident in regard to presidential voting and accounts for the absence of strong evidence of direct media influence on voting choice. Americans have many sources of information available to them in these elections—their personal associates, the interest groups to which they belong, their own and their families' past voting records, and, most critically, their party loyalties. The unique effect of the media, or one media event such as a presidential debate, is therefore likely to be quite limited, for there is a considerable amount of preexisting information, prejudices, and attitudes.

When we examine other contests, greater effects can be seen. In races for the Senate, for example, candidates with greater media exposure generally fare better.[50] In situations involving low levels of information, such as primaries, referenda, and less visible races, the media are more effective in persuading people. Furthermore, even if media messages do not fully determine outcomes, they apparently can change the results by critical margins. A careful study of the press in 1964 concluded that where a newspaper has a monopoly, it can add 5 percent to the vote of a candidate through its editorial endorsement.[51]

Conclusion: Cohesion and Fragmentation

The mass media both exemplify and shape our politics. They tell us who we are, what our leaders are doing, and why the world is the way it seems to be in print and on the screen. When we think of ourselves as Americans, we think in the very language of these mass communications—using their "images," which have been "mediated" through these "channels." The print and electronic press provides the facts and suggests the standards that we need for a common civic life. It does so conscientiously, professionally, and without a controlling political bias. Still, the media do not overcome the fragmentation of American politics.

Though the media provide similar information and interpretation throughout the nation, they do not promote the development of an active mass political community. The press serves its own needs as much as the public's; it neglects controversy and reflects uniformity; and its effects are uncertain and largely indirect. Even when the media do inform the public, they do not promote community, for information is transmitted to private, atomistic observers, not active participants. Television and the press serve spectators, not citizens.

The mass media may be on the brink of a new era. There is increasing diversification in the print media, as specialized publications replace general-interest magazines and newspapers. Technology has opened many new means of electronic communication, such as FM radio, UHF and low-wattage local television, home video recorders, and ever-more important, cable television. In combination with satellite broadcasting, television may soon be able to offer as many as 300 different programs. Specialization, diversification, and special-interest programming are certain to grow. For the public, the new technological benefits are likely to provide a more varied fare of entertainment and programs with greater appeal to particular tastes.[52] The effect on politics will not necessarily be as desirable.

More television channels do not necessarily mean more political communication. Indeed, it may mean less, as each group of the population retreats to its favorite wavelength. More special interests will mean less public consensus, and more entertainment opportunities will mean less political interest. The mass media have not promoted political community, but they have fostered a high degree of social community in the United States. Now, even this unity is challenged by technology. Social fragmentation may then reinforce the effects of political fragmentation. Such developments will create an even greater challenge to our political institutions.

SUMMARY

The mass media are crucial to the shaping of our politics. Reporting events, and defining their meaning, they promote political unity in America. The media tend to homogenize news, because most of their significant stories come from the same limited sources—wire services, a few prestigious newspapers, and, most important, the three national television networks. Competition among these sources centers on the form and speed of presentation, not on diverse interpretations of events.

Organizational features of the media affect the way they operate. Independent of government, they stress their objectivity; the reporting of events takes precedence over interpretation. What is reported, however, does not necessarily give us an accurate picture of political reality. The media are affected by business needs and by operating routines. The most common criterion for choosing stories is their emotional impact. The media present a world of violence, scandal, and simple two-sided conflict.

The press maintains a posture separate from the government, which is involved only in limited regulation of broadcasting. Despite this independence, the media and government are closely related. The press obtains most of its information from official sources, and the government depends on the press to disseminate its messages. The relationship is not always harmonious. Officials want the press to bring only good news to the public; the press, as a critic of government, looks for stories of corruption and incompetence.

The media affect American society generally, providing the information necessary for political activity and furnishing cues—in both entertainment and news programs—for interpreting events. A special effect of television may be *videomalaise*, the negative depiction of political leaders and institutions, which is reinforced by the emphasis on violence. Such treatment can undermine the public's confidence in government generally. However, the media are also used to develop supportive and patriotic feelings.

The media might also influence politics by focusing on certain issues more than others. Research indicates that the media are far more successful in such *agenda setting* when they deal with new or obscure issues rather than familiar ones, for which there are alternative sources of information.

Elections are now conducted largely through the mass media, which cover campaigns in a distinctive manner. *Horserace journalism* focuses on the election game, winning and losing, rather than on the substance of the contest. Instead of policy analysis, the media concentrate on personalities, victory in candidate debates, and quick prediction of elections. Although there is little evidence that television can change people's actual votes, its dominance has greatly changed the kind of candidates we have and the way they campaign.

The media provide crucial information and interpretation for the nation, but they do not promote the development of an active political community. Now, we may be on the brink of a new era in mass communications. Increasing diversification is a possibility in all areas. But more television does not necessarily improve the chances of political communication. As programs cater to more special interests there may be less public consensus.

NOTES

1. U.S. Bureau of the Census, *Statistical Abstract of the United States: 1985* (Washington, 1985).
2. Nielsen Television Index, *Television Audience* (Northbrook, Ill.: Nielsen, appropriate years).
3. James N. Rosse et al., "Trends in the Daily Newspaper Industry, 1932–1973," *Studies in Industry Economics*, no. 57 (Stanford: Dept. of Economics, Stanford U., May 1975).
4. *The New York Times* (Sept. 20, 1969).
5. C. Wright Mills, *The Power Elite* (New York: Oxford U.P., 1956); Herbert Marcuse, *One-Dimensional Man* (Boston: Beacon, 1964).
6. Television and Growing up: The Impact of Televised Violence (Washington: GPO, 1972).
7. Cited by Robert M. Liebart et al., *The Early Window: The Effect of Television on Children and Youth* (Elmsford, N.Y.: Pergamon, 1973), pp. 2–3.
8. David Pearl, "Violence and Aggression," *Transaction/Society*, 21 (Sept./Oct. 1984), p. 21. This article is part of a symposium on the Surgeon General's report.
9. Leon Sigal, *Reporters and Officials: The Organization and Politics of Newsmaking* (Lexington, Mass.: Heath, 1973), pp. 125–28.
10. Timothy Crouse, *The Boys on the Bus* (New York: Random House, 1973), p. 8.
11. Doris A. Graber, *Mass Media and American Politics* (Washington: Congressional Quarterly Press, 1980), pp. 63–65.
12. Dan Nimmo and James E. Combs, *Mediated Political Realities* (New York: Longman, 1983), pp. 28–35.
13. Edward J. Epstein, *News from Nowhere* (New York: Riorden House, 1973), p. 169, emphasizes the impact of point-counterpoint journalism.
14. Richard Neustadt, *Presidential Power* (New York: Wiley, 1960), chaps. 4, 5; Graber, p. 15.
15. Sigal, pp. 129–30.
16. William C. Spragens, *The Presidency and the Mass Media in the Age of Television* (Washington: U.P. of America, 1979); Michael B. Grossman and Martha J. Kumar, *Portraying the President: The White House and the Mass Media* (Baltimore: Johns Hopkins U. P., 1981).

17. *The New York Times* (July 27, 1984); Bruce Owen, *Economics and Freedom of Expression* (Cambridge, Mass.: Ballinger, 1975).
18. *Report of the Commission on Obscenity and Pornography* (New York: Random House, 1971).
19. Tom Smith, "America's Most Important Problem," *Public Opinion Quarterly,* 44 (Summer 1980), pp. 164–80.
20. Herbert E. Krugman and Eugene L. Hartley, "Passive Learning from Television," *Public Opinion Quarterly,* 34 (Summer 1970), pp. 184–90; Stephen J. Fitzsimmons and Herbert G. Osburn, "The Impact of Social Issues and Public Affairs Documentaries," *Public Opinion Quarterly,* 32 (Fall 1968), pp. 379–97; Jay J. Blumer and Denis McQuail, *Television and Politics: Its Uses and Influence* (Chicago: U. of Chicago, 1969).
21. Robert Lane, *Political Life* (New York: Free Press, 1959) p. 285.
22. Michael Robinson, "Public Affairs Television and the Growth of Political Malaise: The Case of 'The Selling of the Pentagon,'" *American Political Science Review,* 70 (June 1976), pp. 409–32.
23. Michael J. Robinson and Margaret A. Sheehan, *Over the Wire and on TV* (New York: Russell Sage, 1983), pp. 110–12 and chap. 5.
24. Maura Clancey and Michael J. Robinson, "The Media in Campaign '84," *Public Opinion,* 7 (Dec./Jan. 1985), pp. 49–54.
25. Austin Ranney, *Channels of Power* (Washington: American Enterprise Institute, 1983), pp. 172–74.
26. Herbert Gans, *Deciding What's News* (New York: Pantheon, 1979), pp. 46, 59.
27. Bernard Cohen, *The Press and Foreign Policy* (Princeton: Princeton U.P., 1963), p. 13.
28. See Bob Woodward and Carl Bernstein, *All the President's Men* (New York: Simon & Schuster, 1974); David Weaver et al., "Watergate and the Media: A Case Study of Agenda-Setting," *American Politics Quarterly,* 3 (Oct. 1975), pp. 458–72; Gladys and Kurt Lang, "Polling on Watergate," *Public Opinion Quarterly,* 4 (Winter 1980), pp. 530–47. The Langs' definitive work is *The Battle for Public Opinion* (New York: Columbia U.P., 1983).
29. G. Ray Funkhouser, "The Issues of the Sixties," *Public Opinion Quarterly,* 37 (Spring 1973), pp. 62–75.
30. Phillip Knightley, *The First Casualty* (New York: Hartcourt, 1975). Peter Braestrup, *Big Story,* vol. 1 (Boulder: Westview, 1977), chaps. 4 and 5; cf. Gary Wamsley and Richard Pride, "Television Network News: Re-Thinking the Iceberg Problem," *Western Political Quarterly,* 25 (Sept. 1972), pp. 434–50.
31. Hadley Cantril, *The Invasion from Mars: A Study in the Psychology of Panic* (Princeton: Princeton U.P., 1940).
32. Daniel Walker, *Rights in Conflict* (New York: Dutton, 1966), p. 20.
33. Lutz Erbring et al., "Front-Page News and Real-World Cues: A New Look at Agenda-Setting by the Media," *American Journal of Political Science,* 24 (Feb. 1980), pp. 16–49; Roy L. Behr and Shanto Iyengar, "Television News, Red-World Cues, and Changes in the Public Agenda," *Public Opinion Quarterly,* 49 (Spring 1985), pp. 38–57.
34. Thomas Patterson, *The Mass Media Election* (New York: Praeger, 1980), chaps. 3–5.
35. Clancey and Robinson, pp. 51–52.
36. Matthews, in Barber, p. 67.
37. F. Christopher Arterton, "The Media Politics of Presidential Campaigns," in Barber, p. 51.
38. Frederick T. Steeper, "Public Responses to Gerald Ford's Statements on Eastern Europe," in George Bishop et al., eds. *The Presidential Debates: Media, Electoral and Policy Perspectives* (New York: Praeger, 1978), p. 85.
39. John E. Jackson, "Election Night Reporting and Voter Turnout," *American Journal of Political Science,* 27 (Nov. 1983), pp. 615–635; Michael X. Delli Carpini, "Scooping the Voter?: The Consequences of the Networks' Early Call of the 1980 Presidential Election," *Journal of Politics,* 46 (Aug. 1984), pp. 866–85.
40. William C. Adams, "Media Coverage of Campaign '84: A Preliminary Report," *Public Opinion* (April/May 1984), pp. 9–13.
41. Robinson and Sheehan, chap. 5 and p. 139.
42. Ibid., chap. 6 and p. 163.
43. Ranney, p. 103.
44. Martin Wattenberg, *The Decline of American Political Parties* (Cambridge: Harvard U.P., 1984), chaps. 4, 6; Richard Trilling, *Party Image and Electoral Behavior* (New York: Wiley, 1976), pp. 222–24.
45. Paul Lazarsfeld et al., *The People's Choice* (New York: Columbia U.P., 1944); Edmund C. Dreyer, "Media Use and Electoral Choices," *Public Opinion Quarterly,* 35 (Winter 1971–72), pp. 544–53; Cliff Zukin, "A Reconsideration of the Effects of Information on Partisan Stability," *Public Opinion Quarterly,* 41 (Summer 1977), pp. 244–54.
46. Paul J. Deutschmann, "Viewing, Conversation, and Voting Intention," in *The Great Debates,* Sidney Kraus, ed. (Bloomington: Indiana U.P., 1962), p. 243; David O. Sears and Steven H. Chaffee, "Uses and Effects of the 1976 Debates: An Overview of Empirical Studies," in *The Great Debates: Carter vs. Ford, 1976,* Sidney Kraus, ed. (Bloomington: Indiana U.P., 1979), p. 244; Douglas D. Rose, "Citizen Uses of the Ford-Carter Debates," *Journal of Politics,* 41 (Feb. 1980), pp. 214–21.
47. Alan Abramowitz, "The Impact of a Presidential Debate on Voter Rationality," *American Journal of Political Science,* 22 (Aug. 1978), pp. 680–90.
48. Joseph T. Klapper, *The Effects of Mass Communication* (New York: Free Press, 1960), chap. 2.
49. Robert B. Techtel, Clark Achelpohl, and Rogers Akers, "Correlates between Observed Behavior and Questionnaire Responses on Television Viewing," in Surgeon General's Scientific Advisory Committee on Television and Social Behavior, *Television and Social Behavior,* vol. 4, p. 294.
50. Gary Jacobson, "The Impact of Broadcast Campaigning on Electoral Outcomes," *Journal of Politics,* 37 (Aug. 1975).
51. Robert Erickson, "The Influence of Newspaper Endorsements in Presidential Elections: The Case of 1964," *American Journal of Politics,* 20 (May 1976), pp. 207–33.
52. Alvin Toffler, *The Third Wave* (New York: Morrow, 1980), pp. 174–83.

CHAPTER 6

The Political Parties

The week before election day, three Americans busily campaign for office.

David Lawrence, a middle-aged Chicago lawyer, is making his first run for elective office, after working for ten years in the Democratic party. Every night, he walks the streets looking for votes in his bid for the city council. With him is the local party committee member, who introduces him to the grocer who is unhappy with garbage collection, a teenager looking for a job, and an elderly woman who boasts of voting for every Democratic candidate since Franklin Roosevelt. David listens carefully, because it is a close race, and every vote counts. If David and his party win, they will be able to appoint a number of people to city jobs and to get more services from the local government.

In a New York suburb, Herbert Lawrence campaigns for the state legislature. Only thirty years old, Herbert became interested in politics through his work as a college instructor of economics. Three years ago, joining with some neighbors, he helped to form a Democratic party club to seek more state control over nuclear energy plants and to get more state aid for the local schools. Tonight, he is going to a meeting of the club to urge members to join in a phone canvass on his behalf and to try to resolve a dispute in the club over U.S. foreign policy in Nicaragua. Afterward, he hopes to have time to prepare a news release on his defense program.

Across the continent, in Los Angeles, Frieda Lawrence is running for Congress. Never connected to a political organization, she tends to think of herself as an independent, although she usually votes for Republican candidates. Because of her reputation as a television newscaster, Frieda was urged to run by a group of local citizens who liked her commentaries on crime control and the national government's budget. Now, Frieda has hired a political consultant and is analyzing opinion polls paid for by the Republican National Committee. In the final week, she will emphasize her tax reduction program in a series of one-minute television advertisements and glossy circulars mailed to the wealthicr parts of the district.

These three fictional candidates share both their last name and an avocation. All are politicians, and all are connected to their political parties, but each has a different relationship. The theme of this chapter is the differences in these relationships.

The political parties are part of the general pattern of American politics, the fragmentation of power. Sometimes they promote cohesion in our political life, but at other times they exemplify America's general dispersal of power. By simplifying most electoral choices to a Republican against a Democrat, by posing issues along the lines of the two major parties' programs, by organizing Congress on partisan dimensions, the parties, like bipolar magnets, bring some order to the scattered political filings of the nation. Simultaneously, the parties are themselves often decentralized, incohesive and unclear in their policy positions. Because they are neither consistently united in their organization nor always agreed on their policies, they are unable or unwilling by themselves to achieve the full mobilization of power for public purposes in the United States.

In this chapter, we will return to these themes as we deal with six aspects of the parties:

1. The general character of the political parties.
2. The American party systems, national and state.
3. The organization of the parties.
4. The nomination of candidates to public office.
5. The role of parties in forming public policy.
6. The changing character of the parties.

What Do Parties Do?

A **political party,** simply put, is a group that tries to elect public officials under its label. Sometimes, other definitions are used. In speaking about the Republican party, for example, we could mean ordinary voters who cast a Republican ballot (the *party-in-the-electorate,* considered in the next chapter), or the officeholders who call themselves Republicans (the *party-in-government,* which will be dealt with later and in Chapter 9). In this chapter, we are mostly interested in the *party-as-organization,* those people who are active in arranging party meetings, conducting campaigns, raising money, and nominating candidates.

Three Theories of Parties

Three different interpretations have been used to explain and evaluate American political parties. We can characterize these different theories as Progressive, participatory, and competitive. These theories deal both with normative questions—What should the parties do?—and with empirical descriptions—How do the parties actually operate?*

PROGRESSIVE The Progressive theory is inherently hostile to parties. It sees the purpose of government as the pursuit of a single "common good," and looks askance at organizations that promote particular interests. Parties are generally criticized as hierarchical organizations that distort the popular will. Individual citizens are seen as fully capable of understanding public issues and of making their wishes effective without the aid of intervening institutions.

The ideal form of government for the Progressives would be direct democracy, and they believe that the institutions of the modern large state should approach that ideal as closely as possible. Historically, the Progressive attitude can be traced to the turn of the century. Parties were both generally corrupt and noncompetitive, and the only means to control them seemed to be to limit their power. The Progressive movement of the time adopted the slogan, "the cure for the ills of democracy is more democracy," and tried to eliminate all barriers between the individual voter and the formal institutions of government.

Progressive ideas are now part of our political procedures, such as the referendum and initiative by which voters directly decide on legislation. For the parties, the most important change was the institution of **direct primaries,** by which candidates are nominated through mass elections, not by party organizations. Although this theory is founded largely on normative grounds, it also has had a great impact on the day-to-day functioning of American parties. Frieda Lawrence's campaign is a good contemporary example of how Progressive ideas have affected these organizations.

PARTICIPATORY The concept of the participatory party gives particular stress to the active members and to the achievement of public policy objectives. As seen in Herbert Lawrence's campaign, the goal of parties is realizing a party program; the means are citizen activity—but activity within the party. Great emphasis is placed on internal party democracy as the way to accomplish the membership's programmatic goals. Generally, advocates of this view often hope to accomplish a "responsible party system," where the parties "bring forth programs to which they commit themselves" and "possess sufficient internal cohesion to carry out these programs."[1]

Advocates of this system sometimes recognize that it would require considerable centralization of the parties so that they could establish and carry through a unified program. At other times, however, they attempt to achieve this goal with an increased degree of membership participation at the local level. Broad participation will lead, it is argued, to a coherent party doctrine that will then be put into effect by leaders and candidates democratically chosen by the active membership. The participatory theory, like the Progressive, emphasizes grass-roots activity. It is different, however, in

*For a more elaborate classification, see Judson L. James, *American Political Parties in Transition* (New York: Harper, 1976), chaps. 1, 2. The categorization used here is derived from the excellent discussion of William E. Wright, *A Comparative Study of Party Organization* (Columbus, Ohio: Merrill, 1971), pp. 17–54.

POLITICAL PERSPECTIVE

COMMENTING ON POLITICAL PARTIES

A political party is a body of men united, for promoting by their joint endeavors, the national interest, upon some particular principle in which they are all agreed.

—Edmund Burke, English statesman, *Thoughts on the Cause of the Present Discontents,* 1770

Politics, noun. A strife of interests masquerading as a contest of principles. The conduct of public affairs for private advantage.

—Ambrose Bierce, American humorist, *The Devil's Dictionary,* 1906

Party serves always to distract the public councils and enfeeble the public administration. It agitates the community with ill-founded jealousies and false alarms; kindles the animosity of one part against another; foments occasionally riot and insurrection. It opens the door to foreign influence and corruption, which find a facilitated access to the government itself through the channels of party passions.

—President George Washington, Farewell Address, 1796

Every difference of opinion is not a difference of principle. We have called by different names brethren of the same principle. We are all Republicans, we are all Federalists.

—President Thomas Jefferson, First Inaugural Address, 1801

When the principles of contending parties are supported with candor, fairness, and moderation, the very discord which is thus produced may in a government like ours, be conducive to the public good.

—President Martin Van Buren, *Autobiography,* 1814

channeling that activity within the party and in its emphasis on coherent partisan programs.

Competitive A third interpretation emphasizes the role of party leaders, candidates, and formal organizations. Largely empirical in content, it also has important normative implications. Parties are viewed as competing power-seeking organizations that encompass broad coalitions seeking support wherever they can. Political activity often arises from private, even selfish motives, and incentives must be provided to arouse political enthusiasm. The emphasis for the party is on its own electoral success, not mass participation, or the purity of its ideology. David Lawrence is a good example.

In this interpretation, parties are seen as serving public interests indirectly. From our viewpoint, politicians can be considered as interested simply in winning elections.* But in order to win elections, they must do other things that are of benefit to the entire society, such as organizing the choice of candidates and policies. Democratic rule is found, in this theory, in the choice between parties, not in their internal structures or in unstructured mass participation. As the theory has been summarized, democracy is basically a system in which "individuals acquire the power to decide by means of a competitive struggle for the people's vote."[2] As an empirical description of America's parties, the competitive theory provides great understanding.

*Anthony Downs, *An Economic Theory of Democracy* (New York: Harper, 1957), builds an important theory of parties and government upon this premise. It is elaborated by Joseph Schlesinger, "On the Theory of Party Organization," *Journal of Politics,* 46 (May 1984), pp. 369–400.

Party Functions

Political parties are basic institutions of the American political community. Although they are not mentioned in the Constitution, they are blatantly evident throughout our government. Without parties, we would be unable to select our most important officials, winnow policy alternatives, and bring our energies and loyalties to bear on social goals. In general, parties are critical links between our private and public lives. Specifically, they carry on the functions listed in Table 6.1.

MANAGING ELECTIONS *Parties manage the machinery of elections.* They nominate the candidates or at least provide a party label for ambitious individuals. Parties canvass the electorate, bring voters to the polls, and administer the casting and counting of ballots. Particularly for less prominent offices, parties conduct campaigns, raise money for electioneering, and group candidates together on a party ticket.

COLLECTIVE ACTION *Parties overcome the limited power of isolated individuals* by uniting them in a collective movement to achieve power. A single person is unlikely to win his or her goal, whether the objective is election to the student council or passage of a national education law. By common action, success is possible.

EMOTIONAL LOYALTIES As they seek power, *parties provide the emotions and personal loyalties essential to politics.* Without these affections, government would be dull, or neglected, or confined to abstract philosophers. Through parties, citizens develop strong ties to other Americans, as they bring their hearts as well as their heads to political action.

SIMPLIFYING CHOICES In nominating candidates, *parties organize public opinion,* giving the voters a simple and understandable choice. In most elections there are only two major candidates for an office and two accompanying programs. As we will see, party identification is a major element in voting. This partisanship provides the intellectual construct by which the voters can bring the blurred, confusing world of multiple candidates for multiple offices into sharper focus. Without party labels, it would hardly be possible

TABLE 6.1 What Political Parties Do

Functions	Examples
Manage elections	Nominating candidates
Foster collective action	Party mobilization of voters
Promote emotional loyalties	Personal involvement in campaigns
Simplify choices	Party labels on ballots
Broker differences	Compromises in legislation
Link opinion to policy	Party programs and platforms
Coordinate government	Presidential meeting with Congress

Parties rally voters behind their candidates. Here, Robert Price of Grundy, Virginia, poses with political buttons that he has been collecting for years as he prepares to attend the Republican National Convention in Detroit. *(AP/Wide World Photos)*

for the American electorate to choose the half-million persons elected to public office. With party labels, instead of a series of unknown names, the voters have a ready guide on the ballot itself to the affiliations and likely beliefs of aspiring politicians.

Brokering To achieve unity, *parties act as "brokers" between different interests,* often moderating their varying demands. Because they are gathered together under the same party banner, competing politicians or social groups may compromise their differences to promote the common cause. Blacks and whites may join in a single "balanced ticket," just as business and labor factions may adjust their economic programs. By such brokerage, parties can reduce social conflict.

Linkages *Parties may contribute to the linkage of public opinion to public policy.* By presenting programs—sometimes specific and sometimes vague, sometimes similar and sometimes different—they allow the electorate, at least partially, to make its wishes felt. This linkage is basic to effective democratic rule.

Coordination *Parties promote coordination in government.* Partisanship can be a bridge across the separation of institutions and a means of overcoming the fragmentation of our multiple checks and balances. Parties provide a president with a link to Congress through his group's leaders and members in the House and Senate. Similarly, they provide important ties among office holders at the national, state, and local levels.

These functions are ideal and do not necessarily describe the actual functioning of American parties. Moreover, there is considerable doubt that parties, even if they wish, can actually perform all these functions. By examining the ways in which our parties operate, we will be able to judge how well they perform these functions and to speculate on likely future developments.

The Party Systems

American parties sometimes have strange names—such as "Bull Moose" or "Know Nothing"—and sometimes support unpopular ideas—such as those of the Libertarians or Socialist Workers. Despite these oddities, there are regular patterns in the way the parties affect the nation.

National Party History

American political history is often divided into five periods of party competition. There are two common characteristics in each of these periods. First, there have been two parties that have held almost all of the offices, although the names and characters of these two parties have changed greatly from one period to another. Second, in most of the periods, one party has been stronger than the other, although subject to defeat on particular occasions. The pattern is summarized in Table 6.2.

TABLE 6.2 National Party Eras

Years	Parties	Major Presidents
1796–1816	Federalists, Republicans	Jefferson, Madison
1828–1852	Democrats, Whigs	Jackson, Van Buren
1860–1892	Republicans, Democrats	Lincoln, Cleveland
1896–1928	Republicans, Democrats	McKinley, T. Roosevelt, Wilson
1932–1964?	Democrats, Republicans	F. D. Roosevelt, Eisenhower, Kennedy

Federalists and Republicans Party politics began in the United States after the adoption of the Constitution. The first American political party was organized by James Madison and Thomas Jefferson and became known as the Republican, then as the Democratic-Republican party. These two founders became increasingly disturbed by the policies of John Adams and of Alexander Hamilton, who was leader of the national administration under George Washington, and of the Federalist majority in Congress. Madison and Jefferson began to organize opposition, first in Congress and then through correspondence with other leaders throughout the young nation.[3] For the election of 1800, they struck an alliance with Aaron Burr and the new political organization in New York, Tammany Hall. By the time of the election, party discipline was complete in the Electoral College,* giving Jefferson and Burr identical majorities. Because of this tie, action by the House of Representatives was needed to choose Jefferson as president and Burr as vice-president. The Twelfth Amendment was added to the Constitution to prevent this problem in the future.

This first party system showed characteristics that would recur in all later periods. First, the political conflict between Federalists and Republicans was also partially a social and regional conflict, in this period between the Eastern commercial interests of the Federalists and the Southern agrarian interests of the Republicans. Second, the party battle also involved policy differences, particularly the Federalist desire for stronger central institutions versus the Republican preference for states' rights. Third, in the interests of victory, the opposition Republicans united diverse politicians.

A Federalist cartoon against Jefferson, who is shown attempting to pull down the Federal Government of Washington and Adams. He is helped by the devil and fortified by a bottle of brandy. *(From the collection of Gerald M. Pomper)*

Democrats and Whigs After two decades, Republicans achieved total control of the government so that by the election of 1820 no effective opposition existed. Disagreement inevitably arose, however, leading to the second party system. John Quincy Adams and Henry Clay led the National Republicans, who won the last election settled by the House in 1824. Those discontented with their policies formed a new party, centered on the leadership of Andrew Jackson, which eventually became the modern Democratic

*The formal vote for President and Vice-President is cast by electors, not the ordinary voters. See Chapter 7 for more details.

party. In turn, the opponents of Jackson organized the Whig party, which first appeared in the 1832 presidential election. Until the onset of the Civil War, these two parties conducted close competition, both nationally and in the states, although the Democrats were victorious in most presidential contests.*

The second party system was greatly affected by social changes in the nation. The extension of the vote to virtually all white men brought new groups into politics. The party conflict became more centered on class and ethnic divisions, with the Democrats the party of many workers and Catholics as well as Westerners, and the Whigs more the party of planters and business. Policy differences were also important. Whigs favored a national program of economic development, whereas Democrats backed small entrepreneurs and agriculture.

Republicans and Democrats The slavery controversy divided the parties as well as the nation. A new Republican party arose to challenge the extension of slavery to the Western territories, and replaced the Whigs. In only its second national election, in 1860, the Republicans elected Abraham Lincoln as president and transformed the nation's politics. Aided by the extension of the vote to the newly freed slaves and by Reconstruction governments established after the Civil War in the Southern states, the Republicans won all but two presidential elections to the end of the nineteenth century.

This period was one of sharp political conflict. The parties divided on issues such as tariffs on imported goods, the power of the central government, and policy toward blacks and the conquered Southern states. Repub-

*For this period, see Richard P. McCormick, *The Second Party System* (Chapel Hill: U. of North Carolina, 1966). For a more general review of party history, see the collection edited by William N. Chambers and Walter Dean Burnham, *The American Party Systems,* 2nd ed. (New York: Oxford U. P., 1975).

Shown here is a wood engraving that appeared in an 1874 issue of *Harper's Weekly.* Based on an original drawing by Thomas Nast, a famous political cartoonist of the time, the engraving shows the first use of the elephant as the symbol of the Republican party. *(Library of Congress)*

licans won their presidential victories only by narrow margins, and Democrats battled to near equality in contests for the House.

Republican Majority At the end of the nineteenth century, leaders unhappy with the growing dominance of industrial capitalism created the Populist party and succeeded, in 1896, in having many of their ideas adopted by the Democrats, led by William Jennings Bryan. The nation, however, was not prepared generally to accept these ideas. In 1896, with William McKinley as their candidate, the Republicans finally won a decisive victory. The fourth party system created in that election ensured their dominance until the great stock market crash of 1929.

In this period, the parties competed nationally, but most states were dominated by one party—the East and Midwest by Republicans, the South by Democrats. In Washington, the Republicans (now becoming known as the GOP for "Grand Old Party") succeeded in moving national policy toward high tariffs and other means of capitalist development. Democrats were a distinct minority comprising such groups as Southern whites and some urban Catholics. By rigging the laws and by force, blacks had been excluded from voting in virtually all of the South. Women won the suffrage through constitutional amendment in 1920, but this had no immediate affect on the party balance.

The New Deal The economic depression of the 1930s transformed the party system, leading to a Democratic majority for close to fifty years. Newly enfranchised immigrants and their children, blacks and Jews abandoning their Republican traditions, and a newly unionized working class led to five straight Democratic victories in the presidential race, party dominance in Congress, and consistent Democratic leads in voter loyalties. Led by Franklin Roosevelt, the Democrats' legislative program was known as the **New Deal.**

The depression of the 1930s made the Democrats, led by Franklin Roosevelt, the majority party in the nation. Here, the president visits a Civilian Conservation Corps camp in Shenandoah Valley, Virginia. *(Franklin D. Roosevelt Library)*

The electoral basis of American politics was changed in this time, from one based primarily on regionalism to one based more on social class. The policies of the United States were also changed, inaugurating a welfare state, in which the government assumes responsibilities for certain social needs, and increasing the power of the national government. Although the New Deal period still shapes our party politics, there are signs of the emergence of a new, sixth party system. We shall return to this important question in the next chapter.

Why Two Parties?

The most striking fact about the American party system is that it usually includes only two parties with any chance of victory. There are occasional members of Congress or a rare governor or a fraction of state legislators who are not Republicans or Democrats, but their number is small and their significance even less. Since the establishment of our present two major parties at the time of the Civil War, the average (median) number of persons outside of their ranks has been only one in the Senate and two in the House. "Third party" representatives have been chosen for the Electoral College in significant numbers (more than 5 percent of the total) only three times in the last thirty presidential contests.

Public Opinion There are a number of explanations for the restriction of the party competition to only two parties. Probably the most important is the distribution of public opinion that tends to concentrate within a small range of policy positions. For example, most Americans favor an economic system of **welfare-state capitalism:** most business is run privately, but government provides aid for such groups as the elderly and the unemployed. More extreme parties have little chance of victory whether they advocate socialism or a completely unregulated economy.

Institutions Furthermore, institutional reasons help to account for the lack of long-term success for third parties. A principal explanation is found in the presidency, the single national elected office, which is decided strictly on a win-or-lose basis. Parties cannot share power or divide up the seats in the executive cabinet, as they can in a system of parliamentary government. Their desire for victory brings competing groups to cooperate and to submerge their differences in a common effort. If they fail to unite, they only make it more likely that their common enemy will win the great power of the presidency. Thus, in 1980, John Anderson lost almost two-thirds of the voters who actually thought him the best candidate. About half of these defectors preferred Reagan to Carter, and about half had the opposite view, liking Carter more than Reagan.[4] They were agreed only on the futility of "wasting" their vote on Anderson and so cast ballots for their second choice. This logic of the presidential election has also contributed to the demise of other third-party movements and to the maintenance of unity within the two major parties.

Election Systems Specific electoral systems also contribute to the restriction of competition to two parties. On the local and state level, representatives are usually elected in single-member districts by plurality vote. This means that only one person is normally chosen to represent a particular area in a governmental institution: there is only one representative from each district, for example, and the person elected is whoever gets the most votes, even if he or she does not get a majority of the total vote. Just as with the presidency, this means that power cannot be divided among a number of parties in each district and that there is considerable incentive for competing groups to unite behind a single candidate.

On the national level, the Electoral College makes the presidential election in reality a series of state contests. In each state, the parties play under *winner-take-all* rules. Having broad support is not enough. To get electoral votes, parties have to come in first in some states. The effect is to penalize candidates without a distinct regional base, such as Robert LaFollette who, in 1924, won a sixth of the national vote but only carried a single state.[5]

But winning some states, even by large margins, also isn't good enough. Since each state is separate, a candidate has to have enough appeal to win different kinds of states. A candidate such as George Wallace in 1968 can therefore win electoral votes in the South but still not affect the national results. The total system works to the advantage of broad and moderate parties.

Election Laws These factors have been reinforced by deliberate actions of the parties themselves. In writing state and federal laws governing elections, the major parties try to protect their own interests. They make it more difficult for minor parties to win a place on the ballot by devices such as setting an early date for closing nominations, insisting that there be a vice-presidential as well as presidential candidate, prescribing complicated forms and high fees, and requiring a large number of petition signatures. John Anderson, in 1980, had to spend months and much of his limited budget to win a place on all state ballots, thereby weakening his direct electioneering.

Nationally, although Congress provides money for the presidential campaigns of the major parties at the beginning of the campaign, minor parties only receive funds after the election is over and only if they receive at least 5 percent of the total vote. This distinction has been upheld as reasonable by the Supreme Court, but its effect is to handicap any new party.[6] Election law, however, can sometimes work to the advantage of third parties. This is its effect in New York state, where minor parties are allowed to endorse major party candidates and have their votes count as if cast for a Republican or Democrat. This system has helped three "third" parties to survive—the Conservatives, the Liberals, and a "Right-to-Life" organization.

Tradition Finally, tradition itself sustains the two-party system. Most Americans still identify as either Democrats or Republicans, and the remaining Independents are not members of another party but simply not psychologically identified with these two giant groups. The two-party system is sometimes even identified by Americans as a necessary feature of any democratic system, despite the prevalence of multiparty systems in other countries. The Democrats and Republicans are united in fostering and benefiting from these sentiments.

DOONESBURY **by Garry Trudeau**

Copyright 1980, G. B. Trudeau. Reprinted with permission of Universal Press Syndicate. All rights reserved.

Third Parties Under the dominant pattern of two-party politics in American history, there is another, if subordinate, pattern. Third parties appear frequently, and important insurgent movements can be found in every generation. Altogether, thirty distinct and significant parties have contested for the presidency alone, running from Prohibitionists to Communists. In the 1980 election, John Anderson won nearly 7 percent of the national vote as an independent. Not long before, in 1968, George Wallace and the American Independent party won twice that proportion of the vote, while carrying five Southern states.[7] In 1984, however, no significant third parties appeared.

Although they are all called third parties, the minor parties in U.S. history have been very different.* Some have arisen to advocate particular programs. Examples are the Free Soilers of 1844, who advocated the abolition of slavery from the territories; the nuclear disarmament advocates of the Citizens party in 1980; or the recurrent parties of economic protest, such as the Populists of 1892 or the Progressives of 1924. Another group of these parties are factions that secede from a major party because of discontent with its leaders or policies. For example, opposition to Democratic civil rights parties stimulated the Dixiecrat party in 1948, as well as Wallace's campaign twenty years later. There are also minor parties whose overall ideology is far different from the moderate programs of the major parties. They currently include a variety of Marxist groups and the Libertarian party.[8]

Party Organizations

Within the environment of a competitive two-party system, the Democratic and Republican organizations attempt to perform their various functions. The varying theories of parties raise different expectations about their structure. To the Progressives, parties are generally undesirable, and they

*A full listing of all parties in American history can be found in Congressional Quarterly, *Guide to U.S. Elections* (Washington, 1975), pp. 189–95.

should be restricted so as to provide fuller opportunity for individuals to exercise direct political power. In the participatory theory, parties are accepted, but the effort is to make them internally democratic and to promote members' control over leaders. The competitive theory seeks to structure the party to promote election victories. This emphasis may lead to incohesion or to unity, depending on which arrangement best promotes success at the polls for particular candidates. Elements of each of these theories can be found in the real workings of the parties.

In the United States, parties are considered different from other organizations, which decide on their own membership rules or internal structure. For most purposes, parties are regarded as a semipublic group that should be democratically controlled by the electorate at large and, if needed, legally regulated. Thus, a party cannot discriminate among members on the grounds of race.[9] Indeed, when it comes to nominating candidates, it cannot set any entrance rules so that any persons who care to call themselves members earn the right to participate in these most critical decisions. This enforced openness and the other extensive legislation governing parties reflect the Progressive theory. Since Progressives distrust parties, they are unwilling to let them conduct their own affairs. The power of the state must be invoked to ensure full and free participation.

Formal Organization

In this section, we will be concerned with the party in the narrower sense of a formal organization with an identifiable membership. Among all voters, fewer than 5 percent can be considered party members in this sense. As a formal group, "the party is described as a political enterprise conducted by a group of working politicians *supported* by partisan voters who approve of the party but are merely partisans (not members of a fictitious association)."[10] These informal supporters have the same relationship to the party organization as baseball fans have to their favorite club or as retail customers have to a favorite department store.

State Parties The formal structure of a political party, usually specified in state law, contains multiple and overlapping bodies. (An example is shown in Figure 6.1, the diagram of the party structure in Texas.) The basic component is the precinct, or election district, a small neighborhood unit of about 500 voters. In each of these precincts, the party voters, through either caucuses or the same direct primaries that nominate candidates, select party precinct representatives, usually one man and one woman. If all of these positions were filled throughout the nation (but about a quarter are not), the result would be the choice of over half a million persons constituting the formal party leadership at the grass-roots level.

From this base are constructed a series of larger and more important party committees. The precinct representatives usually meet together in their local town and county and constitute the town and county (and sometimes state legislative district) committees. They establish party rules for these respective areas, sometimes endorse candidates for public office for these jurisdictions, and are responsible for maintaining contact with the

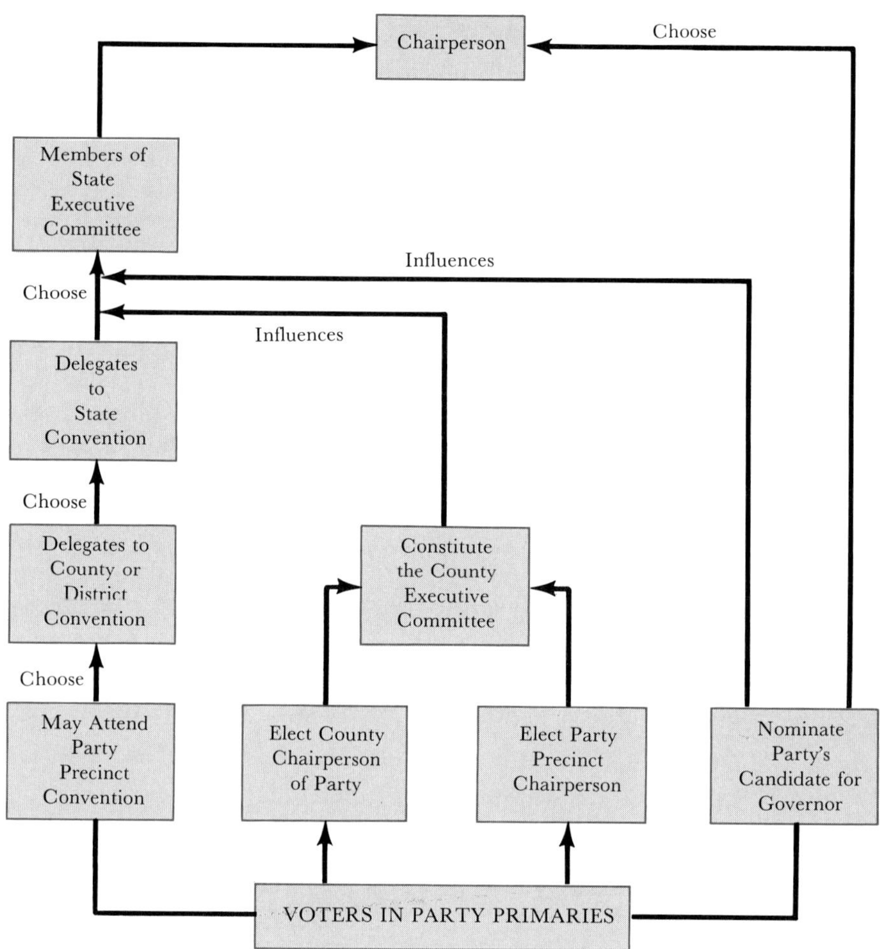

FIGURE 6.1
Party Structure in Texas
(Reprinted by permission from Texas Politics *by James W. Lamare; Copyright © 1981 by West Publishing Company. All rights reserved. Page 73.)*

voters and campaigning for party nominees. It is their responsibility to choose the town and county chairman and/or chairwoman. It is the latter officials, however, who wield whatever real power a party has, because it is only at the town and county level that there are any significant governmental functions and spending that the party can influence.

Given its local base, political party organization is inherently fragmented. This characteristic is even more evident at the state and national levels. There is no uniform pattern to the organization of state parties or any consistent degree of power exercised by the heads of these organizations. State party committees exist everywhere, but they are chosen in diverse ways: sometimes by voters directly in primaries, sometimes by selection from the county committees, sometimes (most notably in California) by the party's candidates and officeholders.[11]

National Committees At the top of the party structures are the national committees, made up of persons from each state and some affiliated groups. Its chairman, a full-time professional, is chosen by the committee, but the president will actually choose this person for the party that holds the White House. The committees have their own buildings in Washington, employ sizable staffs, raise money, and provide publicity and services for candidates running under the party label.

Until the last two decades, these committees were powerless bodies concerned primarily with preparing the presidential nominating conventions. More recently, they have taken on significant roles. For example, the Democratic National Committee has required changes in state party rules to promote affirmative action, while the Republican National Committee has become involved in state legislative races around the nation.[12] These changes are part of the general trends in American politics which we will consider at the end of the chapter.

Effects of Party Organization These details reveal structures that are essentially slack. America does not have parties that are hierarchically arranged, with strong central power or with clear lines of authority. Some positions are not filled; other offices see frequent changes. There are many centers of power and few means of command available for those at "the top" of a decentralized organization. Since the parties are themselves fragmented, they cannot easily be the instrument for overcoming the other fragmentations of American politics in order to enact a policy program. Those who hope to use parties for this purpose, such as the advocates of the participatory theory, face considerable obstacles.

Cohesion in American parties is handicapped by the lack of a powerful central body. In contrast to European parties, there is no national committee that can make authoritative decisions on nominations, financing, and policy. The president does have great influence in his or her camp, and the national parties do have their national committees. But decisions at this apex of the party are made by persuasion, bargaining, and compromise, not by command. Federalism, which fragments power generally in the United States, is also reflected in the structure of the parties.

Party Varieties

The real life of political parties is not found in formal organizational charts, but in the lives of the men and women in them. They join and work in parties for the same reasons people are active in other groups—some see a chance to make money, some want to further a cause, and some enjoy being with others. At the local level, parties vary from the rare disciplined "machine" to the more common loose organization in which commitment is voluntary and hard to maintain.

The Machine A **machine** is a party organization that recruits its workers by providing material incentives, such as patronage or public jobs. Although much fabled, it is virtually extinct. One of the last major strongholds of a traditional machine was the city of Chicago. In 1983, this powerful organization was overthrown. Congressman Harold Washington was elected mayor, following the mobilization of black community groups and the registration of over 100,000 new black and Hispanic voters.

The machine embodies the theory of parties as competitive power-seeking organizations. Those who bring out the vote are compensated by jobs

The strong political machine in Chicago was defeated when a black-led coalition in 1983 elected Harold Washington as mayor. *(UPI/Bettmann Newsphotos)*

on the public payroll or other monetary rewards. In its heyday, the Chicago machine found a job for all of the ward leaders, and for a large proportion of the precinct delegates as well.[13] When operating efficiently (and this happened less often than legend has it),* rewards were proportional to effort. Those who brought in the most votes from their districts got the best jobs, perhaps positions as important as a judgeship, perhaps unskilled jobs as the "hole inspector," whose only duty was to determine whether manhole covers were in place.

Patronage, however, does not explain the success of the machine because jobs provided rewards only for the party workers, not for the far more numerous voters who supported the machine at the polls. In some cases, machine organizations used fraud to win elections, buying votes or casting ballots on behalf of the dead. More often, machines would use money acquired from business corporations seeking favors from the city government. But most important were the services that machines provided. Particularly among the poor and immigrants, machines provided both material welfare (Thanksgiving turkeys, winter coal) and, just as important, an emotional anchor for people loosed from traditional moorings. For all classes, the machine worker could provide intervention with government, a personal tie to overcome the cold formality of bureaucracy. As Martin Lomasny of Boston explained, "I think that there's got to be in every ward somebody that any bloke can come to—no matter what he's done—and get help. Help, you understand; none of your law and your justice, but help."[14]

The kind of help the machine could provide is detailed in the accompanying boxed excerpt from a Tammany district leader at the turn of the century, George Washington Plunkitt. In these ways, the machine acted as a primitive social service state.

The Volunteer Party A different kind of party, almost the exact opposite of the machine, is that of the "reformer" or "amateur." In keeping with the participatory theory of parties, this group is made up largely of volunteers who are primarily motivated by the desire to achieve particular policy goals. The reward for activity is not a patronage job but the satisfaction of advancing the "public interest," as the member defines it. Because the parties have only a small and diminishing supply of material incentives, they must rely more on these intangible rewards of policy satisfaction.

As a result, there is a more ideological character evident among party activists today than was true in the past. Delegates to the Republican National Convention, for example, overwhelmingly call themselves conservatives, while Democratic delegates are very heavily liberal. Among ordinary voters in both parties, however, the predominant groups are the moderates.

Similar ideological differences exist in the states. In California, for exam-

*See W. Robert Gump, "The Functions of Patronage in American Party Politics," *Midwest Journal of Political Science,* 15 (Feb. 1971), pp. 87–107; Frank Sorauf, "Patronage in a Rural County," *American Political Science Review,* 50 (Dec. 1956), pp. 1046–56; and Michael Johnston, "Patrons and Clients, Jobs and Machines," *American Political Science Review,* 73 (July 1979), pp. 385–97.

POLITICAL PERSPECTIVE

TO HOLD YOUR DISTRICT

What tells in holdin' your grip on your district is to go right down among the poor families and help them in the different ways they need help. I've got a regular system for this. If there's a fire in Ninth, Tenth, or Eleventh Avenue, for example, any hour of the day or night, I'm usually there with some of my election district captains as soon as the fire engines. If a family is burned out I don't ask whether they are Republicans or Democrats, and I don't refer them to the Charity Organization Society, which would investigate their case in a month or two and decide they were worthy of help about the time they are dead from starvation. I just get quarters for them, buy clothes for them if their clothes were burned up, and fix them up till they get things runnin' again. It's philanthropy, but it's politics, too—mighty good politics. Who can tell how many votes one of these fires brings me? The poor are the most grateful people in the world, and, let me tell you, they have more friends in their neighborhoods than the rich have in theirs.

If there's a family in my district in want I know it before the charitable societies do, and me and my men are first on the ground. I have a special corps to look up such cases. The consequence is that the poor look up to George W. Plunkitt as a father, come to him in trouble—and don't forget him on election day.

Another thing, I can always get a job for a deservin' man. I make it a point to keep on the track of jobs, and it seldom happens that I don't have a few up my sleeve ready for use. I know every big employer in the district and in the whole city, for that matter, and they ain't in the habit of sayin' no to me when I ask them for a job.

Source: W. I. Riordon, *Plunkitt of Tammany Hall* (New York: Dutton, 1963), pp. 27–28.

ple, 90 percent of Democratic activists favored the Equal Rights Amendment, compared to only 29 percent of their Republican counterparts. (Among the voters, opinions were much closer—both 74 percent of Democrats and 55 percent of Republicans supported the ERA.) Generally, a study of state politicians shows that party differences are meaningful throughout the country. In all of the 11 states examined, Democratic leaders were considerably more liberal, on both economic and social issues, than Republicans. In fact, the most conservative Democrats (Oklahoma) were still more to "the left" than the most liberal Republicans (Maine).[15]

Volunteer parties are likely to become more widespread. Traditional patronage rewards are very limited in modern bureaucratic government, so parties must rely more on voluntary workers, who demand fuller participation and a greater emphasis on issue appeals. Once involved in politics, these workers can be quite effective, as shown by the successes scored by such diverse groups as Reaganite conservatives and black voting leagues. These groups' stress on issues may also help them to mobilize an electorate that is less tied to traditional party loyalties.

Social Rewards in Parties In both machines and volunteer groups, material and ideological incentives are supplemented by a third kind, the desire for social contact, friendship, and affection. Many people join parties for the same reasons they join the Lions Club or drop in to a singles bar: to meet people, to help a friend, to find a use for leisure time. Indeed, these emotional reasons are mentioned most often when party activists are asked

George Wallace, once a strong opponent of racial integration, changed his attitudes as blacks registered and voted. Here, Wallace is shown greeting constituents following his fourth-term election as governor of Alabama. *(Diego Goldberg/Sygma)*

why they originally became interested in politics.* At times, the emphasis on the social benefits of parties may even come to predominate over the political so that parties exclude persons who are not of the "right" social groups.

The Irish encountered this attitude in the nineteenth century, when their growing numbers were at first ignored by the Protestant Anglo-Saxons who dominated politics. Eventually, the Irish took over urban party organizations, running them as extended mutual-benefit societies, where "men were bred from childhood to an urgent and overriding feeling of family duty and parochial loyalty."[16] When new immigrants came to the cities, particularly Italians and blacks, the Irish, in turn, found it difficult to give up the social benefits of close political organizations, even if their exclusiveness meant the loss of potential votes.

A similar effect could be seen in traditional Southern politics, where blacks were excluded not only from the dominant and segregationist Democratic organizations, but also from the vote-starved Republican groups. Maintaining racial purity was more important than seeking new support. In this case, however, parties have overcome their inhibitions. With the passage of federal voting rights laws and the consequent expansion of the black electorate, some of the previous barriers have been overcome. As Atlanta Mayor Andrew Young wryly observed:

> It used to be Southern politics was just "nigger" politics, who could "outnigger" the other—then you registered 10 to 15 percent in the community and folks would start saying "Nigra," and then you got 35 to 40 percent registered and it's amazing how quick they learned to say "Nee-grow," and now that we've got 50, 60, 70 percent of the black votes registered in the South, everybody's proud to be associated with their black brothers and sisters.[17]

*Among the illustrative works in a large literature are Richard Hofstetter, "Organizational Activists: The Basis of Participation in Amateur and Professional Groups," *American Politics Quarterly*, 1 (April 1973), pp. 244–76; Margaret Conway and Frank Feigent, "Motivation, Incentive Systems and Political Party Organization," *American Political Science Review*, 62 (Dec. 1968), pp. 1153–73; and Robert Salisbury, "The Urban Party Organization Member," *Public Opinion Quarterly*, 29 (Winter 1965–66), pp. 553–66.

Parties as Communities Parties are a special kind of social group, which is becoming rare in the increasingly homogenized society of the United States. Parties function—or at least did function at some times—as small political communities. They provided, and still can provide, a place where individual interests and isolated concerns are combined into more general enterprises.

This quality of parties is evident in Alexis de Tocqueville's description of political activity in America generally at the time of his visit: "The American learns to know the laws by participating in the act of legislation; and he takes a lesson in the forms of government from governing. The great work of society is ever going on before his eyes and, as it were, under his hands."[18] What Tocqueville saw was more than people voting or talking about politics. Even more critical was that they participated in some common activity centered around public questions. The political party has been the largest enterprise of this sort in our history. Although less than a tenth of the electorate today is likely to attend a political rally, or work for a party, this is still more than 15 million persons.

Parties as communities are probably the most democratic associations in the nation. Their active membership is diverse, reflecting the variety of the country and its neighborhoods. (The accompanying box sketches three Chicago precinct captains in 1936.) In a Manhattan party club, a university professor may be found working together with a welfare mother. Since parties aim, first of all, to capture votes, their self-interest leads them to expand their membership—at least where there is meaningful competition. They thus express the egalitarian principle that is the root belief of democracy. This commitment is evident in party rules, such as those requiring equal participation of women and men. Similarly, parties have been important means for the assimilation of immigrant groups and their upward mobility within American society. Among the early Irish immigrants, "politics as a career not only required a minimum of education, preparation and money; . . . for the few who had the requisite talents it produced its rewards relatively quickly."[19] The emerging black leadership in urban areas evidence similar effects.

By enlisting women and men in a cause beyond their own private lives, parties can teach people how to practice democracy, and in ways far more effective than school lessons. The desire for victory requires compromise, consideration of others' views, a tolerance of diverse ethnic groups when these other groups have votes, a recognition of the limits on pure selfishness. In the ideal political party, as a Democratic newspaper put it in 1836, the credo becomes, "Union, harmony, self-denial, concession, everything for CAUSE. Nothing for men."[20]

Party Finance

"Money is the mother's milk of politics," and the politicians and voters of the United States need a lot of nourishment. Altogether, over $18 is spent on each voter at all elections. Just for the national House and Senate, 1984 candidates spent $400 million, and the 1984 presidential election cost over $300 million.[21] The costs of politics are high and rising faster than the

POLITICAL PERSPECTIVE

THREE PRECINCT CAPTAINS: CHICAGO, 1936

At the time of the 1936 election [John] Grady was one of the prize precinct captains of his ward. He was going to one of the larger law schools in the city, working his way through by means of a pay-roll job, i.e., a position which did not make great inroads upon the time which he needed for his studies and his political work. It happened that there was a very large gambling place in his bailiwick, and in accordance with prevailing custom he was able to place several of his political workers as employees of this outlawed business. He also claimed that he was able to place some of his constituents in public utility jobs, in city hall jobs, and in hotels, theaters, and business establishments within the precinct that "worked with the organization." One of the hotels had a questionable reputation. Pressure was brought to bear upon the taverns to contribute to all the political benefits. In his canvassing work Grady was a master at adjusting himself to the peculiarities of the persons addressed. A tall, handsome young man with a glib tongue, he could fall into the lingo of the tavern, the dance hall, the gambling den, the church festival, or the political backroom at will. As far as could be ascertained, Grady never attempted any direct bribery by voters by means of money, nor did he engage in any stealing of votes. With his persuasive manner and through canvassing work, he did not need to stoop to these lowest of all political devices.

The case of Joe Czech shows that it is not necessary for a precinct committeeman to have an extensive formal education in order to acquire a social point of view. Joe was a short, stout, rugged, well-spoken Hussite who was born in Bohemia fifty-two years ago. . . . Now he is well read, and on his desk appeared the latest copy of the *Atlantic Monthly* and Papini's *Life of Christ*. Joe longed for an out-of-door life, and he went into politics in 1928 in order to get on the forest-preserve staff. . . .

In his precinct Joe's main interest was in seeing what he could do to make life easier for the poor. He started on this topic by saying that in this country we think we have freedom and strength and wealth, but in actuality there is no such thing as freedom except for a favored few. "For the vast majority of workingmen," he added, "the constitutional guarantees of freedom are a mere mockery in the hands of exploiting capitalists" . . . His fear was not for the older people, who, he said, no longer really mattered, but for the younger people, who were now coming up without anything to do or any way of earning a living. When "kids" were caught stealing as a result of sheer idleness, he always tried to get them off because he felt they were not really to blame. He worked hard for the Democratic party because he thought that it was doing something to alleviate the youth problem. . . .

The methods of woman precinct captains may be illustrated by the case of Mrs. Smith, an official co-captain of a precinct in the Fifteenth Ward and a veteran of many political battles. This neat, elderly, garrulous woman was responsible for the women's votes only, and left the rest of the work to the male captain. For many years she had been an active feminist. In fact, she took part in the agitation for woman suffrage in Illinois before 1913. . . . In those early days, when a woman pleaded she could not vote because she was washing or had to look after the baby, Mrs. Smith would help finish the washing or mind the baby. . . .

A separate women's organization was set up because Mrs. Smith found that a woman could do a lot more to get other women to vote than a man could. Some men even did not like to have the male precinct captain talking to their wives. The women organized card parties and dances. One dance was held at a downtown hotel at which the attendance reached seven hundred. The men always contributed to the expenses of such functions. Mrs. Smith was soon interested in political work for its own sake. She enjoyed getting out and talking to people and thought that many more women would like it if only they once tried it. At the card parties the women started to gossip about politics among themselves and thus acquired a desire to have something to say about how things are run. . . . Once women got used to taking an active part, there was no difficulty whatsoever in keeping them interested and seeking ways to be of service.

Source: Harold Gosnell, *Machine Politics: Chicago Model*, 2nd ed. (Chicago: U. of Chicago, 1968), pp. 58–63.

national rate of inflation because of unusual rises in the cost of such campaign items as airplane fares, consultants, and television commercials.

Election costs have been paid in various ways: by the party itself, with the aid of indirect and hidden public subsidies; by individual and group contributions to the parties or candidates; and by direct public subsidies, given primarily to candidates rather than parties. In recent years, the trend is toward increasing reliance on the last two sources of money.

Party Contributions Patronage jobs, in effect, are a hidden government subsidy to parties and their candidates. Employed on the public payroll, patronage appointees spend some of their time campaigning and contribute some of their salary to the party. This system worked best when campaigning was done primarily by local party loyalists securing the votes of their friends and neighbors, as in the days of Plunkitt. Patronage workers are far less useful in modern times, when campaigning is not done face-to-face for most offices but through impersonal presentations of the candidate's image and through the mass media. Furthermore, fewer patronage jobs are available as civil service and court decisions restrict their availability,* and these basically unskilled jobs are less plentiful or attractive in a modern economy. New sources of funds have become necessary.

Individual Contributions Individual and group contributions are now the principal means of financing politics. Some persons contribute to political campaigns for relatively altruistic reasons because they like candidates personally or favor their policy causes. More often, they are trying to advance some personal interest, such as consideration for a government appointment or the adoption of legislation favorable to an oil company or a construction union. Although simple bribery is relatively rare and, of course, illegal, those who contribute large amounts to a campaign do expect at least to have their claims given consideration by the persons they help to elect and to gain access to them.

The potential dangers in political contributions were dramatically illustrated by the financing of Richard Nixon's reelection campaign in 1972. Operating independently of the Republican party through a Committee to Re-Elect the President (dubbed CREEP by his opponents), Nixon's supporters collected over $60 million, some illegally and some from persons with very immediate interests at stake, such as the nation's milk producers who wanted higher prices for their basic food. The revelation of the abuses of financing and the other elements of the Watergate scandal led to the adoption of new laws regulating election finances.

In regard to individuals, the new emphasis is on small contributions. Taxpayers are encouraged to donate to the parties by being permitted to designate $1 or $2 of their income tax to a presidential campaign fund. Between 25 and 30 percent of taxpayers choose this option each year. Furthermore, citizens are given credit against their taxes for up to $200 in contributions to any party or candidate. Individuals are limited in their total political contributions to no more than $1,000 per election for any individual candidate and no more than $25,000 totally.[22]

Abuses of campaign financing in the 1972 election led to new political finance laws. Here, former U.S. Attorney General John Mitchell prepares to serve a prison sentence for his role in the Watergate cover-up that involved some of these abuses. *(AP/Wide World Photos)*

*In *Branti* v. *Finkel,* 63 L.Ed. 2nd, 574 (1980), the Supreme Court virtually declared party patronage to be unconstitutional, despite its long history in the United States.

Political Action Committees Large individual contributions to candidates have been curtailed by these laws. In their place, a new form of political financing has arisen: the **political action committee (PAC).** These groups collect individual donations (from stockholders of a corporation, members of a labor union, or advocates of a particular policy). They then give sizable contributions, up to $5,000 each, to the candidates they prefer. Alternatively, they can spend the money independently, and without limit, on behalf of their favorites, so long as there is no coordination with a candidate's own efforts.

PAC money has become critical in national elections. By 1984, there were nearly 4,000 of these organizations, providing $105 million in contributions to House and Senate candidates—a threefold increase in six years. The average House candidate received a third of his total contributions from these groups, with incumbents particularly favored, and powerful legislators even more likely to receive donations. (The pattern is pictured in Figure 6.2.) Warned Representative Mike Synar of Oklahoma, "We are evolving very quickly into the best Congress money can buy. You don't buy a Congressman with a contribution, of course, but you buy access and access is the name of the game."[23]

Many commentators are concerned that PACs and the "single-interest groups" they represent will undermine the ability of the parties and legislators to compromise among the various groups interested in government policy.[24] A further problem is the effect of the PACs on the parties themselves. Since they already contribute more than four times as much money to candidates than the parties do, PACs may soon reduce the role of parties in electioneering to insignificance.

Public Subsidies A third means of financing politics would be through direct public subsidy. The post-Watergate reforms provided partial public

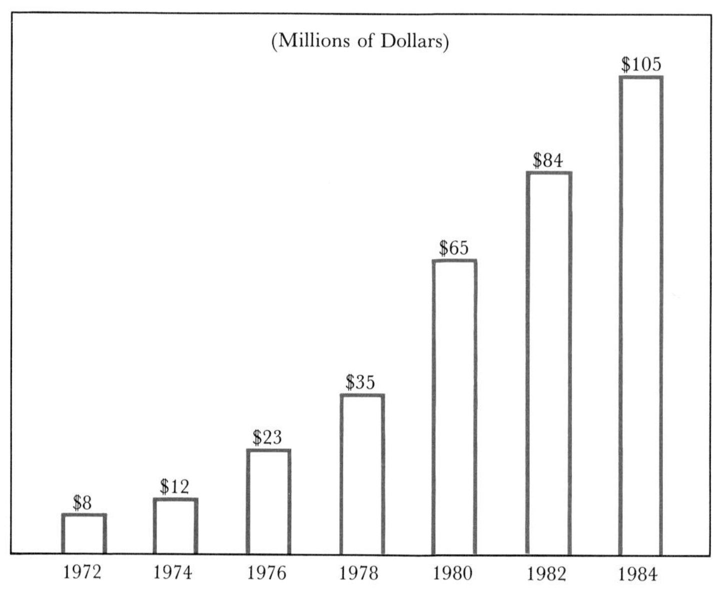

FIGURE 6.2
PAC Contributions to Senate and House Candidates
(Federal Election Commission, as reported in National Journal, *17 [May 25, 1985], 1235.)*

POLITICAL PERSPECTIVE

YOU CAN TAKE YOUR PICK OF PACS GALORE

Just as the song says, there is somebody for everybody. And there seems to be a political action committee (PAC) for everybody.

There is a BeefPAC, CattlePAC, CigarPAC, CoalPAC, EggPAC, FarmPAC, FishPAC, FlatironPAC, FurPAC, LardPAC and, yes, a BackPAC. In Macon, Ga., there is even an ImPACT.

For sports lovers, there are the American Fishing Tackle Manufacturers Association PAC, the Aspen Skiing Company Employees PAC, the California Motorcyclists PAC and the Hawaii Golfers for Good Government.

Beer drinkers are represented by the Coors Employees PAC, the Stroh Brewery Co. PAC and, appropriately, by SixPAC; gamblers by the Casino Employees PAC, Caesar's Palace Corp. PAC, Harrah's PAC and River Boat Casino Inc. PAC; stock investors by Merrill Lynch PAC, Paine Webber Fund for Better Government and Salomon Brothers Inc. PAC; and lawyers by Manatt, Phelps, Rothenberg & Tunney PAC and Dickstein, Shapiro & Morin PAC.

There are segments of society that are concerned enough about public affairs to have organized into PACs, among them Concerned Romanians, Concerned Italian Americans for Better Government, Concerned Professionals, Concerned Businessmen and Concerned Texans.

Some groups strike an upbeat note, including committees for A Stronger Future, A Voice in Energy Policy, Better Political Choices, Honesty and Integrity and Morality and Decency. One visionary organization is called Committee for the Twenty-First Century.

Other groups, however, seem to have expectations that exceed reality, as, for instance, the Committee to Promote Senate Competence for the 80s, the Committee Urging Reduced Bureaucracy, the Council for a Livable World and Prune the Federal Government, which seems inappropriately located in Los Angeles.

For fast-food fans, there is the Burger King PAC, Dr. Pepper Co. PAC, Coca-Cola Bottling Co. PAC, and the Oscar Mayer Employees Better Government Fund Inc. PAC.

And, finally, there is an Oral and Maxillofacial Surgery PAC.

Source: *National Journal,* 14 (Oct. 30, 1982), p. 1835.

support for presidential races. Public funds are made available to individual candidates during the primaries (after they raise $100,000 in small contributions), with the Treasury matching all individual contributions up to $250. The government also pays all expenses in the general election. This public support, if voluntarily accepted by candidates, is accompanied by restrictions on their expenditures, no more than $20.3 million during the nomination effort and no more than $40.4 million during the general election. State and local parties may spend their own funds above the general election limit. These new laws have eliminated the obvious financial abuses evident in the presidential election of 1972, but they have also created administrative tangles and have sharply limited the freedom of national candidates to spend as they wish.

The finance laws do not fully regulate congressional elections. No subsidies are provided at this level, and no limits exist on expenditures. Since national legislative candidates must raise their own money for the most part, there is the potential danger that they will become dependent on their contributors. Another problem is the disparity between incumbents and challengers. Incumbents find it much easier to raise money, for example, receiving five times as much money from PACs. With incumbents already enjoying more visibility by virtue of their official activities, challengers often need to spend more money to make an effective race, but the existing limits on individual contributions make it difficult to raise a large war chest. Public subsidies for congressional candidates have been suggested as the way to overcome both of these problems, but congressmen have been understandably reluctant to provide funds for their opponents.

Political finance again illustrates the decentralization of American parties. For the most part, candidates must raise their own money. Recent statutes may change this pattern, but it remains true that the formal party organizations provide relatively little support, while PACs press their special interests even as they send checks. The reform laws have even aggravated the situation because they provide subsidies to individual presidential candidates and thus allow candidates to wage campaigns independently of the established party channels. Only in limited situations is any money provided to the party organizations—the federal government pays $8 million toward the cost of the national party conventions, and nine states provide direct party subsidies. In general, election finance reinforces the pattern of fragmented parties. It is one more obstacle to the achievement of cohesive and policy-oriented parties, the goal of the participatory theory.

Nominating Candidates

Nominations, the selection of candidates to run in the general election, are the most important function performed by the political parties. Its importance is shown in the fact that every state lists candidates for national and state office with their party labels, and provides automatic access to the ballot for parties that have secured a specified minimum of the vote in previous elections (typically 1 to 5 percent). Nominating candidates, indeed, is the unique task of American parties.

Nominations are treated differently in the three theories of parties. The Progressive view clearly favors nomination by direct individual vote, without any significant involvement of the party organization. The participatory theory would support nomination by party activists, through an internal but broadly democratic process, with a stress on prospective candidates' policy stands. In the competitive theory, parties would be left to make their own selection of candidates. They would nominate persons who would be most likely to succeed at the polls, giving less consideration to issue positions. In actual practice, American nominations show some Progressive, some participatory, and some competitive features.

Nominations can be even more important than the final elections. For example, almost any mature, native-born American is legally eligible for a party nomination as president. In the general election, on the other hand, voters can only effectively choose either a Democrat or a Republican, or throw away their votes on a third candidate. For Congress, nominations can be even more critical, because two-party competition is limited. In House elections, about a tenth of the seats have only one major-party candidate. In most of the others, one party has a decided advantage, winning with at least 55 percent of the vote.[25]

The Direct Primary

For most offices, the formal means of nomination is through a special nominating election, called a **direct primary.** Candidates enter this primary by submitting a petition signed by a designated number of voters, or by paying a filing fee.

OPEN AND CLOSED PRIMARIES Those eligible to vote in the primary differ from one state to another. In most, participation is restricted to those who declare themselves members of the party, and the contest is therefore called a **closed primary.** However, this test of membership is not usually very stringent. Although in New York a person must announce his or her membership at some time before the primary election, in other states such as Iowa, the statement of membership can be made on election day itself. In a few states, such as Wisconsin, there is an **open primary,** meaning that the voter decides in the voting booth whether to participate as a Republican or Democrat.

Even more freedom is permitted in the unique "blanket primary" of Washington and Alaska, where the voter can select nominees of one party for one office, and then nominees of the other party for a different office. A further variation is the "runoff" primary, widely used in the South, in which nominations require an absolute majority of the votes cast. If no candidate wins this majority, a second contest is held between the two leading persons in the first poll.

EFFECTS OF PRIMARIES The direct primary is the most obvious institutional expression of the Progressive theory. It emphasizes popular participation and deliberately seeks to weaken the ability of party activists to control nominations. This effect exists even when participation in the primaries is legally confined to party members, for there is no real test applied to assess their loyalty. In open primaries, there is not even a pretense of restricting participation so that Republicans, for example, are free to affect the choice of their Democratic opponent. Obviously, the authority of the formal party organization is weakened. Runoff primaries also promote incohesion. This system allows factions and individuals to compete freely in the first primary, knowing that it is not likely to be decisive. Before the runoff primary, the various factions can bargain with each other and still maintain their separate existence.*

The United States is the only democracy in which voters at large participate in the selection of party nominees. In other nations, this power is reserved to the party members, and membership entails some significant obligations, such as paying dues and participating in an ongoing organization. In these countries, the party is seen as a distinctive body that should

*The effect of these primary systems on the parties is shown by Richard Tobin and Edward Keynes, "Institutional Differences in the Recruitment Process," *American Journal of Political Science,* 19 (Nov. 1975), pp. 667–82; and by Bradley Canon, "Isolating Causes of Factionalism in the South," in Robert Steed et al., ed., *Party Politics in the South* (New York: Praeger, 1980), chap. 2.

have the opportunity to consolidate its strength for the battle with the opposing forces. These parties select their nominees through internal processes, such as caucus meetings among leaders or conventions of the membership. Similar practices were in fact used by American parties as well, until the end of the nineteenth century, and some vestiges remain here, most notably in the presidential nominating conventions. For the most part, however, the formal power to control nominations has passed out of party hands.[26]

Informal Techniques Although the direct primary is formally used in all states, sometimes informal processes are more important. In a few areas, the party organization may be overwhelmingly strong. Occasionally, a city or county "boss" has the power to emerge from a closed caucus, announce the party's choices, and be confident that there will be no effective challenge in the primary itself. More often, even if there is a relatively active party, its endorsement of candidates comes only after a prolonged period of negotiations, and a party ticket is only assembled after competing claims are reconciled. The contending factions must determine, for example, whether a seat should go to the urban or suburban area of a combined district, whether a Catholic candidate is needed to "balance" the ticket, and, overall, which combination has the highest potential for victory.

Jack Kemp's fame as a football quarterback helped him to be elected a New York House representative. *(UPI/Bettmann Newsphotos)*

Individual Campaigns Most candidates must win their own nominations, since party endorsements are usually either unavailable or ineffective. They must themselves recruit a staff, write advertisements and literature, raise money, arrange meetings, canvass voters, and supervise the balloting. Typical American political campaigns are run like small businesses, not like branch outlets of a national conglomerate. Candidates must be individual entrepreneurs who enter the business of politics by offering their wares to a fickle public.

Congresspersons aptly illustrate this individualism. In a cohesive structure, such as that envisaged by the participatory theory, these national figures would be closely integrated into the state and national parties. In reality, representatives are loyal to the party at election time, but they operate independently of it. As one legislator put it bluntly:

> The party is no damn good . . . They can't organize and they can't raise money . . . I don't have anything to do with the party organization . . . They have their function. They give you a vehicle to run on. The real function of the party is to have someone to meet the candidate for Congress when he comes into a strange town.[27]

Essentially dependent on their own efforts to win a nomination, political aspirants use whatever resources are at hand. Glamor acquired as an athlete [Congressman and former Buffalo Bills' quarterback Jack Kemp] or as an astronaut [Senator John Glenn] is one resource. The services of nonparty consultants is another. Personal wealth is always useful, as Senator Frank Lautenberg showed in spending $3 million to be nominated and elected as senator from New Jersey. Widows, such as former Senator Muriel Humphrey, have sometimes benefited from their husbands' fame, but women are now achieving public notice on the basis of their own nonpolitical achievements. For example, former beauty queen Martha Layne Collins was elected governor of Kentucky in 1983.

Presidential Nominations

The American president is unique not only in the power he or she holds, but in the way he or she is nominated. Contradictions abound. Although the leader of the Republican or Democratic party, the presidential candidate is not selected by a deliberative choice of its leaders, or by the total party membership, but by a complicated, exhaustive, and expensive process. Although the personal representation of party unity, his or her nomination demonstrates the increasing fragmentation of these organizations. Although the formal method is the same as in the past 150 years, the reality of this process has changed considerably.

The essential point about presidential nominations is that they typically result from the ambitions and campaigning skills of individuals and their personal associates, not from the considered action of the parties as coherent organizations. They create coalitions of ideological, social, and personal interests that compete for the temporary leadership of the parties. The result of the struggle among these ambitious individuals is, to be sure, designation as the official Republican or Democratic candidate. The party, however, is little more than an arena in which the contest of individual gladiators takes place, rather than a decision-making body in its own right.

Historical Development In the earliest years of American history, presidential nominations were made by agreement among a party's national leaders. The formal mechanism was a congressional caucus, in which the party's representatives and senators met to select a single candidate who would receive the electoral votes won by the party in the several states. In use until 1824, this procedure resulted in the nomination and election of the "Virginia Dynasty" of presidents Jefferson, Madison, and Monroe. Potentially, the caucus might have developed into a parliamentary system, such as Britain's, in which the executive is chosen from, and responsible to, the legislative branch of government. When the selection of the president was removed from Congress, however, and came to be almost a direct popular choice, the separation of the branches became a political fact as well as a constitutional principle.

The replacement for the congressional caucus as a method of presidential nomination was the national nominating convention. First held before the 1832 election, the convention system was a more democratic means of nominating candidates but was still a party process. In form, although not in reality, it has remained the same up to the present. Delegates are apportioned among the states by formulas previously established by their national committees. The Republicans use the Electoral College as a base for this apportionment and then add "bonus" delegates to states that have voted for previous party candidates. The Democrats distribute votes among the states in accord with two factors, their total population and the total vote given to the previous presidential candidate.

In their heyday, the national party conventions were the scene of intense negotiating among the delegations from the various states. Each delegation would come to the party meeting with a fairly united block of votes, and prepared to bargain for some gain for itself—perhaps one of the nominations for its "favorite son," or promises of favorable treatment in jobs from the next administration, or a desired provision in the party platform. Negotiations might go on for days, sometimes requiring meetings in "smoke-filled" rooms (without air conditioning) or a series of ballots of the delegates before the required majority could be obtained. The legends of these conventions are among the more colorful in American history, a good example being the negotiations that led to Franklin Roosevelt's first nomination in 1932. Roosevelt, then governor of New York, had a majority of the delegates but lacked the required two-thirds support. He could obtain victory by adding the delegates supporting John Nance Garner, Speaker of the House. The managers of these two candidates met at a hot-dog stand at the convention, after the third ballot. They struck a deal to place Garner on the ticket as vice-president. Sealing this alliance, Garner's representative concluded, "We can iron out the details during the day. And will you pass the mustard?"[28]

Selection of Delegates The contemporary nominating convention is a mass gathering of party activists—about 4,000 Democrats and 2,000 Republicans—chosen according to the provisions of party rules and state laws. (Table 6.3 provides some data on 1984 delegates.) An absolute majority of all delegates is required to name the candidates for president and vice-president. (Until 1936, the Democrats required a two-thirds majority, causing frequent deadlocks.) The conventions also write a platform for the party, establish its national organization and rules, and begin the parties' campaigns for the White House.

The delegates are chosen in many different ways, and no two states are exactly the same. The principal methods are *presidential primaries* and *party caucuses or conventions.*

The presidential primaries are different from direct primaries, because the voters do not choose the actual presidential candidate. Instead, they choose delegates to the national conventions, or rate the popularity of potential candidates. They are used in twenty-five states and territories, as well as in three states where they are nonbinding "beauty contests."

In the typical primary, the voters choose among potential delegates who are pledged to support a particular presidential candidate at the convention. Then, the actual delegates are selected to reflect the proportional support given to each presidential hopeful, with the leading candidate often getting some bonus delegates. For example, when Walter Mondale won 36 percent of the vote in the 1984 Alabama primary, he received twenty-three of the state's fifty-two delegates to the Democratic convention.

Where party caucuses are used, local party meetings are held, open to any persons who consider themselves party members. These local meetings choose representatives, reflecting the meeting's proportional support for the presidential candidates. These representatives then go on to state party meetings or conventions, where the national convention delegates are finally chosen. In addition, some people are given the right to go to the

TABLE 6.3 National Convention Delegates in 1984

	Democrats	Republicans
Who They Were		
Men	50%	54%
Women	50	46
White	76	95
Black	18	4
Under 40 years old	37	19
Over 60 years old	22	11
Protestant	53	74
Catholic	32	22
Jewish	9	3
College graduate	70	63
Advanced degrees	44	29
Family income over $50,000	44	57
Family income under $25,000	16	10
Belong to labor union	27	5
Lawyers	14	10
Housewives	5	14
Blue-collar workers	3	1
Government worker or official	19	18
Labor leader	6	0
Business executive	13	32
Teachers and professionals	19	15
Attended previous conventions	29	34
Hold a party office	42	62
Hold a public office	29	28
What They Believed		
Philosophy		
Liberals	50	2
Moderates	42	22
Conservatives	5	76
Favor		
Decreased military spending	93	39
Nuclear freeze	90	62
Equal Rights Amendment*	92	29
Increased public employment spending	91	24
Affirmative action with quotas	41	6
Affirmative action without quotas	55	56
Increased spending on welfare	72	8
Increased spending on education	97	49
"Moral Majority"	9	52

Source: New York Times Delegate Survey, *The New York Times* (July 15, 1984); Los Angeles Times Poll, *Los Angeles Times* (July 15, Aug. 19–20, 1984).
*Poll of national party committees, cited in Martin Plissner and Warren Mitofsky, "Political Elites," *Public Opinion*, 4 (Oct./Nov. 1981), p. 49.

convention because they hold an important party office (such as national committee member) or an important public office (such as governor).

Changes in Nominations Important changes in the presidential nominating system have occurred in the past two decades. Beginning with a commission headed by George McGovern in 1969, the Democratic party has established five groups to revise party rules, and the Republicans have followed suit but less extensively. Resulting changes in party rules and state laws mean that more delegates are now chosen in state primaries rather than through internal party means. Where only a third of the delegates were selected by primaries in 1968, fully three-fourths were picked this way in 1980, and a substantial majority in 1984.

Rules changes have reduced the ability of the conventions to be flexible and to bargain among the groups present. Most of the delegates are elected as pledged to a particular candidate, and votes of each state are not united, but divided among the presidential candidates. To promote a different kind of representation, quotas or goals are established for such groups as women (guaranteed half of the Democratic delegate slots), racial minorities, and youth. Other groups, such as unions and teachers, make their own efforts to elect members as party delegates.

The major exception to these principles is the new Democratic rule, allocating 566 seats (14 percent) to unpledged party and elected officials. This change, instituted in 1984 and expanded in 1988, may allow the convention some room for maneuvering by party leaders. In general, however, emphasis—particularly among Democrats—has shifted from the convention as a gathering of party leaders to the convention as a representation of party groups and activists.

The national conventions have become giant television rallies, instead of places for making decisions. Here, First Lady Nancy Reagan reacts to seeing her husband, President Reagan, on a video monitor after her speech to the Republican National Convention in Dallas. *(AP/Wide World Photos)*

POLITICAL PERSPECTIVE

THE INFLUENCE OF INTEREST GROUPS ON PRESIDENTIAL NOMINATIONS

The influence of interest groups on presidential nominations became particularly strong in the Democratic party in 1984. Walter Mondale took an early lead in the race after he was endorsed by the AFL-CIO, the first time the labor federation had ever united in support of a candidate before the conventions. Women, as represented by the National Organization for Women, were another vital part of Mondale's coalition, and they strongly urged the nomination of a woman for vice-president. Threatening a convention floor fight, they won their goal when Mondale selected Geraldine Ferraro as his running mate, the first female candidate on a major party's national ticket. Blacks also showed their power in 1984, providing almost unanimous support for Reverend Jesse Jackson, the first significant black candidate for president. Although Jackson never had a serious chance to win the nomination, he did win concessions in the party platform and gained new respect for blacks within the party.

The Nominating Campaign The national nominating system has now become a race between individuals, in which persons operate largely outside of the established party organizations and seek victory by attracting a combination of attention from the mass media, popular support in direct state primaries and caucuses, and high standing in public opinion polls. These three rings of the nominating circus have replaced the single arena of the nominating convention. Yet, this is a circus in which the activities in each of the rings affects the others. Candidates who receive attention from the media—particularly the television networks and the weekly newsmagazines—rise in the public opinion polls and are more likely to win state electoral contests; similarly a victory in an isolated primary will increase a candidate's media coverage and poll standing.*

The visible nominating season takes several months. State primaries usually begin in New Hampshire in February and conclude in California in June. Iowa holds the first local caucuses in February, and these meetings continue through the spring. The process culminates with four-day conventions, held in July (usually for the party out of power, which needs more time to campaign) and August (for the party in power, the Republicans in 1984).

Contemporary nominating campaigns in many ways resemble an elimination contest in sports. Candidates who do poorly in one or two states are likely to run short of funds, to decline in the polls, to be written off by the media, and soon to drop out of the race. The formal process also allows little opportunity for a candidate to recover. In 1984, selection of nearly a majority of delegates had been substantially completed by March 20th—ten months before the next presidential inauguration. As in 1980, this rush to judgment left the parties no way to change their minds if political circumstances changed.

*Recent important works on the new system of presidential nominations are John Aldrich, *Before the Convention* (Chicago: U. of Chicago, 1980); William Crotty, *Party Reform* (New York: Longman, 1983); Scott Keeter and Cliff Zukin, *Uninformed Choice* (New York: Praeger, 1983); and Thomas Marshall, *Presidential Nominations in a Reform Age* (New York: Praeger, 1981).

A convention almost always knows its presidential candidate before it even meets, and no party conference has required more than a single ballot since 1952. Instead of making this choice, the convention devotes itself to rousing the spirits of the party and uniting behind its chosen candidate. A vice-presidential candidate remains to be designated, and this task usually falls to the presidential nominee. He or she consults with other party leaders and then suggests a candidate to the convention who can bring some added strength to the national ticket. Rarely is this choice challenged.

Problems in Presidential Nominations The new system of presidential nominations evidences both the progressive and participatory theories of parties. Progressive elements are present in the increased importance of the mass electorate in choosing delegates and thereby indirectly naming the candidate. Most Americans, according to opinion polls, would prefer to go even further and institute a national presidential primary. Participatory elements can be found in the requirements for the representation of demographic groups and in the stress on programmatic objectives for many delegates.

The new system of presidential nominations, with its stress on participation, raises two kinds of problems. Although more people are involved in the process, it is not clear that the result is truly democratic. Only about a quarter of those eligible actually vote in primaries. Moreover, they are not fully representative of the population, being drawn disproportionately from persons with more education, higher social class, and, sometimes, more distinctive policy views. The quality of popular decisions in primaries is also uncertain. A detailed study shows that relatively little voter learning is accomplished in these contests and that the system is one "in which chance and circumstance play an important role in determining which candidates succeed and which ones fail."[29]

For the parties themselves, the result of these changes is further fragmentation. A party that cannot itself choose its national leaders can hardly be expected to be effective in implementing a policy program. When presidents can win nominations with little assistance from other party leaders, such as governors, senators, and representatives, this method limits their ability to work together, making the party weaker as a bridge between governmental institutions. Furthermore, party leaders provide a kind of "peer review," a knowledgeable assessment of the ability of individuals to handle the difficult task of governing the United States. The participatory theory, carried to an extreme, would eliminate peer review, promoting a "disjunction between the qualities required to win the presidential nomination of one's party and the qualities required to be a good president."[30]

Parties and Policy

Elections are the most obvious work of American parties. Less frequently and less obviously, the parties also affect policy results. This influence is not as direct as in other matters, such as their effect on nominations. Our parties are too fragmented to be able to present and enact an ideological program in the way available to such foreign organizations as the British Conservatives or the French Socialists. Still, amid many other influences we discuss throughout the book, the parties do make a contribution.

Progressive theory gives little weight to the policy functions of parties, since it emphasizes unmediated ties between the individual citizens and their elected officials. In the participatory theory, policy issues are a major concern, and parties are intended to be vital links between mass opinion and government action. The competitive theory is not directly concerned with such programs. However, in this theory, as parties pursue their primary goal of electoral victory, they inevitably affect the policy decisions of government.

Governmental Coordination

The governmental structure of the United States, as we have stressed, fragments power among the branches of government, the states and the national government, and public and private authorities. Common party loyalty often provides a glue to join these dismembered parts. Instances of such cooperation include the weekly meetings between the president and the leaders of his party in the House and Senate, the party caucuses in each chamber of Congress, the frequent sessions of the Democratic or Republican governors, and the two parties' national committees.

Party Cooperation The various officials in government need to cooperate because the multiple checks and balances of the political system require their agreement before any action is taken. The political party is one structure that eases this cooperation. It has the advantage for this purpose of being more than an impersonal bureaucracy. Officeholders tend to have strong emotional ties to their party. They join it early, spend many years campaigning under its banner, share friendships in it, and are grateful for its support.

Self-interest reinforces these emotional ties. Whether they like the fact or not, politicians' careers are affected by the public's general evaluations of the Republican or Democratic parties. Electoral tides tend to sweep out to sea or to bring safely to shore persons floating on the same party raft, even if they actually agree little in their programs.

One of the strongest influences in congressional elections, along with economic conditions, has been the relative unpopularity of the president.[31] When the public is unhappy with the chief executive, it tends to vote against candidates of his or her party. This has led to such results as the defeat of twenty-six incumbent Republicans during the economic recession of 1982 and the ouster of thirty-three Democrats amid the Carter defeat of 1980.

Coattails When a popular individual is in office or on the party ticket, other candidates hope that they can be carried along to victory, by holding on to the leader's **coattails.** This interest also makes candidates look for an attractive candidate to head the ticket, a person who will bring added votes to all of them. As a legend has it, a Democratic local leader in Brooklyn assured a minor candidate that his success was guaranteed by Franklin Roosevelt's position as the ticket leader:

> Listen. Did you ever go down to the wharf to see the Staten Island Ferry come in? You ever watch it, and look down in the water at all those chewing-gum wrappers, and the banana peels and the garbage? When the ferryboat comes into the wharf, automatically it pulls all the garbage in too. The name of your ferryboat is Franklin D. Roosevelt—stop worrying![32]

As candidates have become individual campaigners, however, the length of a popular candidate's coattails has shortened considerably, and most candidates today must pull themselves to victory by their own bootstraps. In House elections, the factor of incumbency has become dominant, protecting officeholders in both good and bad times. Able to use the considerable perquisites of office to ride above party tides, nearly 95 percent of incumbents have been able to win reelection each year.* With their own safety virtually ensured, Representatives have less reason to support the programs of their party leader, the president.

Party Platforms

Another means by which a party influences policy is through the **party platform,** a projected plan of action adopted at the national convention. In writing their platforms, parties evidence their function as brokers. In an effort to win group support, they make promises to diverse interests, and often compromise contending claims. In contemporary times, the party documents run to dozens of pages and are likely to include over 500 pledges of future action, each designed to win support from one group or another. Government loans may be promised for small business or college students, Irish-Americans may be courted by advocacy of Ulster's unification with the Republic of Ireland, while the conflict over school segregation may be evaded by a bland declaration that "The supreme law of the land is embodied in the Constitution, which guarantees to all persons the blessings of liberty, due process, and equal protection of the laws."†

These statements of party principles have often been condemned as structures "to run on, not to stand on." As Barry Goldwater reiterated the conventional wisdom, "platforms are written to be ignored and forgotten. Drafters search for God and Motherhood declarations calculated to please everyone and offend no one . . . Like Jell-O shimmering on a dessert plate, there is usually little substance and nothing you can get your teeth into."[33]

*See Barbara Hinckley, "The American Voter in Congressional Elections," *American Political Science Review*, 74 (Sept. 1980), pp. 641–50; *Congressional Elections* (Washington: Congressional Quarterly Press, 1981), chap. 3; and George Edwards, "The Impact of Presidential Coattails on Outcomes of Congressional Elections," *American Politics Quarterly*, 7 (Jan. 1979), pp. 94–108.

†This statement is from the 1956 Republican platform and was matched by the Democrats' evasiveness in recognizing "the Supreme Court of the United States as one of the three Constitutional and coordinate branches of the Federal Government." Donald B. Johnson, ed., *National Party Platforms, 1840–1976* (Urbana: U. of Illinois, 1978), pp. 542–44. Since then, both parties have strongly endorsed the Supreme Court's decision and school desegregation. They have also taken relatively clear and distinct positions on a more current civil rights issue, school busing.

Platform Content Despite this reputation, the platforms actually are given a great deal of attention. The parties now begin preparing their statements early in the presidential year, hold public hearings throughout the nation, and spend weeks before the national convention in preparing the documents. Interest groups make great efforts to have their favored policies included, and once in office, the administration and bureaucracy use the platform as one of the sources from which they develop specific governmental programs.[34] At times, in fact, the platforms may cause more controversy within parties than the nomination of the president and vice-president. In 1984, the fiercest argument at the conventions concerned the platforms. Mondale made concessions to his opponents on foreign policy and affirmative action, while Republicans were sharply divided over the party's failure to endorse the Equal Rights Amendment.

Detailed analysis of platforms has shown that only about one out of six statements consists of "hot air" or "rhetoric," such as "Ethnic Americans have enriched this nation with their hard work, self-reliance and respect for the rights and needs of others." Twice as common are statements that evaluate the parties' policies, particularly those of the incumbents, as exemplified by the Republicans' 1984 statement, "Despite Democratic opposition we succeeded in reducing the tax rates of all taxpayers by about 25 percent," and the Democrats' counterattack on "the huge tax cuts to benefit the wealthy."

The largest part of the typical platform, about half, consists of pledges of future action, sometimes as vague as promises of "peace and liberty" but more often relatively precise statements on such matters as defense bases, tax rates, or the union shop. Overall, party promises tend to be vague in regard to such abstract and distant matters as foreign policy or economic management. By contrast, where there are particular voting blocs and organized interest groups at hand, platform pledges tend to be quite detailed. The parties will then commit themselves to specific policies in regard to such matters as labor policy, social welfare, natural resources, and agriculture.[35]

Platform Action Once adopted, the platform often serves as the basis for governmental policy. Officeholders know that their platforms—even if ignored by most voters—are read by the opposition, and that they will be held to account in the next election. President Carter's staff compiled a list of campaign promises as a guide to legislative action, and President Reagan has frequently cited his election victories as "mandates" for enactment of the party's platform.

Detailed analysis shows that platforms do mean something. Even in the politically incohesive period of 1968–1978, two-thirds of the promises made by the party holding the White House were acted on, and this record of fulfillment was even better in earlier years (1944–1966), when four of every five promises by the "in-party" were redeemed.[36] Just as Jimmy Carter rejected the B-1 bomber and closed some tax loopholes, as the Democrats promised in 1976, so Ronald Reagan had substantially increased defense spending and reduced income taxes, as his party pledged in 1980. These data show that party leaders often do what they say—a result surprising only if we think of politicians as unusually dishonest.

Party Differences

A frequent characterization, and complaint, of the two major parties is their basic similarity on public issues. Even Tocqueville admitted, "To a stranger all the domestic controversies of the Americans at first appear to be incomprehensible or puerile, and he is at a loss whether to pity a people who take such errant trifles in good earnest or to envy that happiness which enables a community to discuss them."[37] More angrily, George Wallace complained that there wasn't "a dime's worth of difference" between the parties.

The parties' desire for victory results in a lessening of their differences, as each seeks to take those middle positions on which most Americans stand.[38] Their actions are similar to those of automobile manufacturers, who produce cars that are very similar to one another as they seek to capture the mass market. Yet, it is not true that the parties are identical, just as car buyers find differences between Fords and Chevys. Issue differences can be found in the positions taken by presidential candidates, in party platforms, and on the floor of Congress. Thus, in a detailed study of the 1968 election, Page found significant differences between the two major parties' voters on half of the issues, and equivalent differences between the candidates.[39] The most common differences—whether between voters, presidential candidates, or national lawmakers—are on issues of social welfare and economic policy, the longstanding basis of party division. In 1984, further differences were evident on many issues, including ratification of ERA, environmental regulation, defense spending, and economic policy.*

Party Coalitions The causes of party difference are suggested by these data. The candidates of the Republican and Democratic parties take different positions because their supporters have different beliefs (see Table 7.3 in the next chapter). In each election, the candidates must first secure their base and make sure that those identified with their party will actually come to the polls. Therefore, they cannot abandon established party stands. It is especially important that the candidates appeal to the party activists who carry the campaign to the precincts, the contributors who finance the primaries and most general elections, and the interest groups that provide endorsements and workers. Since these groups are likely to have definite issue positions, the party and its candidates must respond to their demands.

Each party is a coalition of many groups, but they are not mirror images of one another. As we will see in Chapter 7, conservatives heavily predominate in the Republican party, whereas liberal opinion is concentrated (but not predominant) within the Democratic party.[40] To mobilize its vote, the party must appeal to these different ideological groups and must hold the support of key population elements. A Democrat can never expect to win nationally without a large union vote, and a Republican must secure strong support from businesspeople. These political necessities guarantee that the parties will differ on such issues as union and business regulation.

Parties in Congress What happens in Congress reflects the two-party character of the American political system. As many as half of the floor votes in the national legislature find a majority of Democrats lined up against a majority of Republicans, creating what are called "party unity"

*See Henry Plotkin, "Issues in the Campaign," in *The Election of 1984,* Gerald Pomper, ed. (Chatham, NJ: Chatham House, 1985), chap. 2.

votes. When these issues arise, Senators and Representatives usually "come to the aid of the party." In 1983, for example, only twenty-seven members voted against their Democratic or Republican colleagues on a majority of these "party unity" roll calls.[41]

Party unity depends on the programs being considered. It becomes more evident on issues, particularly domestic matters, that the president emphasizes. Partisan conflict is particularly likely on issues that call into battle the different interest groups behind each party, such as controversies over fiscal policy, labor, agriculture, and welfare. In recent years, the parties have divided most fully on spending priorities in the national budget. As illustrated in Figure 6.3, Democrats have given greater emphasis to social

FIGURE 6.3
The Parties Do (and Don't) Agree
Party differences in Congress depend on the specific issues under debate. The four issues illustrated here are drawn from key votes in Congress during the 1983 session.* These are not always the final roll call, which may be only a formality. Sometimes the key vote comes on an amendment or even a procedural motion. (*Based on government figures in* Congressional Quarterly Weekly Report, *41 [Dec. 3, 1983], 2551–55.*)

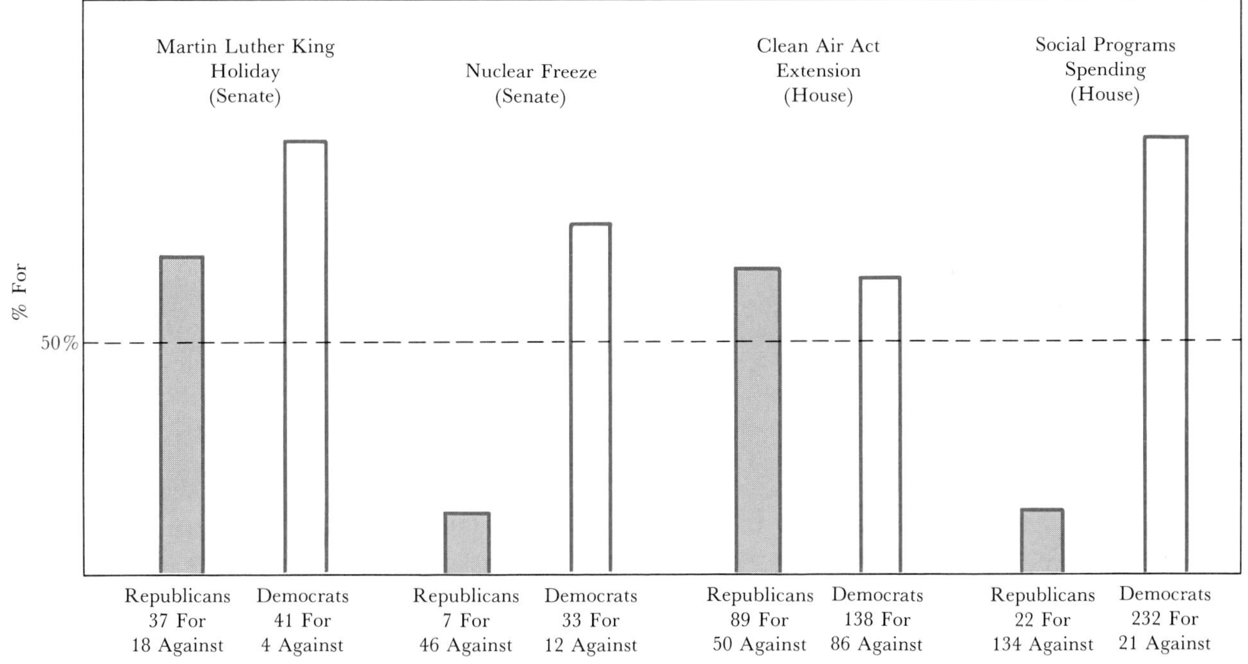

*The four votes we have selected are:

1. Senate passage of a bill (HR 3706) to declare the third Monday in January a legal public holiday honoring the Rev. Dr. Martin Luther King.
2. Senate support of a resolution calling for a mutual, verifiable freeze on U.S. and Soviet nuclear weapons. In the complex parliamentary situation, support for the freeze came in the form of opposition to a motion to kill a nuclear freeze amendment to another bill (HJRes 308).
3. House support for an extension of existing provisions of the Clean Air Act. The actual vote came on an amendment to an appropriations bill (HR 3133), which would extend a deadline for local communities to meet national air standards.
4. House support for adding almost a billion dollars to the federal budget, to be spent on education, job training, energy assistance, and other social programs (HJRes 403).

What do these votes tell you about party unity in Congress?

spending, Republicans to defense expenditures. These differences mean that party differences are also ideological differences.[42]

The parties do not have the consistent and certain cohesion that would be required to make a reality of the policy emphasis desired by the participatory theory. Yet, they show more unity than would be expected if parties were only the power-seeking groups envisaged in the competitive theory. Their ability to affect policy outcomes, however, is reduced by the continuing impact of changes inspired by the Progressive theory. Their future status is the subject of the last section.

The Changing Parties

American parties first arose when the nation had 4 million inhabitants primarily engaged in agriculture. They flourished during the nineteenth century as urbanization and industrialization took hold and the population grew to over 100 million. In the twentieth century, particularly in the last three decades, they have changed in response to the new character of the United States as a nation that is highly developed technologically, a world power, suburban and mobile in its living patterns, and bureaucratic in its organization. In many respects, these changes have meant lessened party effectiveness.

The Decline of Parties

Parties in Elections The evidence for the decline of parties is primarily related to their electoral functions. Voting analysis, which we turn to in the next chapter, shows that fewer voters identify as loyal Republicans and Democrats, with this trend toward independence concentrated in those voters who have come of age since 1960. There is less voting on the basis of party loyalty and more of a willingness to split tickets, choosing a presidential candidate of one party, for example, while casting a ballot for a congressional aspirant of the other party.[43]

With a weaker electoral base, the parties are less important in conducting elections. Presidential nominations are now almost entirely decided through the campaigns of individual candidates. The primary system of nominations for other offices also encourages candidates to wage campaigns separately from the party, while the growing importance of interest group endorsements and funds increases the likelihood of success of this autonomous strategy.

The electoral decline of parties also affects their performance of their other functions. Electoral fortunes provide less of a tie among campaigners than in the past. In some recent elections, a "split-ticket" has been chosen in nearly half of the nation's congressional districts, with the voters choosing presidential and congressional candidates of opposite parties. If representatives, particularly incumbents, receive no help from the president's coattails, they will have less reason to support the programs of the chief executive. Platform fulfillment has dropped in the past decade, and party has also become less important in congressional organization and floor voting. These trends parallel the decline of partisanship at the ballot box.

The emotional attraction of parties also appears to have diminished. Certainly, fewer persons identify with the political parties. Parties no longer provide the central focus for the citizenry's political involvement. Although about a tenth of the nation attends rallies or works in campaigns (often outside of the party organization), far more participate in other forms of politics—trying to persuade others how to vote (37 percent in 1976), giving money, or participating in demonstrations. Other forms of political activity outside of the parties appear to be more common, but party work remains at a low or diminishing level.

Political Consultants The role of parties has also been challenged by a new kind of political strategist, the political consultant. Expert in advertising, polling, and media campaigning, the political consultants gain influence because of these specialized skills, not because of their service to the party. Working primarily for profit, they provide candidates with services that are vital in today's elections. American parties have always been concerned primarily with winning, rather than governing, and the new consultants continue this traditional emphasis. Yet, consultants are also different, because their interests are almost exclusively focused on winning elections, and they have no responsibility for the traditions, leadership, or policy record of the parties. As they take on more of the electoral responsibilities, they further enfeeble the parties' ability to carry on other functions.[44]

Causes of Decline One explanation for party decline is general trends in American society. The cohesion of local communities has been undermined by the assimilation of ethnic groups, the extensive geographical mobility of Americans, family instability, and the low density housing of suburbia. Because they have been rooted in such local communities, parties have particularly felt the effects of these changes. Furthermore, parties have tradition-

Political consultants and advertising specialists have taken on much of the parties' traditional roles in elections. Here, White House Press Secretary Jody Powell (left) talks with Gerald Rafshoon, who was added to President Carter's staff as a presidential assistant for communications. *(UPI/Bettmann Newsphotos)*

ally relied on direct and personal contacts. With a population of more than half a million persons in each congressional district, campaigning inevitably becomes massive in scale and relies on communication through the impersonal mass media. Parties cannot provide either the money or the technical expertise to run such campaigns.*

Beyond these basic social trends, the parties have been weakened by the actions of governments, sometimes unintentionally. A long series of statutes, usually seen as reforms, have limited their capacity. Over the long period of the twentieth century, the most important legal factor in the decline of the parties has been the institution of the nominating primary. By taking the critical function of nominations away from the organized parties, the primary created the likelihood that this system would eventually be used to their own advantage by individualistic candidates, by contributors, and by particular interest groups.

The impulse toward party reform exemplified by the primary has also been evident in other measures. They include restricting or prohibiting the party's endorsement of candidates in the primaries, allowing persons identified with the opposition to participate in an open primary, choosing local government officials on nonpartisan ballots, holding gubernatorial elections in nonpresidential years, eliminating party patronage from the government bureaucracy in favor of universal civil service, forbidding campaign activity or contributions by these government workers, and funneling government's financial contributions to campaigns directly to candidates while bypassing the organized parties.

The Revival of Parties?

To some observers, this gloomy picture of party decline is exaggerated, or even perverse. They see parties changing, adapting to a new environment, but not disappearing. Indeed, they find that the parties are now undergoing renewal. This revival is particularly evident in the organizational structures of the parties, in contrast to their hold on the electorate.

In recent years, the state party organizations have been strengthened, and this development is likely to lead to greater party cohesion. Over the past two decades, full-time state party leadership and professional staffs have been established in virtually every state. The central state parties now provide such technical facilities as computerized voter lists, direct mail services and public opinion polls. Over two-thirds of these organizations now engage in voter registration and turnout campaigns, and half are involved in the development of public policy stands. In contrast to the decline of party loyalty among voters, then, the party organizations have become stronger.[45]

*For analyses of these social trends and of legal developments, see Austin Ranney, *Curing the Mischiefs of Faction* (Berkeley: University of California, 1975), pp. 121–31; Nelson W. Polsby, "The News Media as an Alternative to Party in the Presidential Selection Process," in *Political Parties in the Eighties,* Robert A. Goldwin, ed. (Washington: American Enterprise Institute, and Gambier, Ohio: Kenyon College, 1980); and V. O. Key, *Politics, Parties, and Pressure Groups,* 5th ed. (New York: Crowell, 1964), p. 342.

POLITICAL PERSPECTIVE

A NEW POLITICAL BOSS?

David Garth is one of the most prominent political consultants, and has run campaigns for such major candidates as New York Mayor Ed Koch and Independent presidential contender John Anderson. This portrait sketches his techniques and personality.

Garth talks like Damon Runyon, thinks like Niccolo Machiavelli, and clutches his thin Dannemann cigars like Edward G. Robinson. He combines the personal style of the clubhouse boss with the professionalism required in the new era: he has something more potent to dispense than patronage. It's in such demand that he has become powerful in his own right. He embodies the past in his manner, recalling the denizens of Tammany Hall, while possessing the latest in video politics. When the party bosses went into decline, the media masters filled the vacuum with television commercials. They became the new power brokers. . . .

In political campaigns, Garth deploys a full-service blitz. Some consulting firms consist of a small nucleus that expands during the election season and contracts after the balloting. David Garth and Associates is always pumping at maximum strength. His research staff works year in, year out. A candidate taken on by Garth is investigated to establish the veracity of his claims and to ensure that he is impervious to criticism. Then his achievements are highlighted in the ad campaign and stitched into the overall strategy, which includes research into the opponent's record and statements. Any unsubstantiated remark the opponent may have made can work against him, turning his credibility into an issue itself. Polling is done in-house, too. Garth used to rely on outsiders, but now he prefers his own operation. As a campaign goes down to the wire the polling intensifies. In the beginning there are monthly polls, then weekly polls, then a poll every few days, then daily polls.

Not a single palpitation in public opinion escapes Garth. By running the polling himself, he controls the interpretation of the figures. He insists on consistency. Once the themes are devised the candidate must gallop at Garth's speed. It's a carefully calibrated campaign.

Garth's success has a profound impact beyond his immediate campaigns; he deeply affects politicians and political consultants generally. He is an industry leader. "The emphasis placed on his media wizardry is all wrong," contends his former colleague Jeff Greenfield. "The key to David is that he's a first-rate political analyst. If we were back in 1931 David would still be an invaluable political adviser." There's always a question of whether Garth and his ads are implementing strategy or setting it.

But if others are confused, Garth understands very well what he's doing. "Politicians have always gone where the voters are," he says. "When the voters turned out at local fairs, the pols were there. When the voters listened to the radio, the pols were there. When the voters didn't leave their houses and sat in front of their television tubes, the pols went on television. So the politicians have always gone where the voters have gone. The result has been a real diminution of the power of the parties. What really strikes me now is that a lot of political writers are nostalgic about the bosses, which is really horseshit. As if the machines ever turned out high-quality candidates. Imagery is nothing new. Most of it hasn't happened by accident. Manipulation by publishers and bosses is nothing new. It's the style of manipulation that's new, except for the fact that the voter is more informed with the lousy commercials than he was before."

Source: Sidney Blumenthal, *The Permanent Campaign* (New York: Simon & Schuster, 1982). Copyright © 1980, 1982 by Sidney Blumenthal.

Republicans: The Competitive Party The two major parties have emphasized different patterns of renewal. Among Republicans, change has been in keeping with the competitive theory of parties, aiming to make the party a more efficient contestant in elections. Recent actions include appointing regional directors; hiring by the Republican National Committee of an organizational director for each state; joint fundraising for all party groups, particularly through individual contributions garnered by direct-mail appeals; provision of technical assistance in fundraising, computer processing, polling, advertising, and election analysis; selective registration drives; and active recruiting and training of candidates.

The national party has been fully institutionalized, with its own building in Washington and a staff of over 300 people. Receiving small contributions from nearly 2 million individuals, the national committee now has a two-year budget of $110-135 million. In marked contrast to the past, John Bibby suggests, the Republicans are no longer a party that is decentralized, weak, or obsolete. The party has become an effective competitor in the political marketplace by applying the techniques of modern management.[46]

Democrats: The Participatory Party Change in the Democratic party has been of a sharply different direction, in line with the participatory theory. Procedural innovations have been adopted in an effort to convert the national organization into a representative voice of rank-and-file Democrats. These changes are most evident in the party's supreme bodies, the national convention, and the national committee. They include establishing the authority of the national party to regulate the composition of state party delegations; requiring these delegations to include women, racial minorities, and young people in proportion to their numbers within the Democratic ranks; opening the presidential nominating process to the rank and file, either through presidential primaries or procedural reforms of local caucuses while restricting the role of leaders; making primary decisions binding on convention delegates; and enlarging the national committee and making it more representative. The stress on policy issues was shown in the creation of midterm conventions, consisting largely of locally elected delegates, to adopt a national party charter, or constitution (1974), or to discuss public policy issues (1978).[47] The theory underlying Democratic party revision has been that of the party as a mass movement. In this broad-based party, the job of the party leadership is not to run an efficient organization from above but to represent the views emerging from the membership.

Women have become an important organized group within the Democratic party. Here Betty Friedan speaks to a crowd at an ERA rally. *(Jean-Claude Lejeune/EKM-Nepenthe)*

After their national defeats in 1980 and 1984, the Democrats altered course. Some party leaders felt that the party, in stressing participation, might have neglected electoral effectiveness. Looking at finance alone, the Democrats found themselves consistently in debt, unable to provide a single dollar for state candidates in 1980, and less able to raise small contributions than even John Anderson. To meet the problem, Democrats emphasized centralized funding. Although still outspent 3–1 by the Republicans, the Democrats were able to spend about $100 million through these bodies in 1984.

The Democrats have now turned to a new stress on organizational improvement and electoral effectiveness. Symbolized by the opening of a permanent headquarters in Washington, this new stress was exemplified by devoting the 1982 midterm conference to electoral techniques and limiting it to party leaders, and by canceling a 1986 conference completely. Elected officials and party leaders were given new power in selecting the 1984 presidential nominee and in writing the rules for the 1988 convention, while less recognition was given to specialized groups such as homosexuals, Asian-

Americans, and blacks. In Congress, the party caucus developed a series of policy proposals that formed the basis of the party platform for 1984.[48]

Reflecting the increased homogenization of American life and increased centralization of government, the party organizations are becoming competitive within most states and unified throughout the country. Like large corporations, they are becoming entrepreneurs, cultivating their electoral markets as they seek to win mass loyalties. Their programs and their leadership are now recognizably distinct. They appeal to particular, although overlapping, voter coalitions. Their officials vote differently in Congress and act differently in the White House. Together, these developments suggest the emergence of a truly *national* two-party system.

A Future for Parties?

In the long American discussion of political parties, the focus of debate has been between the competitive model and Progressive model. Although some have urged the participatory model, it has not often either described the real ways parties work or won wide acceptance. The competitive model has been descriptively accurate in many instances, but parties themselves have not enjoyed great popularity.

The Progressive theory has been more widely accepted and continues to affect the parties today. Most of the trends we have discussed in this chapter are either legal embodiments of Progressive thought—such as the direct primary or financial subsidies for individual candidates—or the consequence of broad social developments—such as personalistic campaigning, mass media and interest group influence, and party incohesion within government. Republicans and Democrats have reacted differently in attempting to renew themselves in these conditions, but both are threatened by the dominance of Progressive thought.

There are signs, to be sure, that the parties and some of the public recognize the problem. Republicans are well on the way to creating an efficient vote-seeking organization coordinated and jointly financed from national to state and local levels. The significance of these changes for public policy was shown in the common program and joint campaigning of Ronald Reagan and the party's congressional candidates, and in their unity after the election. Democrats, for their part, are attempting to build a broad-based participatory party and are now taking steps to increase their electoral effectiveness as well. Prestigious groups have called for measures to strengthen the parties "as a means of achieving compromise among the conflicting demands of citizens and as a link between citizens and elected officials."[49] There is growing recognition, then, of the important functions of American parties. Whether the parties can still be rescued remains an open question.

The parties' functions, which we listed at the beginning of the chapter, continue to be essential in American politics, and we know of no other democratic bodies able to take on their role. If parties do not manage elections, they will be incoherent personality contests. If parties do not mobilize collective action, Americans will be more isolated and less potent, particularly the poor and the inarticulate. If parties are unavailable as carriers of emotional loyalties, more threatening cults and antidemocratic movements may take their place. If parties do not structure public opinion, less responsible advertisers, consultants, and the mass media will assume the job. If parties do not broker diverse groups, single interests will expand their fragmenting activity. If parties do not provide a link between voters and public policy, the electorate will become even more repelled by the apparent inattentiveness of government to its needs. If parties fail to coordinate institutions, coherent government action becomes virtually unattainable through the consent of the governed.

Fragmentation pervades the politics of the United States, from the institutional separations of the Constitution to the contentious strivings of policy groups. Parties, too, have reflected and sometimes even reinforced this fragmentation. Yet, many observers believe that "modern democracy is unthinkable save in terms of parties."[50] And parties have also helped to overcome such fragmentation. Unknowingly, sometimes unwillingly, certainly not unselfishly, they have made it easier for millions of citizens to operate a democratic government of multiple conflicts. Will our parties again play this role or will they reinforce fragmentation? This may be the most uncertain question for the future.

SUMMARY

Three different attitudes toward the parties are found in American political thinking. In the Progressive theory, which supports direct democracy, parties are viewed as unnecessary institutions that intervene between the government and the public. Advocates of the participatory theory want to achieve a coherent party program through the activity of enthusiastic partisans. The competitive theory sees parties and politicians as primarily interested in winning elections and gaining power. In this interpretation parties are seen as benefiting society indirectly, since they must serve the public in order to be victorious.

American political parties are most important for their ability to overcome the fragmentation of American life. They manage elections, organize public opinion and link it to government, increase political opportunities for individuals by gathering them in collective movements to achieve power, focus the loyalties of a diverse population, promote a common cause among different interests, and coordinate the institutions of government.

American political history evidences five periods of party competition, from the time of John Adams and Thomas Jefferson to the current contests of Democrats and Republicans. Usually, there have been only two major parties; however, third parties have had significant impacts.

The formal organization of parties begins at the precinct, or local election district, and builds up to the national committees. With its localized roots, the party is characteristically a fragmented organization. There is no uniform pattern to the organization of state and local parties, but the traditional *machine* has largely disappeared.

The parties are finding it ever more difficult to keep pace with the rising cost of election campaigns. Abuses in the system of political contributions led to national laws curtailing individual donations. Replacing them in importance are political action committees (PACs). These powerful organizations, representing narrow interests, threaten to fragment further American parties. Paralleling this change is the shift from party-centered to candidate-centered campaigning. With most nominations to office made through the *direct primary,* individuals usually must win the party label through their own efforts.

Presidential nominations are formally made at national party conventions, but they are no longer critical places for decision making or negotiation. Presidential candidates operate largely outside of the established party organizations and seek victory by attracting a combination of attention from the mass media, popular support in direct state primaries and caucuses, and high standing in public opinion polls.

Parties affect public policy in a number of ways. Officials from the same party work together in government. Party platforms express their programs, and often commit them to detailed action. Although the two major parties tend to gravitate toward the middle, they are divided on issues of social welfare and economic policy. These differences also are evident in the ways members of Congress vote.

Party influence in elections has declined. Fewer voters identify themselves as loyal members. This trend, along with the new role of campaign consultants, encourages independence among candidates and officeholders. At the same time, some observers detect a renewal of the party organizations. The national Republican party, in line with the competitive theory, has become fully institutionalized. Democrats, in keeping with the participatory theory, have attempted to convert their party into a more representative voice of its membership.

NOTES

1. American Political Science Association, Committee on Political Parties, "Toward a More Responsible Two-Party System," *American Political Science Review,* 44 (Sept. 1950), supplement, p. 1.
2. Joseph Schumpeter, *Capitalism, Socialism and Democracy* (New York: Harper, 1950), p. 269.
3. Joseph Charles, *The Origins of the American Party System* (New York: Harper, 1956); Noble Cunningham, "Presidential Leadership, Political Parties, and the Congressional Caucus, 1820–1824," in Patricia Bonomi et al., *The American Constitutional System under Strong and Weak Parties* (New York: Praeger, 1981), pp. 1–20.
4. Kathleen Frankovic, "Public Opinion Trends," in *The Election of 1980,* Gerald Pomper, ed. (Chatham, N.J.: Chatham, 1981), chap. 4.
5. The evolution of the Electoral College is ably analyzed in Richard McCormick, *The Election Game* (New York: Oxford U. P., 1982).
6. *Buckley* v. *Valeo,* 424 U.S. 1 (1976).
7. Jody Carlson, *George C. Wallace and the Politics of Powerlessness* (New Brunswick, N.J.: Transaction Books, 1981), chap. 8.
8. See V. O. Key, Jr., *Politics, Parties and Pressure Groups,* 5th ed. (New York: Crowell, 1964), chap. 4; Steven Rosenstone, *Third Parties in America* (Princeton: Princeton U. P., 1984).
9. *Smith* v. *Allwright,* 321 U.S. 649 (1944).
10. E. E. Schattschneider, *Party Government* (New York: Holt, 1942), pp. 59ff.
11. Malcolm Jewell and David Olson, *American State Political Parties and Elections* (Homewood, Ill.: Dorsey, 1978), chap. 3, especially pp. 55–58; John Owens, Edward Constatini, and Louis Weschler, *California Politics and Parties* (New York: Macmillan, 1970).
12. Cornelius Cotter and John Bibby, "Institutional Development of Parties and the Thesis of Party Decline," *Political Science Quarterly,* 95 (Spring 1980), pp. 1–27; and Cotter and Bibby, *National Party Committees and Political Change* (New York: Longman, 1986).
13. Harold Gosnell, *Machine Politics: Chicago Model,* 2nd ed. (Chicago: U. of Chicago, 1968), chap. 2 and p. 41.
14. Lincoln Steffens, *Autobiography* (New York: Harcourt, 1931), p. 618.
15. Herbert McCloskey et al., "Issue Conflict and Consensus among Party Leaders and Followers," *American Political Science Review,* 54 (June 1960), pp. 406–27; Jeane Kirkpatrick, "Representation in the American National Conventions," *British Journal of Political Science,* 5 (July 1975), pp. 265–322; *Los Angeles Times Poll* (Aug. 2, 1981); Alan Abramowitz et al., "Party Activists in the United States," *International Political Science Review,* 4 (1983), pp. 13–20.
16. William Shannon, *The American Irish,* rev. ed. (New York: Macmillan, 1966), p. 65.
17. Jack Bass and Walter DeVries, *The Transformation of Southern Politics* (New York: Basic Books, 1976), p. 47.
18. Alexis de Tocqueville, *Democracy in America,* Phillips Bradley, ed. (New York: Vintage, 1954), vol. 1, p. 330.
19. Shannon, p. 65; William Glazer and Patrick Moynihan, *Beyond the Melting Pot,* 2nd ed. (Cambridge: MIT Press, 1970), pp. 221–29.
20. Ronald Formisano, *The Birth of Mass Political Parties* (Princeton: Princeton U. P., 1971), p. 70.
21. From Reports of the Federal Election Commission, as presented in the *National Journal,* 17 (May 25, 1985), 1235; *Congressional Quarterly Weekly Report,* 43 (June 8, 1985), pp. 1115–17.
22. The provisions of the original law passed in 1974, and the amendments of 1976 and 1979, may be found in *Congressional Quarterly Almanac,* 30, 612; pp. 32, 459–61.
23. *The New York Times* (Jan. 19, 1983).
24. David Broder, "Let 100 Single Interest Groups Bloom," *The Washington Post* (Jan. 7, 1979); and *The Changing of the Guard* (New York: Simon & Schuster, 1980), p. 121.
25. David Mayhew, "Congressional Elections: The Case of the Vanishing Marginals," *Polity,* 6 (Spring 1974), pp. 295–317; Morris Fiorina, *Congress: Keystone of the Washington Establishment* (New Haven: Yale U. P., 1977), chap. 1.
26. The leading discussion of this history is Austin Ranney, *Curing the Mischiefs of Faction* (Berkeley: U. of California, 1975), chaps. 3, 4.
27. Richard Fenno, *Home Style* (Boston: Little, Brown, 1978), p. 176.
28. Malcolm Moos and Stephen Hess, *Hats in the Ring* (New York: Random House, 1960), p. 130.
29. Scott Keeter and Cliff Zukin, *Uninformed Choice: The Failure of the New Presidential Nominating System* (New York: Praeger, 1983), p. 174. For a general discussion, see Nelson W. Polsby, *The Consequences of Party Reform* (New York: Oxford U. P., 1983), pp. 157–67.
30. Anthony King, "How Not to Select Presidential Candidates,"

in *The American Elections of 1980,* Austin Ranney, ed. (Washington: American Enterprise Institute, 1981), p. 323.

31. Edward Tufte, *Political Control of the Economy* (Princeton: Princeton U. P., 1978), pp. 106–15.
32. Theodore White, *The Making of the President 1960* (New York: Atheneum, 1961), p. 49.
33. Barry Goldwater, *With No Apologies* (New York: Morrow, 1979), p. 111.
34. Paul David, "Party Platforms as National Plans," *Public Administration Review,* 31 (May/June 1971), pp. 303–15; Alan Monroe, "Party Platforms, Public Opinion and Policy Outcomes," paper presented to the Midwest Political Science Association (Cincinnati, 1981).
35. Gerald M. Pomper with Susan Lederman, *Elections in America,* 2nd ed. (New York: Longman, 1980), chap. 7.
36. Ibid., p. 163 and chap. 8.
37. Tocqueville, vol. 1, p. 185.
38. Downs, chap. 8.
39. Benjamin Page, *Choices and Echoes in Presidential Elections* (Chicago: U. of Chicago, 1978), pp. 66, 76.
40. Teresa Levitin and Warren Miller, "Ideological Interpretations of Presidential Elections," *American Political Science Review,* 73 (Sept. 1979), pp. 737–50.
41. *Congressional Quarterly Weekly Report,* 41 (Dec. 31, 1983), pp. 2789–94.
42. Julius Turner and Edward Schneir, *Party and Constituency: Pressures on Congress,* rev. ed. (Baltimore: Johns Hopkins U. P., 1970), chap. 3; Aage Clausen, *How Congressmen Decide: A Policy Focus* (New York: St. Martin's, 1973), chaps. 5, 6; David Mayhew, *Party Loyalty among Congressmen* (Cambridge: Harvard U. P., 1966); William Shaffer, *Party and Ideology in the U.S. Congress* (Lanham, Md.: U. P. of America, 1980).
43. Albert D. Cover, "One Good Term Deserves Another: The Advantage of Incumbency in Congressional Elections," *American Journal of Political Science,* 21 (Aug. 1977), pp. 523–41.
44. Larry Sabato, *The Rise of Political Consultants* (New York: Basic Books, 1981); Stephen Salmore and Barbara Salmore, *Candidates, Parties and Campaigns* (Washington: Congressional Quarterly Press, 1985).
45. James L. Gibson et al., "Assessing Party Organizational Strength," *American Journal of Political Science,* 27 (May 1983), pp. 193–222 and Cornelius Cotter et al., *Party Organizations in American Politics* (New York: Praeger, 1985). See also Xandra Kayden and Eddie Mahe, Jr., *The Party Goes On* (New York: Basic Books, 1985).
46. John Bibby, "Party Renewal in the National Republican Party," in *Party Renewal in America,* Gerald Pomper, ed. (New York: Praeger, 1980), chap. 7. On national party financing, see *National Journal,* 17 (July 20, 1985), pp. 1617–74.
47. William Crotty, *Decision for the Democrats* (Baltimore: Johns Hopkins, U. P., 1978).
48. *Congressional Quarterly Weekly Report,* 43 (June 29, 1985), 1287.
49. U.S. President's Commission for a National Agenda for the Eighties, *Report* (Washington, 1981), p. 93.
50. Schattschneider, p. 1.

CHAPTER 7

Voting and Elections

On November 6, 1984, 93 million Americans chose their leader for the next four years. In churches, school gymnasiums, town halls, and barber shops, they greeted their neighbors, exchanged some gossip, and sampled the wares at the local bake sale. Then, entering a private voting booth, almost three of every five marked ballots for Ronald Reagan, who was reelected president after getting the most votes in every state except Minnesota and the District of Columbia. Walter Mondale, who was chosen by almost all the other voters, phoned Mr. Reagan to congratulate him on his victory, thanked his own supporters, and left on vacation.

Nothing unusual happened. No armed soldiers stood at the polls to interrogate the voters; no tanks waited to roll to keep the Republican party in power; no Democratic party guerrillas stored rifles to storm the White House. Reagan and Mondale awaited the results from television reporters, not from battalion commanders; the candidates prepared to smile or frown, but not to fight.

This much is obvious—in the United States political power comes from the click of a voting lever, not from the click of a rifle trigger. Yet, in 1984, other world leaders were selected in very different ways. In the Soviet Union, upon the death of the nation's leader, his successor was chosen secretly by twelve men of the Communist Party Politburo. In India, the world's largest democracy, the elected prime minister was removed by an assassin. In the Philippines, troops ensured that legislative elections returned a majority supporting the president, who himself had been elected under conditions of martial law. In Guinea, the military assumed direct control of government.

Through voting and elections, Americans peacefully make their most critical collective decisions. They decide most directly on their leadership—who will control the nuclear arsenal, impose and allocate taxes, and regulate social behavior. Through the choice of leadership, voters also indirectly affect these policy decisions. Particularly through political parties, as considered in the previous chapter, they can fix responsibility for programs at the same time that they choose among candidates.

In this chapter, we focus on the theme of voting as collective national decisions. Ultimately, elections do bring us a definite and accepted result. Yet, we will continue also to observe the fragmentation of American politics. Scores of issues and personal attributes enter into the voters' decisions. Thousands of pollsters, media specialists, and canvassers campaign on behalf of candidates for half a million elective offices. Millions vote, but almost as many fail to cast a ballot. Even as it brings a collective decision, an American election is a fragmented process.

In this chapter, we will consider five questions about voting and elections in the United States:

1. Why do and don't people vote?
2. How do voting groups affect elections?
3. How do voters decide in elections?
4. How do campaigns affect voting?
5. What do elections mean?

Participating in Elections

The first decision a citizen has to make is not how to vote, but whether to vote at all. Participation in elections, or **voter turnout,** is not always high, and varies among groups. It is also affected by laws on the structure of elections and on the right to vote.

Voting Turnout

Although casting a ballot is often pictured as the essential act in a democracy, it is not that common. A typical election for a local school board, for example, may draw only a tenth of the electorate to the polls. In the last congressional election, in 1986, only 40 percent of those old enough to vote actually showed up to help choose their House members and senators.

Even for president, barely more than half of all adults (eighteen years and older) participated in the 1984 contest. Moreover, until then, the proportion of the population voting had been dropping regularly since 1960, when some 62 percent of the electorate decided between John Kennedy and Richard Nixon. This decline ended in 1984, but the total turnout was still under 54 percent of the entire adult population. Figure 7.1 charts the voting turnout in U.S. presidential elections since 1896.

OTHER NATIONS Voting participation in the United States appears to be much lower than in other democracies. Turnouts of 80 to 90 percent occur in such nations as France, West Germany, and Israel. Voting in Britain recently declined to 75 percent, still very high by American standards, but this rate was considered deplorable by the English.

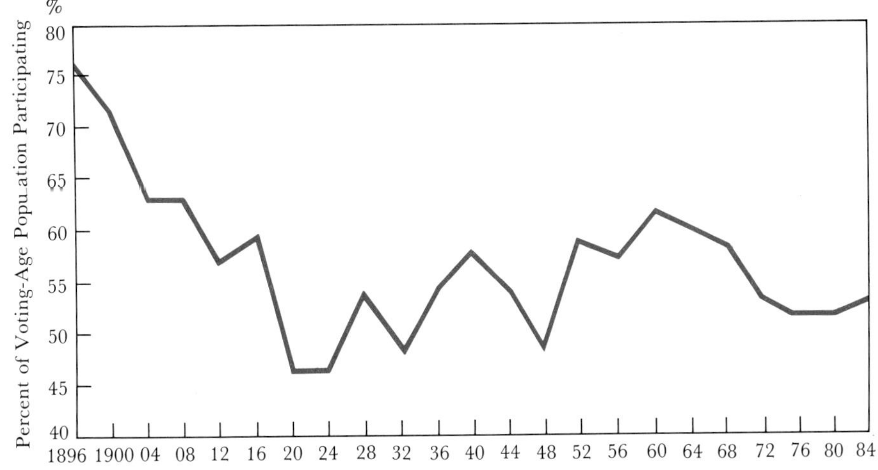

FIGURE 7.1
Voter Turnout in Presidential Elections, 1896–1980
(*For 1860–1928, Bureau of the Census,* Historical Statistics of the United States: Colonial Times to 1970, *pt. 2, p. 107; for 1932–1976,* Statistical Abstract of the United States, 1978, *p. 520; for 1980–1984, Federal Election Commission.*)

The comparatively poor turnout of Americans is widely criticized and seen as politically dangerous. One student of the problem warns, "the vital underpinnings of American democracy are being eroded. The legitimacy of a democratic leadership and the health of the democratic process depend squarely on the informed and active participation of the electorate. Yet the level of political participation is now sinking and the decline seems irreversible."[1]

This pessimistic view is frequently heard, but it may be exaggerated. Figure 7.1 shows that the current voting rates are not spectacularly low for the twentieth century (although they are far less than the rates of participation among the more restricted electorate of the nineteenth century). Many fewer people came to the polls in the 1920s, when women were reluctant to exercise their newly won franchise, and turnout was not much different from today even in the exciting political times of the 1930s.

Statistical Factors Reports of American electoral participation are lowered by statistical factors. Turnout here is calculated as a percentage of all adults in the country, but this base includes many people who are ineligible (aliens) or unable (institutionalized persons) to vote. By contrast, the figures for other countries are reported as percentages only of those who have met the eligibility criteria. Another factor in the United States is the large number of elections. The typical American is asked to vote eleven times over a five-year period; the typical foreigner probably only two or three times.[2]

The Burden of Registration More critically, voting is not simple in this country. It is legally and physically more difficult than in other nations. In the United States (except North Dakota, which has a very high turnout), individuals must personally register to vote before they become eligible to vote. Elsewhere, the government takes responsibility for preparing the electoral list. Thus, an American voter has to take two steps—first registering, then voting—whereas a foreign citizen only has to do a single task. Furthermore, registration is not always easy. In almost every state, it must be done prior to the election (typically thirty days in advance), before voter interest is fully aroused. The times and places for this registration are sometimes inconvenient, and some states lack provisions for absentee enrollment by those who are sick or traveling.

Different legal provisions would increase turnout considerably. If voters could register at the same time as they cast their ballot (as in Minnesota) or register by mail (as in New Jersey), the indications are that many more voters would exercise the franchise. An authoritative estimate is that voting turnout could be raised substantially—about 9 percentage points—by more permissive laws.[3] In 1984, these changes might have brought another 15 million people to the polls. There is some concern, however, that election fraud would be more likely with liberalized provisions.

Probably the most direct way to increase turnout would be to relieve people of the burden of registration. As in other nations, the government could assume responsibility to maintain the list of eligible voters. Colorado recently adopted such a procedure. In that state, when drivers' license renewals are sent out, each driver is also registered to vote. This simple system is likely to reach almost every adult. Similar measures might be used in high schools, at welfare offices, and through the national postal service.

Parties and Turnout Another means to increase voting participation is through registration drives, conducted by the political parties, candidates, and interest groups. Historically, as we saw in the last chapter, parties have stimulated mass participation. This connection still exists today. The weakening of party loyalties has led directly to a decrease in turnout. But, where there is active mobilization by parties, voter turnout goes up.[4]

Registration drives were widespread in 1984, including Jesse Jackson's crusade to enroll Southern and urban blacks, the national Republican party's computerized campaign in sympathetic constituencies and targeted efforts by feminist and Hispanic organizations. These efforts did raise registration substantially—for example, a 20 percent increase in Texas—and certainly helped to increase the total turnout by about 8 million votes over 1980. Among social groups, these drives were especially notable in narrowing the difference between black and white participation, establishing women as a clear majority of the electorate, and adding substantially to the numbers of Hispanic and Fundamentalist voters. Partisan effects, however, were limited. While Democrats registered blacks and Chicanos, their efforts were equaled by Republicans who registered Cuban-Americans or born-again Christians.[5]

Who Votes?

Not everyone votes. But those who do come to the polls are different from those who stay home. Social factors affect turnout.

Age and Turnout Age is one important influence; young people have always voted less frequently than more mature citizens. Recently, this common characteristic of youth has had an exaggerated effect on national turnout rates because there have been more young people in the electorate. Their impact was particularly great in the 1970s when, simultaneously, the postwar "baby boom" matured and the voting age was lowered to 18, altogether adding 25 million persons to the potential electorate. But turnout among those newly eligible was only 52 percent, compared to an impressively high figure, 74 percent, among persons over the age of 35.[6]

Education and Turnout The major demographic determinant of whether a person will vote is not age but education. All other factors are of minor significance compared to the impact of the number of years of schooling. Whether they are young or old, men or women, rich or poor, persons in every category who are more educated vote considerably more often than persons who are less educated. For example, in 1972, among young people without any high school education, only one-seventh voted. By contrast, among people of the same age but who had gone beyond college in their education, nearly six out of seven voted. It is also true that poor people vote less often than the wealthy, and blacks less than whites—but almost all of these differences are due to differences in education, not income or race.

Why does schooling have such a great effect on voting turnout? Fundamentally, according to the most sophisticated writers on the subject, education provides people with basic skills and attitudes that make it easier for them to cope with the demands of politics. "Education increases one's capacity for understanding complex and intangible subjects such as politics, as well as encouraging the ethic of civic responsibility. Moreover, schools provide experience with a variety of bureaucratic problems, such as coping with requirements, filling out forms, and meeting deadlines."[7] These problems are met as much in registering to vote as in registering for courses.

A vigorous Republican drive for new members among Cuban immigrants has increased the party's strength in Florida. Here Vice-President George Bush greets nearly 10,000 people, most of them Hispanics, who are about to take the oath of citizenship. *(UPI/Bettmann Newsphotos)*

Sex and Turnout The relationship between education and voting turnout also helps to explain a major historical change in the relationship between sex and electoral participation. When women were first given the vote, they exercised their franchise considerably less often than men. Today, women constitute not only a majority of the total population but also a majority of those who come to the polls, and the only sex difference in the rate of participation is found among the elderly. As women have gained educational equality, and as they have been given the same civic education as men, they have removed one historic political inequality.

Although we can deflate some of the concern about low turnout in the United States and can discern some of the causal factors, these explanations do not mean there is no problem. It remains true that turnout has fallen generally over the past two decades, at the very time that other changes might be expected to boost voting rates. Registration laws have been simplified; racial discrimination at the polls has been largely eliminated; the average level of education has risen considerably; and women's attitudes have been liberated.

Effects of Nonvoting What are the consequences of lowered turnout? In immediate terms, the impact is surprisingly small. Detailed studies indicate that nonvoters are not much different from voters so that if everyone voted, the results would be pretty much the same. Even though the nonvoters tend to be persons of lower education, and such persons tend to be Democrats, there would be only limited party change with increased voting. There would be the same proportion of Democrats, about 4 percent fewer Republicans, and a similar gain among Independents. The nonvoters would not change issue preferences in the electorate much—since they are not distinctly liberal or conservative—whether the issues involve social welfare questions such as government action to ensure full employment, or matters of morality, such as women's rights.[8] The most obvious characteristic of nonvoters is that they are less interested in politics, and this feature is as evident in their lack of firm positions on issues as in their absence in the polling places.

The long-term consequences of nonvoting are harder to calculate but may be more significant. Certain demographic groups are now underrepresented in the voting population, particularly racial minorities, the poor, and the least educated. Voting less, they may also receive less from government. Currently, the policy positions of these groups are not distinct from those of actual voters, but this similarity is not necessarily permanent. Parties and candidates do not make specific appeals to these groups because of their low turnout; if they voted more frequently, their interests might be given more attention. Certainly, the many feminist appeals now made in elections would be heard infrequently if women did not vote. Conversely, the low voting turnout among the disadvantaged makes it less likely that their interests will be considered in contemporary times, when difficult choices are being made among government spending programs.

Turnout at the polls ultimately also affects the legitimacy of the political system itself. Voting is a secular ritual, one of the ways in which Americans express their faith in the democratic process. When citizens do not perform this ritual, they are also distancing themselves psychologically from the po-

"You've got my vote, sir. But I'm poor, and poor people are notorious for not registering and voting."
Drawing by Dana Fradon; © 1982 The New Yorker Magazine, Inc.

litical community and from its emotions and faith. A neglect of the obligations of democracy can become a disdain for its philosophy and theology. But no people can live long without a system of beliefs. If the rituals of democracy are put aside, authoritarian cults may kindle a harsher devotion.

The Structure of Elections

Voting, or nonvoting, by Americans is affected by the legal structure of elections. These rules are not purely neutral regulations—they have independent effects on politics. For example, we have seen how turnout is reduced by registration requirements. Formal rules also affect voting choice and the parties. Our election laws promote a two-party system, whereas systems of **proportional representation,** in use in other nations, encourage multiple parties. In these other systems, persons are chosen for the national legislature not as individuals but in proportion to the votes cast for their parties.

DECENTRALIZATION Decentralization is the most important characteristic of the legal structure of American elections. From president to Congress to city council, the states make almost all of the major decisions on this subject. They define the eligibility of voters, regulate the parties and their nominating primaries (even for president), and administer the actual polling. National action is largely concerned with setting the times of elections and, most critically, with preventing discrimination.

The actual administration of elections is highly localized and is largely conducted by persons with limited training and clerks chosen by the parties. Different means are used in the casting and counting of ballots. Paper ballots, with penciled votes, are still used in some areas, but voting machines are the most common method. Computer counting of ballots marked by electronically sensitive pens is now being employed in many jurisdictions, particularly in California. San Diego has recently experimented with a mail ballot, which increased "turnout" substantially, and some have even speculated about the possibility of casting votes through coded telephone messages.

The Electoral College The importance of decentralization is seen in the election of the president and vice-president. Although they are the only national officials, they are not chosen by the nation as a unit but in a series of state elections, all held on the same day. To reach the White House, a candidate must obtain a majority in the **Electoral College,** where votes are distributed to equal each states' combined number of senators and representatives (see Figure 7.2). Because every state has two senators, this means that even the smallest state has 3 electoral votes. It also means that the states with the most population, having the most representatives, also have the largest number of electoral votes. Since California has the largest population, it also has the largest bloc in the Electoral College—47 after the 1980 Census—and the greatest impact of any state on the presidential elections.

There is a total of 538 electoral votes—100 equaling the number of senators, 435 the number of representatives, and 3 for the District of Columbia, the latter added to the total by the Twenty-third Amendment. Winning the presidency requires an absolute majority, or 270, of this total. The real battle for the White House is in putting together enough states so that a candidate reaches this magic number.

Under the Constitution, each state determines how its electoral votes will be cast. Today, and for most of our history, almost every state has decided that all of its electoral votes will go to the candidate who receives the most popular votes in that state. When he or she enters the polling booth, a voter

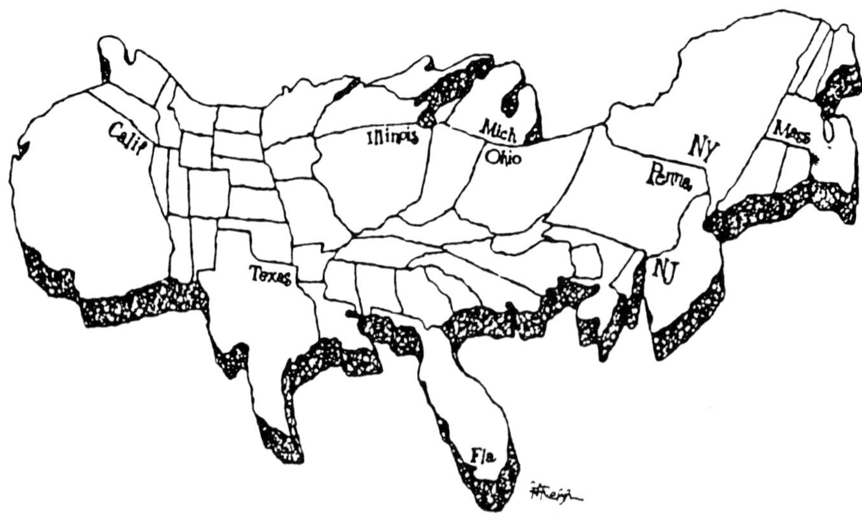

FIGURE 7.2
Electorial College America
The Electoral College makes some states very important, and diminishes the impact of others. These effects distort a map of the U.S. (*"The 1980 Election,"* Congressional Quarterly Special Report, *38 [Oct. 11, 1980], 2968.*)

POLITICAL PERSPECTIVE

ENROLLING A NEW COLLEGE?

In the Electoral College system, it is theoretically possible to elect a president with a minority of the popular vote. This possibility has led to various proposals to change the system.

The smallest change would only eliminate the actual electors and simply award electoral votes mathematically. This would eliminate the occasional problem of the "faithless elector." The legal discretion of the electors is more serious when a third candidate receives a substantial number of electoral votes and then is prepared to bargain with the major candidates for his support. George Wallace hoped to be in this critical position in 1968 but won only forty-six electoral votes, too few to make him a kingmaker.

Another proposal is that one electoral vote be given to the winner in each congressional district and two be awarded from each state to the statewide leader. Although this system was widely employed in the early years of the nation, it is now used only in Maine. By dividing a state's votes between the major parties, it is felt to reduce its national influence.

The most common proposal is to eliminate the electoral votes altogether and choose the president by direct popular vote. This plan has been consistently endorsed by the public in opinion polls and was last seriously advocated by President Carter in 1977. The appeal of the proposal is that it would make the presidency a direct expression of national democracy and legally as well as politically, make the chief executive "the people's president." Opponents see direct election as increasing the possibilities of minority presidents, electoral fraud, and party deterioration. Third parties might also become more common, since each person's vote would be recorded directly, without the need for a minority candidate to win an entire state to have a practical impact. Under the system of direct popular vote, Wallace might have won not 13 percent, but 21 percent (his high in opinion polls) in 1968.

Paradoxically, this proposal is opposed by representatives of both small and large states. The former think the plan would mean total neglect of their interests by candidates emphasizing areas with large concentrations of voters. The latter think (correctly) that they are more advantaged by the present system. Probably, no change will take place unless the Electoral College someday chooses a president who clearly lacks popular support.

technically is not voting for president but selecting a ticket of electors who are pledged to vote for Reagan and Bush or Mondale and Ferraro, for example. Whichever ticket receives the most votes in the state wins. These electors then meet in the state capital a month later and formally cast the electoral votes for their candidate. They are not legally bound to their previous pledge but almost none violate the voters' trust. Later, in January, the electoral votes from all the states are counted in Washington, D.C., by Congress. Only then are all the provisions of the Constitution satisfied and the president and vice-president legally chosen.

Remember that, according to the Constitution, the winning candidates must receive an absolute majority of electoral votes. If nobody has a majority—and this is always possible if more than two candidates win electoral votes by leading in any state—then a special procedure is used. The new House of Representatives then chooses the president, with each state delegation casting a single vote, and an absolute majority of states, twenty-six, is needed to elect. In this vote, however, the House is restricted to the three persons who have received the most electoral votes; it cannot pick a completely new individual. At the same time, the new Senate picks the vice-president, but in this case, each senator has one vote, and the choice must be made from the top two persons with electoral votes. In 1980, with three significant candidates in the running, there seemed to be a real possibility that the Congress would pick the president and vice-president for the first time since 1824.

With victory coming from electoral votes, it is possible for a candidate to win the presidency even though that candidate receives fewer popular votes than his or her opponents. If one person just squeezes by in the big states, while being overwhelmed in the smaller ones, that individual could still win the presidency. The last time this actually occurred in a two-person contest was 1888, when Benjamin Harrison was elected, although he trailed his opponent, Grover Cleveland, by a percentage point. A change of 7,000 votes in New York would have reversed the outcome. In the twentieth century, no president has been elected with fewer votes than any opponent, but Jimmy Carter won in 1976 and a switch of only 9,000 votes in two states would have made Gerald Ford a minority president.[9]

The Right to Vote

Today, we take for granted the right of every adult American to vote. But achieving universal suffrage required many struggles, protests, and laws. In the original Constitution, each state was given complete authority to determine its own electorate. Since then, the Constitution has been amended five times in regard to suffrage, each time extending the vote to a new group. These amendments have enlarged the electorate to include black men (1870), women (1920), residents of the District of Columbia (1961), people who do not pay a poll tax (1964), and youths older than eighteen (1971).

Black Voting Rights Ensuring the right to vote in the case of blacks has required more than a constitutional amendment. Although the freed male slaves did vote for many years after the Civil War, their rights were wrested away in Southern states in the 1890s and later years. Despite the racial equality specified by the amended Constitution, various devices were used to restrict the franchise to whites (and sometimes, only favored whites). Democratic party primaries, the only important elections when the South was a one-party area, were made lily-white. Long residency periods and poll taxes were required, and then enforced in a discriminatory fashion so as to apply only to blacks. **Literacy tests** requiring that voters be able to read and write were used to rule out voting even by well-educated blacks. But illiterate whites were enfranchised, under *grandfather clauses,* giving the vote to persons whose ancestors had been eligible to vote. When these semilegal methods failed, economic pressures, intimidation, and even terrorism were employed.

Black voting revived slowly in the 1940s, through local registration campaigns and lawsuits led by the National Association for the Advancement of Colored People. The civil rights movement of the 1960s quickened the pace of change, with Martin Luther King leading demonstrators throughout the nation, including the historic March on Washington in 1963 and a climactic 1965 march from Selma, Alabama, to the state capitol. Following the publicity and racist murders that occurred in that period, President Lyndon Johnson won passage of the 1965 Voting Rights Act. This law wiped all

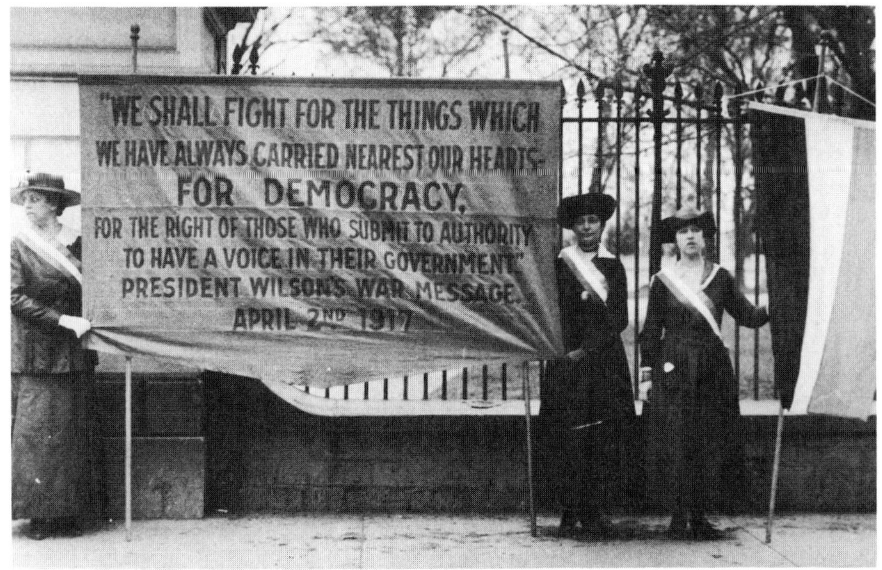

The campaign for woman suffrage extended over decades before the Nineteenth Amendment was passed in 1920. *(Library of Congress)*

discriminatory state legislation off the statute books, provided for federal officials to serve as registrars in the offending states, and required clearance of any new state election legislation in states where blacks were not freely registered to vote. Renewed in 1970, 1975, and 1982, and extended to other minorities, the Voting Rights Act has led to large increases in both the black and white vote in the South, where the two races now vote in almost equal proportions.

Woman Suffrage Until the twentieth century, the right to vote meant only the right of men to vote. The movement for sexual equality at the polls began in 1848, when an historic woman's rights convention was held at Seneca Falls, New York. Leaders such as Susan B. Anthony combined gentle persuasion and public protest over decades to get states—beginning with Wyoming—to extend the franchise to women, and then to pass an amendment to the national Constitution. After 1920, women did not meet much direct discrimination at the polls, but traditional habits of nonvoting took a long time to wear away.

Voters in Groups: Influences on Elections

An election is both obvious and mysterious. It is like a newborn baby. We can immediately tell the size and sex of a newborn child, but the genetic influences on the infant often are unknown. Similarly, in November of 1984 we quickly knew that Ronald Reagan had been reelected president. We knew that he had won over 59 percent of the national popular vote, 49 of the 50 states, and 523 of the country's 538 electoral votes. Figure 7.3 reveals the geographical shape of his victory with exceptional strength in the West, a strong showing in the South and other Sunbelt areas, and lesser support in the Northeast and some states in the Midwest and Pacific Northwest.

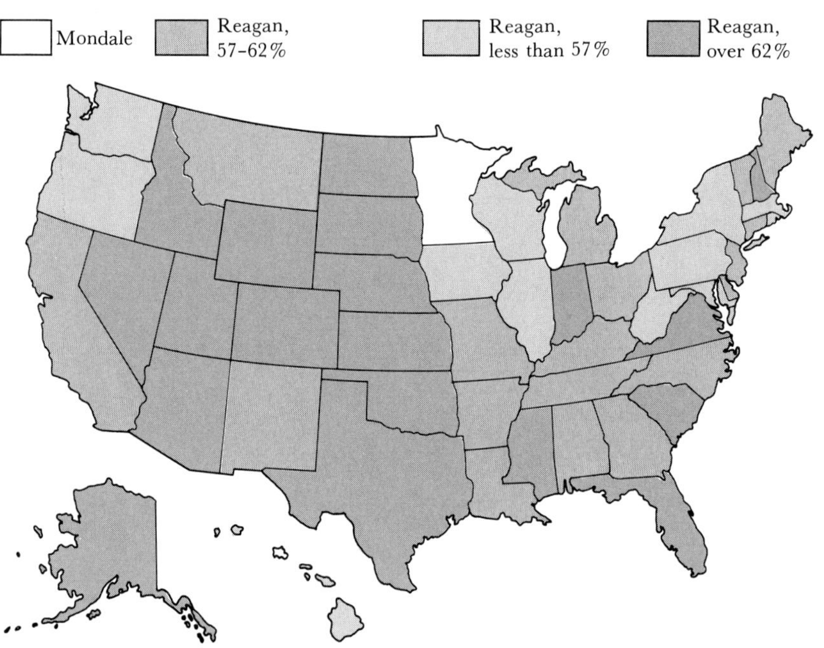

FIGURE 7.3
The National Vote in 1984

We did not know—and will debate for years—the full explanation of this electoral "birth," but there are some clues available. To explain the 1984 and other elections, we first look at the group influences on voters, particularly their party loyalties and their social groups. Then, we examine the ways in which individual voters make up their minds. (A more fanciful way to predict the vote is suggested in the box entitled the Democrats' Stake in '84 Bordeaux.)

Partisanship

Party loyalty, or **partisanship,** is a major influence on the vote. In the 1984 presidential election, Reagan was the choice of nine of every ten Republicans, while three-fourths of the nation's Democrats stayed with their party's losing candidate, Walter Mondale. Even when buried in an electoral landslide, a candidate can count on bedrock support from his or her own party. Republican Barry Goldwater in 1964 and Democrat George McGovern in 1972 each received only 38 percent of the total national vote—but Goldwater still won three out of every four Republicans, and McGovern held on to three of every five Democrats. In congressional elections, party loyalty is even more evident.

Partisanship is the important stable element in any specific election. If there are no unusual influences, most people have in their minds a standing decision in favor of the Democratic or Republican nominee. Stability does not mean blind party loyalty. The voter's decision can be changed by the candidates or issues that become important at a particular time. Much of what happens in a campaign is an effort either to reinforce or to downplay these basic partisan tendencies.

Historical Roots Party loyalty has deep historical roots. It can be traced geographically from the time of original settlement even to the present. The states of the Great Plains, first settled by New England Republicans, still show strong support for the party of nineteenth-century Yankees. In a state such as Oklahoma, removed from settlement until 1890, the northern section of the state drew residents from the Midwest, and displayed both Republican voting habits and county names honoring the party's leaders, such as Lincoln, Garfield, and Blaine. The southern section, settled by Southerners, long evidenced Democratic loyalties in counties named for such partisans as Jefferson, Jackson, and Bryan.[10]

POLITICAL PERSPECTIVE

THE DEMOCRATS' STAKE IN '84 BORDEAUX

Forget about the Ferraro factor, Central America, Texas, the polls, deficits and debates. Why become preoccupied with the irrelevant? The inescapable fact is that events in France, not the United States, will determine who wins in November. *In vino veritas,* in wine there is truth, and the truth is this: When Bordeaux wines have a good vintage year, the Democrats win. When they have a poor one, Republicans win.

This curious but unshakeable link first became apparent in 1956, when one of France's most dismal postwar vintages was followed by Dwight D. Eisenhower's landslide re-election. The obligatory exception to the rule was gotten out of the way in 1960, a disastrous year for Bordeaux. Amazingly, John F. Kennedy won anyway—Cook County being impervious to any laws except those uttered by Mayor Richard Daley, who didn't like wines, especially French. But since then, the trend has been unbroken.

In 1964, a great year, Bordeaux earned a 17 rating out of a possible 20 and Lyndon B. Johnson reaped his landslide. In 1968, after excellent years in 1966 and 1967, Bordeaux suddenly plummeted to a deplorable 6, catapulting Richard M. Nixon into the White House. Things looked good for the Democrats in 1970 and 1971 as the vintages skyrocketed to incredible 19 and 18 ratings. In Paris, they confidently predicted 1972 would be one of the greatest vintages ever, and in this country Democrats around the nation started boasting, "Anyone can beat Nixon."

Then disaster struck. Too much rain and lingering cold caused the whole French wine market to come crashing down, taking George McGovern and the Democrats with it. . . .

The luckless Jimmy Carter fell victim to a late rain that washed precious bacteria off the grapes, and 1980 ended up the worst vintage in the last nine. And so, of course, Ronald Reagan marched into the White House.

Now that you know all this, how can you make it work for you? The beauty of this system is that the crucial months are August and September—and this provides a decided advantage. It means you can get your money down on a sure thing.

Here's what to look for. If France has a hot, dry August with a little bit of rain at the end followed by mild September days—the kind of days politicians think were made for them—talk a lot about fairness and the gender gap: Things will be looking very good for the Democrats.

But if August brings too much rain and is unseasonably cool, or if it is a cold, wet September, you can take up golf and ridicule with impunity the idea of a woman in the Oval Office. . . .

On election day, you'll have to patiently endure the trivial formality of vote counting before you can collect your winnings, pack your bags, and pick up your airline tickets for—where else?—the French wine country to try some of the 1984 vintage for yourself.

Source: Verne W. Newton, *The New York Times* (Aug. 12, 1984). Copyright © 1984 by The New York Times Company. Reprinted by permission.

The late nineteenth century was a time of unusually high party loyalty. From one election to another, a particular community would show identical votes for the two major parties. In one fictional Mississippi community, Democratic loyalty was almost universal. When a Republican ballot was counted, the voting registrar was surprised but complacent. When a second dissenting vote turned up, however, he was outraged, protesting, "The S.O.B. repeated." Throughout the country, partisanship represented a basic psychological tie, with parties being not only electoral organizations but the focus of entertainment, competition, and association. The elections, as Jensen describes, were

> . . . battles in which the two main armies (parties) concentrated on fielding the maximum number of troops (voters) on the battlefield (the polls) on election day. Party organization resembled that of an army (many leaders had been officers in the war), with the head of the ticket as commanding general, the lesser candidates as officers of the line, and party officials as staff officers. Even the language of politics was cast in military terms. From the *opening gun* of the *campaign* the *standard bearer,* along with other *war-horses fielded* by the party, *rallied* the *rank and file* around the party *standard,* the *bloody shirt,* and other *slogans.*[11]

Partisanship is certainly weaker today, as there are other means of entertainment, different outlets for competition and social life, and newer techniques of campaigning. If the ties of party are looser, they still do persist. Most voters do identify with one of the major parties—as many as seven of eight citizens, by some estimates.

"PARTY IDENTIFICATION" Political scientists gauge this loyalty by a measure called **party identification.** It does not mean absolute devotion. Even though a person may vote for someone of the opposite party, that person still identifies as a Republican or Democrat—just as baseball fans sometimes cheer the Phillies although they still consider themselves Dodger rooters. In the last two decades, however, there has been some weakening of loyalty, as fewer people will commit themselves to the major parties. At the same time, there has been no increase in switching from one camp to another. This means people are more ready to go to different ball parks, but few have changed from Dodger to Phillies fans.[12]

Party identification does not imply legal commitment to a party through a formal process of registration or paid membership. Rather, the concept refers to a psychological bond with the party. For decades, this identification has been measured by pollsters by a simple question, "Generally speaking, do you usually think of yourself as a Republican, a Democrat, an Independent, or what?" People who choose either of the two parties are then asked if they are "strong" or "weak" Republicans or Democrats. Those who call themselves Independent are asked if they feel "closer to" one of the major parties.

Because the electorate has been repeatedly asked this question, we can trace national partisanship over a long period of time (see Figure 7.4). Although the two major parties were relatively equal in citizen loyalties until the 1930s, the effects of Franklin Roosevelt's New Deal brought an increasing Democratic predominance. By the time Lyndon Johnson had

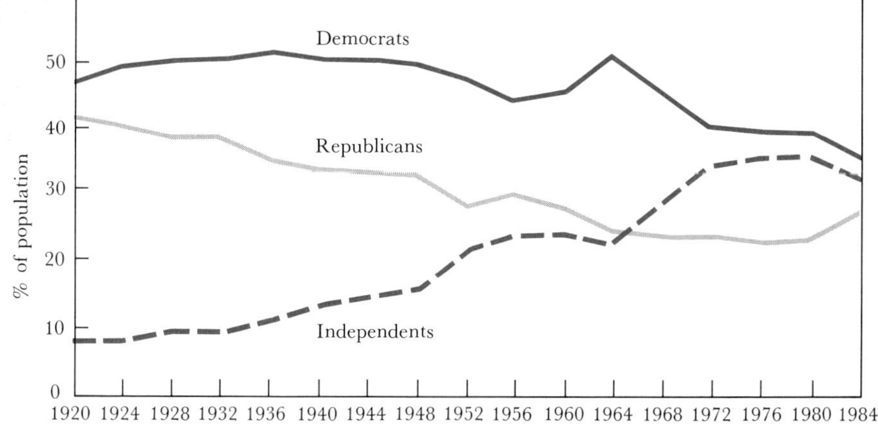

FIGURE 7.4
Party Identification, 1920–1984
(For 1920–1972, Kristi Anderson, The Creation of a Democratic Majority, 1928–1936 *[U. of Chicago, 1979, p. 61]; for 1976–1984, Center for Political Studies and National Election Studies.)*

launched the "Great Society" in the mid-1960s, this advantage grew to a 2 to 1 majority, 60 percent considering themselves Democrats and 30 percent Republicans (including those Independents who felt "closer to" one party or the other).

Changing Party Loyalties

Recent elections, particularly Ronald Reagan's two victories, may have altered the pattern. After the 1980 and 1984 elections, Republican identification began to approach the Democrats. By June of 1985, fully a third of the nation called itself Republican, very close to the 37 percent proclaiming Democratic loyalty. A major shift in the partisan shape of the nation may be underway.[13]

Weaker Loyalties A significant change has been a weakening of the strength of party identification, accompanied by a growth in the proportion of the electorate that considers itself Independent. For thirty years, beginning with the New Deal, the proportion of the electorate that considered itself Independent held quite steadily to about one-fifth. Beginning in the mid-1960s, this proportion rose considerably, and in some surveys reached as high as 40 percent of the total population. This psychological separation of voters from the parties was accompanied by other indications of weakened partisanship. Even those persons who continued to admit party loyalty were more prone to call themselves "weak" partisans. In the voting booth, there was more defection from the party of identification, and more split tickets, such as a Republican vote for president and a Democratic vote for Congress. These trends led many observers to see the "decomposition" or "decay" of the American parties.*

The weakening of party loyalties is certainly real, but it can also be exaggerated. In analyzing the increased proportion of Independents, some qualifications and explanations should be kept in mind. For one thing, this

*Most notably, Walter Dean Burnham, *Critical Elections and the Mainsprings of American Politics* (New York: Norton, 1970), chap. 5.

growth does not mean that the voters are completely abandoning the Republicans and Democrats. Three out of every five persons who call themselves Independents also concede that they feel "closer to" one of the major parties. It is these "leaning" Independents who are especially active and knowledgeable about politics and who provide decisive margins in elections. The "pure" Independents are more likely not to know or care about politics altogether. Therefore, part of the increase in Independents may be accounted for by a change in the way people react to party labels, rather than to a basic shift in their loyalties.[14]

Younger Loyalties Another partial explanation can be found in the large number of new young persons in the electorate. It has always been true that voters are most likely to be Independent during their first adult years, strengthening their partisanship as they become more settled in their jobs, homes, and life styles. In the last two decades, this typical characteristic of youth had an exaggerated impact on the total electorate because of the maturation of the postwar baby boom and the lowering of the voting age to 18 with the passage of the Twenty-sixth Amendment to the Constitution in 1971.

Young voters are not only more numerous. Even more significant is their different attitude toward parties. They have entered the electorate with less commitment to the parties than their parents and have shown more readiness to cast off even these limited ties. Moreover, they do not yet show the common tendency of past voters to become more partisan with the passage of time but have maintained their Independent stance into the 1980s. These trends suggest that the newest generation of voters is also creating a new politics. Because of their large numbers, they are more likely to continue a distinctive style—in politics as much as in music or dress. They also constitute a vast group with the potential for party transformation.*

Causes of Change The change in American party loyalty has two aspects. One one side, there is the decrease in the *affective* or emotional ties to parties, as shown by the smaller proportion that identify with either the Democrats or Republicans. More important is the decline in the *behavioral* relationship—the connection between partisanship and actual voting. In this respect, even where party loyalty still exists, it means less. People vote more often for opposition candidates or split their tickets. For example, many persons in 1984 still considered themselves committed Democrats, even as they cast ballots for Ronald Reagan.

Why? The lesser impact of partisanship in the voting booth, surprisingly, is not because the electorate sees the parties as similar to each other. In fact, on this *cognitive* level, the public sees as many—or even more—distinctions as in the past. By 1980, 58 percent of the electorate thought there were "important differences in what the Republican and Democratic parties stand for."

*The most insightful studies of the relationship of age and partisanship are Philip E. Converse, *The Dynamics of Party Support* (Beverly Hills: Sage Publications, 1976), and Helmut Norpoth and Jerrold Rusk, "Partisan Dealignment in the American Electorate: Itemizing the Deductions since 1964," *American Political Science Review,* 76 (Sept. 1982), pp. 522–37.

TABLE 7.1 Trends in the Public's Evaluations of the Two Major Parties

Year	Negative-Negative	Negative-Neutral	Neutral-Neutral	Positive-Negative	Positive-Neutral	Positive-Positive
1952	3.6	9.7	13.0	50.1	18.1	5.5
1956	2.9	9.0	15.9	40.0	23.3	8.9
1960	1.9	7.5	16.8	41.4	24.2	8.3
1964	4.4	11.2	20.2	38.4	20.6	5.0
1968	10.0	13.8	17.3	37.5	17.4	4.1
1972	7.9	12.6	29.9	30.3	14.7	4.7
1976	7.5	11.8	31.3	31.1	13.7	4.5
1980	5.0	8.6	36.5	27.3	17.7	4.8

Source: SRC/CPS National Election Studies. Reprinted from Martin Wattenberg, *The Decline of American Political Parties, 1952–1980* (Cambridge: Harvard U. P., 1984), p. 61.

The basic explanation is found in how voters *evaluate* the parties. They find the parties less relevant, less salient to their decisions. Voters less frequently believe that parties will deal differently with public policies, despite their differences, and evaluate candidates or presidents more as individuals than as party leaders.

Table 7.1 shows this change. It presents the proportions of negative, positive, and neutral comments made about the two major parties in surveys from 1952 to 1980. Each column represents a different combination of comments; for example, in the first column, unfavorable evaluations of both the Democrats and Republicans. In earlier years, the public had strong feelings, whether favorable or unfavorable. With the passage of the years, the electorate "just no longer has much to say when asked what they like and dislike about the two parties." They are not more hostile to the parties, only more indifferent.[15]

Social Groups

Although party has been the most significant factor affecting voting, much attention has also been devoted to social groups. The Reagan victories, like all elections, gave rise to questions about the electoral preference of different economic, religious, and ethnic groups. Were Catholics turning Republicans? Did blacks remain Democratic? How were women different politically from men?

Group Differences in Voting The data in Table 7.2 show the social divisions in the presidential vote in both 1980 and 1984. They reveal differences in the population bases of the two parties. In these elections, the Democrats do *relatively* better (even if they don't win a majority) among persons with lower income and less education and members of the blue-collar working class; among minority groups, especially blacks and Jews;

TABLE 7.2 Social Groups and the Presidential Vote, 1984 and 1980

Percent of 1984 Total Vote		1984 Reagan	1984 Mondale	1980 Reagan	1980 Carter	1980 Anderson
Party						
38	Democrats	26	73	26	67	6
26	Independents	63	35	55	30	12
35	Republicans	92	7	86	9	4
Sex and marital status						
47	Men	61	37	55	36	7
53	Women	57	42	47	45	7
68	Married	63	37		Not available	
32	Not married	51	47		Not available	
Age						
24	18–29	58	41	43	44	11
34	30–44	58	42	54	36	8
23	45–59	60	39	55	39	5
19	60 and older	63	36	54	41	4
8	First-time voter	60	39		Not available	
Occupation						
30	Professional/manager	62	37	57	32	9
13	White-collar	59	40	50	41	8
14	Blue-collar	53	46	47	46	5
3	Unemployed	31	68	39	51	8
21	Use computer home/job	62	37		Not available	
26	Union household	45	53	43	48	6
Income*						
15	Under $12,500	46	53	42	51	6
27	$12,500–$24,999	57	42	44	46	8
21	$25,000–$34,999	59	40	52	39	7
18	$35,000–$50,000	67	32	59	32	8
13	Over $50,000	68	31	63	26	9

*Family income categories in 1980: under $10,000, $10,000–$14,999, $15,000–$24,999, $25,000–$50,000, and over $50,000.

and in larger communities. Republicans gain more support from upper-status groups—those with more money, more prestigious jobs, and more education; among white Protestants; and in smaller communities and rural areas. These voting differences have been consistent for fifty years since the formation of the **New Deal coalition** during the Great Depression of the 1930s. (The box on page 238 presents other social differences between the parties, as seen from the biased view of the Democrats.)

Other differences are more recent. Catholics are still relatively more Democratic in their loyalties, but the differences are much smaller than in the past. Republicans in 1984 showed an appeal to young voters that might foretell an optimistic future for the party. Most significant may be the **gender gap,** the new tendency for women to be significantly more Democratic (or men significantly more Republican).

TABLE 7.2 (continued)

Percent of 1984 Total Vote		1984 Reagan	1984 Mondale	1980 Reagan	1980 Carter	1980 Anderson
Education						
8	Less than high school	50	49	46	51	2
30	High school graduate	60	39	51	43	4
30	Some college	60	38	55	35	7
29	College graduate	59	40	52	35	11
Race and ethnic group						
86	White	66	34	55	36	7
10	Black	9	90	11	85	3
3	Hispanic	33	65	33	59	6
Religion						
51	White Protestant	73	26	63	31	6
26	Catholic	55	44	49	42	7
3	Jewish	32	66	39	45	15
15	White Born-again Christian	80	20	63	33	3
Region						
24	East	52	47	47	42	9
28	Midwest	61	38	51	40	7
29	South	63	36	52	44	3
18	West	59	40	53	34	10
Community size						
12	Large cities	36	62	35	54	8
55	Suburbs-small cities	57	42	53	37	8
33	Rural and towns	69	29	54	39	5

Source: CBS News/New York Times poll; *New York Times* (Nov. 8, 1984).

The great majority of American black voters have remained loyal to the Democratic party since the time of Franklin Roosevelt. *(Wendy Watriss and Fred Baldwin/Woodfin Camp & Associates)*

POLITICAL PERSPECTIVE

THE PARTY DIFFERENCES: A DEMOCRATIC VIEW

Democrats buy most of the books that have been banned somewhere. Republicans form censorship committees and read them as a group.

Republicans are likely to have fewer but larger debts that cause them no concern. Democrats owe a lot of small bills. They don't worry either.

Democrats give their worn-out clothes to those less fortunate. Republicans wear theirs.

Republicans employ exterminators. Democrats step on the bugs.

Republicans have governesses for the children. Democrats have grandmothers.

Republicans tend to keep their shades drawn, although there is seldom any reason they should. Democrats ought to, but don't.

Republicans study the financial pages of the newspaper. Democrats put them in the bottom of the bird cage.

On Saturday, Republicans head for the hunting lodge or the yacht club. Democrats wash their car and get a haircut.

Republicans raise dahlias, Dalmatians, and eyebrows. Democrats raise Airedales, kids, and taxes.

Republican boys date Democratic girls. They plan to marry Republican girls, but feel they're entitled to a little fun first.

Democrats suffer from chapped hands and headaches. Republicans have tennis elbow and gout.

Republicans sleep in twin beds, some even in separate rooms. That is why there are more Democrats.

Source: *The Democrat,* 8 (Feb. 1968), p. 11; reprinted in the *Congressional Record* and *The New York Times* (July 25, 1984).

THE GENDER GAP In earlier years, the two sexes had voted pretty much the same way, and sometimes women had favored Republicans more than men did. The political split between women and men first became evident in 1980. In 1984, even though Reagan won a majority among both sexes, the "gap" remained and was evident in state elections as well as in underlying party loyalties.

The reasons for these differences are still not clear. "Women's issues," such as abortion or the Equal Rights Amendment, probably are not decisive, since polls show no significant difference between the sexes. More critical may be attitudes on issues such as peace and war or social welfare, where women are more inclined to support the less aggressive and more compassionate policy, often associated with Democratic candidates. Another factor may be economic discrimination against women. Such bias is perceived especially by women at the lowest income levels and by female professionals with high education. These are also the groups where the gender gap is greatest.[16]

POLITICS AND GROUP VOTING Women's electoral behavior illustrates a basic point in voting analysis. The political leanings of a group are not fixed or predestined. They reflect political factors—the history and values of groups, and the varying circumstances and issues of an election. Traditional partisanship is a strong inertial force, but when enough energy, in the form of new political needs, is applied, groups do move.

Most groups do not vote as cohesive blocks (although blacks are a recent exception). We see tendencies toward one party or another, but there is almost always a sizable proportion of the group that prefers the other party.

POLITICAL PERSPECTIVE

A CASE OF BLACK AND WHITE

At one time, blacks were the most loyal of Republicans. In recognition of the historic role of the party in abolishing slavery, blacks typically voted Republican and kept a picture of Abraham Lincoln in the home. This fidelity changed with the Depression and Franklin Roosevelt's support of their economic needs and civil rights. Many blacks agreed with a leader who said, "That debt has been paid. It's time to turn that picture to the wall." As their homes became decorated with pictures of Roosevelt or, later, John Kennedy, black voters became the most steadfast and cohesive of Democratic voters.

Related to the trend among blacks is an opposing one among white Southerners. From the end of Civil War Reconstruction in the 1870s to the beginnings of the modern civil rights movement in the 1950s, white Democrats dominated the solid South. Today, the region has changed enormously, politically as well as socially. Blacks now vote freely, bringing new supporters to the Democrats. This effect has been submerged, however, by the larger trend of white Southerners to vote Republican at the national level. Even Jimmy Carter, a native son, could not win a majority among white Southerners.

One reason for the increase of Southern Republicans is population migration—as Northern Republicans moved from the colder farms and factory towns to the warmer and more prosperous areas of the Sunbelt, and as blacks moved out of the region. Also important has been a gradual transformation in the party loyalties of native white Southerners.

A generation ago, in 1952, 79 percent of this group considered themselves Democrats. In two decades, the proportion dropped to 48 percent. The change was most marked among the younger voters. Soon after the 1984 election, a historical turning point was reached, when the proportion of Republican identifiers among white Southerners surpassed that of the Democrats. If these loyalties are maintained, it is likely to change the basic shape of national politics.[18]

This history shows the impact of political events on group loyalties. Blacks' historic support of the Republicans resulted from a political cause, the party's advocacy of emancipation and racial equality. Blacks changed their party loyalty when Democratic policies in support of civil rights and economic aid to the poor became more important. But as the party changed, so did Dixie. White Southerners have been opposed, generally, to the extension of the power of the federal government—whether for the regulation of the economy or for the protection of civil rights. The Democratic party nationally has come to favor these positions. Now, the disparity between their party loyalty and their issue positions has brought the desertion of millions in the region from the party favored by their parents.

The emotions of the Civil War made the white South a one-party area for over a century. This photograph was taken in 1862 at the Battle of Antietam, in which Southern troops were thoroughly routed. *(Photograph by Alexander Gardener/ Library of Congress)*

It is true that poor people favor the Democrats, and the wealthy the Republicans, but a substantial fraction of each group dissents from this norm and supports what Marxists would call the "class enemy." In American elections, there is "imperfect mobilization of social interests" so that each party contains some people from all groups and therefore will make diverse appeals.[17] Electoral fragmentation is not expressed as the conflict of two cohesive voting coalitions; there are fissures along various social lines within each coalition.

Furthermore, social groups are not fixed in their loyalties. Even in the four-year period between the two presidential elections presented in the table, there were considerable changes. Young voters chose Carter in 1980 (and in 1976), but were strong Republican backers in 1984. In contrast, a majority of Jews in 1980 voted either for Reagan or John Anderson. By 1984, two-thirds of the denomination had returned to their historic Democratic loyalties. Even greater change is evident in the voting of blacks and white Southerners (see box on page 239).

Voters: Deciding in Elections

In a specific election, voters are influenced first by the term factors of party identification and social groups. They, then, respond to the immediate matters: current issues, ideology, and candidates.

Issues in Elections

A large part of a campaign, such as that of 1984, is devoted to policy questions. Different issues are stressed from one election to another. Domestic programs were emphasized in Lyndon Johnson's 1964 triumph; race relations were more important in Richard Nixon's 1968 success; the Vietnam War was a major concern in 1972; the question of honesty in government was stressed in Jimmy Carter's 1976 victory; and inflation and military preparedness were vital in Ronald Reagan's first election. In 1984, the prominent issues included federal spending and taxation, the role of religion in government, and nuclear armament.

Issue Voting Issues (as well as the candidates) are likely to stimulate considerable shifts in the vote from one election to the next. From 1980 to 1984, Ronald Reagan's national vote rose eight percentage points. This increase could not be due to any change in party loyalties or the size of different social groups. To explain these changes, we must look at the way the voters felt about the issues, and how they evaluated the candidates.

In general, the importance of issues in electoral decisions appears to have increased considerably in recent decades. As party loyalists have become less fervent and the ties of social group traditions have waned, voters are more likely to choose candidates on the basis of the policies they advocate. By 1972, 26 percent of the total electorate was voting on the basis of issues alone, while a majority, 53 percent, even if affected by party loyalty, was voting consistently with its position on issues. This behavior represented a considerable change from the period of the 1950s, when pure partisanship or other factors, such as candidate appeal, were predominant. In the last two presidential elections, however, the significance of issue voting has declined again.[19]

Determining the degree of issue voting in specific elections is not simple. A shorthand technique is to compare the attitudes of the public with the policy stances of the winning candidate. If the two positions are in agreement, we might conclude that the voters gave the candidate a mandate to carry out the particular policy. If they did not agree, then no mandate could be claimed. In 1984, for example, we would find that the majority of the voters agreed with Reagan that taxes should not be increased, but—contrary to the president—they favored legalized abortion and a nuclear freeze.[20]

This kind of comparison is simple but misleading. Parallel views on an issue between the national majority and a candidate do not necessarily mean that the issue was the cause of victory. Many voters are unconcerned about a particular issue, or unaware of the candidates' positions, even if they answer a poll question on the topic.

Interpreting elections as mandates has other problems, as discussed in Chapter 4. If the candidates are agreed on a particular policy, there is no choice available to the voters. Thus, in 1984, both Reagan and Mondale favored increased military spending, making that issue moot. Furthermore, a majority of voters usually do not focus on the same issue. If one small group is interested in policy in Afghanistan, another in farm price supports, and another in school prayer, then there is no clear majority demand for any particular public policy.

Issues and Party Identification One way that issues do affect elections is through party loyalties. Republicans are different from Democrats on more than traditional grounds—the adherents of the two parties also take different positions on the issues. As seen in Table 7.3, Democrats are more willing to use government to promote social welfare, and Republicans favor a more assertive foreign policy. However, these differences between the parties are not extreme and disappear on some issues, such as abortion and school busing.

People identifying with the two major parties take different positions on policy issues. Pictured here are ERA supporters at the Democratic national Convention in 1984. *(© Richard Kalvar/Magnum Photos, Inc.)*

Issues in 1984 Although issue positions are related to party leanings, voters do not always give priority to issues in a specific election. For example, Reagan in 1984 still won the votes of a third of the voters who disagreed with his positions on abortion and the nuclear freeze. Even when people explain their vote on the basis of issues, they actually may make their choices on other grounds. Many preferred Reagan because they considered him a better leader, and then said they agreed with his issue positions.

The 1984 election centered on economic issues—but there was no clear mandate in the results. Although the federal budget deficit was mentioned most often as an important issue, it was stressed by only a quarter of the electorate. Voters preferred Reagan's stand against higher spending to Mondale's bold declaration that he would raise taxes, yet, they also acknowledged that even Reagan probably would increase taxes.

The economic issue in 1984 became one of performance rather than promises. As a result, social class differences in the vote were limited. Al-

TABLE 7.3 Party Identification and Issue Positions in 1984

	Issue Positions		
	Liberal	Moderate	Conservative
Government services			
Democrats	49%	33%	18%
Independents	33	32	35
Republicans	20	27	53
Defense spending			
Democrats	43	29	28
Independents	34	32	34
Republicans	16	36	48
Minority aid			
Democrats	41	30	29
Independents	31	31	38
Republicans	21	32	47
Women's equality			
Democrats	49	26	25
Independents	38	31	31
Republicans	24	36	40
Government job guarantee			
Democrats	42	24	34
Independents	35	24	41
Republicans	20	18	62
Abortion			
Democrats	39	49	12
Independents	36	51	13
Republicans	32	52	16

Source: Calculated from National Election Studies, 1984 Pre-Post Study.

Note: Percentages add horizontally, by party identification, to 100 percent. This table shows, for example, that 49 percent of Democrats (upper left entry) favor a liberal position on provision of government services. On all questions except abortion, respondents were presented with the two extreme points identified with a policy. Answers on a seven-point scale are here combined into three categories: the middle point was considered moderate and the points 1–3 and 5–7 either liberal or conservative. The liberal position for each issue is presented below:

Government services: "It is important for government to provide many more services even if it means an increase in spending."

Defense spending: "We should spend much less money for defense."

Minority aid: "The government in Washington should make every possible effort to improve the social and economic position of blacks and other minority groups."

Women's equality: "The government in Washington should make every effort to improve the social and economic position of women."

Government job guarantee: "The government in Washington should see to it that every person has a job and a good standard of living."

Abortion: Four options are presented. The first is considered liberal; the next two are combined as moderate; and the last is considered conservative: "By law, a woman should always be able to obtain an abortion as a matter of personal choice"; "The law should permit abortion for reasons other than rape, incest, or danger to the woman's life, but only after the need for the abortion has been clearly established"; "The law should permit abortion only in case of rape, incest, or when the woman's life is in danger"; "By law, abortion should never be permitted."

though Reagan did get more votes from wealthier people, he still would have won the election even if the only voters were people making less than the average national income. Although concerned about the deficit and the need for new taxes, voters blamed the Democratic Congress as much as the Republican president. And, by a 4–3 margin, they thought that the Republicans would handle the problem better.[21] In reelecting the president, the electorate did not set a course; it placed its trust in the captain of the ship of state.

Ideology in Elections

Ideology is a more general way in which policy questions may affect elections. Rather than vote on the basis of a particular issue such as inflation, the electorate might act on the basis of such broad philosophies as liberalism or conservatism. We have already considered, in Chapter 4, factors that limit the extent and character of ideological thinking in the American public. Nevertheless, over two-thirds of the electorate can be located on a scale of liberalism-conservatism.[22] In regard to the parties specifically, ideology does provide a means for some voters to form a coherent view of the Republicans as conservative and the Democrats as liberal. These attitudes, in turn, are partially related to voting—but to many other voters, these terms have no real political significance.

Ideology and Party Identification To some citizens, the major parties do differ on such philosophical questions as the size of government, the conflict of rich and poor, the desirability of welfare programs, the pace of social change, and the promotion of personal liberty. These people not only place themselves on a liberal-conservative scale but provide some explanation for their positioning. Such ideological thinking has been evident recently in somewhat less than half of the electorate. In 1976, when the most recent sophisticated analyses were done, 26 percent of the citizenry were classified fully as "ideologues," persons who referred to a philosophical distinction between the parties and candidates and backed up their evaluation with reference to particular issues (for example, social security) and groups (for example, big business). Another 15 percent were considered "near-ideologues," who also mentioned philosophical differences but did not add specific references. Such conceptual thinking about politics is considerably greater than in the past—twice as common as in 1956, when political differences were especially muted.[23] Ideology is also related to party identification. The Republican party is an ideologically cohesive group, with ten conservatives for every liberal. Half of the party loyalists are moderates or nonideological. The Democratic party tends more to the left, but it is philosophically divided. For every conservative in the party, there are two liberals—but two-thirds of Democrats are in the middle.*

*Calculated from the *1984 National Election Study*. Persons "leaning" in their partisanship are considered Independents, and those "leaning" in their ideology are considered moderates.

TABLE 7.4 Reagan's Vote: Party and Ideology in the 1984 Election (Percentage of Reagan's Total Vote)

	Democrats	Independents	Republicans	Total by Ideology
	%	%	%	%
Liberal	2	3	3	8
Moderate	7	13	22	42
Conservative	7	12	31	50
Total by party	16	28	56	

Source: Calculated from CBS News/*New York Times* Exit Poll.

IDEOLOGY AND VOTING IN 1984 In 1984, as in most elections, liberals and Democrats voted for the Democratic nominee, Mondale, and conservatives and Republicans for Reagan, the Republican candidate. These results do not show an ideological shift by the voters, since party loyalty already expressed the voters' philosophical leanings. In Table 7.4, Reagan's total support is broken down to show the sources of his overall coalition. We see, for example, that only 2 percent of his vote came from liberal Democrats (the first column in the table). Generally, the table shows that party support was more critical to this victory than ideological support. Republicans, conservative and moderate, were the basic element in the Reagan victory. Support from other groupings were important additions, rather than the foundation of the victory.

Some observers (including one portrayed by Garry Trudeau in the cartoon) have seen the 1980 and 1984 balloting as ideological triumphs of the right. In reality, Reagan received less than half of his support from self-declared conservatives in the two elections. He achieved his victories by assembling broad coalitions, encompassing many moderates and even a small number of liberals. Although there has been a slight increase in the conservatives' proportion of the electorate (they now outnumber liberals by 35–17), the largest proportion of Americans still blandly call themselves moderates. Moreover, ideology cannot explain the vote, since fewer than a tenth of the electorate chose Reagan in either 1980 or 1984 because they saw him as "a real conservative."[24]

Candidates and Voting

Ultimately, voters elect an individual for a political office. Whatever the influences of their party and social group, and whatever their issue preferences, they will select a particular man or woman to be president, senator, and House member. The personal styles of the candidates are an important and relevant part of voter decisions.

CANDIDATE IMAGES Candidate traits have always affected elections. Long before television was available to create favorable "images," William Henry Harrison's campaign leaflets portrayed him as a common man, raised in a log cabin and drinking hard cider—although neither detail was accurate. Other candidates too have used techniques of salesmanship to increase their personal support: Abraham Lincoln grew his famous beard so that he would appear more mature; Franklin Roosevelt flew to Chicago to accept his first nomination, and thereby demonstrate that polio had not limited his physical ability; Jimmy Carter appeared humble but knowledgeable in television commercials showing him dressed in jeans while walking through a peanut field; Ronald Reagan stressed his patriotic appeal in a masterful filmed biography that provided the basic material for his reelection campaign. The president was shown meeting U.S. troops in Korea, walking with his wife into a Western sunset, greeting the Olympic victors, and commemorating the Normandy invasion of the second World War. The film concluded with a new American anthem:

I'm proud to be an American,
Where at least I know I'm free;
And I won't forget the men who died
Who gave that flag to me;
And I'll gladly stand up—next to you—
And defend her still today,
'Cause there ain't no doubt I love this land—
God bless the U.S.A.

TRUST AND COMPETENCE Evaluations of the candidates have become important influences on voting. Much of the success of the president on the

POLITICAL PERSPECTIVE

THE IDEAL PRESIDENTIAL CANDIDATE

He grows up in humble circumstances, enjoying a happy, active boyhood but one that is not without its struggle to rise, through education and hard work, above the station in life into which he had been born. Midway in this climb to success, he is summoned from his peaceful pursuits to defend his country, and covers himself with glory. His country's hour of peril successfully weathered, he resumes his civilian career. . . . He has also taken part in the public life of the nation—not, however, as an occupation, but as a service to his community which, as is its right, has demanded his talents. As he sits before the hearth in his own unpretentious home awaiting the verdict of the people, one sees a plain, simple man of modest means, surrounded by a dutiful, loving wife and adoring children; a man of practical good sense and boundless energy, a man of deep but unostentatious piety, of impeccable moral character, and of sturdy republican virtue.

Source: W. Burlie Brown, *The People's Choice: The Presidential Image in the Campaign Biography* (Baton Rouge: Louisiana State U. P., 1960), pp. 144–45.

job depends on individual traits, so it makes good sense for voters to be concerned with candidates' judgment, experience, compassion, and honesty. For a number of reasons, a candidate's character has become a more important influence on the vote in recent years. Foreign policy decisions are now critical to the United States. Since the president has the most personal power in this area, voters need to consider him or her as an individual. Moreover, presidents have great influence on the resolution of policy issues. As voters have come to be more concerned with issues, they have focused their attention on the nation's chief executive. Similarly, as partisanship and social group memberships have less effect on the vote, personal evaluations have increased impact.

Voters are placing more emphasis on the candidates' perceived trustworthiness and competence. They give considerable weight to the ability of candidates to make good on their promises and assess such related qualities as reliability, sincerity, character, and personal values. Although these standards are not very precise, voters use them to appraise the candidates independently of other factors such as party loyalty or issue preferences. In the final vote, they are most likely to choose the candidate who meets these personal tests.[25]

In 1980, Jimmy Carter had lost his personal popularity, although it revived briefly during the Iranian hostage crisis. The election turned not on issues, but on the performance of the incumbent and the relative competence in the candidates. The critical question was simply whether Ronald Reagan would be considered a satisfactory alternative to an unpopular incumbent president. Reagan himself did not inspire great confidence at the time. Two-thirds of the voters had some criticism to make, and about a third saw a possibility of world war with the Californian in the White House. The Republican campaign, and the pre-election televised debate, reassured voters sufficiently to allow them to vote for Reagan.

As he ran for reelection, Reagan was viewed far more favorably. Although some doubts remained, voters now gave him higher ratings than in 1980 on virtually every criterion. Thus, almost half of the public had doubted in 1980 that Reagan understood "the complicated problems a president had to deal with." Four years in Washington had apparently demonstrated that ability to most voters, and over three-fourths now thought he met this test. The incumbent president's positive evaluations overwhelmed Mondale. The Democrat actually scored better with the public than either Carter or the 1980 version of Reagan, but he was no personal match for an unusually popular president.[26]

Campaigns: Winning Elections

Political campaigns are notable events in American life. They provide excitement for voters, intense commitments for participants, and victory or defeat for candidates. Campaigns have enriched our vocabulary. Small town whistlestops in the days of the railroad have been replaced by propstops and then jetstops in the modern era of air travel. They have been a source of popular culture in songs such as "Rally 'Round the Flag," plays such as "Of Thee I Sing," and movies such as "The Seduction of Joe Tynan."

Hollywood has focused on the glamor and corruption in politics in such films as *The Seduction of Joe Tynan. (Universal City Studios)*

Essentially, however, campaigns are not rituals or amusements but the prelude to power. Men and women engage in campaigns because they lead to the vital electoral decisions—who will govern and for what purposes? Like wars, campaigns are confusing to the combatants, combine careful planning and lucky accidents, and often have unpredicted results. Like wars, too, they are serious matters in which deliberate strategy and tactics are evident, and there are consequences both for the contestants and the noncombatants—the people of the United States.

Campaign Strategy

Political parties provide the framework for campaigns. Nominations are party processes, and may be even more decisive than the general election in areas where two-party competition is limited. Moreover, party loyalty remains a strong influence on the vote, particularly in smaller constituencies where candidates cannot raise much money on their own, or cannot establish an individual campaign. In campaigns for president, statewide offices such as senator and governor, and some House members, much of the party's role has been taken over by campaign consultants, political action committees, and opinion pollsters. Nevertheless, parties still provide the essential structure of elections, and recently they have developed new strength.

CAMPAIGN GOALS The most active persons in campaigns, obviously, are the candidates and their staffs. Essentially, they have three tasks to accomplish: devising a strategy, shaping information for persuasion, and gaining attention. Gaining attention is no problem for a major presidential nominee, but it is often the most difficult task for other candidates, such as those contesting a party primary or the challenger to a well-entrenched House member. Politicians need to do more than simply give speeches to be noticed, and they have shown inventiveness in devising new techniques. Senator Lawton Chiles of Florida, for example, drew attention by walking across the entire state. Others imitated this novel, but tiring, technique.

For presidential hopefuls, the goal is to be mentioned in the national press as a possible nominee. Those who pass the screening of reporters as strong possibilities are then more likely to win the favor of voters, contributors, and the media in primary states. Hiring a well-known political consultant is another way of getting attention. Indeed, the attention gained may be more important than the actual services of a consultant. "A candidate is not merely hiring consultants. He is purchasing acceptance among other politicians, insurance that his campaign will be taken seriously, and favorable mention by journalists."[27]

Basic to campaign success is a strategy—which involves establishing a theme, selecting targets of voting groups and areas that hold the promise of support, setting a schedule of places and times for campaign events, and determining the techniques to be used. For the local candidate, a strategy may mean little more than appearing at the nearest shopping center daily to shake whatever hands are willingly extended. At the presidential level, strategies are as elaborate as war plans.

Campaign Themes Establishing a theme is particularly critical in a campaign. Strategists must decide which of the factors affecting voting they will emphasize. They may try to mobilize a particular social group or stress a salient issue. George Wallace attempted this strategy in 1968, when he based his candidacy on an appeal to white voters disturbed by civil rights policies. Democratic presidential candidates are more likely to appeal to

POLITICAL PERSPECTIVE

CAMPAIGN THEMES IN 1984

Mondale: Look at the record. First, there was Mr. Reagan's tax program. And what happened was this, he gave each of his rich friends enough tax relief to buy a Rolls Royce—and then he asked your family to pay for the hub caps. Then they looked the other way at the ripoffs: soaring utility bills, phone bills, medical bills. . . . When he raises taxes, it won't be done fairly. He will sock it to average-income families again, and he'll leave his rich friends alone.

Reagan: Isn't our choice really not one of left or right, but of up or down: down through the welfare state to statism, to more and more government largesse, accompanied always by more government authority, less individual liberty and ultimately totalitarianism, always advanced as for our own good. The alternative is the dream conceived by our Founding Fathers, up to the ultimate in individual freedom consistent with an orderly society.

From *Penguin Dreams and Stranger Things: A Bloom County Book* by Berke Breathed; copyright © 1985 by The Washington Post Company. By permission of Little, Brown, and Company.

party loyalties, since they represent the national majority, whereas Republicans are more prone to focus on individual candidate's traits and policy satisfaction.

In the 1984 campaign, both parties focused on economic themes and the Reagan record. The Democrats tried to focus the election on the theme of "fairness," claiming that the administration was run for the interests of the wealthy. The Republicans countered with a theme of "opportunity," arguing that their policies were benefiting all groups. The accompanying box shows these differences, as stated when the two 1984 presidential candidates accepted their party nominations.

Campaign Tactics Once established, a strategy must be applied through campaign tactics. The final and critical task facing campaigners is to shape the information received by voters. The candidates' interest is not necessarily in fully educating the electorate but in providing it with interpretations of the world that will help them to get elected.

Candidates will emphasize those personal qualities or issue positions that seem most likely to succeed. Astronauts John Glenn and Harrison Schmitt gained both earth orbit and a political boost from their rocket flights, as Congressmen Christopher Dodd and Barry Goldwater, Jr. benefited from their fathers' political experience. One candidate used a particularly novel technique:

> When a fellow named Gillespie Craighead ran for Congress in Seattle, he asserted he was the only man in the race who could prove he was sane; then he would display his certificate of discharge from a mental hospital. In losing to a former U.S. Senator, he received several thousand votes.[28]

Policy issues provide the framework of most campaigns. Even though voters do not respond only to issues, it is expected that candidates will take positions of some sort on controversial questions. Major candidates now employ their own opinion polling agencies to determine the issues that are of most concern to the voters and the direction of opinion. They do not always simply follow the popular majority, and it is relatively rare for a candidate to take different positions to please different audiences. More commonly, when faced with a contentious or complex issue, a politician will become vague, hoping that the audience will interpret his or her message to its own liking. In 1968, for example, the Vietnam War was a principal issue facing the nation, but neither of the major candidates, Hubert Humphrey and Richard Nixon, took clear positions. For his part, Nixon mentioned Vietnam in only a tenth of his acceptance speech and devoted at most six sentences to future policies.

> Nixon's most specific promises were two: that he would "begin with Vietnam" in making a "complete reappraisal of America's policies in every section of the world"; and that "the first priority foreign policy objective of our next Administration will be to bring an honorable end to the war in Vietnam." The voter could not hope to find much information here—or in the TV spots or stump speeches which echoed the acceptance speech—about what Nixon proposed to do in Vietnam: whether he would "end the war" by massive escalation, by unilateral withdrawal, or by negotiations.[29]

Campaign Advertising Candidates employ techniques similar to advertisers in presenting information about their product: themselves and their positions. Some favor messages with large numbers of statistics to impress voters with their command of the facts; others emphasize appealing visual images and the use of evocative symbols—such as an American flag or the U.S. Capitol in that background. Earnest "spontaneous" interviews with "the person in the street" are meant to present the candidate as "one of the people," whereas a taped message from a home library conveys a message of knowledge and experience in government. A different kind of information is provided when attention is shifted to the opposing candidate, and his or her defects and allegedly injurious policies. Campaign attacks and smears have a long, if not honored, place in American political history. Against Thomas Jefferson, rumors were spread that he had a black mistress, while Grover Cleveland's admitted extramarital liaison with an unwed mother inspired a campaign ditty,

Campaign strategy often relies more on the candidate's personal appeal than on issues. Robert Redford's starring role in the 1972 film *The Candidate* illustrated this point. *(Movie Still Archives)*

> Ma, Ma, where's my pa?
> Gone to the White House, Ha, Ha, Ha.

Negative campaigning continues in the television age, although the forms have become more sophisticated, as two recent examples show. One, in 1964, indirectly attacked Republican Barry Goldwater's alleged willingness to use nuclear weapons. It portrayed an innocent young girl counting petals on a daisy, while the countdown for an atomic explosion was heard in the background. As a nuclear bomb was detonated, the picture disappeared, and Lyndon Johnson was heard: "These are the stakes: to make

POLITICAL PERSPECTIVE

REAGAN TELEVISION COMMERCIALS—1984

Spring of '84

Video: American landscapes.

Audio: This is America. Spring of eighty-four. Just four years ago people were saying its problems were too big and too difficult to be handled by any one president. Yet, today jobs are coming back. Housing is coming back. Hope for the future is coming back. And isn't it interesting that no one, anywhere, is saying the job of president is too big for one person. President Reagan. He's doing what he was elected to do.

Video: President Reagan. Leadership That's Working.

America's Back

Video: Varied occupations, family scenes.

Audio: During the past year, thousands of families have moved into new homes that once seemed out of reach. People are buying new cars they once thought they couldn't afford. Workers are returning to factories that just four years ago were closed. And America is better—with a sense of pride people thought we would never feel again. Now that our country is turning around, why would we ever turn back?

Video: President Reagan. Leadership That's Working.

Peace

Video: Children.

Audio [by Reagan]: In my lifetime, we've faced two world wars, a war in Korea and then Vietnam. And I know this. I want our children never to have to face another. A president's most important job is to secure peace. Not just now, but for the lifetimes of our children. But it takes a strong America to build a peace that lasts. And I believe with all my heart that working together we have made America stronger and prouder and more secure today. And now we can work toward a lasting peace for our children and their children to come. Peace is the highest aspiration of the American people. Today America is prepared for peace. We will negotiate for it, sacrifice for it. We will not surrender for it, now or ever.

Video: President Reagan. Leadership That's Working.

Source: Transcribed from video tape provided by Reagan/Bush '84 Election Committee.

a world in which all God's children can live, or to go into the darkness." An announcer then concluded, "On November 3rd, vote for President Johnson."* Shown only once, this strong message was withdrawn after vehement Republican protests.

The second case came in the 1972 campaign and attacked George McGovern's proposals to limit military spending. The advertisement pictured a map of the world on which were arranged toy ships, planes, and soldiers. As the announcer attacked McGovern's cutback program, the armaments were swept from the map board—implying the inevitable defenselessness of the United States. The commercial ended with a picture of Richard Nixon on a navy ship. As "Hail to the Chief" was played in the background, a voice urged, "President Nixon doesn't believe we should play games with our national security. He believes in a strong America to negotiate for peace from strength."[30]

*Tony Schwartz, producer of this commercial, discusses his work in an article reprinted in Robert Agranoff, *The New Style in Election Campaigns,* 2nd ed. (Boston: Holbrook, 1976), pp. 344–58.

Limits on Campaign Effects

Clever techniques—and the persons who create them—are often credited with winning elections. At the conclusion of a campaign, the winner's advisers are seen as sophisticated Machiavellians who can twist the electorate to their purposes. Politics now has a "star system" for its campaign consultants, with the latest celebrities commanding the highest fees. Despite the acclaim, the importance of campaign techniques is usually greatly exaggerated. In every campaign, after all, for every winner there is at least one loser, who is likely also to have had sophisticated techniques and informed advice. Yet, "there is nothing consultants enjoy more than citing their win-loss records, and as they count them, the records are phenomenally and uniformly successful, rarely falling below 60 to 70 percent triumphant. The numbers are almost always partial or exaggerated citations, winked at by others in the business who understand the polite fictions necessary for self-promotion."[31]

THE LIMITS OF POLITICS There are severe and inherent limitations to campaign effectiveness. The most significant is the prevailing political situation. A campaign does not take place in an isolated world. Before the candidates make a single speech or tape their initial advertisements, much of the vote has already been decided. Thus, in the 1984 presidential contest, the campaign was largely irrelevant, and the relative popularity of Reagan and Mondale hardly changed during the year. Almost half of the voters had made up their minds by the beginning of the year, and only a fourth even waited for the television debates.[32]

In all contests, many important factors are constant. Party loyalties, social group memberships, and objective facts cannot be altered by even the most clever techniques. Whoever is planning his campaign, no Republican will win in a district that is predominantly black, Democratic, and hurt by the Reagan administration's budget cuts. Campaigns only have marginal effects, and often there is no margin in politics.

Furthermore, campaigns are limited by the characteristics and beliefs of the candidates. Candidate personalities cannot be easily transformed. A poor speaker will not become an orator, however many retakes are made of the television spots. Advocates of abortion do not join right-to-life movements, regardless of the latest opinion poll. Strange as it may seem to cynical voters, most politicians do believe in what they say, and they are not likely to change to suit the strategy of the political consultants. These facts further reduce the marginal area within which campaigns can affect election outcomes.

UNCERTAINTY Uncertainty is another limitation. Despite all of the semi-scientific research into campaign techniques, there are no universally valid rules, other than commonsense maxims, such as "Emphasize your strong points" or "Get the largest turnout in areas of your own party." Issue-oriented campaigns work in some races, whereas a stress on personality is successful in others. Television spots are sometimes the best technique, and reliance on door-to-door contacts works at other times. The uncertainty of campaigns is captured by the time-honored conclusion that half of the money spent in campaigns is wasted—but no one knows which half is unnecessary.

Chance adds to this uncertainty. In every campaign, accidental events occur that may have significant impacts. Candidates and their staffs cannot plan these events but must improvise their reactions. Vice-presidential candidate Geraldine Ferraro provides a 1984 example. As the first woman nominated by a major party, Ferraro created great interest in the Democratic ticket, giving it a brief hope of an upset win. The controversy over her and her husband's finances (see Chapter 5), however, dimmed the luster of the Ferraro candidacy, which ultimately gave little significant help to the Democrats. The possibility of lucky breaks and bad bounces hangs over every campaign. Often, a politician is "but Fortune's knave, a minister of her will."[33]

Meaning in Elections

Casting ballots takes only minutes for the individual voter and a day for the nation. Interpreting the results and absorbing the effects of elections requires years, and sometimes decades. At the very least, elections open the gates of power to some individuals in power and lock others out. In doing that, elections also affect the policy decisions of government.

Retrospective Voting

In most elections, future policy directions are unclear and mandates are uncertain. Usually, "the vocabulary of the people consists mainly of the words 'yes' and 'no,' and at times one cannot be certain which word is being uttered."[34] Elections most typically show retrospective voting, judgments on the conduct of the persons and party that has held power. Those who have given satisfaction are confirmed in office; those who are held responsible for the poor performance of the economy or foreign policy failures are dismissed from office.

VOTES OF CONFIDENCE An election, in this respect, can be seen as a national **vote of confidence,** similar to those in parliamentary systems, which determines whether the existing government will continue to hold power. In presidential elections, the voters are making a judgment on the conduct of the chief executive. President Gerald Ford put the case for his own reelection in precisely these terms, asking the voters to decide. "Jerry, you've done a good job. . . . Keep right on doing it."[35] As it turned out, not enough voters were prepared to agree. Four years later, Jimmy Carter became the victim of another vote of no confidence.

The electorate's retrospective judgment is not simply an assessment of individuals but a determination of the quality of their work. Voters need not be expert economists. But they do know about the price of food, and they blame the government when the grocery bill becomes uncomfortably high. Voters indicate their needs and desires, not specific programs; then, election winners must attempt to satisfy these demands. "Governments must worry, not about the meaning of past elections, but about their fate at future elections."[36]

Such retrospective judgments are one of the important ways in which issues affect electoral outcomes. These evaluations of the past also affect individuals' party identification, as well as their views on the future. Morris Fiorina has combined these factors into a general theory of voting behavior. In his model, the vote "is basically a scorecard marked by the citizen while observing and experiencing the world of politics." Party identification is a simple summary of past political experiences. This loyalty is reinforced or changed as citizens are satisfied or discontent with the actions of parties and their leaders. Utilizing the cue of party identification and their retrospective judgments, they then evaluate the alternative future promises.[37]

Retrospective Voting in 1984 When voting is retrospective, ballots are cast mostly on the record of the recent past, not on promises for the future. In 1984, Reagan's overwhelming reelection reflected the voters' belief that the president had done "the two things he was elected to do: curb inflation and restore the nation's sense of military security."[38] Even if they did not understand or even approve of particular policies, they reached a commonsense conclusion of confidence: "If it ain't broke, don't fix it."

Ideology, issues, or campaign tactics did not predominantly determine the election of 1984. Rather, more than any other reason, ballots were decided on the basis of the voters' satisfaction with the first Reagan administration. Three out of five voters justified their votes on the basis of "experience" and "strong leadership." More specifically, they endorsed his economic success. The president had asked the voters, "Are you better off now than you were four years ago?" If voters felt they were better off (45 percent did), six out of seven backed the president. If they felt worse off (only 17 percent), only one of seven voted for Reagan.[39]

President Reagan taking part in ceremonies at the fortieth anniversary of the Allied landing in Normandy. The president won many votes in 1984 because voters saw him as a strong leader. *(UPI/Bettmann Newsphotos)*

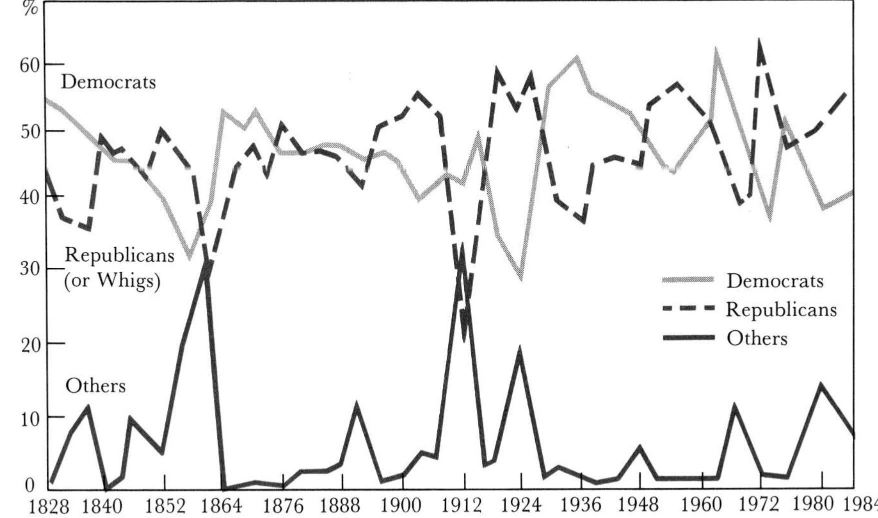

FIGURE 7.5
Party Votes in Presidential Elections
The economic turmoil of the Depression brought Franklin Roosevelt to power in 1932 and put the Democrats into the White House for twenty years. *(Library of Congress)*

Party Realignment

Elections affect parties as well as individuals. In the last chapter, we reviewed the history of the nation's party systems, from the first competition of Federalists and Republicans to the creation of Franklin Roosevelt's New Deal coalition. Typically, in each of these periods, one of the two major parties has been dominant—winning more elections, having more following, and dominating the policy debates of the period. Illustrating these party periods, Figure 7.5 charts the percentage of votes won by each party since 1828.

Realigning Elections Most of the time, the balance between the parties is fairly stable. Even if the majority party loses (as the Democrats did to Dwight Eisenhower in the 1950s), it soon returns to power (as the Democrats did with Kennedy and Johnson). On some dramatic occasions, an election results in more than the victory of one candidate over another. It also alters the basic character of the party balance for a long period of time. In a **realigning election,** the realignment can occur when either the previous minority party becomes the newly dominant party or the previous majority party fundamentally changes its voting coalition.

The last clear realignment of American politics came in the 1930s. The Democrats had long been the minority in the nation, winning only four presidential contests from the time of the Civil War. After the transformations following the Great Depression, the Democrats were clearly dominant—they won most presidential elections, held most seats in Congress, and ranked first in voter loyalty.

The process of party realignment usually occurs at a time of crisis, when the existing parties seem unable to cope with new problems—such as the 1930s economic collapse. Voters are then drawn to new allegiances—or even to a completely new party—in the hope that it will provide a solution to these problems. In the New Deal period, change in the party balance

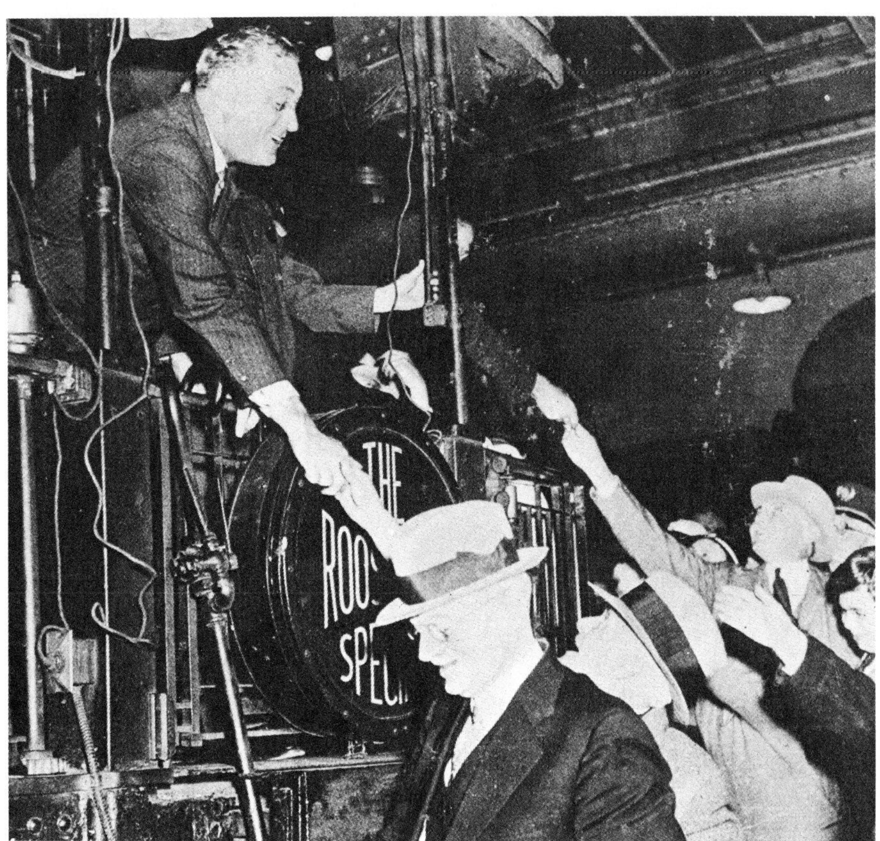

The economic turmoil of the Depression brought Franklin Roosevelt to power in 1932 and put the Democrats into the White House for twenty years. *(Library of Congress)*

came mostly from new voters. Examining this time, Kristi Andersen has shown that there was very little actual conversion of Republican voters during this period. Rather, most of the new support for Roosevelt and the Democrats came from youth and from immigrant and urban groups, who previously did not vote but now entered the electorate in response to party appeals.[40]

Realignment and Policy Change A voting change, however, is not sufficient to create a new party majority. Voters simply provide the opportunity for new policy initiatives by a new party coalition. "Whether or not the potential realignment comes to fruition lies in the hands of the partisan leadership and its ability to make the kinds of policy designs that win the long-term support of newly eligible, weakly identified or unidentified, and formerly apolitical members of the electorate."[41]

A successful realignment changes the nation's public policies. The new majority party is given a chance by the electorate to deal with pressing social problems. Democrats successfully used this opportunity in the 1930s, using the New Deal to create a welfare state and to alleviate the inequalities of a mature industrial nation. Other possible realignments have not come to pass because emerging new coalitions have not carried through successfully. Thus, although Lyndon Johnson in 1964 and Richard Nixon in 1972 both won landslide victories, neither was able to achieve a basic partisan realignment because of unfavorable events, Vietnam and Watergate.

Republican Realignment? The strong Republican victories in 1980 and 1984 suggest that a new party realignment may be in process. Indeed, on the presidential level, the change may have occurred already. The party has won four of the five last campaigns for the White House, losing only in the exceptional circumstances of the post-Watergate election of 1976.

The Reagan years do show some of the characteristics of party realignment. The Republicans gained the presidency because of popular discontent with the existing government, and at a time of increasing economic and international problems. Once in power, the Reagan government made striking changes in national programs, reducing the level of taxation, diminishing government aid to many constituencies, and initiating the largest armament program in U.S. history. The fiscal program appeared to work at least for a time, with the onset of strong economic growth. Even more significantly for the long run, Reagan as president changed the terms of public discourse. The welfare state was not abolished; rather, it was no longer respectable. All politicians came to agree with his philosophy that government should be restricted.

The presidential election returns of 1984 provide additional evidence of a Republican realignment. Notable shifts toward the party occurred in critical constituencies, including some that had been central to the Democratic majority, such as Catholics and White Southerners. Realignments are most likely to be heralded by the younger voters, less tied to the past, and this group—especially among males—gave Reagan strong support. The most critical indicator, party identification, also moved in the Republican direction.

Despite these indications, however, the question of contemporary realignment is still not resolved. Even as Democrats have lost the presidency, they have kept control of Congress in most elections, and they now still dominate the nation's state capitols. There is little reason to believe that there have been fundamental changes in voter ideology, and opinion polls show voter agreement with Democratic party positions on basic issues such as aid to the poor and a nuclear freeze.

Furthermore, the Republicans' successes still seem brittle. An economic downturn would make both Reagan and his party unpopular (as happened in the 1982 recession and congressional elections). Even if prosperity continues, the party must resolve its internal differences between those who focus on economic programs, such as taxation and government spending, and those who emphasize social conservatism, such as school prayers or opposition to abortion.[42]

Party Dealignment Instead of realignment, the United States may now be in a period of **party dealignment,** as voters show less attachment to either party. In this chapter, we have seen many indications of this trend. Party loyalty means less than in the past, as voters rely less on their partisan identification in marking their ballots. Social groups are less anchored to the Democrats or Republicans but shift from one contest to another. Elections are decided on more short-term factors, such as the particular candidates, issues, and strategies of each campaign.

In concluding the previous chapter, we emphasized the contributions parties make to effective democracy. Paralleling the importance of parties as organizations is the significance of party loyalties as an aid to popular control of government. Party identification provides the voters with understandable information that summarizes past performance and provides a usually reliable guide to future action. As its impact declines, voters are more subject to manipulation, forced to depend on uncertain judgments about passing issues and on biased images presented on shadowy television screens.

Elections structured by party identification also facilitate collective responsibility of officeholders. Knowing they will be judged as a group, they will cooperate more in order to ensure their own election. As campaigns center more on individuals, however, incumbents are free to go off on their own and challengers must make personal appeals. "'United we stand' has given way to 'Every man for himself,' and the country is the poorer for it."[43]

Through elections, Americans attempt to make a nation into a political entity. Voting offers us the opportunity to make collective decisions, using the parties' records to judge the past and seek the future. The effort is always difficult in this fragmented society and government. Party dealignment will only worsen the problem and further fragment the politics of the United States.

SUMMARY

Voting is the way we make our collective national decisions. Yet, voting participation in the United States appears to be lower than in other democracies and dropped steadily from 1960 until it increased slightly in the 1984 presidential election. The major determinant of whether a person will vote is education; this factor is far more important than any differences in participation between young and old or between men and women.

Most rules about voting are established by the states; however, the national government has taken action to secure the rights of women and blacks to equal voting participation. The importance of our decentralized election system is seen in the election of the president, who is formally chosen by the Electoral College. Under this system, it is theoretically possible for a candidate to reach the presidency without receiving more popular votes than his or her opponents.

Party loyalty is a major influence on the vote. *Party identification* is the long-standing loyalty people feel to their party. In recent years, there has been some weakening of these loyalties, especially among younger voters. At the same time, the lead of the Democrats in party identification may have disappeared.

The outcome of elections can be explained in part by the voting behavior of social groups. Democrats fare better with minority groups and Republicans with businessmen. Voting differences between men and women, a *gender gap,* have also appeared recently. Social group analyses, however, can be misleading, since any individual can fall into overlapping categories of class, race, sex, and occupation. Election analyses must also recognize that social groups change their loyalties, from one election to the next or from one historical era to another.

With ties between social groups loosened and party loyalties weaker, issues carry more weight with the electorate. Different issues are important in each election; for example, economic policies were most important in 1984. The voters' general philosophies also influence their decisions. Although there is no automatic connection, conservatives are more likely to be Republicans and liberals to be Democrats. Still, to many voters, neither issues nor philosophies are as important as the individual traits of candidates, especially their apparent trustworthiness and competence. Such evaluations provide much of the explanation for both the defeat of President Carter in 1980 and the reelection of President Reagan in 1984.

During a campaign, candidates and their staffs have three major goals: devising a strategy, shaping information persuasively, and gaining attention. To achieve success, they need to establish a theme, target groups that hold the promise of support, and develop advertising that will favorably present the candidate's personality and policies. Even with the best efforts, however, campaign effectiveness is limited by political realities and by uncertainty.

The retrospective judgment of the voters often is the major feature of an election. In this sense, elections function like the votes of confidence in a parliamentary system that decide whether a government will continue in office. In 1984, many Reagan supporters explained their votes this way.

Elections can also affect the balance between the parties. *Realignment* alters their composition or relative strength. Basic policy changes then follow from the realignment. There is some evidence that Reagan's victories have been part of a basic realignment in American politics and may produce a new Republican majority. It is also possible that party decline will continue, accompanied by dealignment in voter loyalties.

NOTES

1. Curtis Gans, "The Empty Ballot Box," *Public Opinion,* 1 (Sept./Oct. 1978), p. 54. Arthur Hadley presents a similar argument in *The Empty Polling Booth* (Englewood Cliffs, N.J.: Prentice-Hall, 1978).
2. See Ronald Moe, "Myth of the Non-Voting American," *Wall Street Journal* (Nov. 4, 1980); Richard Boyd, "Decline of U.S. Voter Turnout: Structural Explanations," *American Politics Quarterly,* 9 (April 1981), pp. 133–60.
3. Raymond Wolfinger and Steven Rosenstone, *Who Votes?* (New Haven: Yale U. P., 1980), chap. 4.
4. Paul R. Abramson and John H. Aldrich, "The Decline of Electoral Participation in America," *American Political Science Review,* 76 (Sept. 1982), pp. 402–21; Samuel C. Patterson and Gregory A. Caldiera, "Getting Out the Vote: Participation in Gubernatorial Elections," *American Political Science Review,* 77 (Sept. 1983), pp. 675–89 and Caldiera et al., "The Mobilization of Voters in Congressional Elections," *Journal of Politics,* 47 (May 1985), pp. 490–509.
5. "Campaign Report 1984," *National Journal,* 16 (Nov. 3, 1984), pp. 2068–73.
6. Wolfinger and Rosenstone, pp. 38, 58.
7. Ibid., p. 102.
8. Ibid., chap. 6.
9. Svend Petersen, *A Statistical History of the American Presidential Elections* (New York: Ungar, 1963), pp. 54, 112.
10. V.O. Key, *American State Politics* (New York: Knopf, 1956), p. 222.
11. Richard Jensen, *The Winning of the Midwest* (Chicago: U. of Chicago, 1971), p. 11.
12. Philip Converse and Gregory Markus, "Plus ça change . . . : The CPS Election Study Panel," *American Political Science Review,* 73 (March 1979), pp. 35–39. The concept originated in Angus Campbell et al., *The American Voter* (New York: Wiley, 1960).
13. CBS News/*New York Times* Poll, May 29–June 2, 1985. Early analysis of the change is found in Seymour Lipset, "The Elections, the Economy and Public Opinion: 1984," *PS,* 18 (Winter 1985), pp. 28–38. A significant datum is found in a 1985 Gallup poll, which found for the first time that the Republicans were considered both better able to assure prosperity (by a 48–32 margin, with 20 percent seeing no party difference) and to ensure peace (by 39–33–28): *The New York Times* (April 4, 1985).
14. Raymond Wolfinger et al., "The Myth of the Independent Voter," Paper presented to the American Political Science Association (Washington, 1977); John Kessel, *Presidential Campaign Politics* (Homewood, Ill.: Dorsey, 1980), pp. 227–31; David Valentine and John Van Wingen, "Partisanship, Independence, and the Partisan Identification Question," *American Politics Quarterly,* 8 (April 1980), pp. 165–86.
15. Martin P. Wattenberg, *The Decline of American Political Parties* (Cambridge: Harvard U. P., 1984), p. 69 and chap. 4.
16. See Scott Keeter, "Public Opinion in 1984," in *The Election of 1984,* Gerald Pomper, ed. (Chatham, N.J.: Chatham House, 1985), pp. 101–106; and Susan Carroll, "Women's Autonomy and the Gender Gap," Paper presented to the American Psychological Association (1984).
17. E. E. Schattschneider, *Political Parties* (New York: Holt, 1942), p. 87.
18. Bruce Campbell, "Patterns of Change in the Partisan Loyalties of Native Southerners: 1952–1972," *Journal of Politics,* 39 (Aug. 1977), pp. 730–61; Carol Cassel, "Cohort Analyses of Party Identification among Southern Whites, 1952–1972," *Public Opinion Quarterly,* 41 (Spring 1977), pp. 28–33; *The New York Times* (April 1, 1985), p. B7.
19. Norman Nie, Sidney Verba, and John Petrocik, *The Changing American Voter,* enlarged ed. (Cambridge: Harvard U. P., 1979), p. 377.
20. Harris poll of July 24, 1984, as reported in *National Journal,* 16 (Aug. 11, 1984), p. 1542; *The New York Times,* Aug. 19, 1984, CBS News/*New York Times* Poll, Aug. 5–9, 1984.
21. CBS News/*New York Times* Poll (Oct. 14, 1984); *Los Angeles Times* Poll (Oct. 16, 1984); Keeter, pp. 93–99.
22. Teresa Levitin and Warren Miller, "Ideological Interpretations of Presidential Elections," *American Political Science Review,* 73 (Sept. 1979), p. 753ff. The figure includes a tenth of the electorate classified as "centrists."
23. Nie et al., p. 115, as corrected in "Communications," *American Political Science Review,* 75 (March 1981), p. 150.
24. CBS News/*New York Times* Exit Polls of 1980, 1984.

25. Jeffrey A. Smith, *American Presidential Elections: Trust and the Rational Voter* (New York: Praeger, 1980), chaps. 5, 6.
26. Gregory Markus, "Political Attitudes during an Election Year: A Report on the 1980 NES Study," *American Political Science Review,* 76 (Sept. 1982), pp. 538–60; Kathleen Frankovic, "Public Opinion Trends," in *The Election of 1980,* Gerald Pomper, ed. (Chatham, N.J.: Chatham House, 1981), p. 103; CBS News/*New York Times* Poll (Sept. 12–16, 1984).
27. Larry Sabato, *The Rise of Political Consultants* (New York: Basic Books, 1981), p. 20.
28. Stimson Bullitt, *To Be a Politician* (New Haven: Yale U. P., 1977), p. 111.
29. Benjamin Page, *Choices and Echoes in Presidential Elections* (Chicago: U. of Chicago, 1978), pp. 153–54.
30. Robert Agranoff, *The New Style in Election Campaigns,* 2nd ed. (Boston: Holbrook, 1976), p. 4.
31. Sabato, p. 18.
32. Kathleen Frankovic, "The 1984 Election: The Irrelevance of the Campaign," *PS,* 18 (Winter 1985), pp. 39–47; *Los Angeles Times* Exit Poll, reported in *National Journal,* 16 (Nov. 10, 1984), p. 2131.
33. William Shakespeare, *Anthony and Cleopatra,* V:ii,3.
34. V. O. Key, Jr., *Politics, Parties and Pressure Groups,* 5th ed. (New York: Crowell, 1964), p. 544.
35. *Congressional Quarterly Weekly Report,* 34 (Aug. 21, 1976), p. 2316.
36. V. O. Key, Jr., with Milton C. Cummings, Jr., *The Responsible Electorate* (Cambridge: Harvard U. P., 1966), p. 77.
37. Morris P. Fiorina, *Retrospective Voting in American National Elections* (New Haven: Yale U. P., 1981), chaps. 4, 5. Also see Charles Franklin and John Jackson, "The Dynamics of Party Identification," *American Political Science Review,* 77 (Dec. 1983), pp. 957–73.
38. William Schneider, "Performance Is the Big Campaign Issue, and That Gives Reagan a Big Edge," *National Journal,* 16 (Oct. 6, 1984), p. 1984ff.
39. Gerald Pomper, ed., *The Election of 1984* (Chatham, N.J.: Chatham House, 1985), p. 99.
40. Kristi Andersen, *The Creation of a Democratic Majority, 1928–1936* (Chicago: U. of Chicago, 1979), pp. 62–69. Also see Robert C. Erikson and Kent L. Tedin, "The 1928–1936 Partisan Realignment: The Case for the Conversion Hypothesis," *American Political Science Review,* 75 (Dec. 1981), pp. 951–62.
41. Jerome Clubb, William Flanigan, and Nancy Zingale, *Partisan Realignment* (Beverly Hills: Sage, 1980), p. 268.
42. Analyses of the realignment implications of the 1984 election include Lipset, "The Elections, the Economy and Public Opinion"; Everett C. Ladd, "As the Realignment Turns," *Public Opinion,* 7 (Dec. 1984/Jan. 1985), pp. 2–7; Michael Nelson, *The Elections of 1984* (Washington: Congressional Quarterly Press, 1985); Pomper et al., *The Election of 1984;* "Special Election Issue," *The Brookings Review,* 3 (Winter 1984); and Nelson Polsby, "Did the 1984 Election Signal Major Party Realignment?," *The Key Reporter,* 50 (Spring 1985), pp. 1–4.
43. Fiorina, p. 211.

CHAPTER 8

Interest Groups

Follow a typical day in Washington. An association of automobile manufacturers urges a congressional committee to restrict foreign car imports. Spokesmen for the television networks seek an administrative ruling to allow more commercials during broadcasts. An attorney files a brief at the Supreme Court opposing federal aid to segregated private schools. The National Organization for Women plans a renewed public campaign on behalf of the Equal Rights Amendment. The staff of the National Rifle Association calmly reads the latest opinion polls favoring limitations on handguns, confident that it will defeat any restrictive legislation. Opponents of nuclear weapons picket the White House.

This is the world of **interest groups,** organizations that seek to influence public decisions. They are not constitutional institutions, such as Congress, the executive, and the courts, but—like political parties—they have considerable influence on the actions of these formal bodies. Indeed, as James Madison wrote in explaining the Constitution, interest groups are inevitably involved "in the necessary and ordinary operations of the government."[1] They are particularly important from our general perspective, the fragmentation of power. The Constitution fragmented the formal powers of government. Interest groups reinforce formal divisions, by expressing the social fragmentations of American life.

In this chapter, we will explore the world of interest groups, surveying five areas:

1. The character and growth of interest groups.
2. The variety of interest groups.
3. Their activities and techniques.
4. Differing evaluations of their power.
5. Means to control interest groups.

The World of Interest Groups: "This Dangerous Vice"

Madison on Interest Groups

James Madison's thought, as we have outlined it in Chapter 1, is critical to understanding politics in the United States. In his major essay, *The Federalist, No. 10,* the "Father of the Constitution" emphasized the role of interest groups, which he called "factions."

Wanting to protect individual liberty and private rights, Madison feared these values would be harmed if government is subject to the "dangerous vice" of the "violence of faction." Today, we may be concerned about the inordinate influence of corporations or labor unions. Similarly, Madison worried about the power of any "faction . . . whether amounting to a majority or minority of the whole, who are united and actuated by some common impulse of passion, or of interest, adverse to the rights of other citizens, or to the permanent and aggregate interests of the community."

Although disagreeable, factions cannot be eliminated, Madison argued, unless liberty itself was eliminated or all people were made identical. Factions flourish because they are "sown in the nature of man." Although they come in many varieties, they are especially evident in conflicts of economic interests. (Madison's own words are reproduced in the boxed excerpt.)

Once established, factions use various activities and resources to gain their ends in "the conflicts of rival parties." Madison built a theoretical means "to adjust these clashing interests." He gave scant attention to minority factions, assuming they would be easily outvoted, and could not predict the enormous growth of specialized interests in a modern society. His

POLITICAL PERSPECTIVE

JAMES MADISON EXPLAINS INTEREST GROUPS

A zeal for different opinions concerning religion, concerning government, and many other points, as well of speculation as of practice; an attachment to different leaders ambitiously contending for pre-eminence and power; or to persons of other descriptions whose fortunes have been interesting to the human passions, have, in turn, divided mankind into parties, inflamed them with mutual animosity, and rendered them much more disposed to vex and oppress each other than to cooperate for their common good. So strong is this propensity of mankind to fall into mutual animosities, that where no substantial occasion presents itself, the most frivolous and fanciful distinctions have been sufficient to kindle their unfriendly passions and excite their most violent conflicts. But the most common and durable sources of factions has been the various and unequal distribution of property. Those who hold and those who are without property have ever formed distinct interests in society. Those who are creditors, and those who are debtors, fall under a like discrimination. A landed interest, a manufacturing interest, a mercantile interest, a money interest, with many lesser interests, grow up of necessity in civilized nations, and divide them into different classes, actuated by different sentiments and views. The regulation of these various and interfering interests forms the principal task of modern legislation and involves the spirit of party and faction in the necessary and ordinary operations of the government.

Source: James Madison, *The Federalist, No. 10* (New York: Modern Library edition, 1941), pp. 55–56.

major concern was a majority faction, such as those without property. To deal with them, Madison had two aims: "To secure the public good and private rights against the danger of such a faction, and at the same time to preserve the spirit and the form of popular government."

Seeking a "cure for the mischiefs of faction," Madison supported the Constitution's fragmentation of power. He argued for representation rather than direct democracy and for a large nation, Federalism, and the division of institutions (see Chapters 1 and 2). Through these legal and social devices, he believed that both liberty and property would be secured, and, thus, he thought he had found "a republican remedy for the diseases most incident to republican government."

Since Madison's time, the United States has changed enormously, producing many more interests. Although we may understand their important functions, we need to be aware of their defects as well.

Functions of Interest Groups Interest groups serve some important functions in our complex society. In many ways, they fill in gaps that arise in the activities of political parties and the formal agencies of government:

1. They enable people to focus on their special needs, instead of compromising with others in advocating a common program.
2. They raise issues that parties and officials ignore or don't understand, providing information that is independent of the bureaucracy.
3. Unlike the vague meanings of elections, they communicate messages about specific issues, and indicate the intensity of feelings on these issues.
4. They provide this information regularly, in contrast to the long periods of time between elections.

Defects of Interest Groups Interest groups are necessary, but this does not mean that they are always desirable. In reviewing the functions of interest groups, critics raise these objections:

1. By focusing on their own needs, these groups ignore the general good of the nation.
2. The information they provide is biased, presenting only their own side of issues.
3. The influence of interest groups can lead to inequality and even corruption, because their power is based on resources such as social prestige or money.
4. Because they are not subject to control in elections, interest groups undermine democracy.

The Growth of Interest Groups

Imagine a motion picture documentary about life in the United States. Such a film would reveal a broad diversity within the nation, from urban centers with 30,000 persons in a square mile to the cattle ranges of the far

Interest groups are often criticized as caring only for their selfish aims. Here, in the movie *Mr. Smith Goes to Washington,* Jimmy Stewart carries on a three-day Senate filibuster to defeat an interest-group-sponsored bill that would use public land for corrupt purposes. *(Movie Still Archives)*

West, with fewer than 3 persons in the same area. The people in this film would include representatives of every ethnic stock in the world, from the Indians of Asia to the native American Indian tribes, and including more Jews than in Israel, more persons of Irish descent than now live in the Emerald Isle, and more blacks than in Zaire. These people operate highly sophisticated computers and pick vegetables by hand, manufacture supersonic airplanes, repair bicycles, sew dresses, and trade gold. They practice hundreds of religions, pursue thousands of leisure activities, and on the average each purchases $15,000 of goods and services every year.

This striking diversity is reflected in and organized by over 17,000 recognized associations in the country, as well as by many more informal groupings. They include large groups, such as the United Automobile Workers, or the 58 different associations connected to the steel industry, as well as less imposing groups. The Committee for Pedestrian Tolls, the American Association of Bovine Practitioners, or the eleven Brooklyn members of JACGUAR (Johns and Call Girls United Against Repression) are some of the smaller groups. There is even an American League of Lobbyists.[2]

These organizations draw considerable membership from the American population. A cross-national study found that 57 percent of Americans, more than citizens of any of the five countries studied, participated in some voluntary association.[3] Furthermore, about a third of U.S. citizens, a larger proportion than in any of seven countries, report that they are active in an organization that is involved in studying community problems. Memberships in groups broadly involved in politics are more common than affiliations with veterans' or church-related organizations.[4]

These groups become political interest groups when they come to the conclusion that they cannot accomplish important ends without the power of government. Groups try to deal with disturbances in their environment, such as changing economic conditions. "As our society has become increasingly complex, however, these disturbances have affected not merely the relationships of widely distributed individuals; they have also created a new problem, by placing the means of adjustment beyond the resources of direct action by the groups involved."[5] Lacking the power to control the environment by themselves, groups turn to the fullest source of power, the government.

Entering Politics: Women The women's movement is a recent example of groups' increased involvement in politics. Individual women have been involved in American government since its beginnings, and they played important roles in abolitionist and settlement house movements. As a feminist action, the most important campaign was to establish women's suffrage, which was achieved in 1920. Changes in society and the economy, however, were also altering the character of women's lives; as more of them entered the labor force, family size diminished, and new contraceptive techniques permitted a wider choice of life styles.

These trends became politically significant in the 1960s. At a White House conference of state Commissions on the Status of Women, a new interest group was formed, the **National Organization for Women (NOW).** This was soon followed by the creation of other organizations, and feminists quickly found that their goals of sexual equality could not be met without government action. A political agenda was established, including adoption of the **Equal Rights Amendment** to the Constitution (prohibiting discrimination on the basis of sex), removal of government restrictions on abortion, equal pay, and the election and appointment of more females to public office.[6] The mobilization of this women's movement also spurred the entrance of other women who opposed these particular goals into politics. Women who were satisfied with a more domestic role found themselves

820
HARPER'S WEEKLY.
[MAY 16, 1868.
HOW IT WOULD BE, IF SOME LADIES HAD THEIR OWN WAY.

Even in the nineteenth century, it was clear that the women's movement implied changes in the structure of family life. *(Library of Congress)*

organizing politically into such groups as Stop ERA. Even to defend a restricted political role, these groups found it necessary to become heavily political.

The opposition was successful in defeating the proposed addition to the Constitution. The response of NOW was to broaden its involvement in politics, by participating more directly in the election process. The organization not only endorsed a presidential candidate, Democrat Walter Mondale, but set out to elect friendly women to the state legislatures. Judy Goldsmith, president of NOW, put it simply in launching the campaign: "The only way for us to achieve real goals for women is to have women in those legislative seats making the decisions."[7]

Social and Political Change As the example of the women's movement suggests, there are two general but separate causes of the growth in the number of interest groups and their increasing involvement in politics. The underlying cause is social and political changes that make politics relevant to persons who share some characteristics and goals. Then, there is an immediate cause, which makes an interest group an active political contestant. This happens by the action of a specific person, group, or government agency. Forming groups is not an easy business, as potential members must be given some meaningful incentive to lend their efforts to the cause.

The development of the United States into a large, industrialized world power guarantees that new interests will arise. As the nation has developed, government has come to have a greater impact on the society, and those affected seek to use government's power to promote their own goals. If the economic development of the nation had been left entirely in private hands (which never happened), those involved in the economy might have kept out of politics. In fact, of course, American government has always been involved. The development of the transportation systems of the nation depended on government aid to canal builders, land grants to railroads, and subsidized contracts for the airlines. The historical tradition continues today as interest groups seek to have government build a barge canal across Alabama, pay for repair of railroad beds, and maintain profitable airplane fares.

As the scope of government activity has increased, there has been a parallel increase in the number and political activity of interest groups. A large part of federal spending today is in programs that provide benefits to various sectors of the population, such as senior citizens, veterans, and the poor. A variety of interest groups have arisen to protect and expand these programs, such as the National Council of Senior Citizens and the Disabled American Veterans.

Creating Interest Groups Government does more than passively respond to the pressures and demands of these groups. At times, government itself helps in the creation of formal associations. An historical example is the American Farm Bureau Federation, long the most important agricultural interest group. It originated in the federal government's county agent system, through which the U.S. Department of Agriculture provided education and technical help to farmers. To provide this help more efficiently, farm bureaus of local residents were created. They developed close ties to the government officials, sometimes even paying their salaries. As these local groups united to form state and national associations, they maintained their close connection to the Agriculture Department, and the interest group became the major source for administrators of farm programs.[8]

Government sponsorship of interest groups continues to the present. The Reagan administration, reflecting its pro-business bent, listened deferentially to the American Business Conference, an association of high-growth companies. It also sponsored the president's Private Sector Survey on Cost Control, a privately funded group of corporate executives that has endorsed such conservative policies as reductions in federal health expenditures.[9] In an earlier time, the antipoverty program of the 1960s included provisions for the creation of local community action agencies. Originating in a desire to promote "maximum feasible participation" of the poor in these programs, the consequence was to create new interest groups making demands on government.[10]

POLITICAL PERSPECTIVE

INTEREST GROUPS IN FICTION

In Allen Drury's novel of Washington politics, *Advise and Consent,* a common view of interest group pressure is presented in two telephone conversations. Excerpted below, these conversations deal with the president's nomination of a prominent liberal as Secretary of State.

> The trouble with the president of General Motors, in the opinion of Roy B. Mulholland, was that he thought he owned the Senators from Michigan, or at least the junior Senator from Michigan, namely Roy B. Mulholland. He didn't try to pressure Bob Munson very often, except indirectly through Roy, but he was always after Roy about something.
>
> "No, God damn it," he was saying vigorously over the line from Detroit, "we don't want a radical like that for Secretary of State. Now do we? Do we?"
>
> "Bill," Senator Mulholland said with a trace of asperity, "I tell you I haven't made up my mind yet."
>
> "Well, make it up, man," the president of General Motors said impatiently. "Make it up. Time waits for no man, you know. And you can tell Bob from me that we're going to be watching his actions on this very closely. Very closely indeed. . . ."
>
> . . .
>
> The trouble with the president of the United Auto Workers, in the opinion of Bob Munson, was that he thought he owned the Senators from Michigan, or at least the senior Senator from Michigan, namely Bob Munson. He didn't try to pressure Roy Mulholland very often, except indirectly through Bob, but he was always after Bob about something.
>
> "Now, God damn it," he was saying vigorously over the line from Detroit, "we want to get organized and get this nomination through as soon as possible. We want to help, Bob. We want you to let us know what we can do. . . . We've got to beat these reactionary bastards at their own game. You're going to need all the assistance you can get, Bob, and we intend to help you. We want you to know that, Bob. Incidentally, what about that lily-livered pantywaist of a colleague of yours? What are they going to scare him into doing?"
>
> "I haven't talked to Roy yet," Bob Munson said, "I imagine on this one he'll make up his own mind."
>
> "Well," said the president of the UAW darkly, "you tell him we're going to be watching his action on this one very closely. *Damn* closely."

Source: Excerpts from *Advise and Consent* by Allen Drury. Copyright © 1959 by Allen Drury. Reprinted by permission of Doubleday & Company, Inc.

Creation of interest groups especially requires some leader or group to take advantage of the social trends and available political opportunities. The individuals who do this usefully can be considered entrepreneurs. Like business innovators, these entrepreneurs see opportunity for change in the existing social situation. They apply their personal talents to creating a formal association for the expression of a group's interests. Without these individual entrepreneurs, some potential interests will be unheard.

In the case of the feminist movement, women's inequality existed centuries before the 1960s. The formation of NOW and its sister groups, however, only came when the women at the White House conference took deliberate action to translate grievances into political strategy.

Entrepreneurs are critical to interest groups. They are the links in a series of exchanges between the group member and the political system. The leader provides benefits for the members, such as governmental programs, and in return receives the rewards of officeholding. He or she makes demands on government, promising support from the group in exchange for favorable action by politicians. The ability of the entrepreneur considerably affects the success or failure of each interest.[11]

In recent years, entrepreneurship has been particularly exemplified by a modern-day legend, Ralph Nader. Acting entirely alone, Nader gained national prominence by investigating the dangers of the Chevrolet Corvair and becoming the target of a defamatory General Motors campaign. After winning a damage suit from GM, Nader created a series of issue-oriented groups to oversee government action on topics ranging from air pollution to tax reform. Revered as an ascetic "secular saint," Nader is now financed by his own income from books and lectures, college student fees through local PIRGs (public interest research groups), and by Public Citizen, an organization whose members contribute money voluntarily but receive no personal benefits, newsletters, or voice in deciding the programs of the association.

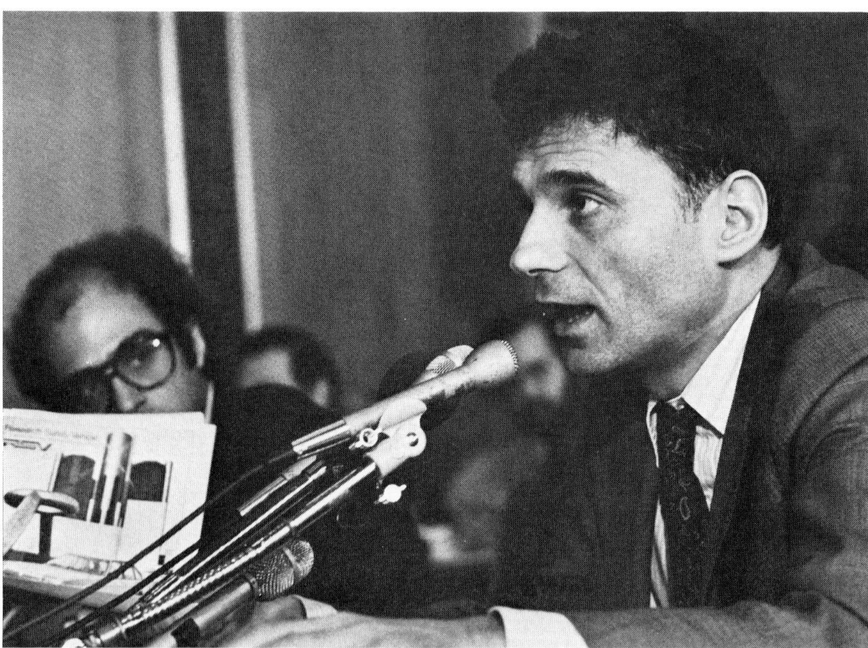

Ralph Nader almost single-handedly created a new consciousness among Americans about consumer issues relating to product performance, health, and safety. *(AP)*

Varieties of Interest Groups: "Sown in the Nature of Man"

Interest groups come in many varieties—large and small, centralized and federated, broad and narrow in purpose. Their diversity is shown in Table 8.1. As Madison expected, the largest proportion of interest groups are concerned with economic matters. Others are organized around issues or common demographic characteristics of their members. They also differ in the importance of different incentives for the members.

Incentives in Interest Groups

All groups face the need to persuade potential recruits to join the organization; maintain the affiliation; and contribute their time, money, and enthusiasm. Since membership is usually voluntary, the leaders of the group must devote considerable effort to gain this support, and provide reasons, or incentives, for continued backing. Even if membership is not entirely voluntary—as in some labor unions or dominant professional groups such as the American Medical Association—leadership still would like members to do more than pay dues grudgingly.

The Need for Incentives For the individual member, however, there are often reasons not to join the group. Activity in an interest group involves

TABLE 8.1 American National Organizations

Focus	Number of Groups 1968	1979
Agriculture	491	640
Athletics	318	476
Chambers of commerce	126	103
Cultural, educational	1,286	2,188
Fraternal, nationality, ethnic	640	448
Governmental, administration, military, legal	301	479
Greek letter societies	351	320
Health, medical	791	1,278
Hobby, avocational	423	759
Labor unions	237	230
Public affairs	446	913
Religious	794	772
Scientific, engineering, technical	488	932
Social welfare	389	848
Trade, business, commercial	2,832	2,992
Veterans, hereditary, patriotic	197	211
Other	189	1,020
Total	10,229	14,609

Source: Encyclopedia of Associations, as compiled in U.S. Department of Commerce, Bureau of the Census, *Social Indicators III* (Washington, 1980), p. 521.
Note: Includes nonprofit organizations of national scope.

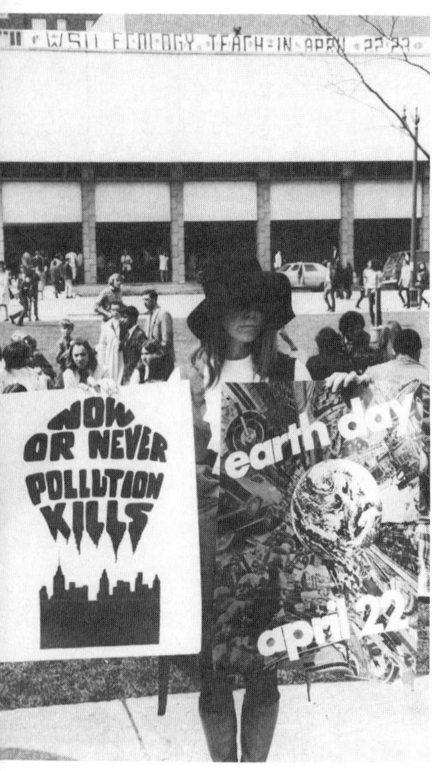

Environmental interest groups use unusual methods to gain members. Earth Day, a day of celebrating the earth and its natural resources, was initiated by several such organizations in 1970 to draw attention to environmental conditions nationwide. *(Benyas-Kaufman/ Black Star)*

costs, such as time and money. The ideal situation for an individual is for others to pay these costs and to make the interest group effective, while he or she gets the benefits. There is a common and understandable desire to "Let George do it." Unions face this problem in the form of the free rider, the plant worker who refuses to join the union, saves monthly dues and meeting time but still gets the benefit of the higher wages and other benefits negotiated by the labor group. Associations seeking more general interests, such as environmentalists, may have even more difficulty in recruiting members. All persons gain if the group wins legislation to promote cleaner air or less polluted water, whether or not they have worked personally toward these goals. Since the benefits do not depend on any particular individuals joining the group, they may leave the hard work to others, while they "go fishing" in the cleaner environment.

To meet this problem, groups use two strategies, as analyzed by Mancur Olson: they can coerce membership in their group, as happens when union membership is required before getting a job (the "closed shop"), or they can provide specific benefits for individuals, so as to induce them to join. Olson's theory of collective action provides a useful basis for classifying groups on the basis of the benefits, or incentives, they provide to the membership. He suggests that groups will be stronger when their benefits are provided only to individuals who support the organization. "An organization that did nothing except lobby to obtain a collective good for some group would not have a source of rewards or positive selective incentives it could offer potential members."[12] Thus, labor unions would gain more membership if their economic benefits were restricted to those paying dues, and environmental groups would recruit millions to their cause if clear air were available only to contributors to Friends of the Earth.

Tangible and Intangible Incentives There are two ways to look at incentives in the form of the benefits provided to group members. The first is the tangible or intangible nature of the incentive. A tangible incentive is one that is seen as real, or material, and can usually be expressed in numbers—higher wages, more profit, better housing, or longer life. An intangible incentive is less direct and may consist of personal psychological satisfaction or the emotional rewards of helping others.

Divisibility of Benefits The second classification of incentives is the divisibility of the benefit, that is, whether it can be given specifically to people

FIGURE 8.1 Varieties of Interest Groups and Incentives

	Tangible Incentives	Intangible Incentives
Divisible Benefits	*Material Rewards* Economic Groups Tax policies	*Status Rewards* Solidary Groups Ethnic policies
Nondivisible Benefits	*Policy Rewards* Issue groups Abortion policy	*Ideological Rewards* Programmatic groups "Good government" policies

in a group while being denied to outsiders, or whether it is impossible, even theoretically, to divide it. Money is the most obvious divisible reward because it can be paid just to the "right" persons. Clean air, on the other hand, cannot be restricted—if a group succeeds in reducing pollution, both members and nonmembers benefit.

Figure 8.1 shows how these two classifications result in four different kinds of rewards and in four common varieties of interest groups. Using this classification, we will now consider some specific interest groups. Note, however, that almost all groups make some use of each kind of incentive.

Economic Groups

The most prominent and numerous interest groups are those that work on behalf of the economic interests of their members. Business groups are the most conspicuous in this category. They include individual firms, giant corporations such as General Motors, and trade associations speaking on behalf of a single industry, such as the Southwestern Peanut Shellers Association or the American Steel Institute. The general interests of business are promoted by such "peak associations" as the inclusive U.S. Chamber of Commerce or the smaller but powerful Business Roundtable, comprising executives of the 200 largest corporations in America.

Other significant economic groups include national labor unions, which are united for political purposes in the American Federation of Labor and Congress of Industrial Organizations; agricultural groups such as the American Farm Bureau Federation and the National Grange; specialized groups for athletes, gas station operators, and civil servants; and professional associations of doctors, dentists, and educators.

Material Rewards The common characteristic of these groups is that their major objective is to promote the material welfare of their members. The incentives they provide for affiliation are certainly tangible, including favorable tax provisions or government subsidies for business, minimum wages for union workers, and increased acreage allotments for farmers. These incentives also are divisible, for persons outside the group may be kept from enjoying the benefits. For example, lawyers in some states may not be admitted to the courts unless they are members of the bar association, or hospitals may require their doctors to be members of the county medical association.

Even organizations that are not primarily concerned with economic objectives are prepared, if necessary, to defend their members' well-being. A notable example came in a little-noticed but significant conflict between book publishers and universities over revision of the copyright laws. These two groups normally share an interest in the dissemination of knowledge. A new technological development—the photocopying machine—disrupted their amicable relationships. Publishers and their authors opposed widespread photocopying, since no book royalties were paid on these copies. Universities, on the other hand, favored freer use of the new technology as a means of adding to their libraries and their students' materials at a relatively low cost. Professors were divided between their personal interest in earning royalties and their educational interest in having more reading material available in the classroom. Ultimately, a compromise was reached limiting universities generally to making only one photocopy of any published work.[13]

Business Interests Although business groups are the most important economic interests, there usually is not a single position advocated by the corporate world on any particular issue. Most issues concern small differences, and on these, business groups are usually divided. Even on a major issue such as foreign trade, a major study found that corporations selling their products abroad generally sought lower import tariffs, whereas domestic industries threatened by foreign competition wanted legislative protection—and that both groups were incompletely mobilized and only partially aware of the issue.[14]

Economic issues usually are not direct clashes between the "haves" and the "have-nots." They are more likely to be conflicts between groups, both of which have something and want more to be allocated to them. In these economic controversies, businesses will often form a coalition with their presumed antagonists, labor unions. Thus, when the Chrysler automobile corporation faced financial distress, a fervent advocate of aid to the manufacturer was the United Automobile Workers.

Issue Groups

A second category of interests are those that are organized to promote particular issues that are not so closely tied to the economic position of their members. A great variety of groups can be placed in this category, such as advocates and opponents of gun control, environmentalists, supporters of a larger expenditure for children's health services, or the American Automobile Association. The issues they support may have implications for the economic position of their members—for example, the AAA favors toll-free highways—but they are not organized on the basis of these economic roles.

To keep their support, interest groups provide special benefits for members. Among the services that the Automobile Association of America (AAA) provides is a list of recommended hotels. *(John Schultz/PAR-NYC)*

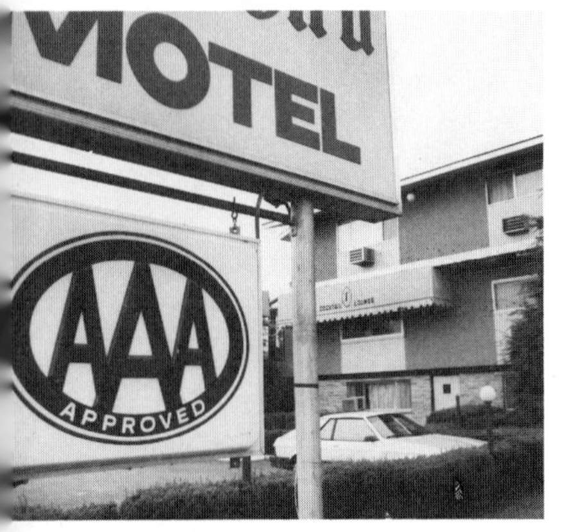

Policy Rewards The incentives provided by these groups to members consist more of policy rewards. The members support the group because it supports easy access to hunting rifles, for example, or wants to restrict the availability of handguns. The emphasis on policy rewards can make it difficult to maintain membership, however, for these rewards tend to be nondivisible in character. If toll roads are eliminated through the efforts of the AAA, all drivers will benefit, whether or not they have paid dues to the group. This situation encourages free riding, in both senses. To combat this tendency, groups will try to develop some benefits that are only available to members, such as providing information on hotels and car routes, or discounts on guns for hunters.[15] The same techniques are used by purely economic groups, but the need is probably even greater for those issue groups that cannot easily promise material gains to their members.

Despite their inherent problems, issue groups have become increasingly important. The rise of such single-interest groups has become widely recognized and widely deplored. Focusing only on their unique concerns, these

POLITICAL PERSPECTIVE

SMOKE GETS IN YOUR AYES

The issue of smoking shows the conflicts between two kinds of interests: economic and issue groups.

Over two decades ago, the Surgeon General, the chief medical officer of the government, issued a report that cigarette smoking is detrimental to health, based on laboratory results showing smoking produces lung cancer and other diseases. Consequently, the Federal Trade Commission, which regulates advertising, attempted to bar cigarette promotions from the mass media. The antismoking effort was supported by issue groups, including the American Cancer Society and ASH (Action on Smoking and Health). The anticigarette groups, however, lacked a constituency that had specific and divisible stakes in the conflict. Those who had already suffered lung cancer were in no position effectively to argue their case, and those who would be hurt in the future were unknown.

In contrast, there were specific groups that had an immediate and identifiable interest in maintaining cigarette usage—tobacco farmers, the state and national governments that obtained considerable revenue from cigarette taxes, the media that relied on advertising for these products, and the consumers who enjoyed the habit. Representatives from tobacco-growing states had major positions of power in Congress, including the chair of the Agriculture Committee, and their lobbyists included prominent Washington attorneys.

When Congress considered the issue, the specific economic interest easily won a law that placed a health warning on cigarette packages and advertising but barred the FTC from any further action. The antismoking groups then trained their lobbying efforts on more sympathetic forums. The Civil Aeronautics Board restricted smoking on planes, other agencies banned cigarettes from offices, and the courts accepted segregation of smokers in public places such as restaurants.

Sources: Based on Elizabeth Drew, "The Quiet Victory of the Cigarette Lobby," *Atlantic,* 216 (Sept. 1965), 76–80; A. Lee Fritschler, *Smoking and Politics,* 3rd ed. (Englewood Cliffs, N.J.: Prentice-Hall, 1983).

groups "are forcing upon elected officials and candidates . . . loyalty tests on wide ranges of peripheral issues," judging politicans "by a single litmus test of ideological purity," according to Senator John Culver.[16] The single-interest groups' influence has been magnified by the decline of the parties, discussed in the previous chapter. By using specialized mailing lists, focusing their contributions on close races, and influencing a marginal proportion of voters, such groups can make an election turn not on the general set of issues or the overall qualities of the candidates but on narrower questions such as gun control or the conflicts of Northern Ireland.

The enhanced significance of single-interest groups has had effects throughout the national government. Administration is more complicated, litigation more frequent, and compromise more difficult. The most significant long-range effect may be further to weaken the political parties. "Our parties have atrophied for many of the same reasons [single-interest] groups have arisen: widespread alienation, a perception of governmental unresponsiveness, and the influence of the civil rights and antiwar movements. . . . Moreover, their success had made it much more difficult for the two major parties to recover."[17]

Abortion The current abortion controversy is a heightened example of the conflict of issue groups. Right-to-life groups seek to limit the ability of women to obtain terminations of pregnancy, even seeking a Constitutional amendment to this end, while the right-to-choice organizations want to remove government from this decision. A related controversy is whether government should pay for abortions for poor women unable to pay their own medical expenses. Right-to-life groups oppose this spending; the right-to-choice organizations support it. Although the effects of government action on this subject are certainly tangible, for neither group are the effects directly relevant to the members. No right-to-life member would be required to have an abortion, regardless of government policy, and few right-to-choice members would be prevented from ending a pregnancy. The issue is therefore solely one over public policy.

Even though self-interest is not at stake, the issue has been as emotional and divisive as any in the past decade, involving deeply religious and psychological sentiments. Compromise is impossible when both sides see an issue as fundamentally moral, and politicians are handicapped when advocates of both sides are ready to decide their votes on the basis of this single issue (see Chapter 4). The groups have clashed in many locales. In Congress, annual battles over the funding of abortions for indigent women have repeatedly delayed funding for the nation's health programs. Bureaucratic agencies have also responded to these groups, as in the Reagan administration's effort to require parental consent to abortions for adolescents. The courts have been petitioned to override these actions, generally supporting the advocates of free choice. The competing groups have also entered electoral politics. When right-to-life groups gained recognition as an independent political party in New York, and affected a number of state and national elections, right-to-choice advocates mobilized their own resources to support their friends.

Programmatic Groups

Closely related to single-issue groups are those that are concerned with a full political program. They have become increasingly important, as more Americans have come to define politics in broad ideological terms, and as loyalties to the political parties have declined.

The programmatic groups include ideological associations such as Americans for Democratic Action among liberals and Americans for Constitutional Action on the conservative side of the political spectrum. There are traditional "good government" organizations, such as the League of Women Voters, and a recent spate of more aggressive groups, such as the Nader conglomeration and Common Cause. Supported by contributions of over a quarter of a million individuals with no obvious personal interest, Common Cause has become one of the most prominent lobbies in Washington and claims (but may not deserve) credit for such actions as structural changes in Congress and passage of the campaign finance reforms of the 1970s.

Ideological Rewards Like the more specific issue groups, these organizations cannot offer their members divisible benefits. Furthermore, their incentives are less likely to be tangible. Although automobile drivers will gain materially from toll-free roads, even if they are not members of AAA, there is no obvious payoff from "good government."

Nevertheless, these groups have attracted considerable support through ideological rewards. They provide members with a simple, cheap means to participate in government. For annual dues of $15 an individual can promote his or her personal beliefs and gain the psychological satisfaction of "doing good." With the decline of other forms of participation, such as party work or even of voting, the general issue groups provide a new outlet for the American citizen's traditional custom "of combining his exertions with those of his fellow creatures and of acting in common with them."[18]

Solidary Groups

In all groups, members develop emotional ties with one another. Indeed, these familial feelings are one of the chief incentives to action, as members participate in fund raising or political action as much to help each other as for the achievement of the ostensible goal of the organization. These sentiments are also employed by leaders of interest groups to increase the effectiveness of the group—labor union members call each other "brothers" and feminist groups rally their "sisters." Hardworking individuals are rewarded with titles and positions within the organization, and national conventions, marked by ritual and fun, reinforce the organizational loyalty.

Status Rewards In one kind of interest group, these sentiments are also the basis of affiliation itself. Known as solidary groups, they are organized on the basis of the attachments people have to general groups in the population. Particularly important here are status rewards, either positions within the organization or political gains for similar kinds of people.

The most notable of these groups are formed around ethnic loyalties, such as the National Association for the Advancement of Colored People, the oldest and largest organization of black Americans; the American Jewish Committee; or La Raza, a Hispanic group. The distinction between solidary and issue groups is not sharp. Many issue groups also are based on solidary ties, such as the multitude of women's organizations. On the other hand, solidary groups are concerned with issues affecting their members, including the economic advancement of blacks and Hispanics, the Jewish concern for the survival of Israel, and the promotion of higher pensions for veterans and senior citizens.

There is a problem inherent in the incentives provided by solidary groups. These groups emphasize the common demographic features of their members, and underline their differences from other groups, such as their race or religion or sex. Political success, however, usually requires alliances with other groups, and therefore a lowered stress on group characteristics. Furthermore, these ties do not in themselves constitute a political program, for the intangible satisfactions of group membership may be satisfied as well by social events as by common action toward policy ends.

Black Groups The varying success of black groups illustrates this point. The NAACP's relative success is partially the result of its historic policy of including whites as well as blacks in its organization and of selecting goals—from the abolition of segregation to government job programs—that went

POLITICAL PERSPECTIVE

A PROGRAMMATIC GROUP IN ACTION

The NCPAC is a conservative programmatic group. In seeking members, it praises its own activities, as illustrated in this excerpt from a leaflet.

The Variety of NCPAC Programs

NCPAC worked with many transition teams to place strong conservatives in important positions within the Reagan Administration.

NCPAC has undertaken a nationwide television effort ($300,000–$500,000) to support President Reagan's Economic Recovery Program and to insure its passage through the Congress in the shortest possible time.

NCPAC is targeting liberal Senators and Members of the House of Representatives for defeat who obstruct the goals of the Reagan Administration. More than $1,000,000 is budgeted.

NCPAC believes that once conservatives are in office, the last thing we should do is forget them.

NCPAC works with Members of Congress on a day-to-day basis, advising on legislation and the strategy to get it passed. NCPAC has helped place key conservatives on Congressional staffs.

NCPAC is currently helping establish pro free enterprise political action committees throughout the Nation.

NCPAC sponsored legislative alerts and lobbying efforts that were instrumental in stopping taxpayer financing of Congressional elections and instant voter registration.

NCPAC maintains a program to assist incumbent conservatives with fund raising and other projects to see that they are re-elected.

NCPAC sponsors regional training seminars all over America to recruit competent candidates and campaign staff. NCPAC aids candidates in running the most professional campaigns possible.

NCPAC sponsors orientation seminars for new conservative Members of the Congress briefing them on how to be most effective.

Source: Promotional material of the National Conservative Political Action Committee (1981).

beyond the assertion of exclusively racial ends. Other black groups, however, placed far more emphasis on solidary goals, such as black pride and black power. These emphases may have increased cohesion within the groups, such as the Nation of Islam or the Student Non-Violent Coordinating Committee in the late 1960s. Yet, this stress on racial solidarity also limited their appeal to whites and made it more difficult to form a politically effective coalition of both races. Ultimately, a group relying principally on solidary rewards can become self-defeating, as it imposes more severe demands on its members and seeks ever more difficult goals. Thus, to SNCC, "an easy victory was no victory at all, for it would mean only that society had yielded at its hypocritical periphery and not changed at its immoral core and that the members involved had proved themselves marginally involved but not totally committed."[19]

By contrast, the NAACP has been able to maintain its position through a combination of careful organization, skilled leadership, deliberate selection of targets, and a shifting system of alliances. The group has used not only solidary incentives but also issues and economic benefits. Although generally in coalition with unions and liberal groups, it has also formed alliances with business organizations. In regard to energy policy, for example, the NAACP has been wary of liberal environmentalists and has supported some increases in energy production within the United States as a means to provide more jobs for minority workers.

Activities and Resources: "The Conflicts of Rival Parties"

Interest groups are busy. Officers, paid staff, and volunteer members rush from Capitol Hill to the regulatory agencies, back to the Supreme Court, and then out to meetings and election campaigns around the country. The range of these activities is evident in Table 8.2. For a representative sample of interests (175 Washington groups), the table shows the percentage which use each of twenty-seven different techniques.

These groups are busier than ever. There are more organizations contending with one another. Of the groups active in Washington, "fully 40 percent of these organizations have been founded since the beginning of the 1960s; in fact, 25 percent have been founded since the beginning of the 1970s." Moreover, old and new groups alike are more active, with eight out of nine reporting that they are doing more than in the past. These increases are presented in the second column of Table 8.2.

These groups have one general goal: access to public officials, the opportunity to present their case. Once access is achieved, the group can then argue its case on the merits or can attempt to convince the official that the interest group can advance his or her own political goals.

We will consider five tactics of interest groups, which are generally arranged in order of the number of people involved: (1) providing information, (2) establishing positions of strength, (3) mobilizing the public, (4) electioneering, and (5) protesting. In all of these activities, the overt goal is to win some benefit from the government for the group and its members.

Sometimes, however, there is another purpose. At times, a group is more concerned with internal problems, such as increasing its cohesion or reinforcing loyalty of members to leaders. Then, testimony before congressional committees or the national party platform committees is undertaken to "show the flag" and to demonstrate that the group is active, not because these presentations are always effective in themselves. The group's leaders also engage in extensive communication with members to reinforce group loyalty.

Providing Information

The most common and extensive activity of interest groups is providing information to government agencies. Originally, this was done face-to-face in the lobby of the legislature, and the people doing so became known as **lobbyists.** Now, various methods are used, including personal communications, letters from the groups' leaders and members, and formal appearances at hearings. Congressional committees will invite specific groups as well as the general public to testify, and formal proceedings before the federal regulatory agencies are publicized in advance.

Direct, personal communication is regarded by lobbyists as their most effective technique and, in turn, is rated as the most important interest group activity by House members. These contacts are as likely to be with officials of the executive branch as with Congress, or with other nonelected persons such as legislative assistants and staff researchers. A detailed study of the activity of lobbyists found it more common for them to communicate with these officials, or with their own members, than with Congress.[20]

Group representatives provide two types of information in these com-

TABLE 8.2 Activities of Interest Groups

	Percentage Using Each Technique	Percentage Using Each Technique More Than the Past
Testifying at hearings	99	66
Contacting government officials directly to present your point of view	98	67
Engaging in informal contacts with officials (at conventions, over lunch, etc.)	95	57
Presenting research results or technical information	92	63
Sending letters to members of your organization to inform them about your activities	92	65
Entering into coalitions with other organizations	90	67
Attempting to shape the implementation of policies	89	56
Talking with people from the press and the media	86	68
Consulting with government officials to plan legislative strategy	85	54
Helping to draft legislation	85	54
Inspiring letter writing or telegram campaigns	84	58
Shaping the government's agenda by raising new issues and calling attention to previously ignored problems	84	54
Mounting grass-roots lobbying efforts	80	59
Having influential constituents contact their congressman's office	80	52
Helping to draft regulations, rules, or guidelines	78	44
Serving on advisory commissions and boards	76	32
Alerting members of congress to the effects of a bill on their districts	75	45
Filing suit or otherwise engaging in litigation	72	38
Making financial contributions to electoral campaigns	58	49
Doing favors for officials who need assistance	56	21
Attempting to influence appointments to public office	53	23
Publicizing candidates' voting records	44	19
Engaging in direct-mail fund raising for your organization	44	31
Running advertisements in the media about your position on issues	31	19
Contributing work or personnel to electoral campaigns	24	18
Making public endorsements of candidates for office	22	14
Engaging in protests or demonstrations	20	9

Source: Compilation of Tables 7.1 and 7.3 (slightly adapted) from *Organized Interests and American Democracy* by Kay Lehman Schlozman and John T. Tierney. Copyright © 1986 by Kay Lehman Schlozman and John T. Tierney. Reprinted by permission of Harper & Row, Publishers, Inc.

munications. There is political information, the preferences of the group, the weight it attaches to the issue, and the effect that the representative's vote on this measure may have on the group's electoral support. House members worry most about "the individual or group armed with information and feeling deeply aggrieved about one vote or one cluster of votes."[21] Lobbyists play on this worry to win their arguments.

The larger proportion of information is on the substance of the issue to be decided. Interest groups represent those with specialized knowledge and concern about a policy matter, whereas elected officials are likely to be less expert. The legislators need to learn the details of a policy issue, and they can gain much knowledge about occupational safety from plant workers or about supersonic flight from aeronautical engineers. Knowledge is power, and because the interest groups have knowledge, they are likely to have power to affect the course of decision making. Most matters that come to Congress immediately affect only small proportions of the population and can be given only limited attention by the representative. He or she must rely on the experts to provide detailed information, and interest groups are one of the major sources of this information, along with the governmental bureaucracy and congressional staff.

Uses and Limits The information provided by interest groups provides a different input to the political process. American governmental structure, and legislative representation, is based on geographical territory—a legislator represents a particular city or a number of counties. However, many problems and policy needs are not related to geography—such as occupational concerns in an industrialized economy or the needs of women, ethnic groups, and consumers. These problems cut across particular territorial areas. The advice of interest groups helps to repair these deficiencies by speaking for these widespread constituencies.

At the same time, we must also recognize that the information provided by interest groups is necessarily limited. However objectively they present their research, they are pleading their own cause. General interests may be neglected. Thus, although Congress may get considerable data from all of the groups immediately affected by the issue of important tariffs, it is less likely to hear from the consumers who will eventually pay the costs of these tariffs, and general considerations of foreign policy are probably not represented by any organization. Decisions based only on the information provided by the interested groups will reflect only the interests of those groups.[22]

After a successful career as the NAACP's lawyer, Thurgood Marshall was appointed to the federal judiciary system and later became a justice of the United States Supreme Court. *(AP/World Wide Photos)*

Establishing Positions of Strength

Groups often seek the advantage of having a direct hand in making government policy. If they have a formal position, they may be able to get the decisions they want more easily. Interest groups also try to use the various institutions of government to their best advantage.

Formal Positions Formal institutional power is illustrated by professional groups. In some states, the Bar Association is given direct authority to pass on the admission of new lawyers to the privileges of the profession, and the same process is evident sometimes for barbers, funeral directors, and other occupations. In the federal government, appointments to the Supreme Court and other tribunals are formally cleared with the American Bar Association, even though this step is not legally required.

Recruitment into government may accomplish the same result as formal

POLITICAL PERSPECTIVE

"PORTRAIT OF A LOBBYIST"

Horace D. Godfrey, 68, takes all aspects of farming interests seriously. His experiences as farmer, administrator and lobbyist have reinforced his view that "farm issues can cover everything—taxes, labor, clean air, immigration bills, among others, in the past year—and we have to provide policy analysis for all of them." They have also made him an outspoken advocate of campaign support for friends of farming.

Godfrey, who runs Godfrey Associates Inc., a Washington lobbying firm that deals with farm issues, has spent his entire professional life in agriculture. Because of his work with farm programs in his home state of North Carolina, he said, "I have known every Secretary of Agriculture since Henry Wallace (1933–40) and know people on every floor at the Agriculture Department." From 1961–69, Godfrey was federal administrator of the Agricultural Stabilization and Conservation Service, the agency that administers farm commodity and other crop programs. He continues to commute nearly every weekend to his farm in Roanoke Rapids, N.C., where he grows peanuts, tobacco, corn and soybeans.

With his assistant Michael D. Morton, Godfrey analyzes all farm legislation and proposed regulations for their effect on his clients. "I like it this size because, with my background, we can render a special service to my clients," he said. "We'll do anything for them" so long as it is not illegal.

Last year, on behalf of Florida sugar growers who use Lake Okeechobee waters, he fought a proposal that would have required a permit for any use of runoff water from facilities controlled by the Army Corps of Engineers. Working with an ad hoc coalition of other farm groups—including fertilizer, cattle, cotton and produce interests—he persuaded the Senate Environment and Public Works Committee to strike the proposal from the Clean Water Act amendments that it was considering. Godfrey, who also represents Texas sugar growers, later worked actively for the dairy price support bill that Congress passed in November, partly to forestall a possible Senate move to cut the sugar price support level. . . .

Godfrey believes that winning on often narrow policy issues requires more than lobbying skills. "If you are going to get legislation, you have to have friends and once you make friends you need to keep them," Godfrey said he tells his clients. "It takes a lot of money to get elected, whether we like it or not. A Member should not have to worry about this. His friends should help him."

As a result, Godfrey helps to organize fund-raising events at the request of many Members, partly because they and their staff lack the needed time and expertise. Morton spends half of his time on this fundraising, he said.

Godfrey believes that fund-raisers are a useful place to share information. "I can sometimes do more work at a fund-raiser than I do in a week because other Members and lobbyists are there," he said. On other occasions, he said, "I go to a fund-raiser keeping in mind that I want help on a fund-raiser the next week."

Godfrey also makes recommendations to members of the Florida Sugar Cane League Political Action Committee, which contributed $74,370 to candidates in 1981–82; of the total, $69,480 went to incumbents and $55,355 to Democrats. "You can't buy a Member with a contribution, but you can buy access and the opportunity to tell your story," he said. "Without that, our members would be adversely affected because their case would not be heard." Because of his work in organizing fund-raisers, he added, his support for candidates "often involves much more than contributions."

Source: *National Journal,* 16 (Jan. 14, 1984), p. 70. Copyright 1984 by *National Journal, Inc.* All Rights Reserved. Reprinted by permission.

power. By drawing many of its administrators from the American Farm Bureau Federation, the U.S. Department of Agriculture made the interest group a semiofficial agency. Moreover, cabinet appointments are sometimes negotiated with the relevant interest group so that a secretary of labor must be satisfactory to the AFL-CIO, or a secretary of commerce with the Chamber of Commerce, to be politically viable.

Often lobbyists for a group are drawn from former members of Con-

DOONESBURY **by Garry Trudeau**

Copyright 1981, G. B. Trudeau. Reprinted with permission of Universal Press Syndicate. All rights reserved.

gress or from former employees of administrative agencies regulating a group's business, and sometimes the movement is in the opposite direction—from the group to the government. The exchange of personnel between administrative agencies and the interests they are intended to regulate creates the possibility of conflict of interest and of special advantages for some groups. (Table 8.3 lists some appointments of President Reagan that illustrate the problem.) An official responsible for buying military weapons, for example, acquires valuable technical knowledge and contacts with other persons in the Pentagon. If she resigns from the government to work for a defense company, she might have an advantage in obtaining contracts. To limit this problem of the "revolving door," restrictions have been imposed on former government administrators, prohibiting them from personal contracts with the agency that they worked for as long as two years.

TABLE 8.3 Businesspeople as Regulators

Agency	Chair	Private Experience
Federal Communications Commission	Mark S. Fowler	Counsel, Virginia Association of Broadcasters
Federal Energy Regulatory Commission	Raymond J. O'Connor	Head of public utility finance, Prudential-Bache Securities
Federal Home Loan Bank Board	Edwin J. Gray	Public relations, San Diego Savings & Loan Bank
Federal Trade Commission	James C. Miller III	Economist, Texas A&M University
Interstate Commerce Commission	Reese H. Taylor, Jr.	Counsel, various trucking corporations
National Labor Relations Board	Donald L. Dotson	Counsel, Wheeling-Pittsburgh Steel Corporation
Nuclear Regulatory Commission	Nunzio J. Palladino	Engineer, Westinghouse Electric Corporation
Securities and Exchange Commission	John S. R. Shad	Vice-chairman, E. F. Hutton Group

Source: "The Decision Makers," *National Journal,* 17 (May 18, 1985).

The Position of Business Even more significant than individual conflicts is the generalized institutional position of some groups. The most dominating is that of business. Because most of the American economy is legally in private hands and controlled by corporations, government cannot make fundamental decisions on the economy on its own. Vital outcomes such as prices, wages, job locations, capital investment, even foreign policy depend on decisions in boardrooms as much, sometimes more, as on decisions in congressional committee rooms. The major corporations, therefore, must be consulted in some manner, even if they do not hold the formal positions of authority. Oil producers are not necessarily a closed elite, but they must be included in the development of a national energy policy. Generally, businesspeople are "functionaries performing functions that government officials regard as indispensable. . . . Collaboration and deference between the two are at the heart of politics in such systems. Businessmen cannot be left knocking at the doors of the political system, they must be invited in."[23]

Policy Subgovernments Institutionalization of interest groups attains its most complete form in the creation of policy **subgovernments** (see "iron triangles" in Chapter 10).[24]In this arrangement, the decisions on policy in a particular area are made, in effect, through a triangular relationship of the relevant interest group, administrative agency, and congressional subcommittee. Other participants are rarely heard from, even though they can legally overturn the decisions of these participants. Veterans' pensions are, thus, decided by negotiations between the American Legion, the Veterans Administration, and the Veterans Affairs committees of Congress, but policy in regard to ocean-borne freight is negotiated between the Maritime Administration, the Merchant Marine committee of the House, and shipping companies and unions. These relationships together make up the "Washington establishment," characterized by Fiorina as a system in which "more and more bureaucrats promulgate more and more regulations and dispense more and more money. Fewer and fewer congressmen suffer electoral defeat. Elements of the electorate benefit from government programs, and all of the electorate is eligible for ombudsman services. But the general, long-term welfare of the United States is no more than an incidental by-product of the system."[25] We shall consider these alliances more fully in Chapters 9 and 11. They graphically show the fragmenting effects of interest groups and the advantages they gain by narrowing the conflict.

The Courts Courts are another institution where interest groups can establish a position of strength. They are particularly appropriate for groups with relatively small memberships that have limited social status. The judicial branch is least likely to be swayed by the public majority, and it provides formal equality for all participants before the bar of justice.

One means by which interest groups enter the courts is by judicial invitation, when they are asked by the courts to present special arguments, called *amicus curiae* ("friend of the court") briefs. More important have been **class actions,** in which an adversary in a lawsuit speaks not only for his or her immediate interests but for all similar persons. One conservationist, for example, cannot claim much personal damage from the construction of a dam in a recreational area, but in a class action she can claim that many persons will be harmed.

Litigation has been used most successfully by the NAACP. In a series of cases beginning in the 1930s, the leading black organization attacked the segregationist doctrine of "separate but equal" facilities for the races, and eventually had segregation itself declared unconstitutional in the landmark school cases of 1954. This example spurred other groups, such as women seeking to protect the right to abortion, the handicapped seeking full access to public facilities, children seeking protection from school discipline codes, environmentalists seeking to limit industrial instructions, and minority political parties seeking to weaken the dominant position of the Democrats and Republicans.

Conservatives have also turned to the courts recently. To justify the military leadership of the Vietnam War, right-wing groups provided millions of dollars in a libel action brought against the Columbia Broadcasting System. The Mountain States Legal Foundation has used lawsuits on behalf of many conservative causes, such as opening Western lands to commercial development and challenging affirmative action programs.

Mobilizing the Public

The scope of interest group activities increases still further when such groups try to mobilize the force of their members and sympathizers. Involving these larger numbers of people, however, is difficult and expensive. This activity will be undertaken when a group's leader sees broader public support as one of its resources but when other methods have not worked.

MAIL CAMPAIGNS The reason mail techniques work, when they do, is that they may affect, openly or indirectly, the representative's chances of election. One gentle technique of this sort is letter-writing campaigns. Although they may not specifically promise or threaten electoral action, letter writers are still voters, and there is an unmentioned political significance to these communications. When members of a group are asked to write to their representatives in support of desired legislation, the hope is to demonstrate a popular groundswell and to convince the legislators that their reelection depends on compliance with the group's demands. The tactic is particularly likely to be used by groups with a relatively large and geographically diffused membership, such as labor unions or citizens' groups. Common Cause has made letter-writing campaigns a habitual action, through a system of "citizen-alerts," calling for mail on active bills.

The technique has its limits. Representatives are disposed to discount these campaigns as consisting largely of "pressure mail," communications that are stimulated by the interest group but which do not reflect deep understanding of the issue itself. Typically, they will claim to be more affected by a single, personal letter than by thousands of identical form letters. Moreover, representatives are more likely to hear from those who agree with them, or to interpret mail in this way, than from the opposition. Such communications simply reinforce the legislator's own position, rather than change it.[26] There is also a social class bias in the mail. Middle-class people and those in occupations requiring higher education are more likely to write than those in lower-status occupations. Ideologically, more conservatives write to their representatives than do liberals so that the legislators get a distorted picture of public opinion.[27]

For the interest group, mail campaigns have their risks as well. By making a conflict open, the group may permanently alienate a legislator whose support it will want on another bill. Moreover, mail campaigns may not succeed, since the membership, busy with its own daily tasks, may not respond in large numbers, and the threat of an aroused public opinion may prove illusory. Letter-writing campaigns are becoming more extensive, bringing a vast increase in the volume of communications to government.[28] They are also increasingly sophisticated, employing computerized direct-mail techniques for targeting.

The most successful mobilization campaign in memory was mounted in 1983 by the nation's banks. To reduce the federal budget deficit, Congress had provided that the taxes due on bank interest would be withheld in advance, just as happens with taxes on ordinary wages and salaries. Persons with low incomes could be exempted from these payments by signing a simple statement at their local bank. Therefore, the only persons who would be severely hurt would be persons who had not been paying the taxes they owed on bank interest. Their personal self-interest was costing the Treasury—and other taxpayers—as much as $20 billion a year.

Although the banks did not want to defraud the government, they did want to avoid the inconvenience and cost involved in calculating tax payments and sending them to Washington. A notice was sent to all depositors, warning them of this "threat" to their savings, and evoking a grim picture of a poor widow deprived of her last dollars. The public reacted strongly, burying House members in an average of 10,000 letters from each district, with sentiment 99–1 against the withholding plan. Facing an aroused, if uninformed, public, all but a dozen members of the two houses of Congress voted to repeal the provision.

Electioneering

Interest groups also intervene directly in the election process, using voting records, endorsements, and campaign contributions.

Voting Records and Endorsements A number of groups now issue annual reports on Congress, selecting "key votes" from each session and judging the representatives' votes as "right" or "wrong." About sixty groups now issue these reports, including relatively narrow groups such as environmentalists and antiabortionists, as well as broad ideological organizations, such as Americans for Democratic Action on the left and Americans for Constitutional Action on the right. The ratings are taken seriously by the members of Congress, who in some cases will attempt to influence the roll calls included in order to achieve a higher score.[29]

Although most of the groups giving ratings are concerned with single or narrow issues, the programmatic groups cover a variety of votes. The ADA and ACA ratings have now come to be a general measure of ideology in American politics. Scores on the two indexes almost mirror each other. For example, Senator Paul Sarbanes received a perfect rating from ADA in 1984, but he failed the ACA test with a flat zero. On the other side of the spectrum, seven Republican senators were considered perfect conservatives by ACA but won no points from ADA.[30]

A major purpose of these ratings is to provide a basis for group endorsements of legislators, or opposition to these candidates. As the role of the political parties in elections has become less central, the support of interest groups has grown proportionately. The record of success for these groups has now become as closely watched as that of the parties. (The 1984 records of six groups are pictured in Figure 8.2.) The broader groups, such as labor and business, will endorse hundreds of candidates, whereas other, narrower groups will confine their attention to a few races in which they can hope to make a difference. Environmental Action, a conservationist group, has used a technique of opposing a selected "Dirty Dozen" of representatives with unfavored records on environmental issues, and concentrating its political activity in their races. Negative endorsements of this kind have become quite common as a technique of single-interest groups. Particularly active have been antiabortionists, who have waged highly emotional campaigns in marginal races against legislators they regard as "antilife." A recent trend is for single-interest groups to concentrate their efforts on senatorial races in the Far West. These states are sparsely populated, and television advertising and other campaign costs are relatively low. A victory for a favored candidate means just as much as a victory in heavily populated New York or California, but the interest group can get "more for its money" in the Western states.

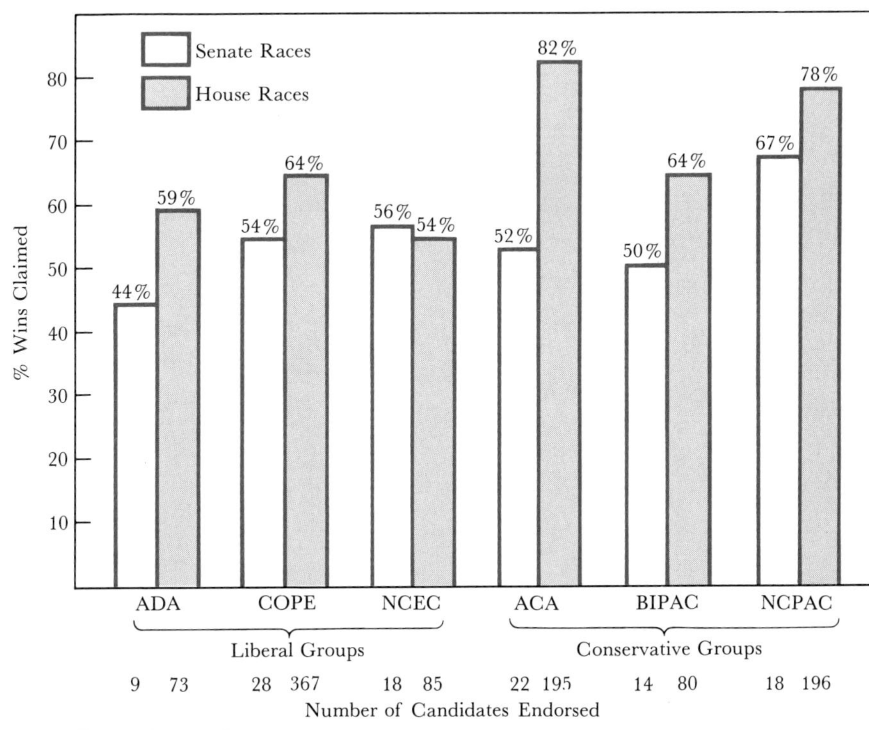

FIGURE 8.2
Interest-Group Scorecard in Elections
The bars show the percentage of winners among candidates for Congress endorsed by six interest groups in 1984. Note the considerable differences in the numbers endorsed by the different groups as they "picked their spots." *(Calculated from tables in* Congressional Quarterly Weekly Report, *42 [Nov. 17, 1984], 2970–76.)*

FIGURE 8.3
Sources of 1984 Campaign contributions
Contribution totals are for the two-year election cycle of House and Senate candidates whose names appeared on general election ballots in November 1984. (Totals do not include contributions from candidates themselves or from party committees.) *(Federal Election Commission as reported in* Congressional Quarterly Weekly Report, *43 [June 8, 1985], 1115.)*

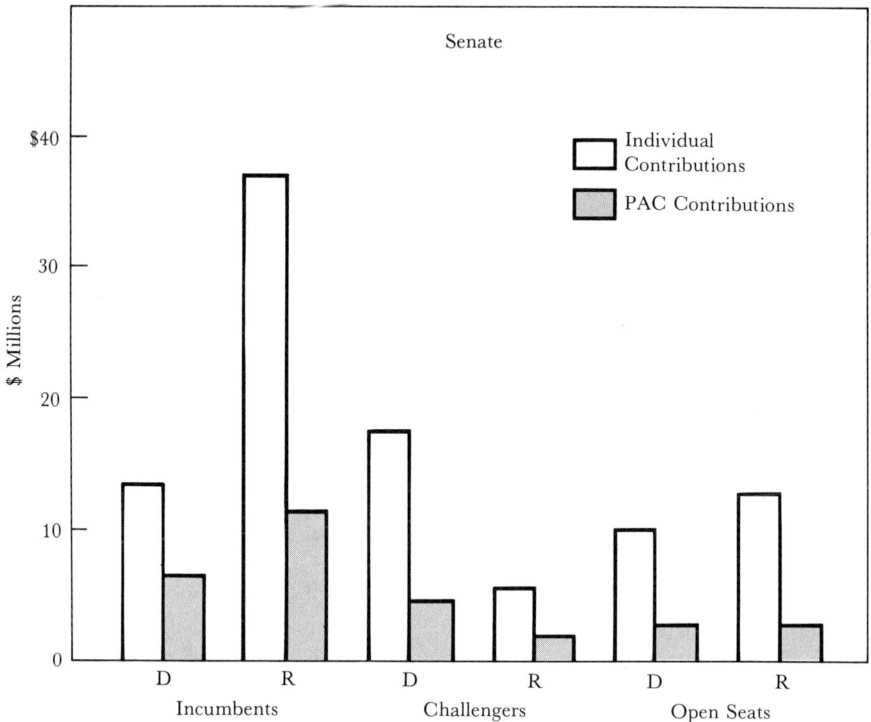

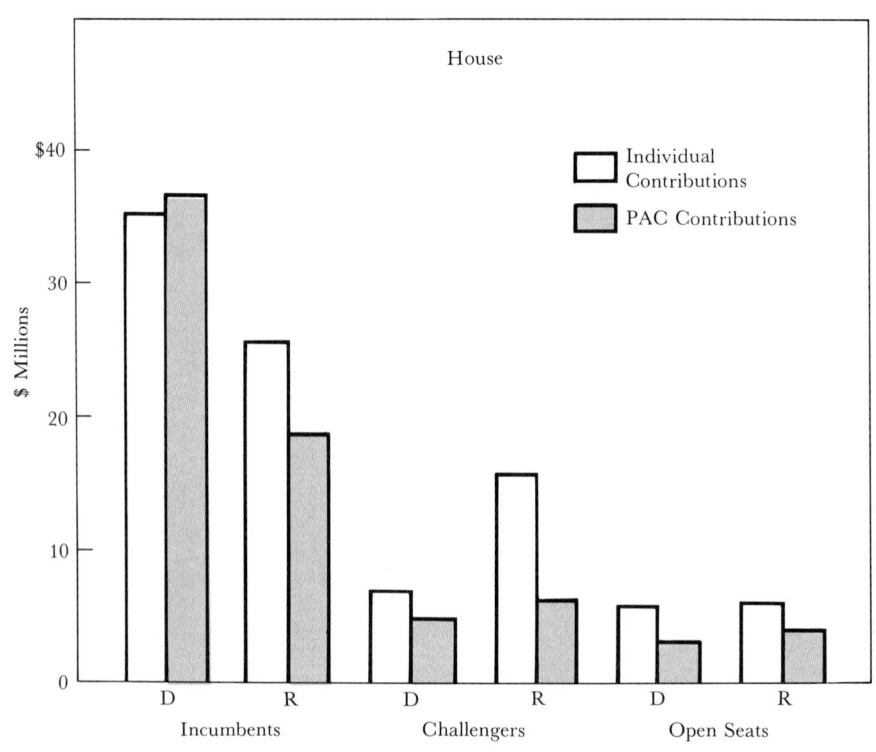

Campaign Contributions Endorsements have tangible value when they are supported by campaign contributions. As we have seen in Chapter 7, the effects of interest groups in elections have been magnified by the growth of campaign spending through their political action committees. Incumbents and committee chairpersons have been particularly favored (see Figure 8.3). For example, members of the important tax-writing committees in Congress received an average in PAC contributions of almost $200,000 for each member of the House and over $500,000 for each senator.[31] A summary view of the relative activity of interest groups can be gained from Table 8.4. It shows the reported election spending of the fif-

TABLE 8.4 Top of the PAC Chart

Political Action Committee	1984	1982	1980
1. Realtors Political Action Committee (National Association of Realtors)	$2,429,552	$2,115,135	$1,536,573
2. American Medical Association Political Action Committee	1,839,464	1,737,090	1,348,985
3. BUILD-PAC (National Association of Home Builders)	1,625,539	1,006,628	379,391
4. National Education Association Political Action Committee	1,574,003	1,183,215	283,585
5. UAW V-CAP (United Auto Workers Volunteer Community Action Program)	1,405,107	1,628,347	1,422,731
6. Seafarers Political Activity Donation (Seafarers International Union)	1,322,410	850,514	685,248
7. Machinists Non-Partisan Political League (International Association of Machinists and Aerospace Workers)	1,306,497	1,445,459	847,708
8. Active Ballot Club (United Food and Commercial Workers International Union)	1,271,974	729,213	569,775
9. Committee on Letter Carriers Political Education (National Association of Letter Carriers)	1,234,603	387,915	44,715
10. National Association of Retired Federal Employees Political Action Committee	1,099,243	564,225	8,200
11. Committee for Thorough Agricultural Political Education of Associated Milk Producers Inc.	1,087,658	962,450	738,289
12. Automobile and Truck Dealers Election Action Committee (National Automobile Dealers Association)	1,057,165	917,295	1,035,276
13. Public Employees Organized to Promote Legislative Equality (American Federation of State, County and Municipal Employees)	905,806	496,400	338,035
14. National Association of Life Underwriters Political Action Committee	900,200	563,573	652,112
15. BANKPAC (American Bankers Association)	882,850	947,460	592,960

Source: Adapted from Federal Election Commission, as reported in *Congressional Quarterly Weekly Report,* 43 (June 8, 1985), p. 11117.
Note: The data are based on a two-year election cycle and only include direct contributions to candidates for the House and Senate. The leading fifteen PACs were selected based on direct contributions to congressional candidates in the 1984 election cycle. For reference purposes, the PACs' aggregate contributions for the 1980 and 1982 election cycles are included.

teen largest political action committees from 1980 to 1984. As we have already seen in Chapter 6, these contributions have increased vastly in recent years.

What does the money buy? Few observers believe that representatives and senators are bribed by these contributions. Not only are most legislators honest, but a "payoff" is not worth the electoral cost. What is purchased is not control of a legislator, but "access" to him or her, the opportunity to meet and present a case. Access itself is important. As every salesperson knows, the biggest step in persuading a customer is getting your foot in the door. House representatives are very busy people, and the lobbyist who can get to see them has a distinct edge over the average citizen.

Protesting

The most dramatic form of interest group activity is protest. Groups take such action as marches, demonstrations, illegal strikes, sit-ins, and takeovers of buildings in order to bring their causes to the attention of the wider public. From the time Boston merchants dressed as Indians in 1773 to throw the Boston Tea Party, to the demonstrations at Wounded Knee, South Dakota, in 1973 by true native Americans, protest has been a recurrent means by which interests are expressed.

Except for actual violence, protest is the highest escalation of political conflict. It will be undertaken by groups only when they have been defeated in more normal activities such as lobbying or electioneering, or when they believe that these alternate means of action are useless for their cause. The purpose of protest is to force people to choose sides, especially those persons in the general public who have not previously been involved. In forcing this choice, moderate positions become less viable and conflict increases.

Among the most notable groups to employ protest in American history have been the nineteenth-century abolitionists, the original feminist advocates of women's suffrage, civil rights activists, and protestors against the Vietnam War. These groups were alike in some characteristics. All shared an intense attitude akin to religious commitment on the moral righteousness of their cause. All believed that they would win majority democratic support, but only if the majority could be aroused to grasp the moral issue involved. And all had been defeated in the more ordinary politics of legislatures and elections.

The Civil Rights Movement The civil rights movement in the 1960s was the most successful and sophisticated protest movement in American history. Although school segregation had been declared unconstitutional in 1954, blacks saw only limited progress in their lives and faced strong political obstacles, including segregationist governments in most Southern states, legislative barriers in Congress such as the Senate filibuster and conservative control of the House Rules Committee, frequent delays in court action, and a minority position in the total national electorate. Protest was a means of changing this political environment.

This sit-in at a Little Rock, Arkansas, lunch counter in 1962 helped focus attention on civil rights issues. *(UPI)*

There was no single civil rights movement, but a variety of tactics and philosophies. The undoubted spokesperson of the movement was Martin Luther King, Jr., who combined a strong moral appeal based on the American premise of equality with considerable skill as a political leader. Following Dr. King, civil rights activists employed different techniques. Sit-ins at lunch counters or freedom rides on segregated buses emphasized the injustices of discrimination. Mass marches first induced attempted repression by local officials and then precipitated intervention by the national government to ensure voting rights.[32] The 1963 March on Washington brought a quarter of a million persons to the nation's capital and forced the issue of civil rights legislation to the top of the congressional agenda. Segregationist laws were deliberately violated so that the law itself could be challenged in court while public attention was captured.

Uses of Protest The success of the civil rights movement brought much imitation. Protest has now become a frequent means of political activity by Americans, and its legitimacy is much greater than in the past. A majority of the nation will now support protest marches, and two-thirds will even condone disruptive activities such as takeovers of public buildings, in some circumstances.[33] The tactics have been used by others with a generalized moral appeal, such as the war resisters and feminists and the antinuclear movement. Younger siblings of those involved in the Vietnam protest now use the same methods to oppose intervention in Central America. Mass action has also come to be employed by those with a more self-interested appeal. Construction workers who once attacked opponents of the Vietnam intervention have conducted their own demonstrations. Farmers seeking higher federal benefits have brought their tractors to Washington to tie up the city's traffic. Groups such as the American Nazi party and the Ku Klux Klan, without the moral appeal of the civil rights marchers, have still paid them the compliment of imitation.

As the Civil Rights Movement has demonstrated, protest is a dramatic way for groups to get attention for their grievances. *(Flip Schulke/Black Star)*

The increased use of protest reflects its success, for protest does accomplish some ends. For the group itself, it is likely to lead to increased internal cohesion. Persons who have shared the emotional experience of a demonstration are more likely to be committed to the group than those who confine themselves to paying dues. These tactics also fit the needs of contemporary political expression. They are visual and present issues in a simplified manner, and therefore are well-suited to television, the major medium today for political communication. Some group leaders have become skilled in staging media events to present their cause. With the decline of political parties as the means to express interests, the influence of the mass media increases.

Probably the chief virtue of protest is that it may alter the agenda of issues. The demands of a group, which may have been previously buried in a legislative committee or unnoticed by the press, now get dramatic attention. When a government official hears the chants of thousands of demonstrators outside his or her window or cannot get into the office, the official must give the group the attention it has not received before. It can hardly be doubted that the national government moved more quickly and sweepingly to ensure black voting rights because of the civil rights protests than it would have without these pressures.

Limitations of Protest Protest also has severe limitations as a political tactic. Demonstrators may win the attention of the media, but they may also be the targets of its condemnation. Persons blocking a street, for example, can be pictured sympathetically as calling attention to problems of traffic safety or can be portrayed as selfishly disrupting civic life. The media tend to regard some groups as more legitimate (such as housewives) and others as less legitimate (such as prostitutes), resulting in different coverage.

Protestors also face a problem in making the compromises that are inevitably necessary to resolve political conflicts. Because they must simplify the issues in order to make them dramatic, they must continue to press nonnegotiable demands, leaving it to a different group to negotiate.[34] When their original demands are not fully met, the protestors often will feel betrayed or ineffective.

Effective protest is generally also limited to those situations in which a group has a clear moral claim or can use protest to win a specific symbolic demand. The cause of blacks for equal voting rights could be furthered through protest, but their claim for better economic opportunities is more complicated and not achieved through demonstrations alone. Even Dr. King, therefore, could not use marches effectively to counteract the subtle forms of discrimination in Northern cities. On the other hand, protest may be effective for groups with concentrated economic power, such as truckers, although this power is not an expression of a moral cause but of a limited economic interest.

Finally, there is always the possibility that protest may become violent. In some cases, as in the voting rights marches, this violence demonstrates the very injustices against which protest has been organized. In other cases, the violence becomes damaging to the group itself, as well as to the lives and property of society in general. Politics has, then, been replaced by power, and expression by repression.

Evaluating Interest Groups: "To Adjust These Clashing Interests"

Interest groups can be seen as either furthering or impeding the fulfillment of democracy. They are based on the freedom of association stated in the First Amendment to the Constitution, and they provide a means by which citizens can influence the government and keep it under democratic control. On the other hand, interest groups only represent their own members and are commonly denounced as "special interests" and "lobbies." Observers can always draw a laugh by condemning Congress as "the best that money can buy," and politicians are prone to present themselves as standing for "the people" against "the interests."

The differing evaluations of the desirability of interest groups are related to differing interpretations of the role of interest groups in American politics. Pluralism is a theory that sees politics in the United States as a relatively open contest between groups which, together, present the position of all elements in the population. In contrast, the theory of elitism sees policy as dominated by a basically closed and continuing group of powerholders.

Pluralist Theory

The pluralistic theory emphasizes the role of interest groups. In one formulation, public policy is the simple result of the differing pressures they exert, with the formal institutions of government only passively responding to, and recording the relative power of, the interest groups. In other formulations, the activity of government itself is recognized, but the emphasis continues to be on interest groups as major participants, and on policy formulation as the result of "a kaleidoscopic and largely irresponsible interplay of ideas, interests, institutions, and individuals."[35]

A basic premise in the pluralist approach is that the process is open to most groups, and that the results are essentially democratic—that is, that the resulting policies are in line with the preferences and interests of the total population. Advocates of pluralism "see American society as fractured into congeries of small 'special interest' groups with incompletely overlapping memberships, widely differing power bases, and a multitude of techniques for exercising influence on decisions salient to them."[36] Power is limited, according to the pluralists, because individuals are members of many overlapping groups and, therefore, will not fully support the demands of any one association. Furthermore, power is always checked. The efforts of business meet the resistance of labor or consumers. All groups are subject to the limits imposed by general social values. If these limits are crossed, "potential interest groups" will mobilize to enforce the "rules of the game."[37]

Problems of Pluralist Theory There are three basic problems with the pluralist theory, relating to the leadership, scope, and resources of interest groups. If interest group politics were fully democratic, the existing groups would be truly representative of their memberships, all groups would be represented, and the relative power of these groups would be proportionate to their membership. In fact, these conditions are not met.

First, the leaders of groups are inherently different from the members, simply by virtue of their leadership position. They must be concerned about the continuing existence of the organization, whereas members can take the familiar course of "Let George do it." Leaders also develop a self-interest in their own position, which may or may not serve the goals of the group. In the simplest example, leaders prefer high salaries for their work, and the members prefer low dues.

Aside from personal matters, influence within groups is not necessarily equal among members. Those factions that are most active, or supply the largest share of funds, are likely to have disproportionate impact on its policies. The National Association of Manufacturers purports to speak for all industries, but its program tends to favor large corporations, which pay higher dues, as against smaller producers. In the American Medical Association, general practitioners have historically been more active than specialized physicians, and the policies of the AMA have been slanted toward the former group, as in its long-time opposition to government health care.[38] Similarly, labor unions have placed great stress on the protection of the seniority rights of concern to their most involved members, although this emphasis might work to the detriment of younger but less active unionists.

Second, the scope of interest groups is also limited. The individual participants and contributors of interest groups are not a representative sample of the population. It is also true that all of the groups together are not fully representative of the diversity of American life. Nearly a quarter of all national organizations speak for business and commercial interests, and a sixth on educational and cultural matters. By contrast, only 6 percent of the associations are social welfare groups and only 2 percent are labor unions (although the membership of unions is often quite large).[39] It is true that many of these groups have small memberships and that simply counting them does not necessarily measure their impact. Yet, to E. E. Schattschneider and other critics, the very fact of limited membership is what makes interest group representation defective. "The flaw in the pluralist heaven is that the heavenly chorus sings with a strong upper-class accent. . . . *Pressure politics is a selective process* ill designed to serve diffuse interests. The system is skewed, loaded and unbalanced in favor of a fraction of a minority."[40]

Numerous but disadvantaged groups are in effect excluded from interest groups politics. There are no significant groups speaking on behalf of migrant farmers, illegal aliens, or—until recently—the handicapped. Diffuse interests are generally disadvantaged when confronted by focused groups—as in the example of smokers and the tobacco industry or, more generally, in the conflict between the interests of producers (farmers, steel companies, and steelworkers) and consumers (eaters, automobile buyers).

Finally, third, as these examples indicate, the relative power of interest groups varies but not necessarily in relation to their numbers. To be fully democratic, larger groups should be more influential than smaller ones, but numbers are not decisive in this form of politics. Labor unions, with hundreds of thousands on their rolls, may be legislatively defeated by business groups representing hundreds. Agricultural programs may increase the income of 3 million farmers while they increase the food costs of 230 million consumers. In some circumstances, a large group may even find its size to be a disadvantage, complicating the process of developing internal unity.

These inherent biases of interest group politics have been partially corrected by the growth of issue groups in the past two decades, such as the Nader investigators, environmentalists, and consumer associations. The needs of some elements previously unheard, such as women, the poor, and the handicapped, are now being voiced and sometimes heeded. Even in these cases, however, success has been largely dependent on providing specific benefits to group members and has tended to be advantageous to members of the middle class. Thus, the women's movement has succeeded in such goals as sexual equality in bank credit, of benefit to middle-income women but has achieved less for women of lower status.[41]

Elite Theory

A sharply contrasting theory of the role of interest groups in American politics is provided by the theory of elitism. In this interpretation, the conflicts of these organizations are only of secondary importance. On the most basic decisions, there is a relatively small and usually united group that has decisive influence. This "power elite" consists of those in command of the "major hierarchies and organizations of modern society. They rule the big corporations. They run the machinery of the state and claim its prerogatives. They direct the military establishment. They occupy the strategic command posts of the social structure."[42]

It is difficult to prove, or disprove, the existence of this elite. If we examine specific issues, such as energy policy or disarmament, it is readily apparent that there is conflict among corporations, among the military services, and among government agencies. There is a long series of individual case studies of policy development in the United States, and these consistently support a pluralist interpretation. The elitist theorists' response to this evidence is that the issues studied are not fundamental and that the unity of the elite is evident on truly vital questions.

Such prime issues include the maintenance of a capitalist economic structure and the basic anticommunist direction of American foreign policy since the Second World War. There is considerable variation in the attitudes of American leaders, but it is certainly true that there is no noticeable sentiment among businesspeople for socialism, nor any obvious support for unilateral disarmament in the military, and that national policy is consistent with these opinions. What is not clear is whether these results prove the existence of an elite. These general policy positions also represent the consensus of mass public opinion. In supporting these policies, then, there is a parallelism between the views of the mass public, the preferences of the presumed power elite, and the actions of the government. The parallelism, however, does not demonstrate a simple cause-and-effect relationship.

Business as an Elite Elitist theory emphasizes the power of business groups. Their predominant role in the economy, and their considerable influence in government, certainly do not easily fit with democratic theory. Although the officers of the 500 largest corporations make vital decisions affecting every American, they are not controlled by either their scattered stockholders or the general electorate. Business interests are visible and ably promoted, and other groups often are unknown and without resources. Although few in number, the combined power of major corporate executives is certainly greater than that of more numerous groups.

There is some development toward more concentrated power within the business community, as evidenced by the creation of the Business Roundtable as a single voice for large corporations. Multinational associations have also developed. The most notable is the Trilateral Commission, which includes government officials, business leaders, and intellectuals from the United States, Western Europe, and Japan. Unified action by such groups would have critical influence, but it is not certain that they can consistently act together.

To demonstrate the elitist theory, we would need to find that an identifiable group or coalition of groups regularly achieved its political goals. When we examine specific outcomes in American politics, we often find conflict within business, not unity. Economic giants such as IBM and AT&T compete not only in the marketplace but for favorable rulings from the Federal Communications Commission. Smaller businesses may be disadvantaged financially, but they can sometimes defeat larger corporations in government. For example, smaller companies achieved deregulation of the airline industry.

Business interests are certainly always significant in American politics, because our economy is run by private corporations. Yet business, even when it is united, does not always achieve its goals. Major programs such as the progressive income tax, antitrust prosecutions, the social security system, union recognition, and environmental regulation were largely opposed by dominant economic groups but were still achieved through mass political action. Although business does well in American government, it does not run the government. As *Fortune* magazine grudgingly admitted, "Its leaders go to Washington with an attitude very much like the one that politicians take there themselves. They usually find something to praise and accept as well as something to refine or reject; they are willing to do deals and strike bargains; they never go away mad."[43]

Pluralism vs. Elitism

Is the United States "really" pluralist or "really" elitist? The simple answer is that it's not that simple, but rather American government is both. As elite theory suggests, some groups have more advantages than others. As pluralist theory suggests, the power of an interest groups shifts from one policy area to the next. Veterans groups, for example, have a major impact on pension policy but have little impact on foreign affairs. The Defense Department, on the other hand, can strongly influence American foreign involvement but cannot get veterans' benefits reduced. The best description of American politics may be *plural elitism,* a combination of the other theories.[44]

Especially important in explaining the outcome of a political dispute is the **scope of conflict,** the number of people and groups involved. Interest groups usually are most successful when they can restrict the scope of conflict, so that decisions are made by small groups with limited controversy. Interest groups do best when a congressional subcommittee decides on closing military bases, a lower-level administrative agency rules on railroad freight charges, or the group itself has the power to decide on professional certification. "The pressure system makes sense only as the political instrument of a segment of the community. It gets results by being selective and biased."[45]

As conflict expands further, broader segments of the population become involved, as in presidential decisions, full congressional debates, and elections. Then, the power of any particular interest group will be diminished. Other groups that are normally disadvantaged are likely to become more visible and better able to bring the influence of their membership to bear. Thus, poor people do not exert much influence in the typical competition between interest groups, but they will be given more attention when political conflict becomes manifest in the mass activities of elections, protests, and marches. Interest group politics is the politics of small numbers. It arises from the fragmentation of the political system, and it is to the benefit of interest groups to maintain that fragmentation.

The Control of Interest Groups: "Curing the Mischiefs of Faction"

Interest groups affect American politics at every stage, from the development of political attitudes among school children to the implementation of statutes by administrative regulation. We should emphasize that interest groups are both inevitable and, in many ways, desirable. They arise because citizens have special needs and wants and, in a free society, they are able to express these desires. Without such formal organizations, citizens would have to rely on the uncertain goodwill and knowledge of officials for protection. Interest groups provide the government with surer knowledge of the population's needs and wants, and with a measure of the intensity of these differing demands. The only way to eliminate the competition of interest groups fully, as Madison wrote, would be the authoritarian methods of "destroying the liberty which is essential to its existence" or "by giving to every citizen the same opinions, the same passions, and the same interests."

Legislative Controls

Instead of eliminating interest groups, an impossibility in a democracy, efforts have been made to control them. Some of the means of control are through legislation, others through more general social restraints. Both types of control evidence defects.

Regulation of Lobbying Legislatively, the principal attempt to control interest groups came in the 1946 Federal Regulation of Lobbying Act, which was passed as part of a general reorganization of Congress. The law required that lobbyists register with Congress and report their expenditures quarterly. These requirements apply to "any person" who receives compensation "to aid . . . the passage or defeat of any legislation by the Congress." In the 1983 Congress, about 6,000 individuals and organizations registered under its provisions and reported a total annual spending of over $43 million—equal to $81,000 devoted to each legislator.[46]

The purpose of the lobbyist regulations law was not to eliminate interest groups but to provide for a public disclosure of their activities, on the premise that publicity itself would prevent any abuses. It is generally agreed that the statute has had little effect in either deterring improper conduct or even achieving full disclosure. The law itself is not clearly written and contains several loopholes. A major limitation is that the law applies, according to the Supreme Court, only to those groups whose principal purpose is affecting legislation.[47] Since most organizations have multiple purposes, including internal servicing of their members, they can consider themselves exempt from the registration requirements. Thus, the National Association of Manufacturers, certainly a major business interest group, has consistently refused to comply with these provisions. Inconsistencies in reporting lead to misleading results, with Common Cause, an advocate of reporting, appearing to be a major lobby and the NAM appearing to exert no influence on the federal government. Another problem is that the lobbying law applies only to Congress. The major activities of interest groups, particularly those based on economic goals, are directed toward the executive branch and its administrative agencies. These solicitations need not be reported.

GRASS-ROOTS LOBBYING The most complicated issue involved in the regulation of lobbying is the broad public activity of interest groups, known as **grass-roots lobbying.** The present statute deals only with direct contacts with Congress, such as personal visits to representatives. Increasingly, as we have seen, interest groups attempt to influence legislation by enlisting outside pressure through public relations, electioneering, or mass demonstrations. Although efforts to influence elections through campaign contributions are separately regulated under the election finance laws, the other means of public activity are not covered. Yet, more money is probably spent on grass-roots lobbying than in direct contact.

Finally, weak as it is, the lobbying act has not been enforced. Reports are filed with congressional employees, but there is no regular mechanism for verifying their accuracy or of investigating those groups that do not report. There has been only one successful prosecution under the act. In 1954, two unregistered lobbyists gave an unsolicited contribution to a senator who favored their position on the deregulation of natural gas. The lobbyists were fined $2,500, and their employer, Superior Oil of California, was fined $5,000. These mild penalties have hardly induced more widespread compliance.

Efforts to regulate interest groups raise difficult questions. If the purpose of this legislation is simply disclosure, it is not clear that disclosure will have any effect in altering the techniques or relative power of these groups. If the purpose is to prevent abuses, such as outright bribery, this goal is probably better accomplished by laws specifically directed toward that end. In any case, simple corruption of this sort is probably very rare. Most legislators are more interested in winning election than in taking bribes. If there is corruption in Congress, it is far more subtle than a cash payment in exchange for a floor vote. It is more likely to result from a campaign contribution to a sympathetic legislator. The contribution is not a bribe to get the legislator to do something he or she personally opposes but an expression of appreciation for that legislator's action.

American Artists: American Politics

American political events and political circumstances have inspired generations of artists. Often the subject has been nationalistic, a homage to the growth of nationhood. But just as often—and with a reassuring democratic humanism—the subject has been one expressing the American political community. To many artists, the monument of the American nation is the American individual and the interdependence of the individual and government.

In 1803 the United States doubled its geographical extent by purchasing the Louisiana Territory from France for fifteen million dollars. The significance of the sound central government established by the Constitution in 1787 increased as the country expanded dramatically throughout the first half of the nineteenth century.

***Raising the Flag* (1803) by Dethulstrup.**
(Courtesy of the Louisiana State Museum.)

In a frontier nation, centers of population grew fast, faster than cultural refinements such as theater and music could reach them. Elections and stump-speaking campaigns not only served a political end but filled an entertainment vacuum.

***Verdict of the People* (1852) by George Caleb Bingham.**
(Courtesy the Art Collection of the Boatmen's National Bank of St. Louis.)

The Civil War almost overturned the fundamental principles of the Constitution. Nevertheless, eleven years after the end of that bloody conflict, Erastus Salisbury Field could symbolize the triumph of the Republic in a fantastic architectural wedding cake reaching the clouds.

Historical Monument of the American Republic **(c. 1876) by Erastus Salisbury Field.**
(Courtesy The Museum of Fine Arts, Springfield, Massachusetts.)

American politics often mixed boisterous fun with differences on issues. Here the Republican candidate, who has lost a bet as well as an election, pulls his victorious Democratic opponent through the streets in a cart.

The Lost Bet, after a painting by Joseph Klir in 1892.
(Courtesy the Chicago Historical Society.)

The United States entered the First World War in April of 1917. American troops arrived in Europe barely in time to counterbalance Russia's withdrawal from alliance with France and Britain and to defeat a renewed German offensive. When the peace treaty was signed at Versailles, the United States had clearly emerged as a world power.

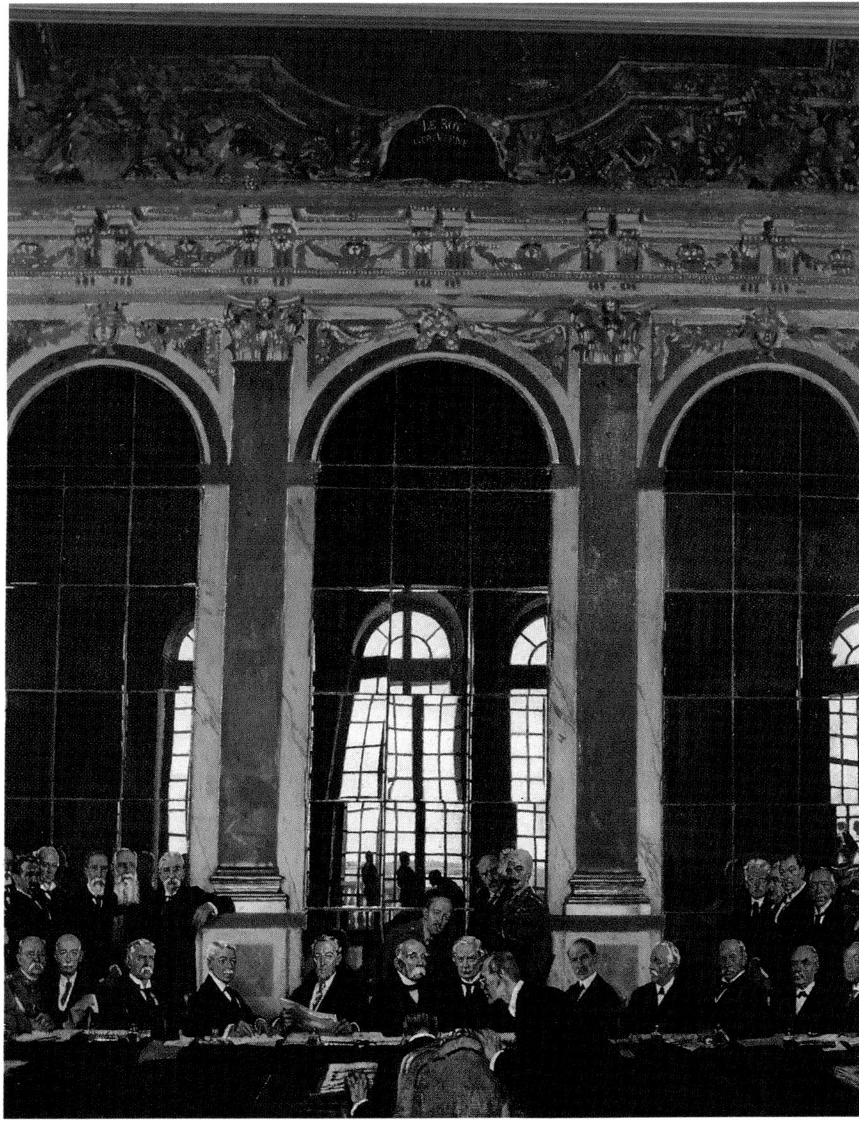

Signing of the Peace **(1919) by Sir William Orpen.**
(Courtesy The Trustees of the Imperial War Museum, London.)

This cartoon of Roosevelt's inauguration in 1933 caricatures the chief political figures of the time and also reflects the exuberance of hope for a reversal of the Great Depression in the victory of the Democrats over the Republican party, which had dominated the government since the 1890's.

COPYRIGHT, 1933, THE CONDÉ NAST PUBLICATIONS, INC

THE INAUGURATION OF FRANKLIN D. ROOSEVELT

AN HEROIC PANORAMA DEPICTING THE HIGH CEREMONY ON THE CAPITOL PLAZA AT WASHINGTON ON MARCH 4TH, 1933

Done Into Full Colour, In The Memorial Manner, By Miguel Covarrubias, Painter Extraordinary and Historiographer to the Court on the Potomac

ENGRAVED IN THIS YEAR OF OUR LORD 1933 AND INCLUDED IN THE MARCH NUMBER OF VANITY FAIR, THE GENTRY'S GAZETTEER OF ARTS AND MANNERS

PUBLISHED AT THE SIGN OF THE GRAYBAR BLDG. (WHICH IS HARD BY ST. BARTHOLOMEW CHURCH MEWS AND OLD TONY'S TAVERN IN THE CITY OF NEW YORK)

1. **PRESIDENT** Franklin D. Roosevelt
2. **CHIEF JUSTICE** Charles Evans Hughes
3. Mrs. Franklin D. Roosevelt
4. **VICE-PRESIDENT** John N. Garner
5. **EX-PRESIDENT** Herbert Hoover
6. Mrs. Herbert Hoover
7. **EX-VICE-PRESIDENT** Charles E. Curtis
8. Alfred E. Smith
9. James Farley
10. Raymond Moley
11. Louis Howe
12. **SENATOR** Joe Robinson
13. Bernard M. Baruch
14. Owen D. Young
15. **SENATOR** William G. McAdoo
16. **GOVERNOR** Albert C. Ritchie
17. **SENATOR** Claude Swanson
18. **SENATOR** Pat Harrison
19. **GOVERNOR** Herbert Lehman
20. **SENATOR** Thomas Walsh
21. John W. Davis
22. **SENATOR** Carter Glass
23. Norman Davis
24. Newton D. Baker
25. Henry L. Stimson
26. Andrew Mellon
27. Ogden L. Mills
28. J. P. Morgan
29. **AMBASSADOR** Paul Claudel
30. **AMBASSADOR** Sir Ronald Lindsay

31, 32. Oriental Ambassadors

33. Mark Sullivan
34. Walter Lippmann
35. Gentlemen of the Press
36. **GENERAL** John J. Pershing
37. The **FORGOTTEN** Man
38. The **U. S.** Navy

Inauguration of FDR.
(Courtesy the Franklin D. Roosevelt Library.)

Despite the election of Franklin D. Roosevelt and the emergence of New Deal policies, the effects of the Great Depression yielded only slowly to improvement. As the hopeless expressions of the artist's subjects show, jobs were still scarce in 1937.

***The Employment Agency* (1937) by Isaac Soyer.**
(Collection of the Whitney Museum of American Art.)

One hundred years after Bingham painted *The Verdict of the People*, the association of politics and entertainment still prevails. Now, however, the entertainment is less a celebration of democracy than a somewhat wearisome social obligation with the participants over- or under-dressed.

***Election Night* (1954) by Jack Levine.**
(Oil on canvas. Collection, The Museum of Modern Art, New York. Gift of Joseph H. Hirshhorn.)

Regulation of interest groups raises questions about individual freedom. These organizations have a constitutional foundation in the First Amendment's guarantee of the "right of the people to petition the Government for a redress of grievances." Restrictions on grass-roots lobbying comes close to restricting the political process itself. Even simple disclosure may have a chilling effect on individual freedom, argue the opponents of such legislation. Some women, for example, may not want it known that they have contributed to a group favoring abortion, or Southern blacks may fear economic retribution if their support of the NAACP is publicized. Even if individuals are protected, the costs of bookkeeping and reporting may be a burden to groups and thereby reduce their ability to petition the government. Such objections have led the proponents of interest group regulation to oppose most controls over grass-roots lobbying.

Social Restraints

A more general means of controlling interest groups is through social restraints. In his exposition of the theory underlying the federal Constitution, Madison recognized that the growth of interest groups was inevitable in a free society and could be eliminated only "by destroying the liberty which is essential to its existence." Madison's solution was, instead, to allow, even to encourage, a flourishing of interest groups so that no one "faction" could predominate. The diversity of society in a large nation would result in a multiplicity of groups, providing a system of checks and balances within society.

Majority Factions Today, with nearly two hundred years of experience, there is reason to doubt that Madison's solutions are completely effective. To him, the principal problem was an interest group that comprised a majority of the population, particularly those without property. By fostering multiple groups, he believed that a majority interest group would either be impossible to create or would be unable to act cohesively. In this regard, Madison has been proved correct. There is no interest group that remotely approaches a popular majority. The political parties, which might be able to aggregate large groups, are unable to enact decisive policies.

Minority Factions Minority factions were given little consideration by Madison, who dismissed the problem by reference to "the republican principle, which enables the majority to defeat its sinister views by regular vote." In fact, the problem is not dismissed so easily. If majorities cannot be assembled to accomplish their own purposes, it is at least as difficult to assemble them to defeat other groups. The characteristics of interest group politics favor small factions. The incentive structure promotes activity by members of organizations with distinct and self-interested goals, while discouraging activity by members of general groups. The narrow scope of most issues gives an advantage to those who are interested in these policies and have an institutional base to promote their concerns. The pattern of participation in organizations and the nature of financing campaigns gives a boost to persons and groups of higher social status.

Single-issue groups complicate the process of policymaking. *(Jean-Louis Atlan/Sygma)*

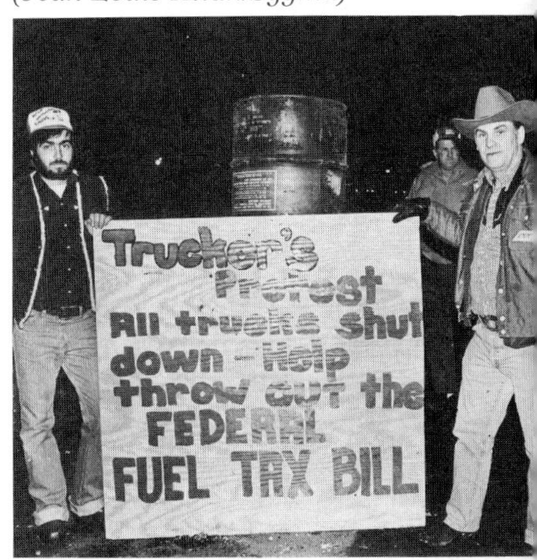

Contemporary features of American politics create opportunities for minority factions that Madison never could have foreseen. Specialization within Congress gives rise to policy subgovernments, which narrows the scope of conflict, limits any intervention by the general public, and gives affected interests a clear target for their efforts. Lobbyists are more expert, better trained, and more necessary than ever, although sophisticated direct-mail techniques and media-oriented protests enable a group to mobilize its supporters throughout the nation. Meanwhile, the decline of political parties as integrating institutions means that it is more difficult to compromise competing claims and to establish a program for the common good.

Our problem today is not Madison's concern, the control of an "interested and overbearing majority." Our problem is the overbearing power of the single-interest group, pursuing causes "adverse to the rights of other citizens, or to the permanent and aggregate interests of the community." We still require institutions that will assert these general interests. Lacking these institutions, interest groups will continue to reflect the general character of American politics: the fragmentation of power.

SUMMARY

Interest groups are vital expressions of the diversity of American life and of the freedom of our politics. They regularly provide information to government about the special needs of different groups and they raise issues that may be ignored or disregarded by government. But, because interest groups are self-interested and unequal in their influence, they may undermine the general good.

People associate with one another for many purposes. As seen in the women's movement, they turn to government when they find they cannot deal with social and political change by their own efforts. As government has taken on more roles, more interest groups have attempted to enlist its aid. Individual leaders, acting as entrepreneurs, have furthered this development.

All interest groups face the common problems of gaining their members' time, money, and attention and of getting individuals to work for collective goals. Different groups emphasize economic goals, specific issues, general programs, or solidary goals. Along with these differences, they vary as to whether their principal rewards are material gain, policies, ideology, or status.

The activities of these organizations vary with the resources they have. Those that represent the more advantaged segments of society are likely to have more money, prestige, and skill and, therefore, are more likely to win their goals. But there also are opportunities for other groups. Their activities include providing information as in lobbying, establishing position of strength in government, mobilizing the public as in mail campaigns, electioneering (including campaign endorsements and PAC contributions), and—as illustrated by the civil rights movement—protesting.

Two different theories attempt to evaluate interest groups. The pluralist theory argues that groups generally promote democratic control. The theory is flawed, however, because these organizations are not fully democratic, some groups are not represented, and there are distinct advantages for higher-status groups. The elitist theory sees American politics dominated by a small unified group, especially big business. Empirical evidence does not show consistent control by any single combination of interest groups. Generally, the power of an interest group is greatest when it succeeds in keeping the scope of conflict limited.

Efforts to control interest groups include formal legislation and more indirect social restraints. Laws to regulate interest groups have not been effective and may be improper limitations of individual freedom. Social restraints, the other means of control, do not deal with the problems created by small special interests. The general fragmentation of power in the United States means that the theoretical democratic principle of majority rule is not always followed in practice. In the clash of interest groups, the overall public good often can be defeated or simply forgotten.

NOTES

1. *The Federalist, No. 10* (New York: Modern Library, 1941), p. 56. Subsequent quotations of Madison are from the same essay.
2. Denise S. Akey, ed., *Encyclopedia of Associations 1984* (Detroit: Gale Research, 1984). A useful source of lobbyists in the national capital is Arthur C. Close, *Washington Representatives* (Washington: Columbia Books, published annually).
3. Gabriel A. Almond and Sidney Verba, *The Civic Culture* (Boston: Little, Brown, 1965), p. 247.
4. Sidney Verba and Norman H. Nie, *Participation in America* (New York: Harper, 1972), pp. 31, 42; Sidney Verba, Norman H. Nie and Jae-on-Kim, *The Modes of Democratic Participation* (Beverly Hills: Sage, 1971), p. 58.
5. David B. Truman, *The Governmental Process* (New York: Knopf, 1951), p. 104.
6. On the development of NOW, see Jo Freeman, *The Politics of Women's Liberation* (New York: McKay, 1975), chap. 2.
7. *Congressional Quarterly Weekly Report,* 42 (Feb. 18, 1984), p. 296.
8. Grant McConnell, *Private Power and American Democracy* (New York: Vintage, 1966), chap. 7; Charles M. Hardin, *The Politics of Agriculture* (Glencoe, Ill.: Free Press, 1952); O. M. Kile, *The Farm Bureau through Three Decades* (Baltimore: Waverly, 1949).
9. *The New York Times* (May 22, 1983); *Congressional Quarterly Weekly Report,* 42 (Jan. 14, 1984), pp. 47–48.
10. Theodore J. Lowi, *The End of Liberalism,* 2nd ed. (New York: Norton, 1979), pp. 207–36; Francis Fox Piven and Richard A. Cloward, *Regulating the Poor* (New York: Vintage, 1971).
11. Robert H. Salisbury, "An Exchange Theory of Interest Groups," *Midwest Journal of Political Science,* 13 (Feb. 1969), pp. 1–32.
12. Mancur Olson, Jr., *The Logic of Collective Action* (Cambridge: Harvard U.P.), p. 33.
13. *Congressional Quarterly Almanac,* 32 (1976), p. 497.
14. Raymond A. Bauer, Ithiel de Sola Pool, and Lewis Anthony Dexter, *American Business and Public Policy* (New York: Atherton, 1963).
15. Olson, p. 51.
16. David Broder, "Let 100 Single-Issue Groups Bloom," *The Washington Post* (Jan. 7, 1979).
17. Jeffrey M. Berry, "Public Interest vs. Party System," *Society,* 17 (May/June 1980), 47; also *Lobbying for the People* (Princeton: Princeton U.P., 1977).
18. Alexis de Tocqueville, *Democracy in America,* vol. 1. (New York: Vintage, 1954), p. 203.
19. James Q. Wilson, *Political Organizations* (New York: Basic Books, 1973), p. 125.
20. Lester Milbrath, *The Washington Lobbyists* (Skokie, Ill.: Rand McNally, 1963), p. 117.
21. Richard Fenno, *Home Style* (Boston: Little, Brown, 1978), p. 142.
22. E. E. Schattschneider, *Politics, Pressure, and the Tariff* (Englewood Cliffs, N.J.: Prentice-Hall, 1935), chap. 2.
23. Charles Lindblom, *Politics and Markets* (New York: Basic Books, 1977), p. 175.
24. J. Leiper Freeman, *The Political Process,* rev. ed. (New York: Random House, 1965).
25. Morris T. Fiorina, *Congress: Keystone of the Washington Establishment* (New Haven: Yale U.P., 1977), p. 49.
26. Leila A. Sussman, *Dear FDR: A Study of Political Letter-Writing* (Totowa, N.J.: Bedminister, 1963); Lewis Anthony, *The Sociology and Politics of Congress* (Skokie, Ill.: Rand McNally, 1969), p. 152.
27. Philip E. Converse, Aage R. Clausen, and Warren E. Miller, "Electoral Myth and Reality: The 1964 Election," *American Political Science Review,* 59 (June 1965), pp. 321–36.
28. James N. Rosenau, *Citizenship Between Elections* (New York: Free Press, 1974), p. 81.
29. *Congressional Quarterly Weekly Report,* 38 (April 26, 1980), pp. 1112–13.
30. *Congressional Quarterly Weekly Report,* 43 (April 20, 1985), pp. 741–49.
31. *Congressional Quarterly Weekly Report,* 43 (Feb. 16, 1985), p. 302.
32. Charles E. Fager, *Selma 1965* (New York: Scribners, 1974).
33. Warren Miller, Arthur Miller, and Edward Schneider, *American National Election Studies Data Sourcebook, 1952–1978* (Cambridge: Harvard U.P., 1980), p. 226.
34. Michael Lipsky, "Protest as a Political Source," *American Political Science Review,* 62 (Dec. 1968), pp. 1144–48.
35. Stephen K. Bailey, *Congress Makes a Law* (New York: Columbia U.P., 1950), p. 240.
36. Nelson Polsby, "How to Study Community Power: The Pluralist Alternative," *Journal of Politics,* 22 (Aug. 1960), p. 474.
37. Truman, chap. 16.
38. Theodore R. Marmor, *The Politics of Medicare* (Chicago: Aldine, 1973).
39. U.S. Department of Commerce, Bureau of the Census, *Social Indicators III* (Washington: GPO, 1980), p. 521.
40. E. E. Schattschneider, *The Semi-Sovereign People* (New York: Holt, 1960), p. 35. Italics in original.
41. Joyce Gelb and Marian Lief Palley, *Women and Public Policies* (Princeton: Princeton U.P., 1982).
42. C. Wright Mills, *The Power Elite* (New York: Oxford U.P., 1956), p. 4.
43. Walter Guzzardi, Jr., "A New Public Face for Business," *Fortune,* 101 (June 30, 1980), p. 50.
44. See Thomas R. Dye and L. Harmon Ziegler, *The Irony of Democracy,* 2nd ed. (North Scutiate, Mass.: Duxbury, 1972), pp. 10–12.
45. Schattschneider (1960), chap. 1 and p. 34.
46. *The New York Times* (June 5, 1983).
47. *U.S.* v. *Harriss,* 347 U.S. 612 (1954).

PART 3

The Institutions of Government

What picture do you see when you hear the word "institution"? If you think of a large, granite building with columns, your image is probably in line with that of most Americans. If you've been to Washington, D.C., you know that the Capitol, the White House, and the Executive Office Building, for example, physically fit that description. They also house, in whole or in part, some of the major institutions of our national government: Congress, the presidency, and the bureaucracy. But even if these institutions of our national government were housed in circus tents or high school gymnasiums, they would still be respected. This is true because of the important roles the Constitution gives them and because they are basic to the operation of the political system.

As we know, the Constitution is a document that is not easily changed or amended—not like an ordinary act of Congress that can be repealed by a majority vote of the members. In the same way, the institutions established under the Constitution were not designed to be changed easily or casually. The framers of the Constitution knew that once serious changes are begun, institutions may end up not being able to perform the functions for which they were established. It's not that the framers were arrogant enough to believe that they had created perfect institutions. Rather, they felt that changes ought to be undertaken cautiously, after considerable discussion and with a high degree of agreement among citizens.

We have already implied that our national institutions are not simply those elements of government set forth in the Constitution. The Constitution itself has changed over the years, through both the formal process of amendment and the less formal process of adapting to changing times. Some features of American government that we could refer to as institutions were either not mentioned in the Constitution or just alluded to in a vague way.

Although we dealt with political parties in Part 2, The Political Process, they could just as well have been included in this part of the book, in our discussion of government institutions. As we said in Part 2, parties were not even mentioned in the Constitution, yet they have been a crucial factor in providing structure for American politics. Likewise, the committees of Congress are not spoken of in the Constitution; yet, it would be difficult to imagine the House and Senate operating without them. They, too, can justly be referred to as institutions. Then, there is the bureaucracy of government, which has attained institutional status despite the most oblique reference to it in the Constitution. Institutions, therefore, may or may not have specific constitutional sanction. Some not mentioned in the Constitution may be more important than some prominently mentioned, such as the Electoral College.

In Part 3, we will examine the three institutions of the Congress, the presidency, and the bureaucracy and take note of how well they are operating. Something so basic to the political system should be fulfilling its role. We want to make sure that the powers of these elements of government are not so fragmented that they are unable to function in proper harmony with other institutions and with one another. We want to see if these institutions are striking a balance between accessibility to the public and an ability to assert the national interest over special interests. The accessibility of Congress is impressive, but its vulnerability to internal fragmentation makes it a less effective defender of the common good than it should be.

The presidency is the institution in which the common good should most eloquently and effectively be asserted. Generally, this is so. But the presidency is sometimes used as a place from which to advocate divisive causes. In addition, the authority of the president over the bureaucracy can be uncertain: Agencies of the president's own executive branch have important allies in Congress, and interest groups there can prevent the president from achieving objectives. Although this is not always bad, the one individual elected by all of the people must not be consistently stymied in carrying out his or her mandate and policies.

Part 4 will examine how another institution, the federal court system, does its job as the guardian of our civil liberties and civil rights. The section on the courts will serve as a kind of bridge between the section on institutions and the section on public policies, because our discussion of the courts will show how one set of institutions influences those policies relating to the most precious and delicate legacy we have as Americans: our liberties and rights.

CHAPTER 9

The Congress

It seemed a noble and timely idea: In March 1984, the House of Representatives overwhelmingly passed a bill providing $60 million in aid for victims of drought-ravaged Africa. Under our system of government, however, that money could not be spent until the same bill also passed the Senate and was approved by the president.

When the bill reached the Senate, some senators, seeing the bill's popularity and obvious good cause, decided to add their own worthy amendments. Senator Alan Dixon, an Illinois Democrat, added an amendment to spend $100 million on summer jobs for American youth. Other senators joined in, and the bill gained 35 amendments, including money for such things as a highway tunnel in Kentucky, parks on Long Island, land reclamation in Montana, and funds for the Corporation for Public Broadcasting. A bill that began with a single objective and a modest $60-million price tag finally arrived at the White House in July loaded down with 22 major provisions, for a cost of $1.1 billion.

Before going to the White House, however, the amended bill had to be returned to the House for action on the Senate amendments—some of which were deleted and others modified. This process necessitated a conference between the two houses to iron out the differences. By the time the president finally signed the bill, many Africans who might have survived with more timely aid had died.[1]

Could the framers of the Constitution possibly have foreseen such a result? Here, a simple, compassionate gesture was diluted by a complicated, slow-moving legislative process that all but canceled the original intent of the bill. Obviously, the framers did not design the legislative system to promote action. Indeed, they specifically wanted to discourage haste, fearing that any lawmaking system that was too simple might be used to oppressive ends. Still, not even James Madison or Alexander Hamilton could have imagined the federal government paying for a town park or a highway. Clearly, the scope of government activities is much broader now than it was in 1789.

Fragmentation of Legislative Power: The Many Voices Influencing Congress

To help us understand what happened to the famine bill, we must first realize that senators and House members come to Washington with the goal of looking after their interests. Members of Congress aim to satisfy the voters whose ballots enable them to remain in office. Thus, a senator from Florida or a representative from Texas will want to please as many members within their constituencies as possible.

There are a great many other voices that members of Congress must heed in addition to those of their constituents. Having been elected as either Democrats or Republicans, new members quickly discover that both Houses of Congress are organized along partisan lines.

Nor do the claims on the member's attention end there. A multitude of organized and unorganized interest groups on a regional and sometimes nationwide basis clamor for representation: farmers wanting government loans; professions (such as the medical) regulated by the federal government demanding changes in the rules; defense contractors lobbying for the continuance of a weapons system that Congress wants to eliminate; or movie stars upset over the environmental threat posed by a change in logging policy announced by the U.S. Forest Service. All of these problems are dealt with, to a greater or lesser degree, by Congress.

Finally, the president, as we shall see in Chapter 10, is a major actor in the legislative process. Usually, the most important bills that Congress deals with are those that the president submits.

Not surprisingly, the time and the attention of members of Congress are fragmented. Members are bombarded with a multitude of messages from a multitude of sources; in response, they introduce some 15,000 bills in each two-year session. Obviously, no member can be familiar with—or even aware of—15,000 bills. For this reason, a system of committees and subcommittees covering the range of public policy filters through and reduces somewhat the number of bills that reach the floor of either house. But changes over the years have made the committee system less efficient than it once was. To chair a committee or subcommittee of the House or Senate brings prestige and power, and the demand by younger members for chair positions in the 1970s produced an increase in the number of subcommittees in the House. The result is that power has been parceled out in smaller and smaller portions. Today, 300 House and Senate committees hold hearings and mold legislation.

This, then, is a very general picture of how our Congress works. Before we take an in-depth look at the intricacies of its operation, however, let us examine the membership of Congress—the people who represent us and the challenges they face.

The Membership of Congress

The Constitution decrees that each state shall have two senators represent it in Washington and at least one representative in the House. Every American, except for residents of Washington, D.C., has at least three representatives: two **Senators** and one **House member.** We call them U.S. Senators and U.S. Representatives. (The terms *representative, House member*, and *congressman/woman* are interchangeable.)

Representation vs. Lawmaking

Does the discrepancy between the background of the voter and the background of the members described in the box on page 305 mean that citizens are poorly represented? Paradoxically, the answer is no. As Maine Senator Edmund Muskie put it, "The people are unhappy with Congress because it represents them too well." The members are well aware of what is going on in the minds of the voters in their states and districts and in the groups that

POLITICAL PERSPECTIVE

DEMOGRAPHIC FEATURES OF MEMBERS OF CONGRESS

Age

Members of Congress are younger today than they were twenty years ago. The average is slightly more than 49 years old; in 1958, the average age was about 53. House members, at an average age of 45.5, are somewhat younger than the average senator, who is 53.4. The median age of Americans is now 30.2.

Occupation

The tendency for people in high-status occupations and professions to predominate in Congress suggests that our national legislature is not the portrait in miniature of the American people that John Adams said it should be.

Lawyers predominate in the House and the Senate; in recent years, the proportion has hovered around 50 percent in both houses. In the 1970s this figure declined somewhat, but the trend was reversed in the 98th Congress (1981–1983). Though they run a poor second, bankers and business executives form the next largest occupational group. And while there is a rancher, a funeral director, and an interior decorator in Congress, there is a distinct absence of people in blue-collar occupations.

Religion, Nationality, and Gender

Protestants of northern European stock are estimated to make up 56 percent of the population but constitute 62 percent of Congress. Catholic ethnics—people of Italian, Slavic, Irish, or German stock—comprise 26 percent of the national population but only 21 percent of Congress. Jews constitute about 3 percent of the nation's population but, with thirty-seven members of both houses, they make up about 8 percent of Congress. Blacks, by contrast, are 12 percent of the American population, but with twenty voting members (the one nonvoting black member is the delegate from the District of Columbia) all of whom are in the House, they made up just over three percent of Congress in 1984. The greatest underrepresentation is by gender: there are only twenty-two women, about 4 percent of Congress, even though 52 percent of the national population is female.

Source: Based on statistics in *How Congress Works* (Washington: Congressional Quarterly, 1983), p. 2; and *Congressional Quarterly Weekly Report,* 41 (Jan. 1985), pp. 34–41.

Many members of Congress, especially House members, spend at least one day a week in their constituency. Representative Romano Mazzoli is shown here talking to a constituent in Louisville. *(Paul Conklin)*

make up their constituencies. Many spend at least one day a week in their constituency, and so many spend more time back home that Congress usually works a three-day week.

Members are also on call when state or district delegations come to Washington. They meet with them during the business day and then have to appear at the group's evening cocktail party. Since most depend on their own personal campaign organizations at home and have no strong party group to rely on, they are obliged to go home to encourage and mobilize support. This need is felt particularly keenly by House members, who must run for office every two years. With so much time spent in the constituency sounding out the voters, mending political fences, and attending social functions—all of which are aimed at holding on to their seats—the task of being a national legislator often takes a backseat.

The Bullet Vote As the discipline that parties formerly placed on issues (see Chapter 6) has eroded, and public policy has been fragmented into a collection of single issues, members often become fearful of losing their seats as a result of a single wrong vote. For example, the failure to vote to kill a dam project that threatens a plant or animal on the endangered species list can bring down the wrath of environmental groups on a member whose previous voting record was 90 percent proconservation. This is known as the **bullet vote.**

Any unhappy group can mount a campaign in a member's state or district to defeat him or her for a solitary vote which, from their point of view, is wrong. The single-issue group is much better able to target the member because of the dramatic increase in recorded votes and the opening up of committee meetings. In the mid-1960s recorded votes averaged about 100 a session. Today, the number is more than 800. The likelihood is that every important vote members cast will be recorded and used as evidence against them by one group or another. Opening committee meetings to the public has made it easier for lobbyists to keep tabs on members. Ordinary citizens, for whose benefit meetings were opened, rarely attend.

U.S. Post Office at York, Pa.
secured through the efforts of
Congressman D.F. Lafean.
UNITED STATES POST OFFICE
STANDS ON HIS RECORD
Vote for Daniel F. Lafean for Congress

Representative Daniel F. LaFean wanted no one in York, Pennsylvania, to be in the dark as to who was responsible for the Post Office building. LaFean, a Republican who served from 1903 until 1917, had these postcards printed up to remind voters to express their gratitude on election day.

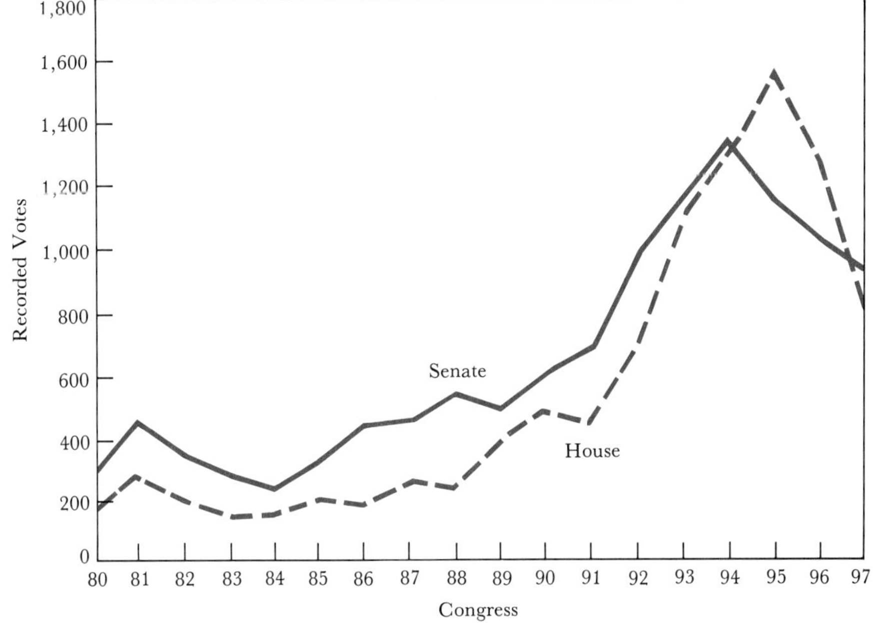

FIGURE 9.1
Recorded Votes in the House and the Senate, 80th–97th Congresses, 1947–1982
Although the number of recorded votes has tailed off in recent years, the 800 or so votes in which "aye" or "nay" goes down next to a member's name is four times greater than it was in the 1950s. (*Norman Ornstein, Thomas E. Mann, Michael J. Malbin, Allen Schick, and John F. Bibby,* Vital Statistics on Congress, 1984–1985 *[Washington: American Enterprise Institute, 1984], p. 149. Used with permission.*)

Fragmentation and the Dispersion of Power How do the members of Congress respond to this confusion of messages on major issues of national policy? One response is to maximize their representational role and minimize their role as national lawmakers; in other words, to base reelection on their noncontroversial activities—their casework and success in procuring **pork** [federal projects for home districts]—rather than on lawmaking activities, which divided their districts. Members involved in controversial matters of national policy find themselves compelled to answer at the roll call and risk antagonizing voters. Therefore it is safer, if reelection is the goal, to be a "rainmaker" rather than a "wave-maker."

The members' outlooks, attitudes, and behavior are what might be expected of people who have won their seats by dint of individual effort and whose objective is mainly to be reelected by the voters of a single state or congressional district. Members of Congress are intensely individualistic, keenly competitive, and wary of their lawmaking role. Because members owe little to their political party or its leaders in Congress, it becomes difficult to move Congress in a single direction.

The emphasis on representation, rather than lawmaking, has caused a marked amount of fragmentation in national policy and a broad dispersion of power within Congress as an institution. As a result, Congress is much weaker as an initiator of national policy than is the president and produces policies that lack the powerful national impact they might have.

We must bear in mind that members of Congress are not solely responsible for this fragmentation. They are responding to the expectations of the public that government provide services, benefits, and solutions. The national public agenda has become crowded with issues that were once dealt with elsewhere, or not at all. In addition, the democratization of the Congress, in which power is more evenly distributed among the membership, and the oversight of a bureaucracy as fully decentralized as Congress itself add up to a Congress that is the very essence of fragmentation.

Senator Rudy Boschwitz talks with staff members on the Capitol steps following an important vote. *(Paul Conklin)*

Congressional Staff

Members of Congress do have resources that enable them to handle the increased load of business. Staff is one of the principal resources at a member's command. The rise in the number of congressional staff from about 10,000 in 1970 to about 18,000 in 1980 reflects the members' increased workload and a diminishing amount of time to deal with it. Employed intel-

TABLE 9.1 Staffs of Members of the House and the Senate, 1891–1983

Year	Employees in House	Employees in Senate
1891	Not available	39
1914	Not available	72
1930	870	280
1935	870	424
1947	1,440	590
1957	2,441	1,115
1967	4,055	1,749
1972	5,280	2,426
1976	6,939	3,251
1977	6,942	3,554
1978	6,944	3,268
1979	7,067	3,593
1980	7,371	3,746
1981	7,487	3,945
1982	7,511	4,041
1983	7,606	4,059

Source: Norman J. Ornstein, Thomas E. Mann, Michael J. Malbin, Allen Schick, and John F. Bibby in *Vital Statistics on Congress, 1984–85* (Washington: American Enterprise Institute, 1984), p. 121. Used with permission.
Note: This chart will give you an idea of the enormous growth of congressional staff. The big increase came between 1967 and 1977 when staff doubled.

ligently, congressional staff people are sources of information and advice, and, in some instances, they even serve as a member's alter ego. Standing at the door of the chamber before a vote, they are prepared to offer a quick briefing of what is being voted on, or even to flash a thumbs-up or thumbs-down signal on how the member ought to vote. Armed with a member's authority, they do much negotiating on his or her behalf.

Each House member is entitled to a staff of twenty-two, which can be divided between Washington and the district offices. Staff salary allowances are apportioned to senators according to the populations of their states. Senators can hire any number of staff aides within the dollar limits imposed by their state's population.

With so many people working long hours to boost members' political fortunes, it is not surprising that much activity is aimed at building political reputations. It is true that the growth of public business does warrant more staff support for Congress; yet adding staff often does little more than generate more business, as staff members seek out new projects that will help the political fortunes of senators and House members.

POLITICAL PERSPECTIVE

BENEFITS, PERQUISITES, AND INCUMBENCY

Given the enormous pressures on members, how is it that we never run out of people to run for Congress? There are as many different answers to the question "Why did you run for Congress?" as there are members. For some, the satisfactions come from a commitment to public service and a desire to influence national policy, and for others, a keen sense of the prestige that attaches to being a member of the world's foremost legislative assembly. There are other, more tangible, benefits that not only make the members' lives more comfortable but add greatly to their ability to defend their seats against challengers. The perquisites (perks) of office are considerable. Here are but some of them:

1. A basic salary of $75,100 to which is added a contributory life insurance policy, health insurance, the services of the attending physician of the Capitol, legal counsel, and the ability to augment one's salary with fees for speeches and honorariums. There is also a liberal retirement plan and special living allowances for the time spent in Washington.
2. Recreational and dining facilities are also available to members. There are gymnasiums on both sides of the Capitol as well as private dining rooms that are heavily subsidized to keep down the cost of members' meals.
3. Perquisites that give members a decided edge over challengers and greatly enhance their ability to defend their seats include the *franking privilege,* which enables a member to send out certain types of mail with a facsimile of his or her signature instead of regular postage on the envelope; newsletter, telephone, and telegraph allowances, which enable members to communicate with their constituents; travel allotments, which allow as many as thirty-two round trips a year between Washington and the member's state or district; and the use of the House and Senate recording studios to make films and tapes for use in TV and radio spots in the state or district. These recordings are billed to the member at cost; challengers must pay the going commercial rate for the same services.

Congressional Committees

The authority to create committees can be found in Article 1, Section 5, which gives each house the power to make its own rules.

By 1795, the House had four standing, or permanent, committees to replace the temporary committees that had existed previously. It was not until 1822, however, that committees were given the power to consider legislation before the rest of the house and to make recommendations to the full membership on proposed legislation. Even at this early date, it was clear that congressional members were busy with issues that pertained to their own districts and could not be experts on every subject that came before them. Smaller and more specialized groups drawn from the membership were needed to develop expertise in various areas of policy.

Because members must make policy decisions in more than a dozen major areas, it is impossible for anyone to be expert in all or even most. And so members defer to the expertise of committees. The assumption is that members of the Armed Services Committee know more about battleships than people on the Agriculture Committee; members on Agriculture assume that their knowledge of soybean prices is superior to that of their colleagues on Armed Services.

Committees process and screen legislation. It would be rare for any bill today to be debated and voted on by all 100 senators and 435 House members without having first been acted on and recommended by a committee.

Types of Committees

Today, there are four types of committees in Congress.

SELECT OR SPECIAL COMMITTEES **Select committees** and **special committees** (the terms are interchangeable) are set up to investigate or study a particular problem. Once their specific task is completed, they are usually disbanded at the end of the two-year Congress in which they are created. The role of most select committees is to investigate problems that do not fit readily into the jurisdiction of the standing committees. They do not report out legislation for action by the entire House or Senate but rather propose ideas or plans. The best-known recent examples of select committees were the Senate Select Committee on Campaign Activities, which was the Watergate investigating committee headed by Sam Ervin (D-N.C.), and the Senate Select Committee on Government Operations with Respect to Intelligence Activities, which investigated the CIA under the chairmanship of the late Frank Church (D-Ida.). Sometimes permanent select or special committees are created that last beyond the life of a Congress, such as the Permanent Select Committee on Aging, whose continuation is supported by powerful groups representing the elderly.

JOINT COMMITTEES **Joint committees** are composed of members of both the Senate and the House in equal numbers. Typically, they are special committees set up temporarily to examine a particular problem, but there are a few permanent joint committees, such as the Joint Economic Committee. The chair and vice-chair positions of joint committees rotate between houses from Congress to Congress so that when a senator holds the chair, the vice-chairperson is a representative—both, of course, from the majority party in their respective houses. As with select committees, joint committees make recommendations rather than report out specific legislation.

STANDING COMMITTEES **Standing committees** are permanent; they continue from Congress to Congress. Some, like the Senate Foreign Relations Committee, have remained unchanged in both name and subject matter since the early nineteenth century. So powerful were these committees by the late 1880s that Woodrow Wilson could say without exaggeration that, "ours [is] a government by the Standing Committees of Congress."

Standing committees enjoy the unique power of reporting out bills for the entire membership of each of the houses to vote on. Members of Congress tend to defer to the specialized knowledge of the standing committees, and if a committee reports out a bill, there is a strong tendency to follow its recommendations. So, although it is true that "Congress does not affirm every committee decision . . . the committee's negative powers are nearly absolute; the bills they do not report out to the floor usually die."[2] Currently, there are fifteen Senate standing committees and twenty-two in the House.

SUBCOMMITTEES **Subcommittees** are exactly what the name implies—subgroups of larger standing committees, select committees, or joint committees. There are 132 House subcommittees and 94 Senate subcommittees. A Congress in which power is distributed among so many subcommittees, each with its own little slice of the legislative pie, is institutionally fragmented and, on the whole, weaker and less able to formulate unified positions on particular issues.

Environmental Protection Agency personnel test toxic waste barrels during an EPA "Superfund" cleanup in Pennsylvania in 1984. *(Tom Kelly)*

The Problem of Overlapping Jurisdiction The jurisdiction of each committee and subcommittee is set forth in the rules and precedents that govern each house. (See Table 9.2 for the jurisdiction of the Senate Committee on Environment and Public Works.) Sometimes, however, the responsibilities of each committee are not so clear-cut, and other committees claim their right to hold hearings or write legislation on that subject. The temptation to raid another committee's jurisdiction is especially strong when the issue is likely to attract newspaper and television coverage.

During the scandal over mismanagement of the toxic waste cleanup program "Superfund" by the Environmental Protection Agency (EPA) in 1983, six committees or subcommittees were holding hearings on the EPA. They were bombarding a single agency for information, taking testimony from the same witnesses, and coming up with six separate sets of recommendations on toxic waste. The beleaguered bureaucrats of EPA had some grounds for consolation, however: The total number of committees and subcommittees that could claim some jurisdiction in the issue was actually forty-four.

The Problem of Fragmentation The fragmentation of power and jurisdiction among committees and subcommittees has come about quite recently. In 1971, House Democrats adopted a rule that made it impossible for any-

TABLE 9.2 Jurisdiction of the Senate Committee on the Environment and Public Works

1. Air pollution
2. Construction and maintenance of highways
3. Environmental aspects of Outer Continental Shelf lands
4. Environmental effects of toxic substances, other than pesticides
5. Environmental policy
6. Environmental research and development
7. Fisheries and wildlife
8. Flood control and improvements of rivers and harbors, including environmental aspects of deepwater ports
9. Noise pollution
10. Nonmilitary environmental regulation and control of nuclear energy
11. Ocean dumping
12. Public buildings and improved grounds of the United States generally; federal buildings in the District of Columbia
13. Public works, bridges, and dams
14. Regional economic development
15. Solid waste disposal and recycling
16. Water pollution
17. Water resources

Note: Such committee shall also study and review, on a comprehensive basis, matters relating to environmental protection and resource utilization and conservation, and report thereon from time to time.

one to be chair of more than one subcommittee. This rule limited the power of senior members, who often presided over several, and opened up committee leadership positions to younger members. Since Democrats controlled the House and all the chairs, this amounted to an institutional reform rather than just a party reform.

In 1973, a subcommittee bill of rights was adopted, giving Democrats on all subcommittees the right to elect chairs. For most of this century, chairs of the standing committees controlled all committee business. Also established was a fairer procedure for assigning members to subcommittees so that senior members would not get all the choice assignments.

In 1974 subcommittees were strengthened by a Democratic proposal incorporated into House rules that required standing committees to have at least four subcommittees. This meant that more people could call themselves "Mr. Chairman" or "Madame Chairman"; it dispersed leadership positions and made the House more egalitarian.

The "Problem" of Democracy "And isn't democracy good in itself? Perhaps, but democracy has its cost. In particular, those who applaud internal democratic reforms should not criticize Congress for inefficiency, shortsightedness, and foot-dragging. For example, public interest groups applaud the democratization of Congress, on the one hand, and deplore Congress' failure to formulate a national energy policy, on the other. There is something of an inconsistency here."[3]

Committees and Seniority

Although it is no longer the rule—in the House at least—that chairs go automatically to those members of the majority party who have served the longest on the committee, that is generally the way chairs are selected in Congress. Despite reforms in the House that have made chairmanships elective, the practice of **seniority** usually prevails. This means that the person elected is the member of the majority party who has been the longest on the committee.

The system of giving chairs by seniority was looked upon by congressional reformers as a backward system that rewarded nothing but political survival. House members from the solid Democratic South came to dominate congressional chairs. Since they were never defeated, and often not even challenged for their seats by candidates of the weak Republican Party organizations of the South, they were able to build up the seniority needed to be first in line for committee chairs.

To chair a congressional committee means planning the agenda, calling meetings and hearings, hiring and firing the staff, and otherwise managing the affairs of the group. The chair usually works closely with the ranking minority member, who is the senior committee member of the minority party. Should the minority become the majority in a house of Congress, it usually is its ranking member who takes over the chair.

"It's A Hell Of A Way To Run A Railroad"

This cartoon attacking the seniority system appeared in 1948 when the solidly Democratic South sent members to Congress who were never defeated because the Republicans were so weak in the region. The seniority system has been defended with the argument that those who have been on a committee the longest have the most knowledge and ought to lead the committee. Sometimes this results in chairmen who are clearly past their prime. (*From* The Herblock Book *[Beacon Press, 1952]*.)

Changes in Senate procedures for selecting chairpersons have been far less dramatic than those in the House: seniority generally prevails. Senate Democrats made the choice a little less automatic in 1975 by requiring that a list of all chair nominees be submitted to all Senate Democrats, who may then check the names of those nominees they feel should be elected by secret ballot. They return the unsigned list to the Democratic Steering Committee, and if 20 percent of the members request a vote on a candidate, it is taken within two days. The Republicans followed a similar procedure when they took control of the Senate in 1981. Despite these changes in the rule of automatic seniority, members in both houses still favor the most senior of their colleagues for the chairperson positions.

Committee Assignments

When it comes to committee assignment, members try to be placed on committees that will meet their individual needs. Richard Fenno cites four needs that govern their choice of committee assignments: (1) reelection, (2) influence within the chamber, (3) the opportunity to make good public policy, and (4) ambition for higher office. There is no single ranking of priorities. In the House, at least, "the opportunity to achieve the[se] . . . goals varied widely among committees. House members, therefore, match their individual patterns of aspiration to the diverse patterns of opportunity presented by House committees."[4]

The choice of committee assignments is very individualistic with a number of factors entering into the selection. When Democrat John J. Cavanaugh of Nebraska arrived in the House as a freshman, he discussed what went into his preference for Banking, Finance, and Urban Affairs:

> My first consideration was to try to obtain a committee on which I could be most effective. . . . I'm a generalist. The economy will be the strongest issue. To have input into the banking system, into the whole area of housing, would be good for me. Omaha is a strong banking community serving the interests of Nebraska agriculture, and cities the size of Omaha, and smaller ones, need some voice in housing legislation.[5]

When there are more applications for a committee than there are vacancies, some applicants will be disappointed. Failure to get your first choice usually means that you must wait two years for a new Congress to convene unless there is a death or a resignation in the interim. When New York Democrat Herman Badillo was in the House, his choice for a committee assignment was Banking, Finance, and Urban Affairs. He took an assignment on Labor when he could not get Banking but missed his second shot at Banking as well and took Judiciary. On his third try, Badillo finally got Banking—the committee whose jurisdiction over matters relating to urban areas was appropriate for his South Bronx district. Badillo paid a price, however. Having switched committees twice, he lost seniority. He chose instead an assignment closer to the needs of his district.

Finally, it appears that the most important factor considered by the House committees that make the committee assignments is the preference

The Senate Health and Scientific Research Subcommittee hearing on health implications from the Three Mile Island nuclear accident. *(Arthur Grace/Sygma)*

of the member. Even freshmen find that they are placed on committees in which they have some interest, though it might not be their first choice. However, when a freshman vies with a senior member for a choice seat, the veteran tends to win out.

In both chambers and in both parties, there are committees that assign members to committees. These committees are either controlled directly or influenced by the party leadership. Assignment of new members to committees or shifting veteran members from one committee to another is one of those few times in which party leaders can reward loyalty or punish those who have consistently supported the opposition. Members of Congress are entitled to serve on a committee, but whether they get their first choice depends to some extent on how supportive they have been of the party leadership and how impressed are the senior members of the committee they hope to join.

Certain forms of influence can be used to get a favored committee assignment. Regional support is important, as is support from a member's own **state delegation**—that is, all of the members in either congressional house who come from one state. Those wanting to be assigned to a committee try to enlist the support of the chair of that committee and other ranking members. Sometimes the argument that the member's state has no members on an important committee is persuasive.

Interest Group Influence Committee assignments and chair-holding are not wholly an internal matter. Special interests also attempt to influence the personnel and leadership of congressional committees. Interest groups involve themselves in the committee assignment and chair selection by encouraging freshman members to seek seats on committees and subcommittees that are crucial to the special interest, by lobbying chairpersons and

POLITICAL PERSPECTIVE

COMMITTEE PRESTIGE

In Congress right now, some committees are hot. The House and Senate Appropriations Committee, the House and Senate Budget Committee, the House Ways and Means and the Senate Finance Committees, the House Energy and Commerce Committee, the Senate Foreign Relations Committee, and the House Rules Committee are examples.

But some are not—such as the House Education and Labor and the Senate Labor and Human Resources Committees, the House and Senate Judiciary, the Senate Rules Committee, the House Standards of Official Conduct and the Senate Select Ethics Committees, the House Administration Committee, and the House District of Columbia Committee.

The prestige of committees rises and falls over time; a committee that was important at one point can lose its prestige and attractiveness to members at a later time.

For most of the 1960s, the House committee on Education and Labor was a hive of activity as programs to fight poverty were being pushed by the Johnson administration. By the 1980s, however, the emphasis was on cutting money from social programs, not authorizing or appropriating funds for new ones. As a result, Education and Labor lost its attractiveness and prestige. Members left for traditional powerhouse committees, such as Ways and Means and Budget in the House, and Budget and Finance in the Senate, both of which initiated the spending and tax cuts.

In 1973–74, when it held hearings on the articles of impeachment against President Richard Nixon, the House Judiciary Committee drew media attention and praise for the quality of its deliberations. By the 1980s, it was the graveyard for many items on the conservative social agenda, such as school prayer, the balanced budget amendment, and abortion restrictions. It was badly polarized between its liberal majority, presided over by Representative Peter Rodino, and the Republican minority. A similar split between liberals and conservatives has made the Senate Judiciary Committee less attractive to senators because the moral issues that come up in the committee are not easily subject to compromise, and positions on both sides tend to be inflexible. This makes for conflict within the committee.

Predicting the rise and fall of congressional committees is not easy. The Senate and House committees dealing with the space program were quiet backwaters until the *Challenger* disaster in 1986. A single dramatic event can propel a committee into the spotlight, but long-term trends such as a decline in government spending can affect committee prestige over time.

senior committee members to support for seats members friendly to those interests, and by lobbying state delegations and regional caucuses to nominate friendly members for seats.

Interest groups are usually more successful in their efforts to place friendly members and elect friendly chairpersons in the House than they are in the Senate. The efforts of a single-interest group simply count for more in a congressional district than in an entire state, where there are so many other interest groups.

Party Leadership in Congress

The Constitution mentions only three leadership positions in the Congress: the vice-president in his role as president of the Senate, the president *pro tem* of the Senate, who presides in the vice-president's absence, and the speaker of the House. The vice-president rarely presides in the Senate except when his vote is needed to break a tie. Even the **president pro tem** of the Senate, the most senior member of the majority party in terms of Senate service, rarely presides. Usually, this chore falls to the most junior members. The **speaker of the House,** however, is quite a different position. The speaker is a true presiding officer because the House is a body so vast that a strong leadership is needed to transact business.

The Speaker and the House Leadership

The term "speaker" comes down to us from the English parliament: the member who was selected from the body to go and speak with the king. The speakership is generally not a jumping-off place for higher office. Only one speaker, James K. Polk, has ever become president. In modern times, the speaker has been a veteran member: Speaker Thomas P. O'Neill was a member of the House for twenty-four years before his election in 1977. Despite the fact that the speaker must preside over a house with very complex rules of order, those with knowledge of the rules are rarely elected. What Speaker Champ Clark said in 1920 is true today:

> It is a peculiar and interesting fact that no man was ever elected Speaker chiefly because of his knowledge of parliamentary law. Speakers are elected by reason of the possession of other qualities. The quality of leadership is usually the thing which enables a man to win the glittering prize.[6]

In the job of presiding over the House, the speaker has the power to recognize members who wish to address the chamber. Although he may leave the details of scheduling the activities of the House to the majority leader, the speaker does have the final word on scheduling. The speaker wants the business of the House to flow smoothly but also to flow according to his own plan. The speaker is, in short, the chief strategist, and controls the pace and sequence of House activities in order to increase his chances for success. The speaker may put off a vote on a major piece of legislation

T. B. R.
THE CZAR IS DEAD.
LONG LIVE THE CZAR.

Today's party leaders in Congress could only dream of the power enjoyed by nineteenth-century Speaker Thomas B. Reed, referred to by friend and foe alike as Czar Reed.

Former Speaker of the House Tip O'Neill swearing in a new member in 1983. *(Dennis Brack/Black Star)*

for weeks in order to line up enough support for it, or may withdraw a bill from the schedule if he or she thinks that support is lacking.[7]

The speaker can get support from members by building loyalty. He can perform a broad range of services for members: from helping them to gain a seat on a committee that they want (through his influence with the committee that assigns members to committees), to preventing important votes when they are absent or sparing them from controversial votes at sensitive times. For example, Speaker O'Neill postponed the vote on an immigration bill until after the California primary because of opposition to the bill among members of Hispanic origin in that state.

Perhaps the most important of the speaker's roles is supervision of a large intelligence network that he runs with the majority leader and the assistant majority leaders. If the same party controls both the House of Representatives and the White House, the speaker is the chief liaison officer to the president and attempts to develop support for administration programs in the House. Given the tendency of House members to vote the way they feel the voters in their districts wish them to vote rather than the way the president or the party leadership would like them to, this role sometimes involves bringing the president the bad news that his programs do not have enough votes to pass the House.

As with all leadership posts, a speaker's success is often largely the result of personal skill. But when the inducements at a speaker's disposal are limited, when the nature of the institution is not conducive to strong leadership, and when party loyalty is weak, even the most charming and forceful person may not achieve his ends. Right now, the tools of reward and punishment available to the speaker are not so great as they were in the heyday of strong speakers like Sam Rayburn. Party loyalty counts for a good deal less than it did thirty years ago, and the decentralized nature of power and individualism erodes the influence of the speaker as well as of the entire leadership.[8]

The House Majority Leader and the Whips

The **House majority leader** is the majority party's second-in-command in the House. The fact that this official and his minority party counterpart are often referred to as "floor leaders" suggests that it is their job to circulate among their party colleagues on the floor while the speaker is presiding. The majority leader's job is to share the legislative strategy making with the speaker and to carry it out. He is the eyes and ears of the speaker in the party's information-gathering network and is aided by an assistant floor leader, or **whip.**

The majority leader and the whip are selected by party caucus or conference, and the whip appoints several assistant whips. The whip system is the real key to bringing a bill to a vote at just the right time. To do so, the whips must have an accurate picture of how members plan to vote. This is known as a "whip count," and if it shows that a bill supported by the leadership does not have enough votes, the speaker may withdraw it rather than suffer an embarrassing defeat. The whips also "whip" the supporters into line, that is, make sure that supporters are present for votes. In the days when party loyalty in the House was stronger, this system of advance warning was less important than it is now. But the whip count has been used more widely in recent years because of the larger number of issues and the inability of the leaders to have House members conform to their wishes.

The Senate Majority Leader

Robert J. Dole (right), the Senate majority leader of the 99th Congress, at press conference with Robert C. Byrd, Senate minority leader. *(Dennis Brack/Black Star)*

The **Senate majority leader** controls the legislative schedule and is his party's chief strategist and spokesperson. Whether or not the majority leader succeeds in these tasks depends less on this individual's formal powers than on the trust and confidence he establishes with colleagues. Democrats have concentrated more power in their leaders than Republicans have. The Democratic leader is chairman of the Senate Democratic Conference (the Senate equivalent of the party caucus in the House). He also chairs the Committee that makes committee assignments for Democrats. The Democratic majority leader chairs the Policy Committee that plays a major role in coordinating party positions on legislation. On the Republican side, these leadership posts are filled by different individuals: in the 99th Congress, the Senate Republican Conference was chaired by Senator John H. Chaffee of Rhode Island, and William L. Armstrong of Colorado chaired the policy committee.

Personal style greatly influences what the Senate majority leader accomplishes in the job. As majority leader, Lyndon Johnson put enormous pressure on colleagues, developed a loyal group of followers, and was capable of great ruthlessness. His successor, Mike Mansfield, was a solemn, softspoken Montanan who was reluctant to apply pressure. Robert Byrd, who followed Mansfield, was neither as passive as Mansfield nor as hard-driving as Johnson. Howard Baker was an easy-going consensus builder, and Bob Dole an energetic leader during their tenures. It is rare for a majority leader of the Senate to have the power and influence enjoyed by a speaker.

For this reason, we can see why Johnson developed so muscular a style. He had slim majorities to work with, and for six years of his incumbency there was a Republican president at the other end of Pennsylvania Avenue. This made Johnson the unchallenged spokesman of Senate Democrats who defined where the party stood on legislative programs in that chamber.

The Minority Leader

The tasks of the minority leaders in both houses are much like those of the majority leaders. Like the majority leaders, those at the head of the minority party must see that their troops are on the floor to vote, especially on matters on which the party has taken a position. Although they do not generally involve themselves in committee hearings or bill drafting, they must be prepared to deal with legislation as it comes out of the committees. If their party supports a bill, they must develop the majority to pass it. If the party is opposed to the bill, they must work to see that it is defeated.

The Party in Congress

Loyalty to a party's national platform often competes, in the mind of the senator or representative, with the interests of the state or district and the personal goals of the legislator. Party leaders in Congress have few positive incentives to offer members to go along with party positions and they can inflict even fewer negative sanctions. When a Democratic member of the House Ways and Means Committee cosponsored a major piece of tax legislation supported by Republican President Ronald Reagan in 1981, the only punishment he could recall was that the little wheels were taken off his swivel chair in the committee hearing room, causing him to sit about three inches lower than the other members. Nevertheless, members vote more often than not with their fellow partisans.

The Party as a Source of Leadership Even though party influence has weakened (see Chapter 6), parties are instruments for cohesion. As Barbara Sinclair points out, "The only centralized leadership is based on party. Speakers, floor leader, whips, and conference and policy chairpersons owe their selection and continuing support to the members of their congressional party."[9] Without some loyalty beyond that to a member's district or state, there would be, in effect, 535 separate political parties and no overall policy for which anyone would be responsible. Party programs give a semblance of structure to national policy.

The problems that have driven a wedge between members of Congress and their party do not afflict Republicans and Democrats equally. The Democrats have tended to be a more diverse party with distinct Northern-liberal and Southern-conservative wings. These regional and philosophical differences are less important among Republicans, and as a result President Reagan was able to get support among congressional Republicans for his economic recovery program early in his first term. Virtually all congressional Republicans supported the president's budget cuts and tax cuts and brought a large number of Southern Democrats with them. There were only a handful of Republican members who supported the Democratic alternatives.

A popular president of his or her own party is an asset to members of Congress, but they will shun an unpopular or ineffective president even to the extent of avoiding joint appearances with that individual. Members who defend the policies of an unpopular president of their own party can suffer defeat for their loyalty. This happened to Republicans during the recession year of 1982. Yet by 1984, when prosperity had returned, Reagan was again an asset and Democratic congressional candidates were now putting distance between themselves and Democratic presidential candidate Walter F. Mondale.

The Legislative Process in Congress

For a bill to become law, it must pass many hurdles, but basically every measure, except those dealing with internal matters of the Senate and House, must pass both houses of Congress in identical form and be approved by the president. As straightforward as that sounds, the reality is

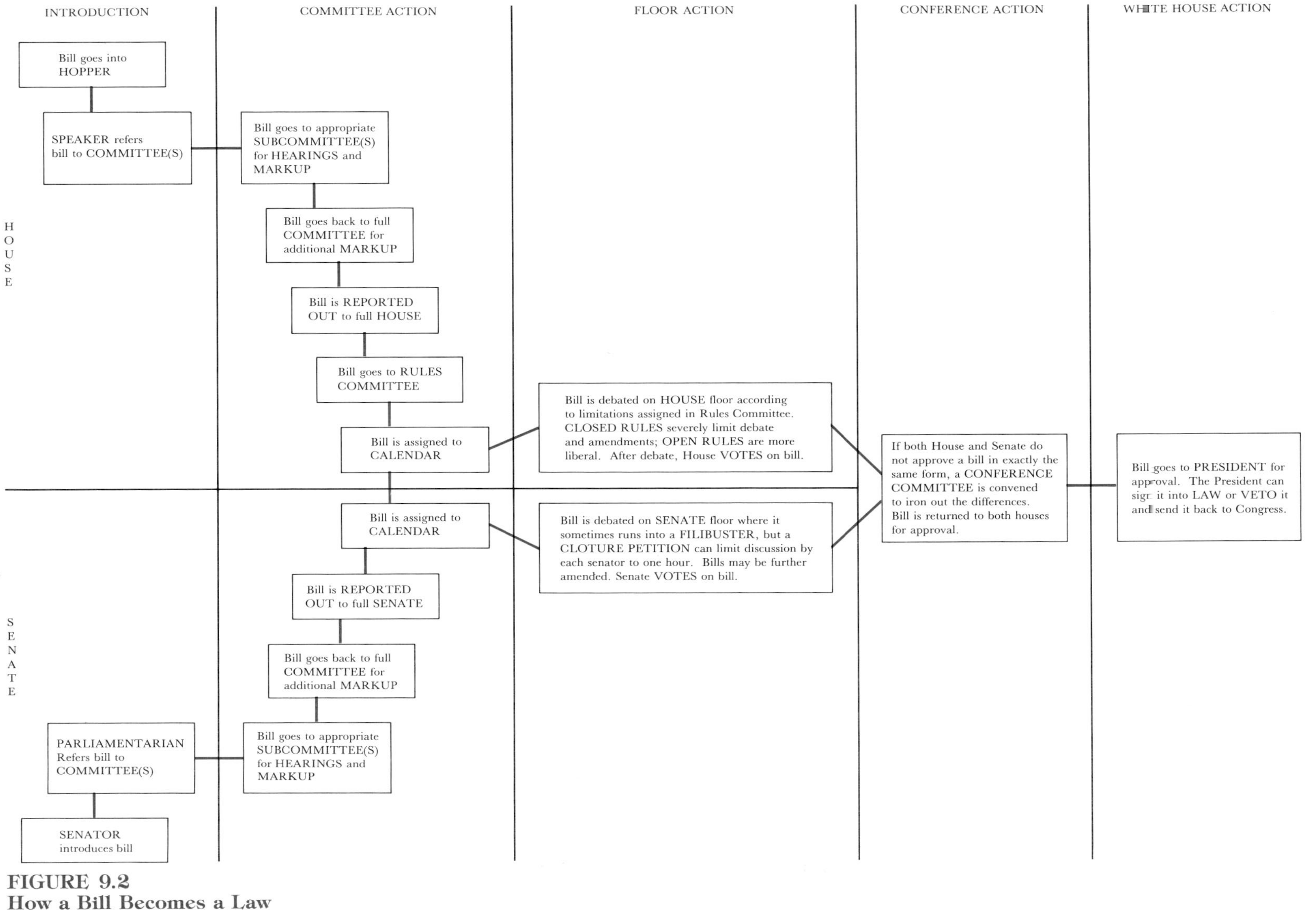

FIGURE 9.2
How a Bill Becomes a Law

much more complicated, mainly because of differences between the House and Senate. Each house does some things better than its counterpart: Senate rules allow for more thorough debates than in the House; House members have more limited and specialized committee assignments and are better versed in the details of legislation. (Some of the differences between the House and Senate are listed in Table 9.3.)

Introducing a Bill

Introducing a bill is the simplest thing a member of Congress can do. House members deposit bills in a hopper at the front of the chamber; senators ask for recognition from the chair and introduce the bill on the floor. Sometimes a bill will carry only the name of the **sponsor,** the member

TABLE 9.3 House-Senate Differences

	Senate	House
1. Member's term of office	6 years	2 years
2. Size of house	100 senators	435 members + 1 resident commissioner from Puerto Rico and 4 delegates (all nonvoting)
3. Constituency	Whole states	Congressional districts of roughly 550,000
4. Role in treaty ratification	Sole power	No power
5. Confirmation of executive appointments	Sole power	No power
6. Initiation of tax legislation	May amend freely any tax bill coming from House	Constitutional power to initiate tax measures (no longer important)
7. Distribution of power	Very broad, with senators having considerable personal power; highly individualistic	Power concentrated in the hands of the institutional leaders and committee chairs; little for junior members
8. Nature of legislative process	Informal, slow-moving, extended debate, few rules	Numerous and more rigorous rules, more restrictions on debate; fast-moving
9. Nature of leadership	Difficult to lead due to great power enjoyed by individuals	Easier to lead due to formal powers held by speaker
10. Distribution of committee assignments	Senators average 10 committee assignments; all have seats on key committees	House members average 6 committee assignments but smaller percentage on key committees
11. Policy expertise	More difficult to achieve with senators needing to cover several areas	With fewer committee assignments, mastery of single area is easier
12. Role of staff	Considerable delegation of functions to staff	More limited, but considerable delegation to staff
13. Political advantage of incumbency	Average reelection rate of incumbents 74.9%	Average reelection rate of incumbents 90.9%

who introduced it. Other bills carry the names of numerous **cosponsors,** who want to be associated with the bill. Popular bills, such as the bill to provide famine relief for Africa, pick up scores of cosponsors—the more cosponsors, the more potential votes for the bill. Although cosponsors are not obliged to vote for the bill in the final form, which may differ substantially from the original bill, lots of cosponsors help launch a bill and get it serious consideration.

Members solicit cosponsorships with "dear colleague" letters that inform all of their colleagues of their intention to introduce a bill. The offices of senators and House members are flooded every day with dear colleague letters for everything from a resolution calling for a day of recognition for Father Junipero Serra, founder of the California missions, to a resolution designating the month of May as "National Tap Dance Appreciation Month." (A copy of this Dear Colleague letter can be seen below.)

Though it takes little legislative skill or political courage to bestow an honor on a priest who died in 1784 or to praise tap dancing, it is just this kind of activity that gives members visibility at home and cements the bond between them and the voters in their districts and states. Many of these resolutions are introduced by House members and senators as a courtesy to

EDWARD P. BOLAND
SECOND DISTRICT, MASSACHUSETTS

COMMITTEE
APPROPRIATIONS

Congress of the United States
House of Representatives
Washington, D.C.

January 31, 1984

Dear Colleague,

On November 17, 1983, I introduced H. J. Res. 433, a bill which would designate the month of May, 1984 as "National Tap Dance Appreciation Month." I would like to invite you to join me as a cosponsor.

Tap dancing is a uniquely American art form. The development of tap dancing embodies the spirit of this nation. It blends elements of all forms of dance and a wide range of cultures, tradition and imagination, into an expression of personal style and freedom. Tap dancing is a celebration of individuality.

In recognition of the valuable contribution tap dancing has made to American art and entertainment, I urge you to join me in this tribute to a vital and creative cultural achievement.

Please join me and the growing list of cosponsors in support of H. J. Res. 433. Hope Wernick will be pleased to provide additional information and enlist your support for this resolution at extension 55601. Thank you.

Sincerely,

Edward P. Boland

EDWARD P. BOLAND
Member of Congress

EPB:sw

a constituent and are not taken too seriously. On more important or controversial bills, cosponsorship is undertaken only after the political consequences have been explored fully.

Once introduced, the bill is given a number with an "H" prefix letter if introduced in the House, or an "S" if introduced in the Senate. It, then, is sent off to be printed.

Public and Private Bills There are two general classes of bills: private and public. Public bills deal with general legislative matters. Private bills, now about one-tenth of the total of bills passed by Congress, are for the benefit of individuals. One example is a bill that was introduced in the House to waive for tennis star Martina Navratilova the five-year residency required of aliens who wish to apply for citizenship. About the same time, on the other side of Capitol Hill, Alabama's two senators were introducing a private bill to pay almost $100,000 to the family of Harry Eugene Walker of Anniston, Alabama, who was eaten by a grizzly bear in Yellowstone National Park in 1972. His heirs reasoned that since Walker was attacked on federal property, the federal government was in some way responsible for his death.

Administration bills that are part of the president's legislative program are introduced "by request." The actual introduction of an administration bill is usually by the chairman of the committee or subcommittee that would have jurisdiction over the measure.

Consideration by Committee

Deciding which of the many committees in either house a bill shall be sent to is a fairly routine job, performed in the Senate by the **parliamentarian,** who is an employee rather than a member. In the House, the speaker refers bills to committees. Once in committee, usually a standing committee, the bill is referred to an appropriate subcommittee, which is responsible for scheduling and holding hearings on the bill. With complex bills, usually administration bills that have many components, several subcommittees may be involved in holding hearings. Increasingly, bills are referred jointly to two or more committees at the same time or sequentially to one and then another. The subject matter of bills has become so complicated that rarely does a major bill fit today within the jurisdiction of a single committee. Not surprisingly, the more committees and subcommittees involved, the longer it takes for the bill to make it through the committee process and the more chances for it to be killed or greatly modified.

The Hearing The hearing is used to acquaint members with the bill and to allow citizens or representatives of interest groups to testify for or against it. The mark of how seriously a bill is being taken is whether the representatives of the executive branch testify on the bill.

After the hearings the bill is altered and amended and often substantially rewritten in a process known as a **markup.** Markup sessions in subcommittee usually attract large numbers of lobbyists who sit in and try to influence the changes through contacts with members or their staffs. After subcommittee markups, the bill is passed on to the full committee, where additional markups take place. The full committee then votes either to report out the bill to the full Senate or House or to kill the bill by not reporting it out.

Reporting Out The bill, as it is reported out, has a committee report attached to it. This explains the bill to all the members who have not had the chance to study it as closely as the committee members and gives the reasons for the amendments that were added in markup. Minority reports are usually attached as well. These explain the negative votes of the committee's minority and are, in effect, an appeal to the full house to reject the committee's endorsement of the bill. When acts of Congress come up for constitutional challenge before the courts, as is sometimes the case, the committee reports are used to determine exactly what Congress had in mind when it passed a bill. The courts call this "legislative intent."

Failure to report out a bill usually means that it is dead. Such is the fate of most bills. If the sponsors are determined to see the bill enacted, they may reintroduce it at the next session of Congress, but they may also attempt to rescue it from the committee by the use of a **discharge petition.** The full House and Senate are usually reluctant to reject the decision of the committee by demanding that it be reported out. This is because of the assumption that the committee knows more about the bill than those who have not studied it so thoroughly. Most recent efforts at discharge have involved controversial bills on subjects such as school prayer and busing, but this technique is not often used. It is difficult to get the 218 votes needed in the House—an absolute majority—to get an unreported bill to the floor. In the Senate, a single member can move to discharge a bill; but here again, it is a rarely used device.

Scheduling: Calendars and Rules

As we have said, scheduling is the responsibility of the leaders of the majority. In both chambers, all bills reported out of committee are assigned to **calendars** or categories, depending on the nature of the bill. Many bills are put on the calendar, but few are actually called up. In the Senate, the decision to call up a bill rests with the leadership—principally the majority leadership.

In the House, the larger and more unwieldy body, bills face an additional obstacle after clearing the committee but before calendaring can take place. In the House, but not in the Senate, each bill must receive a rule from the House Rules Committee. A rule stipulates (1) the amount of time a bill can be debated on the floor and (2) whether amendments to the bill can be made on the floor of the House by members not on the committee that reported out the bill. Highly restrictive rules that severely limit an amendment on a bill are known as **closed rules.** More liberal debate and amendment limitations are **open rules.** Purely routine matters in the House are not required to receive rules to be considered by the full membership.

The house leadership uses the Rules Committee to try to control which bills reach the floor for a vote. The Senate's method for getting quick floor action on a bill is by a **unanimous consent agreement,** which, as the name implies, requires the assent of all senators. Bills taken up under unanimous consent agreements are usually noncontroversial.

Members of the Democratic leadership debate a bill on the House floor. *(Dennis Brack/Black Star)*

Floor Action

Except in the case of taxing and spending bills, there is no requirement that either house be the first to vote a bill up or down; the House gets the first crack at revenue or spending bills. Procedures do vary between the House and Senate in regard to floor action. Senators address the floor at length from their seats; House members walk up to the podium for their few minutes of debate set by the rules. Since all debates are recorded at the time by stenographers on the floor, a member need not even be present for the debate but may read it the following morning when a copy of the *Congressional Record* is placed on his or her desk by a young employee known as a "page."

Amendments from the floor are made more readily in the Senate than in the House, where a rule attached to a bill may stipulate no floor amendments. A unanimous consent agreement in the Senate can function like a rule does in the House by specifying the ground rules of debate.

In the House, floor debate is rigidly scheduled by the Rules Committee. This is not so in the Senate, where there is unlimited debate. The extreme form of this unlimited Senate debate is the **filibuster,** whereby a senator or group of senators attempts to block the other business of the Senate by monopolizing the floor with lengthy speeches. When there is other business that must be voted on and when the end of a session or a recess is near, this can be effective in killing a bill. Rather than risk an adjournment without dealing with other pressing matters, the sponsors of a bill that is being talked to death by filibuster may feel pressure to withdraw it rather than see the Senate brought to a halt. Even the threat of a filibuster can block a bill coming to the floor for a vote. If supporters of a Senate bill that is being filibustered are determined to stop discussion and have their bill come to a vote, they must get the signatures of one-sixth of the membership on a **cloture petition.** If the petition is supported by three-fifths of the members (now sixty senators), a one-hour time limit is imposed on the discussion by each senator speaking on the bill.

Senator Strom Thurmond, famous for leading the anti-Civil Rights filibuster in 1957. *(AP)*

Floor debate in both houses, but particularly in the Senate, is notable for its extreme, almost excessive, politeness. Typically, one member will address another as, "My distinguished colleague and good friend." Though in fact there may be no love lost between the two, in a body as fiercely competitive as Congress, with political futures riding on the outcome of a vote, such gestures help to maintain decorum. Tempers do flare, and some members say things in the heat of passion that they may come to regret. Hence, members are allowed to edit their remarks before they are printed in the *Record.*

Voting

In Congress most important bills or amendments are subject to a **recorded vote.** The member must vote "yea" or "nay," which is recorded next to his or her name. It is not always in the political interest of a member to be recorded on a vote. On highly controversial measures in which there is a nearly even split in opinion among constituents or a vote is likely to be

POLITICAL PERSPECTIVE

STATEMENTS FOR THE *RECORD*

You may be surprised to learn that everything printed in the *Record* was not necessarily spoken on the floor. "Statements for the *Record*" or "extension of remarks" are printed under a member's name, even though they are usually not publicly uttered in the chamber. Concerned lest they be thought deceitful, members of Congress voted to place a black dot or "bullet" in front of any statement not actually delivered on the floor. Several years later, the House voted to print unspoken messages of members in boldface type, thus making the unspoken statements more conspicuous in the *Record* than those actually delivered. The Senate retained the bullet. These statements for the *Record* require no formal vote but are used to expand on a point or to flatter constituents by putting their names and accomplishments in the *Congressional Record.*

unpopular with the voters, a vote so recorded may take a lot of explaining. Yet these are the very bills and amendments on which record votes take place or can be demanded by one-fifth of the members.

The fact that a member votes "yea" on a roll call may not tell us everything about how he or she actually stands on the matter. For example, a member may well have supported previous procedural motions to **recommit** or send the bill back to committee in order to avoid having to vote on it at all. He or she may vote for amendments to be added to the bills that are so unpopular that they doom the basic measure. But even if those efforts fail and the member must take sides publicly on the bill and vote for it knowing that the vote may alienate some constituents, he or she can always point to those procedural votes and "killer" amendments and convince constituents who opposed the bill that it was the best the member could do.

The Conference Committee

If both houses pass the same bill, one would expect the successful measure to go right to the president for approval. In practice, however, the House and Senate versions of the same bill often turn out to be different from each other. On simple or routine bills, one house may simply accept the version sent to it by the other house. It may even attach a minor amendment and send the bill back to the originating house and have it accepted. On major, complicated, or controversial bills, legislative volleying can go on forever. When one house does not simply accept the bill of the other house or add amendments readily acceptable to the originating house, a **conference committee** is convened to come up with a bill that is acceptable in all particulars to both houses. We saw one example of how this works at the beginning of the chapter.

The device of the conference committee was inherited from the British Parliament as a means of resolving House-Senate differences on legislation after the first Congress met in April 1789. Currently, about 25 percent of all laws enacted by Congress are products of conferences. Lewis Froman estimated that in the mid-1960s only about one-tenth of enactments were

POLITICAL PERSPECTIVE

A LETTER WRITER'S GUIDE TO CONGRESS

Lawmakers often learn about the views of the voting public through letters, rather than face-to-face discussions. Writing effective letters to your senators and representative is not a difficult task. Here are a few guidelines that will make writing to your lawmakers even easier:

1. Write on your personal or business stationery, if possible. And sign your name over the typed signature at the end of your message.
2. Be sure that your return address is on your letter, not just on the envelope. Envelopes sometimes get misplaced before the letter is answered.
3. Identify the subject of your letter clearly. Give the name of the legislation you are writing about. Use the appropriate House or Senate bill number, if possible.
4. State your reason for writing. Your own personal experience is your best supporting evidence. Explain how the legislation would affect you or your family, business, or profession—or what effect it would have on your state or community.
5. Avoid trite phrases and sentences. Cliches make your letter appear to be part of an organized "pressure" campaign—and, thus, minimize the impact of your message.
6. Be reasonable. Don't ask for the impossible. Don't threaten. Don't say "I'll never vote for you unless you do. . . . " That will not help your cause; it may harm it.
7. Be constructive. If a bill deals with a problem that you admit exists, but you believe that the bill takes the wrong approach toward solving that problem, explain what you believe the right approach is.
8. Don't pretend to wield vast political influence. Write your member as an individual, not as a self-appointed spokesperson for your neighborhood, community, or industry. Unsupported claims of political influence only cast doubt upon the views you express.
9. Don't become a constant "pen pal." Quality, rather than quantity, is what counts. Don't try to instruct your members on every issue that comes up. And don't nag them if their votes do not reflect your thinking every time. Remember, each member has to consider all of his or her constituents and all of their points of view.
10. Concentrate on your own delegation. Your district's representative and your state's senators cast your votes in Congress and want to know your views. Don't undertake writing to all 435 representatives and all 100 senators, who cast their votes in the interests of other districts and other states.
11. Ask your legislators to explain their position on the issue in reply. As a constituent, you're entitled to know how and why your members feel as they do.
12. Consider timing. Try to communicate on a bill while it still is in committee. Your senators and representative usually will be more responsive to your views at that time—rather than later on, when the bill has already been shaped by committee.
13. Thank your members if they please you with a vote. Everybody appreciates a complimentary letter—and remembers it. On the other hand, if they displease you, don't hesitate to communicate your displeasure—that too, will be remembered.

Suggested Addresses and Salutations

The Honorable John Doe
House of Representatives
Washington, D.C. 20515

Dear Mr. Doe:

The Honorable John Doe
United States Senate
Washington, D.C. 20510

Dear Senator Doe:

the products of conferences. The increase suggests that institutional differences between the House and Senate are greater now than they were twenty years ago. Certainly, in the case of the annual debates on federal funding of abortions that took place through much of the 1970s, there were distinct differences between House and Senate positions, as there were on the Simpson-Mazzoli Immigration Bill in the 98th Congress. The controversy between the two houses over specific provisions of the immigration bill was heightened because President Reagan supported the Senate version and threatened a veto if the conferees accepted the House version. The shadow of the presidential veto is in the background of many conference committees.

Technically, the conference committee is a joint committee but is obviously not a standing one, since it is formed only to deal with a particular bill on which there is a difference of opinion between the two houses. The committee is composed of senators and House members, although not necessarily in equal numbers. A majority of each delegation is from the party that is in the majority in its chamber.

The final product of a Conference Committee is called the "conference report." When the conferees agree on the report, it goes back in identical form to both houses for final passage. If both accept it, it goes to the White House for presidential action. If either house rejects the conference report or adds amendments, it must go back to conference until there is agreement by both full House and Senate or until one house backs off. In recent years, most conference battles have been won by the Senate. According to one interpretation, this is because Senate conferees usually have broader backing from their own chamber than do House conferees, who tend to represent narrower committee positions.[10]

The Appropriation and Budget Process

On bills requiring the appropriation of money, there are two complete legislative cycles of the manner just described. The first cycle is the authorization process, consisting of committee hearings, markups, and floor votes. The authorization process establishes a program, the approximate amount of money required to carry out the program, what the program should achieve, and what its general direction should be. Once the authorization process is completed, the appropriations cycle, in which a specific amount of money is set aside to carry out the program, starts. An important difference between the two processes is that appropriations take place every year, while authorizations are often open-ended or for a period of several years.

The Budget Act Before 1975, when the *Congressional Budget and Impoundment Control Act* took effect, the appropriation of money by Congress was guided by no overall plan or strategy. The Budget Act was an attempt to centralize the budget process and to limit its fragmentation in Congress by creating budget committees in both the House and Senate to set ceilings for overall expenditures. In theory, all appropriations have to conform to the overall spending limits, and expenditures have to be in line with what the federal government can reasonably expect in the way of revenues.

Some years, however, the end of the fiscal year arrives and Congress has not passed appropriations for certain agencies. In 1981 and 1984 this resulted in a partial shutdown of the federal government. More typically, Congress averts this embarrassing spectacle by passing *continuing resolutions,* which enable the agencies to continue to operate at the previous year's level of funding. If agencies run out of money, they can request from Congress a *supplemental appropriation.* Agencies can also ask for "a supplemental" if they encounter unforeseen expenses.

HOW POWERFUL IS THE POWER OF THE PURSE It is simply easier for Congress to spend money and make friends than it is to cut spending and make enemies. Presidents talk economy too; but they also can develop lavish spending habits, such as the military buildup spree of President Reagan. Congress's aversion to cutting spending and presidential extravagance created huge budget deficits in the 1980s. In response to mounting deficits, Congress passed the **Gramm-Rudman Act** in 1985, which forced spending restraint in a very radical way. It declared that if the president does not propose, and the Congress does not enact, cuts in the budget sufficient to eliminate the deficit, the Comptroller General (head of Congress's General Accounting Office) will withhold funds already appropriated. This law met an immediate Supreme Court test because of its delegation of the power of the purse to an unelected official who is removable by a simple resolution of Congress and the enforcement provision was ruled unconstitutional.

Congressional Oversight

Having passed a law, established a new program, or appropriated money for a program already in existence, does Congress then sit back and let the executive branch "take care that the laws be faithfully executed," as it says in Article II of the Constitution?

The answer is no—Congress cares very much how the programs it establishes are working, and individual members want to shape the manner in which policies are carried out by the executive branch bureaucracies. If a senator, for example, works hard to get colleagues' votes to retain a program the White House wants to kill and then fights to get on the conference committee in order to prevent the House from deleting it, you can bet that that senator will not trust someone in the executive branch to carry it out without congressional supervision. We call the process by which Congress checks up on the bureaucrats **oversight.**

Congressional oversight of the executive branch usually has two objectives. First, it attempts to ensure that the original intentions of Congress are being followed by the agencies it has created and that the programs it has authorized are functioning properly. It can also be a device that members of Congress use to intervene in the administration of government on behalf of constituents or special interests.

Ideally, the committees of Congress ought to be overseeing continually the executive branch agencies over which they have legislative or appropriations jurisdiction, but oversight rarely has political payoff for members. Most members would prefer to be back in the district and visible to the voters than to sit in a stuffy hearing room grilling bureaucrats. Voters give

MY CONSTITUENTS HAVE EVERY REASON TO BE OUTRAGED OVER CONGRESS' SHAMEFUL BUDGET RESOLUTION...
...AND IF I WERE THEM, I'D KEEP SENDING ME BACK TO WASHINGTON UNTIL I GOT IT RIGHT!
©1985 THE ORANGE COUNTY REGISTER
MShelton

One of the reasons for Congress's lack of success in producing a unified budget plan can be traced to the zeal with which members defend special interests and blame the institution when processes break down. *(Illustration by Mike Shelton; reprinted with special permission of King Features Syndicate, Inc.)*

members very little credit for having dissected the State Department budget or exposed shoddy practices at the Small Business Administration. Nor is it obvious how much oversight hearings contribute to improved government operations. As Rep. Patricia Schroeder of Colorado has noted:

> When we have oversight hearings, we hear that everything is terrific. When you listen to the witnesses, it is like you have died and gone to heaven. We go back feeling very happy. But you find you left the transom open and it is like there has been a snowstorm overnight. You hear, "They did not talk about this; you did not ask the question right; that is why they were able to duck that;" and so forth and so on. It becomes a nightmare.[11]

As our previous discussion of the EPA toxic waste scandal suggested, there can be too much oversight when the chairs of committees with overlapping jurisdictions battle for the attention of the media. There can also be too little when the problem is less newsworthy or the bad practices too closely identified with interests that members want to cultivate.

From the point of view of gaining ready access to the media—important to members for reelection—the normal run of oversight hearings is less profitable than calling for investigative hearings to look into reports of wrongdoing by government officials. Because outright wrongdoing is rare, normal oversight usually takes place well beyond the range of TV cameras.

Tools of Oversight

Congress does have four important constitutional tools for influencing the conduct and operation of the bureaucracy.

Budget Control Congressional control of executive branch budgets is by far the most important tool of oversight. Oversight through the power of

In a 1979 example of congressional oversight, Defense Secretary Harold Brown and members of the Joint Chiefs of Staff give testimony to Congress that prevented the passage of Carter's Salt II arms limitation treaty with the Soviet Union. *(Consolidated News Pictures)*

the purse can be brought to bear when the agency requests an authorization during the appropriations process, and even after the agency has received its operating funds for the year. Congress has, in its investigation arm, the General Accounting Office (GAO), an organization that can examine the books of any agency of the executive branch.

Confirmation Powers In its constitutional power to confirm the president's nominees for the leadership of executive branch agencies, the Senate can influence the conduct of the agency.

Investigative Hearings Although not specifically mentioned in the Constitution, the investigative role of Congress is inherited from the British House of Commons, which functioned as "the grand inquest of the nation." The theory behind congressional investigations is that they enable Congress to gather facts to assist members in the lawmaking process. Since 1972, there have been more than 600 congressional investigations, many of which have had as their focus the operation of the executive branch. Among the most famous were the Senate Watergate Committee, which examined abuses by the Nixon White House, and the Senate and House Committee that looked into the assassination of President John F. Kennedy.

The Legislative Veto Given what we know about the doctrine of separation of powers, the term "legislative veto" strikes us as a very strange one indeed. The legislative veto enabled Congress to delegate authority to an agency of the executive branch or to a regulatory agency and say, in effect: "We'll see how you exercise the authority we've given you. If we don't like what you're doing, we'll tell you to stop. If you don't hear from us, you can proceed." The legislative veto is not a general power given to Congress by the Constitution, as is the presidential veto, but one that Congress wrote into specific bills when it delegated authority.

One form of the legislative veto enabled a single house of Congress to halt an agency action. Another form required action by both houses. Some even permitted committees of Congress to exercise the veto. Most of the 200 laws written since 1932 that contained the legislative veto had to do with matters of federal regulation, but some very important laws, such as the 1974 Budget Act and the War Powers Act, contained veto provisions. One provision of the **War Powers Act,** by which Congress hoped to regain some control over the use of military forces, said that U.S. troops sent into combat without authorization by Congress could be withdrawn by a resolution of both houses of Congress, without a presidential signature.

On June 23, 1983, the Supreme Court dealt a major blow to the congressional veto when it handed down its decision in the case of *Immigration and Naturalization Service* v. *Chadha.* The court ruled the legislative veto unconstitutional because it violated the doctrine of separation of powers. The justices felt that the Constitution entitled only the president to have a veto. Following the *Chadha* case, the experts speculated that Congress had received a serious setback in its efforts to hold the executive branch accountable. They feared that the only way Congress could ensure that the bureaucrats were hewing to its wishes was to write laws so detailed and specific that agency people had no discretion. The experts also doubted whether Congress even had enough technical knowledge to write such precise laws.

With the passage of time, however, expert opinion seems to be that Congress has not suffered a mortal blow. Congress can still control agencies through the appropriations process or by modifying an agency's authorization or the areas over which it has jurisdiction. It can even exert control over the agencies with **joint resolutions** of both houses of Congress that require a presidential signature, but it would be unusual for a president to sign a bill that limited the authority of agencies in the executive branch.

Congress and the President

Given the fragmentation of Congress produced by the strong pulls on members and senators to their districts and states, and by the institutional fragmentation of the committee structure and the decline in influence of party leaders, someone has to keep them in touch with the larger picture. Under our system of government, that job falls to the president. Congress is not always happy with this situation.

Some conflict between presidents and Congress is based on the issues at hand or the personalities involved, but even when the issues are the most compelling and the personalities most compatible, certain institutional conflicts come into play. Nelson Polsby has pointed to three of them. The first is that presidents are in a hurry. They have, at most, eight years to accomplish their objectives. There are no term limitations on members of Congress, and, given the success that incumbents have in gaining reelection, they tend to be around for a long time. Their approach to issues is more casual and less urgent than the president's. Second, the president is both a unifying and a partisan figure. The president can rarely disregard the members of the other party in Congress and may have to woo members of the other party who are more crucial to the attainment of goals than fellow partisans. Finally, the president wants early commitments to his or her programs, whereas members of Congress like to keep their options open—especially when it comes to assessing the effects that presidential plans will have on the interests and constituencies that are vital to the members.[12] In this clash of unifying and fragmenting forces lie the tensions between the president and Congress.

SUMMARY

Though the membership of the two houses of Congress is hardly a representative sample of the American people, Congress does a good job of representing the American people and looking after the interests of the states and congressional districts. What is less clear is that Congress is quite so effective in legislating in the national interest.

Members of Congress receive pay well above the national average and enjoy benefits and perquisites, including large staffs to assist them. The increase in congressional staff reflects the increased scope of government activity, yet staff may also generate activity of their own in order to make their bosses look good to the voters.

Paramount in the decisions a member of Congress has to make is the choice of committee assignments. It is in these committees that the real business of Congress is accomplished. It is also where members develop the expertise needed to deal with complex legislation, but the role of the committee in giving members access to political resources for reelection should also be stressed.

The multitude of committees, in which most important decisions are made, keep power fragmented and prevent the possibility of policies being cohesively formulated. Furthermore, House members often concentrate more on the complicated legislative procedure itself than on substantive issues, which obstructs attempts to achieve a more centralized legislative process.

There are four types of congressional committees. The powerful standing committee is permanent. The select or special committee is established temporarily to investigate a particular problem. Joint committees are composed of members from both houses. Subcommittees are subgroups of any of the other committees.

Chairs usually go to members of the majority party who have served longest on a party committee. Appointments for membership are made by two special committees established by the parties in both houses of Congress.

The speaker of the House has a lot of power, although it has declined since the heyday of strong party loyalty. The speaker's is the final word on scheduling, which he can manipulate effectively, since he is the head of a large intelligence and persuasion network. The Senate majority leader controls the legislative schedule and acts as his party's chief strategist and spokesperson. Minority leaders in both houses function in much the same way as their majority party counterparts.

After a bill has been referred to a committee, it is sent to an appropriate subcommittee for hearings. Amendments to bills are then made in markup sessions. The bill is returned to the full committee, which may or may not report it out to the full House or Senate. Before a bill is debated on the floor, it must be calendared. During this process, the House Rules Committee determines the length of time a bill can be debated and any stipulations about floor amendments. There are no limitations placed on Senate debate, which often results in the delaying process called a **filibuster.**

When the two houses fail to agree on the final form of a bill, a conference committee composed of both senators and representatives is established to reach a compromise. If passage through Congress eventually takes place, the bill proceeds to the president for presidential action.

In addition to legislation, Congress is responsible for overseeing the executive branch to ensure that agencies and programs are operating as they were originally intended to. Four important tools Congress has for checking up on the bureaucracy are the power of the purse, the power to confirm presidential nominees, the power to hold congressional investigations, and the power of legislative veto, which was widely used by Congress but was held unconstitutional by the Supreme Court. Congress now may have to rely more on its traditional power of the purse, confirmation powers, and more tightly written laws.

The built-in conflicts between Congress and the presidency can be mitigated by some degree when they agree on issues or when personalities are compatible. But the president's need to see things in larger, national terms and Congress's attention to more parochial and specialized interests make conflicts likely between presidents who must accomplish their objectives in eight years at most and members of Congress who can serve for long periods.

NOTES

1. Gregg Easterbrook, "What's Wrong with Congress?" *The Atlantic Monthly,* 254 (Dec. 1984), p. 62.
2. Ted Siff and Alan Weil, *Ruling Congress* (New York: Penguin, 1977), p. 70.
3. Morris P. Fiorina, *Congress: Keystone of the Washington Establishment* (New Haven: Yale U.P., 1974), p. 64.
4. Richard F. Fenno, Jr., *Congressmen in Committees* (Boston: Little, Brown, 1973), p. 1.
5. Martin Tolchin, "Congressmen Must Also Campaign in Congress," *The New York Times* (Jan. 23, 1977).
6. Champ Clark, *My Quarter Century of American Politics,* vol. 1 (New York: Harper, 1920), p. 208.
7. Barbara Sinclair, "Majority Party Leadership Strategies for Coping with the New House," *Legislative Studies Quarterly,* 6 (June 1981), p. 403.
8. Joseph Cooper and David W. Brady, "Institutional Context and Leadership Style: The House from Cannon to Rayburn," *American Political Science Review,* 75 (June 1981), pp. 423–24.
9. Sinclair, p. 405.
10. David Vogler, *The Politics of Congress,* 2nd ed. (Boston: Allyn, 1977), p. 212.
11. U.S. Congress, House, Committee on Rules, *Congressional Oversight of Federal Programs,* 97th Cong., 1st and 2nd Sess., 1981–82, p. 109.
12. Nelson W. Polsby, *Congress and the Presidency,* 3rd ed. (Englewood Cliffs, N.J.: Prentice-Hall, 1976), pp. 180–83.

CHAPTER

10

The Presidency

We realize how imperfect our understanding of the presidency is when two presidents do virtually the same thing, but their acts are treated differently because the time, the circumstances, and the personalities are different. Sometimes the actions of presidents even involve violations of the Constitution.

Abraham Lincoln, the choice of most experts as our greatest president, violated the Constitution in 1861 when he suspended the writ of *habeas corpus* (a writ that prevents long detention without trial). That is a power that the Constitution gives only to Congress and even then in only very restricted circumstances. Franklin D. Roosevelt, another great president, probably violated the First and Fifth Amendments when he ordered Japanese-Americans into internment camps after the attack on Pearl Harbor in 1941. And Richard Nixon violated the Constitution when he approved the notorious "Huston Plan" that called for the FBI and the CIA to spy on American citizens who the president felt were a threat to national security.

How is it, then, that we name monuments after Lincoln and put Roosevelt's likeness on a coin but regard Nixon with dread and embarrassment? Lincoln faced an emergency situation that was without precedent in U.S. history—the open rebellion of a dozen states against the authority of the government. Roosevelt was responding to the first attack by a foreign power on American soil since the War of 1812. Nixon faced neither of these challenges; his violations of the Constitution were part of a pattern of illegality and abuse of power that came to define his term in office.

Is the institution of the presidency, then, totally shaped by the personality of the individual who happens to occupy the Oval Office and the circumstances that happen to come up? We recognize how important the character of the president is and how important events can be, but the powers of the presidency itself are also considerable.

Obviously, there is an interplay between the institution, the times,

Ceremonial duties enable the president to accomplish important political objectives. In this scene, President John F. Kennedy is shown dedicating a postage stamp to Eleanor Roosevelt. Standing to Kennedy's left is Adlai E. Stevenson, whom Mrs. Roosevelt favored over Kennedy for the Democratic nomination in 1960. The purpose of this ceremony was not only to honor the memory of a great American but also to foster unity within the Democratic party. *(UPI/Bettmann Newsphotos)*

and the person who is president. Some presidents manage to dominate the institution, and a temporary situation then exists in which people think of the presidency as an "imperial office." But there are other times—probably more numerous—when a president does not seem able to achieve objectives and we wonder if the office should have been given more power. That topic—the cycle of the imperial presidency and the imperiled presidency—will be reserved for the final section in this chapter.

Our first order of business will be to ask, "What makes the president so powerful? We will answer it by discussing the president's many roles: chief executive; policy expert; the person who appoints and removes high administration figures; the head of a particular political party; and the person who sets out foreign policy and acts as commander-in-chief of the armed forces. Some of these roles are dictated by the Constitution; others have evolved.

The next major section will deal with the special relationship between the president and Congress and the various weapons in the presidential arsenal to persuade Congress to see things the president's way. Effective use of media is crucial.

The third major topic will be on those who assist the president: the cabinet, the White House staff, and the vice-president. The discussion of the vice-presidency will set the stage for consideration of **presidential succession**—when a president dies, becomes too ill to serve, or is removed by impeachment or resignation.

The final section raises the question, "How much presidential power is enough?" Clearly, we do not want the presidency to dominate and overshadow all the other institutions of our government

Paul Szep, 1967. Reprinted courtesy of *The Boston Globe.*

Concern over an "imperial presidency" is not a new thing. Among others, Andrew Jackson was given the "royal treatment" in the nineteenth century and Lyndon B. Johnson in the twentieth.

and to become an instrument of oppression. But we also want to avoid the more likely risk of having the one office responsible to all the people, and charged with looking out for the common good, lacking sufficient power. In that event the forces of fragmentation built into the Constitution can get dangerously out of control. The result can be drift and deadlock in government and an inability to meet the challenges of the modern world.

What Makes the President So Powerful?

The writings of the seventeenth-century British philosopher, John Locke, had a considerable impact on the framers of the Constitution. Locke looked on executives as the guardians of the public good. He put the case for the executive in his *Second Treatise on Government,* thus:

> . . . Legislators not being able to foresee and provide by laws for all that may be useful to a community, the executor of the laws, having the power in his hands, has by common law of Nature a right to make use of it for the good of society.

The President as Head of State

We have in the president an individual elected by a majority of the people, but a representative of all the people and very much the personification of the state. The idea of a symbolic head of state who performed ceremonial functions with leadership of the government vested in someone else was not an idea that had much appeal to the framers.

As a result of this decision, the United States stands virtually alone among the major powers of the world in joining in one office the symbolic role of head of state and the political role of head of government. No one, not even the vice-president, who is also elected by the people, is held to represent adequately the nation as fully as does the president. This was brought home quite forcefully in May 1980 when Vice-President Mondale was dispatched to represent this country at the funeral of Yugoslavia's leader, Marshal Tito. The Yugoslavs were deeply offended. For them, only the president could have fulfilled the role of this country's first mourner.

The president's ceremonial functions are many, but whether or not he regards these tasks as burdensome really depends on what kind of person the president is. The performance of ceremonial duties can help a president to build coalitions and enhance his or her prestige and reputation. The president can use these ceremonies to confer honors on representatives or constituencies that he would like to cultivate or to pay off those who have helped win the White House, and "with the added prestige that goes with ceremonial leadership the President can be more effective when he defends the national interest against selfish and parochial concerns."[1]

The President as Chief Executive

The president of the United States as chief executive presides over a bureaucratic empire consisting of 1,900 federal agencies employing more than 2 million people. Although most of these elements consist of the thirteen cabinet-level departments, there are also independent agencies, regulatory commissions, and boards of various kinds. So that the president may, in the words of the Constitution, "take care that the laws be faithfully executed," he is theoretically responsible for the conduct of each and every one of these people as they carry out the laws passed by Congress. Again, in theory, the president as their boss can pick up the telephone and order any one of these 2 million people to do his or her job in the manner the president desires. The practice, however, is far less certain and predictable than the theory.

We must bear in mind that the programs for which the employees of the executive branch are responsible are primarily the result of acts of Congress. It may be that Congress has enacted these programs on the basis of recommendations from the president, but the laws that are being faithfully executed have been authorized by Congress and paid for by congressional appropriation. This simple fact means that the members of the executive branch are not responsible exclusively to the president. The congressional power of the purse, power to confirm the president's nominees for leadership of executive agencies, and the oversight by the House and Senate automatically create divided loyalties for those in the executive branch.

POLITICAL PERSPECTIVE

PARADOX OF PRESIDENTIAL POWER

Lawrence F. O'Brien, a high-ranking aide to President John F. Kennedy, tells two stories that underscore both the power and limitations of the presidency:

In the first, the president found himself on the threshold of a showdown with Rep. Carl Vinson of Georgia, powerful Chairman of the House Armed Services Committee over money for a bomber that Vinson wanted the Air Force to order. Most of the components of the bomber were built in Vinson's own state of Georgia. Kennedy, on the advice of his Secretary of Defense, Robert S. McNamara, opposed ordering the plane, but realized that flat opposition to Vinson's favorite plane might jeopardize the entire Kennedy defense program because of Vinson's important role in the House.

A compromise was proposed by the White House whereby a limited but still considerable amount of money would be spent for further testing and development of the plane but nowhere near the amount Vinson wanted. Vinson then proceeded to add an amendment to a Defense Department appropriations bill "directing" the Secretary of the Air Force to spend the money. To oppose the measure was to alienate Vinson and jeopardize defense policy.

Kennedy sent a number of high-ranking Defense Department officials to plead with Vinson, including the Secretary of Defense himself. Finally, Kennedy invited Vinson to the Oval Office at the White House and the two took a walk in the Rose Garden where Kennedy made his appeal directly. Vinson not only dropped the amendment after the conversation, but also boasted, "I feel good about this . . . because I really want to help the President." Presidential persuasion and the magical surroundings of the White House had won the day.

Kennedy was not so lucky with Rep. D. B. Saund of California who wanted to prevent the Veteran's Administration from closing a V.A. hospital in his district, despite the fact that the facility had been condemned as unsafe. When the V.A. refused to reconsider its decision and was backed up by the White House, Saund retaliated by introducing an amendment to a bill denying the President long-term borrowing authority. Kennedy dug in his heels and refused to reconsider the hospital question, and Saund's amendment passed the House. Kennedy's retaliation against Saund was rather pathetic: when Saund sent in a photograph of his grandson with Kennedy for the President to autograph, a White House staffer managed to "lose" it behind a sofa—a feeble gesture of revenge from the world's most powerful individual against a not-very-powerful member of Congress.

There are some ironies to these two stories. Both Vinson and Saund were Democrats—members of Kennedy's own party. Vinson was powerful, yet gave in; Saund was a rank-and-file member, yet thwarted the president. In the case the president won, he was up against a House member in an area in which Congress is in a commanding position—authority to spend money. In the case the president lost, he was on turf in which presidents usually have the upper hand—discretion given him by Congress to close down a military facility if he sees fit. He is, after all, the commander-in-chief of the armed forces. Yet he won where he probably should have lost and lost where, by all rights, he should have won. Such is the paradox of the presidency—a paradox that flows from the fragmented nature of power at the national level.

Source: Based on Lawrence F. O'Brien, *No Final Victories* (Garden City: Doubleday, 1974), pp. 117–20.

Part of the reason that Congress is often so effective in denying to a president his objectives is that Congress is an institution that is open to external influences. Constituents, interest groups, and even the president's own executive branch bureaucracy find Congress the ideal place to stake their claims or defend what benefits they already enjoy. It is the very fragmentation of Congress into committees, subcommittees, and caucuses that gives outsiders so many points of access. Access to Congress can even be achieved through influential individual members. The presidency is not so easy to penetrate, especially with matters that are narrow or parochial.

The President as Expert The question of how much policy expertise the president must have in leadership of the executive branch is an intriguing one. There is little evidence to suggest that all the American people want of a president is that he be steeped in the details of policy. However, a 1983 CBS News/*New York Times* poll indicated that about 10 percent of the people surveyed said they would like the president to have some knowledge of foreign affairs.[2] The record of presidents who were preoccupied with the details and intricacies of policies has not been a good one. Detail-oriented presidents like Herbert Hoover and Jimmy Carter were not conspicuously successful; yet intensely political presidents like Lyndon Johnson also ran into serious problems.

Jimmy Carter immersed himself in the details of energy policy and was probably as knowledgeable about specifics as anyone in government, but he often lost sight of the large picture. He concerned himself with the day-to-day trivia of running the White House to the point where he was scheduling the use of the White House tennis court—hardly a productive use of time for a person with so many important concerns.

Ronald Reagan showed himself to be quite the opposite type of president. His strong point was the selling of policies to Congress and the public through his superb use of television, his one-on-one persuasion of House members and senators, and his willingness to make the compromises necessary to get proposals enacted into law.

Mastery of the art of politics does seem more crucial to the president's ability to control fragmentation than a mastery of the minutiae of policies, but the president cannot ignore the content of policy. A good balance between the extremes would seem to be a president familiar enough with the content of policy to make his goals clear and skilled enough in the art of politics to succeed in those goals.

Appointment and Removal One thing the president can do to increase the chances for success as the chief executive is to appoint people of quality to the major posts in the administration and to remove those who are either incompetent at the jobs or seriously at odds with presidential policies. The 2,700 presidential appointees who are not civil servants and can be fired at any time are the president's leadership team. They supervise and guide the 2 million civil servants, and it is their job to see that the bureaucrats carry out the laws. These 2,700 individuals run the gamut from cabinet secretaries to members of obscure boards and commissions.

The term "appointment," as we have learned, is technically imprecise as it applies to the president's power. It is the advice and consent of the Senate that converts a nominee into an appointee. Although the president may indeed make temporary or **recess appointments** while Congress is not in session, all noncareer choices except those on his White House staff must come before the Senate. As far as cabinet choices are concerned, the Senate is inclined to allow the president great discretion in choosing an "official family"—those thirteen individuals who head the major departments.

Presidents use appointments to pay off important segments of the constituencies that helped them in their election. In nominating a prolabor person to the labor board, Carter was reciprocating to organized labor, which aided him in his 1976 campaign; Reagan, who had the wholehearted

When President Reagan nominated Thomas Enders as a special envoy to Latin America, the Senate refused to make him an appointee. Enders supported military aid to the Contras in Nicaragua, which the Senate—at the time—did not. *(Liaison)*

POLITICAL PERSPECTIVE

PRESIDENTS WHO WERE GOVERNORS

Being governor of a state is one of the ways that executive experience is acquired. Fifteen of our forty presidents have served as governors. It is a very impressive list that contains the names of some of our greatest presidents: Jefferson, the two Roosevelts, and Woodrow Wilson. But there are also names like Andrew Johnson and Rutherford B. Hayes who were not notably successful.

Jefferson—Virginia
Monroe—Virginia
Van Buren—New York
Tyler—Virginia
Polk—Tennessee
A. Johnson—Tennessee
Hayes—Ohio
Cleveland—New York
McKinley—Ohio
T. Roosevelt—New York
Wilson—New Jersey
Coolidge—Massachusetts
F. D. Roosevelt—New York
Carter—Georgia
Reagan—California

support of conservatives, was acknowledging their help in his nominations to the federal courts.

Presidents rarely make appointments that antagonize important elements of their electoral constituencies or indeed any major interest group. President Carter who, in 1976, announced that, "I owe the special interests nothing," was singing a different tune in the summer of 1979 when his overall approval score according to one public opinion poll was at 26 percent. With the Democratic convention a year away, Carter took his chief advisers to Camp David and shuffled his cabinet. He accepted the resignations of cabinet members with minimal ties to major constituencies and replaced them with people who were clearly identified with groups whose support Carter wished to cultivate. This prompted one Democratic party official to comment that, "The president has put together about as solid a cabinet as I have ever seen in terms of touching the bases."[3]

The president can provide better centralized direction, coordination, and coherence of his policies when a cabinet is composed of people with no strong ties to the constituencies of their departments. Those with strong constituency support often turn out to be special pleaders for the interest they represent, and policy fragmentation tends to result.

Although those political appointees who serve strictly at the pleasure of the president—as opposed to members of regulatory commissions appointed for a term of years and federal judges who serve for life—can be legally fired at any time, such dismissals can create political problems for the president. Appointees from a previous administration—especially of a president from the other party—usually submit meekly to their fate, since the 2,700 so-called **"schedule C" jobs** are the only high-level patronage of the new president. But firing one of his own appointees, especially when a member of Congress is involved, can cause embarrassment (see box on page 343).

The removal power, where it applies, is shared with Congress through its power of impeachment. This is not a widely used power: only thirteen officials have been impeached by the House since 1789 and only four, all federal judges, were convicted and removed from office. The right of the president to fire an appointee was established in 1926 in the case of *Myers* v. *United States*[4] which held that the Tenure of Office Act, which had been passed by Congress to prevent President Andrew Johnson from dismissing officials, was unconstitutional. The act itself had been repealed by Congress in 1887, but the *Myers* case established the right of the president to remove noncivil-service officials of the executive branch. A limitation on the president's power of removal was established in the Supreme Court's decision in the case of *Humphrey's Executor* v. *U.S.*,[5] which denied presidents the power to fire members of independent regulatory commissions established by Congress.

Executive Orders, Executive Agreements, and Pardons Although it is true that the president has no lawmaking powers, he may issue proclamations that have the force of law. Some of these executive orders may be issued by the president pursuant to some statute enacted by Congress. Of the 1,769 such orders issued from 1945 to 1965, 83 percent were issued under specific statutory authority of Congress.[6] In other cases, Congress has acted to ratify, in effect, executive orders not issued pursuant to some statutory authority. The constitutional authority for the issuance of these orders, like so much having to do with the president, is hard to pin down. The U.S. Supreme Court and presidents themselves have favored a broad view of executive power that says, in effect, that there are certain powers that are inherent or implied in the role of executive. Presidents also point to two clauses in Article II that state that, "executive power shall be vested in a President of the United States of America," that the "President shall be

POLITICAL PERSPECTIVE

DORNAN IS "DUMPED" TO SAVE MX

Political calculations are at the forefront both of presidential appointments and removals. A good example of this was President Reagan's decision to appoint former Congressman Robert K. Dornan of California to a job with the Arms Control and Disarmament Agency in 1983. Dornan was a critic of arms control who favored a military build-up, but Mr. Reagan was under pressure from his conservative supporters to find a job for the ex-congressman. No sooner was the appointment made, however, than the Republican member who was leading the fight for the MX missile for Mr. Reagan in the House called to say that the appointment of a hardliner like Mr. Dornan would play into the hands of opponents of the MX. In the hope that the MX could be saved, Mr. Dornan was dumped. Dornan complained, "The White House threw me to the wolves." The White House Chief of Staff, James A. Baker III was more philosophical. He was reported to have said, "We had to do what we had to do. The MX was just too important."

Source: Based on Robert Tinberg, "An Angry Dornan Says White House Hired, Then Dropped Him to Save MX," *Baltimore Sun* (June 12, 1983).

POLITICAL PERSPECTIVE

REAGAN IMPOSES EMBARGO ON NICARAGUA BY EXECUTIVE ORDER

What form does an executive order take? This one issued by President Reagan imposed an embargo on the country of Nicaragua. You will note in the first paragraph that the president cites as authority for the embargo powers previously given to the president by Congress.

By the authority vested in me as President by the Constitution and laws of the United States of America, including the International Emergency Economic Powers Act (50 U.S.C. 1701 et seq.), the National Emergencies Act (50 U.S.C. 1601 et seq.), Chapter 12 of Title 50 of the United States Code (50 U.S.C. 191 et seq.), and Section 301 of Title 3 of the United States Code,

I, Ronald Reagan, President of the United States of America, find that the policies and actions of the Government of Nicaragua constitute an unusual and extraordinary threat to the national security and foreign policy of the United States and hereby declare a national emergency to deal with that threat.

I hereby prohibit all imports into the United States of goods and services of Nicaraguan origin; all exports from the United States of goods to or destined for Nicaragua, except those destined for the organized democratic resistance, and transactions relating thereto.

I hereby prohibit Nicaraguan air carriers from engaging in air transportation to or from points in the United States, and transactions relating thereto.

In addition, I hereby prohibit vessels of Nicaraguan registry from entering into United States ports, and transactions relating thereto.

The Secretary of the Treasury is delegated and authorized to employ all powers granted to me by the International Emergency Economic Powers Act to carry out the purposes of this order.

The prohibitions set forth in this order shall be effective as of 12:01 a.m., Eastern daylight time, May 7, 1985, and shall be transmitted to the Congress and published in the Federal Register.

Commander in Chief of the Army and Navy," and that, "he shall take Care that the Laws be faithfully executed."[7]

The Emancipation Proclamation of Abraham Lincoln was an executive order, as were Executive Order No. 9981 barring racial segregation in the armed forces issued by President Truman on July 26, 1948, and Executive Order 11063 of President Kennedy, which prohibited discrimination in federal housing. President Reagan in 1981 issued an order that subjected all federal regulations to review in terms of their cost effectiveness. In the first three cases, Congress passed subsequent laws either ratifying or expanding on what the president had proclaimed.

Since the power of presidents to make treaties is subject to the ratification of the Senate, they have resorted, in recent years, to **executive agreements** (agreements between heads of state having the force of law) when Senate ratification of a formal treaty was held unlikely. Many of the post-World War II agreements for American military bases to be established on foreign soil were without Senate ratification. Perhaps the most spectacular of all examples of the use of executive agreements was the one in which President Franklin Roosevelt traded fifty overage U.S. Navy destroyers to the beleaguered British in 1940 in exchange for U.S. base rights on British territories in the Western Hemisphere.

As the chief executive, the president can also be a kind of court of last resort. The president may issue pardons, reprieves, and amnesties in all federal criminal cases except those of officials impeached and convicted. Presidential pardons are not statements of innocence; they are merely statements of forgiveness for crimes that may or may not have been committed. Pardons can be broad, such as Andrew Johnson's pardon of most Confederate soldiers and Jimmy Carter's blanket pardon of Vietnam-era draft evaders.

The President as Chief Diplomat

In 1932, war broke out between the South American countries of Paraguay and Bolivia. Without domestic sources of weapons, the two warring powers began to look abroad for munitions. The closest potential major arms supplier was the United States. Fearing that weapons from this country would prolong the conflict, Congress, on May 28, 1934, delegated to the president the power to prohibit American arms companies from selling weapons to either side if, in his judgment, such an embargo would hasten the end of the conflict. Congress said that if the president exercised this power to ban arms sales, it would be illegal for any American company to sell them to either Paraguay or Bolivia. The day after Congress acted, the Curtiss-Wright Export Corporation, a subsidiary of an aircraft and arms company, sold fifteen machine guns to Bolivian agents in the United States. Prosecuted under this law, Curtiss-Wright brought suit on the grounds that this act of Congress was an improper delegation of congressional power to the executive.

Ultimately, the case reached the Supreme Court. Speaking for the majority of the Court in its finding against Curtiss-Wright, Mr. Justice Sutherland wrote:

> It is quite apparent that if, in the maintenance of our international relations, embarrassment—perhaps serious embarrassment—is to be avoided and success for our aims achieved, congressional legislation . . . within the international field must often accord to the president a degree of discretion and freedom from statutory restriction which would not be admissable were domestic affairs alone involved.[8]

In his role as chief diplomat, President Roosevelt reviews Mexican troops in 1943. *(OAS)*

What the Court was saying was that so far as congressional delegation of congressional lawmaking power to the president was concerned, foreign affairs was in a separate category from domestic policy—a category in which the president could be given more discretion to act.

Aaron Wildavsky has gone so far as to speak of "The Two Presidencies"—"One presidency is for domestic affairs, and the other is concerned with defense and foreign policy. Since World War II, presidents have had much greater success in controlling the nation's defense and foreign policies than in dominating its domestic policies."[9]

What's the Attraction of Foreign Affairs for Presidents? Several factors come together to push the president in the direction of foreign policy activity:

1. Constitutional provisions and court decisions that make it clear that in this area the president is preeminent.
2. Congressional recognition that the conduct of foreign policy is, by its very nature, an executive responsibility, especially in a nuclear age when quick decisions may be called for.
3. A tendency on the part of special interests to shy away from challenging the president in this area.
4. The fact that presidents simply relish their role as chief diplomat and given the choice would rather spend their time on that than on the infinitely more contentious areas of domestic policy.

Since the Vietnam War, Congress has been less willing to defer automatically to presidents on foreign policy questions. Many in Congress have felt that if they had been more skeptical of the war aims of Presidents Kennedy, Johnson and Nixon and more disposed to question their assertions, the Vietnam tragedy might have been averted. In passing the War Powers Resolution (limiting the president's ability to deploy U.S. troops without express congressional approval beyond a period of ninety days), in passing the Arms Export Control Act (which makes it possible for Congress to block the sale of military equipment overseas if both House and Senate vote resolutions of disapproval), and in refusing to grant military aid to rebels in Nicaragua, Congress has provided us with evidence of this new combativeness on its part.

Nevertheless, the president does have impressive informal powers of persuasion when he looks a member of Congress straight in the eye and tells that individual that the nation is facing a crisis overseas and that Congress should not tie the president's hands or embarrass the president in dealings with foreign governments.

Does Politics Really Stop at "the Water's Edge"? The president has also tended to enjoy good public support in foreign crisis situations. There is a tendency for the public to rally to the chief executive at such times, and popular support usually rises even when the outcome of a crisis is unfavorable to the United States. Harry Truman picked up about ten points in his job rating after the Korean War broke out; Eisenhower's highest standing in all of 1958 came after he dispatched Marines to Lebanon. The Cuban

Missile Crisis added another 13 points to John Kennedy's approval ratings in 1962 after the crisis that was deemed to be an American triumph. His highest rating for his entire time in office came not after a success but a failure (the Cuban Bay of Pigs invasion). Jimmy Carter's approval ratings went up after the seizure of the U.S. Embassy in Teheran and also after the failure to have the hostages rescued. As Kenneth Waltz has observed, there is little time for opposition to develop in a short, sharp crisis, but prolonged and frustrating foreign involvements (such as Korea and Vietnam) tend to erode support for presidents.[10]

Presidents have the power to extend **diplomatic recognition** to foreign countries or to withdraw such recognition. This means that they can establish or break diplomatic relations on their own. It is little wonder that in this policy area where the president has the power, almost unilaterally, to command that something be done and to risk few serious challenges is one that is immensely appealing. Public support and support from Congress, at least in the short run, give validity to the old saying that "politics stops at the water's edge."

Iranians celebrate the three-month anniversary of their forcible occupation of the U.S. embassy in Teheran by burning the American flag. *(Alfred/Gamma)*

The President as Commander-in-Chief

The president receives war powers from Article II, section 2, of the Constitution. Although Congress can declare war, the last time Congress exercised its constitutional power to do so under Article I, section 8, was on December 8, 1941, the day after the Japanese attack on Pearl Harbor. Since that time, American troops have been in large-scale combat in Korea (1950–1953) and Southeast Asia (1962–1973). Smaller-scale commitments of American combat troops overseas have been made in Lebanon (1958), Santa Domingo (1965), and in Cambodia in 1975 after the seizure of the American merchant vessel *Mayaguez,* and in the landings on Grenada on October 25, 1983. We suffered 137,000 military casualties in Korea and 200,000 in Southeast Asia without a formal declaration of war. Indeed, in our entire history, war has been formally declared only five times (the War of 1812, the War with Mexico in 1846, the Spanish-American War in 1898, and the two World Wars).

These costly military actions by the United States in the absence of a formal declaration of war reflect the fact that the war-making power of the United States is largely in the hands of the president. Presidents may commit American troops overseas to protect American lives and property and have done so on at least 150 occasions by virtue of their power as commander-in-chief of the armed forces. One distinguished scholar of the presidency stated quite flatly, "As for the power to make war, there [has] never been much question of the clear primacy of the executive."[11] Others argue that most of these 150 incidents were minor affairs that cannot be used to defend unilateral presidential action in such major conflicts as Vietnam.[12]

Presidents, in their decisions to commit American troops, did not usually do so in total disregard of Congress. Since World War II, presidents have managed to secure congressional approval for military actions that were already underway or were being contemplated. President Lyndon B. Johnson secured the **Tonkin Gulf Resolution** from Congress in August 1964. It

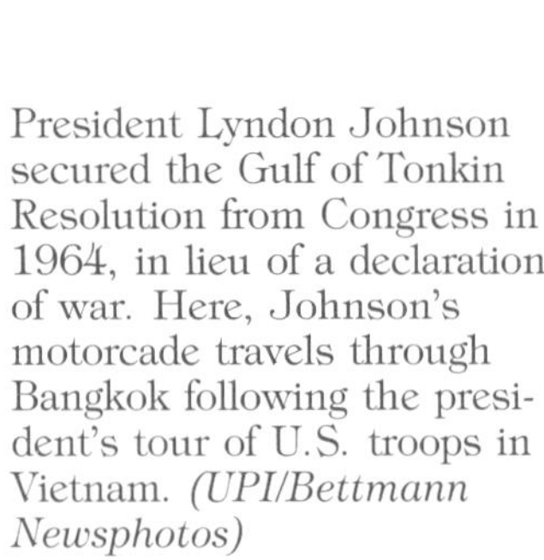

President Lyndon Johnson secured the Gulf of Tonkin Resolution from Congress in 1964, in lieu of a declaration of war. Here, Johnson's motorcade travels through Bangkok following the president's tour of U.S. troops in Vietnam. *(UPI/Bettmann Newsphotos)*

authorized Johnson to use whatever force was necessary to repel attacks on U.S. forces in Vietnam. Congress passed the resolution in the aftermath of an attack by North Vietnamese naval units on U.S. warships. The resolution would be described, at a later date, by Undersecretary of State Nicholas Katzenbach as "a functional equivalent" of a declaration of war. The ultimate result was the sending of 536,000 American troops to Southeast Asia.

In the case of the Cambodian incursion of 1970, there was not the slightest prior consultation with Congress, let alone a formal expression of support. In the case of the mission to rescue the American hostages in Iran, President Carter hinted to Senate Majority Leader Robert C. Byrd that a rescue mission was being planned but did not alert him to the fact that it was just a few days off. The mission provoked a debate over whether the president had complied with the most recent attempt by Congress to control the president's war-making power, the War Powers Act of 1973. President Carter argued that he could not inform Congress as required by the Act for fear that secrecy would be breached. He also denied that the Act was even applicable by describing the operation as "humanitarian." There seemed little feeling in Congress that the president ought to be challenged. This does not mean, however, that the Congress might not at some later time vote to cut off funds for a presidential commitment of troops lasting longer than ninety days.

The classic story of the president's advantage over Congress in his employment of the armed forces is when Theodore Roosevelt decided to "show the flag" by sending an American naval fleet around the world. Senator Nelson Aldrich, Chairman of the Senate Finance Committee, refused to authorize payment for the cost of the voyage and believed that he had been able to stop the fleet from sailing, but Roosevelt had the last word.

> . . . I got to work on the job of digging up funds out of unexpended balances in different departments. . . . We finally found enough money to take the fleet around South America to Japan and China—possibly a little further. It would then be halfway around the world. I made up my mind to send the ships that far and then let Aldrich take the responsibility for leaving them there at anchor or appropriate the funds to bring them back. I felt sure the country would not stand for ordering the ships back across the Pacific; Aldrich would have no option; he would have to bring them home by way of the Atlantic, which was exactly what I wanted.[13]

The President as Chief Politician

Although the president is the undisputed leader of his or her political party, we must hasten to point out that one of the major sources of the erosion of party influence must be laid at the door of recent presidents. Candidate-centered politics—which is the story of contemporary presidential election—is the negation of the party's role in the electoral process. Presidential candidates seem much more concerned with building electoral constituencies loyal to them than in drawing on the traditional sources of party support. The culmination of this was the Committee to Re-Elect the President—Richard Nixon's personal campaign organization in 1972. A Republican party official, when asked by the *Washington Post* reporter Carl Bernstein if Watergate burglar James W. McCord, Jr., worked for the Republican National Committee, confided, "What he has been doing, I assume, is taking care of security for the Committee to Re-Elect. All they care about at CRP is Richard M. Nixon. They couldn't care less about the Republican Party. Given the chance, they would wreck it."[14]

Nixon may have carried this tendency to an extreme, but the practice of presidents to treat the party lightly was not restricted to him. As Joseph Califano wrote:

> I doubt that any recent president has set much priority on strengthening his political party except for his own short-term purposes, however vigorously partisan his campaign or after-dinner political rhetoric. The problems of incumbency tend to focus presidential attention on congressional and special-interest politics, not partisan party politics.[15]

Democratic and Republican national party chairs are the creatures of Democratic and Republican presidents; if a president is displeased by the performance of his or her party's national chair, that person had better start looking for another job.

Presidents have always favored people from their own party when it came to making political appointments, but being of the president's party does not guarantee that you will be favored if you happen to be from a faction of the party that the president doesn't like. People who were identified as being supporters of Senator Edward M. Kennedy were not well treated when Jimmy Carter became president because Kennedy was a long-time political rival to Carter.

Conflicts in the President's Personal and Partisan Agendas Presidents reward people from those groups that contribute to their victories. As we noted previously, when the president begins to think about reelection, his appointments policy is guided by those groups that will, or could be encouraged to, support that individual's bid for a second term.

A Republican president, for example, will generally make campaign appearances at rallies and fund raisers for Republican congressional candidates but may make only token efforts on behalf of Republicans running against those Democratic members who have supported the president's legislation. This is because a friendly Democrat in the Congress may be of greater value to the president than a Republican of uncertain loyalty.

When she endorsed Ted Kennedy for president in 1980, Chicago Mayor Jane Byrne offended the Carter White House and thereby jeopardized Chicago's "share" of discretionary funds. *(UPI/Bettmann Newsphotos)*

On October 24, 1983, President Reagan sent thank-you letters to 145 House Democrats who had voted in favor of increasing U.S. aid to the International Monetary Fund. The Democrats had demanded the letter after they had been assailed by House members of the president's own party for supporting an international agency that made loans to "communist dictatorships." These letters, in effect, immunized the Democrats against campaign attacks by Republican challengers seeking to use the IMF vote against them. The Democrats could simply pull the thank-you note from the Republican president and wave it in the face of their Republican opponents.[16]

This may seem like strange conduct for the person who is the titular head of his party, but, as in the case of ex-Congressman Dornan who lost his job because he was seen as jeopardizing the president's chances for getting House passage of his MX missile program, presidents have personal agendas quite apart from their partisan obligations.

The role of the president as a partisan figure, then, is not clear-cut. Presidents will do what they can to foster the fortunes of their own parties but only when those fortunes tend to coincide with their own objectives. As we shall see in our later section on presidents' uses of patronage and preferments in their skirmishes with Congress, a certain amount of political leverage comes with the office that can be used to good advantage by politically astute presidents, and nowhere are the political skills of presidents tested so exactingly as in their relations with Congress.

The President and Congress

Given what we have learned about the separation of powers, it seems peculiar to speak of the legislative role of the chief executive, but to a very great extent the most important matters of business on which Congress acts are proposals from the White House. As we saw in the previous chapter, the size, specialization, and attention to local or special interests makes Congress far less able to develop comprehensive policies than the president.

The messages that the president sends to Congress, to request the enactment of certain bills, receive far greater attention than any other initiative from outside the Congress. To a large extent, it has become a measure of greatness whether a president is able to see major parts of his or her legislative program enacted. Indeed, as Clinton Rossiter has said, "the refusal or inability of the president to serve as [legislative] leader results in weak and disorganized government."[17]

Although Article II, section 3, of the Constitution empowers the president to call Congress into special session, it is not this rarely used power that is the measure of the president's ability to give Congress its marching orders. For Congress, to a remarkable degree, is simply dependent on the White House for information on which to act. In the previous chapter, we mentioned that bills on which administration spokesmen decline to testify are not taken seriously, since it is the executive branch that must carry out acts of Congress. If presidents think so little of measures that they order their officials not to comment on them, this tends not to be taken seriously.

The sheer ability of the executive branch to gather data in support of, or in opposition to, a piece of legislation is magnitudes greater than that of Congress. When the total number of employees of the Congress—and that includes personal and committee staffs and employees of the support agencies of Congress—is added up, it comes to roughly 40,000 people. The executive branch has that many people in a single job category: computer specialists.[18]

Not only can the executive branch overwhelm the Congress with information; it can also withhold information. Hearings and investigations by Congress are successful largely because of the information they uncover and publicize. If the president's branch has exclusive custody of information, as it so often does, and refuses to release it in a timely fashion, congressional committees have little grist for their investigative mills.

Can a president simply dig in his heels and refuse to provide Congress with any information it seeks? In extreme cases where the White House was determined not to let Congress get its hands on information that the president wanted withheld, the doctrine of **executive privilege** was invoked. Presidents have claimed this as an inherent power of the executive based on the separation of powers.

President Richard Nixon claimed executive privilege to avoid having to turn over to Congress tape recordings made in his office that contained allegedly criminal material. The Supreme Court, in the case of *U.S.* v. *Nixon,*[19] ordered Nixon to surrender the tapes but at the same time said that such a thing as executive privilege did exist. So although Nixon was forced to turn over the tapes, other presidents withholding information under different circumstances might not have to surrender their sources of information.

In 1974, President Richard Nixon failed in his bid to invoke "executive privilege" when Congress demanded the Watergate tapes. *(UPI/Bettmann Newsphotos)*

President vs. Congress: Who's on Top?

It may sound as if it is the president who usually prevails in this ongoing contest with Congress, but we can point to only a few instances in modern times in which Congress enacted every major measure submitted by a president. In none of these cases did presidential dominance last very long, especially in the area of domestic policy, where constituent interests lie close to the surface.

Franklin Roosevelt was able to dominate Congress between 1933 and 1936 when the House and Senate were willing to give him virtually any tool he wanted to pull this country out of the Great Depression. Similarly, Lyndon Johnson pushed through a remarkable amount of Great Society social legislation in the aftermath of his crushing defeat of Barry Goldwater in 1964. He was also helped by his claim that he was redeeming the pledges of his assassinated predecessor John F. Kennedy. More recently, Ronald Reagan achieved remarkable success with budget and tax cuts with the 97th Congress in 1981 after his smashing triumph over Jimmy Carter. Reagan's masterful appeals to the American people that he possessed a mandate for far-reaching change strengthened his hand with Congress.

But observe, these were all unusual circumstances—an economic calamity, an assassination followed by a lopsided victory, and an election performance so strong that one house of Congress changed hands for the first time in twenty-six years. These events do not often occur.

The President vs. the "Iron Triangles"

Congress has some important allies in its contest with the president. Most committees and subcommittees of Congress have intimate relationships with the agencies of the executive branch whose programs they authorize and for whom they appropriate money. The committees and the bureaucrats from the agencies have permanent and close relationships with interest groups that want to influence the policies of government. These three-sided combinations of members of Congress, bureaucrats, and interest groups have been referred to as **iron triangles** because of their ability to stop presidents in their tracks. Name a policy area from defense to agriculture and you will find an iron triangle. When President Reagan, for example, proposed selling the Federal Housing Administration (FHA) to private interests, the outcry from the organizations of home builders and mortgage bankers and the committees of Congress with jurisdiction over the FHA was so great that the White House backed off by saying that the proposal needed further study.

These iron triangles usually outlast the four or eight years of a single presidency. Presidents may come and go, but the civil servants of the executive branch can have careers spanning forty years; and their relationships with members of Congress and interest groups are more permanent fixtures of national government than presidents' careers. Accordingly, presidents are eager to see their programs enacted, since their time in office is limited by the Constitution. Presidents, moreover, try to accomplish most of their objectives early in their term. As second terms proceed, they are seen as **lame ducks** with little influence—since they cannot succeed themselves.

As a consequence, it is often easier for a bureaucrat to defy a president than to cooperate with a president in defying Congress, which, after all, keeps the bureaucratic ship afloat with appropriations. One way in which presidents have sought to break up the iron triangles is by proposing reorganizations of the executive branch with the goal of bringing similar programs scattered among a variety of federal departments into a single agency. From the president's point of view, this permits a more rational approach to a single national problem. If a unified approach to a problem is desirable and a fragmented one less likely to achieve success, one might imagine that no right-minded person could oppose it. Fragmentation does, however, have its defenders. Unhappily, for the president, many of these are in Congress. But even if hampered in controlling the machinery of the executive branch of government by allied forces of bureaucrats, special interests, and Congress, the president still has an array of weapons, including the veto power, patronage and preferments, and appeals to the public.

The Veto Power

The power of the veto set forth in Article I of the Constitution is a major weapon in the presidential arsenal. With the exception of joint resolutions proposing constitutional amendments, every other bill or joint resolution must come to the president's desk. The president can sign it, allow it to become law by taking no action, or veto it and send it back to Congress within ten days. Only by a two-thirds vote of both houses can a presidential veto be overriden. When Congress passes a bill with fewer than ten days left in the legislative session and the president fails to sign the bill, it is known as a **pocket veto.**

Overriding a presidential veto is no easy matter for Congress, especially if the Congress is of the same party as the president. To block an override, that is, to sustain a veto, all the president needs is the support of one-third plus one member of a single house. The other house may be able to muster well in excess of two-thirds, but it does not matter. For this reason, overrides are extremely rare: only 6 percent of all presidential vetoes have been overridden.

You will notice from the list of presidential vetoes in Table 10.1 that it was not until after the Civil War that the veto was widely used. It has also not been extensively used since the administration of Dwight D. Eisenhower.

Most bills that suffer the presidential veto are private bills, such as the ones we discussed in Chapter 9. Rarely are major tax and appropriations bills vetoed because modern presidents have usually tried to compromise with Congress in advance on these major measures. Even if presidents find objectionable provisions in these bills, they usually sign them anyway. The same applies to public works bills that contain the pet projects of members of Congress. The president might forfeit important congressional support if he denied members one of the surefire devices they use to win reelection. Presidents have increasingly made their veto decisions based on a desire to reward or punish individual members of Congress.

Finally, presidents often do not have to resort actually to the use of the veto to deal with provisions of bills that displease them. They can use the threat of the veto to get Congress to modify things they do not like, because members of Congress will drop a provision in a bill that a president objects to rather than seeing the entire bill vetoed.

TABLE 10.1 Presidential Vetoes

President	Total Vetoes	Regular Vetoes	Pocket Vetoes	Vetoes Sustained or No Attempt to Override	Vetoes Overridden
Washington	2	2	0	2	0
J. Adams	0				
Jefferson	0				
Madison	7	5	2	7	0
Monroe	2	1	1	1	1
Jackson	12	5	7	12	0
Van Buren	0				
W. H. Harrison	0				
Tyler	10	6	4	9	1
Taylor	0				
Fillmore	0				
Pierce	9	9	0	4	5
Buchanan	7	4	3	7	0
Lincoln	6	2	4	6	0
A. Johnson	28	21	7	13	15
Grant	92	44	48	88	4
Hayes	13	12	1	12	1
Garfield	0				
Arthur	12	4	8	11	1
Cleveland (1885–1889)	414	304	110	412	2
B. Harrison	44	19	25	43	1
Cleveland (1893–1897)	170	42	128	165	5
McKinley	42	6	36	42	0
T. Roosevelt	82	42	40	81	1
Taft	39	30	9	38	1
Wilson	44	33	11	38	6
Harding	6	5	1	6	0
Coolidge	50	20	30	46	4
Hoover	37	21	16	34	3
F. Roosevelt	631	371	260	622	9
Truman	250	180	70	238	12
Eisenhower	181	73	108	179	2
Kennedy	21	12	9	21	0
L. Johnson	30	16	14	30	0
Nixon	43	24	19	38	5
Ford	66	48	18	54	12
Carter	22	9	13	21	1
Reagan (first term)	39	17	22	35	4

Patronage and Preferments

Patronage, the practice of distributing public jobs or privileges for reasons of politics rather than merit, is a less potent presidential weapon than it used to be. At one time all postmasters were political appointees, and grants and contracts were given out with political support in mind. Since 1970 when the U.S. Postal Service was established as an independent agency free of political influence, this form of patronage has no longer been available to presidents. Most federal grants, moreover, are given out on the basis of formulas written into law, so that states and localities get their funds automatically when they meet certain conditions.

The president enjoys excellent leverage against Congress in the area of grants-in-aid, contracts, and the location of government facilities. If a decision is to be made on whether or not to close down a number of air force bases, or where the Department of Energy will locate a solar energy laboratory, or which company will receive a contract for glassware for the U.S. Public Health Service, it will often be made with congressional support in mind. A member of Congress who is anxious to deliver a federal facility, grant, or contract to his state or district to help his reelection chances can be persuaded to support bills favored by the president. The president also stands to gain political support from the creation of a federal program or facility or from saving it from being closed down. These areas in which presidents have discretion in where money is spent are known as **preferments.**

Presidents can also retaliate against those who do not show a cooperative spirit. Fifteen minutes after the Senate Foreign Relations Committee voted, 9 to 8, against a military sale proposed by President Reagan, one of the nine negative voters, Senator Rudy Boschwitz of Minnesota, learned that the air force would close down a facility in his state.[20]

Going Public: The President and the Media

The president's trump card in the struggle with Congress is the ability to go directly to the people to make his case. Nelson Polsby cautions us that this is not as simple as it sounds, because the president really doesn't want to put the public in the position of having to choose between the president and their elected representatives. What the president really wants in going public is to alert the media and relevant interest groups to the position he favors.[21]

But there is considerably more to the president's resort to using the media than just a way to go over the heads of Congress, although it is certainly a major weapon in the president's competition with Congress. As one observer of the presidency has said, "Whether the president attempts to generate public support [for his programs] through direct appeals or through the mere reporting of his activities, he must do so through the national media."[22]

The president, of course, is a person whom journalists love to write about. They just can't get enough stories with a White House dateline. When you combine the journalist's need to file an interesting story with the president's need for journalists to get his message out, you have a relationship that is both symbiotic and adversarial. This stems from a situation in which presidents want the media to carry the good news about what they are doing, whereas the press covers all White House stories whether they are good for the president, or not. Some presidents suspect that the journalists actually prefer the bad ones.

Presidents in the electronic era do very little that is not influenced by media considerations. So, although the Constitution calls for the president to be inaugurated on January 20, President Reagan put off the formal

President Ronald Reagan is the only president to have made a living in front of the cameras before coming to the White House, but every president has been mindful of what the media can do *for* and *to* him. *(Daniel Simon/Gamma-Liaison)*

swearing-in for a day so as not to compete with the telecast of the Super Bowl. His visit to Normandy to commemorate the fortieth anniversary of D-Day landings was impressive in terms of its visual impact. The news footage of the event showed the president delivering an emotional speech at the base of the cliffs at Pointe du Hoc while cameras cut away to the tear-streaked faces of men who, in their youth, had braved German fire to scale those very cliffs. So effective was Reagan in recapturing the event and identifying himself with their heroism that the veterans could easily forget that he had spent the war in Hollywood making training films. The footage of the Normandy commemoration was used extensively in Mr. Reagan's 1984 reelection campaign.

President Reagan is our only president to have made a living in front of the cameras before coming to the White House, but every president has been mindful of what the media can do *for* him and *to* him. During two events in 1983—the destruction of the U.S. Marine barracks in Beirut, Lebanon by a terrorist bomb and the invasion, a week later, of the island of Grenada by U.S. forces—White House strategy with the media was to protect the president from being associated with negative developments. When Reverend Jesse Jackson succeeded in freeing a U.S. Navy pilot who had been shot down over Lebanon and held by the Syrians, the approach was to associate the president as closely as possible with Jackson's successful effort. This was done by inviting Jackson and the flier to the White House and making it appear that somehow the president had played a role in getting the prisoner released.[23]

What we rarely see is the test of wills between journalists anxious for a breath of scandal or intrigue and the presidential press secretary who, like all press agents, has the job of making his or her boss look good. A particularly acerbic exchange between presidential press secretary Larry Speakes and NBC reporter Chris Wallace took place over whether an "investigation" or a "review of documents" was the proper term to describe a particular White House activity (see box entitled "Choice of Words Sparks Speakes"). It is a superb example of the tensions that exist between journalists who thrive on controversy and press spokespersons who shun it.

By and large, presidents have remarkable control over what is written and said about them. This is not necessarily a result of manipulating or "managing" the news so much as it is a kind of advantage that inheres in the presidency. In foreign affairs in particular the president enjoys this advantage. Important events can occur in remote corners of the world that the president can be alerted to by our embassies, armed forces, or intelligence agencies. Even the most far-flung TV or newspaper correspondents cannot monitor the globe like the people who report to the White House. As commander-in-chief of the armed forces, moreover, the president can simply rule that an area of conflict is out of bounds to the press. There was virtually no independent press coverage of the Grenada invasion, and the great bulk of the combat footage available was shot by army camera personnel.

Even in those situations in which you might expect some give-and-take, such as at televised press conferences, the president enjoys built-in advantages. The president can choose to recognize or not recognize a reporter and generally knows who the friendly ones are. The president can allow or rule out follow-up questions. And, finally, if the president has said all he has to say or the going gets rough, the president can nod to the press

POLITICAL PERSPECTIVE

CHOICE OF WORDS SPARKS SPEAKES

White House spokesman Larry Speakes, during his morning briefing with reporters yesterday, insisted on using the term "a review of documents" to define the White House probe of contacts with the Environmental Protection Agency.

But he said once, "Any of these allegations which have been raised . . . are being investigated by the Justice Department, by the FBI, by the White House and by numerous congressional committees."

The exchange concerning the EPA that took place yesterday morning between Speakes and reporters:

"Who in the White House is investigating?" a reporter asked.

Speakes corrected himself, saying, "Review, or however you want to say it—the Fielding review."

Washington Post reporter David Hoffman then read a question from a transcript of Thursday's official briefing in which the question was asked, "Is the White House conducting any kind of internal investigation to find out the nature of the contacts between [White House aide Craig] Fuller and [President Reagan's counselor Edwin] Meese on the one hand and [fired EPA assistant administrator Rita M.] Lavelle on the other?" He read Speakes' answer of, "No, not that I'm aware of."

NBC reporter Chris Wallace then complained that reporters had been given "bum information on what [White House counsel Fred F.] Fielding was doing."

Wallace to Speakes: You think that that's a frank and candid answer to that question, that you were unaware of this, when everybody was being asked to turn over information on contacts?

Speakes: Sure.

Wallace: Well, I don't consider that a candid answer. I consider that misleading.

Speakes: Screw you then.

Wallace: I really do. I consider it a lie, frankly.

Speakes: Wait a minute. That's the most serious charge that you can level at me. It was not a lie. It was the word "investigation" that was used. Fielding is not doing an investigation. He is not doing anything but receiving reports. Do you want to call that a lie?

Wallace: If that is an accurate reflection of the question that you were asked.

Speakes: Do you want to call that a lie?

Wallace: Let me make my statement.

Speakes: Go ahead and make your statement, because you have said something that I consider very, very, very serious. That's the most serious thing you can level at me. And you're dead wrong. Make your statement and see if you want to stick by the word "lie."

Wallace: You were asked whether or not there was an investigation going on of the contacts between Fuller and Meese and the EPA, and you said no, not that you know of.

Speakes: That's right. Are you calling that a lie?

Wallace: I consider that misleading, yes.

Speakes: You call that a lie?

Wallace: You knew that this had been asked?

Speakes: Sure.

Wallace: Yes. I do.

Speakes: Okay, that's it then. Good enough.

As the morning briefing ended, Wallace approached Speakes, "I'm not having anything to do with you, Chris," Speakes said with a glare. "You're out of business as far as I'm concerned."

Source: United Press International in *The Washington Post* (Feb. 20, 1983). Reprinted with permission of United Press International, Inc.

secretary who will shout, "Thank you very much, Mr. President," and terminate the press conference.

Presidents also have little ways of retaliating against journalists who offend them. President Kennedy canceled the White House subscription to the *New York Herald Tribune,* Richard Nixon put some journalists on his "enemies list," and other presidents have stricken the names of unfriendly reporters from the list of invitees to state dinners. Presidents can also take advantage of the ability to isolate themselves by simply not being available to the press. This does not mean they disappear from sight, but rather that they appear and speak at times and places of their own choosing. Presidents Nixon and Reagan often preferred to speak at small church-affiliated colleges or in towns with sizable populations of military families because they thought such groups were more supportive of their policies. Such practices have troubled some observers who see in them, "a growing fragmentation of politics [when] presidents are speaking to specialized groups more than to national audiences and . . . creating attention-focusing situations more than sustained educational campaigns."[24]

Presidents believe that only if they could speak directly to the American people and not have their words filtered and interpreted by the networks and the major newspapers—"a tiny and closed fraternity of privileged men elected by no one," in the words of former Vice-President Spiro T. Agnew—support for the president's policies would surely follow. But one need only visit a country with a controlled press to appreciate the value of an aggressive and combative press. In such places, one reads only the most dreary and monotonous praise for leaders and their policies. No president, even the most thin-skinned, should aspire to that.

Perhaps the greatest disservice done to the presidency by the press has little to do with what is said or written about any given president or his policies, but rather the tendency to suggest that presidents can work miracles and that solutions to most problems can be found within the Oval Office. This raises expectations about what is possible and sets the public up for disappointment when solutions are not found. The irony is that the press is in the vanguard of both puffing up the expectations and prophesying doom when the expectations aren't fulfilled.

Those Who Assist the President

The Presidential Cabinet

The **cabinet** is the president's "official family" in the executive branch. Its members provide the president with advice in the thirteen policy areas over which their departments have jurisdiction. They are also responsible for carrying out the president's policies. A great deal of attention is paid to the people selected as cabinet officers, since the nature of the institution is said to be a signal of the direction in which an administration will go. Although not mentioned by name in the Constitution, the cabinet is nevertheless an enduring but highly controversial element of American government.

The controversy relates to fragmentation of responsibility. Appointed by the president and confirmed by the Senate, the members of the cabinet are also seen as spokespersons for the interest groups within their jurisdiction. They are, in addition, required to make the case for their departmental authorizations and appropriations to both houses of Congress and are expected to be responsive to both. Richard Fenno sums up the problem admirably:

> As a group the Cabinet draws its life breath from the President, but as individuals the Cabinet members are by no means dependent upon him . . . [I]n order for the Cabinet member to be of real help to the President in one of his leadership roles, the member must have non-presidential "public" prestige, party following, legislative support, or roots of influence in his department. . . . For his part, the President's influence over the Cabinet member becomes splintered and eroded as the member begins to respond to political forces not presidential in origin or direction.[25]

The problem of the individual cabinet member and the cabinet as a whole has been summed up in the single word, **clientelism**—a too great dependency of cabinet members on the approval and support of the interest groups or clients with which their departments deal and an insufficient loyalty to the programs of the president. Some departments are held to be worse than others. The State Department does not have clients in foreign governments in the same sense that Labor has clients in the AFL-CIO and the large independent unions, Agriculture has in the National Farm Bureau Federation, or Education in the National Education Association.

The cabinet members, then, can find themselves serving different masters. Is a cabinet member the president's emissary to the interest groups when the chief executive wants to mobilize these groups behind programs? Is the cabinet member the messenger of the interests, carrying their demands and complaints to the president, and their agent inside the official family? Do cabinet members address themselves to Congress who pays their bills or to the president who sets their policies? Are cabinet members, moreover, most valuable only for the political influence they can bring to the cabinet or for their expertise? The answer to all of these questions, depending upon the circumstances, is yes.

Cabinets have also been vulnerable to jurisdictional disputes such as those that saw the Labor Department, the Department of Housing and Urban Development, and the Department of Health, Education, and Welfare (now Health and Human Services) fighting over who would get the largest portion of President Johnson's Great Society social programs. Each secretary and his supporting clients wanted the lion's share of the action. Another problem with the cabinet acting as a unit to make policy across a broad range of subjects is that not all members are equally interested in the business at hand. Discussion on defense policy will involve the secretaries of State, Defense, and possibly Treasury, but not the others. Discussions of agriculture policy will be of little interest to the Secretary of Labor or the Secretary of Education. President Reagan's use of cabinet committees as "little cabinets" dealing with issues of common interest to a few secretaries was an effort to get around this problem. As a general proposition, however, broad policymaking by the entire cabinet is a little like bringing together a pig, a serpent, a tiger, and an ox and telling them to produce offspring.

President Reagan in 1981 with "little cabinet" members Murray Weidenbaum, Donald Regan, and David Stockman. *(O. Franken/Sygma)*

With cabinets fragmented and cabinet members cross-pressured by the loyalty to the president or their department's clients and with the uncertainty of presidential control over the bureaucracy, it is not at all surprising that presidents turn to people they can better control and whose loyalty is never in doubt: the members of the White House staff. This is particularly the case when presidents feel very strongly about a problem or a program and want to ensure that their policies are carried out as faithfully as possible. It is to those groups and individuals that we now turn.

The White House Staff and the Executive Office of the President

No part of the executive branch has experienced such dramatic growth over such a short period of time or acquired influence so dramatically as the Executive Office of the President. Prior to 1939 there was not even such an organization as the Executive Office. Lincoln guided the nation through the Civil War with what amounted to an administrative staff of two young secretaries—journalist John G. Nicolay and lawyer John Hay. Aside from a small housekeeping staff, that is all he had under the same roof. Prior to Lincoln's time there was not even that. As late as the Wilson administration, the president often answered his own telephone. For the first seven years of the Roosevelt presidency when the nation was in the grip of depression, the same situation prevailed.

It was only in 1939 when the country faced the additional challenge of world war that Congress finally provided help as part of a bill to allow the president to reorganize the executive branch subject to congressional veto. The bill formally recognized the Executive Office of the President, assigned to that office the Bureau of the Budget, which had previously been part of the Treasury Department, and authorized the president to hire six administrative assistants. In September 1939, with Europe already at war, Roosevelt issued Executive Order No. 8248, which formalized the Executive Office of the President and placed within it the White House Office, "to serve the President in an intimate capacity in the performance of many detailed activities incident to his immediate office," and the Bureau of the Budget—two of the most important divisions of the Executive Office.

The Executive Office of the President and its most significant component organization, the White House Office and policy staffs, have grown over the years. In 1980, the White House staff consisted of 350 presidential assistants, 70 people detailed from the cabinet departments, and 540 people in the Office of Management and Budget (OMB), the successor to the Bureau of the Budget.

The current organization of the Executive Office of the President is a good indicator of those areas of policy that the president considers most important: economic policy (OMB, Council of Economic Advisers); general domestic policy, which necessarily involves economic policy as well (Domestic Policy Staff); national security and foreign policy (National Security Council, Intelligence Oversight Board, Special Representative for Trade Negotiations); environmental policy (Council on Environmental Quality);

and science and technology (Office of Science and Technology). In addition to these policy areas are the politically important Assistant to the President for Congressional Liaison; Office of the Press Secretary to the President; special assistants to the president for liaison to various constituencies in the public—such as consumers, women, blacks, Jews, and Hispanics; and those responsible for the management of the staff and the administration of the Executive Office of the President.

The Vice-President

One individual who assists the president can be either an important partner in helping the president achieve objectives or an unhappy and isolated person. As Mr. Dooley—the fictional barroom philosopher of the early part of this century—tells the story, the vice-president calls at the White House every morning to inquire of the president's health. "When told that the president was never better, he gives three cheers and departs with a heavy heart."

Vice-presidential success or failure seems to depend very much on the personal rapport that he or she can establish with the president. Although the most recent vice-presidents have been able to establish that bond, "the verdict of history is harsh on the vice-presidency. The office has done only one thing well, solving our succession problem, and it is open to question whether it has done even that well enough."[26]

The Constitution assigns the vice-presidency very little—hardly enough to keep a grown person busy. There is not much need for the vice-president to preside over the Senate; the vice-president does this rarely anyway, and most senators would just as soon have one of their own number (preferably a very junior one) do the job. Breaking tie votes in the Senate? That is part of the vice-president's constitutional role, but tie votes in the Senate seldom occur—on the average of once a year. A clear and immediate successor for a dead or disabled president seems to be the most useful formal role for the person "one heartbeat away."

The most useful political role for the vice-president is as a candidate rather than an incumbent. Historically, the vice-president has been a ticket-balancer—someone from a state distant from that of the presidential candidate or from a wing of the party that the presidential candidate does not belong to. This is a time-honored tradition going back to Virginia presidents and Massachusetts or New York vice-presidents in the early nineteenth century. George Bush was put on the ticket by Ronald Reagan as a gesture of reassurance to those who might have been put off by Reagan's strong conservatism. Bush was seen as a solid, establishment-type figure. Presidential candidates without congressional experience tend to choose running mates who have been either in the House or Senate. Franklin Roosevelt selected Speaker of the House John Nance Garner and later Senator Harry Truman. Eisenhower took ex-Congressman and Senator Richard Nixon. Vice-President Bush had also been a House member.

George Bush and his predecessors in the vice-presidency have had only as much authority as the president wished to grant them. *(Cynthia Johnson/Gamma-Liaison)*

In recent years, presidents have tried to make better use of their vice-presidents by assigning specific projects to them. Carter assigned Mondale

"Here He Comes Now"

President Eisenhower often used Vice-President Nixon to perform unpleasant tasks that he did not want to be associated with publicly. Such a role did little for the image of Nixon, who is shown here emerging from a sewer in one of the most devastating American political cartoons. (*From Herblock's Special for Today [Simon & Schuster, 1955].*)

the job of being the administration's spokesperson on Africa. Mondale also played a key role in the effort to get loan guarantees for the financially troubled Chrysler Corporation in 1980. George Bush has been used as a roving ambassador and has filled in a good deal for President Reagan at political appearances. He was also designated to head the White House crisis-management team.

Presidents tend to use vice-presidents to do things they themselves would not stoop to do or say things presidents would not like to utter. When Vice-President Mondale called into question the patriotism of Senator Edward M. Kennedy during the 1980 primary campaign, he was performing such a role.

Proposals for reforming the vice-presidency range from making the vice-president a member of the cabinet to abolishing the office altogether. Neither of these suggestions is likely to be adopted. What is more likely is that the powers and importance of the office will depend very much on who is president and how much confidence that person has in the person who is number two.

The one clear role that the vice-president does have is as what Nelson Rockefeller (the unhappy occupant of that office) referred to as "standby equipment." It is with this in mind that we turn to the mechanisms for presidential succession.

Arrangements for Presidential Succession

Impeachment and Removal

The Constitution provides that the president can be impeached by the House of Representatives by a majority vote for "Treason, bribery, or other high crimes and misdemeanors" and can be removed from office if found guilty of those charges by two-thirds of the Senate. The Chief Justice of the Supreme Court presides at a Senate trial of an impeached president.*

One president, Andrew Johnson, was impeached in 1868 by the House and escaped conviction by a single vote. Two other presidents faced less serious impeachment moves—John Tyler in 1843 and Herbert Hoover in 1933. The most recent brush with impeachment by a president was Richard Nixon's in 1974, when the House Judiciary Committee voted three articles of impeachment against the 37th president for obstruction of justice, violating the constitutional rights of American citizens through the use of illegal break-ins and wiretaps, and for refusing to provide Congress with tapes and other materials that they had subpoenaed. Before the full House had the opportunity to vote on the report of the Judiciary Committee, Nixon resigned.

The framers had a rather different view of impeachment than we have today. They saw it as a political weapon and intended that it be used as such. They had no dispute at all about its use when a president broke the criminal laws, but beyond that they also saw it as a defense against the abuse of executive power. Madison felt that it should not be brought to bear for simple differences of opinion over policy but only for "great and dangerous offenses."

Presidential Death and Disability

The death of a president in office does not involve the same kind of constitutional crisis as an impeachment. What was, until recently, a murky area was the question of presidential disability. The Twenty-fifth Amendment [ratified on February 19, 1967] does provide a mechanism for the replacement of a president who is physically or mentally unable to fulfill his duties, but is yet to be tested by an actual crisis of presidential capacity.

Eight presidents have died in office, and in all cases the vacancy was immediately filled by the vice-president, as provided for by the Constitution. Four of these vice-presidents who succeeded to the office were not subsequently reelected in their own right and never had a vice-president. One, Gerald Ford, who succeeded to the office after Nixon's resignation, acquired a vice-president through the mechanism of the Twenty-fifth Amendment, which we will discuss shortly. Six vice-presidents died in office and two (Calhoun and Agnew) resigned—Calhoun because of differences over tariff policy with President Andrew Jackson and Agnew in disgrace after pleading "no contest" to charges of bribery and tax evasion.

The first test of the Twenty-fifth Amendment's provision for filling a

*Note that impeachment is not the same as removal, which occurs only after a president is found guilty by the Senate.

POLITICAL PERSPECTIVE

THE EIGHT WHO DIED IN OFFICE

Name	Date of Death	Cause of Death
William Henry Harrison	April 4, 1841	Pneumonia
Zachary Taylor	July 9, 1850	Typhoid fever
Abraham Lincoln	April 15, 1865	Assassination
James A. Garfield	September 19, 1881	Assassination
William McKinley	September 14, 1901	Assassination
Warren G. Harding	August 2, 1923	Apoplexy
Franklin D. Roosevelt	April 12, 1945	Cerebral hemorrhage
John F. Kennedy	November 22, 1963	Assassination

Eight of our presidents died in office and one—Woodrow Wilson—was incapacitated for more than a year. Cleveland, Eisenhower, and Reagan had serious medical crises during their terms which removed them, for a time, from the Oval Office. It is a sad commentary on the sometimes-violent nature of American politics that half of all the deaths in office of presidents were caused by assassinations.

vice-presidential vacancy came with the Agnew resignation in October 1973. The amendment calls for the president to nominate a vice-president, who takes office after confirmation by a simple majority of both the House and Senate.

Contrary to his statement at the time of the attempted assassination of President Reagan in 1981, Secretary of State Alexander Haig was only fourth in line to succeed the president. *(Pierre Perrin/Gamma)*

How Does the Twenty-fifth Amendment Work When Presidents Can't The question of presidential incapacity was also addressed by the Twenty-fifth Amendment. It provides that the vice-president can become *acting president* if the president communicates in writing to the speaker of the House and the president pro tem. of the Senate that he cannot discharge presidential duties. The president can also be declared incapacitated if the majority of the cabinet and the vice-president certify in writing that the president cannot carry out his or her duties.

The president can reclaim office at any time after that unless the president's assertion that he is fit to resume the duties of office is challenged by the vice-president, a majority of the cabinet, or "such other body" as Congress provides. Should that kind of dispute arise, Congress would have to convene within forty-eight hours and determine within three weeks whether or not the president can resume duties or whether the vice-president will continue as acting president. It requires a two-thirds vote of Congress to settle the matter, and in the three-week period that they are deciding what to do, the vice-president continues to hold the office on an acting basis. If Congress decides that the president is no longer incapacitated, the president may resume the duties of office right away.

Although statisticians have calculated that the death of both president and vice-president in the same administration might occur only once in 840 years, there have been succession laws on the federal statutes providing for this eventuality since 1792. The most recent, The Presidential Succession Act of 1947, with amendments in 1955, places the line of succession as follows: (1) speaker of the House, (2) president pro tem. of the Senate, and (3) cabinet secretaries in order of the establishment of their departments. Currently, this would mean that the secretary of state would be first in line among cabinet secretaries and last would be the secretary of education, since this is the most recently established cabinet department. Accordingly, Secretary of State Alexander Haig's statement in the White House after the assassination attempt on President Reagan on March 30, 1981, that "I have taken charge" was not only bad manners but bad law as well, since Vice-President George Bush, Speaker O'Neill, and President Pro Tem. Senator Strom Thurmond were still very much alive.

It was to avoid this type of confusion that President Reagan handed over power to Vice-President Bush in July 1985 when Reagan entered the hospital for a cancer operation. Reagan did not formally invoke the Twenty-fifth Amendment but followed the spirit of the amendment in a letter to the president pro tem. of the Senate and the speaker of the House (see box entitled "President Informally Invokes the Twenty-fifth Amendment").

POLITICAL PERSPECTIVE

PRESIDENT INFORMALLY INVOKES THE TWENTY-FIFTH AMENDMENT

The second test of the Twenty-fifth Amendment came in 1985 when President Reagan underwent surgery for a cancerous growth in his intestine. Although the president did not formally invoke the amendment, he followed the procedures set forth by the amendment. Among the reasons given for not formally invoking the Twenty-fifth Amendment were that the White House did not want to overdramatize the surgery and cause undue concern among Americans. In addition, using an informal procedure relieved the president of having to inform the leaders of Congress when he was ready to resume his duties.

Text of President Reagan's letter:

BETHESDA, Md., July 13, 1985

I am about to undergo surgery during which time I will be briefly and temporarily incapable of discharging the constitutional powers and duties of the office of the President of the United States.

After consultation with my counsel and the Attorney General, I am mindful of the provisions of Section 3 of the 25th Amendment to the Constitution and of the uncertainties of its application to such brief and temporary periods of incapacity. I do not believe that the drafters of this amendment intended its application to situations such as the instant one.

Nevertheless, consistent with my longstanding arrangement with Vice President George Bush, and not intending to set a precedent binding anyone privileged to hold the office in the future, I have determined and it is my intention and direction, that Vice President George Bush shall discharge those powers and duties in my stead commencing with the administration of anesthesia to me in this instance.

I shall advise you and the Vice President when I determine that I am able to resume the discharge of the constitutional powers and duties of this office.

May God bless this nation and us all.

Sincerely,
Ronald Reagan.

Fragmentation and the Presidency

Elected by the American people and not merely by the citizens of a state or a congressional district, the president is unique in having as a constituency the entire nation. This has been both a blessing and a curse to presidents. They have been blessed insofar as people look to them to deal with problems of national scope and societywide urgency. They have been cursed because, as other institutions come to suffer more acutely from fragmentation, people turn with even greater urgency to the White House for solutions. We spoke earlier in this chapter of the role that the media have played in fostering these expectations. Presidents and people running for the presidency promote expectations as well by overpromising. Hugh Heclo places the blame on,

> . . . a more politically volatile public, a less manageable Congress, a disappearing party hierarchy, proliferating groups of single-minded activists which merge with . . . networks of policy experts . . . All these add up to a shifting political base of support for presidents . . . It is rampant pluralism, with groups crosscutting the political landscape into incoherent patterns . . . Rampant pluralism produces what we in fact have: unnegotiable demands, political stagnation, and stalemate.[27]

This "rampant pluralism" is what we call fragmentation, and in dealing with it, presidents have tended to invite fragmentation into the organization and operation of the White House. Presidents have tried to build reliable bases of political support by formalizing their ties to the various interest groups that have supported them or are crucial to the success of presidential programs. They have done this by creating within the White House itself a portrait in miniature of the interest groups whose help they need. Sometimes it is just adding a staff person to deal with the needs of a particular interest group; sometimes it is adding a whole office.

The Carter administration offered an example of this problem in the controversial area of abortion and women's rights. The president had said that he opposed the use of federal Medicaid funds to pay for abortions for poor women. At the same time, he wanted the support of feminist groups, who favored the broadest possible availability of abortions. Carter appointed as his special assistant for liaison with various interest groups a woman named Midge Costanza who did not share the president's views on abortion funding. Costanza proceeded to call a meeting at the White House of prominent women in the Carter administration to urge the president to change his position and began readying a petition to present to him. A cabinet member recalled, "I was incredulous that a White House staffer would organize such a meeting . . . [and] was appalled at Costanza's judgment and seriously questioned her loyalty to Carter."[28] Examples of this kind of internal friction led people to conclude that far from serving as a force for national cohesion, the presidency was having trouble containing fragmentation within its own domain.

Without question, the first term in office of President Reagan saw an imposition of internal discipline in the White House that few thought possible. He accomplished this through a centralized management structure, a very cohesive staff of senior advisers who followed the president's priorities single-mindedly, and the careful selection of political appointees to bring the bureaucracy into line with Reagan's policies. President Reagan also took care to ensure that his relations with Congress were in good shape.[29]

In his first term at least Ronald Reagan was also able to circumvent many of the "iron triangles" of which we spoke earlier in the chapter. This ability to flank these groups that had been able to dominate their own domain of public policy was, in some ways, President Reagan's most impressive achievement.

But for all of the control that he was able to impose on an institution that had been adjudged imperiled just a few years before and for all his ability to innovate in policy areas believed to be off limits to presidents, there remain areas of concern.

The very personal success of Mr. Reagan and the praise lavished upon him as "the Great Communicator" raised the question of whether his successes were institutional as well as personal. President Reagan was criticized from within his own party for not campaigning vigorously on behalf of Republican congressional candidates in 1984 until he was certain that he would crush Walter Mondale easily. Reagan was also faulted for forming temporary alliances with blocs in Congress for the purpose of passing individual pieces of legislation rather than trying to form permanent coalitions.

Whatever history's ultimate verdict on President Reagan, he did demonstrate that the presidency was not an "endangered species" and that presidents could lead, innovate, and enjoy consistently high levels of public support (see Figure 10-1). While giving due credit to the extraordinary personality of the man who reinvigorated the institution, we believe that the true test of a strengthened presidency is that the office of chief executive remain strong and not merely reflect the qualities of the person who is occupying it. In a government "of laws and not of men," especially one that depends on the functioning of strong institutions, our concerns are for periods longer than eight years.

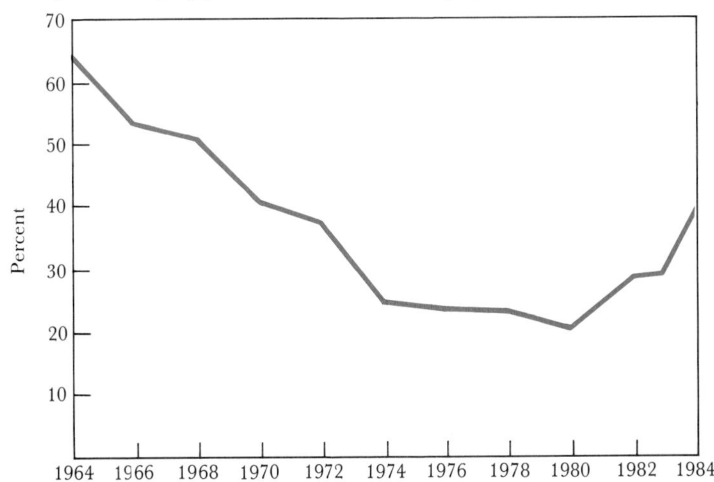
"Would you say the government is pretty much run by a few big interests looking out for themselves, or that it is run for the benefit of all the people?" Percentage of respondents saying government benefits all the people.
Percent
70
60
50
40
30
20
10
1964 1966 1968 1970 1972 1974 1976 1978 1980 1982 1984

FIGURE 10-1
Does Government Benefit All the People?

According to one public opinion poll, President Reagan succeeded in reversing a twenty-year decline in citizens' views on who benefits from the activities of the federal government. The percentage of those thinking that government worked for all the people rather than just for special interests was higher in 1984 than at any time since before the Watergate scandal of 1972. *(Data based on a CBS/New York Times poll. Copyright © 1984 by The New Times Company. Reprinted by permission.)*

Conclusion: Changing Views of the Presidency

In the fall of 1980, about the time of the presidential election, there appeared in the prestigious journal *Foreign Affairs* a lengthy and thoughtful article by Lloyd M. Cutler, counsel to President Carter.[30] The article said that it had become impossible for presidents to carry out their programs because of the political compromises they had to make to win reelection. Cutler proposed a number of radical constitutional changes—among them, a single six-year presidential term. This, he argued, would free presidents from politics and enable them to think only of the national interest.

Such ideas have been around since the days of Andrew Jackson and seem to crop up when presidents are stymied by Congress in their ability to achieve their objectives. Ironically, Cutler's proposal was made only seven years after Arthur M. Schlesinger, Jr.'s *The Imperial Presidency* that warned of "a compulsion towards presidential power rising out of deep-running changes in . . . society."[31]

Within the space of less than a decade, then, we had gone from a preoccupation over a runaway presidency to an obsession with a powerless one. After the passage of another half-decade, we seemed to have come almost full-circle to the 1970s. Although few suggested the reappearance of an imperial presidency under Ronald Reagan, most observers felt that he had laid to rest much of the talk of an ungovernable country.

That a single institution with an unchanged Constitutional mandate can vary so much in its performance over the period of a single decade might seem remarkable in a mature political system such as ours until you recall that that period of ten years saw four different people occupying the Oval Office. One influential school of thought in presidential studies argues that the character and personality of the president is far more influential in determining the performance of the institution than the formal powers enjoyed by presidents.[32] Another prominent treatise[33] cited three sources of presidential influence, two of which were traits associated with individuals and only one with the formal powers of the office.

Americans may feel uneasy with such an important institution so dependent for its success on the personal qualities of an individual who occupies it temporarily. But though it is true that there are stronger presidents and weaker ones, the *institution* of the presidency has moved much more consistently in the direction of greater complexity and size, and perhaps in this respect has gained a strength of its own.

SUMMARY

The president is both the symbolic and the political head of the United States. A powerful individual, the president is responsible for the operation of the bureaucracy's agencies and employees. But the programs for which the bureaucratic machine exists are primarily the result of congressional acts. Thus bureaucrats and members of the executive branch are not answerable solely to the president who frequently finds his or her policies hampered by a triangle of administrators, special interests, and Congress.

To cope with the forces that might ally themselves

against these policies, a number of means are available to the president. The president can appoint people to, and remove them from, major posts in the executive branch, veto congressional legislation, award contracts and grants-in-aid, and locate government facilities.

The president has no lawmaking powers, but can issue executive orders, in response to congressional statutes, that have the force of law. The president may also issue pardons, reprieves, and amnesties in federal criminal cases.

Although the Vietnam War made Congress more reluctant to defer automatically to the chief executive on foreign policy issues, the president is given much more leeway in this area than in domestic policy. The support of the Constitution and the courts, the need for quick decisions in times of crisis, and the reluctance of special-interest groups and the public to meddle in international relations encourage the president to shape foreign policy according to his own plan. The war-making power of the United States is also largely in the hands of the president.

The primary role of the parties in presidential elections has been supplanted by candidate-centered politics. Those who aspire to the presidency appeal more to electoral constituencies than to parties for support, and those who contribute to a president's election or reelection receive the spoils of victory.

The president can initiate legislation by proposing a program to Congress for approval. The president's ability to get a program through the House and Senate without its being butchered is one measure of his or her success. If Congress proves unresponsive to presidential pressure, the chief executive can always make a direct appeal to the people. Use of the mass media by presidents is broader than simply a device to influence Congress. Presidents use the media to publicize and press for their programs and objectives with domestic and foreign audiences alike. A complex relationship prevails between presidents and the media involving the use by presidents of journalists to get their story told, and the need by journalists for good stories, even those that might embarrass the White House.

Because cabinet heads are increasingly prone to listen to the voices of special-interest groups, presidents have been looking to their White House staffs for unqualified loyalty. Since 1939 the Executive Office has grown dramatically. So has tension between cabinet heads and the president's key policy advisers.

The vice-president has never been invested with much power. Historically, the vice-president's most significant role has been to rally support in areas where the presidential running mate is weak.

If the vice-presidency is insignificant, the presidency is the most important office in the land. The chief executive is the official most likely to advance the public good, to resist the overtures of myopic single-issue groups, and to counteract the fragmentation of American politics by speaking with one voice.

The Constitution contains a loose definition of presidential power. The success of any president can be determined in part by the extent to which this individual takes advantage of the flexibility allowed the executive office by the Constitution. As a result, some presidents can stretch the powers of the office even to an extent that threatens the separation of powers, whereas others preside over an apparent shrinkage of executive power. These extremes have given rise to proposals to make constitutional changes. Given the ability of the institution to adapt to new challenges, these alterations are probably unnecessary.

NOTES

1. Marlin Gustafson, "Our Part-Time Chief of State," *Presidential Studies Quarterly*, 9 (Spring 1979), pp. 166–67.
2. Phil Gailey, "Poll Cites Qualities of Ideal President," *The New York Times*, (Oct. 9, 1983).
3. David S. Broder, "Drawing for Aces: Cabinet Shuffle Strengthens Carter's Political Hand," *Washington Post* (July 29, 1979).
4. 272 U.S. 52 (1927).
5. 292 U.S. 602 (1935).
6. Ruth Morgan, *The President and Civil Rights* (New York: St. Martin's, 1970), p. 5.
7. Ibid., p. 8.
8. 299 U.S. 304 (1936).
9. *Trans-Action*, 4 (Dec. 1966).

10. Kenneth N. Waltz, "Electoral Punishment and Foreign Policy Crisis," in James N. Rosenau, ed., *Domestic Sources of Foreign Policy* (New York: Free Press, 1971), pp. 272–73.
11. James MacGregor Burns, *Presidential Government* (Boston: Houghton Mifflin, 1966), p. 13.
12. Arthur M. Schlesinger, Jr., *The Imperial Presidency* (Boston: Houghton Mifflin, 1973), p. 51.
13. Henry L. Stoddard, *As I Knew Them* (New York: Harper, 1927), p. 298.
14. Carl Bernstein and Bob Woodward, *All the President's Men* (New York: Warner, 1975), p. 29.
15. Joseph A. Califano, Jr., *A Presidential Nation* (New York: Norton, 1975), p. 159.
16. Clyde Farnsworth, "Reagan Thanks Democrats," *The New York Times* (Oct. 25, 1983).
17. Clinton Rossiter, *The American Presidency* (New York: Harcourt, 1960).
18. "Just How Big is the Federal Government?" *U.S. News and World Report* (June 11, 1979), p. 57.
19. 418 U.S. 683 (1974).
20. Charles Mohr, "White House is Keeping AWACS Alive by All Means," *The New York Times* (Oct. 18, 1981).
21. Nelson W. Polsby, *Congress and the Presidency*, 3rd ed. (Englewood Cliffs, N.J.: Prentice-Hall, 1976), p. 187.
22. Robert E. DiClerico, *The American President*, 2nd ed. (Englewood Cliffs, N.J.: Prentice-Hall, 1983), p. 171.
23. Francis X. Clines, "At Reagan Press Office, It's Avoid The Negative," *The New York Times* (Oct. 28, 1983).
24. William W. Lammers, "Presidential Attention-Focusing Activities," in Doris A. Graber, ed., *The President and the Public* (Philadelphia: Institute for the Study of Human Issues, 1981), p. 168.
25. Richard F. Fenno, Jr., *The President's Cabinet* (Cambridge: Harvard U. P., 1966), p. 248.
26. Thomas E. Cronin, *The State of the Presidency* (Boston: Little, Brown, 1975), p. 232.
27. Hugh Heclo, "The Changing Presidential Office," in Arnold J. Meltsner, ed., *Politics and the Oval Office* (San Francisco: Institute for Contemporary Studies, 1981), p. 169.
28. Joseph A. Califano, Jr., *Governing America* (New York: Simon & Schuster, 1981), p. 65.
29. Lester M. Salamon and Alan J. Abramson, "Governance: The Politics of Retrenchment," in John L. Palmer and Isabel V. Sawhill, eds., *The Reagan Record* (Cambridge: Ballinger, 1984), pp. 40–41.
30. Lloyd N. Cutler, "To Form a Government," *Foreign Affairs*, 59 (Fall 1980), pp. 126–27.
31. Schlesinger, p. 417.
32. James David Barber, *The Presidential Character* (Englewood Cliffs, N.J.: Prentice-Hall, 1972).
33. Richard E. Neustadt, *Presidential Power* (New York: Wiley, 1980).

CHAPTER 11

The Federal Bureaucracy and Regulators

Holidays are difficult periods at American airports. Millions of people clog the terminals and jam the parking lots. But New Year's week of 1983 was an especially harrowing time at Miami International Airport. The combination of holiday crowds and the necessity for travelers arriving from overseas to pass through two separate inspections—one by customs agents and the other by immigration officials—resulted in passengers having to wait for periods up to four hours. After a while, however, the travelers infuriated by the delays rushed the inspection aisles and manhandled the officials. The whole episode might have been avoided if a proposal to merge the two inspections into one, which had first been made thirty years before, had been acted on by government officials.[1]

In the bewildering world of the federal government, such reforms are more easily proposed than carried out. For one thing, the U.S. Customs Service is part of the Treasury Department and is charged with ensuring that taxes are paid on imported goods and that no illegal articles or substances are brought into this country. The Immigration and Naturalization Service (INS) is located within the Justice Department and is responsible for intercepting people trying to get into the United States illegally. Getting these two functions to be performed at the same counter for the convenience of passengers is a more difficult task than you might imagine.

A compromise was proposed at one point that called for both inspection jobs to be performed by the INS, only, at the highway checkpoints on the U.S.–Canada and U.S.–Mexico borders. Customs would perform both functions at airports in the United States that handled flights from overseas. A real basis for a compromise, right? Yes, except for the fact that the deal also required the exchange of personnel between customs and INS in which the Customs Service would lose 282 people. Treasury Secretary Donald T. Regan was having none of that. An official who tried to put the

On a not-so-crowded day, members of the U.S. Customs Service inspect baggage for imported goods at John F. Kennedy International Airport in New York. *(© 1983 Robin Moyer/Black Star)*

compromise together, only to see it fall apart, lamented life in the federal bureaucracy: It's wrangling for personnel, resources, and jurisdiction. Bureaucrats won't let you change, and congressional committees won't let you change. They all want as much of the world to rule as they can. They forget the convenience of the passenger.[2]

It may be difficult for us to accept the needs of the public at large being sacrificed to bureaucratic leaders' desires not to come out on the short end of a personnel swap with another department. It is, after all, desirable for travelers to enter this country as effortlessly as possible. The first impression that a foreigner might gain of this country after waiting four hours to be processed by two government agencies is not likely to be favorable. Such an ordeal is also not a very nice "welcome home" for Americans returning from abroad. So why doesn't the president simply step in and force these warring agencies to do the right thing? These two agencies are right within the executive branch of government. Or, why doesn't Congress force them to cooperate? Congress approves the budgets of these agencies. And where are the courts in all of this? Is there any Constitutional authority to force two agencies of the federal government to cooperate with each other in the public interest?

What the framers of the Constitution would have thought of this situation can only be imagined because they included only the most ambiguous authority for the creation of a structure that now numbers 1,245 separate agencies with almost 3 million federal workers. There is only a scattering of clauses in the Constitution that applies even remotely to the administering of government policies. One simply enables the president to require the written opinions of the principal officers of the executive branch on matters under that jurisdiction.

Also relevant is the passage of Article II, section 2, which empowers the president to appoint, with the advice and consent of the Senate, . . . "all other officers of the United States, whose Appointments are not herein otherwise provided for, and which shall be established by Law." It goes on to say that "the Congress may by Law vest the Appointment of such inferior Officers, as they think proper, in the President alone, in the Courts of Law, or in the Heads of Department." Not a word appears about a Department of Education and certainly nothing about an aeronautics and space agency. As for the idea that 11,000 Americans might be teaching school overseas to the dependents of a far-flung military, it would have struck them as preposterous. Indeed, the word *bureaucracy* had not even been coined in 1789.

What Is a Bureaucracy?

Although there are many definitions of **bureaucracy,** they all seem to agree on the fact that first and foremost it is a large organization. The vast majority of people who work in this large organization are full-time individuals who are dedicated to the organization. These people are hired and promoted according to a standard of performance or expected performance. They are not elected nor are they chosen by such ascribed traits as family connections, race, religion, or social class. Finally, the work that they do is not judged by its ability to sell in some market outside the organization: the products of a bureaucracy are intangible. We might also add that bureaucracies are hierarchical; they are organized so that there is a complex chain of command from the top to bottom and a chain of reporting that tends to run from bottom to top. Bureaucrats, the individuals within this organization, are career personnel whose functions and activities are governed by rules that dictate what they can and cannot do.[3]

Our concern here is not just with any bureaucracy but with the bureaucracy of the federal government. It is a public sector bureaucracy as are those at the state and local levels, but there are private bureaucracies as well. Any sizable corporation will have one, although the bureaucratic part of a large industry may not account for most of its employees. Most of the federal bureaucracies that we will concern ourselves with in this chapter are in the executive branch.

The creation of the federal bureaucracy is a joint enterprise of the president and Congress. It is another example of the principle of checks and balances, since it is Congress that must provide the authority to set up these agencies of the executive branch, to organize them, to specify their purposes, and to pass on the qualifications of those whom the president nominates to lead them. At the same time, however, these organizations are within the president's branch of government under the terms of Article II, which places the executive power in the presidency and imposes on it the obligation to "take care that the laws be faithfully executed." But by allowing for the creation of organizations that, in effect, serve two masters, the control of both branches over the bureaucracy is often uncertain.[4]

The greatest uncertainty, perhaps, exists in the relationship between the president, who must take care to see that the laws are faithfully executed,

POLITICAL PERSPECTIVE

JUST HOW BIG IS BIG GOVERNMENT?

WASHINGTON, Nov. 22—The Federal Government is, indeed, Big Business, spending more than $91 million an hour, 24 hours a day, and handling more than $1,700 billion in receipts and outlays annually.

So says the President's Private Sector Survey on Cost Control, a panel established by President Reagan on June 30, 1982 to examine ways to increase efficiency and reduce costs of Government.

The Federal Government, according to some calculations made recently by the panel, does these things:

¶Employs 2.8 million people.

¶Purchases more than $130 billion annually in goods and services.

¶Owns one-third of the United States land mass, an estimated 744 million acres, equal to all of the states east of the Mississippi River, plus Texas.

¶Occupies 2.6 billion square feet of office space, the equivalent of all the office space in the 10 largest cities in America times four.

¶Provides $95 million subsidized meals a day.

¶Has more than 17,000 computers, 332 accounting systems and 319 payroll systems.

¶Issues 4.8 billion publications annually.

¶Delivers medical care to 47 million people.

"To effectively discharge these massive responsibilities," the report said, "the Federal Government needs a comprehensive and integrated strategy; an efficient and well-managed organizational structure; effective and responsive management systems; and competent, qualified and properly motivated employees.

Source: *The New York Times* (Nov. 23, 1983).

and the bureaucrats over whom presidential supervision must extend. The president and chief cabinet officers sometimes find themselves at odds with the bureaucrats of the executive branch and moving in quite separate directions.

These uncertain situations give us a clue to why the Customs Service and the Immigration and Naturalization Service fought each other to a standstill, and the public turned out the loser. Committees of Congress authorize these agencies to operate, appropriate money for those operations, and oversee the agencies as they carry out the operations. Members of Congress don't like to see agencies under the jurisdictions of their committees lose even 282 people. That shrinks the committee's domain. At the same time, the warring departments of Justice and Treasury can call on the help of interest groups served by them to use their influence with Congress or the White House. Sometimes, one agency clearly has stronger allies than another and forces the weaker bureaucracy to yield bureaucratic "turf." In other cases, the forces are more nearly equal and a stalemate results—in this case with adverse effects on air travelers. Sometimes, the president can do little more than stand by as a bemused observer because his or her own supporters, contributors, or constituent groups are in opposite camps.

In general, there are four reasons why the president's control over the federal bureaucracy may be shaky:

1. The president governs for a maximum of eight years and, therefore, he is impermanent. Bureaucrats, protected since 1883 by civil service laws, hold their jobs until death or retirement. There are few grounds for firing a civil servant. They are, in a very real sense, "the permanent government."

2. Civil servants do not pursue careers in the civil service in general but in a particular agency. It is unusual for a civil servant to begin a career in Agriculture and move on to Interior or State. This makes civil servants the reigning experts in highly specialized fields. They tend to be committed to particular bureaus rather than to the government per se, the executive branch, or even the president.
3. The federal bureaucracy is neutral in terms of partisan politics, but that does not mean that bureaucrats are political neuters. People are often attracted to government service by presidents whose policies they esteem. They may find, however, that they are serving under a president with whose policies they do not agree. President Eisenhower commanded a bureaucracy filled with people who had come into government service under Democratic presidents. Their careers were shaped under relatively liberal administrations, yet they were required to carry out more conservative policies. They did not always do this wholeheartedly. The situation creates conflicts for them and frustrations for the president.
4. The top bureaucrats are more familiar and comfortable with the chairs of committees of Congress that have jurisdiction over their agencies and programs and with representatives of the interest groups that are the clients of their agencies than they are with the president or presidential aides.[5]

The cumulative effect of this is the "iron triangle" phenomenon we encountered in Chapters 9 and 10, where congressional committees, bureaucrats, and interest groups band together around a policy and frustrate presidential efforts to change the policy. Some people seem to suggest that if the framers of the Constitution could have foreseen the development of a huge federal bureaucracy, they might have designed the Constitution somewhat differently. They argue that the powers held by the president under Article II are really insufficient for the president to control the bureaucracy and let it to respond to such control. They point out that the

All data gathered by Social Security—the branch of the bureaucracy that administers six income-maintenance and hospital-insurance programs, including Medicare/Medicaid—are stored on computer memory tape in a special library. *(Social Security Administration)*

mixed parentage of bureaucracies that are created by Congress (often at presidential urging), but located in the executive branch, leaves agencies open to congressional interference and enables bureaucrats to use friends in Congress and the interest groups to shield them from presidential efforts at control.[6]

Some senior bureaucrats have such strong support in Congress that any attempt by a president to remove them would create political problems for the president on Capitol Hill. One of John Kennedy's first acts as president-elect in 1960 was to announce that two such "superbureaucrats"—FBI Director J. Edgar Hoover and CIA Director Allen W. Dulles—would be kept on in their jobs. The political cost of not reappointing two officials so popular and influential in Congress would have been too great for Kennedy.

The Organization of the Federal Bureaucracy

Part of the president's problem in gaining control over the federal bureaucracy is not only its size, but that rather than being a single unit it is three distinct types of agencies: *cabinet departments; independent executive agencies;* and *independent regulatory* agencies. The president is likely to know the heads of the cabinet department rather well, since they serve in the cabinet. The president may even know some of the directors of the better-known executive agencies such as the Director of the Central Intelligence Agency, who briefs the president on intelligence matters and sits on the high-level National Security Council, but is not likely to know well, or even see very much, the five commissioners on the Federal Maritime Commission or the two cochairs of the Appalachian Regional Commission. They are appointed and can be fired by the president, but the chief executive's interest in their day-to-day activities is not very intense.

Even directors of agencies of considerable size such as the 288,000-worker Veterans Administration or the 650,000-person U.S. Postal Service rarely see the president.

We will discuss the independent regulatory agencies later in the chapter when we consider the regulatory functions of government, but we can say that these are the most peculiar cousins in the president's bureaucratic family. They are not part of any of the three major branches of government. The heads of these commissions are appointed by the president with the advice and consent of the Senate, but they do not report to the president. The president selects the chairperson, who will usually be from the president's own party, but the membership of an independent regulatory commission cannot by law be entirely composed of either all Democrats or all Republicans. The commissioners, moreover, cannot be removed by the president but serve for a fixed term of years.

Another characteristic of the organization of the federal bureaucracy that makes presidential control more difficult is that it is geographically dispersed. Of the almost 3 million employees of the executive branch, only about 10 percent actually work in Washington. Philadelphia alone boasts almost 50,000 civil servants in federal activities ranging from naval supply facilities to regional offices of the Department of Housing and Urban Development. The policies that these bureaucrats follow may be laid down in Washington, but on any given day they are more likely to be carried out in New York or San Antonio than they are in Washington. In some states like Alaska, Utah, and Oklahoma, federal employees constitute more than 3.5 percent of the nonagricultural work force. Not surprisingly, members of Congress take a special interest in these federal workers and the U.S. government facilities in which they work. The civil servants are voters and constituents and the federal facilities in which they work contribute greatly to the economies of the states and congressional districts.

Because of the size, complexity, and dispersion of the federal government, a great deal of discretion in carrying out policies must necessarily be left to bureaucrats. Such decisions can of course be overruled by appeals to citizens' elected representatives, by going to court to block such decisions or by forming associations to publicize and protest these bureaucratic decisions; but even with these checks, the ability of bureaucrats to exercise discretion in the interpretation, application, and implementation of federal policies is very great.

Characteristics of a Bureaucracy: Ideals and Reality

The sociologist Max Weber saw bureaucracy as the ultimate in rationality. Unlike more primitive forms of authority that rest on the military prowess or force of personality of a single individual or the religious or magical powers of priests or medicine men, bureaucratic organization was the ideal mechanism for dealing with the multitude of complex problems that face modern industrialized states.

With its characteristics of (1) a well-established chain of command, (2) the ability to apply rules without regard to personalities, (3) use of standard operating procedures, and (4) possession of specialized knowledge, the bureaucracy can provide the stability and predictability required for the carrying out of policies. These ideals, however, are often at variance with practice.

The carrying out of policies can often bog down in a lengthy chain of command. Rules can be applied mindlessly. Standard operating procedures can produce paperwork but no action, and expertise can be used to obstruct the implementation of a policy as easily as it can facilitate it.

There are certain features of American bureaucracy that Weber did not consider, since he did not have the United States particularly in mind. Specifically, the relationship between bureaucrats and elected and appointed political officials is one of great subtlety. The president and the people the president appoints are entrusted by the people with carrying out the policies for which they voted. To a great extent, however, their success in carrying out those policies depends upon the skill, knowledge, and expertise of the nonelected career bureaucrat. This gives the bureaucrat considerable leverage against the political official, but the political official has an important attribute that the bureaucrat lacks, and that is political legitimacy. In a political system in which ultimate power rests in the people, one way in which popular sovereignty is expressed is through elections.

In the United States, then, bureaucracies must be under political control in the same way that the military is under the civilian control of a popularly elected president. But, does this mean that both the bureaucracy and the military are simply political instruments to be used for whatever goals are sought by the party temporarily in power? Do we want to thwart those objectives of our elected officials that the bureaucrats think are wrong?

What we want is a bureaucracy that can bring to bear its ability to translate policies into action through its mastery of complex tasks, its specialized knowledge, and its impartiality. In short, we expect effectiveness. At the same time we do not want a bureaucracy that uses these skills to obstruct the policies of our elected officials, to substitute their own judgment on what is best for the judgment of those who we have elected, or to oppress us by the arbitrary and high-handed application of rules and hide behind their protected status as career officials. We want them to be responsive to us and to the people we have elected but not so much so that they become contaminated politically in the process.

Striking the proper balance between effectiveness and responsiveness in the bureaucracy is complicated by a reality that we discussed earlier in the chapter. The president, the president's appointees, and the membership of Congress cannot be looking over the shoulder of each and every civil servant to ensure that the laws they enforce and the policies they implement are being applied in a fair and reasonable manner. Leaving to the bureaucrats the responsibility for filling in the blanks and applying general principles to specific cases necessarily involves giving them a good deal of discretion. Having a bureaucrat check back with Congress or the White House on every last detail would simply be an unworkable situation. Although there are legal and political checks on bureaucratic action, they can often be used only after someone has gotten embroiled in a serious dispute. How our bureaucratic ideals of effectiveness and responsiveness work in light of the reality of bureaucratic discretion can be seen in the box entitled: "The Regulator and the Calculator."

Within the limits laid down for them by Congress, federal bureaucrats do have considerable authority. As we pointed out in Chapter 9, senators and House representatives cannot oversee the daily operations of the agencies they create or the programs that these agencies are authorized to execute. Often, the manner in which bureaucrats perform their legal tasks is not the subject of universal approval. Expecting bureaucrats at the same time to be impartial, responsive, and efficient may be unrealistic. There are clearly tensions between what we expect of bureaucrats and what they can reasonably deliver.

The Evolution of the Federal Bureaucracy

How did it happen that an institution barely mentioned in the Constitution has managed to establish itself as what is, in fact, a Fourth Branch of Government?

The bureaucracy under the first six presidents grew in a more or less haphazard fashion until, in the 1820s, it numbered slightly more than 7,000 individuals.

The bureaucracy during this period was essentially an elite corps of better-educated people whose views were more or less in accord with the party in power. As more frontier territories were brought into the union, the upper-crust character of the employees of the executive branch became something of a sore point. When Andrew Jackson, the first president who was a product of the frontier, came to office in 1828, he was determined to change this situation.

Jackson's "Spoils System"

Jackson was a firm believer in the principles set forth by his ally, Senator William Learned Marcy, that, "to the victor belong the spoils." The **spoils system** means giving out public jobs or contracts to those who are politically loyal to you, rather than on the basis of merit.[7] Jackson also reformed the

POLITICAL PERSPECTIVE

THE REGULATOR AND THE CALCULATOR

There is a small firm in Northbrook, Illinois, called JS&A, which manufactures pocket calculators and markets them through advertisements in newspapers so that consumers can order them by mail. In January 1979 a dual calamity befell JS&A. A huge snowstorm struck Northbrook, and most of its people were snowbound at home including almost all of JS&A's employees. At the same time, the firm's computers broke down. Together, the two disasters made it impossible for JS&A to fill their mail orders for calculators.

The Federal Trade Commission (FTC) was given the power by Congress to protect consumers from fraud and has jurisdiction over mail-order firms that ship their products between states. Like many other regulatory agencies set up by Congress, the FTC was given a broad delegation of authority. Congress said, in effect, to the FTC when it was set up: Your general power is to protect consumers from unscrupulous businesses. The particular way you go about doing this is left to you, subject to our oversight. Over the years, the FTC had made a rule that stated that anyone paying for a mail-order item by check must receive the product within 30 days or be notified and allowed to cancel the order.

JS&A was falling behind in filling its orders because of the blizzard and computer malfunction, and some buyers complained to the FTC, which slapped a $100,000 fine on JS&A for not meeting the 30-day deadline. Fearing that the costs of fighting the fine in the courts would be too costly, JS&A's president, Joseph Sugarman, attempted to settle the case by paying a lesser amount in fines. The FTC demanded that JS&A sign a "consent decree," a tacit admission of wrongdoing. The company's president argued that no one had really suffered any damages and that the calculators would all be mailed. He decided to fight the fine despite the large legal costs involved.

Were the FTC bureaucrats doing their job in the JS&A case? It would appear that they were on solid ground in carrying out the letter of the law. But what about its spirit? Was JS&A really trying to defraud the public? Our reaction was that it wasn't. But what if the FTC people had said, "Let's make an exception in the case of good old Joe Sugarman." What kind of rating would we give them for impartiality and effectiveness? Sugarman took his case to the public and to political officials in a series of pamphlets called "JS&A/FTC Battle Reports." He appealed to Congressman John D. Dingell of the House Subcommittee on Oversight and Investigations and to Vice-President George Bush. Would we feel better about the episode if the FTC backed off under political pressure or if they resisted the pressure and refused to treat JS&A as a special case? If the FTC officials were fired or reassigned, would we rejoice and feel uneasy that next time the bureaucrats would be less energetic about protecting us against genuinely fraudulent advertising?

When Andrew Jackson instituted the "spoils system" in 1829, it was a worthy reform that allowed humble citizens to vie with the better-educated and the wealthier for jobs in the federal bureaucracy. *(Library of Congress)*

bureaucracy through political selection of administrators. This enabled Jackson to reward those who were his political allies and to hold out to others the prospect of a job in return for future support. Since political faithfulness was the only test for a job applicant, humble citizens could vie for jobs and stand at least as good a chance of getting one as a person of wealth.

Parties seeking loyal supporters found the new system delightful. If 7,000 political payoffs were good, double that number was even better. By the time Jackson left office, this had come to pass. The Whig party that came to power in 1841 showed itself no less eager to take advantage of this political innovation.

All manner of jobs were available to reward the faithful. The extent of these political resources in a single city on the eve of the Civil War gives some indication of how many people might be deployed on behalf of a political party:

> In New York City and Brooklyn were the customhouse, two post offices, and the navy yard. The size of the port required many employees at the customhouse; and its system of bonded warehouses meant numerous carters and freight handlers . . . were susceptible to political influence. The post offices handled tremendous quantities of foreign and domestic mail; therefore their clerks were almost legion. Also their revenues were immense, and the postmaster upon occasion might loan some of them for party purposes between quarterly accounting periods.
>
> The navy yard had fifteen hundred civilian employees under a dozen or so master workmen. Each of the city Congressmen was allotted some of these foremen, who in turn employed laborers capable of showing some political enthusiasm. At election time employees were excused for party duties, and additional men were taken on as a reward for loyalty or as an inducement to political labor. Supplies were purchased from generous campaign contributors, and this item at the Brooklyn Navy Yard was tremendous.[8]

As Whigs and Democrats alternated in the presidency, the rotation in office that Jackson desired came to pass. So effective was the rotation, in fact, that when a Democrat of one faction occupied the White House he often ousted members of a rival Democratic faction and replaced them with his own loyalists.

Some jobs were considered "plums"; others were more menial. In the latter category were those that came to be filled by women. These jobs, typically, were "copyist" positions in the U.S. Patent Office. In the days before the photocopier, it was necessary to make duplicates by hand. This was a time-consuming job that was considered "women's work." Other women were employed in the same department making two-dimensional renderings of models that had been submitted for patenting. When the Civil War broke out, many women, who wanted to be close to their husbands or male friends, flocked to Washington, which was the staging area for the Union Army. These jobs, menial as they were, enabled the women to maintain themselves in the wartime capital.*

*For a fuller treatment of the origins of female employment in the federal government, see: Ross K. Baker, "Entry of Women into the Federal Job World—At a Price," *The Smithsonian,* 8 (July 1977), pp. 82–91.

The Civil War swelled the federal work force to almost 37,000 in 1861. With the cost of the war running to $1.5 million a day and with the men under arms nearing a million, a huge supporting bureaucracy was needed. To deal with War Department contracts alone required a huge work force. The Civil War established a precedent: when the nation faced a grave danger—either domestic or foreign—power tended to flow to Washington, and power flowing to Washington meant, by extension, that it flowed to a bureaucracy that swelled to meet the challenge.

The problem was that no one gave this trend much thought. It was somehow simply assumed that government could operate more or less as it had in Jackson's day. The logic of Jackson's spoils system, however, was being increasingly undermined by the realities created by the war and its aftermath. For one thing, the noble objective of rotation in office became increasingly irrelevant inasmuch as the Republicans totally dominated post-Civil War national politics. Within the party itself the so-called "stalwart" wing controlled patronage. Anxious to maintain the incredible profits from government contracts that had prevailed during the war, unscrupulous businesspeople struck corrupt deals with government officials. High officials of the Grant administration actually auctioned off well-paying government jobs to the highest bidder. As the price for a position as an Indian Agent at Fort Sill, Oklahoma, Secretary of War William Belknap had a trader pay Mrs. Belknap $12,000 annually.[9]

The Pressure for Reform

Pressure began to build in the late 1860s for some kind of federal **civil service,** a system of hiring government employees on the basis of merit or qualifications rather than political loyalty. Throughout the 1870s, reformers tried desperately to get Congress to pass a civil service law, but members of Congress were reluctant to give up this valuable political resource, for they too had patronage to give out. It was typical for a president to participate in the doling out of jobs with cooperative members of Congress and also to "clear" with them the names of nominees for federal posts in their states or congressional districts. It was a system that benefited many people, but the public as a whole became increasingly unhappy with a federal bureaucracy that had become a sinkhole of corruption.

The quest for comfortable, well-paying federal jobs grew quite hectic, and it was the act of one who failed to get a federal job that demonstrated dramatically that the system had to be changed.

On July 2, 1881, President James A. Garfield on his way to a college reunion was shot and mortally wounded by an unsuccessful job applicant. The death of Garfield three months later accelerated the campaign for reform, and in 1883, Garfield's successor, Chester A. Arthur, signed into law the Pendleton Act creating a civil service based on merit. From this point on, most federal jobs were awarded on the basis of performance in a competitive examination. Civil servants would also be virtually immune from being removed from their jobs solely for political reasons, and federal civil service was organized on a nonpartisan basis.

Government was developing to match the developments in the private sector, but its growth was not merely in size; the functions and scope of

After the assassination of President Garfield in 1881 by a disappointed job applicant, President Chester A. Arthur (shown here) helped create our modern civil service system, based on merit rather than patronage. *(UPI)*

One of the reasons for the growth of the federal bureaucracy has been the increased interdependence of local and national economies. Here, a group of turkeys has been placed under quarantine by the U.S. Department of Agriculture and the state of Pennsylvania in an effort to protect this food source against the fatal avian flu virus. *(© Tom Kelly)*

government were also expanding as cries from discontented groups began to be heard in regard to price gouging by railroads and operators of grain storage facilities, restrictive money policies, and the corruption of the civil service. These protestors, like many in later years, were turning to the federal government for action because there was nowhere else to turn. A national economy in which states and regions were becoming more interdependent meant that problems that had once been handled locally or not at all had to be addressed nationally.

The Growth of Bureaucratic Power

Where government is limited in what it does and restricts itself to such activities as it did in the time of Thomas Jefferson, it has little need for large bureaucracies. For the first 100 years of our federal government, the concept of **limited government** was well established. Thomas Paine referred to government as a "necessary evil." What government did in the early nineteenth century did not exceed by much the literal commandments of the Constitution: defense, tax collection, coining money, delivering mail, tak-

The transition from limited government to positive government has expanded the federal bureaucracy to almost unmanageable proportions. (*Illustration by Reg Manning. Reprinted with permission of* The Arizona Republic.)

ing the census, and meting out justice. That government would, 175 years hence, be setting standards for the amount of lead in house paint or that one-third of all Americans would be receiving monthly payments from the federal government, would have been situations beyond the comprehension of Jefferson or Paine (see Table 11.1).

History overtook the limited government concept and replaced it with the notion of **positive government**—a government that actively intervenes to protect, regulate, set standards, and otherwise smooth out the conditions of the lives of the citizens. (Chapter 16 gives a fuller discussion of the concepts of positive government and limited government.) The transition from limited government to positive government—the result of world wars, depressions, scientific innovations, and changes in popular attitudes as to the proper role of government—has brought bureaucracy along in its wake. To say that government ought to tackle a problem is to say that the bureaucracy should be expanded.

Congress, as we have seen, was unwilling and unable to write detailed laws containing specific guidelines for bureaucratic behavior or to involve itself on a daily basis in the actual implementation of the policies it enacted. It delegated these responsibilities to bureaucrats but provided them with little specific direction on how to carry out these policies. Decisions, for

TABLE 11.1 Breakdown of Benefits

	Monthly Recipients (in thousands)	Percent of Population
Those who received benefits from one or more programs	66,454	29.0
Social Security	31,710	14.1
Medicare	26,711	11.9
Veterans' compensation and pensions	4,622	2.1
Education assistance	3,624	1.6
Unemployment compensation	3,040	1.4
Railroad retirement	759	0.3
Workers' compensation	702	0.3
Those who benefitted from one or more means-tested programs*	42,061	18.8
Food stamps	18,662	8.3
Medicaid	17,508	7.8
Aid to Families with Dependent Children	9,323	4.2
Public or subsidized rental housing	8,465	3.8
Federal Supplemental Security Income	3,205	1.4
Women's-Infant-Children Nutrition Program	2,429	1.1
Other cash assistance	2,311	1.0

Source: U.S. Census Bureau, 1983.

Note: Nearly 30 percent of the U.S. population is receiving benefits from federal programs.
*Awarded on the basis of total assets.

example, on whether the freight rates charged by a railroad were "fair and reasonable" or the decision to destroy a state's cattle herds because they were infected with hoof-and-mouth disease were essentially political questions. The very vagueness of the standards set down by Congress to guide the behavior of bureaucrats added greatly to their political power. Certain bureaucrats now enjoy powers that the Supreme Court has dubbed "quasi legislative," and in a series of cases the Court gave its approval to the delegation by Congress of considerable policymaking discretion to bureaucrats even when the standards were vague.*

Beginning in the late 1920s, members of Congress became concerned about giving so much discretion to the bureaucrats and, as we saw in Chapter 10, began to use the legislative veto. The Supreme Court ruling in the *Chadha* case (see Chapter 9) may mean that Congress will have to spell out its intentions more clearly and use tools such as oversight more aggressively.

Governmental Regulation: Symbol of Bureaucratic Power

Perhaps no activity so clearly symbolizes positive government and bureaucratic power as does regulation. Not every bureaucrat regulates, and not every agency of the executive branch has regulatory functions, but the granting to nonelected government employees the power to make rules that have the force of law, to make a determination as to whether an individual or corporation is complying with those rules, and to enforce those rules constituted a major change in the way American government worked. These three regulatory functions of *rule making, rule adjudication,* and *rule enforcement* must legally come from a grant of power from Congress, but Congress has usually given regulatory bureaucracies a good deal of latitude in what they do.

Government regulation was not always a function of the federal government. As Theodore Lowi has written:

> Between 1795 and 1887 the key Federal policies were tariffs, internal improvements, land sales, and land grants, development of a merchant fleet and coastal shipping, the post offices, patents and copyrights, and research on how the private sector was doing.[10]

The "Revolution" of 1887: Creation of the ICC

The year 1887 marked the beginning of a revolution as profound, in many ways, as the decision 100 years before to establish a three-branch federal government. The revolution of 1887 did not establish what amounted to a fourth branch but accelerated the trend in that direction. What Congress did that year in the creation of the Interstate Commerce Commission (ICC) was to admit, in effect, that it could not oversee, on a day-to-day basis, the transportation industries, which had produced so many abuses. It delegated this function to an administrative agency (the ICC), which was cre-

*See *U.S.* v. *Rock Royal Cooperative,* 307 U.S. 533 (1939), and *U.S.* v. *Darby,* 312 U.S. 100 (1941).

ated specifically for the purpose of regulating certain aspects on interstate commerce.

The mandate that the Congress gave to the members of the ICC in 1887 was that they go about their regulatory duties so that what they did responded to "public convenience and necessity." The ideal in this was that certain important decisions be transferred from the highly political arena of congressional politics into the newly cleansed area of the civil service. These important decisions would be made by "experts" who would exercise discretion in making them within legal boundaries set forth by Congress.

The ICC was a modest beginning by government in the area of regulation and it was not quickly duplicated. Early in the twentieth century a furor developed over conditions in the meat-packing industry as the result of some sensational exposés by Upton Sinclair and other reformers. Some scholars give a good deal of credit to Theodore Roosevelt for the law requiring mandatory inspections of meat. According to one interpretation, Roosevelt was instrumental in forcing Congress to pass the measure over the objections of the meat-packing industry.

Other scholars argue that the meat-packing industry, or at least the larger members, not only welcomed regulation but worked actively to achieve it. The large meat packers could afford to implement government sanitary standards if they were imposed, whereas the smaller meat packers could not. Unable to meet the standards, they would be forced out of business, leaving the big packers with a larger share of the market. According to this interpretation, then, government regulation would have the effect of limiting competition.[11]

A similar theory has been put forth to explain the creation of the Federal Reserve System. In this case small banks who were operating on a shoestring were seen as damaging the reputation of the industry with slipshod practices. The big banks saw regulation by the federal government as cleaning up the banking business but also driving out small competitors.

But public pressure and industry's desire to restrict competition were not the only sources of demands for regulation; pressure from within the government itself was also a factor in some cases. It came not only from reformer presidents, such as Theodore Roosevelt and Woodrow Wilson, but from within the bureaucracy.

Bureaucrats wanting to extend their authority also pressed for regulation and inspection. An Agriculture Department chemist named Harvey W. Wiley assembled a coalition of interest groups—grocers, dairymen, brewers, and candymakers—who were concerned with deceptive food labeling. Wiley and his allies drafted, and lobbied for passage of the bill that ultimately established the Food and Drug Administration. Wiley's reward was the directorship of the new Board of Food and Drug Inspection.[12]

Regulation—A Dangerous Trend?

Some conservatives saw danger signals in the regulatory powers of the federal government. Some opposed government intervention on principle, saying that it interfered with the free operation of markets and tampered with the laws of supply and demand. Others had very specific problems with the practice of the government's setting rates and standards for industries. They feared that it would lead to a situation in which regulatory decisions would be made for political reasons. In arguing against the Hepburn Rate Bill, which expanded the rate-setting power of the ICC, Congressman Samuel C. McCall (R-Mass.) warned that "With the Government fixing rates, constituencies would inevitably carry their grievances into politics . . . [and] you will have the different parts of the country knocking at the door of the National Government for favors. . . .[13]

The fear of conservatives that the regulatory process would become tangled up with politics quickly was borne out. Understaffed regulatory agencies often became dependent for information on the industries that they were charged with regulating. Once a regulatory agency was established—especially one that industry itself had called for—industry members were not content to sit back and leave the business of regulating to civil servants.

When presidents nominated members to the ICC—and the other regulatory agencies as well—the regulated industries developed a virtual veto power over these appointees.

Regulated industries would use their considerable influence on Capitol Hill to ensure that only those commissioners who would see the industry's point of view were confirmed. The industries would provide political resources to members of Congress to ensure their cooperation. Commission members were given incentives to "behave" in the form of jobs with the

The unseen holders of the reins in this cartoon are the industries that are supposed to be regulated but actually exert considerable control over the federal regulators. *(From Herblock's Special for Today [Simon & Schuster, 1958].)*

regulated industries when they left office. The process was even more neatly executed when the regulators were actually recruited from the ranks of the regulated industries.

The constituencies of regulatory agencies are not merely the industries they regulate. The ICC's constituency network includes, for example, the International Brotherhood of Teamsters, one of this country's largest independent unions. It is composed of truck drivers and warehouseworkers employed by the regulated trucking companies.

Along with the railroads and the unions of engineers and trainmen are the barge industry and the unions of watermen who crew the barges, and the pipeline industry and the oil workers' unions whose operations are also under the jurisdiction of the ICC. All of these groups have their own friends in Congress who oversee the ICC.

The Development of Regulatory Agencies

The creation of regulatory agencies came in a series of waves: the first from the end of the 1880s to the time of the first World War, the second in the period immediately after the Great Depression, and the third in the 1960s and 1970s. The first two waves arose out of abuses in particular industries. They were sometimes created as much out of businesspeople's concern for imposing some semblance of order or regularity on their industries, sometimes as the result of public outcries for protection against the excesses of business, and sometimes from pressure from within the government itself. Moreover, the regulatory agencies created during the New Deal era tended to be "initiated by particular groups to deal with specific evils as they arose, rather than inspired by any general philosophy of government control."*

The most recent wave of regulation began in the 1960s and was directed principally at social problems such as job discrimination against minorities, health hazards in the work place, the safety and fitness of consumer products, and threats to the environment. The wave of social regulations grew in the 1970s when such targets as ensuring equality of educational opportunity for women and racial minorities was added along with equal access to public facilities for the handicapped.

The decisions to involve the federal government in these areas were made by the top-level policymakers: the president, the Congress, and, on occasion, the courts. The actual carrying out of the day-to-day enforcement or application of these top-level decisions were left to bureaucrats. It was inevitable because the expansion of the scope of government in its movement into new areas of activity does not multiply the number of House members and senators or give rise to a demand for a dozen assistant presidents. It does, however, create new bureaucracies and hosts of civil servants to carry out the mandates of the top policymakers. The powers of these bureaucrats are considerable, and in a very real sense their powers are as political as those of the Congress or the president.

*See Marver H. Bernstein, *Regulating Business by Independent Commission* (Princeton: Princeton U. P., 1955).

Environmental regulations are important safeguards against air pollution and toxic wastes. Those who take the position that all regulation is an economic burden on industry overlook the value of regulation to protect the lives and health of our citizens regardless of the economic costs. (*Illustration by Bennett for* The Fayetteville Times.)

From Regulation to Deregulation By the mid-1970s the debate over regulation took on a new tone when economists pointed to the inflationary impact of **economic regulation,** such as the kind that was applied to the railroads in the freight rates and schedules they were required to maintain. The airline industry was a particularly glaring example of regulation adding to inflation. The Civil Aeronautics Board (CAB) told airlines what cities they had to serve, how many flights they could schedule, and how much they could charge for tickets. In exchange, the CAB limited the number of airlines and set minimum prices for tickets.

The reason this kind of regulation fueled inflation was that the customer could no longer shop around for the best price for a ticket. The CAB required United, TWA, and American Airlines to charge identical fares from New York to Chicago and airlines were reduced to competing over who had the best snacks or the most polite cabin attendants.

Similar regulations pushed up the cost of shipping by truck by requiring that trucks return empty to their point of origin after dropping off their loads. The FCC also had the power to permit applicants a trucking license or deny it.

Beginning with President Ford in 1975, presidents tried to curb this kind of mindless regulation. In 1978, President Carter's Executive Order 12044 tightened White House control over regulators within the executive branch. President Reagan took deregulation a giant step further by requiring that all regulatory agencies in the executive branch, not independent regulatory agencies, to submit **cost-benefit analyses** for every major regulation they proposed (see a listing of those regulatory agencies in the executive branch and the independent regulatory agencies in Table 11.2). Cost-benefit analysis is a calculation that balances the benefits that come from a regulation against the costs of implementing it. These analyses would then be submitted to the office of Management and Budget (OMB).

TABLE 11.2 Major Federal Regulatory Agencies

Independent	Executive Branch
Consumer Product Safety Commission	Drug Enforcement Administration (Justice Department)
Equal Employment Opportunity Commission	National Highway Traffic Safety Administration (Transportation Department)
Federal Communications Commission	Occupational Safety and Health Administration (Labor Department)
Food and Drug Administration	National Oceanographic and Atmospheric Administration (Commerce Department)
Federal Deposit Insurance Corporation	Wage and Hour Administration (Labor Department)
Interstate Commerce Commission	

Note: The independent regulatory agencies are the most peculiar cousins in the president's bureaucratic family. They are not part of any of the three major branches of government. The heads of these commissions are appointed by the president with the advice and consent of the Senate, but they do not report to the president. The president selects the chairperson, who will usually be from the president's own party, but the membership of an independent regulatory commission cannot by law be entirely composed of either all Democrats or all Republicans. The commissioners, moreover, cannot be removed by the president but serve for a fixed term of years.

President Reagan wanted Congress to acquiesce in his proposal to extend the cost-effectiveness screening by OMB to *all* regulatory agencies. Congress balked for two reasons. First, members of Congress knew that Americans wanted protection of their air and water and safety and health whether or not it was cost effective. Second, they did not want to turn over such sweeping powers to OMB. The White House decided not to press ahead with this proposal in the face of congressional opposition and turned to the more traditional approach of appointing regulators who shared the president's views and who would enforce the rules in a manner in keeping with his philosophy.

On January 1, 1985, the existence of the Civil Aeronautics Board came to an end after forty-six years. Pictured above is the last board meeting, presided over by the chairman, the vice-chairman, and a Marine Corps honor guard. *(AP/Wide World Photos)*

To Deregulate or Not to Deregulate There have been winners and losers with deregulation, and some of the losers did not anticipate the consequences of the process when it began. Deregulation of the airline industry allowed for the entry into the market of cut-rate airlines such as People Express. Competition for the air traveler's dollar has forced more established airlines to cut fares to compete. Some critics of the industry have charged that airlines will cut back on the maintenance and repair of aircraft to reduce costs and to make themselves more competitive with the cut-rate carriers. These carriers are often nonunion companies that have lower labor costs. Some airlines have simply gone out of business in response to the pressures of competition. Others have eliminated some towns from their routes because the CAB can no longer tell them where to fly. So for those who are concerned about airline safety more than the price of the ticket or who come from a town cut off from air service, deregulation is certainly a mixed blessing.

Political Fragmentation and Bureaucratic Power

The legacy of political fragmentation handed down to us by the framers of the Constitution and their obsession not to put too much power in any one set of hands provided the ground rules in which bureaucracy, once established, could thrive. Both separation of powers among the three branches of the national government and the division of powers between the states and national government—the system of federalism—were insurance against the concentration of power. The authors of the Constitution could not have foreseen that the system they established in the interests of limiting the scope of government has had the ironic effect of providing the preconditions for its expansion.

But the formal fragmentation of power could not alone have produced the bureaucratic growth of recent years. The evolution of Congress as an institution played a major role. In the early days Congress was less specialized than it is now, and both houses would take up bills that had not been scrutinized by experts. When it became clear that Congress as a whole could not possibly consider in detail every piece of legislation, specialized committees were established. Citizens with interests in legislation, then, could target their efforts very efficiently on a single committee in the knowledge that members of both houses respected the specialized knowledge of the committees and were likely to follow their recommendations. With the growth of formal interest groups, lobbying could be directed to individual committee members. As congressional power was dispersed even more to the subcommittees, policy areas became still more fragmented and legislative expertise more specialized.

When Congress began, in the late nineteenth century, to delegate policy decisions to bureaucrats, interest groups promptly recognized that they would have to diversify their activities to include not only the committees and subcommittees that wrote the laws but the bureaucrats who enforced them. If bureaucrats were given discretion by Congress in carrying out its general policies, interest groups wanted that discretion to work in their favor.

The Revolving Door Process

One way of ensuring that federal bureaucracies were sympathetic to industries within the jurisdiction of a federal agency was to influence the makeup of an agency's leadership.

We saw how this worked in the case of members of independent regulatory commissions who are nominated by the president with the advice and consent of the Senate and then serve for a term of years. Regulated industries not only strongly influence the choice of regulatory personnel (play a major role in clearing regulatory personnel before confirmation) but also tend to hire these same people after they leave government service. In this **revolving door process,** regulatory personnel who a short time before were making rules to regulate industry showed up before the same agencies on which they had served, pleading the case of regulated industries as lawyers and lobbyists.

Defense Contracting

The revolving door phenomenon does not merely affect those bureaucrats with regulatory duties. In fact, it can often be seen most clearly in agencies without regulatory functions such as the Department of Defense, where retired military personnel take jobs with defense contractors who are only too happy to hire ex-officers because they know the ins-and-outs of the Pentagon. They have many friends there whom they have made in twenty years or more of military service and can easily get access to them. Officers with an eye toward retirement may favor a particular company with a contract worth billions of dollars and shortly thereafter go on the payroll of that company.

This, of course, raises serious questions about whether our armed forces are getting the best possible equipment with which to defend us or whether the decision to acquire one weapon over another is based on cronyism and what is know as "the buddy system."

Defense contractors are politically astute and always ensure that members of Congress will not be prompted to object. The Navy's F-18 fighter, for example, has components made in 44 states. This means that 88 senators and a substantial number of House members will have constituents working on the F-18. If there are problems with the quality of the plane—even serious ones—these members will be less apt to raise objections for fear that the cancellation of the project will lead to the loss of jobs among voters in their states and districts. When Congressman Thomas Downey, who represents a district on New York's Long Island, began to probe the quality and effectiveness of the F-18, colleagues quickly accused him of sour grapes because not only did no factory in his district have a contract for F-18 parts, but one of the largest employers there had been a competitor to the company that became the prime contractor.

The president, then, may be commander-in-chief and provide overall direction of military policy, but many of the important decisions on how that policy is carried out, and with which military tools, are left to contract

"AT LAST! A WEAPONS SYSTEM ABSOLUTELY IMPERVIOUS TO ATTACK: IT HAS COMPONENTS MANUFACTURED IN ALL 435 CONGRESSIONAL DISTRICTS!"

By John Trever, *The Albuquerque Journal.*
Reprinted by permission of News America Syndicate.

officers and procurement personnel at the Pentagon who may choose one company over another for personal and even self-serving reasons. They will be supported in these decisions by members of Congress who may benefit either by the infusion of jobs into their states and districts or by the campaign contributions of contractors. The "iron triangle" composed of industries, bureaucrats of the executive branch, and members of Congress can often make policies quite different from, and even opposed to, what the president might prefer.

The bureaucracy's external relations with the two other sides of its triangle are a source of great bureaucratic power. It is a relationship of great mutual advantage to the other partners. Government bureaus provide goods and services to organized interest groups, but they need resources to do so. The committees of Congress provide those resources, but they need political support to have their way in Congress, and this is provided by the interest groups. The interest groups need the goods and services that the bureaucracy provides so that they can satisfy their members. What results is a closed system that can operate apart from politics. It operates best, however, out of the glare of publicity and away from the attention of the general public. Once attention becomes focused on the policy that ties the subsystem together, it becomes more difficult to satisfy each member's needs.*

*See Randall B. Ripley and Grace A. Franklin, *Congress: the Bureaucracy and Public Policy*, rev. ed. (Homewood, Ill.: Dorsey, 1980), pp. 94–119.

The Internal Sources of Bureaucratic Power

We have seen how the bureaucracy and its allies in Congress and the interest groups manage to capture important policy decisions from the president, but these sources of political support outside the bureaucracy itself are only a part of the enormous power enjoyed by civil servants. There are distinct advantages that support bureaucratic power that flow from the very nature of bureaucracies themselves.

Expertise as a Source of Power

One of the principal reasons for the growth of government bureaucracy in the United States is that this country is a very complex place. Bureaucracy is, in a very real sense, government's response to growing complexity. When complexity created problems and the intervention of government was demanded, its response was to set up a bureaucracy to deal with that specialized problem. As we have seen, the problems that developed with the railroads resulted in a regulatory bureaucracy (the ICC), which required the services of economists who knew something about freight rates. The creation of the Food and Drug Administration to safeguard the public against tainted meat and bogus medicines called forth the need for chemists, pathologists, and pharmacologists. The advent of modern wars and periods of international tensions produced a defense establishment replete with physicists, weapons experts, aeronautical engineers, intelligence analysts, and cryptographers.

Bureaucracies are highly differentiated one from the other. The Department of Agriculture might boast hundreds of soil chemists but have no one who knows one end of a recoilless rifle from another. The Defense Department certainly has lots of recoilless rifle experts but no one who knows anything about the soil acidity level required for the proper cultivation of soybeans. The various bureaucracies, then, are mines of specialized knowledge.

The various bureaucracies are mines of specialized knowledge. Here, a soil chemist from the Department of Agriculture is shown giving information to farmers in rural Nebraska. *(Soil Conservation Service /USDA)*

It is not unusual to find that a civil servant within a government bureaucracy is the outstanding expert in a single area. No president or even 535 members of Congress with all of their staffs can compete with the specialized and detailed knowledge of the federal bureaucracy.

In 1975, for example, Senator Edward Kennedy became concerned over the amount of lead in oil-based house paints. He had received reports that children in Boston had eaten chips of paint that had fallen from ceilings or had chewed on woodwork that had been finished with paints high in lead content and had suffered brain damage. The prevailing maximum for lead content in house paint in 1975 was 0.5 percent. Kennedy demanded that the maximum be 0.06 percent. No one in the U.S. Senate wanted little children to suffer brain damage, but there was opposition to Kennedy's proposal for economic reasons. It was pointed out, for example, that a standard of 0.06 percent would virtually eliminate oil-based paint and drive out of business the farmers who raised flax for linseed oil.

But Kennedy was adamant. He wanted the more stringent standard. The members and staff of the Committee on Human Resources, however, did not know enough about paint to make an intelligent judgment, so they turned the matter over to a regulatory bureaucracy, the Consumer Product Safety Commission, to conduct tests and to make the decision that the Senate did not have enough knowledge to make. The issue of whether or not to ban lead-based paint was also a political hot potato that senators preferred to avoid.

It follows from an example such as this that the bureaucracy has knowledge and expertise not available to our elected representatives, who have neither the time nor the inclination to familiarize themselves with such details as the properties of house paint. This specialized knowledge gives the bureaucrats protection against the politicians who might try to control them. Bureaucrats were most useful to the politicians here, since they could turn this controversial issue over to them and let experts take the heat if the public was aroused by the decision.

How does it happen that bureaucrats are better able to master information and expertise than members of Congress? For one thing, they are simply better specialists. Despite Congress's own efforts at specialization in the committee system, a member's attention is spread over several committee and subcommittee assignments, the necessity to attend to needs of constituents, and the political problems in states and districts related to the member's reelection. Although members have personal staff and committee staff at their disposal and can draw on the services of the Congressional Research Service of the Library of Congress, the General Accounting Office, the Congressional Budget Office, and the Office of Technology Assessment, the amount of this staff support is miniscule when compared to the numbers of bureaucrats assigned to particular policies and programs.[14]

The Language of Bureaucracy If the functions of bureaucrats are specialized, so is their language. As Ralph Hummel has said, the function of **bureaucratese** (the language of bureaucrats) is to make outsiders feel powerless. Superficially, bureaucratese resembles English but is loaded with jargon.[15] In the box on page 396 you will see one of the authors' attempts to translate the Declaration of Independence into bureaucratese. Compare it to the original of the Declaration in the Appendix. But even that parody is lucid prose compared to one Pentagon bureaucrat's version of the jargon used to sell military programs on Capitol Hill:

> We go to Congress and tell them that our WWMCCS has got to have a BMEWS upgrade, our fuzzy sevens have to be replaced by PAVE PAWS, we want to keep PARCS and DEW in operation, we have to harden the NEACP, and we have to improve our MEECN with more TACMO and begin planning to replace AFSATCOM with Triple-S.[16]

The effect of the use or misuse of such language on Congress and the clients of bureaucrats is to further strengthen the hand of the bureaucrat in his or her dealings with them.

Rules, Routines, and Red Tape as a Source of Power

Recruits entering the U.S. Army are usually told during the course of basic training that there are three ways to do something: the right way, the wrong way, and the Army way. According to this logic, then, it is possible to do something "right" and still have it be "wrong" because it is not done according to the formula prescribed by the Army. What is right or wrong can often be disputed; what can never be disputed are Army regulations. The same can be said for the rules and **standard operating procedures** that lay out the precise way to perform a task that bureaucrats can rarely depart from.

The rules are usually simple enough to facilitate easy learning and unambiguous application. Since procedures are "standard," they do not change quickly or easily. Without such standard procedures, it would not be possible to perform certain concerted tasks. But because of them, organizational behavior in particular instances appears unduly formalized, sluggish, and often inappropriate.[17]

The reasons for these procedures is to limit as much as possible the discretion of bureaucrats in such things as imposing a fine on a mail-order house for failure to deliver calculators when it was obvious that the company could not be held responsible for an act of God.

By establishing these procedures, however, the bureaucracy is given the power to change drastically the pace and effect of decisions made by policymakers. The bureaucrat is charged with the implementation of decisions made by presidents and cabinet members who want their decisions carried out rapidly. This conflicts with the need for bureaucrats to operate according to established procedures, a practice that usually takes a great deal of time. Sometimes the pace at which bureaucrats carry out presidential policies amounts to outright defiance of a president's will.

On some occasions there is a head-on clash between presidents and bureaucrats, such as when President Nixon ordered American diplomats to cease visiting Americans who were jailed in foreign countries on drug-related charges. They simply ignored Nixon's order and continued to make the visits.

This suggests that the standard operating procedures of a bureaucracy

POLITICAL PERSPECTIVE

WHY JEFFERSON FAINTED

Following is an executive summary of a declaration of independence as it has surfaced after having been signed off on by all of the appropriate bureaus, agencies and departments of the Continental Congress.

When at a given point in time in the human events cycle, the phase-out of political relationships is mandated, a clear signal needs to be communicated to the world as to why we are putting independence on-line.

Truthwise, it has been apparent for some time that human resources should be accorded equal treatment and that they are eligible for certain entitlements, that among them are viability, liberty and the capability of accessing happiness.

That, to secure this package of benefits, governments are normally established, but only after adequate levels of citizen participation.

If that government begins to impact adversely on the citizens, it is their right to modify the entire structure and come up with a new set of options that will have a significant positive effect. Governments can usually hold the line when they are counterproductive or even when they tilt toward tyranny. Citizens will typically not phase-out governments over issues that are on the margins. But when a picture begins to emerge of a government that wants to go forward with a program of despotism, there is a clear mandate to terminate that government and to begin long-range planning for the out-years.

These Colonies have engaged in flexible dialogue with the Government of Great Britain, but the latest set of guidelines to emerge from London does not seem workable. The track record of the current King is one that is chronically in a state of noncompliance. The data to support these charges are presented below so as to facilitate the assessment of a candid world.

He has refused to facilitate credible and meaningful legislation.

He has forbidden his Governors to crank in crash programs unless he has first interfaced with them.

His scheduling of legislative sessions is counterproductive time frame-wise.

He has refused to provide us with guidance on immigration and naturalization policy.

He has assumed a low profile on funding the justice system.

He has caused shortfalls to occur in the salaries of judges.

He has authorized a proliferation of new administrative slots and sent those staffers here to harass us and to over-utilize our resources.

can have the beneficial effect of blunting ill-considered and rash acts by presidents. They can, of course, have the opposite effect such as the six weeks it took the State Department to draft a reply to Soviet Premier Nikita S. Khrushchev's note to President Kennedy after the two had met for the first time in Vienna in 1961. "No one in the White House, least of all the President, would ever understand why this not very exacting assignment proved so difficult."[18] If it is often difficult to prod bureaucrats into the process of implementation, it can be as difficult to stop them once they have begun.

The ability of bureaucrats to thwart the implementation of new policies and their tendency to persist in implementing policies that have been discarded is a major source of frustration to executives, but it has also caused them to consider more fully the techniques they will have to rely on for carrying out their policies. This becomes part of the decision-making process. We can truly sympathize with Chief Justice John Marshall who handed down a decision of the Supreme Court that involved action by an executive branch headed by President Andrew Jackson, who disagreed with the court's decision. Jackson was reported to have said, "John Marshall has made his decision; now let him enforce it."

He has upgraded troop strength without legislative input.

For assigning substantial numbers of British service personnel to duty stations in American households;

For holding them harmless and granting them immunity from the judicial process;

For capping our trade with all parts of the world;

For enhancing his revenues without our consent;

For cutting travel orders for us to offshore destinations where we would be put at risk by foreign juries;

For modifying the parameters of our governmental system.

Military options have been prioritized and peaceful options downgraded by him.

He has begun, at this point in time, to task teams of uninformed third parties, operating under a consulting agreement with the Grand Duke of Hesse-Darmstadt, for insertion into this country for the purpose of terminating us with extreme prejudice.

The lives of Americans of all age groups have been prematurely curtailed by members of an armed minority group deployed at his direction.

A King with such a performance record is not cost-effective as the supervisor of a free people.

We generated a number of proposals and communicated them. We presented the big picture to them and attempted to fine-tune our negotiations based on our common ethnicity. But they refused to monitor our grievances and backed off from an in-depth evaluation of the outstanding issues that divide us. Countermeasures, accordingly, should be directed against them.

We, therefore, representatives of the States in Congress assembled, appealing to the Supervisor of All Manpower, declare the termination of all further political relationship between these Colonies and Great Britain, to be implemented at the close of business today; that, as free and independent states, we have the full power to conduct and/or terminate military operations, maximize foreign trade and develop such other projects, programs and activities as independent states may of a right do. And, to come quickly to the bottom line, with a significant input in the form of forecasts and projections from the Office of Divine Providence, we mutually pledge to each other our support services, our resource bases and our sacred credibility.

Source: Ross K. Baker, *The New York Times* (July 4, 1984). Copyright © 1984 by The New York Times Company. Reprinted by permission.

Paperwork Clients of federal bureaucracies, such as Social Security recipients, people receiving veterans' benefits, or industries subject to government regulation, are all required to fill out federal government forms. The work of government is conducted mainly on paper, and the paperwork generated by the federal bureaucracy is no less frustrating to conscientious bureaucrats, who see the red tape as an obstacle to carrying out their real duties. As one worker in the Veterans' Administration expressed this frustration, "We spend 35 percent of our time logging files in and out rather than actually getting benefits for veterans."[19]

Paperwork is in one sense, however, evidence of government activity. A government that does little will need little in the way of documentation. So, when President Reagan's Presidential Task Force on Regulatory Relief first announced that it had eliminated hundreds of millions of hours of paperwork required of individuals and corporations, there was cause for joy. But how much rejoicing would there have been if we had discovered that the paperwork being eliminated was the requirement that chemical companies document each drop of toxic waste and how it was being disposed of? This is not to say that proper government activities are necessarily accompanied

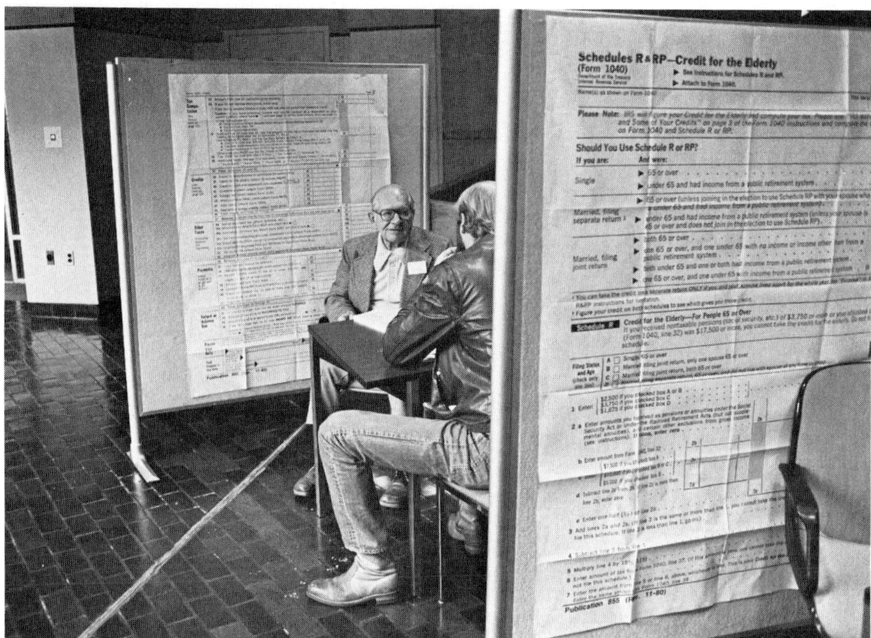

Every year most Americans are required to fill out at least one government document—the federal income tax form. *(Delia Flynn/Stock Boston)*

by vast amounts of paperwork, but one must always be skeptical of simple-sounding solutions that may end up replacing one evil with a worse one.

Bureaucratic Accountability and Responsiveness

Accountability is the key term in understanding how to make the bureaucracy effective in serving the people with fairness and as much simplicity as is possible from organizations that will always be large. The problem of how to hold bureaucrats accountable for their performance stems, ironically, from the Pendleton Act of 1883, which was designed, of course, to protect civil servants from removal from office for political reasons. As time went on, it became clear that it was almost impossible to remove them for any reason at all. A person who cannot be removed from office for anything but outright thievery cannot, ultimately, be held accountable. Outright thievery by bureaucrats, however, is rarely a problem these days. Accountability is, and the bureaucrat who serves two masters has, in effect, no masters at all.

Protecting bureaucrats from politically motivated attacks is the key element in an impartial civil service, but sometimes the protections also insulate the incompetent bureaucrat who should be removed. Rewarding the capable bureaucrat and punishing the lazy and ineffective ones is not as easy a job as it sounds. An attempt by Barbara Blum, deputy director of the Environmental Protection Agency early in the Carter administration, to get evaluations of the performance of civil servants in her agency produced a report showing that 97 percent of the workers were rated satisfactory. Throughout the 1970s, 99 percent of all federal workers received merit pay increases. The federal government's rate of firings for inefficiency is one-seventh of 1 percent. Imagine a class of 100 students in which the failure rate is less than 1 percent and in which 99 out of 100 students receive a grade of "A."[20]

Federal bureaucrats have tended to be relatively well paid, and, in general, working conditions are pleasant. It is not surprising, then, that they want to hold on to their jobs.

Currently, the average pay for all federal employees (white-collar and blue-collar workers included) is $26,140. The top pay for the regular federal employees is $68,000. These regular employees are categorized according to the GS (or General Schedule) scale. The largest group of federal employees are in the relatively low-ranking GS-5 category. This category of employee makes between $15,000 and $18,000 a year. The second-largest category consists of the relatively well-paid GS-12s whose earnings can go as high as $41,000. Topping all federal employees are those in the Senior Executive Service (see page 402) who can make as much as $72,300 because of the job security they are willing to forego.

The most serious threat to a bureaucrat's well-being is if his or her agency suffers a budget cut or, in the extreme, is eliminated outright. Bureaucrats are very resourceful in their efforts to stave off budget cuts. They are even more resourceful in enlarging their agency's budget. To understand the heroic lengths that bureaucrats will go to in order to avoid a budget cut for their agency, it is important to recognize that no agency will spend less than Congress has budgeted for it. If an agency turns back unused funds to the Treasury at the end of a fiscal year, there is a presumption that it was given too much money to begin with and that its next year's budget should be cut. If, on the other hand, all funds are expended by the end of September, a case can be made that the agency ought to get at least as much for the following year and more if possible.

As September 30 draws near each year, there is an activity known as **"hurry up spending"** or "use it or lose it." In 1978, the Young Adult Conservation Corps camp in Missouri came down to the wire with $1 million in unexpended funds and went on a real buying spree: 1,072 pairs of chaps, 3,736 pairs of work gloves, 112 stepladders, 54 wheelbarrows, and 1,059 desk calendars—all for the use of 135 YACC trainees.[21]

Proposals to bring the federal bureaucracy under control and to make it more responsive to the people and their elected representatives run up against a number of problems. Certainly, we want unelected bureaucrats to follow the dictates of our elected officials, but what of the defiance of Richard Nixon's order by American diplomats and their determination to continue visits to jailed Americans overseas irrespective of the causes of their imprisonment? Isn't that worthy of praise? How does the need for responsiveness square with Richard Nixon's attempt to use the Federal Bureau of Investigation in 1970 to spy on Americans, open their mail, and break into their homes in the interests of "internal security affairs"?

There is no easy answer to this problem of the need to bring responsiveness to the bureaucracy. First of all, who is the bureaucracy to be responsive to? The president is constitutionally the head of the executive branch of government, but the role of Congress is appropriating money, confirming presidential appointments, and being the institution to which the independent regulatory agency reports could make a good claim that the bureaucracy ought to be responsive to the House and Senate. The fragmentation of power of the national government makes the question of bureaucratic responsiveness a thorny one.

Ways the President Can Make the Bureaucracy More Responsive

There are four ways that the president can make the bureaucracy more responsive to presidential power: (1) by reorganizing the executive branch to reduce the number of agencies, (2) by tax and budget cutting, (3) by expanding patronage appointments, and (4) by instituting civil service reform.

Reorganization of the Executive Branch Reorganization of the executive branch by presidents has not fared well over the years. The effort by Jimmy Carter to reduce the number of agencies from 1,900 (his figure) to just a handful was largely unsuccessful. He did manage to consolidate a number of energy-related agencies in the Department of Energy and to do the same with scattered education bureaucracies in the Department of Education.

These two bureaucracies were at the top of President Reagan's list of candidates for elimination when he took office. Reagan learned what previous presidents have learned and that is that bureaucracies—even new ones—develop constituencies that do not want to see them abolished. Although he did transfer some of the functions of Energy and Education to other agencies and even abolished a few functions, his basic strategy for making the bureaucracy conform to his view of government was through budget and tax cuts and by appointing people who shared his views. Although Reagan's conservative nominees ran into trouble with Congress and some interest groups, most were able to reorient their agencies. The most spectacular successes of all, however, were with the use of tax and budget cuts to reduce the size and scope of the bureaucracy.

Budget and Tax Cutting The reduction or elimination of programs or agencies enables a president to cut the costs of government and to eliminate or scale down activities that conflict with the president's overall policies. In this effort the president has at his or her disposal a powerful weapon in the Office of Management and Budget.

The OMB is the checkpoint through which all executive branch funding requests must go before they are presented to Congress. A determined president and an equally determined OMB director can make the budget requests of executive branch agencies comply with the president's overall spending goals. The OMB director is not always popular with cabinet members who do not want their requests slashed, or with committee chairs in Congress who want to protect their favorite bureaucracies and programs. Given the right circumstances, however, a budget-making process centralized in the presidency can produce dramatic results.

If spending is slashed for a program, the agency in charge may respond with a reduction in force, known as a "rif" by bureaucrats. The results of riffing by the Reagan administration in Reagan's first term can be seen in Table 11.3.

Expansion of Patronage There are two more approaches to consider, a return to patronage and civil service reform:

TABLE 11.3 The Results of "Riffing" in Reagan's First Term

	1980 Average	September 1983	Percentage of Change
Defense Department	958,716	1,016,467	+ 6.0
Postal Service	664,096	663,027	− 0.2
Veterans Administration	232,168	236,257	+ 1.8
Health and Human Services Department	157,235	143,097	− 9.0
Treasury Department	129,299	123,574	− 4.4
Agriculture Department	127,420	122,786	− 3.6
Interior Department	80,961	78,621	− 2.9
Transportation Department	71,791	62,174	−13.4
Justice Department	55,727	57,943	+ 4.0
Tennessee Valley Authority	51,146	37,181	−27.3
Commerce Department	48,000	35,283	−26.5
General Services Administration	37,010	29,214	−21.1
State Department	23,525	23,890	+ 1.6
National Aeronautics and Space Administration	23,396	22,534	− 3.7
Labor Department	23,495	18,859	−19.7
Energy Department	21,168	17,000	−19.7
Housing and Urban Development Department	17,709	12,953	−26.9
Environmental Protection Agency	14,088	11,170	−20.7
Panama Canal Commission	8,622	8,356	− 3.1
U.S. Information Agency	8,095	7,974	− 1.5
Office of Personnel Management	8,344	6,322	−24.2
International Development Cooperation Agency	6,148	5,398	−12.2
Education Department	7,256	5,226	−28.0

Source: Reprinted from *U.S. News and World Report* (Jan. 30, 1984). Copyright 1984, U.S. News and World Report.

> It is widely assumed that the patronage system will result in a government run by unqualified people. Let's take a look at that assumption. Why do political appointees *have* to be unqualified? A politically appointed typist could be required to type the same number of words per minute as the civil service typist. . . .
>
> Isn't it possible that government jobs might best be filled by politicians who are interested in putting together an administration that will do a good enough job to get them re-elected? The same principle applies to most of the decisions that government employees make. Why shouldn't they be made on a partisan basis if the motive behind them is doing a good enough job to be re-elected?[22]

Since the passage of the *Hatch Act* in 1939, it has been illegal for civil servants to run for national or state office or to serve in any partisan post. It is also illegal to fire a federal bureaucrat for purely political reasons. Unleashing more than 2 million bureaucrats for political activities—especially in these days of lengthy presidential campaigns—might not produce a dividend of effectiveness along with the desired accountability, since bureaucrats would likely be out campaigning madly for the party that gave them their jobs.

Most experts consider a return to patronage on the federal level most unlikely, but one major civil service reform technique is already in use.

Civil Service Reform A greater degree of bureaucratic accountability was achieved with the Civil Service Reform Act of 1978. This did not remove federal workers from the protection of civil service laws but rather created a Senior Executive Service of roughly 8,000 high-level individuals who can choose to participate in a program that gives them financial incentives to give up some of their job security in a government agency. They can be shifted from department to department more easily by the president and agree that their salaries can be raised or lowered depending on their performance.

Ironically, the first beneficiary of the 1978 act was the Reagan administration. Until the law went into effect, a top-level civil servant had ironclad job protection for the particular job he or she held, so long as the money had been appropriated for the job, the job needed doing, and the job was being done properly. Under the 1978 law, the president's political appointees were given the power to reassign top bureaucrats. This power was used aggressively by the Reagan administration against those not in sympathy with the policies of the White House.

Although outright firing was not common, a number of dissenting bureaucrats were given the choice of a transfer out of Washington or loss of their job. A senior pathologist with the Environmental Protection Agency was transferred from his prestigious Washington post to a tiny and remote facility because he had criticized his supervisors for being in collusion with a chemical company to get an insecticide approved. He had shown himself out of step with the Reagan administration's efforts to remove the regulatory burden from industry when he criticized what he thought was a too-close relationship between his superiors and the chemical company in getting approval for the pesticide.[23]

Bureaucrats who are dealt with in this manner often take their cases to Congress where they can find sympathetic chairpersons with whom they have dealt over the years. Sometimes, the threat of intervention by a congressional committee is sufficient to save the top-level bureaucrat from transfer or dismissal; in other cases, the politically appointed leadership of the agency digs in its heels.

This type of situation may raise some ambivalent feelings in us. We certainly want civil servants, especially those at the highest levels, to be responsive to the policies of those we have elected, but we also want some assurance that people acting honestly and on the basis of their expertise are not exiled or dismissed by people whose motives are political. We might applaud when senators or House members protect a bureaucrat who is being persecuted by a political appointee, but do we really want massive intervention from Capitol Hill on personnel matters any more than we want members of Congress to urge the continuation of an obsolete weapons system just because its parts happen to be made in their district or state?

Efforts by Congress to Control the Bureaucracy

Efforts by Congress to gain control of the bureaucracy through the use of oversight, sunset laws, the ill-fated legislative veto, hearings and investigations, and the confirmation process were discussed in Chapter 9. But it is an open question as to whether the 535 men and women of Congress are really able to supervise the bureaucracy very effectively or even to write laws that lay down very specific guidelines as to how bureaucrats should implement the laws that Congress passes and administer the programs that Congress establishes. Can Congress play a constructive role in establishing bureaucratic responsiveness? Presidents who attempted to reorganize the executive branch learned that Congress could be a barrier to efforts to make the bureaucracy more responsive to the White House, but as Richard Neustadt has pointed out, referring to "Congress" is dealing in abstractions. "And what is Congress?" Neustadt asks:

> Congress is a chamber and a hall, four sets of party leaders, 300 subcommittees, 535 members, 15,000 professional staff members. Yet, the executive departments and their programs are at least as much servants of "Congress" as of presidents—properly so; indeed constitutionally. If one seeks in the executive establishment of more integration of objectives, better coordination, more effectual administration, and the like, a good cry would be "strengthen the congressional leadership," give some reality to Congress as an entity—and thereby give the president some colleagues he can bargain with for help in jointly superintending agencies downtown.[24]

The most effective effort to date to bring the federal bureaucracy into line with presidential objectives came about as the result of President Reagan's tax and budget cuts in 1981 and the Gramm-Rudman-Hollings Budget Law of 1985. These measures cut the federal government off from the tax revenues it needs to operate and require cuts in the budgets of federal agencies in the interest of a balanced budget. Both the size and scope of federal government activity were curtailed and a number of government services that people considered important were eliminated.

The drastic cuts in federal programs in the mid-1980s raises the question of whether there isn't some compromise position between a bloated and extravagant federal government and one that is passive and helpless. "What most citizens want is better government. What they have too often gotten is more government or less government with one set of favored beneficiaries replacing another. Under these circumstances, public disillusionment about the process may grow."[25]

SUMMARY

Although the Constitution refers to the administration of government policies in the vaguest terms, over the last century a bureaucratic empire composed of 1,245 agencies and 3 million federal workers has arisen in response to an increasingly complex technological society. The person reigning over this vast organization is the president, whose responsibility to execute faithfully the laws has been largely relegated to the ranks of the bureaucracy. Explanation for this can be found in the authority of Congress to organize and fund agencies, which means that the bureaucracy is, in effect, answerable to two branches of government. Career bureaucrats are often more familiar with the committees in Congress that have jurisdiction over their agencies than they are with presidents whose administrations span no more than four or eight years. Moreover, a bureaucracy as large and as geographically dispersed as America's is impossible to oversee closely, either by the president or by Congress.

Starting with President Jackson's administration, appointments to the bureaucracy were made through political selection. After President Garfield was assassinated by an unsuccessful job applicant, a nonpartisan system of awarding positions based on performance in a competitive examination was established.

The growth of a national economy and the corresponding expansion of government—the transition from limited to positive government—resulted in the need for regulation. Congress, unwilling and unable to lay out specific guidelines for the execution of laws, left the details for the bureaucracy to work out. This freedom to fill in the legislative blanks has been advantageous to the more powerful bureaucrats, who have been granted policymaking discretion that often has the force of law.

There are three basic types of agencies: cabinet departments, independent executive agencies, and independent regulatory commissions. The latter function in three ways, as rule makers, rule adjudicators, and rule enforcers. Historically, these regulatory powers are the offspring of public pressure, industry's desire to restrict competition, and the bureaucratic goal of extending authority. Industrial abuses generated the first two waves of regulatory fever in American history; the most recent wave, which began in the 1960s, was primarily the outcome of social problems.

The bureaucracy derives its power from a number of sources. The backing of interest groups and regulated industries gives agencies the leverage they need in dealing with the executive and legislative branches. The revolving door process, whereby industries clear regulatory personnel before confirmation and hire them upon retirement from the government, indicates how strong the connection is between the regulators and the regulated. The bureaucrat's expertise also exerts great influence over a Congress of representatives who have little time to research the details of thousands of different issues. Bureaucratic jargon incomprehensible to many elected officials, is nevertheless an asset to the administrator who wants to bury the questionability of a particular project or agency branch. An intangible power is contained in the bureaucracy's profusion of rules and paperwork, by which a civil servant can delay the implementation of policymakers' decisions and shun accountability for almost any action. A bureaucrat, moreover, does not have to cooperate completely with a president if he or she does not care to—the Pendleton Act protects civil servants from being fired for political reasons.

The bureaucracy has become the focal point of a battle over the scope of government. Believing that the federal government has attempted to do far too much to equalize conditions among Americans and to meddle excessively in the private sector, the Reagan administration has attacked the size of the bureaucracy as a way of limiting government's scope.

NOTES

1. Leslie Maitland Werner, "Agencies Battle to Control U.S. Border Inspections," *The New York Times* (May 7, 1984).
2. Ibid.
3. Anthony Downs, *Inside Bureaucracy* (Boston: Little, Brown, 1967), pp. 24–26.
4. Ibid.
5. Rowland Egger, *The President of the United States* (New York: McGraw-Hill, 1972), p. 45
6. Peter Woll, *American Bureaucracy* (New York: Norton, 1963), pp. 143–44.
7. Paul Van Riper, "American Civil Service Reform," in Michael T. Dalby and Michael S. Wertman, eds., *Bureaucracy in Historical Perspective* (Glenview, Ill.: Scott, Foresman, 1971), p. 125.
8. Roy F. Nichols, *The Disruption of the American Democracy* (New York: Macmillan, 1948), p. 83.
9. Edwin Palmer Hoyt, Jr., *Jumbos and Jackasses* (Garden City, N.Y.: Doubleday, 1980), p. 81.
10. Theodore J. Lowi, *The End of Liberalism* (New York: Norton, 1969), p. 128.
11. Gabriel Kolko, *The Triumph of Conservatism* (Chicago: Quadrangle, 1963), pp. 98–112.
12. Ibid., pp. 108–10.
13. *Congressional Record,* 59th Congress, 1st Session (Feb. 2, 1906), p. 1972.

14. Peter Woll, pp. 130–33.
15. Ralph P. Hummel, *The Bureaucratic Experience* (New York: St. Martin's, 1977), p. 147.
16. Richard Halloran, "Pentagon Aide Rates a GRAPE Waging War on Acronyms," *The New York Times* (Dec. 18, 1979).
17. Graham Allison, *Essence of Decision* (Boston: Little, Brown, 1971), p. 83.
18. Arthur M. Schlesinger, *A Thousand Days* (Boston: Houghton Mifflin, 1964), pp. 383–84.
19. *U.S. News and World Report* (June 19, 1979), p. 53.
20. Charles Peters, *How Washington Really Works* (North Reading, Mass.: Addison-Wesley, 1980), p. 49.
21. Spencer Rich, "Spending Spree by New Year's Eve Is Bureaucratic Custom," *The Washington Post* (Sept. 28, 1980).
22. Charles Peters, p. 49.
23. Paul Taylor, "Frictions Crest in Civil Service in Reagan Era," *The Washington Post,* (Jan. 19, 1983).
24. Richard F. Neustadt, "What to Do with the Bureaucracy," *The Washington Post* (Oct. 12, 1980).
25. John L. Palmer and Isabel V. Sawhill, eds., *The Reagan Record* (Cambridge, Mass.: Ballinger, 1984), p. 30.

PART 4

The Courts, Civil Liberties, and Civil Rights

The federal courts are also institutions, basic to the operation of government, just like the presidency, the Congress, and the bureaucracy. But the courts are institutions of a special kind. Under the Constitution, the powers and limits of institutions are determined by law, but it is up to the courts to define what the law *is*.

Of course, the courts are bound by, and have a duty to enforce, the Constitution itself. Yet, when the federal courts engage in judicial review—when they declare that a law is or is not constitutional—they are exercising a power that is only hinted at in the Constitution. Similarly, the way we think about what the Constitution says and requires is strongly influenced by the decisions of the courts.

The courts mark out the boundaries between institutions, and they draw the line between the proper concerns of government—the public sphere—and matters that should be left to private associations and individuals. The courts are a unique institution because they have a special responsibility to figure out and protect the design and balance of the constitutional system as a whole, and in that sense, we argue that they are a barrier against fragmentation.

We will examine the ways in which the federal courts—and especially, the Supreme Court—have played this role in American political history and the ways in which they are playing it today, including the ways in which courts decide cases and interpret law. But we emphasize that political life plays a vital part in defining the role of the courts. Fragmentation in other institutions makes Americans more likely to look to the courts for solutions. People are also apt to appeal to the courts if they feel at a disadvantage in other institutions. For both reasons, racial groups, women, and various minorities have turned to the courts to advance their claims to equality; and, in general, the courts have become increasingly visible in politics, chiefly as the definers and defenders of rights. Many Americans are critical of this tendency, but we find no evidence that the trend toward the courts is likely to abate.

Like most Americans, we are particularly concerned with the courts as defenders of our rights and liberties. We want to examine the ways in which courts think about and try to protect our civil liberties—our protections against government—and our civil rights—our claims on government. We will be especially interested in the tension between private liberties, like the right of property, and our public life as a political society. Do the liberties we enjoy as private individuals, by fragmenting power, prevent us from doing public business? Or, to rephrase the question, do our rights as private individuals weaken or get in the way of our rights as citizens?

The answers that federal courts give to these questions define the limits of legitimate public policy and set the terms on which other institutions lawfully are entitled to address public problems. In this sense, our discussion of the courts is a bridge to Part 5: the federal courts are sometimes architects and always building inspectors in the construction of public policy.

CHAPTER 12

The Courts

The federal courts play a paradoxical role in American politics. In a country that prides itself on democracy, judges are appointed and hold their positions, for practical purposes, for life. In a constitutional system based on "checks and balances," the Supreme Court and the federal courts under it have supreme authority in interpreting the Constitution and the right to overrule the legislature and the executive. As we will argue, the courts are an exception to the framers' strategy of fragmentation though onc intended by the framers themselves. Despite all these peculiarities, the federal courts seem to

The Supreme Court may rule only on actual "cases and controversies" arising from differing interpretations of the Constitution. *(ISP-PSI/Jack Schneider)*

fit the American system. Appearances to the contrary, there are ways in which the courts are more democratic than the elected branches, and the courts are part of the vital center of American political life.

Courts and Politics

The Federal Judiciary

Because of federalism, there are two court systems in the United States, the federal judiciary and the fifty state judicial systems. In this chapter, we will emphasize the federal judiciary, but it is important to remember that most cases are dealt with by state courts. And although all state courts are similar and are governed by common legal doctrines, each state judiciary has its own special legal traditions, procedures, and principles.

The federal judicial system derives from Article III of the Constitution, but that article is relatively open. The framers clearly felt that the structure of the federal courts should be something Congress could define and vary with political experience and the needs of the country. Article III provides for the jurisdiction of federal courts and establishes a Supreme Court. It leaves inferior courts and other matters to Congress's discretion.

The basic outline of the federal judiciary was established by the *Federal Judiciary Act of 1789.* At the base of the system are the ninety-three federal District Courts; above them are the thirteen Courts of Appeal, each with from three to nine judges; at the top of the system is the United States Supreme Court. All of these **constitutional courts** are established under Article III, and as it provides, the judges hold their office "during good behavior." In other words, judges serve until they die, resign, or are removed by impeachment. Impeachment is extremely rare: only seven district court judges and one justice of the Supreme Court (Samuel Chase, in 1804–1805) have even been impeached, and only four district court judges have ever been convicted. For practical purposes, judges in the constitutional courts hold office for life.

Article III also limits these constitutional courts to "cases and controversies" arising between conflicting parties (later, we will discuss this restriction at length). Congress cannot ask the Supreme Court if a given law is constitutional; the federal courts cannot tell the United States Attorneys how they would rule on some point of law if it were presented to them; the constitutional courts cannot be asked to help administer statutes.

Congress has, however, established certain **legislative courts** under Article I, section 8 (that is, the power "to constitute tribunals inferior to the Supreme Court). These courts are not limited by Article III: the judges need not have life tenure, and the courts may be allowed to give advisory opinions or administer statutes. One such court is the Court of Military Appeals, established under the power to "make rules for the government and regulation of land and naval forces," which handles appeals from military courts. Similarly, the independent regulatory commissions, like the Interstate Commerce Commission, are classed as "quasi-judicial" bodies, although they exist to administer particular laws.[1] Legislative courts may be changed into constitutional courts if Congress wishes, as happened in the case of the Court of Claims in 1953, the United States Customs Court in

1956, and the Court of Customs and Patent Appeals in 1958.* Legislative courts are clearly a secondary part of the federal judiciary. The heart of the judicial system is still the basic structure established in the early years of the republic.

The Framers and Judicial Review

Judicial review (see Chapter 2), the power to declare laws unconstitutional, is the most remarkable prerogative of the federal courts. It is noteworthy, consequently, that the framers seem to have taken judicial review for granted. They did not provide for it explicitly because, given the principles of constitutional government, the logic of the argument for judicial review struck them as inescapable. If the Constitution is the supreme law, it must prevail whenever it conflicts with lesser laws. If courts exist to determine the law, then courts must define the Constitution. If there is a Supreme Court, then its interpretations must govern all lesser courts. In the Constitutional Convention, even delegates who later opposed ratification observed that the Constitution necessarily gave the judges a power of review over all ordinary laws.[2]

Nor were the framers unduly disturbed by the power this gave the courts. Alexander Hamilton explained this position in *The Federalist,* No. 78. There are, Hamilton observed, two great dangers to the constitutional unity of a federal regime. First, there is likely to be a conflict between state and federal law, especially because a "local spirit" is likely to influence state courts when they interpret the Constitution. Second, the legislature and other agencies of the federal government are likely to go beyond the limits of their authority, and they are even more likely to be influenced by "cabals" and "factions" and "momentary inclination." The government, in other words, is likely to sacrifice the public good to private interests and the long term to the short. And each branch of government is likely to violate the design of the Constitution as a whole while pursuing its interest as a part.

The problem, of course, is who to trust with the task of protecting the political society as a whole. The people, Hamilton argued, have final authority but are too often preoccupied with their own concerns, which makes them unaware when officials endanger public liberty. Constitutional government needs "an intermediate body between the people and the legislature to keep the latter within the limits assigned to their authority." But why should the people rely on the courts to be this sort of watchdog?

Hamilton answered that the courts, unlike the executive and the legislature, "have neither FORCE nor WILL but only judgment." The judiciary commands no armies, levies no taxes, and coins no money. Judges issue orders and sentence criminals to prison, but these commands are only so many words unless the executive is willing to enforce them and the legislature respects them. In any conflict with the legislature or the executive, the courts can win only if they have the support of the people, and the courts'

*In 1982, as part of a reform that created the United States Court of Appeals for the Federal Circuit, a new Court of Claims was established as a legislative court.

only means of winning that support are words and judgments. Courts make arguments about the meaning of justice and right conduct, and these arguments are "forceful" only if they are persuasive.

Since courts depend on opinion for their force and power, a divided public opinion weakens the court, just as it limits the effectiveness of law. Courts, consequently, have an interest in a unified public opinion. Hence, Hamilton argued, courts can be trusted with the interest of political society as a whole because the courts are interested that political society should be a whole. Courts are most powerful when they speak to, and on behalf of, a public that holds common values and beliefs and that cares about the Constitution and the laws. The interest of the courts, in other words, disposes them to promote political aggregation. Particular judges and courts may deviate from this tendency, but the history of the Supreme Court shows how characteristic it is of the Court as an institution.

The Supreme Court in Political History

The "Marshall Court" Prior to the appointment of John Marshall as Chief Justice, the Supreme Court was not regarded as a particularly important institution. Marshall, a forceful person with a coherent philosophy of law, made the court a crucial part of the American political scene. The *Marshall Court* (1801–1835) insisted on (1) the supremacy of the federal government over the states, since Marshall argued that the Constitution was established by the sovereign "people of the United States" rather than the separate states. Marshall also held that (2) the ability to respond to change was a first principle of any constitution "intended to endure" and, consequently, that the Constitution should be interpreted broadly, giving the government the power and flexibility required to meet new needs and changing times.[3]

For more than three decades, Chief Justice John Marshall spearheaded a strong role for the Supreme Court. *(Library of Congress)*

The "Taney Court" Under Marshall's successor, Roger B. Taney, the Supreme Court followed most of the lines Marshall had laid down, but the *Taney Court* (1836–1864) was more inclined to respect the Jeffersonian principles of states's rights and "strict construction." But Jeffersonian and Jacksonian theory also emphasized democracy and government according to the political values of the majority. These two aspects of Jeffersonian and Jacksonian theory were increasingly at odds with one another. The slavery question, posing a conflict between the states' rights and the ideal of equality, was the most obvious example of this tension, and the Supreme Court's effort to settle the issue in the Dred Scott case was the greatest failure of the Taney Court.[4]

The Taney Court had little better success in dealing with the rise of corporations as part of the growth of a national, industrial economy. The Constitution makes certain crucial aspects of economic life into federal questions outside the authority of the states, and the Taney Court illustrated this when it held that corporations were "citizens" with a right to appeal to the federal courts.[5] But public values demanded that corporations be regulated, especially since large corporations were coming to be wealthier and more powerful than some state governments. Corporations, Justice John Campbell observed, are inclined to slight "moral or political principles" in favor of private profit and power.* The Court was not willing to say, however, that if states cannot regulate corporations, the national government has the constitutional duty and power to do so.

The "Waite Court" The Civil War confirmed national supremacy in law and politics, and industrialization made more and more Americans demand some form of regulation over economic life. At first, the *Waite Court* (1874–1888) showed some sympathy for the efforts of states to control their economies, but gradually, the Court changed its views. Justice Stephen Field persuaded the majority of the Court that a corporation was a "legal person," entitled to the protection of the Fourteenth Amendment against the states.[6] By the end of the nineteenth century, the Court, influenced by laissez-faire economics and the Social Darwinist principle of "survival of the fittest," had become hostile to all government regulation of the economy. It sought to limit, as far as possible, the authority of the federal government over commerce, despite the "modern conditions" that were making the economy into a unified whole, and the Court was especially antagonistic to efforts to regulate the conditions and terms of labor.†

President Roosevelt and "Court Packing" The Great Depression, however, greatly strengthened the demand for regulation by accentuating the unreliability of change and the injustice of the ways—most notably, mass unemployment—by which the private sector dealt with economic crisis. The Supreme Court did show some sympathy for state efforts to mitigate the depression, but with very few exceptions the Supreme Court struck down the crucial measures by which President Roosevelt's New Deal hoped to manage the economy.‡ The Supreme Court seemed to define itself as an undemocratic "judicial oligarchy," and President Roosevelt sought to overcome the Court's opposition by a bill that would have allowed the president to appoint an additional justice (up to a total of fifteen) for every justice who failed to retire at age seventy. But although most Americans supported Roosevelt's economic program, his "Court-Packing" Bill stirred opposition because Americans also valued the independence of the Supreme Court. Roosevelt's bill might not have been passed anyway, but two moderate members of the Court, Chief Justice Hughes and Justice Roberts, deserted the conservatives and sided with those members of the Court who took a more generous view of the government's power. The Court upheld the Social Security Act and the Wagner Labor Relations Act, and this "switch in time" persuaded the decisive members of Congress that

*See Campbell's dissent in *Marshall* v. *Baltimore & Ohio Railroad,* 16, How. 314 (1853); and *Dodge* v. *Woolsey,* 18 How. 331 (1855).

†For example of the Court's reasoning during this period, see *U.S.* v. *E. C. Knight,* 156 U.S. 1 (1895); *Swift and Co.* v. *U.S.* overruled the Knight case. On the conditions of labor, see *Lochner* v. *N.Y.,* 195 U.S. 45 (1905); *Coppage* v. *Kansas,* 236 U.S. 1 (1915); *Hammer* v. *Dagenhart,* 247 U.S. 251 (1918); and *Bailey* v. *Drexel Furniture,* 259 U.S. 20 (1922).

‡The crucial rulings against the New Deal included *Schechter Poultry* v. *U.S.,* 295 U.S. 495 (1935); *Panama Refining* v. *Ryan,* 293 U.S. 388 (1935); and *U.S.* v. *Butler,* 297 U.S. 1 (1936). One of a small number of New Deal victories was *Ashwander* v. *T.V.A.,* 297 U.S. 288 (1936).

the "Court-Packing" Bill was unnecessary.* The conflict between the Court and the New Deal indicates that the Court bows to public opinion, but also that public opinion may support the Court even against a supremely popular president.

THE "NEW DEAL COURT" In 1937, President Roosevelt was able to make his first appointment to the Court, and by the end of his long term in office, he had appointed all but two of the justices. The *New Deal Court* (1937–1953), as one would expect, took a very advanced view of the powers of the federal government. It almost never held a federal law unconstitutional, and it was extremely sympathetic to the argument that change requires expanding the government's power to respond to events.

THE "WARREN COURT" When Earl Warren became Chief Justice, the Court continued to support the government's power to govern the economy. However, the *Warren Court* (1953–1969) became increasingly suspicious of any interference with individual liberty and more and more active in extending its attack on segregation into a demand for racial equality. Over the energetic protests of a minority on the Court, the Warren Court seemed bent on "constitutionalizing" America, extending constitutional law and regulation into more and more spheres of life.[7]

Earl Warren guided the Supreme Court into far-reaching decisions affecting all Americans, particularly in the areas of civil rights and criminal justice. *(UPI)*

THE "BURGER COURT" Many people expected a repudiation of the Warren era when Chief Justice Warren Burger succeeded Earl Warren and President Nixon named three additional conservatives to the Court. In fact, the *Burger Court* (1970–1986) refused to extend, or narrowly construed, precedents set by the Warren Court. From time to time, it indicated a new sympathy for the states and a greater respect for the decisions of legislatures.[8]

The Burger Court was also more lenient with law enforcement authorities and more inclined to limit the rights of suspects and accused persons.[9] The appointment of Justice Sandra Day O'Connor accentuated the Court's shift to the right, since O'Connor regularly sided with Justice William Rehnquist, the Court's most conservative member. When Chief Justice Burger resigned in 1986, President Reagan named Rehnquist to replace him, a move which may strengthen this shift to the right. By subsequently selecting Judge Antonin Scalia to replace Burger, Reagan substituted one conservative for another. If Reagan is given the chance to make additional appointments, the change in the court may become decisive if not radical. The Burger Court, though undeniably more conservative than its predecessor, left the major decisions of the Warren Court intact, and only slowed, not stopped, the intrusion of courts into new areas of life.[10]

In general, the political history of the Court suggests that the Court will tend to sustain, with some periods of resistance, the *supremacy of the national government* and the *ability to respond to change,* following the course that Justice Marshall established early in its history. It also indicates that the Court *depends on opinion* and must either persuade the public or, in a relatively

*Alpheus T. Mason, *The Supreme Court: Vehicle of Revealed Truth or Power Group* (Boston: Boston U.P., 1953), pp. 36–37; the crucial Court decisions were *National Labor Relations Board* v. *Jones and Laughlin,* 301 U.S. 1 (1937); and *Helvering* v. *Davis,* 301 U.S. 619 (1937).

POLITICAL PERSPECTIVE

LINE-UP OF BURGER COURT

Conservatives	Centrist or Swing Bloc	Liberals
Sandra Day O'Connor	Byron White	Thurgood Marshall
William Rehnquist	John Paul Stevens	William Brennan
Warren Burger	Lewis Powell	
Antonin Scalia	Harry Blackmun	

short time, be compelled to follow it. As Hamilton remarked, the people will always hold the scales of justice in their hands, and ultimately all constitutional government depends on their firmness and their wisdom.[11]

The Courts and Interest Groups

The Court's history also reminds us that, directly or indirectly, every case that comes before a court affects economic and social interests. When the Supreme Court decided that the freedom of speech included the right to ask people to join a union, it was effectively siding with unions and against antiunion employers.[12] When the Court gave a broad construction to the Antitrust Acts, it limited the ability of all large corporations to acquire others.[13] When the Court ruled that a state could not deny contraceptives to unmarried people if it gave them to married couples, it allied itself, for practical purposes, with "new lifestyles" against the traditional family.[14]

Beginning with this fact, some political scientists have gone on to conclude that the judicial process can be reduced to the competition between interest groups. The courts, in this view, are best interpreted in terms of the conflicts and coalitions of "pressure politics."[15]

Interest groups certainly do attempt to sway court decisions, but the courts do not follow the ordinary logic of interest-group politics. Numbers and money, translated into voting strength and campaign contributions, are the stuff of interest-group power. Such resources, however, are less influential on federal judges, who serve during "good behavior," than they are on elected officials. (Even at state levels, where judges are often elected, votes and money are less important to judges than they are to other officials.) Because of this, in part, even powerful interests may weigh less with the court than the broader issues of constitutional government. It would be hard to think of a group with less political influence than convicted criminals, but the courts are far more likely than the legislature to see beyond the convict at the bar to the concern we all have in due process of law.*

In this sense, *interest groups are far more equal in the courts than in other branches of government* or sectors of society. Groups that are small, unpopu-

*See, for example, *Gideon* v. *Wainwright*, 372 U.S. 335 (1963).

lar, and relatively poor get a better hearing in the courts. The Jehovah's Witnesses, for example, have appealed repeatedly to the courts to sustain their right to refuse to salute the flag, to ring doorbells in order to disseminate their message, and so on. Between 1938 and 1958, the Jehovah's Witnesses were involved in 55 cases and won 45 of them, a record they could not have hoped to equal in another part of the political process.[16] Courts are slow and have fewer resources than the other branches, and consequently interest groups are inclined to turn to the courts only when other political channels are closed or have failed. That, however, only emphasizes the courts as the best hope of the otherwise disadvantaged.

However, this equality is limited. Obviously, groups have a better chance in court if their interests are embodied in statutes or in the Constitution. In that sense, courts are especially favorable to groups that once had enough power to shape the law. If a group still had that kind of power, it would probably turn to Congress or the president to protect its interests. Groups that look to the courts are likely to be those that have lost or are losing political power. In the late nineteenth century, for example, as corporations became the object of more and more public resentment, they turned to the courts, and there was often a close, quasi-conspiratorial relationship between judges and corporate executives.[17] This "conservatism" of the courts, however, can work in favor of any group that has lost power or fallen out of favor. The NAACP emphasized the law, for example, because blacks had little power or popular support in the early decades of the twentieth century, but the law—or at least, the Thirteenth, Fourteenth, and Fifteenth Amendments—reflected the far more favorable climate that had existed at the time of the post-Civil War Reconstruction.

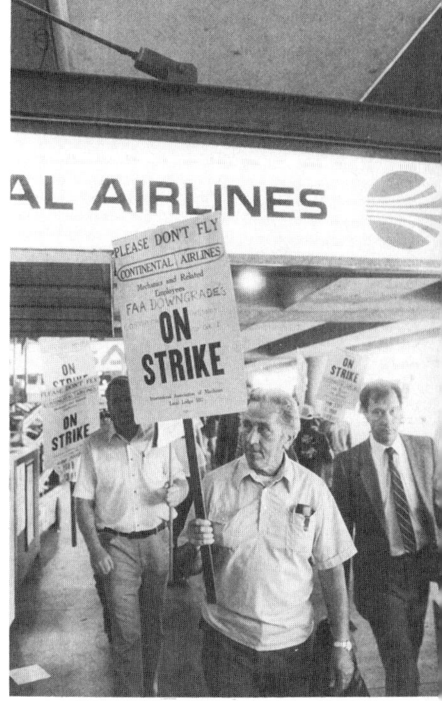

By holding that peaceful picketing and union organizing are included in free speech, the Supreme Court helped promote the organization of labor.
(B. Nation/Sygma)

Choosing Judges

The politics of judicial selection is another limit on the equality of interest groups before the law. Persuading a judge is obviously a good deal easier if he or she is already favorably inclined, and powerful interest groups have their usual advantage in influencing judicial selection. All of the resources of a group can be brought to bear on the president or the Senate, and the normal processes of interest group politics are far more likely to apply than they are in litigation.

This is as the framers expected. The Constitution, of course, provides that judges shall be appointed by the president with the advice and consent of the Senate, but this was not the method that Madison preferred. Madison wanted the president alone to have the choice of judges. Any "numerous body," Madison argued, would be too much governed by faction and private interest; the legislature, in other words, would be too little concerned with the good of the whole.[18] Madison and his allies were able to win the power to name judges for the president, but they had to compromise with those delegates who feared that the president would choose judges only from his state or section and who insisted on the "advice and consent" of the Senate in order to guarantee that membership on the bench be "diffused." Madison persuaded himself that this concession was acceptable, but James Wilson thought it would make the president into a "minion of the Senate."[19] In practice, the truth has been somewhere between Madison's hopes and Wilson's fears, but the Constitution's method of selecting judges is *more open to interest politics* than Madison would have liked.

Of course, interest groups would have been powerful even if the Senate did not have a veto on the president's choices. Presidents can only choose those possible judges who have come to their attention. Presidents sometimes choose people they know personally, as Harry Truman did when he named Fred Vinson to the Court, or as John Kennedy did when he selected Byron White (see Table 12.1). More often, however, a judge is called to the president's attention: the Attorney General and his deputies, Justices of the

TABLE 12.1 The Supreme Court Since 1945

	Party Affiliation	Appointed By	Home State	Years on Court
Harlan F. Stone (Chief Justice)	Republican	Coolidge	N.Y.	1925–1941 (Assoc. Justice) 1941–1946 (Chief Justice)
Owen J. Roberts	Republican	Hoover	Pa.	1930–1945
Hugo L. Black	Democrat	F.D.R.	Ala.	1937–1971
Stanley F. Reed	Democrat	F.D.R.	Ky.	1938–1957
Felix Frankfurter	Independent	F.D.R.	Mass.	1939–1962
William O. Douglas	Democrat	F.D.R.	Conn.	1939 1975
Frank Murphy	Democrat	F.D.R.	Mich.	1940–1949
Robert H. Jackson	Democrat	F.D.R.	N.Y.	1941–1954
Wiley B. Rutledge	Democrat	F.D.R.	Ia.	1943–1949
Harold H. Burton	Republican	Truman	Ohio	1945–1958
Fred M. Vinson (Chief Justice)	Democrat	Truman	Ky.	1946–1953
Tom C. Clark	Democrat	Truman	Tex.	1949–1967
Sherman Minton	Democrat	Truman	Ind.	1949–1956
Earl Warren (Chief Justice)	Republican	Eisenhower	Calif.	1953–1969
John M. Harlan	Republican	Eisenhower	N.Y.	1955–1971
William J. Brennan	Democrat	Eisenhower	N.J.	1956–
Charles Whittaker	Republican	Eisenhower	Mo.	1957–1962
Potter Stewart	Republican	Eisenhower	Ohio	1958–1981
Byron R. White	Democrat	Kennedy	Colo.	1962–
Arthur Goldberg	Democrat	Kennedy	Ill.	1962–1965
Abe Fortas	Democrat	Johnson	Tenn.	1965–1969
Thurgood Marshall	Democrat	Johnson	N.Y.	1967–
Warren Burger (Chief Justice)	Republican	Nixon	Minn.	1969–1986
Harry Blackmun	Republican	Nixon	Minn.	1970–
Lewis Powell	Democrat	Nixon	Va.	1971–
William Rehnquist (Chief Justice)	Republican	Nixon	Ariz.	1971–1986 (Assoc. Justice) 1986– (Chief Justice)
John Paul Stevens	Republican	Ford	Ill.	1976–
Sandra Day O'Connor	Republican	Reagan	Ariz.	1981–
Antonin Scalia	Republican	Reagan	Ill.	1986–

Supreme Court and other federal judges, and the president's own political associates exert varying degrees of influence. Attorneys who want to be judges "campaign" to be noticed; they become active in party politics, contribute money, and in general, try to make themselves discreetly visible. And interest groups use all their resources to bring forward their own nominees. In general, judges must have contacts in the upper levels of politics or their profession. They tend, consequently, to come from upper-middle-class families and to be well off themselves. In a broad sense of the term, the judiciary tends to be composed of the elite.

Byron White was personally acquainted with President John Kennedy before being appointed to the Supreme Court. *(UPI)*

Party in Judicial Selection Political party plays a vital role in the selection of judges in at least two ways. First, with very few exceptions, presidents select members of their own political party. President Carter scorned traditional party politics, but nearly 95 percent of the judges he chose were Democrats. In this century, President Ford made the largest percentage of these selections from outside his party, and that was a slim 21 percent.

Second, party influences the kind of people a president notices and selects. Democratic presidents, for example, have been much less likely than Republicans to name corporate lawyers and much more likely to nominate attorneys who have held positions in government.[20]

Ethnicity sometimes plays a role in the selection of judges. Franklin Roosevelt named Felix Frankfurter to the Supreme Court, in part, because he wanted to replace Justice Benjamin Cardozo with another Jew, and Roosevelt also chose a Catholic, Frank Murphy, to replace a coreligionist, Justice Butler. President Johnson was eager to name a black to the Court, and President Reagan selected Justice O'Connor because he wanted to name a woman. But ethnic influences vary greatly depending on the political party in power. Democratic presidents created the impression that there was a "Jewish seat" on the Supreme Court: Roosevelt chose Frankfurter; Kennedy replaced Frankfurter with Arthur Goldberg; Johnson named Abe Fortas to replace Goldberg. Since Fortas resigned in 1969, however, Republican presidents have not named a Jew, although they have had five chances to fill a vacancy on the Supreme Court. (The only Democratic president since 1969, Jimmy Carter, had no opportunity to make an appointment to the Court.) President Carter emphasized affirmative action (see Chapter 14), and his judicial appointments included a relatively high percentage of blacks, other minorities, and women, but such considerations appear to have little weight in President Reagan's selection of judges. Similarly, about one-third of the district court judges appointed by Johnson and Carter were Catholics; less than one-fifth of the judges named by Nixon and Ford were members of that church.[21]

Ideology and Judicial Selection In part, presidents name members of their own parties or choose judges from particular groups, in order to strengthen their political positions. President Nixon, for example, was eager to name a Southerner to the Court as part of the Republican strategy of wooing the Sunbelt states. Presidents are even more concerned, however, to choose judges who share their views about the Constitution and public policy. Presidents tend, in other words, to choose those members of their party who share their philosophy or ideology, and sometimes they will

Presidents usually name judges to the Supreme Court who are members of their own party, or who share their political philosophy. An exception was Herbert Hoover's choice of Justice Cardozo, who was a Democrat and a liberal. *(Library of Congress)*

go outside their party to select a judge whose ideas are sympathetic. Taft and Harding, for example, named conservative Democrats (Lamar and Butler) to the Supreme Court, and Franklin Roosevelt elevated a liberal Republican, Justice Stone, to the rank of Chief Justice.

There are only a few exceptions to this rule (one was President Hoover's selection of Justice Cardozo, who was known to be a liberal). It is much more frequent that presidents are mistaken in supposing that a judge agrees with them. On the bench, a judge is freed from many of the constraints and pressures that previously affected his or her views, and he or she is exposed to new constituencies and concerns. President Wilson was unpleasantly surprised by the extreme conservatism Justice McReynolds displayed on the Court, and President Eisenhower undoubtedly did not expect Earl Warren to be an activistic liberal. Moreover, even a judge who generally conforms to the president's expectations may surprise him with this or that decision: Justice Holmes outraged Theodore Roosevelt, who had named him to the Court, with a dissenting opinion critical of "trust busting."* These cases, however, are exceptional; presidents are generally successful in identifying judges who share their convictions and beliefs.

The Senate: Senatorial Courtesy Since the Senate must "advise and consent" to presidents' appointments, it has a good deal of influence on their choices, especially in the lower courts where the custom of **senatorial courtesy** applies. Senatorial courtesy means that the Senate will not confirm a judge (or any other appointment) for a post in a state if the appointee is "personally obnoxious" to a senator from that state who is also a member of the president's party. (If both senators are members of the president's party, the "courtesy" is normally granted to the senior senator.)

This tradition helps strengthen state party organizations. Evidently, it also tends to fragment the process of judicial selection, and it makes the bench far more susceptible to the influence of locally powerful interests. For practical purposes, the fifty state organizations of the president's party can veto judicial nominees in their states (in fact, in states where the president's party has no senator, the president frequently gives the state party the equivalent of senatorial courtesy).[22]

The Supreme Court, however, is another matter. The Senate does reject appointees rather frequently: 28 out of 137 appointments, about one in five, have been vetoed in one way or another. The Senate rejected President Hoover's nomination of John Parker because of the feeling that he was antiblack and antilabor, and President Nixon's selection of Clement Haynesworth was not confirmed because of similar doubts. The grounds for rejection, however, must necessarily turn on national, rather than local, political values and interests, and senators who oppose a nominee must be prepared to make a reasoned case.[23]

Interest groups probably have their greatest impact on judicial selection in the Senate Judiciary Committee. Sometimes, they can be effective merely by informing the committee about a nominee. President Nixon seems to

***Northern Securities Co.* v. *U.S.*, 193 U.S. 97 (1904); on the process of selection generally, see David Danelski, *A Supreme Court Justice is Appointed* (New York: Random House, 1964).

have believed, for example, that there were no embarrassments in the past of G. Harold Carswell, but civil rights groups unearthed Carswell's earlier support for white supremacy and his role in drawing up contracts to permit a golf club to remain segregated. Groups will also try, of course, to use whatever clout they have to support or oppose a nomination. In general, groups that depend on the courts—like civil rights organizations—are likely to be extremely active in this sort of lobbying.

The American Bar Association (ABA) plays a rather special role in judicial selection. In one sense, the ABA reflects the interest of lawyers in professional standards and competence and can bring unusual expertise to the problem of choosing judges. Its committee on the Federal Judiciary rates the competence of judicial nominees, and a candidate is seriously damaged if he or she is rated "Not Qualified." Politically, however, the ABA is a very conservative group. Democratic presidents, consequently, pay less attention to its ratings than Republicans, and liberal senators are not inclined to let the testimony of the ABA outweigh other considerations.[24] Moreover, despite his own conservatism, Ronald Reagan did not consult the ABA before announcing the appointment of Justice O'Connor. Nevertheless, the influence of the ABA is considerable, and its role is one dimension of the peculiar qualities of judicial politics.

The Jurisdiction of Federal Courts

Jurisdiction: Getting a Hearing

Selecting judges, however, only sets the stage; the real drama takes place in court. Even before that, however, one must get into court. Courts will not hear every case, and there are special limitations that apply to the federal courts. Getting a hearing, in fact, may go a long way toward winning a case. Persuading a court to take jurisdiction and grant a hearing, moreover, is a political process and, implicitly, it requires courts to make decisions about the nature and purpose of American politics.

Article III limits the jurisdiction of the federal courts in three ways: (1) it limits the courts to "cases and controversies"; (2) it limits them by subject matter to "cases arising under" the Constitution, treaties, and federal laws, or under Admiralty and maritime law; and (3) it restricts them to cases in which the United States is a party, as well as those which involve more than one state, or the citizens of more than one state (see Table 12.2).

Congress, however, can and does limit even further the exercise of this authority. It has provided, for example, that cases between citizens of different states ("diversity of citizenship" cases) where less than $10,000 is involved will be decided by state courts. Congress may also decide to allow **concurrent jurisdiction,** in which both federal and state courts share the authority to hear a case. Examples are bank robbery and embezzlement. Federal agencies are involved because of federal laws governing banking; state courts are empowered by laws against larceny.

In cases of concurrent jurisdiction, it is theoretically possible for a criminal to be prosecuted in both state and federal courts and to be subject to a

TABLE 12.2 Jurisdiction of the Federal Courts

Federal Jurisdiction	No Federal Jurisdiction
Under Article III of the Constitution, federal courts have jurisdiction in:	
All cases "arising under" the Constitution, treaties, or federal laws	
All cases involving ambassadors or diplomatic personnel	
All cases of Admiralty or maritime law	
In addition, federal courts have jurisdiction in "cases and controversies" in which:	
The United States is a party (is suing or being sued by someone else)	
A state is suing someone	A state is being sued by private persons or by foreign governments (Eleventh Amendment)
A state is being sued by another state	
The parties are citizens of different states	
The parties are citizens of the *same* state, but the suit involves land claimed under titles from *different* states	Under most circumstances, in cases involving citizens of the same state

kind of double jeopardy.* Government policy, however, is to avoid such prosecutions except in "unusual circumstances."

A similar problem was posed by the fact that states have rules of evidence different from those that apply in federal courts. For a long time, for instance, state courts were permitted to use evidence that had been obtained by illegal searches and seizures, so long as there was provision for punishing the officers who conducted the search.[25] Moreover, state officers could give this sort of evidence to *federal* officials, who could then introduce it in federal court, although it would have been inadmissable if federal officers had acquired it in the same way. This "silver platter doctrine" was eventually overturned in *Elkins* v. *Ohio* in 1960. In *Mapp* v. *Ohio* (1961), the Supreme Court extended the "exclusionary rule," which bars the admission of il-

***Barthus* v. *Illinois,* 359 U.S. 121 (1959); a very slight doubt was raised on this point by *Waller* v. *Florida,* 397 U.S. 387 (1970).

legally obtained evidence, to state courts.[26] The controversies about this sort of evidence, however, illustrate the kind of problem that is bound to occur given the overlapping jurisdiction of federal and state judicial systems.

Nominated by Lyndon Johnson to be Chief Justice, Abe Fortas underwent extensive questioning by the Senate. *(UPI)*

The Jurisdiction of the Supreme Court

Ordinarily, a federal case originates in a district court; if appealed, the case goes first to a circuit court and then to the Supreme Court. The Constitution, however, gives the Supreme Court original jurisdiction in cases (1) involving ambassadors and diplomats, and (2) those "in which a state shall be a party." Congress, however, has granted concurrent original jurisdiction to lower federal courts in cases involving diplomats and many cases in which a state is a party. Suits by states against citizens of other states and even suits by the United States against a state may now originate in district courts. Consequently, the Supreme Court retains relatively exclusive original jurisdiction only in controversies between states.*

The reason for this change is clear: the Supreme Court had too much work for it to handle all the cases over which the Constitution gives it original jurisdiction. As Congress recognized, the Court had to reserve itself for the most important cases, delegating others to the lower federal courts. Much the same thing has happened to the Supreme Court's appellate jurisdiction.

Most cases are appealed to the Supreme Court from either the state supreme courts or the federal Courts of Appeal (see Figure 12-1). In some cases, however, which the Supreme Court believes are of "such imperative public importance" as to demand "immediate settlement," it may permit an appeal directly from a district court. During the Watergate scandal, President Nixon refused to surrender tapes of his conversations to a United States District Court that was hearing the prosecution of several people involved in the Watergate burglary. Nixon challenged the constitutionality of the district court's subpoena, claiming the confidential conversation was an "executive privilege" under the Constitution. The case seemed even more imperative because impeachment proceedings against Nixon were pending in the House of Representatives. Consequently, the Supreme Court permitted a direct appeal from the district court, eventually insisting that Nixon "forthwith" obey the subpoena.[27]

Cases are appealed to the Supreme Court in three ways: (1) by a writ of *certiorari,* (2) by appeal "as of right," and (3) by certification. The last method, certification, is extremely rare. It occurs when a lower court—not one of the parties to the case—asks the Supreme Court to answer certain questions of law that must be answered in order to reach a correct decision.

In a writ of *certiorari,* the Supreme Court will hear a case when four justices believe that the public issues raised by the case are important enough to be worth consideration by the Court. Only about 10 percent of the petitions for *certiorari* are granted. When it decides whether to grant *certiorari,* the Court exercises **judicial discretion,** reserving its scarce time

*For example, *Arizona* v. *California,* 373 U.S. 546 (1963).

FIGURE 12–1
How Cases Get to the Supreme Court

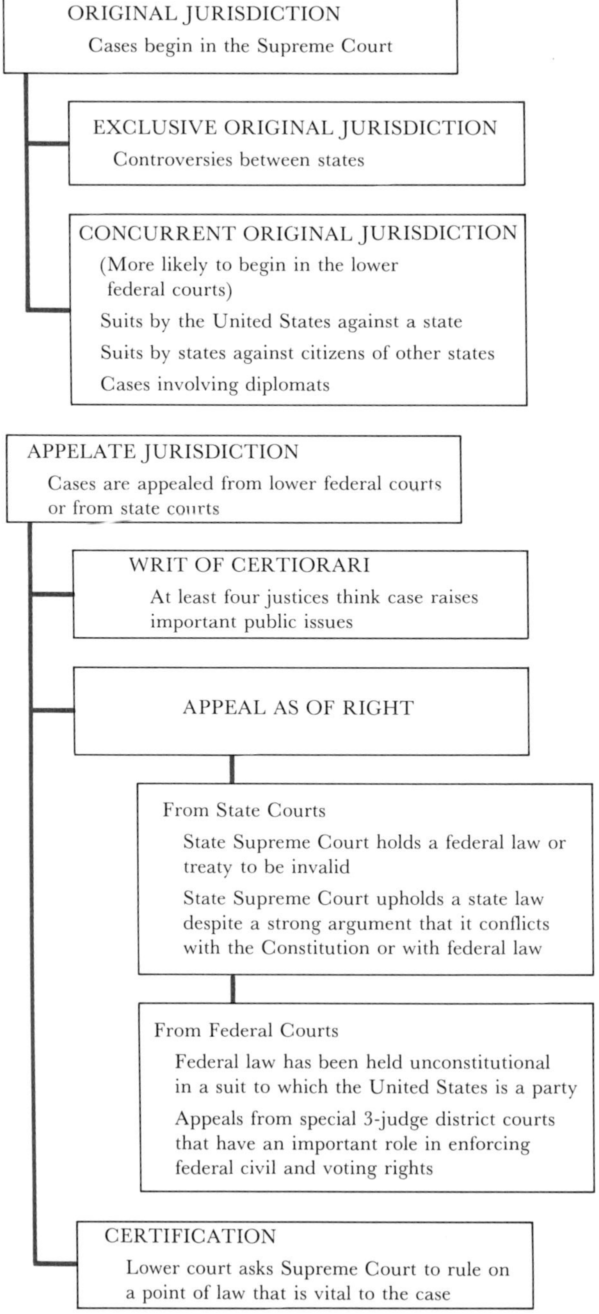

for those problems and controversies it thinks are vital to constitutional government in America.

ORIGINAL JURISDICTION
Cases begin in the Supreme Court
EXCLUSIVE ORIGINAL JURISDICTION
Controversies between states
CONCURRENT ORIGINAL JURISDICTION
(More likely to begin in the lower federal courts)
Suits by the United States against a state
Suits by states against citizens of other states
Cases involving diplomats
APPELATE JURISDICTION
Cases are appealed from lower federal courts or from state courts
WRIT OF CERTIORARI
At least four justices think case raises important public issues
APPEAL AS OF RIGHT
From State Courts
State Supreme Court holds a federal law or treaty to be invalid
State Supreme Court upholds a state law despite a strong argument that it conflicts with the Constitution or with federal law
From Federal Courts
Federal law has been held unconstitutional in a suit to which the United States is a party
Appeals from special 3-judge district courts that have an important role in enforcing federal civil and voting rights
CERTIFICATION
Lower court asks Supreme Court to rule on a point of law that is vital to the case

Appeal as a right is more similar to *certiorari* than one might suspect. Congress has granted a "right" to appeal to the Supreme Court from state courts when (1) a state supreme court has upheld a state law against a substantial argument that the law conflicts with the U.S. Constitution, treaties, or federal law, or (2) a state supreme court holds a federal law or treaty to be invalid. The "right" of appeal also includes appeals from federal courts when a federal law has been held unconstitutional and the federal government is a party to the suit. There is also a "right" of appeal from certain special, three-judge district courts when the federal or state regulations involved in the case are alleged to be unconstitutional. (These special courts are particularly important in the area of civil and voting rights.) There are other, less important examples of the right to appeal. In fact, however, the right of appeal is greatly limited in practice. Congress has granted the right of appeal in too many cases for the Court to hear them all, and in 1928, Congress authorized the Court to refuse to hear those cases in which it does not think there is a substantial federal question. In fact, the Court rules out about 50 to 60 percent of all appeals "as of right."

The Court, in other words, has what amounts to *complete discretion to decide what cases it will hear* based on its judgments of those cases that raise "important" issues or "substantial" questions for constitutional government. Since, as we have observed, a case must get into court before one can win it, this decision is the most crucial stage in litigation before the Supreme Court.[28]

GRANTING JURISDICTION This vital decision requires the Justices of the Supreme Court to turn to an explicit or implicit theory of constitutional government that defines the essential qualities of our form of government and determines what questions are "important" or "substantial." Before it hears a case, the supreme Court attempts to separate the politically essential from the accidental. It is, in summary, outlining our political identity as a people.

If it refuses to hear a case, the Court leaves the question to be decided by private organizations or by more or less specialized public agencies (such as committees of Congress, bureaucratic agencies, and local bodies) that are likely to be responsive to a narrow range of values and private interests.[29] A judicial ruling, by contrast, is always an attempt to apply the **principle of aggregation,** settlement by a common rule. When the Court declines to hear a case, it is also defining the limits of our commonality.

CASES AND CONTROVERSIES As we have observed, the Constitution limits the constitutional courts to "cases and controversies." As a result, the federal courts will not rule on abstract principles of hypothetical cases. They will only rule in specific cases involving at least two parties whose claims are in conflict.[30]

Many of the framers opposed this restriction. Madison, for example, wanted the Court to share the veto power with the president, (1) because it would help keep unconstitutional laws off the books, and (2) because laws can be "unjust, oppressive, or pernicious" without being unconstitutional. This position, however, went too far for most delegates to the Constitutional Convention. The majority preferred to limit the judiciary to particular cases, trying to hold the courts to the role of arbiters between interests. The "case and controversy" clause, in other words, strengthened the strategy of fragmentation.[31]

There are other reasons, however, for limiting the courts to cases and controversies. Judges rely on the competition between contestants. A great deal of their information must be brought to them by the parties to a suit, who are at least familiar with the relevant facts. Conflict gives judges some protection against biased or partial information: the courts trust that opposing lawyers will challenge any debatable or misleading assertions. For this adversary system to work, however, there must be a real clash, a contest that both parties want to win.[32]

Nevertheless, the Court will sometimes allow a suit where the parties do not really disagree if the Court wants to rule on the case and is satisfied that it has all the information it needs. For example, in *Carter* v. *Carter Coal Co.*, a stockholder (Carter) asked the Court to forbid the company to obey certain federal regulations. The company itself did not want to obey these rules, but it did not want to risk defying them; in fact, Carter was suing the company with its support. In this case, however, the Court felt it had enough information to relax the "controversy" rule.[33]

The **case and controversy rule** means that the Court must wait, on the whole, for a case to arise. Unlike Congress or the president, it is very hard for the Court to take the initiative in raising a public question. Judges can and do encourage cases; in their opinions, they can hint, sometimes pointedly, that a particular argument would be successful. For example, several justices of the Supreme Court suggested that they might be disposed to rule that the death penalty in cases of rape was "cruel and unusual punishment," even though that question was not before them.* But even if someone takes the hint and brings suit in the way the Court suggests, the judicial process takes time, and it will be a long while before the Court can rule. The case and controversy rule makes the Court relatively passive and slow moving, and it always leaves open the argument that in a different case, the Court's ruling would not apply.

STANDING TO SUE One derivative of the "case and controversy" rule is the Court's decision that only certain parties have **standing to sue.** This means that in order to bring suit, someone must have a personal interest in the outcome greater than the interest of the public at large. In a sense, all citizens have an interest in the outcome of all cases: it affects us if unjustice is done or the Constitution is violated. However, most cases affect us only indirectly or in small ways, and as a result, we do not care very much about them. If someone is denied a hunting license unfairly, for example, it affects our right to fair treatment from government agencies, but this will not upset us very much if we don't hunt. Nonhunters, in other words, could not be trusted to spend the time, energy, and money it takes to make the best case on behalf of the hunter's right to a license. Similarly, if the hunter in question were denied his or her license because that individual is black, white hunters could not be trusted to make the best case.

A **litigant** (a party to a suit), in this sense, is a kind of representative of all those whose interests are at stake in the case. The Court observes that such people have a right to be well represented, to have the case argued by a litigant who cares enough to guarantee that it is presented ably and with force. For example, the Court ruled that the interest of an ordinary tax-

*See Justice Goldberg's opinion, which Brennan and Douglas joined, in *Snider* v. *Cunningham*, 375 U.S. 83 (1968).

payer in the moneys in the Treasury is too "minute" to give such a taxpayer standing to sue. To sue, a taxpayer would have to show that his or her interest is substantial.[34]

In recent years, the Court has defined "substantial interest" in a more inclusive way. The Warren Court held that taxpayers might have standing to sue if there was a logical relationship (or "nexus") between being a taxpayer and the constitutional provision under dispute. If Congress has violated its power to tax and spend, the Court reasoned, taxpayers are the parties whose interests are most clearly affected. What matters, the Court argued, is not how great the interest is, but whether there is enough "personal stake" to guarantee "concrete adverseness" between the parties.[35]

The Court also expanded the definition of "interests" to include the concern of citizens and groups for public values and policies. Previously, the Court had insisted that for judicial purposes, the only interests that counted were those recognized by the Constitution and by statutes. When the Tennessee Valley Authority began to compete with privately owned power companies, it certainly hurt them severely, but the Court ruled that the private companies had no legal right to be free from competition.[36] Now, by contrast, the Court does not require that an interest or right be explicitly acknowledged by law. It is sufficient if policies or values are "arguably" within the "zone of interests" that Congress or the Constitution aimed to protect. An "interest," then, is defined by public purposes and goals as evinced in the political process, rather than the specific provisions of a statute.[37]

Political Questions When the Court denies "standing," it may be saying that a particular litigant lacks the "substantial interest" that another might have. But it may also be asserting that no litigant would be appropriate and that the case does not lend itself to adjudication. A number of reserve officers opposed to the Vietnam War sought to challenge the right of reservists

The Supreme Court now includes several conservative justices appointed by Presidents Nixon, Ford, and Reagan—virtually reversing the composition of the Warren Court. *(UPI)*

and members of the National Guard to sit in Congress, pointing out that the Constitution forbids a member of Congress holding "office" under the United States (Art. I, sec. 2, clause 3). The Court ruled, however, that the Reservists to Stop the War did not have standing because its members were not specifically injured by reservists serving in Congress. In all probability, no litigant could ever show such an injury. The Court was ruling, in effect, that any remedy had to be sought "politically," that is, through public opinion and through the other branches of government.[38]

As this implies, the Court will not rule on those controversies it defines as political questions. When the Court classifies a question as "political," it is saying that the controversy raises matters outside and beyond the reach of law.

The rule of law presupposes common standards and basic institutions. The authority of the Court, for example, cannot extend further than the Constitution, and consequently, the Court has ruled that the conduct of foreign relations is a "political question."[39] Similarly, the Court does not feel empowered to decide cases in which the Constitution itself is in doubt. Ordinarily, this is not a problem: we agree about what the Constitution says, and we ask the Court to decide what it means. Sometimes, however, there is doubt about whether an amendment to the Constitution has been ratified. State legislatures that initially approved an amendment sometimes want to rescind their ratification. Does the original ratification "count" toward the three-quarter vote of the states necessary to adopt the amendment? Or can a state change its mind so long as the process is still going on? This question, for example, arose in relation to the proposed Equal Rights Amendment. The Court has ruled that such disputes about the due ratification of constitutional amendments are "political questions."[40]

Similarly, where there is lack of consensus on basic principles, the Court sometimes terms the issue "political." In 1842, a large number of people in Rhode Island tried to overthrow the existing, rather undemocratic, constitution and set up a new regime. The Supreme Court refused to decide which government was the legitimate government of Rhode Island. Although the Constitution does guarantee every state a "republican form of government," Chief Justice Taney observed that, within broad limits, people disagree about the meaning of those terms, and the Constitution does not tell us how to decide between defensible theories of republican government or how to determine the "will of the people."[41] Many years later, the Court refused, on similar grounds, to decide whether the initiative and referendum were forms of "direct democracy" at odds with a "republican form of government."[42]

Consensus, however, is a changing standard. In 1946, the Court ruled that the apportionment of legislatures was a political question; there was, apparently, no single theory of representation that all states were compelled to adopt. In 1962, however, the Court began to rule that states were obliged to apportion legislatures on the basis of "one person, one vote." Justice Harlan, among others, was outraged and wrote bitter dissenting opinions. Nevertheless, the Court's decisions have been broadly accepted and seem to have reflected a growing consensus among Americans that apportionment by population was the only legitimate method for designing legislative districts.[43]

This discussion should indicate that "political questions" are hard to define, especially since the meaning of the term changes over time. By holding that some questions are "political," however, the Court does recognize that there are areas that are outside its competence and authority.

Interest Groups and Litigation

Even if a case passes all the tests and gets by all the obstacles we have discussed, it is not assured of a hearing. Taking a case to court costs money for lawyers and research, and it is very expensive to pursue a constitutional issue all the way to the Supreme Court. The case of *Brown* v. *Board of Education,* which ruled against segregation in the schools, cost the plaintiffs $200,000 in 1954, and inflation has multiplied costs since then. In other words, ordinary citizens as individuals cannot take a case through the federal courts. They need the pooled resources and support of interest groups to make their rights effective.[44]

It would be easy to thwart civil rights if each individual had to go to court to win his or her rights; cost and inconvenience would act as major deterrents, especially since there is no certainty of winning in the end. Local governments in the South, for example, used the tactic of forcing each individual to go to court to try to frustrate black demands for equality. Moreover, some money claims are too small to be worth the cost of taking them to court. Small shareholders and ordinary customers, consequently, have few effective rights if they act on their own. Whether we are talking about civil rights or commercial claims, it is necessary to consolidate cases in order to get judicial protection for the rights of ordinary citizens.[45] Even well-to-do citizens often find such consolidation advantageous. The Mountain States Legal Foundation represents businesspeople and others who want to open public lands to oil drilling, grazing, and commercial development. James Watt, Ronald Reagan's first—and controversial—Secretary of the Interior, once served as the Foundation's chief counsel.

The Supreme Court made it easier for interest groups to act on behalf of such citizens when it relaxed its standard for *class action suits.* In such cases, someone who has been injured is allowed to sue on behalf of all similarly injured persons. Groups (and individuals) that could not afford a multitude of suits may be able to afford one; small shareholders or customers may get the benefit from suits brought by larger claimants. Liberalized rules for class action expand the access of ordinary citizens to the courts and, consequently, lessen the power of large-scale organizations and interests.

Between 1970 and 1975, encouraged by the Court's more friendly attitude toward such actions, class action suits nearly doubled. As the Court has become more conservative, it has become more suspicious of class action suits, insisting on a narrower and more specific definition of the class of persons and the injuries they are alleged to have suffered.[46] This restrictive attitude, obviously, reduces the citizen's access to the courts and makes large organizations and highly organized interests relatively invulnerable.

Groups also participate in litigation in another way. An organization like the American Civil Liberties Union or the National Association for the Advancement of Colored People often petitions to be allowed to enter a case in which it has an interest but which it has not brought. It asks to be admitted to the case as *amicus curiae* (a "friend of the court"), submitting arguments on legal points that are within its area of expertise and concern. Courts tend to grant such requests, since judges want the best information and analysis they can get. An organization's reputation for ability and reliability may make judges attend to its arguments, and the support of such groups is an important resource in the judicial process.

Outcomes: How Courts Decide

The Mechanics of Supreme Court Decision

In its weekly Friday Conference, the Supreme Court meets to discuss, privately, the cases it has heard recently. There is every effort to preserve confidentiality: no one except the justices is present, and no formal records are kept of their discussion.

The Court decides by majority rule. The Chief Justice, if he or she voted with the majority, assigns someone to write the opinion of the Court. If the Chief Justice was on the losing side, the senior associate justice who voted with the majority will assign the opinion. A justice is chosen to write an opinion, in the first place, because it is thought that he or she will say what must be said in order to hold the majority together. An opinion of the Court is not necessarily the opinion of the justice who writes it: it must reflect the common ground on which the majority agreed.[47]

Second, a justice may be selected to write an opinion because it is believed that he or she will add to the authority of the Court's decision. The Chief Justice may decide to write an opinion, for example, because this stature gives evidence of the Court's concern. Similarly, a judge may be chosen because his or her political beliefs would ordinarily incline him or her to take the other side. A liberal justice supporting a decision restrictive of civil liberty or a conservative siding with the right to an abortion is persuasive because he or she must have felt the argument very compelling, and such a justice is likely to be heard respectfully by those who are displeased with the decision.*

In extremely important cases, the Court hopes for unanimity to make the decision seem certain and irreversible. John Marshall, for example, strove for unanimous opinions as a way of establishing the Court's authority early in its history and even wrote opinions contrary to his own judgment in order to preserve the appearance of unity. In such vital cases, any justice who has doubts or questions may be able to dictate the grounds on which a case is decided. In 1941, for example, Chief Justice Stone wanted a unanimous decision against a California law that restricted the right of migrant workers to enter the state. Most judges felt that the law was contrary to the "privileges and immunities" clause of the Fourteenth Amendment. Justice Byrnes, however, announced that he would dissent unless the Court decided the case on the basis of the commerce power. Moreover, James Byrnes insisted on writing the opinion himself. Justice Jackson was

*Justice Black, a liberal, wrote the opinion that sustained the relocation of Japanese Americans (*Korematsu* v. *U.S.*, 323, U.S. 214 [1944]). Justice Blackmun, a conservative, spoke for the Court on the question of abortion (*Roe* v. *Wade*, 410 U.S. 113 [1973]).

outraged by Byrnes's opinion which, he said, must "result in . . . distorting commercial law or denaturing human rights," and other justices agreed. Justice Stone, however, thought unanimity worth the price.*

THE IMPORTANCE OF OPINION Why do the justices care so much about the Court's opinion? For the people involved in the case, after all, it is the Court's decision, not its reasons, that determines winners and losers, assigns damages, or sends culprits to jail. For the *political society,* however, the Court's *argument is far more important than the outcome* of the case.

Simply deciding a case does not establish a rule. Every case is different, in some respects, from every other case. Suppose that the Court has just decided a case somewhat like one that concerns me. Will it rule in the same way in my case? Or are the differences between the cases so important that I have reason to fear (or hope) that the Court will rule differently? I can only make such a prediction by knowing what factors the Court thought were important in the earlier case and what it thought trivial or accidental. I need to know the Court's reasoning before I can know whether one case establishes a precedent for my own. The Court's opinion establishes a standard of likeness or unlikeness in different cases; it is the *argument* of the Court that creates a *general rule* applicable to all cases.

This has vital political consequences. When an attorney advises us on what the law forbids or permits, he or she is predicting what courts will decide. When the police arrest a suspected criminal, search a car, or inquire into our conduct, they are assuming that the courts will sustain their actions. When citizens insist on their right to attend an integrated school or to say things that offend their neighbors, they ordinarily rely on support from the courts. Such predictions involve an element of risk, but we feel we have reasonable grounds for hope. By influencing what lawyers, officials, and attentive citizens expect, the courts can shape what they advise and do; the opinions of courts, consequently, can have an important impact on public behavior.

We are most influenced by court opinions that are clear and articulate because confusing opinions lend themselves to differing interpretations. We are also more inclined to rely on a well-argued opinion, both because it persuades us and because it makes it seem less likely that judges will be persuaded to change their minds. Finally, as we have observed, consensus on the Supreme Court and among other courts makes an opinion more forceful because it disposes us to believe that the decision is permanent. Whenever the Court speaks clearly, with forceful reasoning and with considerable consensus, we are likely to change our behavior to adapt to the law.

DISSENTING AND CONCURRING OPINIONS As this suggests, however, whenever there is confusion or disagreement among judges, the force of law is weakened, especially if **dissenting opinions,** those that disagree with the majority, seem to have the better of the argument. Dissenting opinions hold out the hope for change, especially in 5 to 4 decisions where one justice

*On Marshall's view, see Donald Morgan, *Justice William Johnson* (Columbia: U. of South Carolina P., 1954) pp. 181–82; on Byrnes's role in *Edwards* v. *California,* 314 U.S. 160 (1941), see Alpheus T. Mason, *Harlan Fisk Stone: Pillar of the Law* (New York: Viking, 1956), p. 501.

holds the balance, and even one or a few dissenters may be able to shape the future of law if they state their case well. **Concurring opinions,** in which a judge accepts the decision of the majority but departs from its reasons, also weaken the impact of a court's decisions. They suggest that given different circumstances or different arguments, the majority might fall apart. A great many lawyers, in fact, criticize concurring opinions as no more than expressions of personal pride that undermine the certainty of law.[48]

By contrast, most lawyers and legal scholars seem reconciled to dissenting opinions. Thomas Jefferson argued against John Marshall that it was a mistake for the Court to issue opinions that concealed disagreements between judges. It would be better, Jefferson reasoned, to give the public—the ultimate authority—the best arguments for and against a decision.[49] After all, any majority on the Court is made up of a small number of fallible human beings, and it can easily be mistaken. Whenever the Court misconceives the nature of the United States as a political society or does violence to our identity as a people, as it did in the Dred Scott case, it is desirable that some voices on the Court should remind us of the truth of the matter. The history of American constitutional law would be poorer, and the Court less honorable, without the great dissents.

How the Courts Decide on Interpretation of the Constitution and of the Laws

The most important task of the federal courts is upholding the Constitution of the United States, a task that requires them to interpret it. Sometimes the language of the Constitution is clear and beyond debate. It would be hard to argue, for example, about the provision that the Senate "shall be composed of two Senators from each state, chosen . . . for six years; and each Senator shall have one vote." (Art. I, sec. 3, clause 1). But other phrases are evidently more ambiguous. A term like *the freedom of speech* involves *clear* meanings—for example, one's right to make a reasoned argument about public issues to a peaceful meeting. It also has *possible* meanings, such as the right to utter obscenities or urge violent revolution, about which Americans disagree.

The Court does not rule on cases involving the clear meanings of the Constitution; it deals with issues in which there is a good argument on both sides. The clear meanings, however, are the foundation of interpretation. Within the area of disagreement (possible meanings), the Court is trying to mark the line that separates *permissible* and *impermissible usage.* For example, the Court has ruled that "the freedom of speech" authorizes an organization to refuse to disclose its membership to a legislative committee, but free speech does not permit demonstrators to obstruct the normal operations of government. The Supreme Court and the lower federal courts *school public language* by establishing the range of *legitimate meanings* that can be attached to the language of the Constitution.*

**Gibson* v. *Florida Legislative Investigation Committee,* 372 U.S. 539 (1936); *Adderley* v. *Florida,* 385 U.S. 39 (1967); on the general point, see Ralph Lerner, "The Supreme Court as Republican Schoolmaster," in Philip Kurland, ed., *The Supreme Court Review, 1967* (Chicago: U. of Chicago, 1967), pp. 127–80.

The Intent of the Framers In doing so, the Court will consult the intention of the framers and the way in which the framers understood the terms of the Constitution. Contemporary Americans take their institutions more or less for granted. Political culture is a matter of habit, and many Americans have no idea of the promises or implications of the Constitution. The framers, by contrast, thought seriously and spoke articulately about these matters. In that sense, the framers made explicit much of what has become implicit in American life, and we consult them in order to better understand ourselves.

Public Purpose But the intent of the framers is not always clear. Sometimes they disagreed or spoke ambiguously. The Constitution, for example, gives the federal government power to regulate "commerce among the several states." The framers' goal seems clear enough: they believed that "interstate commerce" was desirable and that it ought not to be burdened by local regulation. It is harder to tell how far they wanted federal authority to extend. Is there some point at which commerce "among" the states leaves off and commerce "within" a state begins? What is the distinction, in other words, between "interstate" and "intrastate" commerce? Scholars and judges have wrestled with this question for a long time and probably will continue to do so. In general, however, the Supreme Court has held that a *public purpose implies all the power needed to accomplish that purpose.* In Chief Justice Marshall's famous statement,

> It must have been the intention of those who gave these powers to insure . . . their beneficial execution. This could not be done by confiding the choice of means to such narrow limits as not to leave it in the power of Congress to adopt any which might be appropriate and which were conducive to the end.[50]

Congress has the authority, under this doctrine, to control intrastate commerce if it needs to do so in order to control interstate commerce. Thus, the authority of Congress varies with time: it depends on the nature of interstate commerce and the things necessary to control it. Hence, the expansion of commercial relations and the unification of the national economy extend the scope of the commerce power.[51] From time to time, the Court has quarreled with this approach and has tried to find some permanent, restrictive definition of interstate commerce. On the whole, however, the Court has followed Marshall's rule that in the absence of specific prohibitions, ends define means and public purpose conveys authority.

The Spirit of the Laws The Court also relies on philosophical ideas and doctrines drawn from the tradition of political theory. The case for such unwritten first principles depends on one or more of the following arguments: (1) they were doctrines held by the framers and, hence, implicitly part of their intent; (2) they are part of the spirit of the Constitution as distinct from the letter; or (3) they are derived from nature, specifically from human nature, and take precedence over all human-made law. These arguments are related. The framers certainly believed, for example, that a body of laws had a "spirit" or quality that characterized the whole of a political society as opposed to its parts. Hamilton carefully avoided a direct answer to the charge that the Constitution empowered the federal courts "to construe the laws according to the spirit of the constitution." He observed that the Constitution does not directly give the courts such power, but he went on to say that the "general theory of a limited constitution" does give such a power, arguing only that this is also "applicable to . . . the state governments" and their judiciaries.[52] Hamilton argues, in other words, that the *idea of limited government* is a "spirit" or basic premise that pervades our Constitution, and that this spirit conveys to the courts the power of judging according to the "spirit of the constitution." The Court, too, has from time to time appealed to the "spirit of our free institutions" or the "essence of ordered liberty."[53]

The idea that there is a spirit of the laws implies that a whole is more than the sum of its parts, a very complicated (and debatable) philosophical thesis, and it confirms that interpretations of the Constitution depend on theories of politics. For example, the Constitution says very little about foreign policy. It provides for the way in which ambassadors are to be appointed and in which treaties are to be made and ratified; it gives Congress the power to regulate trade and to declare war. Otherwise, it is silent. When questions about the conduct of foreign policy arose, the Supreme Court appealed to the **theory of sovereignty,** the argument that a "political society must have a supreme will somewhere," at least in foreign affairs. Sovereignty in foreign affairs (and with it, a certain "delicate, plenary and exclusive" power vested in the president) *does not depend on the Constitution,* the Court argued. It inheres in the *nature of political society* and *international politics.* Outside our boundaries, the Court declared, the United States is endowed with a "right and power" equal to that of other nations; logically, then, this "sovereign power" is not defined by what the Constitution says but by what other nations do.[54] Among other things, sovereignty has been held to give Congress an "absolute and unqualified" right to admit and expel aliens. In this crucial respect, aliens residing in the United States are not protected by the Constitution. This worries the Court, and it has limited Congress's power over aliens in some respects. Nevertheless, the Burger Court recently held that the Immigration Service may use illegally obtained evidence in order to deport aliens, and has indicated that in general, aliens can expect only limited protection from the Fourth and Fifth Amendments. The basic position of aliens is still defined by "sovereignty," a theoretical notion that the Court derived from nature as the Court understands it, not the words of the Constitution.*

Precedent Above all, courts try to follow *precedent* (see Chapter 2), adopting the interpretation or rule that has been used in similar cases in the past. This applies to nonconstitutional as well as to constitutional cases. Precedent has a value in itself, quite separate from the wisdom of earlier decisions. It makes people secure if they believe that the rule of law will be the same tomorrow as it is today. It gives them stable expectations about their rights and duties, encouraging them to exercise or assert their rights, and it encourages them to make long-term commitments. Consequently, courts

**Fong Yue Ting* v. *U.S.*, 149 U.S. 698 (1893); for later limits, see *Hampton* v. *Mew Sung Wong,* 426 U.S. 88 (1976). The Burger Court's rulings on evidence may be found in *INS* v. *Lopez-Mendoza,* 52 L.W. 5190, June 26, 1984, and *INS* v. *Delgado,* 52 L.W. 4436, April 17, 1984.

will try to follow the rule of precedent (or *stare decisis*) even if judges do not entirely agree with previous decisions. Justice Brandeis wrote, "in most matters, it is more important that the applicable rule of law be settled than that it be settled right."[55]

But there are crucial qualifications to this principle. First, as Justice Brandeis also observed, the Court has greater reason to overrule precedents in cases involving constitutional law. If Congress does not like the Court's interpretation of a statute, it can pass a new one that sets matters straight, but it is much harder to pass a constitutional amendment. Consequently, Brandeis argued, the Court is under great pressure to correct its own mistakes in constitutional interpretation, whatever damage this does to the rule of precedent.

Second, it is not always easy to determine which precedent, out of many possible precedents, to apply, and it is not always clear that there is any precedent. Since all cases are different, involving different parties, different circumstances, and different times, it is always easy for the Court to distinguish cases, arguing that two cases are so different that the earlier rule is no precedent for the present case, at least without modification.

This ability to distinguish cases allows the Court to change a rule of law gradually, allowing people to revise their expectations little by little, minimizing any damage to their sense of security. By the 1930s, for example, the Court had become dissatisfied with the doctrine that permitted racial segregation so long as "separate but equal" facilities were available to both races. Racial segregation, however, was entrenched in parts of the North as well as the South, and the Court was not inclined to challenge so established an institution directly. Rather than argue that separate facilities could never be equal, the Court upheld "separate but equal," but it began to find that particular forms of segregation were not in fact equal. Missouri, for example, admitted only whites to its university law school, but it paid tuition for black students at law schools in neighboring states. The Court ruled that this was not "equal protection of the laws" because a state was obliged to give equal protection "within its boundaries."[56] A decade later, the Court ruled that it was not equal to admit blacks to a law school but require them to sit in a separate row in classrooms. The Court also ruled that a separate black law school was not equal because the university law school had more prestige and a more distinguished faculty.[57] After these decisions, very little was left of "separate but equal." The Court had chipped away at the doctrine so much that it was not a great surprise when the Court, in *Brown* v. *Board of Education,* finally argued directly that segregation was incompatible with equal protection. Even in that case, however, the Court denied that its earlier ruling was wrong. It distinguished cases: the "place" of public education in American life had changed, the Court argued, and "psychological knowledge" about the effects of segregation had improved. Even in that landmark case, the Court tried to damage the rule of precedent as little as possible.[58]

Interpreting the Constitution is evidently not a simple or mechanical task. And although the Court will try to respect the rule of precedent, it is by no means bound by it. The Court's role is philosophical and theoretical, not technical, and although this applies to the Supreme Court with particular force, it is true of the lower courts as well. Each judge must answer the questions and puzzles posed by the problem of interpretation.

Limits on Judicial Power

Internal Limits

On all the great questions of law, there is room for disagreement, so it is no surprise that there are differences between lawyers and judges on the proper interpretation of the Constitution and the laws. It is also to be expected that interpretations are influenced by feelings and by political beliefs. Over the years, observers have found it useful to classify judges as "liberals" and "conservatives." *Liberals*—Justice Brennan, for example—tend to uphold the constitutionality of social and economic legislation and are inclined to take a broad view of the rights guaranteed by the First and Fourteenth Amendments. *Conservatives*—for example, the arch opponents of the New Deal, Sutherland, VanDevanter, McReynolds, and Butler—hold the contrary convictions. In general classifications like these are clearly useful in understanding the courts.[59]

But the "liberal" and "conservative" labels are tricky. Justice Frankfurter was very "liberal" in matters of economic and social legislation, but he was "conservative" on questions of civil liberty. An extreme conservative, Justice Sutherland, took an extremely "liberal" view of executive power in foreign affairs and wrote a landmark opinion expanding the meaning of the Fourteenth Amendment.[60] Each judge tends to take pride in his or her own very personal notion of the law, something that makes the "blocks" on the Supreme Court very loose and unstable.[61]

In 1981, President Reagan appointed the first woman to sit on the Supreme Court—Sandra Day O'Connor. *(Wide World Photos)*

This only emphasizes that judges, and especially justices of the Supreme Court, have a great deal of discretion in interpreting the Constitution and laws. Charles Evans Hughes had this in mind when he remarked that the Constitution "is what the judges say it is."* This fact leads some scholars to argue that judges simply "make up" the Constitution out of their own beliefs and feelings. In this relativistic view, judicial opinions are only "rationalizations," efforts to justify and disguise what are, essentially, nothing more than the judge's biases, convictions, and interests. Edward H. Levi wrote that constitutional interpretation is fundamentally only judicial discretion "concealed either as the search for the intention of the framers or as a proper understanding of a living instrument, and sometimes as both."[62]

The private, subjective side of a judge's role, however, is only part of the story. A judge is a public person engaged in a public task. If a judge is deciding my case I care about his or her public decision, not the private feelings that led to it. If I am influenced by a court's opinion, it will be the reasoning and rhetoric of the opinion, not its origins and development, that persuade me. In law and politics, the public dimension is decisive. And, in fact, a judge's discretion is severely limited.

In the first place, judges are part of a profession with its own traditions and its own ways of reasoning and talking. Judges are influential only if they argue in those terms.

The pressure of the legal profession is more than intellectual. At local levels, lawyers are likely to work frequently with one another and to develop social ties and common interests. Groups like this are likely to share attitudes toward law and toward court decisions, and these opinions will have a

*Hughes made this remark in a speech at Elmira, N.Y., May 3, 1907.

vital effect on what the law means in practice.[63] Courts, moreover, can never ignore other courts. Lower courts are crucial in carrying out decisions; higher courts may reverse the holdings of a lower court unless they are persuaded that its decision was sound. The court hierarchy, then, exerts strong pressures on a judge's decisions and on the reasons he or she gives for them. Second, courts are part of a political society with its own on-going purposes, ways of speaking, and customs, and a court is necessarily limited by this fact.

Political Limits on the Court

Justice Holmes was right: courts can and do "legislate," but only in the gaps left open by the legal tradition, our political culture, and the place of the court in constitutional politics.[64] In fact, the Supreme Court is reluctant to rule on constitutional questions at all. If a case can be resolved without reaching a question of constitutional interpretation, the Court has tended to do so. It would trivialize the Constitution, the Court reasons, to appeal to it in cases where lesser laws suffice.

The Court will also try to avoid ruling that any statute is unconstitutional. It presumes that laws are constitutional until the contrary is proved (although the Warren Court was highly suspicious of any statute that seemed to infringe on civil liberty). If there are two possible interpretations, one of which will save a statute and the other not, the Court is inclined to declare that Congress "intended" the former. Sometimes, in fact, the Court "saves" a statute only by making it ineffective or meaningless. The Smith Act, for example, prohibited conspiracies to "teach or advocate" the violent overthrow of the government. Clearly, Congress intended to outlaw the dissemination of communist doctrine. In *Yates* v. *U.S.*, however, the Court was able to rule that the Smith Act was constitutional only by interpreting it to permit the "theoretical" advocacy of revolutionary violence.[65] Even so, the effort to save statutes or avoid constitutional questions indicates the Court's reluctance to appeal to its own authority.

The Supreme Court must always be aware that it has the "last say" only in a very limited sense. The Court can hope to lead or educate majority opinion. It must recognize, however, that majority opinion will ultimately prevail.

In the first place, if a majority of Americans are discontented with the Court's opinions, and if that dissatisfaction is expressed in voting, majority opinion will make itself felt as members of the Court die or retire. Change of personnel, moreover, is only one of the ways—a slow but sure one—by which majority opinion can alter the rulings of the Court.

In cases where the Court has interpreted a statute, it can be overruled by new legislation. If the Court declares a law unconstitutional, it is always possible to pass an amendment reversing its ruling. The Eleventh and Sixteenth Amendments resulted from just such a situation.* The amending

**Chisholm* v. *Ga.,* 2 Dall. 419 (1793) resulted in the Eleventh Amendment; the Sixteenth Amendment grew out of the protest against *Pollock* v. *Farmers' Loan and Trust,* 158 U.S. 601 (1895).

process, of course, is cumbersome and can be frustrated by any sizable minority, but majority opinion has other weapons.

It is always possible to change the number of judges on the Court. In 1863, for example, Congress raised the number of justices to ten in order to provide a more militant Unionist majority. During Andrew Johnson's term, Congress lowered the number of justices to seven in order to keep Johnson from making any appointments; when Johnson left office, Congress again set the number at nine. The public tends to be suspicious of this sort of tampering, as Franklin Roosevelt discovered, but that only emphasizes the dependence of the Court on opinion.

Moreover, apart from the original jurisdiction of the Supreme Court, which is specified in the Constitution, Congress can always withdraw or modify jurisdiction. After the Civil War, Congress deprived the Supreme Court of jurisdiction over cases under the Habeas Corpus Act of 1867 in order to prevent the Court from interfering with the Reconstruction.[66] Recently, opponents of abortion and advocates of prayer in the public schools have sought to persuade Congress to deny to the federal courts jurisdiction over both issues.

In the extreme case, people who find court decisions intolerable can always resist or refuse to comply with them. Resistance is most serious when the executive refuses to carry out the commands of the courts. During the Civil War, Chief Justice Taney issued a writ of habeas corpus ordering a military commander to release a prisoner (Merryman, a Southern sympathizer). The general in question, acting under presidential authority, refused to obey or even to appear in court. Taney wrote a stinging opinion attacking the president, but he could do nothing else. President Lincoln did, eventually, release Merryman, but he did so in his own time.[67]

More frequently, the courts meet with resistance from state and local governments. Local police departments have resisted court decisions granting new rights to suspected criminals; the effort of the courts to desegregate the schools has also met with a prolonged effort to find ways of avoiding or slowing integration.[68] On the whole, however, state and local agencies have complied even with court decisions they disliked intensely. This is especially

Police in Boston helping to enforce court-ordered busing. When there is resistance to their decisions, courts depend on executive authority to enforce the law. *(Wide World Photos)*

true if the cost of noncompliance is high: police officers would rather read a suspect his rights than see him go free, and school districts would rather integrate than lose federal aid.[69] In an even more important sense, however, the record of compliance is an indication of public support for the courts.

The Courts and Public Opinion

The authority of courts, as Hamilton observed, is always fragile and vulnerable. A hostile public has no shortage of ways to resist, modify, or overturn the rulings of the courts, and a determined majority will prevail over the courts sooner or later. Even a minority opposed to the courts forces the judiciary to rely on the executive to enforce its rulings, and the executive, in turn, is chosen by, and depends on, the support of public opinion. Alexis de Tocqueville was impressed by the power of judges in American politics, but he went on to state:

> Their power is enormous but it is clothed in the authority of public opinion. They are the all-powerful guardians of a people which respects law; but they would be impotent against public neglect or popular contempt.[70]

Activism and Self-Restraint Tocqueville's comments warn the courts against opposing deeply held public values. Yet equally, Tocqueville indicated the danger of failing to support public values and demands. As Tocqueville himself put it,

> The force of public opinion is the most intractable of agents, because its exact limits cannot be defined, and it is not less dangerous to exceed than to remain below the boundary prescribed.[71]

In other words, the courts are always in danger of doing too little or too much, and to do either they would endanger the public support on which they depend.

During the Warren years, this dilemma was the subject of a sharp debate on the Supreme Court. The majority of the Court, led by Chief Justice Warren, became more and more "activist." The Court took a more aggressive role in the pursuit of racial equality, demanding measures to promote equality rather than contenting itself with striking down discriminatory laws. The Court also expanded the rights of suspects in criminal cases, extended the meaning of the First Amendment, and discovered a "right to privacy." All of these activities stirred considerable, sometimes very militant, opposition and many people—including several justices on the Court—argued that the Court had gone too far.

Justice Felix Frankfurter was the most notable spokesperson for the school that urged **judicial self-restraint,** the doctrine that the Court is an essentially undemocratic institution and should not mistake its view for public values. In his view, the elected branches of government more perfectly reflect the public will. For the Court to oppose the judgment of elected officials puts it in a position that is at least vulnerable.* In addition

*See Frankfurter's concurring opinion in *Dennis* v. *U.S.*, 341 U.S. 494 (1951).

Otherwise considered a liberal, Justice Felix Frankfurter was conservative on questions of civil rights, believing in "judicial self-restraint." *(UPI)*

to this practical danger, there is a *moral* objection to an aggressive role for the courts. Even if there are real abuses that need to be corrected, if the courts take over the task of reform, they teach citizens to rely on the courts rather than on their own political participation. Judicial activism protects people against the consequences of bad citizenship, and to that extent it discourages individuals from taking the trouble to become good citizens. James Bradley Thayer warned many years ago against the risk that courts, in becoming too strong, might "dwarf the political capacities of the people."[72]

Chief Justice Warren and his allies, however, saw compelling reasons for **judicial activism,** the belief that the elected branches of government are not necessarily suited to reflect the values and the opinions of their constituents. The forces of fragmentation are powerful: legislatures are attentive to narrow and highly organized groups, and they are much more certain to represent our private interests than they are to articulate our public values. Moreover, given the "checks and balances" of our system, minorities often find it easy to block majorities; the most graphic example was the use of the filibuster in the Senate to stop civil rights laws. Consequently, to defer to the elected branches may slight public values.

Most people, for example, care about political liberties: they want and value freedom of speech, the right of assembly, and the right to vote. Most of us, however, find the world so complicated and confusing that it is difficult enough to take care of matters that touch us directly, here and now, and we neglect threats that are not pressing and that—at the moment—affect other people. The danger that we will allow public rights to be nibbled away is especially serious because some violations of our rights are subtle and covert.[73] The Court, judicial activists argued, may have to protect people against their own inattentiveness. This, after all, is what the framers intended: that the courts should act as an "intermediate body" between the public and its government.[74]

There is something to be said for both sides of this argument. Advocates of self-restraint are right that the courts cannot ignore opinion, even short-term opinion. They are also correct in observing that the courts are always in danger of mistaking their own dogmas for public values. Judicial activists, however, are right to argue that the courts must concern themselves with broader public values, especially since the public, as a general rule, wants and expects the courts to protect its liberties. As Justice Jackson wrote, "The people have seemed to feel that the Supreme Court, whatever its defects, is still the most detached, dispassionate and trustworthy custodian that our system affords. . . ."[75] Even so, the courts must take care: if they protect the people too well, both the people and the courts may forget that it is the public that is the ultimate safeguard of constitutional government.

SUMMARY

The United States has two court systems, the federal judiciary and the state judicial systems. The federal judiciary is composed of constitutional courts, which are limited to hearing cases between conflicting parties. There are ninety-three district courts, thirteen courts of appeal, and one Supreme Court in the federal judiciary. The judges that preside over these courts serve for life unless they resign or are removed by impeachment.

The Supreme Court and the federal courts under it have the authority to interpret the Constitution and to overrule the legislative and executive branches. The federal judiciary was entrusted with an amount of power that is relatively large for a constitutional system of checks and balances because the courts embody neither the force nor the momentary will of the people.

Federal judges are appointed by the president with the advice and consent of the Senate. The chief executive chooses people who support his or her political positions and share his or her views about the Constitution. Interest groups are able to influence judicial selection, particularly through the channel of the Senate Judiciary Committee. Partisan ties play a role as well, since presidents usually pick judges from their own party.

Most cases originate in a district court. The Supreme Court retains exclusive original jurisdiction only in controversies between states. Cases are appealed to the Supreme Court by a writ of *certiorari,* an appeal "as of right," or by certification. The Court has the right to determine which cases are significant enough for it to hear. The Court will not rule on controversies it defines as political questions, such as the conduct of foreign relations.

The Court has decided that in order to have standing to sue, the party to a controversy must have personal interest greater than the interest of the public at large. A litigant is considered a representative of all those whose interests are at stake in the case. The suer can be a group rather than an individual if that group proves to have a sincere concern for particular areas of policy.

The Supreme Court decides by majority rule; a tie vote sustains the decision of the lower court. Once a ruling has been made, a justice is chosen to write an opinion, which must set forth the argument of the majority. For political society, the argument is more important than the outcome of a case. The Court's opinion influences what lawyers, officials, and citizens expect, and therefore it can direct what they advise and do.

The federal courts, being charged with interpreting the Constitution, establish the range of legitimate meanings that can be attached to its language. The Supreme Court has a guideline for performing this most important function. Justices follow precedents, a practice that gives society stable expectations about their rights and duties. The Court may also appeal to the framers' intent, the spirit of the Constitution, or fundamental laws of human nature for authority. Justices often seek assistance from Chief Justice Marshall's rule, which says that in the absence of specific constitutional prohibitions, the end defines the means and public purpose conveys authority.

The authority of the courts is fragile and vulnerable. Majority opinion will ultimately prevail for a number of reasons. For example, if the Court interprets a statute, it can be overruled by new legislation. Congress also has the power to withdraw or modify the Court's jurisdiction.

The courts are always in danger of losing public support by doing too little or too much. They must find the right balance between judicial restraint and judicial activism at any period in history. Activism is good to the extent that it protects the people from the less detached branches of government; restraint is desirable insofar as it maintains the people as the ultimate safeguard of constitutional government.

NOTES

1. *Humphrey's Executor* v. *U.S.,* 295 U.S. 602 (1935).
2. Edward S. Corwin, *The Doctrine of Judicial Review* (Princeton: Princeton U. P., 1941), p. 17.
3. Robert K. Faulkner, *The Jurisprudence of John Marshall* (Princeton: Princeton U. P.), 1968.
4. *Scott* v. *Sandford,* 19 How. 393 (1857).
5. *Louisville, Cincinnati & Charleston Railroad* v. *Letson,* 2 How. 478 (1844).
6. *Santa Clara County* v. *Southern Pacific Railroad,* 118 U.S. 394 (1886).
7. A. E. Dick Howard, "The Burger Court," *Law and Contemporary Problems,* 43 (1980), p. 22.
8. *National League of Cities* v.*Usery,* 430 U.S. 833 (1976).
9. *New York* v. *Quarles,* 52 L.W. 4790, June 12, 1984; *U.S.* v. *Leon,* 52 L.W. 5155, June 26, 1984.
10. Benno C. Schmidt, Jr., "As Burger Continues, His Court Becomes Unstable," *The New York Times* (Sept, 30, 1984), p. E19; Justice O'Connor sided with Justice Rehnquist on 26 of 29 close decisions during the 1983–1984 term of the Court. Linda Greenhouse, "Conservatives on Supreme Court Domi-

nated Rulings of Latest Term," *The New York Times* (July 8, 1984), pp. 1, 18.

11. *The Federalist,* no. 31.
12. *Thomas* v. *Collins,* 323 U.S. 516 (1945).
13. *U.S.* v. *du Pont,* 353 U.S. 586 (1957).
14. *Eisenstadt* v. *Baird,* 408 U.S. 438 (1972).
15. Jack Peltason, *Federal Courts in the Political Process* (Garden City, N.Y.: Doubleday, 1955).
16. Anthony Champagne, Marian Neff, and Stuart Nagel, "Laws, Organizations, and the Judiciary," in *Handbook of Organizational Design* (New York: Oxford U. P., 1981), p. 189; David Manwaring, *Render Unto Caesar: The Flag Salute Controversy* (Chicago: U. of Chicago, 1963), pp. 33–34.
17. C. B. Swisher, *Stephen J. Field: Craftsman of the Law* (Washington: Brookings, 1930), pp. 243–44.
18. James Madison, *Notes of Debates in the Federal Convention in 1787,* A. Koch, ed. (Athens: Ohio U. P., 1966), p. 68; see also p. 315.
19. Ibid, pp. 315, 588.
20. John R. Schmidhauser, *The Supreme Court* (New York: Holt, 1961, pp. 44ff.; Howard Ball, *Counts and Politics* (Englewood Cliffs, N.J.: Prentice-Hall, 1980), p. 161.
21. Ball, p. 163.
22. Kenneth Richardson and Richard Vines, *The Politics of Federal Courts* (Boston: Little, Brown, 1970).
23. Henry J. Abraham, *Justices and Presidents* (New York: Oxford U. P., 1975).
24. Harold Chase, *Federal Judges: The Appointing Process.* (Minneapolis: U. of Minnesota, 1972), pp. 148–50.
25. *Wolf* v. *Colorado,* 388 U.S. 25 (1949).
26. *Elkins* v. *Ohio,* 364 U.S. 206 (1960); *Mapp* v. *Ohio,* 367 U.S. 643 (1961).
27. *U.S.* v. *Nixon,* 417 U.S. 683 (1974).
28. Schmidhauser, pp. 132–33.
29. Karen Orren, "Standing to Sue: Interest Group Conflict in the Federal Courts," *American Political Science Review,* 70 (1976), pp. 723–41.
30. *Hayburn's Case,* 2 Dall. 409 (1792).
31. Madison, pp. 340–43, 487, 539.
32. *Chicago and Grand Trunk Railway* v. *Wellman,* 143 U.S. 339 (1892).
33. *Carter* v. *Carter Coal Co.,* 298 U.S. 238 (1936).
34. *Frothingham* v. *Mellon* and *Massachusetts* v. *Mellon,* 262 U.S. 447 (1923).
35. *Flast* v. *Cohen,* 392 U.S. 83 (1968).
36. *Tennessee Electric Power Co.* v. *T.V.A.,* 306 U.S. 118 (1939).
37. Orren, pp. 732, 739–40; *Association of Data Processing Service Organizations* v. *Camp,* 397 U.S. 150–52, 157 (1970).
38. *Schlesinger* v. *Reservists to Stop the War,* 418 U.S. 208 (1974).
39. *Foster* v. *Neilson,* 2 Pet. 253 (1829).
40. *Coleman* v. *Miller,* 307 U.S. 433 (1939).
41. *Luther* v. *Borden,* 7 How. 1 (1849).
42. *Pacific States Telephone and Telegraph Co.* v. *Oregon,* 223 U.S. 118 (1912).
43. *Colegrove* v. *Green,* 328 U.S. 549 (1946); *Baker* v. *Carr,* 369 U.S. 186 (1962); *Reynolds* v. *Sims,* 377 U.S. 533 (1964).
44. Lucius Barker, "Third Parties in Litigation," *Journal of Politics,* vol. 29 (1967), pp. 41–69; Clement Vose, *Constitutional Change* (Lexington, Mass.: Lexington Books, 1972).
45. Orren, p. 725; Richard Kluger, *Simple Justice* (New York: Random House, 1977).
46. *Oppenheimer* v. *Sanders,* 437 U.S. 340 (1978).
47. Walter F. Murphy, *Elements of Judicial Strategy* (Chicago: U. of Chicago, 1960), pp. 59, 185.
48. Schmidhauser, pp. 141–44.
49. Paul L. Ford, ed., *The Writings of Thomas Jefferson* (New York: Putnam, 1899), pp. 223–24.
50. *McCulloch* v. *Maryland,* 4 Wh. 316 (1819); see also *Charles River Bridge Co.* v. *Warren,* 11 Pet. 420 (1837).
51. *Hood* v. *DuMond,* 336 U.S. 69 (1949).
52. *The Federalist,* no. 81.
53. *Fletcher* v. *Peck,* 6 Cr. 87 (1810); *Palko* v. *Connecticut,* 302 U.S. 319 (1937); *Gilbert* v. *Minnesota,* 254 U.S. 325 (1920).
54. *U.S.* v. *Curtiss-Wright Export Corp.,* 299 U.S. 304 (1936).
55. *Burnett* v. *Coronado Oil and Gas Co.,* 285 U.S. 293 (1932).
56. *Missouri ex rel. Gaines* v. *Canada,* 305 U.S. 337 (1937).
57. *McLaurin* v. *Oklahoma,* 339 U.S. 637 (1950); *Sweatt* v. *Painter,* 339 U.S. 629 (1950).
58. *Brown* v. *Board of Education,* 347 U.S. 483 (1954).
59. C. Herman Pritchett, *The Roosevelt Court* (New York: Macmillan, 1948), pp. 239–63.
60. *Powell* v. *Alabama,* 287 U.S. 45 (1932).
61. Joel Grossman, "Dissenting Blocs on the Warren Court," *Journal of Politics,* 30 (1968), p. 1090.
62. Edward H. Levi, "An Introduction to Legal Reasoning," *University of Chicago Law Review,* 15 (1948), p. 506.
63. James Eisenstein and Herbert Jacob, *Felony Justice* (Boston: Little, Brown, 1977).
64. *Southern Pacific* v. *Jensen,* 244 U.S. 205, 221 (1916).
65. *Yates* v. *U.S.,* 354 U.S. 298 (1957).
66. *Ex parte McCardle,* 7 Wall. 506 (1869).
67. *Ex parte Merryman,* 17 Fed. Cas. 144 (1861).
68. Walter Murphy and C. Herman Pritchett, *Courts, Judges and Politics* (New York: Random House, 1961); "Interrogations in New Haven: The Impact of Miranda," *Yale Law Journal,* 49 (1967), p. 1519.
69. Theodore Becker, ed., *The Impact of Supreme Court Decisions* (New York: Oxford U.P., 1972); Otis Stephens, *The Supreme Court and Confessions of Guilt* (Knoxville: U. of Tennessee, 1973).
70. *Democracy in America,* vol. 1 (New York: Schocken, 1961), p. 166.
71. Ibid.
72. James Bradley Thayer, *John Marshall* (Boston: Houghton, 1901), p. 107.
73. *Allen* v. *State Board of Elections,* 393 U.S. 544 (1968).
74. *The Federalist,* no. 78.
75. Robert H. Jackson, *The Supreme Court in the American System of Government* (Cambridge: Harvard U.P., 1965), p. 23.

CHAPTER 13

Civil Liberties

When Americans say that the United States is a free society—and when they complain that it is not—they have two different ideas in mind. First, they are talking about individual or private liberty, the right of Americans to do as they please in large areas of life. We are free in this sense because no government can tell us what to do, nor can anyone else. Second, however, Americans refer to political or public liberty. In these terms, the United States is a "free society" because its government is democratic, chosen by us rather than imposed on us. Politically, we are free even when government tells us what to do because we have had a say about the government and its policies. As a people, we would feel oppressed if we were ruled by outsiders or dictators even if they allowed us a great deal of individual freedom. (British rule in 1776, for example, respected most individual liberties.) As individuals, we often feel restricted and oppressed by the laws and regulations imposed by a freely elected government.

Public Rights and Private Liberties

Civil Liberties and Civil Rights

This chapter and the next follow the conventional distinction according to which **civil liberties** are areas of life in which we are protected against interference by government, and **civil rights** are those things in which we are entitled to government's active support. In this usage, constitutional government defends our civil liberties by acting as a "shield" against unlawful interference by government officials. In relation to civil rights, constitutional government is a "sword," forcing private persons as well as officials to treat us fairly and with due respect.[1] In political speech, we associate civil liberty with freedom, and civil rights with equality.

It is important to state right away that this familiar and useful distinction is also misleading, concealing the many ways in which civil rights and civil

Contracts, like this agreement between the United Steelworkers and the Wheeling-Pittsburgh Steel Corporation, are the legal basis of economic and social life in America. *(Jim Hermann-UPI/Bettmann Newsphotos)*

liberties are intertwined and inseparable. Distinguishing between our rights and our liberties obscures a more fundamental disagreement about the meaning of civil freedom.[2]

Liberty, Public and Private

The framers thought of human beings as free by nature, private beings endowed with natural rights. Government, they held, is created to secure and enhance these rights. Political society is valuable, in these terms, only because it makes possible the safe and full enjoyment of **private liberty.** Freedom is largely negative, the "absence of restraint."

If we think this way, the kind of government we have will not matter, provided that it leaves us alone. The proverb, "that government is best which governs least," implies that a weak monarchy is better than a strong democracy. We may decide that democracy offers the best protection of our private liberties, but fundamentally, we will be concerned about our immunities as private individuals, not our freedom as citizens. Democracy is valuable, in this view, only as a way of achieving our private purposes.

By contrast, thinkers like Aristotle and Tocqueville argue that freedom is not something we have "before" political society; it develops in and through political life. Aristotle felt confident in asserting that by nature the *polis* is "prior to the individual," by which he meant that genuine individuality can unfold only in a political society that fosters our individual talents and qualities.[3] Since we are, in this sense, parts of a political whole, we are self-ruled only when we have a say about and a share in public decisions. From this perspective, being left alone can easily amount to being left out. **Public**

liberty—the citizen's right to share in a free political life—matters more than private freedom. Democracy is only one possible way of protecting private rights; it is inseparable from public liberty.

The difference between the two ideas can be illustrated in relation to the freedom of the press. If we care about private liberty, our first concern is likely to be the right of *publishers* to print what they choose without governmental restraint. If public liberty matters more to us, we will be inclined to stress the right of the *people* to a responsible press that will print whatever they need in order to be informed citizens.[4]

Most Americans are convinced that both kinds of liberty are vital and valuable. In practical politics, we argue about whether we need more of one sort of liberty and less of the other. Nevertheless, conflicts over civil rights and civil liberties in America do involve a difference of first principles, a continuing tug-of-war between the defenders of private liberty and the partisans of public freedom.

Civil Liberty and the Bill of Rights

The conflict between the natural rights of individuals and political ideas of liberty was central to the disagreement among the framers about the value of a Bill of Rights.

The omission of a Bill of Rights from the original Constitution was not casual. Supporters of the Constitution knew that the lack of such a bill would be the strongest argument, politically, against ratification. Nevertheless, advocates of the Constitution like Alexander Hamilton argued that a Bill of Rights was undesirable because it would imply that the inalienable, natural rights of the individuals were granted or conferred by the Constitution and by membership in a political community.*

Madison, for example, conceded that a Bill of Rights would be useful in educating the public about its rights and alerting it to usurpations. Hence, the English Bill of Rights of 1689, like similar proclamations, had been useful in Great Britain because it helped protect the community against the king and the aristocracy. But in America, where political power derives from the majority, Madison thought it far more necessary to protect the individual against the public. A majority faction would not be deterred by mere words. The real safeguard of individual liberty did not lie in the parchment barriers of a Bill of Rights, but in the strategy of fragmentation that divided power and made majority factions all but impossible.

Although Madison thought a Bill of Rights insufficient, he did not consider it harmful. In fact, he observed, a long-established Bill of Rights may "become incorporated with the national sentiment," restraining passions and interests when they conflict with individual rights. Such sentiments could not be relied on, but they would be a useful, auxiliary protection for the rights of the individual, and, as Jefferson commented, a declaration of rights put a check into the hands of the courts. Combined with the political

***The Federalist* no. 84; see also Robert A. Rutland, *The Birth of the Bill of Rights* (Chapel Hill: U. of North Carolina, 1955), pp. 120–58.

POLITICAL PERSPECTIVE

From The Virginia Declaration of Rights

1. . . . (A)ll men are by nature equally free and independent, and have certain inherent rights, of which, when they enter into a state of society, they cannot, by any compact, deprive or divest their posterity; namely, the enjoyment of life and liberty, with the means of acquiring and possessing property, and pursuing and obtaining happiness and safety.

June 12, 1776

From The Declaration of Independence

We hold these truths to be self-evident, that all men are created equal, that they are endowed by their Creator with certain inalienable Rights, that among these are Life, Liberty, and the pursuit of Happiness.

July 4, 1776

pressure for a Bill of Rights, such considerations eventually persuaded Madison to champion the first ten amendments in the House of Representatives.*

Nevertheless, the framers designed the Constitution to protect individual rights and private liberties, and Madison helped to phrase the Bill of Rights in the language of negative liberty. As Justice Black once remarked, the Bill of Rights is a "collection of 'Thou shalt nots.'"[5]

The very existence of a Bill of Rights, however, indicates that the framers did not have matters all their own way. Ideas of public liberty were deeply embedded in American political culture. The English Bill of Rights, as Madison had observed, speaks of political rights to free elections, free debate in parliament, and the right of petition; it provides for government under law and for certain judicial rights; it assures Protestants of the right to bear arms. But it does not refer to individual rights to freedom of speech or religion.[6]

The Declaration of Independence represents a compromise with these older views. The Virginia Declaration of Rights refers to human beings as "equally free and independent" by nature, endowed with certain rights that they cannot give up when they "enter" society, including the "means of acquiring and possessing property." By contrast, the Declaration of Independence refers to human beings as "created equal," suggests that governments are "instituted" without implying that there was ever a prepolitical "state of nature," and does not mention property among the inalienable rights of humankind. The Declaration, in other words, makes human beings more political and less private than they appear to be in the Virginia Declaration of Rights.[7]

The idea of public liberty is also apparent in the belief that government, as well as individuals, has inherent and inalienable rights. Among these, in the American tradition, are **eminent domain,** the public's right to take property for public purposes, and the **police power,** the right to legislate for the health, good order, and general welfare of the political society as a

*Julian Boyd, ed., *The Papers of Thomas Jefferson,* vol. 14 (Princeton: Princeton U. P., 1950), pp. 19–20, 659; see also Rutland, pp. 195–218.

whole.[8] The Fifth Amendment, of course, follows Magna Carta in providing that property may not be taken without "just compensation" and "due process of law."[9] This constitutional provision implies, however, that the right of the community to command the private properties (and the lives and liberties) of its citizens for public purposes is unlimited unless specifically curtailed. The individual's right to compensation is itself a political right granted by the law. Consequently, before the Fourteenth Amendment, the Supreme Court held that states were not required to pay when they took property under eminent domain, and at first, the Court denied that even the Fourteenth Amendment obliged the states to do so. In the era when laissez-faire notions were strongest, the court did make "just compensation" part of the due process guaranteed by the Fourteenth Amendment, and so it remains.[10]

Moreover, government can tax property or regulate it under the "police power" without providing compensation at all. The line between "taking" property and "regulating" it is difficult to draw: regulations change the value of property and sometimes make it valueless.[11] The public, however, does have the right to prevent the noxious or wasteful use of property because such uses harm the public. Consequently, the public can regulate pollution or forbid vice, and the more that private property is involved in public life, the more it is subject to regulation. (Public accommodations, like hotels and restaurants, are obvious examples of highly regulable property.)[12] The right of private property, in other words, is limited to rightful uses, uses that are truly private and do not substantially affect public rights.

The Obligation of Contract

Private Rights: Property, Privacy, and Consent

The theory of the framers stressed that the primary purpose of political society is making secure private rights, with which the individual is already endowed. In one respect, however, they believed that political society does add to the liberty of the individual. They reasoned that civil government is preceded by savage competition between self-seeking individuals, a "state of war" in which no individual can trust another. Since advanced economies require interdependence, they presume a reasonable reliance on the promises of others. Economic life "before" civil government, consequently, is primitive and poor. Government, by enforcing our contracts, makes it easier—or so the framers argued—for people to trust one another. The *freedom to make secure contracts*, consequently, is the great, positive contribution of government; in the framer's view, the freedom to contract safely is the civil liberty par excellence.

Recently, the Supreme Court reasserted this doctrine, holding that relationships of trust and confidentiality in the business world are a "most fundamental human right." Such relationships, the Court declared, involve the "basic decency of society" as well as the "life and spirit of the commercial world."[13]

Reflecting these ideas of the framers, the Constitution forbids states to make laws "impairing the obligation of contracts" (Art. I, sec. 10). In a crucial decision, the Marshall Court ruled that a charter of incorporation, granted by a state, was a "contract." Hence, once a state had created a corporation, it could not change or take away the rights created by that charter.[14] This, obviously, greatly restricted the ability of states to regulate economic life, and it greatly strengthened the position of private as opposed to public rights.

However, the Marshall Court agreed that a state could reserve the right to change corporate charters by making that right part of the original "contract."[15] Moreover, the Marshall Court argued—with Marshall himself dissenting for the first time—that though a state could not "impair" an existing contract by passing new laws, it could pass laws restricting or regulating contracts made in the future.[16]

The Taney Court went further. In *Charles River Bridge* v. *Warren Bridge* in 1837, the Court ruled that a corporation acquires no rights not explicitly granted to it. The Charles River Bridge Company had no right to a monopoly for its toll bridge even though its charter implied a monopoly and the company's investors had relied on this implicit promise. Taney argued that public rights are paramount and private rights bear the burden of proof whenever they seek to limit public power.

> The object of all government is to promote the happiness and prosperity of the community by which it is established . . . A state is never to be presumed to surrender this power because . . . the whole community have an interest in preserving it undiminished . . . While the rights of property are sacredly guarded . . . the community also have rights and the happiness and well being of every citizen depend on their faithful preservation.[17]

Following this doctrine of "paramount rights," the Court ruled that there are certain rights the government cannot surrender, including eminent domain and the police powers.[18] Moreover, the Court has argued that states may change the terms of a valid contract so long as they do not take away any "substantial rights."[19]

"Due Process" and the Freedom of Contract

But the "contracts clause" is not the only constitutional protection of private rights. The Fourteenth Amendment provides that no person may be deprived of "life, liberty, or property" by a state without **due process of law.** During the nineteenth century, in fact, the Court made that clause the most important bastion of private rights through the doctrine of **substantive due process.** Basically, substantive due process means that the Court will go beyond asking, "Did the state use lawful *procedures* [due process] in depriving you of life, liberty or property?" It will also ask, "Did the state have a legitimate *purpose* in so depriving you [substantive due process]? Is the *result* of the process just to you? Does it give you your 'due'?"

In the nineteenth century (and the first decades of the twentieth), the Court approached and answered these questions in terms of individualistic theory. When it asked, "Is there really a public purpose?," the Court assumed that government exists to protect private rights and should be limited to the smallest possible sphere. In *Lochner* v. *New York*, the Court ruled that due process forbade "unreasonable, unnecessary, and arbitrary legislation."* The laws in question, regulating the hours of bakers, were clearly not arbitrary nor could they really be called "unreasonable," but they could be termed "unnecessary," and that severe test underlay many of the Court's rulings against economic regulation.

The Court argued that the pursuit of one's chosen occupation is part of the liberty protected by the due process clause. This liberty, the Court reasoned, entails the right to sell one's labor or product, to purchase materials, to hire others, and generally to enter into all contracts related to one's calling. This **freedom of contract** was not to be violated except in cases of public necessity. The states could not legislate minimum wages because to do so would prevent people from working for less. The states could not standardize loaves of bread or mattresses because such laws restricted the freedom to buy and sell. And so on.†

Freedom of contract, however, came on hard times during the New Deal era. The demand for economic regulation created by the Depression was reinforced by the long-evident fact that workers or consumers, as individuals, had little power relative to employers or corporations. Their freedom to negotiate contracts often came down to "take it or leave it" in circumstances where one could not afford to leave it. Workers and consumers—and ordinary citizens generally—often needed government regulation to protect their right to organize or to establish their freedom to contract on some sort of equal basis.‡

Partly because of such considerations, the Court relaxed the standard for substantive due process. It rejected the notion that it had the right to reject "unwise" or "unnecessary" legislation. Instead, the Court established the rule it still applies in cases involving economic rights: if the state is pursuing a legitimate public goal, it need only show a "reasonable" relation between ends and means.[20] Today, the Court almost never strikes down an economic regulation as a violation of substantive due process, and the rights of property—including the "freedom of contract"—seem to have been subordinated to public purpose. In this area at least, public rights have won priority over private liberties.

The Right to Privacy

Private rights, however, extend beyond the economic sphere. Aristotle argued, in fact, that even in private terms, property is only a means to the end of family and friendship. From a very different perspective, a conservative Supreme Court included the right "to marry, to establish a home, and bring up children," the right to freedom of religion and the right to "acquire useful knowledge" among the liberties protected by substantive due process.[21]

**Lochner* v. *New York,* 198 U.S. 45, 56 (1905).

†*Allgeyer* v. *Louisiana,* 165 U.S. 578 (1897) proclaimed the "freedom of contract"; *Adkins* v. *Children's Hospital,* 261 U.S. 525 (1923) ruled out minimum wages; on standardized products, see *Weaver* v. *Palmer Bros.,* 270 U.S. 402 (1926).

‡For an earlier anticipation, see *Holden* v. *Hardy,* 169 U.S. 366 (1898).

Since the New Deal Court distrusted the idea of substantive due process, it did not expand on, or appeal to, such notions. In 1952, however, the Court ruled, in *Rochin* v. *California,* that police could not forcibly pump the stomach of a suspect in a drug case. Justice Frankfurter, speaking for the Court, did not argue that the police had denied any specific procedural right of the prisoner, such as his protection against compulsory self-incrimination. Rather, Frankfurter maintained, the police had denied the prisoner the essence of due process by breaking into his "privacy" in a way that "shocks the conscience" because of its brutality.[22]

The impact of this decision has been limited. The Court subsequently held that a state could impose a compulsory blood test to determine whether a driver was intoxicated because its interest in reducing the "mortal hazard" of drunk driving outweighed the "right of the individual that his person be held inviolable."[23] Moreover, the Court eventually confirmed that the freedom from compulsory self-incrimination granted by the Fifth Amendment does not protect the body in the absence of the kind of brutality that appalled the Court in the Rochin case. Only "personal communication" is protected against self-incrimination, and the police may fingerprint suspects, require them to give samples of writing or speak for purposes of identification, and the like.[24] Nevertheless, the Court had held that the "privacy" of one's "person" is a liberty entitled to the protection of due process.

In 1965, the Court went a good deal further when it struck down a Connecticut law against the prescription or use of birth control materials. In *Griswold* v. *Connecticut,* the Court held that a right to privacy in married life could be found as part of a "penumbra" of various provisions of the Constitution. Justice Douglas appealed to the framers' belief that there are

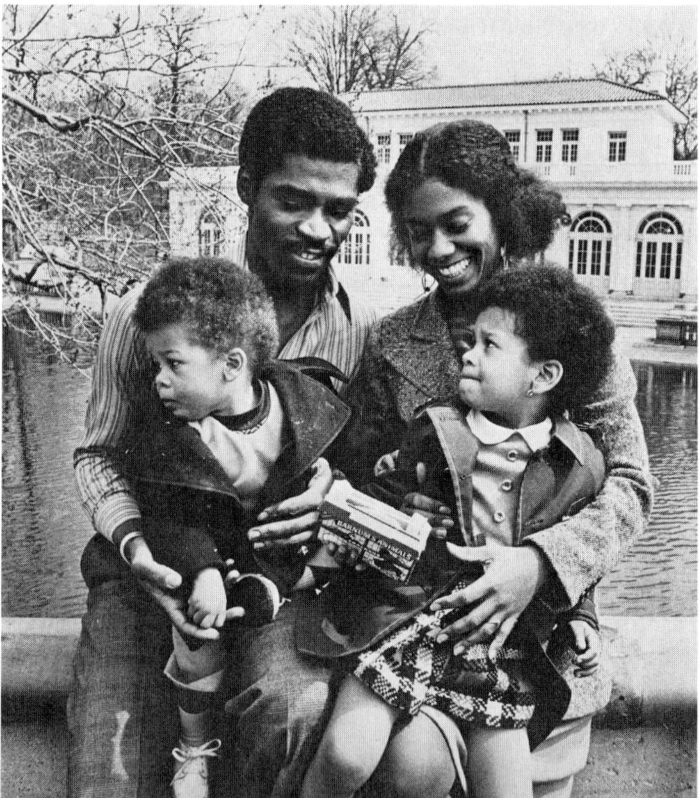

The protection and promotion of family life is recognized as a valid concern of government at all levels. *(Chester Higgins, Jr./Photo Researchers, Inc.)*

certain "fundamental" rights, "older than the Bill of Rights," including the freedom of "family life" from interference by the state.[25] As the language suggests, the Court's doctrine in *Griswold* reflects the framers' theory that "society" precedes the state.

There was, however, another side to the Court's opinion in the Griswold case: Justice Douglas referred to the rights of marriage as a relationship, a whole distinct from the individuals who compose it. Douglas emphasized the right of privacy in *associations,* at least those of a particularly intimate kind, rather than the rights of individuals. In this view, Douglas turned from the framers to thinkers like Aristotle and Tocqueville who regarded families and friendships as natural to humankind, the foundations of personality and individuality. Such groups strengthen us against "tyranny of the majority."

In point of fact, the state does sanction certain relationships. It recognizes marriage and gives marital couples and their children certain special rights and duties: for example, a spouse cannot be compelled to testify against his or her partner. The Court has also held that states may forbid or refuse to acknowledge marriage between persons of the same sex and may outlaw private homosexual relations between consenting adults.[26] Whatever one thinks of the wisdom of such decisions, they indicate the Court's belief that the public has a vital interest in the organization and conduct of these crucial areas of private life.

In one case, *Beauharnais* v. *Illinois,* the Court upheld an Illinois law that made it a crime to defame racial or religious groups. The Court understood that the honor and dignity of individuals may be inextricably tied to that of the groups to which they belong. Although recent decisions of the Court have undermined the Beauharnais opinion, it has never been overruled.*

Nevertheless, decisions and policies that treat primary groups and communities as entitled to public support are the exception to the rule. It soon became clear, for example, that the Court preferred to interpret the right of privacy in individualistic terms. In *Eisenstadt* v. *Baird* in 1972, it denied that a state could provide contraceptive materials to married persons and deny them to unmarried individuals. Marriage, the Court argued, "is not an independent entity with a mind and heart of its own, but an association of two individuals." Hence, the right of privacy must be the right of an *individual* to be free from "unwarranted governmental intrusion into matters so fundamental to the person as whether to bear or beget a child."[27]

The Court's Ruling on Abortion The Court's reference to "bearing" a child pointed unmistakably in the direction of its decision, a year later, that the "concept of personal liberty," to which the "right of privacy" belongs, extends to the right to procure an abortion.[28] Originally, the Court discovered this right among "activities relating to marriage," including, in addition to procreation, family relations, child rearing, and education. The Court soon made it clear, however, that it regarded abortion as an individual right, not part of a privacy owed to close relationships between people. It struck down a Missouri law that required that a husband (or a parent, in

**Beauharnais* v. *Illinois,* 343 U.S. 250 (1952); recent decisions that run against Beauharnais include, most notably, *Collin* v. *Smith,* 439 U.S. 916 (1978).

the case of an unmarried minor) consent to an abortion, arguing that a state cannot "delegate to a spouse" a power to interfere with individual liberty that the state itself does not possess.[29]

Subsequent decisions have confirmed that the Court interprets this right in negative terms as the right of individual women to be free from state interference. States may not "unduly" burden the right to abortion, but they need not finance it, nor must city hospitals provide abortions. A woman may decide to terminate her pregnancy, but the public has no obligation to enable her to carry out her choice.[30] Many people have observed that this means that the poor are denied a right, allegedly fundamental to the person, which is available to the well-to-do. That sort of discrimination, however, is the consequence of individualistic theory. It seems a mockery to defenders of public liberty, however, whatever their opinion of abortion.

Private Liberty and Mass Society

In individualistic doctrine, each person naturally pursues his or her self-interest in a more or less rational way. When someone consents to something, he or she is presumed to have acted voluntarily unless there has been a physical threat to life, liberty, or property. Consent, like contract, is free and we are responsible for it. The theory that we are political animals, on the other hand, tells us that human beings are vulnerable to emotional and spiritual, as well as to physical, coercion and need support, advice, and counsel in order to be free.

Part of the Supreme Court's willingness to abandon the "freedom of contract" derives from a recognition that individuals are vulnerable in mass society and, in isolation, are likely to feel baffled and powerless. The Court, consequently, has come to insist that consent is free only when individuals are protected against psychological forms of coercion. In mass society, private liberty is not enough.

In 1940, the Court held that prolonged isolation from friends and counsel, combined with "third-degree" tactics, were forms of compulsion that invalidated any confession.* Nevertheless, the police were still permitted to question a suspect in the absence of an attorney, and so long as they acted within reason, any confession they obtained was presumed to be valid.

The Miranda Doctrine In 1964, however, the Supreme Court held that being under suspicion is bound to create anxiety, making the individual vulnerable to psychological coercion unless he or she has the support of counsel. Moreover, the Court went on, individuals cannot be presumed to be aware of their rights, especially given the confusion inherent in being arrested.[31] A little later, in *Miranda* v. *Arizona,* the Court held that any suspect in custody must be advised of his or her rights, including the right to be silent, that any statements suspects make can be held against them,

**Chambers* v. *Florida,* 309 U.S. 227 (1940); the police are permitted, however, to use psychological pressures and tricks, such as offering a suspect reassurance (*Stein* v. *New York,* 346 U.S. 156 [1953]).

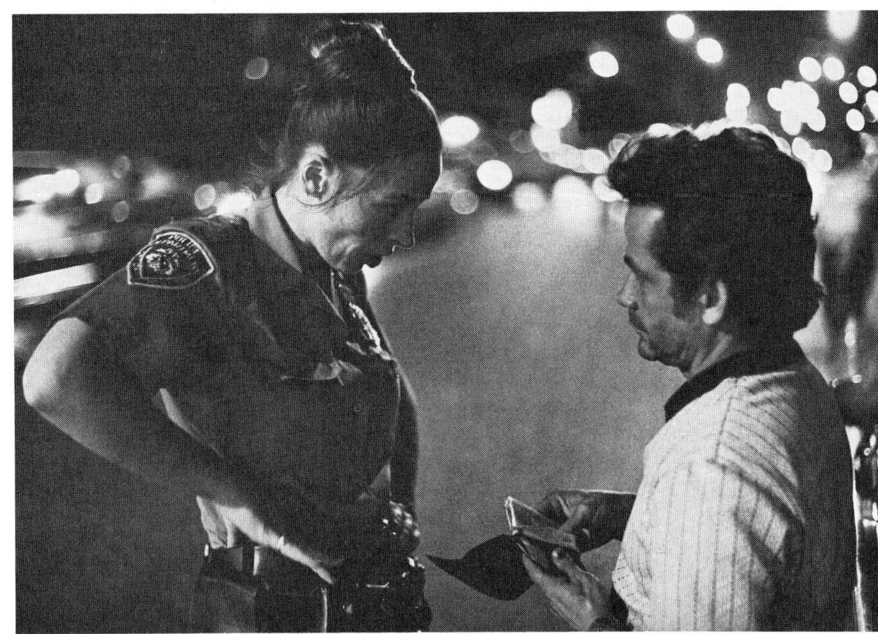

The courts now require the police to observe proper procedures in any dealings with citizens. *(Sepp Seitz/Woodfin Camp & Associates)*

and the right to have an attorney present during questioning.[32] Subsequently, the Court has ruled that if a suspect gives up the right to counsel and confesses, the police must demonstrate that it was done knowingly.[33] The Burger Court weakened the **Miranda doctrine,** but it upheld the rule itself.* Individualist theory assumed that consent is knowing and voluntary; the Court now holds that isolated human beings must be presumed to be neither rational nor free.

"UNREASONABLE SEARCHES AND SEIZURES" This sensitivity to the vulnerability of individuals in modern society helps account for the Court's concern to shore up the right of privacy by limiting searches and seizures (see Table 13.1, Amendment IV) in any place where the individual has a "legitimate expectation of privacy." The police do not need a warrant to search a person or the immediate vicinity when making a legal arrest, and with "probable cause" they may search a vehicle. The Court has held, however, that unless the police have a warrant, nothing short of an emergency justifies them in entering a home.†

* *Tague* v. *Louisiana,* 444 U.S. 469 (1980) reflects the Court's support for the Miranda rule. It has held, by contrast, that if an accused person takes the stand, things he or she said to the police without an attorney present may be used to cast doubt on contrary testimony (*Oregon* v. *Hass,* 420 U.S. 714 [1975]). The Court has also ruled that a suspect may be questioned without being advised where "overriding considerations of public safety" are involved. *New York* v. *Quarles,* 52 L.W. 4790 (1984).

† The basic rule is defined by *U.S.* v. *Robinson,* 414 U.S. 218 (1973); on the "legitimate expectation of privacy," see *U.S.* v. *Chadwick,* 433 U.S. 1 (1977); the rule for entry into homes was proclaimed in *Payton* v. *New York,* 455 U.S. 573 (1980). Unfortunately, the Court's sensitivities do not extend to the poor: it has upheld "bedchecks" by welfare agencies, conducted without a warrant, to see whether recipients of family assistance are being visited by their spouses (*Wyman* v. *James,* 400 U.S. 309 [1971]).

TABLE 13.1 Amendments to the U.S. Constitution

	Amendment	Date Ratified	Provisions
The Bill of Rights	I	1791	Freedom of speech, press, assembly, and religion; prohibits religious establishment; gives right to petition
	II	1791	Right to keep and bear arms as part of a "well-regulated Militia"
	III	1791	No quartering of soldiers during peacetime (or during wartime, except as prescribed by law)
	IV	1791	Prohibits "unreasonable searches and seizures"
	V	1791	Protects against double jeopardy or compulsory self-incrimination; forbids trial for major crimes without indictment by Grand Jury; no person may be deprived of life, liberty, or property without "due process of law," and private property may not be taken without "just compensation"
	VI	1791	Right to trial by jury in criminal cases; right to speedy trial, to be informed of charges, and to confront and secure witnesses
	VII	1791	Right to jury trial in civil cases
	VIII	1791	Forbids excessive bail, fines, and "cruel or unusual punishments"
	IX	1791	Rights listed in the Constitution do not deny other rights "retained by the people"
	X	1791	Powers not delegated to U.S. government are reserved to the states or the people
	XI	1795	Federal judicial power does not extend to suits brought against a state by citizens of another state (overrules *Chisholm* v. *Ga.* 2 Dall. 419,[1793])
	XII	1804	Separate ballots for the election of president and vice-president

Similar concerns have contributed to the Court's rulings on wiretapping. In 1928, the Court held that if "bugging" a phone did not involve a physical intrusion into a home or office, it was not an illegal "search."[34] In concerning itself only with physical intrusions on private persons and property, the Court neglected the necessary interdependence of modern society, and it ignored the human need for private relationships. In the 1960s, by contrast, the Court held that the Fourth Amendment protects "people, not places," although it ruled that wiretapping and electronic surveillance were permissible with a warrant.[35]

Yet, criminals can also employ new technologies, just as they can take advantage of the fact that our more fragmented way of life makes detection

TABLE 13.1 *(continued)*

	Amendment	Date Ratified	Provisions
The Reconstruction Amendments	XIII	1865	Abolishes slavery or involuntary servitude
	XIV	1868	Defines citizenship; protects the "privileges and immunities" of citizens of the United States; forbids states to deny "equal protection of the laws" or to deprive any person of life, liberty, or property without "due process of law"
	XV	1870	Right to vote shall not be denied because of race, color, or previous condition of servitude
The Progressive Era Amendments	XVI	1913	Permits a federal income tax
	XVII	1913	Direct election of senators
	XVIII	1919	Prohibition
	XIX	1920	Right to vote shall not be denied because of sex
	XX	1933	Changes terms of president, vice-president, and Congress to eliminate "lame duck" sessions
	XXI	1933	Repeals Eighteenth Amendment
	XXII	1951	Limits presidents to two terms
	XXIII	1961	Allows the District of Columbia to vote in presidential elections
	XXIV	1964	Outlaws the poll tax in federal elections
	XXV	1967	Provides for filling the office of vice-president in case of a vacancy; provides measures for circumstances in which the president is unable to carry out his or her duties
	XXVI	1971	Right to vote of citizens eighteen years or older shall not be denied because of age

difficult. It is hard to deny the government the right to respond in kind. For just such reasons, the Burger Court proved increasingly inclined to relax the rules governing search and seizure, especially in cases involving organized crime or the traffic in illegal drugs. Even this conservative court, however, sought to limit this new latitude to more or less exceptional circumstances.

In 1982, overturning earlier rulings, the Court held that if the police have reason to believe that a car contains "contraband," they may search it without getting a warrant. Such a search is "limited by its object": if the police are looking for something, like illegal drugs, which can be hidden in small places, they may search almost anywhere, but a search for illegal aliens would not justify opening a briefcase.[36] Similarly, the Court agreed that a sociopsychological "profile," describing the behaviors and characteristics of probable drug carriers, provides enough basis for suspicion to justify narcotics agents in intercepting airline passengers. Nevertheless, the Court held that such suspicion does *not* justify prolonged interrogation.[37]

The Supreme Court also has found more reason to be tolerant of electronic surveillance.[38] Nevertheless, the Court held unconstitutional those provisions of the Omnibus Crime Control Act of 1968 that made a warrant unnecessary in cases involving national security or "conspiratorial activities characteristic of organized crime." Such intrusions are impermissible in domestic life, the Court argued, because they violate the need to protect "citizen dissent and discussion in private conversation."* The Court has not abandoned that basic position. The most valuable and inviolable of private rights, as the Court implied, are those that are essential to public liberty.

Public Rights: Preferred Position and the Bill of Rights

Preferred Position

From the New Deal era to today, the Supreme Court has been inclined to presume the constitutionality of limitations on the right of property. It has been much more suspicious of any infringement of our liberties under the First Amendment, our rights to justice in criminal cases, and our right to vote. Some scholars have criticized this "double standard," asking why property is less valuable as a personal right.[39]

Part of the answer to that question was provided by Justice Benjamin Cardozo when he listed "freedom of thought and speech" as fundamental rights "implicit in the concept of ordered liberty" and, in fact, the condition of all other forms of freedom.[40] Cardozo gave thought and speech their higher rank, in other words, because he regarded them as essential to a free political society, rights pertaining to the regime as a whole as opposed to the liberties of individuals.

In broad outline, the Court has continued to apply Cardozo's doctrine. Put simply, the Court believes that no free government is possible without the First Amendment and without other judicial and political rights, but it considers that a free political society is possible with at least major restrictions on the right of property. Property is largely if not entirely a private right, dependent on, rather than essential to, the polity as a whole.[41]

Justice Harlan Stone shaped this view with his argument that certain rights enjoy a **preferred position** in American government. First, Stone argued, the specific prohibitions of the Bill of Rights require that the Court be highly suspicious of any infringing legislation. These restraints, in Stone's view, are essential not only to freedom of the "mind and spirit," but also to "justice and moderation." Stone's terms suggest that the prohibitions of the Bill of Rights are necessary to any just government.† So far, Stone

**U.S.* v. *U.S. District Court,* 407 U.S. 297 (1972).

†For Stone's view, see *U.S.* v. *Carolene Products,* 304 U.S. 144, 152–53 (1938), and *Jones* v. *Opelika,* 316 U.S. 584 (1942). See also Martin Shapiro, *Freedom of Speech* (Englewood Cliffs, N.J.: Prentice-Hall, 1966).

extended but followed the outline of Cardozo's principle of "ordered liberty." Second, however, Stone held that the political processes required by democracy and necessary to protect minorities merit equally watchful judicial protection. Stone emphasized, in other words, the rights essential to political democracy—citizenship, free deliberation, and fair elections. In this, he went beyond Cardozo, asking for a specific, democratic kind of "ordered liberty," which Stone regarded as a defining characteristic of the United States as a political society. Stone's argument implies that in addition to the more negative liberties made explicit by the Bill of Rights, citizens have a positive right to participate in political life.

The theory of "preferred position" has been opposed by two major competing doctrines. Justice Black went further than Stone, contending that the First Amendment and similar provisions of the Bill of Rights are "absolutes," resting his case on the text of the Constitution and what he regarded as the intent of the framers. This absolute quality, however, is confined to speaking and writing, according to Black; it does not extend to conduct.[42]

By contrast, a school of thought associated with Justice Frankfurter argues that the liberties of the Bill of Rights must be balanced against the public interest in order, security, and well-being. This balance is more or less a matter of judgment, and unless the liberty sacrificed clearly and greatly outweighs the public interests being served, the Court should not substitute its judgment for that of the legislature.* These competing theories have prevailed from time to time and in this case or that, but "preferred position" remains the dominant theory of the Court.

The Freedom of Speech

Free speech can refer to either a public right or a private liberty. Professor Alexander Meiklejohn argued, for example, that the "freedom of speech" refers only to speech about public affairs. Free speech is an aspect of democratic citizenship, essential to self-government and democratic deliberation, and does not extend to matters of private concern. Freedom of speech allows me to discuss the question, "Should obscene speech be permitted?" It does not permit me to utter obscenities. Private speech has constitutional protection, Meiklejohn maintained, but only as part of the "liberty" entitled to "due process of law." In Meiklejohn's theory, by contrast, freedom of public speech is an absolute that cannot be infringed at all.[43] Meiklejohn's ideas and phrasing have found their way into many opinions of the Court and were virtually adopted by the Court in recent decisions dealing with the freedom of the press.†

Americans, however, have increasingly adopted a more individualistic view of free speech. Most people today, for example, treat "free expression" as a synonym for free speech, but the two terms differ in an important respect. "Speaking" at least suggests an audience whose "hearing" must be

*On Frankfurter's position and his conflict with Black, see Wallace Mendelson, *Justices Black and Frankfurter: Conflict in the Court* (Chicago: U. of Chicago, 1961), and Mark Silverstein, *Constitutional Faiths* (Ithaca: Cornell U. P., 1984).

†For example, *Rosenbloom* v. *Multimedia,* 403 U.S. 29 (1971).

considered; "self-expression" is wholly self-concerned. To "express myself" freely, I cannot consider anyone else because to do so would constrain the authenticity of my self-expression.

The Court has adopted a good deal of this privatistic view. Originally, the Court denied that motion pictures were protected by the First Amendment. Movies, the Court argued, were a "spectacle" conducted for private profit and designed for private entertainment; they were a "business pure and simple," private speech relatively open to regulation. In 1952, however, the Court reversed itself, arguing that movies—and eventually, theater in general—are forms of "free expression."[44]

Similarly, the traditional doctrine of the Court held that advertising is simply commercial activity subject to regulation. In 1976, however, the Burger Court ruled that commercial speech, and hence advertising, is protected by the First Amendment. The Court made an exception for professions like law and medicine that provide such specialized and complex services that it would be easy to deceive or confuse the public. In 1977, however, it extended "free speech" to cover advertising by lawyers about simple services such as drafting a will. There is no right to print ads that are fraudulent or contrary to public policy, such as a job listing for "Men only," or which promote unlawful acts. With those exceptions, however, "commercial speech" no longer has second-class status.*

Justice Brennan raised the obvious problem posed by these decisions: since the government has lost most of its power to regulate advertising, the mass media will be free to prefer commercial speech over controversial speech. In establishing the people's right to commercial information, the Court may have weakened the public's likelihood of being informed about public issues.†

The freedom of speech also goes beyond words to include certain forms of conduct. For example, peaceful picketing is speech because it is a means of telling the public about a strike and about other matters of public concern.[45] The First Amendment also protects any number of forms of symbolic speech, such as the right of students to wear black armbands to protest the Vietnam War and the right of Jehovah's Witnesses to cover the motto, "Live Free or Die" on New Hampshire's license plates.[46] However, even the Warren Court saw limits to "symbolic speech." Sit-in demonstrations cannot obstruct the lawful functions of government or the use of its property.[47] Thus, since the government has the right to establish selective service and to require registration for it, it was not lawful for antiwar protesters to burn their draft cards. Similarly, the military may, as part of its lawful functions, restrict the First Amendment rights of service personnel.[48]

There are, moreover, limits to what one may say. Certain terms, the Court observed in *Chaplinsky* v. *New Hampshire*, are so provocative and insulting that they are "fighting words." Calling someone a "damned Facist" is not necessary to "any exposition of ideas" (unless, perhaps, one is speak-

**Valentine* v. *Christensen*, 316 U.S. 52 (1942) states the original position. The Burger Court's rulings are found in *Virginia Board of Pharmacy* v. *Citizen's Consumer Council*, 425 U.S. 748 (1976), *Bates* v. *Arizona*, 433 U.S. 350 (1977), and *Pittsburgh Press* v. *Pennsylvania Commission on Human Relations*, 413 U.S. 376 (1973). The Court has made some modest allowance for professional standards in *A.M.A.* v. *F.T.C.*, 455 U.S. 676 (1982).

†Dissenting in *Columbia Broadcasting Corp.* v. *Democratic National Committee*, 412 U.S. 94 (1973).

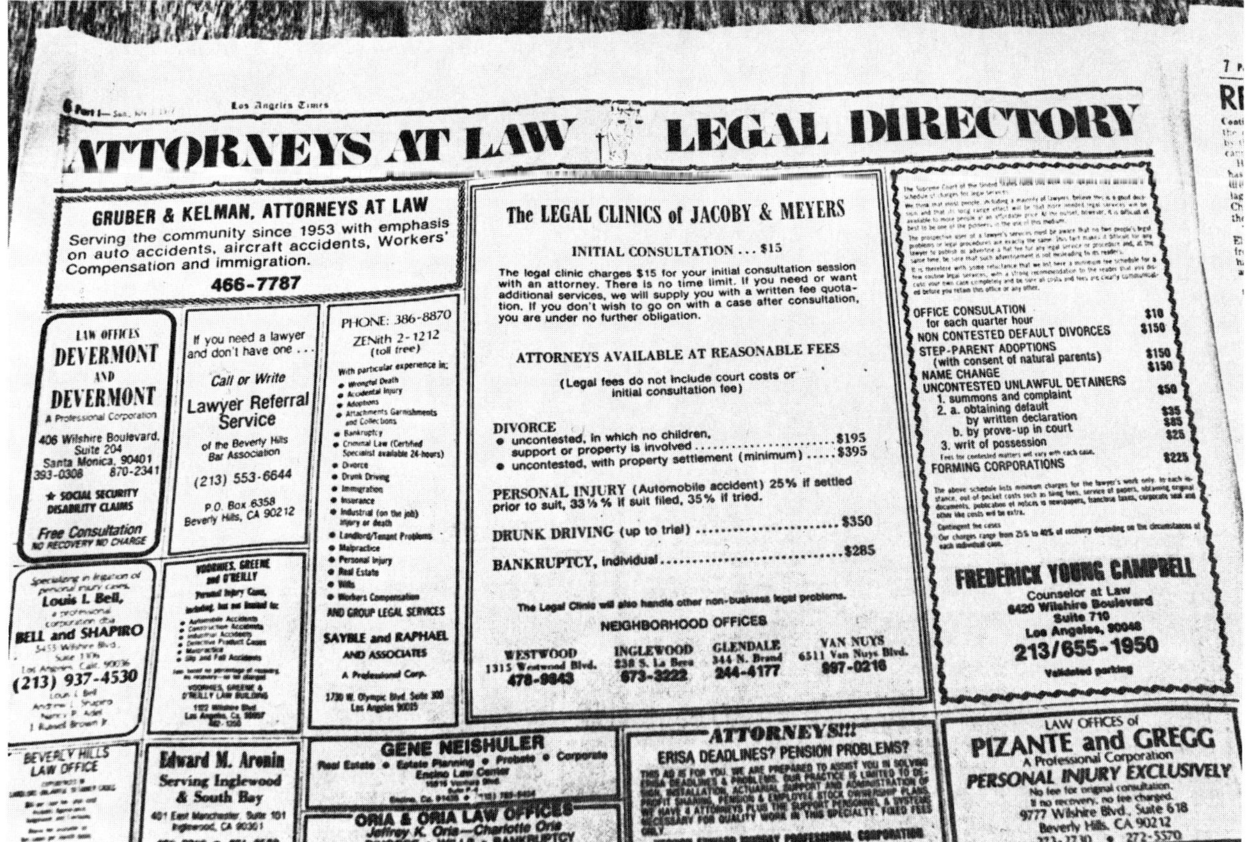

Los Angeles Times

ATTORNEYS AT LAW LEGAL DIRECTORY

GRUBER & KELMAN, ATTORNEYS AT LAW
Serving the community since 1953 with emphasis on auto accidents, aircraft accidents, Workers' Compensation and immigration.
466-7787

LAW OFFICES
DEVERMONT AND DEVERMONT
A Professional Corporation
406 Wilshire Boulevard, Suite 204
Santa Monica, 90401
393-0308 870-2341
★ SOCIAL SECURITY DISABILITY CLAIMS
Free Consultation
NO RECOVERY NO CHARGE

If you need a lawyer and don't have one . . .
Call or Write
Lawyer Referral Service
of the Beverly Hills Bar Association
(213) 553-6644
P.O. Box 6358
Beverly Hills, CA 90212

PHONE: 386-8870
ZENith 2-1212
(toll free)
AND GROUP LEGAL SERVICES
SAYBLE and RAPHAEL AND ASSOCIATES
A Professional Corp.

The LEGAL CLINICS of JACOBY & MEYERS

INITIAL CONSULTATION . . . $15

The legal clinic charges $15 for your initial consultation session with an attorney. There is no time limit. If you need or want additional services, we will supply you with a written fee quotation. If you don't wish to go on with a case after consultation, you are under no further obligation.

ATTORNEYS AVAILABLE AT REASONABLE FEES

(Legal fees do not include court costs or initial consultation fee)

DIVORCE
- uncontested, in which no children, support or property is involved $195
- uncontested, with property settlement (minimum) $395

PERSONAL INJURY (Automobile accident) 25% if settled prior to suit, 33⅓% if suit filed, 35% if tried.

DRUNK DRIVING (up to trial) $350

BANKRUPTCY, individual $285

The Legal Clinic will also handle other non-business legal problems.

NEIGHBORHOOD OFFICES

WESTWOOD	INGLEWOOD	GLENDALE	VAN NUYS
1315 Westwood Blvd.	238 S. La Brea	344 N. Brand	6511 Van Nuys Blvd.
478-9843	673-3222	244-4177	997-0216

OFFICE CONSULATION for each quarter hour	$10
NON CONTESTED DEFAULT DIVORCES	$150
STEP-PARENT ADOPTIONS (with consent of natural parents)	$150
NAME CHANGE	$150
UNCONTESTED UNLAWFUL DETAINERS	
1. summons and complaint	$50
2. a. obtaining default by written declaration	$35
b. by prove-up in court	$85
3. writ of possession	$25
FORMING CORPORATIONS	$225

FREDERICK YOUNG CAMPBELL
Counselor at Law
6420 Wilshire Boulevard
Suite 710
Los Angeles, 90048
213/655-1950
Validated parking

Louis L. Bell,
BELL and SHAPIRO
(213) 937-4530

BEVERLY HILLS LAW OFFICE

Edward M. Aronin
Serving Inglewood & South Bay

GENE NEISHULER

ORIA & ORIA LAW OFFICES

ATTORNEYS!!!
ERISA DEADLINES? PENSION PROBLEMS?

LAW OFFICES of
PIZANTE and GREGG
A Professional Corporation
PERSONAL INJURY EXCLUSIVELY
No fee for original consultation.
If no recovery, no fee charged.
9777 Wilshire Blvd., Suite 618
Beverly Hills, CA 90212

Since 1977, lawyers and doctors have been permitted to advertise their services. *(Wide World Photos)*

ing to someone who really is a Fascist), and the same might be said of demeaning terms about either sex or any racial or ethnic group. Consequently, using such terms is not speaking to someone; it is an attack on the dignity of the person addressed so severe as to amount to violence. It follows, the Court declared, that a law that is carefully written to forbid only "fighting words" is not a violation of the freedom of speech.[49]

Public authorities cannot, by contrast, interfere with a speaker merely because what he or she says "stirs the public to anger." The idea that a hostile audience reaction justifies the police in breaking up an otherwise legal meeting is called a **"heckler's veto";** if it were permitted, there would be no effective constitutional protection for unpopular ideas. A speaker may talk about whatever he or she pleases, even if he or she advocates nonsensical or outrageous ideas like racism; "fighting words" refers to the manner and not the content of the speech. We have no right to incite overtly an audience to riot or to overthrow the government, but we have a right to advocate just such ideas if we do so theoretically.[50] In fact, we have great latitude even in the way in which we choose to speak. For example, the Court has ruled that four-letter vulgarities come under the protection of free speech.[51]

Free Speech and National Security National security, however, sometimes justifies major restraints on First Amendment freedoms. In 1919, Justice Holmes addressed the question, "May the government, in time of

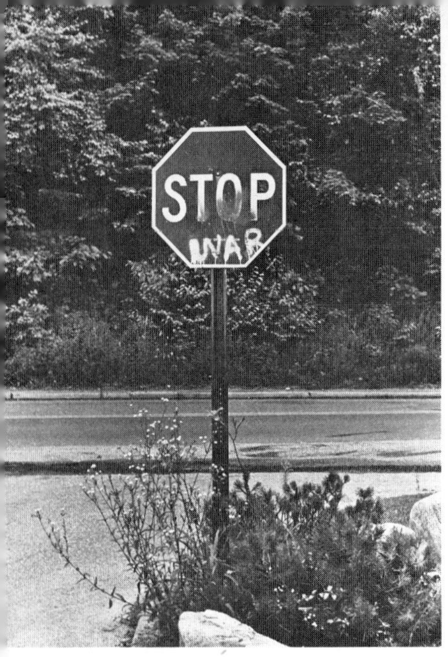

"Free speech" has to stop somewhere, and vandalism is not a proper exercise of one's constitutional liberties. *(Rhoda Galyn/Photo Researchers, Inc.)*

war, prevent communications intended to interfere with the draft and cause insubordination in the armed forces?" He answered that it could, at least in any case where

> the words used are used in such circumstances and are of such a nature as to create a clear and present danger that they will bring about substantive evils that Congress has a right to prevent. . . . When a nation is at war, many things that might be said in time of peace are such a hindrance to its effort that their utterance will not be endured . . . and that no court could regard them as protected by any constitutional right.[52]

In this test, Holmes tried to be guarded: he spoke of a nation at war, and he insisted that any danger be "clear and present." After World War I, however, the superpatriotic atmosphere persisted, heightened by fears aroused by the success of the Bolshevik Revolution in Russia. Repeatedly, with Holmes and Justice Brandeis now dissenting, the Court sustained the restriction of speech when the danger was neither clear nor present. Finally, in 1925, the Court explicitly went beyond Holmes's test. If the government waits for a revolutionary threat to become clear and present, the Court reasoned, it will be too late to prevent violence and possibly to prevent revolution itself. The government has a right to suppress the danger of revolution "in its incipiency."[53]

The Court grew hostile to this "bad tendency" test during the New Deal years, especially as Justice Stone developed the doctrine of "preferred position." World War II, however, necessarily restricted civil liberty, and in the years after the war, the Cold War and anti-Communist zealotry created new pressures to limit "conspiratorial" Communist activities.

In 1985, John A. Walker, Jr. admitted heading a ring that sold naval secrets to the Soviet Union. The military importance of technological secrets greatly increases the danger of espionage and the need for security measures. *(UPI/Bettmann Newsphotos)*

In 1951 (*Dennis* v. *U.S.*), the Supreme Court upheld the constitutionality of the Smith Act of 1940, which made it a crime to "teach" or even to "conspire to teach and advocate" the "duty or propriety" of overthrowing the government by violence or unlawful means. Chief Justice Vinson acknowledged that there was little present danger of any attempt to overthrow the government; he did not even argue that there was any foreseeable danger. Vinson, however, contended that "clear and present danger," properly interpreted, requires the Court to weigh "the gravity of the evil, discounted by its improbability." Any attempt at violent revolution is a life and death matter, and Vinson insisted that Communists would make such an attempt whenever they thought the "time was ripe." Hence, "the existence of the conspiracy creates the danger."[54]

The doctrine in the Dennis case might be called the "bad intention" test: it presumes that Communists have dangerous hopes and aims, and their lack of means to realize those ends is, therefore, relatively unimportant.

The Warren Court, however, retreated from this extreme position, very quickly asserting the right to engage in the "theoretical advocacy" of violent revolution. In one sense, the Warren Court returned to Justice Holmes's formula, permitting any speech not closely related to some overt, unlawful act, but it applied Holmes's test with sensibilities shaped by the idea of "preferred position." In fact, the Warren Court eventually required that the danger of lawless action be *imminent,* as opposed to merely "present."[55]

It remains true, however, that it is very hard for any court to oppose the judgment of the president in time of war. As the Supreme Court remarked in 1944, "the power to protect must be commensurate with the threatened danger."[56] Since modern weapons unimaginably magnify the danger of war, they also increase the need for executive power to avert war. Modern war makes national security into a permanent concern, leaving the nation in what amounts to a continuous state of emergency. Moreover, modern military technology makes secrecy more necessary than it was in the past. All these factors make the Court unwilling to oppose executive demands for secrecy and discretion. The courts realize that even secret judicial hearings are likely to "leak" in ways that could endanger security, and judges know how limited their information about foreign affairs is when compared with that of the president.[57]

Nevertheless, constitutional government requires the courts to examine the president's claims. The Supreme Court ruled, for example, that the appeal to "national security" was not sufficient to prevent the publication of the "Pentagon Papers," which included secret documents about the origin and conduct of the Vietnam War. To make its case, in time of peace at any rate, the government would have had to show that "immediate and irreparable harm" would result from publication in order to prevent it.[58] The Court, in other words, applied a very restrictive version of the clear and present danger test. The public's right to deliberate implies a right to know that is not to be limited except in cases of genuine necessity. That, however, does not undo the fact that thermonuclear weapons and rapid change make such necessities all too likely.

Nor is the public's right to know always easily compatible with other civil liberties. For example, any ability to check the president in matters relating to national security requires that Congress have broad powers to inquire into such affairs. It demands, consequently, that congressional committees be able to subpoena witnesses and documents, and cite for contempt any witness who refuses to testify. Of course, a witness need not engage in self-incrimination, but Congress can compel even such a witness to testify by granting immunity from prosecution.[59]

Periodically, congressional committees abuse these powers, engaging in sensational "investigations" that have little purpose apart from grabbing headlines. During the 1950s, especially, legislators like Senator Joseph McCarthy (and Representative and Senator Richard Nixon) engaged in inquiries into "subversion" that were no more than attempts to try Communists and their alleged sympathizers in the "court of public opinion," without the safeguards of judicial procedure. Eventually, the Warren Court ruled that a witness need not answer questions that are not pertinent to some valid legislative purpose. A committee must, in other words, tell a witness *why* he or she has been called and, if asked, explain what its questions are getting at. "Exposure for the sake of exposure," moreover, is not a valid purpose.[60] The cost of these decisions to Congress's ability to get information has been small, but they have contributed a good deal to an atmosphere in which citizens feel free to speak their minds about matters of common concern.

During the 1950s, legislators such as Senator Joseph McCarthy abused the power of congressional committees by engaging in sensational "investigations" of alleged communists in the State Department. *(Wide World Photos)*

Private Rights and Free Speech The exercise of the freedom of speech sometimes conflicts with private rights. A quiet neighborhood cannot be expected to be happy if a political sound truck broadcasts in its streets, but such sound systems are protected by the First Amendment. Fortunately, the Court has held that communities may prohibit "loud and raucous" sound systems, but such statutes must be written carefully, excluding the nuisance without limiting the right.[61]

Similarly, the First Amendment protects religious missionaries who distribute literature door-to-door.[62] Property owners do not have to answer the door, but they do have to put up with their bells being rung.

A related decision upheld the right of the Jehovah's Witnesses to distribute literature on the streets of a "company town." The Gulf Shipbuilding Corporation owned the real estate in the town and rented it to workers and tenants. The Court ruled that this privately owned town functioned like every other town and public space performed the same role it did in other communities. Consequently, public rights took precedence in public space; private title was immaterial.[63]

In recent times, there have been very few company towns, but more and more Americans have deserted traditional "downtown" shopping areas in favor of privately owned shopping centers and malls. Accordingly, in 1968, the Supreme Court held that there was a right to picket in a shopping center because it was the "functional equivalent" of the business district of a traditional community.[64] The Burger Court, more sympathetic to private rights, retreated from this doctrine. In 1976, it flatly overruled the 1968 decision, holding that a shopping mall is not essentially similar to a municipality. For private property to become public, the Court ruled, it must have all the "attributes of a town" including, presumably, residential areas and municipal services.[65] This opinion has the effect of radically restricting access by citizens to their fellows in the places such as malls where, in the real world of the late twentieth century, public life is really lived.

The Burger Court may have had second thoughts. The California Supreme Court held that California's state constitution protects speech in shopping centers so long as the right is exercised in a reasonable way. When this decision came before the federal Supreme Court, Justice Rehnquist argued for a unanimous court that the rights of property owners under the federal constitution are not strong enough to keep a state from preferring and extending the rights of public speech, as California had done. In a very limited way, in other words, the Court was conceding that public freedoms, even in shopping centers, have some priority over private rights.[66]

Obscenity A related problem is posed by the widespread desire to censor or prohibit pornography and obscenity. The possession of pornography, the Court has ruled, is a private right.[67] A great many people worry, however, about the public impact of pornography, especially its tendency to portray sexuality as casual or exploitative, and about the deteriorative impact of "adult" theaters and bookstores on community life. The Supreme Court is sensitive to these concerns: it has held, for example, that communities may zone "adult" movie theaters into a small section of town, and that states (partly on the authority of the Twenty-first Amendment) may ban bars featuring nude dancing. These concessions do not go far enough, however, for towns that want to ban pornography altogether. This is especially true since the Court recently held that nude dancing "is not without its First Amendment protection" in places less likely than bars to be associated with sexuality.[68]

Except as a private right, obscenity is not protected by the First Amendment. It is hard, however, for the Court to find a satisfactory definition of obscenity, especially given the breakdown of traditional moral codes and the divergence of sexual ethics among Americans. The Court's definition still rests on its opinion in *Roth* v. *U.S.*, written in 1957. In that case, the Court held that obscenity is an appeal to "prurient interest" (that is, an attempt to arouse sexual desire) as understood by "the average person, applying contemporary community standards." This obscenity must be the "dominant theme" of a work, not characteristic of a few passages only. Even if it is obscene by all these standards, a work may not be banned or censored if it has any "redeeming social importance."[69]

When the Court referred to an "average person" and "community standards," it was referring to Americans as a whole. That doctrine was sensible enough in 1957, but given the changes of the 1960s, the Roth doctrine meant that there was almost no way to establish the obscenity of a book or movie. Americans differed so much that there were virtually no standards to apply, and willy-nilly, more traditional communities were compelled to accept the standard of the most permissive as a lowest common denominator.

In 1973, in *Miller* v. *California*, the Court took a less tolerant position in relation to pornography. The Court held that local communities could apply their own standards. Second, it ruled that material could be classified as obscene if it was without "serious" literary, artistic, or political value, a much more relaxed standard than the requirement that such materials be "utterly without" such value. The Miller decision almost certainly will not satisfy advocates of individual liberty nor those who contend for public rights, but it may provide a workable compromise for this period in American political culture.[70]

The Freedom of the Press

In two ways, the freedom of the press involves a collision between public and private claims. The private side of freedom of the press implies that the media may not be hampered or restricted by the government in what they print or say, and we expect this to be the ordinary rule. Even indirect regulation is suspect; a tax on newsprint, for example, is impermissible because it lays a special burden on the press.[71] But these private rights of the press exist for a public purpose.

In the first place, most of us are concerned with the media as readers, listeners, or viewers interested in an adequate exposition of public affairs. For us, a free press means a press that is not prevented from telling the truth, but it also means a press that is free from deceptions and distortions. Freedom of the press in this public dimension is a positive right to know those things a democratic citizen needs to know. It is not enough for the government to let the media alone; we may look to the government to help ensure a responsible press. The public meaning of a free press, however, is obviously at odds with the liberty of those who own and control the press to print and say what they please.[72]

THE PRESS AND NATIONAL SECURITY In wartime, for example, the press has been censored, and there may be reasons for restraining the press in time of peace. When the government sought to halt publication of the "Pentagon Papers" (see Chapter 17) because of the classified material they contained, the Supreme Court held that the government failed to meet the "heavy burden" of justifying such a restriction on the press. The Court's reasoning, however, indicated that there *are* circumstances in which **prior restraint** would be justifiable, and five justices implied that even if the newspapers involved in the case could not be censored, their publishers could be prosecuted and punished.[73]

In 1980, the Burger Court went farther. Frank Snepp, a former CIA agent, published a book which drew heavily on his experiences in the Agency. The book did not contain any classified information, but Snepp did not obtain clearance from the CIA before publishing the book, as his contract with the Agency had required. The Supreme Court held that this contract did not violate Snepp's First Amendment rights, and it ruled that by breaking it, Snepp had caused irreparable harm to his former employers. He was ordered to give up all his profits from the book and to submit any further writings to the CIA before publishing them. The Court's decision means that anyone employed in sensitive work by the CIA acquires public responsibilities which permanently limit his or her rights to freedom of the press.[74] Yet the fidelity that officials owe to government, the Court's concern in *Snepp* v. *U.S.*, is only one side of their duty; public officials also have a responsibility to see that citizens are informed of the things they have a need and a right to know.

THE PRESS AND "PUBLIC FIGURES" A second problem, however, inheres in the public role of the media. The effort to inform the public leads the media to intrude on the lives of individuals, sometimes injuring their reputations and welfare. Traditionally, individuals who were damaged by false statements in the press could sue for libel. The Court reasoned, however, that the threat of libel suits can persuade the media to withhold information from the public and dampens the "uninhibited, robust and wide open" controversy to be desired in democratic politics. In *The New York Times* v. *Sullivan* in 1964, the Court held that public figures voluntarily expose themselves to attacks and defamations as a part of public life. In order to sue for libel, they must do more than show that published statements are false: public figures must demonstrate that whoever published the falsehood acted with "malice," either knowing that the statement was false or showing a "reckless disregard" for the truth.[75] For example, in 1985, a jury found that *Time* had falsely defamed General Ariel Sharon by asserting that the Israeli minister had connived at the massacre of Palestinians in Beirut in 1984. But it also held that Sharon had failed to show that *Time* acted with malice, and the General lost his suit.

The Court has revised the Sullivan doctrine, holding that the public has an interest in events rather than persons. Consequently, even a private individual involved in a matter of "public or general concern" would have to show malice in any suit for libel, even though he or she was only involuntarily part of the public realm.[76] Apparently, however, the Court has now retreated from this position. In 1974, it held that a private citizen "elevated to sudden prominence" by events need not show malice in order to sue.[77]

The Burger Court continued to chip away at the rule promulgated in *The New York Times* v. *Sullivan.* It held, logically enough, that a scandalous divorce does not make someone into a public figure; it would be difficult to show a legitimate public interest in the extramarital affairs of a private citizen.[78] Public figures, in the Court's definition, are persons who thrust themselves "into the forefront . . . of public controversies" and can be said to have surrendered voluntarily some of their ordinary private rights. It is not enough to be involved in public business. A corporation is not a public figure because it advertises widely; neither is a government contractor or a professional political advisor.[79] Even public figures, moreover, must be permitted to question broadcasters or the press about their motives and editorial policies in order to give them a fair chance to demonstrate malice.[80] The Court, in other words, seems to be showing a growing sympathy with individual claims to privacy, and a greater suspicion of assertions of a putative public right to know.

When CBS wanted to air possibly incriminating tapes of John DeLorean before his trial, the television station acted on the basis of the public's right to information. Judge Takasugi thought, however, that airing the tapes could have interfered with DeLorean's right to a fair trial. *(L.A. News Service/ Sygma)*

Media Coverage of Trials Similar problems are posed by media coverage of trials. The media have almost unlimited freedom to criticize judges and court officials.[81] Publicity that makes it impossible for an individual to receive a fair trial, however, is another matter. The Court will reverse any conviction obtained in a "poisoned" atmosphere, and it has warned that the media that act as "poisoners" cannot expect to be immune.[82] Moreover, in cases of "great notoriety," the Court has ruled that television is incompatible with a fair trial.

In 1976, in *Nebraska Press Association* v. *Stuart,* the Court struck a major blow for news coverage when it ruled that a judge may not forbid the publication of information about a criminal trial, even in the interests of a fair trial.[83] The Court hastened to qualify that decision: for example, judges may bar reporters from pretrial proceedings if there is a "reasonable probability" of damage from their presence to the right of fair trial. But trials are part of the functioning of government, a public activity about which the public has claims to be informed. The Court's position seems to be that though it is not impossible to justify excluding the media, the public's right to information is so compelling that such justification is difficult indeed.[84]

It is important to emphasize that the Court's chief concern is the public's right to know, not the private liberties of the press. Consequently, the press cannot refuse to provide grand juries with the names of their sources without facing citations for contempt.[85] Newspeople argue that confidentiality is essential to their ability to get information for the public. Juries, however, need information in order to do justice here and now, and the public is allowed to prefer these immediate considerations to conjectures, however reasonable, about the long term. By contrast, as we have observed, the government cannot keep the media from disseminating matters affecting national security without showing that "immediate and irreparable" harm will result. The public right to information outweighs the claims of the government, at least as long as that claim remains conjectural. The Court, in other words, seems to judge the press and the government by the same rule, holding both accountable to the public at large.

In relation to radio and television, in fact, the Court upheld the right of the Federal Communications Commission to require "fairness," giving the

POLITICAL PERSPECTIVE

PUBLIC RIGHT OR PRIVATE LIBERTY: FREEDOM OF THE PRESS VS. JOHN DE LOREAN'S RIGHT TO A FAIR TRIAL

The possibility of the press's jeopardizing one man's right to a fair trial was evident in the case of John De Lorean in 1983. Only nine days before his trial, CBS-TV aired video tapes showing De Lorean's apparently enthusiastic acceptance of $24 million worth of cocaine from undercover government agents. Since the key issue in the case was whether or not De Lorean had been "framed" by government agents, the tapes could have unduly influenced the public and the jury against De Lorean. CBS executives justified the airing by saying that there was nothing new in the tapes that hadn't already been described in detail and concluded that there would be little impact on De Lorean's ability to get a fair trial.

After he learned that CBS planned to show the tapes before the trial, De Lorean's chief defense attorney, Howard Weitzman, demanded a temporary restraining order from the judge who was to preside over the trial. Judge Robert Takasugi complied, but the order was struck down by an appeals court. Judge Takasugi responded by denouncing CBS for their "interference" in the judicial process and by postponing the trial.

Defenders of CBS's action said that the network had a Constitutional right to broadcast the tapes: the case was highly newsworthy—and the public had a right to know. Critics, although they agreed that CBS was within legal bounds, said that the network, nevertheless, acted irresponsibly and out of baser motives than the public's right to information.

Source: Based on "The Case of the Purloined Tapes," *Time* (Nov. 7, 1983), p. 82.

interest of listeners and viewers priority over the rights of broadcasters.[86] The Burger Court, however, has been unwilling to go further. It ruled that a newspaper may be required to print retractions of defamatory statements, but it cannot be required to print replies to editorials. Moreover, the Court ruled that neither the First Amendment nor the Federal Communications Act requires the media to accept political advertising. Dissenting, Justice Brennan argued that such decisions endanger the right of democratic citizens "not only . . . to hear the debate, but also the right to participate in that debate." Chief Justice Burger, however, rejoined that access by advertising might be monopolized by the wealthy, and that the regulatory authority of the FCC was a better guarantee of adequate debate.[87] Both Burger and Brennan, however, began with the recognition that at least the electronic mass media are private governments, crucial in shaping public alternatives and opinion. (Print media are more diverse and more numerous, and their situation differs significantly if not in kind.) The terms of access to the media will define the contemporary meaning of citizenship and democratic deliberation, matters too important to America as a whole to be left in the sphere of private right.

The Freedom of Association

The "right of the people peaceably to assemble" may be our most important public liberty. It implies the freedom to associate, at least for the purposes of political action ("to petition the government for a redress of grievances"), and, as Tocqueville realized, in a country as large and complex as the

United States, association is almost the only means of effective citizenship and the only protection of genuine individuality.*

Two dangers threaten the freedom of association. In the first place, the government may attempt to forbid certain forms of organization on the grounds that they are not "peaceable" or that they lack a legitimate public purpose. That, certainly, was the intent of the Smith Act, which included the "conspiracy to organize the American Communist party" among the conspiracies it outlawed. When the Court, in the interest of freedom of speech, interpreted the Smith Act to permit citizens to advocate the "abstract idea" of revolution, it did so by emphasizing the propriety of those sections of the act that restricted overt acts, specifically the organization of a conspiratorial party. The Court strengthened freedom of speech, not the freedom of association.[88]

In 1961, however, the Supreme Court observed that the Communist party, even in the most critical eyes, had two aspects: (1) a political movement devoted to advocating and advancing the Communist cause through more or less legal means, and (2) a conspiracy devoted to violent revolution. It was entirely possible, the Court observed, for an individual to join the Communist party because he or she supported the first, while being ignorant of, or opposing, the second. Membership in the party cannot be made criminal, the Court argued, unless the government is prepared to show that it is knowing, active, and involves a specific personal intent to overthrow the government.[89] The mere fact of association is not enough. By the same token, though the government may forbid violent or illegal acts, it cannot outlaw any association that has legitimate public purposes and concerns. Organizing a nonviolent economic boycott to exert political pressure, for example, is protected by the First Amendment even if the organizers use "emotionally charged rhetoric."[90]

This only means, however, that government cannot make membership a crime punishable in courts of law. By itself, that limitation might be very little comfort to members of an unpopular association, since they would still be exposed to the second danger to free association, economic *and* social sanctions. For example, in 1952, the Supreme Court ruled that New York had a right to dismiss teachers who were members of subversive organizations. The New York law, Justice Sherman Minton wrote, did not violate the First Amendment because it left the dismissed teacher free to think and associate as he pleased. The law set reasonable conditions for public employment; the teacher in question, one Adler, was free to comply or "go elsewhere." Admittedly, Minton reasoned, the "Feinberg Law" made Adler's job the price of his beliefs, but the Constitution does not promise that one's political associations will have no costs.[91] The Court's opinion in the Adler case spoke the language of private liberty; it emphasized that Adler was "free to choose" and discounted the restriction of his right of association inherent in threatening his job.

With the ebbing of Cold War hysteria, the Court reversed its field. It now argues that a state may inquire into the associations of employees only when they are related to fitness and competence on the job.[92] The *Adler*

*Alexis de Tocqueville, *Democracy in America,* vol. 2 (New York: Schocken, 1961), pp. 128–33; see also *N.A.A.C.P.* v. *Alabama,* 357 U.S. 449 (1958).

decision was overruled in 1967 because the Feinberg Law penalized membership without showing any "specific intent to further the unlawful goals of the organization." Mere membership in a subversive organization is not enough, the Court argued, especially given the "special concern" of the First Amendment for academic freedom.[93] The Court has gone even further, arguing that a Communist cannot be excluded from employment in a defense plant without inquiring into the "quality and degree" of his or her membership, and showing some relationship between the individual and possible acts of sabotage.[94]

A state may still ask employees to refrain from illegal and unconstitutional means of opposing the government. It may not, however, cross the line that separates the control of actions from the control of associations. This doctrine also vitally affects those most exalted of associations protected by the freedom of religion.

The Free Exercise of Religion

Even before the Bill of Rights was adopted, Article VI of the Constitution prohibited any religious test as a qualification for office, and the First Amendment added the familiar provisions denying Congress any power to legislate "respecting an establishment of religion" and requiring it to permit "the free exercise thereof."

For the framers, the right to "free exercise of religion" was as absolute as any human right could be. There was, however, more disagreement on the question of religious establishments and aid to religion. Madison thought religion an inalienable natural right, wholly outside and exempt from civil society, but Madison did not have his own way.[95] A majority of states had some form of religious test or establishment, and many members of Congress were eager to protect the right of states to aid religion as the foundation of civil and republican morality. The "no establishment" clause prevents Congress from legislating about religious establishments at all: it can neither set up a church nor forbid states to do so.[96] There the matter rested until the Supreme Court declared, in 1947, that the Fourteenth Amendment makes the prohibition on religious establishment binding on the states.[97]

The terms of the early debate suggest that the freedom of religion may be divided into (1) free exercise, a nearly absolute individual right, and (2) the prohibition on legislating "respecting" establishment, which forbids an official church or public assistance to "religion."

Each freedom has its own difficulty. Certain forms of conduct are necessary to the "free exercise" of religion, but religious belief will not justify every form of conduct. The "no establishment" clause, for its part, forbids aid to "religion" but leaves religion undefined. It is clear that the government may not support religious worship or indoctrination, but may it give aid to other church-related activities that have secular value? Is a mathematics class in a parochial school, or a church-sponsored basketball league, "religion"? Paradoxically, the ban on an establishment of religion requires the courts to establish an official definition of religion and to make the boundary that divides religious and secular affairs.

POLITICAL PERSPECTIVE

MADISON ON CHURCH AND STATE

In 1784 1785, the Virginia legislature considered a bill that proposed to "restore and propogate the holy Christian religion" by paying the salaries of Episcopal clergymen. Madison and several associates wrote a "Memorial and Remonstrance" in opposition to the bill, which opens with the following arguments:

> The religion . . . of every man must be left to the conviction and conscience of every man, and it is the right of every man to exercise it as these may dictate. This right is in its nature an unalienable right. It is unalienable because the opinions of men, depending only on the evidence contemplated by their own minds, cannot follow the dictates of other men. It is unalienable also because what is here a right towards men, is a duty towards the Creator. It is the duty of every man to render to the Creator such homage, and such only, as he believes to be acceptable to him. This duty is precedent, both in order of time and degree of obligation, to the claims of Civil Society. Before any man can be considered as a member of Civil Society, he must be considered as a subject of the Governor of the Universe. . . . We maintain therefore that in matters of religion no man's right is abridged by the institution of Civil Society, and that religion is wholly exempt from its cognizance. . . .
>
> [I]f religion be exempt from the authority of the society at large, still less can it be subject to that of the Legislative Body. The latter are but the creatures and viceregents of the former.

Source: Gaillard Hunt, ed., *The Writings of James Madison,* vol. 2 (New York: Putnam, 1900–1910), pp. 183–84.

The right to free exercise of religion allows people an almost unlimited liberty to speak on religious matters. It will not, however, protect certain dangerous or noxious rituals, like handling poisonous snakes as part of a religious ceremony.[98] The public is also entitled to forbid certain forms of conduct, most notably polygamy, which some religious teachings encourage or command. Although adults have the right to refuse medical treatment (such as transfusions, vaccinations, or tranquilizers) on religious grounds, the public *may* insist on such treatments for children.*

The public's interest in the health, education, and welfare of children imposes the most severe limitations on religiously inspired conduct. Public authorities can forbid the use of children in "preaching," which includes the door-to-door sale of literature, because a democratic society rests on the "healthy, well-rounded growth of young people into . . . citizens, with all that implies."[99] The public's right to educate citizens, and the right of citizens to be educated for public life outweigh many of the claims to religious conduct. Hence, although parents have a right to send their children to religious schools, the state has a right to insist that all children attend an accredited school. In deciding what schools to recognize, the state may inquire into the character and qualifications of teachers, require the teaching of subjects "plainly essential to good citizenship," or forbid the teaching of subjects "manifestly inimical" to public welfare.[100] Despite the qualifying terms, this amounts to a massive public right to constrain the private liberties of religious schools. Recently, for example, the Burger Court upheld the authority of states to enforce closing of unaccredited religious schools.[101]

* *Reynolds* v. *U.S.*, 98 U.S. 145 (1878) deals with polygamy; on medical treatment for adults and children, see *Jacobson* v. *Massachusetts,* 197 U.S. 11 (1905).

Two exceptions need to be noted. First, the government may not require children in any school to salute the flag if their religious beliefs forbid it. The Court changed its mind on this matter, first thinking of the flag salute as an acceptable promotion of good citizenship but later ruling that the freedom of conscience includes that freedom to be silent.* Second, the Court has recently held that Amish parents, given their long-established belief that secondary education teaches "worldly" values hostile to their religion, need not send their children to such schools. This is at best a curious decision, and Chief Justice Burger was careful to limit its terms. The Court made its judgment, Burger argued, because the Amish had demonstrated the ability to rear useful human beings, and the state had not showed that the lack of secondary education would impair the physical or mental health of the children or their ability to be self-supporting. The decision would not apply, Burger pointed out, to "faddish new sects and communes."[102] This opinion, however, turns on the argument that Amish children can lead useful private lives without secondary education: it ignores the difference between being healthy and self-supporting and being a citizen. Implicitly, in other words, Burger's opinion treated education in less public and more private terms.

In another vital area, conduct arising from religious motives is protected by the First Amendment. An employer cannot discharge a worker for refusing to work on Saturday (or, presumably, any other day) because of religious conviction. To confront a worker with a choice between employment and religious belief, the Court reasoned, imposes too great a penalty on religious freedom.[103] Similarly, a worker who quits because his or her religious beliefs forbid helping to manufacture weapons cannot be denied unemployment insurance. If such workers were denied unemployment insurance, they would have to choose between religion and destitution.[104]

Yet, the Supreme Court also ruled that Sunday closing laws are legal.

**Minersville* v. *Gobitis,* 310 U.S. 586 (1940) was overruled by *West Virginia Board of Education* v. *Barnette,* 319 U.S. 624 (1943).

The Court has recently held that Amish parents, given their long-established belief that secondary education teaches "worldly" values hostile to their religion, need not send their children to secondary schools. *(John Launois/Black Star)*

The Court was chiefly concerned to argue that such laws are not an "establishment of religion" because their contemporary meaning is secular. Nevertheless, the Court's decision meant that businesspeople whose religion requires them to close on Saturday may be required to suffer a competitive disadvantage as the price of their beliefs, since they would be able to do business only on five days of the week.[105] It almost seemed as if the Court had given employees a right to free exercise that it did not extend to employers. The Court appears to have reasoned, however, that the loss of one day's business is not comparable in severity to losing one's job. People may, in other words, have to pay a price for their beliefs so long as the Court does not consider the cost to be crushing or unfair.

The Establishment of Religion

In similar terms, Justice Wiley Rutledge contended, in a 1947 case involving aid to religious schools, that all such aid is an impermissible "establishment of religion." Parents, Rutledge argued, have a right to educate their children religiously, but they must be willing to pay the "price" of their convictions.[106] In Rutledge's view, like Madison's, religious liberty is a private, negative liberty. The First Amendment, in these terms, lowers the price we can be asked to pay for our beliefs by ruling out religious persecution; it does not rule out a price in money, even a very high one.

That doctrine, however, has obvious problems. It lays an unequal burden on the religious beliefs of the poor. Like a worker forced to choose between keeping a job and keeping the Sabbath, poor Americans who believe in religious education may confront an intolerable choice between basic well-being and religious belief. Refusing to help low-income families send their children to religious schools protects America against an establishment of religion at the cost of burdening the free exercise of religion. If government may require us to pay a price for our beliefs, to what extent must it do so? How far may the public share with its fellow citizens the burden of their religious liberty?

Conscientious Objection Certainly, the public has supported the religious freedom of pacifists by allowing them the privilege of **conscientious objection,** the refusal to take part in military service. This privilege is not required by the First Amendment: when Madison proposed to exempt the "religiously scrupulous" from militia service, he was voted down.[107] Conscientious objection can only be regarded as the public's contribution to religious freedom, since military service not performed by pacifists must be assumed by others.

In the Warren years, the Court worried that the legislation providing for conscientious objection—and which speaks of "religious training and belief" and convictions about a "Supreme Being"—might constitute an "establishment of religion." It took pains, consequently, to define "religion" as including convictions based on secular teachings if those beliefs are held firmly enough, even if the person in question denies that his or her beliefs are "religious."[108]

This inclusive definition, however, did not solve the problem. Conscientious objection grants a privilege to those opposed to all war that it denies to those who are conscientiously opposed only to unjust wars. It is not hard to see the secular reasons for such a discrimination: pacifists are a small minority, unlikely to inconvenience military policy, but exempting selective objectors might make it hard for the military to meet its demands for personnel. Political reasons of this sort apparently convinced the Supreme Court when it ruled that Congress had not established a religion by excluding selective objectors.[109] This decision, however, turns on the proposition that Congress may discriminate between beliefs when such distinctions are reasonably related to secular purposes.

Public Schools and Religion The cases dealing with conscientious objection point to still another conclusion. If firmly held beliefs derived from history, sociology, and philosophy are "religious," as the Court held, then any education in the social sciences and humanities has a religious dimension. In these terms, even public education is "religious." Since the "no establishment" clause forbids the government to prefer one religion to another, a good case can be made that the government must provide an equal place for religion in the public schools or give equal support to religious schools.[110]

It is hard to argue against the Court's decision that the "no establishment" clause prohibits official prayers in the schools, even if they are nondenominational, simply because an official prayer creates an official creed.[111] On similar grounds, the Court ruled against devotional Bible-reading in public schools.[112] These decisions occasioned bitter protest, but they seem almost unanswerable as a matter of law. Reasons of the same sort, though less compelling ones, led the Court to rule against voluntary classes in religion on public school premises, though it upheld "release time" programs that dismiss classes so that students may attend religious instruction elsewhere.[113]

The Supreme Court finds cases involving prayer in the schools more than a little troublesome. *(AUTH, by Tony Auth. © 1985 Philadelphia Inquirer. Reprinted with permission of Universal Press Syndicate. All rights reserved.)*

Concern for the equal rights of religious associations, however, has led the Court to some relaxation of its rule regarding the use of public school property. It now appears that voluntary religious groups may be allowed to use public school facilities before or after regular school hours, on the ground that there is no "establishment" so long as such groups meet at a time when children are not under the control of school authorities.[114] An even more difficult question may soon come before the Court: Can a school that permits secular groups to use its facilities during school hours rightly exclude religious groups? Does the "no establishment" clause, in other words, permit or require schools to discriminate against religion? Any exceptions the Court may make on behalf of the freedom of association, however, do not seem likely—despite the Reagan administration's pressure to erode the ban on official school prayer.

Religious Schools and State Aid There is a better case, however, for public assistance to the secular functions of religious schools. The Court first applied the "no establishment" clause to the states in a case in which it ruled that a state may provide buses to take children to religious schools because their safety is an appropriate public objective.[115] Similarly, the Court has held that it is permissible to loan secular textbooks to students in religious schools.[116]

The Court is wary of such proposals, however, because aid to religious schools, even for secular instruction, releases resources that can be used to support religious instruction. The effect of such aid is to support religion even if its purpose is secular. The Court is especially suspicious of any program to grant money, whether to religious schools themselves or to parents in the form of grants. Even where money grants are carefully tied to secular goals—giving parents the money to buy textbooks, for example—the court fears that such assistance would foster an "excessive entanglement" and a relation of dependence between public money and religious education.[117] The Court upheld sending public school teachers into religious schools to provide special services to "disadvantaged" children, but it struck down a New York law aimed at providing money assistance to religious schools serving low-income families as well as tuition reimbursement for the families themselves.[118]

In 1983, however, the Court upheld a Minnesota law that allowed a deduction for "tuition, textbooks, and transportation" paid to *any* school, public or private. Of course, parents with children in public schools were allowed very few deductions—the most important seem to have been the cost of renting musical instruments and some expenses associated with driver education. But the fact that such benefits were available to all parents—Justice Rehnquist argued for a narrow 5 to 4 majority—was enough to establish the deduction as a support for education rather than a support to religious schools. Justice Marshall, for the dissenters, saw no distinction between the Minnesota law and forms of tuition assistance that the Court had struck down. The question is by no means closed. The number of families sending their children to private and religious schools is growing, increasing the pressure on government to provide some form of aid.[119]

The "Wall" of Separation between Church and State Decisions dealing with the "establishment of religion" often seem like quibbling, but the

Court has a difficult task. Every so often, a justice uses a ringing phrase like the "wall of separation between church and state" when attempting to define the ban on religious establishments. In fact, no such wall exists: ministers, to cite one obvious example, have a right to seek and hold public office.[120] Religion plays too important a role in American political culture to be excluded from public life. The government employs chaplains in the armed services and in state legislatures; the pledge of allegiance asserts that the United States is "under God"; the public schools are allowed to observe religious holidays.[121] The Burger Court grew more and more tolerant of such public recognition of "beliefs widely held by the people of this country": in 1984, it upheld by a 5 to 4 majority the right of local governments to include a Nativity scene as part of an official Christmas display.[122]

In material terms, the fact that churches and church schools are exempt from taxation is the most important breach in the "wall" between church and state.[123] Granting this exemption also requires government to decide which institutions are and are not "religious" within the meaning of the law. The state of New York was overruled by the courts when it maintained that the Rev. Sun Myung Moon's Unification Church was chiefly an economic and political, as opposed to a religious, organization.[124] But New York was upheld when it denied a tax exemption, on grounds of fraud, to the 200 (out of 236) residents of Hardenburgh, New York, who claimed to be ministers—based on mail-order degrees—and set themselves up as "churches."[125] Similarly, over President Reagan's objections, the Supreme Court upheld the Internal Revenue Service in denying tax exemptions to religious colleges that discriminate on racial grounds, observing that a charitable institution must "serve a public purpose and not be contrary to public policy."[126] Yet, distinguishing between religious institutions that "serve" a public purpose and those that do not comes very close to an establishment of religion.

The Court is operating in a world of fine distinctions, attempting to separate "excessive" entanglement from permissible relationships. As Americans grow more anxious about moral confusion and social decay, they can be expected to increase their demands for public recognition of religion and aid to religious institutions. The task of the Supreme Court is likely to grow more difficult rather than less.

SUMMARY

The interplay between private liberty (including exercise of rights of property) and public liberties (such as the right to have accurate public information, to speak freely, to petition, and associate with others) is central to American political debate.

The arguments for the supremacy of private rights reflect the individualist views of the framers—government follows the establishment of society and exists to give citizens their private liberties. But many Americans have agreed with Aristotelian theory that private freedom must be subordinated to the public good.

The Bill of Rights reflects the private and public notions of civil liberties. Though the Bill of Rights would help preserve private liberties, the framers were reluctant to accept it because acceptance implied that the rights were conferred by the state, and not held naturally by individuals.

The Bill of Rights also contains "public" rights—the rights to speak, associate, petition, and have free elections. These, and freedom of the press, have been deemed "preferred rights" by the Supreme Court because they are essential to a free society. The Constitution also gives government inherent rights, such as *eminent domain* and *police powers,* which give communities power over private property for public goals.

The Constitutional protection of private liberty includes the freedom to make secure contracts and the right to life, liberty, and property. In the nineteenth century, the latter was strongly defended by the doctrine of *substantive due process,* which meant the Supreme Court examined not only the means but the end of a state action to deprive an individual of life, liberty, or property. Today, however, the rights of property generally take a back seat to public purpose.

Substantive due process protects our right to marry, to establish a home and raise children, and to pursue the religion of our choice. These rights are part of our right to privacy, which in recent years has been carefully guarded by a Supreme Court sensitive to the vulnerability of individuals in modern society. For example, the conducting of searches and seizures in private places has been sharply curbed.

The Supreme Court is most restrictive of governments' limits on private discussion and dissent. Speech can be limited only to the extent that it provokes immediate violence, either privately or against the government, although speech involving national security or "conspiracy" has been curtailed at times.

The nature of press freedom brings a collision of public and private liberties. In the first place, this freedom means a citizen has the right to information necessary to the operation of a democracy; in the private domain, however, the owner of a newspaper has the right to print what he or she pleases. A second point of contention is that to obtain information, the media often intrude on the privacy of individuals. In regard to the first problem, the Burger Court appears to hold the media accountable to the public at large; regarding the second, the Court has shown a growing sympathy for individual claims to privacy.

The freedom of religion implies both free exercise and the prohibition of both an official church and public assistance to religious establishments. Yet, the government continues to treat religious associations differently than others—churches are tax-exempt. As Americans grow more anxious about social decay and moral confusion, the task of the Court in determining the relationship between church and state is likely to become more difficult. For instance, does the no establishment clause permit or require public schools to discriminate against religious groups?

NOTES

1. Robert K. Carr, *The Federal Protection of Civil Rights* (Ithaca: Cornell U.P., 1947).
2. Carey McWilliams, *Witch Hunt: The Revival of Heresy* (Boston: Little Brown, 1950), pp. 8–10.
3. Aristotle, *Politics,* p. 6.
4. Itzhak Galnoor, ed., *Government Secrecy in Democracies* (New York: Harper, 1977), pp. 3–39.
5. *Reid* v. *Covert,* 354 U.S. 1, 9 (1957).
6. Howard, vol. 1, pp. 30–31.
7. Ibid., vol. 1, p. 58.
8. J. A. C. Grant, "The 'Higher Law' Background of the Law of Eminent Domain," *Wisconsin Law Review,* 6 (1931), pp. 67ff.; *West River Bridge Co.* v. *Dix,* 6 How. 507 (1848); *Atlantic Coast Line* v. *Goldsboro,* 232 U.S. 548, 558 (1914).
9. Howard, vol. 1, p. 210.
10. *Davidson* v. *New Orleans,* 96 U.S. 97 (1878) restates the Court's original position. The new doctrine was enunciated in *Chicago, Burlington and Quincy Railroad* v. *Chicago,* 166 U.S. 226 (1897).
11. Joseph Sax, "Takings and the Police Power," *Yale Law Journal,* 74 (1974), pp. 26–37.
12. *Mugler* v. *Kansas,* 123 U.S. 623 (1887); *Champlin Refining* v. *Corporation Commission,* 286 U.S. 210 (1932).
13. *Kewanee Oil Co.* v. *Bicron.,* 416 U.S. 470, 481–82, 487 (1974).
14. *Dartmouth College* v. *Woodward,* 4 Wh. 518 (1819).
15. Ibid., p. 708.
16. *Ogden* v. *Saunders,* 12 Wh. 213 (1827).
17. *Charles River Bridge* v. *Warren Bridge,* 11 Pet. 420 (1837).
18. *West River Bridge* v. *Dix* 6 How. 507 (1848); *Stone* v. *Mississippi,* 101 U.S. 814 (1880).
19. *Bronson* v. *Kinzie,* 1 How. 311 (1843).
20. *Ferguson* v. *Skrupa,* 372 U.S. 726 (1963); *Williamson* v. *Lee Optical,* 348 U.S. 483, 491 (1955).
21. Aristotle, pp. 18–22; *Meyer* v. *Nebraska,* 262 U.S. 390, 399 (1923).
22. *Rochin* v. *California,* 342 U.S. 165 (1952).
23. *Breithaupt* v. *Abram,* 352 U.S. 432 (1957).
24. *Schmerber* v. *California,* 384 U.S. 757 (1966).
25. *Griswold* v. *Connecticut,* 381 U.S. 479, 488 (1965).
26. Edward Bloustein, "Group Privacy," *Rutgers-Camden Law Journal,* 8 (1977), pp. 228–29; *Baker* v. *Nelson,* 489 U.S. 810 (1971); *Doe* v. *Commonwealth Attorney,* 425 U.S. 901 (1976). The Court reaffirmed the rights of states to prohibit homosexual acts and other forms of sodomy in a highly publicized case in 1986. See *Bowers* v. *Hardwick,* 54 L.W. 4919 (1986).
27. *Eisenstadt* v. *Baird,* 405 U.S. 438 (1972).
28. *Roe* v. *Wade,* 410 U.S. 113, 153 (1973).
29. Ibid., pp. 152, 153; *Planned Parenthood* v. *Danforth,* 428 U.S. 52 (1976).

30. *Belotti* v. *Baird,* 443 U.S. 622 (1979); *Harris* v. *McRae,* 448 U.S. 297 (1980); *Akron* v. *Akron Center for Reproductive Rights,* 103 S. Ct. 2481 (1983).
31. *Escobedo* v. *Illinois,* 378 U.S. 478 (1964).
32. *Miranda* v. *Arizona,* 384 U.S. 436 (1966).
33. *Faietta* v. *California,* 422 U.S. 806 (1975).
34. *Olmstead* v. *U.S.,* 277 U.S. 438 (1928).
35. *Katz* v. *U.S.,* 389 U.S. 347, 351 (1967).
36. *U.S.* v. *Albert Ross,* 102 S. Ct. 2157 (1982), overruling *Robbins* v. *California,* 453 U.S. 420 (1981).
37. *Florida* v. *Royer,* 51 L.W. 4293 (1983).
38. *U.S.* v. *Caceres,* 440 U.S. 741 (1979); *U.S.* v. *Knotts,* 103 S. Ct. 1081 (1983).
39. Henry J. Abraham, *Freedom and the Court* (New York: Oxford U. P., 1977), pp. 9–32.
40. *Palko* v. *Connecticut,* 302 U.S. 319, 325 (1937).
41. *Baltimore and Ohio R.R.* v. *U.S.,* 386 U.S. 372, 478 (1967).
42. Hugo Black, "The Bill of Rights," *New York University Law Review,* 35 (1960), pp. 866–67.
43. Alexander Meiklejohn, *Free Speech and Its Relation to Self-Government* (New York: Harper, 1948).
44. *Mutual Film Corp.* v. *Industrial Commission,* 236 U.S. 230 (1915); *Burstyn* v. *Wilson,* 343 U.S. 495 (1952).
45. *Thornhill* v. *Alabama,* 310 U.S. 88 (1940).
46. *Tinker* v. *Des Moines Independent Community School District,* 393 U.S. 503 (1969); *Wooley* v. *Maynard,* 430 U.S. 705 (1977).
47. *Adderley* v. *Florida,* 385 U.S. 39 (1966).
48. *U.S.* v. *O'Brien,* 391 U.S. 367 (1968); *Brown* v. *Glines,* 444, U.S. 348 (1980).
49. *Chaplinsky* v. *New Hampshire,* 315 U.S. 568 (1942); in recent years, the Court has defined "fighting words" in a very narrow way, preferring some risk of violence to a constraint on speech. For example, see *Gooding* v. *Wilson,* 405 U.S. 518 (1972).
50. *Terminiello* v. *Chicago,* 337 U.S. 1 (1949); *Yates* v. *U.S.,* 354 U.S. 298 (1957).
51. *Cohen* v. *California,* 403 U.S. 15 (1971).
52. *Schenck* v. *U.S.,* 249 U.S. 47 (1919).
53. *Gitlow* v. *New York,* 268 U.S. 652 (1925).
54. *Dennis* v. *U.S.,* 341 U.S. 494, 510–11 (1952).
55. *Yates* v. *U.S.,* 354 U.S. 298 (1957); *Noto* v. *U.S.,* 367 U.S. 290 (1961); *Brandenburg* v. *Ohio,* 395 U.S. 444 (1969).
56. *Korematsu* v. *U.S.,* 323 U.S. 214, 219–20 (1944).
57. *U.S.* v. *Reynolds,* 345 U.S. 1, 10 (1953).
58. *The New York Times* v. *U.S.,* 403 U.S. 713 (1971).
59. *Ullman* v. *U.S.,* 350 U.S. 422 (1955).
60. *Watkins* v. *U.S.,* 354 U.S. 178 (1957); *Barenblatt* v. *U.S.,* 360 U.S. 109 (1959); *Braden* v. *U.S.,* 365 U.S. 431 (1961).
61. *Saia* v. *New York,* 334 U.S. 558 (1948); *Kovacs* v. *Cooper,* 336 U.S. 77 (1949).
62. *Martin* v. *Struthers,* 319 U.S. 141 (1943).
63. *Marsh* v. *Alabama,* 326 U.S. 501 (1946).
64. *Amalgamated Food Employees* v. *Logan Valley Plaza,* 391 U.S. 308 (1968).
65. *Hudgens* v. *National Labor Relations Board,* 424 U.S. 507 (1976).
66. *PruneYard Shopping Center* v. *Robins,* 447 U.S. 74 (1980).
67. *Stanley* v. *Georgia,* 394 U.S. 557 (1967).
68. *California* v. *LaRue,* 409 U.S. 109 (1972); *Schad* v. *Mt. Ephraim,* 452 U.S. 61 (1981).
69. *Roth* v. *U.S.,* 354 U.S. 476 (1957).
70. *Miller* v. *California,* 413 U.S. 15 (1973).
71. Walter Berns, "The Constitution and a Responsible Press," in *The Mass Media and Modern Democracy,* Harry Clor, ed. (Chicago: Rand McNally, 1974), pp. 113–36.
72. *The New York Times* v. *Sullivan,* 376 U.S. 254 (1964).
73. *Time, Inc.* v. *Hill,* 385 U.S. 374 (1967); *Rosenbloom* v. *Metromedia,* 403 U.S. 29 (1971).
74. *Gertz* v. *Robert Welch, Inc.,* 418 U.S. 323 (1974).
75. *Time, Inc.* v. *Firestone,* 424 U.S. 448 (1976).
76. *Loudon Times Mirror* v. *Arctic Co.,* 449 U.S. 102 (1981); *Moss* v. *Lawrence,* 451 U.S. 1031 (1981).
77. *Herbert* v. *Lando,* 441 U.S. 153 (1979).
78. *Hutchinson* v. *Proxmire,* 443 U.S. 111 (1979); *Wolston* v. *Reader's Digest,* 443 U.S. 157 (1979).
79. *Pennekamp* v. *Florida,* 328 U.S. 331 (1946); *Smith* v. *Daily Mail,* 443 U.S. 97 (1979).
80. *Irvin* v. *Dowd,* 366 U.S. 717 (1961); *Sheppard* v. *Maxwell,* 384 U.S. 333 (1966).
81. *Estes* v. *Texas,* 381 U.S. 532 (1965).
82. *Nebraska Press Association* v. *Stuart,* 423 U.S. 713 (1976).
83. *Gannett Co.* v. *De Pasquale,* 443 U.S. 368 (1979).
84. *Richmond Newspapers* v. *Virginia,* 448 U.S. 555 (1980); *Press Enterprise* v. *Superior Court,* 104 S. Ct. 819 (1984).
85. *Branzburg* v. *Hayes,* 408 U.S. 665 (1972); *The New York Times* v. *New Jersey,* 439 U.S. 997 (1978).
86. *Red Lion Broadcasting* v. *F.C.C.,* 395 U.S. 367 (1969).
87. *Columbia Broadcasting System* v. *Democratic National Committee,* 412 U.S. 94 (1973); *Miami Herald* v. *Tornillo,* 418 U.S. 241 (1974).
88. *Yates* v. *U.S.,* 354 U.S. 298 (1957).
89. *Scales* v. *U.S.,* 367 U.S. 203 (1961); *Noto* v. *U.S.,* 367 U.S. 290 (1961).
90. *N.A.A.C.P.* v. *Claiborne Hardware,* 102 S. Ct. 3409 (1982).
91. *Adler* v. *Board of Education,* 342 U.S. 485 (1952).
92. *Shelton* v. *Tucker,* 364 U.S. 479 (1960).
93. *Keyishian* v. *Board of Regents,* 385 U.S. 598 (1967).
94. *U.S.* v. *Rober,* 389 U.S. 258 (1967); *Schneider* v. *Smith,* 390 U.S. 17 (1968).
95. Howard, vol. 1, p. 291.
96. Walter Berns, "Religion and the Founding Principle," in Robert Horwitz, ed., *The Moral Foundations of the American Republic* (Charlottesville: U. of Virginia, 1977), pp. 162–63.
97. *Everson* v. *Board of Education,* 330 U.S. 1 (1947).
98. *State* v. *Bunn,* 336 U.S. 942 (1949).
99. *Prince* v. *Massachusetts,* 321 U.S. 158 (1944).
100. *Pierce* v. *Society of Sisters,* 268 U.S. 510 (1925).
101. *Faith Baptist Church* v. *Douglas,* 454 U.S. 803 (1981).
102. *Wisconsin* v. *Yoder,* 406 U.S. 205 (1972); despite this fondness for the Amish, their members—exempted from the Social Security tax by federal statute—must pay it and other taxes demanded of employers, even though part of their belief is that taxpaying is a sin. *U.S.* v. *Lee,* 455 U.S. 252 (1982).
103. *Sherbert* v. *Verner,* 374 U.S. 398 (1963); however, in order to accommodate the religious beliefs of a junior worker whose convictions forbid work on Saturday, an employer need not force more senior workers to work in his place. *TWA* v. *Hardison,* 432 U.S. 63 (1977).
104. *Thomas* v. *Review Board,* 450 U.S. 707 (1981).
105. *Gallagher* v. *Crown Kosher Market,* 366 U.S. 617 (1961).

106. *Everson* v. *Board of Education,* 330, U.S. 1, 59 (1947).
107. Edward Dumbauld, *The Bill of Rights and What It Means Today* (Norman: U. of Oklahoma, 1957), p. 207.
108. *U.S.* v. *Seeger,* 380 U.S. 163 (1965); *Welsh* v. *U.S.,* 398 U.S. 333 (1970).
109. *Gilette* v. *U.S.,* 401 U.S. 437 (1971).
110. Wilbur Katz, *Religion and the American Constitutions* (Evanston: Northwestern U. P., 1964).
111. *Engel* v. *Vitale,* 370 U.S. 421 (1962).
112. *Abingdon School District* v. *Schempp,* 374 U.S. 203 (1963).
113. *Illinois ex rel. McCollum* v. *Board of Education,* 333 U.S. 203 (1948); *Zorach* v. *Clauson,* 343 U.S. 306 (1952).
114. And in colleges and universities, where attendance itself is voluntary, religious groups have the same rights as secular organizations. *Widmar* v. *Vincent,* 454 U.S. 263 (1981).
115. *Everson* v. *Board of Education,* 330 U.S. 1 (1947).
116. *Board of Education* v. *Allen,* 392 U.S. 236 (1968).
117. *Lemon* v. *Kurtzman,* 403 U.S. 602 (1971); *Essex* v. *Wolman,* 409 U.S. 808 (1972); *Marburger and Griggs* v. *Public Funds for Public Schools,* 417 U.S. 961 (1974); *Meek* v. *Pittenger,* 421 U.S. 349 (1975).
118. *Wheeler* v. *Barrera,* 414 U.S. 908 (1974); *Committee for Public Education* v. *Nyquist,* 413 U.S. 756 (1973).
119. *Mueller* v. *Allen,* 103 S. Ct. 3062 (1983).
120. *McDaniel* v. *Paty,* 435 U.S. 618 (1978).
121. Justice Brennan summarized many of these institutions in *Abingdon* v. *Schempp,* 374 U.S. 203, 296–303 (1963). See also *Florey* v. *Sioux Falls,* 449 U.S. 987 (1980) and *Marsh* v. *Chambers,* 103 S. Ct. 3330 (1983).
122. *Lynch* v. *Donnelly,* 79 L.E.D.2d 604 (1984).
123. *Walz* v. *Tax Commission,* 397 U.S. 664, 1970; *West* v. *Mt. Lebanon School District,* 412 U.S. 967 (1974).
124. *The New York Times* (May 7, 1982); similarly, the courts struck down a Minnesota law, aimed at the Unification Church, which required churches to report the sources of their income if more than 50 percent was derived from nonmembers. *Larson* v. *Valente,* 457 U.S. 111 (1982).
125. *Hardenburgh* v. *N.Y.,* 154 U.S. 958 (1981).
126. *Bob Jones University* v. *U.S.,* 103 S. Ct. 2017 (1983).

CHAPTER

14

Civil Rights

Civil rights are the foundations of citizenship. We have civil rights even if we are not citizens; some rights belong to us simply because we are members of civil society. (The Fourteenth Amendment, for example—see Table 13.1—proclaims that all "persons," not merely all citizens, have a rightful claim to due process and equal protection of the laws.) Civil rights open the door to participation in social and economic life and, hence, may be binding on private persons as well as on public authorities. Moreover, civil rights entitle us to be treated with civility and afforded a minimum of dignity and respect.

In the United States, however, civil dignity and participation are incomplete—and more or less insecure—without citizenship. The American political tradition, G. K. Chesterton observed, teaches Americans that "no man must aspire to be anything more than a citizen, and no man shall endure to be anything less."[1] Civil rights, in the full sense of the term, include political rights.

In fact, in order to protect civil rights, it is necessary for the federal government to extend the rule of equality which the Constitution ordains for national citizenship. Civil rights set limits to federalism and to private liberty. States and localities are self-governing and can differ, but not in ways that are incompatible with civic equality. Nebraska may have a one-house legislature, but that legislature must be apportioned on the principle of "one person, one vote." Our private liberty permits differences of wealth, association, power, and taste, but not if such inequalities are incompatible with equal citizenship or are exercised in ways that are unacceptable in civil society. People are entitled to spend their money pretty much as they please, but bankers may not refuse to extend credit to prospective borrowers simply because they are women. Our debates about civil rights involve, fundamentally, arguments about what is necessary for a decent life in civil society and what it means to be a citizen of the United States.

The Right to Citizenship

Public Rights: Citizenship

The original Constitution—the document as the framers wrote it, before any amendments—refers to citizens of the United States, but it does not define them. It gives Congress a fairly unlimited power to establish a "uniform rule of naturalization" (Art. I, sec. 8). It requires that members of Congress be citizens and have been so for seven years, in the case of the House, and for nine years, in the case of the Senate. It provides that the president must be "natural born" or a citizen "at the time of the Adoption of this Constitution." It is otherwise silent.

These provisions do contain an *implicit* idea of citizenship. Those people who were American citizens under the Articles of Confederation—"at the time of the Adoption of this Constitution"—are automatically citizens under the Constitution. Subsequently, citizenship must be acquired by native birth or naturalization. Given the existence of slavery, however, not *all* native-born persons were citizens, and the framers preferred not to acknowledge that sad exception. They also hesitated to declare openly that the states have no role in defining or granting citizenship in the United States, although that seems to have been the framers' intent. They left such contradictions and ambiguities to be resolved by political practice.

Citizenship was not given a more explicit definition until the Fourteenth Amendment, which declares that "all persons born or naturalized in the United States" are "citizens of the United States and of the state wherein they reside."

In recent decades, the Supreme Court has defined citizenship as the premise of all rights—a "right to have rights"—and has made it impossible for Congress to deprive a person of citizenship. In *Trop* v. *Dulles,* decided in 1958, the Court held that to deprive a person of citizenship, even for desertion in time of war, is **cruel and unusual punishment**[2] (see Table 13.1, Amendment 8)—that is, punishment that is too severe to be appropriate for the crime. In 1963, in a case that took on great importance during the Vietnam War, the Court ruled that citizenship cannot be taken away from a person who leaves the country to avoid military service.[3] The Court carried the logic of these decisions to its conclusion in 1967, denying that Congress has any power to take away citizenship. Citizenship can be lost only if the citizen freely and explicitly renounces it.[4]

National Citizenship and the Bill of Rights

For most of the history of the United States, the Bill of Rights limited only the federal government, not the states. Speaking for the Supreme Court in the case of *Barron* v. *Baltimore,* John Marshall argued that the Constitution was ordained by the "people of the United States," and the states were "distinct governments, framed by different persons and for different purposes." Americans were citizens of the United States and of their respective states, and with very few exceptions the Constitution deals—Marshall argued—only with the rights and duties of the former. Except for those clauses that specifically mention the states, the limitations on government in the Constitution refer, the Court ruled, to the federal government alone.[5]

This idea of **dual citizenship** came under attack after the Civil War. Despite a long debate among scholars, it seems clear that the Fourteenth Amendment aimed to subordinate state citizenship to national citizenship. The amendment makes state citizenship derive from national citizenship; persons who are U.S. citizens are also citizens of the state "wherein they reside." This language is directly contrary to *Barron* v. *Baltimore*; the people of a state are not a separate public but a part of American people as a whole. To emphasize the point, the authors of the Fourteenth Amendment provided that no state should abridge the "privileges and immunities of citizens of the United States."

The Supreme Court, however, resisted so radical a transformation of the federal system. In the *Slaughterhouse Cases* in 1873, Justice Miller insisted that so long as there was any doubt, the Court should reject any interpretation that involved a "far reaching and pervasive" change in the "structure and spirit of our institutions" or that would "fetter and degrade the state governments."[6] Accordingly, the Court reaffirmed the principle of dual citizenship. It defined the "privileges and immunities of citizens of the United States" as those that "owe their existence to the Federal government, its national character, its Constitution or its laws." In general, any right possessed by Americans before the adoption of the Constitution was excluded from the "privileges and immunities" of national citizenship. Those privileges, the Court ruled, include the right to hold federal office and to visit the capital, the right to use navigable waters and have access to seaports, and the right to protection in foreign affairs. The Court did add the right to assemble and petition and the privilege of habeas corpus to its list. With these exceptions, it left the protection of civil rights to the states.

The **privileges and immunities clause** never recovered from the *Slaugh-*

The Supreme Court has ruled that state and local police must respect the rights granted by the Constitution. *(©Tom Kelly)*

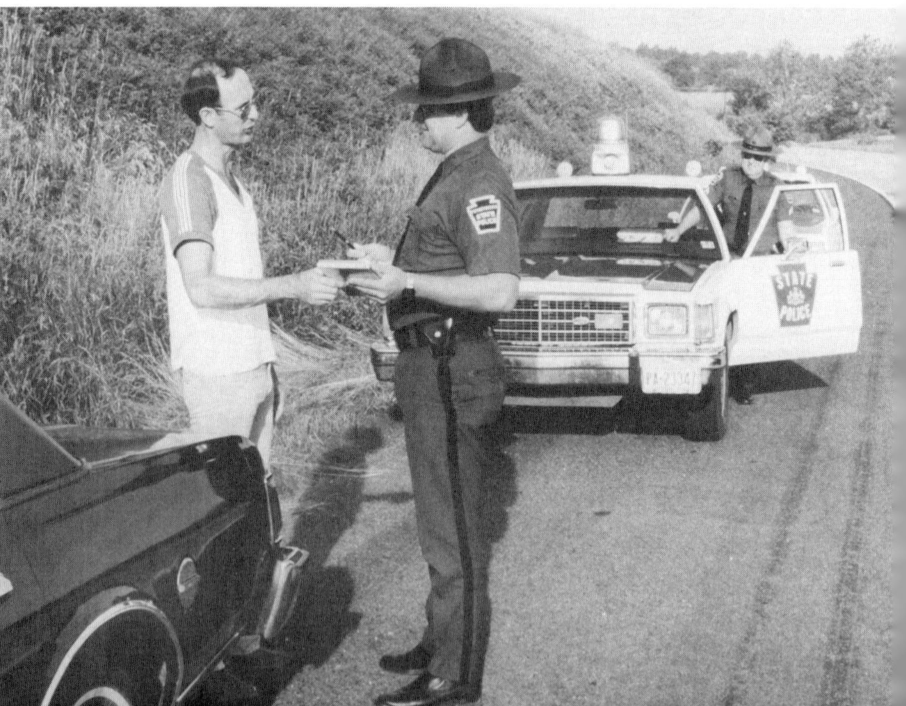

terhouse Cases. Moreover, the Court was equally restrained in interpreting the provision that no state may deprive any person of "life, liberty, or property" without "due process of law." In *Hurtado* v. *California* in 1884, the Court specifically rejected the idea that the Bill of Rights is a part of due process. But, devoted to the rights of property, the conservative Court did make one exception: it ruled that due process includes the right to compensation when a state takes private property for public purposes.[7] The Court explained this by arguing that principles "founded in natural equity" or "essential to free government" are part of due process. It was not inclined to add to the list of such principles. Compensation aside, it seemed clear that the Bill of Rights did not apply to the states.

In 1925, however, the Court asserted, rather off-handedly, that the freedom of speech and the press were among the liberties protected by due process. This comment was confirmed in subsequent cases, and in 1931 the Court declared that the relation between the liberty of speech and press and due process of law "is no longer open to doubt."[8] During the 1930s, the Court expanded the list of rights protected by due process to include the right to counsel in capital cases, the free exercise of religion, and the right of petition and assembly.[9] The Court maintained the position, however, that only "fundamental" rights were part of due process. As we have observed, Justice Cardozo argued in 1937 that only those rights "implicit in the concept of ordered liberty" are incorporated into due process. The protection against double jeopardy, the right at issue in *Palko* v. *Connecticut,* was not among those fundamental rights, Cardozo argued, because a "fair and enlightened system of justice" could be imagined without it.[10]

During the late 1940s, the Court defined certain judicial procedures, such as the right to a public trial, as parts of due process. It was very hesitant: in *Wolf* v. *Colorado,* the Court held that the ban on **unreasonable searches and seizures**—the Fourth Amendment clause that limits search and seizure in any place where a person has a "legitimate expectation of privacy"—applied to the states; but it allowed the use of evidence obtained by such searches. The decision meant only that an individual whose rights had been violated could sue the offending officers for damages.[11] The Court became convinced, however, that such suits were not a sufficient deterrent to illegal searches and the seizures. In 1961, in *Mapp* v. *Ohio,* the Court ruled that no illegally obtained evidence could be admitted into state courts. This "exclusionary rule" has been much criticized, since it clearly subordinates concern for the truth to the rights of the individual.[12] The Burger Court became increasingly hostile to the exclusionary rule. It held that illegally acquired evidence *may* be introduced if the police obtain it in "good faith," believing that constitutional standards have been observed.[13] Similarly, evidence that "inevitably" would have been discovered by legal means may be introduced even if, in fact, it was found illegally.[14] And several justices appear to be ready to abandon the rule altogether. Nevertheless, it remains the ruling principle of law.

After *Mapp* v. *Ohio,* the Warren Court proceeded to incorporate almost all of the remaining provisions of the Bill of Rights into the due process clause. In 1962, it extended the ban on cruel and unusual punishment to the states; in 1963, it insisted that states honor the right to counsel in all criminal cases where the accused faces a prison term; in 1964, the Court overturned an early ruling and held that due process includes protection against compulsory self-incrimination.[15] Before the 1960s ended, the Warren Court had added the right to confront and subpoena witnesses, the right to speedy trial, and the right to trial by jury in criminal cases. Finally, in 1969, it overturned *Palko* v. *Connecticut,* holding that a state could not try an individual twice for the same offense.[16]

Only a few provisions of the Bill of Rights have not been incorporated into due process. States are not obliged to indict by grand jury or to grant jury trials in civil cases; the Supreme Court has not applied the ban on "excessive bail" to the states, although lower federal courts have done so. There has been no violation of the Third Amendment, and hence no opportunity to apply its prohibition on quartering troops to the states. The right "to keep and bear arms," however, clearly does not limit the states. In the first place, this right is extended to "the people" collectively, as a part of a militia and does not refer to individual rights. Moreover, the Second Amendment gives states the right to order the militia and, consequently, the right to regulate the use and possession of arms.[17]

For practical purposes, the Warren Court fulfilled the aim of the authors of the Fourteenth Amendment, extending the Bill of Rights to the states. The Burger Court, in its typical pattern, narrowed the Warren Court's ruling in minor respects but left the basic principles intact. In 1972, in fact, the Burger Court ruled that the death penalty as then administered was an unconstitutional "cruel and unusual punishment." Later, the Court ruled that the death penalty might be constitutional if a law were carefully written and confined to cases where life had been taken, and many states responded by restoring the penalty.[18] Increasingly conservative, the Burger Court became more and more tolerant of the death penalty.[19] Nevertheless, the Court has gone beyond the death penalty to hold that a sentence is "cruel and unusual" if it is too severe to be proportionate to the offense: a person convicted of a series of petty crimes cannot be sentenced to life without parole.[20] These rulings are one indication of how far the Court will intrude, under the authority of the Fourteenth Amendment, into the life of the states. National citizenship became the law of the land.

Equality and Civil Rights

In everyday speech, Americans associate civil rights with equality, and with reason. Equality is a civil right in at least two ways: all citizens are equal in respect of their citizenship, and the Fourteenth Amendment adds that all persons have a right to "the equal protection of the laws."

Civil equality does not mean, however, that we all must be treated identically. The laws cannot protect us without treating criminals and their victims in different ways. The equality of all citizens establishes that each of us has the right to be treated as an equal, not that we must be treated equally.[21]

Our civil right to equality does mean that any distinction between citizens must be justified. When a law or policy treats one class of persons differently from another, the government must be prepared to show (1) that this distinction is significantly related to a valid public purpose and (2) that the persons within each classification are treated in a reasonably equal way.[22] For example, when a state university sets standards for graduation, it discriminates in favor of those students who meet the standards and against those who do not. It is within its rights so long as these inequalities are reasonably related to its educational purpose and so long as it applies its standards in a fair and evenhanded way.

Even in relatively clear cases, however, the appeal to public purpose raises a number of difficult questions of evidence and philosophy. In 1983, the New York legislature raised the state's drinking age—discriminating against New York's younger citizens—in the interest of reducing serious automobile accidents. The new law presumes both that the relationship between legal teen-age drinking and traffic accidents is sufficiently clear to justify treating young New Yorkers differently from their elders and that the public purpose—preventing traffic fatalities and serious injuries—is sufficiently strong to outweigh the damage done to the civil equality of younger citizens of New York. Most of us would agree on both points, especially given the fact that the right to drink is hardly essential to citizenship. Yet, the Court must satisfy itself on the same two counts whenever it attempts to define **equal protection of the laws** (see Table 13.1, Fourteenth Amendment)—that is, the clause in the Fourteenth Amendment that forbids states to deny protection of the law to anyone. And, of course, in the cases that come before the Court, the answers are not so clear.

"Separate but Equal" and the Civil Rights Movement For many years, the Supreme Court was inclined to accept almost any discrimination so long as it was "reasonably" related to a public purpose. In 1896, in the case of *Plessy* v. *Ferguson,* the Court upheld the right of a state to impose racial segregation in public places on the ground that there was a reasonable relationship between racial separation and public order. In the Court's view, the argument that keeping the races apart would reduce the likelihood of racial conflict was sensible enough to sustain segregation. Civic equality, the Court asserted, would be sufficiently protected if segregated facilities were "separate but equal." Dissenting, Justice Harlan protested that racial equality is *itself* a public purpose so strong as to override the sort of reasoning on which the Court relied. "Our Constitution is color-blind, and neither knows nor tolerates classes among citizens."[23] At the time, Harlan's argument went unheeded.

Blacks, already exposed (by the decision in *The Civil Rights Cases,* which we will discuss later in this chapter) to discrimination by private persons, were also subjected to discriminatory state laws, especially in the South. Black Americans knew that if they attempted to assert their rights under the federal Constitution or their claims to civil equality, at best they could expect harassment and threats to their livelihood. They were never free, moreover, from the menace of public and private violence; over 5,000 blacks were lynched in the United States between 1880 and 1950.

Despite this, the struggle for equal rights went on, slowly eroding some of the bases of racism. As we have seen (in Chapter 12), in the 1930s the Supreme Court began to chip away at "separate but equal" until there was almost nothing left, and *Brown* v. *Board of Education,* decided in 1954, rejected the old doctrine altogether.[24]

Despite the constant menace of public and private violence, the Civil Rights Movement continued slowly to erode some of the bases of racism. *(Charles Moore/Black Star)*

The decision in *Brown* v. *Board,* moreover, helped to set the stage for what we have come to call the **Civil Rights Movement,** the series of actions during the 1950s and 1960s intending to end policies and practices of racial segregation. Late in 1955, Rosa Parks, riding a bus in Montgomery, Alabama, refused to surrender her seat in the section of the bus reserved for whites. She was tired, and she had reached the limit of her willingness to put up with offenses to her dignity. Mrs. Parks' arrest—she was fined $10—led to a year-long boycott of Montgomery's bus system in which Dr. Martin Luther King, Jr. first gained national prominence. The Montgomery boycott ended when a federal court issued an injunction forbidding the segregation of buses. This victory helped inspire similar protests against segregation. In 1960, black students in Greensboro, North Carolina, demanded equal access to a Woolworth lunch counter, continuing to occupy seats—"sitting in"—even though they were denied service and even though, as the days went on, they were subjected to harassment and violence. The movement spread, developing new tactics to dramatize the injustices of segregated society. In 1963, Dr. King led a march in Birmingham, Alabama, involving mass, nonviolent defiance of "Jim Crow" laws; the repressive measures of Police Commissioner "Bull" Connor, shown on national television, inspired widespread indignation. Not long after, a black church was dynamited in Birmingham, killing four girls who were attending Sunday school, and white Americans outside this region were confronted with the cruelty underlying racial segregation and inequality.

Also in 1963, a coalition of civil rights organizations in Mississippi sponsored a Freedom Ballot, intended to make clear the barriers of law and violence that kept blacks from voting in that state. Despite intimidation, thousands of blacks, denied the right to vote, cast unofficial ballots. Increasing demands for the protection of voting rights culminated, in 1965, with a march from Selma, Alabama, to Montgomery; state troopers attacked and attempted to disrupt the march until President Johnson intervened.

The political momentum generated by the Southern Civil Rights Movement resulted in a series of federal laws designed to protect civil rights, most notably the Civil Rights Act of 1964 and the Voting Rights Act of 1965. This federal intervention against legally imposed segregation and overt racial repression did not, of course, end de facto segregation or the less visible, deeply embedded patterns of racism in American society. President Johnson once remarked that American race relations had only moved "from D+ to C−." The rights of women and other disadvantaged groups had scarcely been addressed at all. Nevertheless, the passage of federal civil rights laws signaled a minor revolution in American politics and law.

The New Equal Protection and Affirmative Action Today, the Supreme Court has virtually adopted Harlan's reasoning. The Court now regards racial and ethnic classifications as "suspect," so contrary to public purpose under ordinary circumstances that a state must show a "compelling" interest to justify using them.

Affirmative Action programs are the most important reflection of such a compelling interest. As a political society, the United States has an "affirmative duty" to try to undo the wrongs of the past, an obligation so strong as to be "compelling."[25] Affirmative Action policies attempt to compensate racial minorities—and other groups, like women, with similar claims—for the inequalities they suffered in the past by encouraging employers, schools, and other institutions to make a special effort to include and accommodate disadvantaged groups. An exception to this use of racial classifications to combat racism and "inequality" to promote equality was demonstrated in *Regents* v. *Bakke* in 1978.[26] (See the accompanying box entitled "Affirmative Action and 'Reverse Discrimination'" on page 484.)

Subsequently, the Supreme Court has given affirmative action even stronger support. In 1979, it approved a voluntarily adopted private plan for correcting the racial imbalance in "traditionally segregated job categories" even though the program involved quotas and did result in some discrimination against whites. Although the Civil Rights Act of 1964 forbids all racial discrimination, the Court denied that Congress intended to forbid "voluntary, private, race-conscious efforts to abolish traditional patterns of segregation and hierarchy." The next year, the Court upheld a provision of the Public Works Employment Act of 1977 which required that 10 percent of federal funds granted for local public works projects be spent in hiring or buying supplies from minority-owned businesses. In his concurring opinion, Justice Powell argued that this case was different from Bakke's because (1) Congress has constitutional authority to remedy discrimination, whereas in *Bakke,* the regents of the university had only "educational functions," and (2) Congress had found, and was attempting to remedy, past discrimination, whereas the regents made no such claim. In any case, the Court's opinion gave Congress a broad charter to mandate affirmative action in the interest of equality.[27]

"Suspect Categories" and Fundamental Rights Race and ethnicity are not the only "suspect categories" requiring a "compelling" public purpose. Classifications distinguishing aliens from citizens are similarly suspect, especially in relation to the states. Traditionally, the law held that a state had a special obligation to nurture and care for citizens, and consequently, a special interest in reserving public resources for their benefit.[28] The Fourteenth Amendment weakened that idea, and in 1971, the Supreme Court ruled that states cannot discriminate against aliens in relation to welfare assistance because alienage is a **"suspect category,"**[29] a classification in it-

POLITICAL PERSPECTIVE

AFFIRMATIVE ACTION AND "REVERSE DISCRIMINATION"

Critics charge that Affirmative Action creates "reverse discrimination" against whites and men, and in 1978, that issue came before the Court. The medical school of the University of California at Davis reserved 16 out of 100 places in its entering class for minority students. Allan Bakke, a white applicant, claimed that he had been denied admission, despite fairly high test scores, because of this "special admissions" quota. It helped Bakke's case that the Supreme Court had already held that federal civil rights laws dealing with employment forbid discrimination against *any* race and that the use of standardized tests is legitimate even if blacks and other minorities tend to receive lower scores than whites.

In the end, the Supreme Court did rule in Bakke's favor, but the arguments made by the justices were more important than their decision. The Court was sharply divided: four justices wanted to approve the university's program, quotas and all, and four justices supported Bakke's position. Justice Powell's compromise opinion maintained that it *is* legitimate to use racial classifications to promote equality, in this case, by increasing the diversity of the student body. But in pursuing equality, Powell reasoned, such policies must give some consideration to people, like Bakke, who may be shut out. Affirmative action must be carried out in a way that minimizes the threat to the rights of those citizens who, effectively, are asked to bear the burden of America's past injustices. Quota systems, like that which helped to exclude Bakke, fail to meet this standard: they are too rigid, too impersonal, too inconsiderate of those they exclude. With that important qualification, Powell's opinion sustained affirmative action.

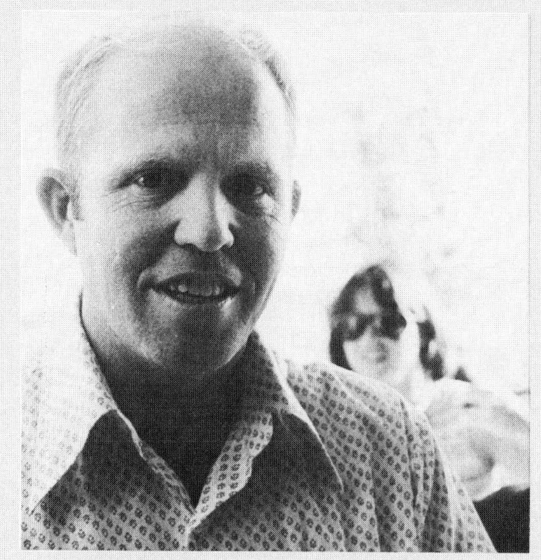

Medical student Allan P. Bakke. *(Wide World Photos/AP)*

self so contrary to public goals under ordinary circumstances that government must have a "compelling" interest to use it at all. However, the federal government's powers over immigration and naturalization still leave it relatively free to make "reasonable" distinctions between citizens and aliens, provided that they are made by statute rather than administrative decisions.[30]

A similar suspicion applies to any attempt to limit the fundamental rights of citizens as those rights are defined by the Supreme Court. These fundamental rights include the ability to participate in political life, which will be discussed later on. Also included among the fundamental civil liberties is the right to travel between states. Since states may not abridge this right without a compelling interest, a state may not make an extended period of residence a condition for receiving welfare because such a rule would make it difficult for indigent people to move into that state (which, ordinarily, is a major purpose of such laws).[31]

Economic distinctions, by contrast, are not "suspect classifications." In general, states may discriminate on an economic basis if such inequalities are "reasonably" related to a "legitimate" public purpose. The poor do have a limited number of rights to civic equality: they are entitled to court-appointed counsel in criminal cases, for example, and they cannot be sent to jail simply because they lack the money to pay a fine.[32] Nevertheless, poverty by itself is not a "suspect classification."[33] And although states may not discriminate against racial minorities in housing, they may adopt regulations that discriminate against the poor. Justice Thurgood Marshall protested this reasoning but without avail.[34] Just as poverty is not a suspect classification, moreover, the necessities of life are not "fundamental rights." Neither is education, which allows states to tolerate a great disparity between rich and poor school districts in the amount of money spent on each pupil.[35]

The Court's reasoning appears to run something like the following. First, the "equal protection of the laws" forbids any violation of the citizen's equality as a citizen or a person's equality as a person. Consequently, the states may not deny the political essentials of citizenship. Similarly, they must respect personal dignity, the equal respect we owe one another as part of civility and humanity. Race and ethnic classifications are suspect because they imply that there are essentially superior and inferior people, and alienage is tainted by the same flaw. Economic distinctions, however, are not judgments about the virtue or worth of a person; they speak only to his or her wealth, a more or less accidental quality. Differences in housing, education, and welfare may be undesirable or unwise, but they are not forbidden; so long as there is a legitimate public purpose, the law may favor the rich as well as the poor.

One evident problem with this implicit doctrine is the status of education. Education is not essential to the moral worth of a person, but it is of

In 1971, the Supreme Court ruled that states cannot discriminate against aliens in relation to such public resources as welfare assistance and education, because alienage is a "suspect category." *(U.S. Department of Health and Human Services)*

Though the poor have a limited number of rights to civic equality, poverty is not a "suspect classification," and states may discriminate on an economic basis. *(Martha Tabor/Working Images Photographs)*

crucial importance to the ability to be a citizen. Jefferson thought the right to an education was implicit in the idea of citizenship, and the Court made virtually the same argument when it struck down racial segregation in the schools.[36]

The Rights of Women

Since gender is irrelevant to the worth of a person or the role of a citizen, the Court's failure to include discrimination on the basis of sex among the suspect classifications is a striking gap in its reasoning. In the 1970s, under the impact of feminism, the Court began to look more closely at such distinctions, and in 1973, the Court came close to holding that gender is a suspect classification. In a case involving the benefits due to personnel in the armed services, four justices held that gender is a suspect category, but they fell short of a majority.[37] The Court inched closer in 1976, ruling that sex is a "semisuspect" classification that requires the government to show "important" (as opposed to merely "legitimate") public purposes to which the classification is "substantially" (as opposed to "reasonably") related.[38] And in 1982, deciding that men could not be excluded from a state-financed school of nursing, the Court declared that any discrimination on the basis of sex requires an "exceedingly persuasive justification."[39] The Court has been unwilling to go further.

Despite this reticence, the Burger Court was rigorous in opposing formal discrimination in public institutions. The Warren Court had upheld the right of states to exempt women from jury duty on the ground that so many women have pressing duties in the home; the Burger Court declared such exemptions a violation of equal protection.[40] Similar reasons helped lead the Burger Court to decide that states may not establish different ages of maturity for the sexes, making women adults at an earlier age than men. Despite a considerable body of evidence that women do mature before men, the Court scorned such "old notions," perhaps because different ages of maturity would imply differences in readiness for citizenship.[41]

A major reason for the Court's unwillingness to declare gender a suspect classification—especially given the Court's own increasing conservatism—lies in the fact that women's claims to civic equality extend into areas, like the family, traditionally regarded as part of the private sphere. The problem of sexual harassment provides a striking illustration. Women justly complain that their civil equality is hampered by the fact that so often they are the objects of unwelcome sexual advances from superiors or clients, made with the implication—or the open suggestion—that compliance is the price of employment, promotion, or favor. Regulations of the **Equal Opportunity Commission,** promulgated during the Carter administration, forbid sexual harassment, although many feminists argue that existing regulations do not go far enough.[42] Nevertheless, in deciding whether a woman was in fact sexually harassed by her employer, it is necessary to decide whether she was exploited by him or, whatever she claims now, encouraged his advances because she was drawn by his social position or other attractions. Making such judgments demands an evaluation of *motives* and *meanings*. The law cannot forbid sexual harassment without becoming, to some extent, the censor of our personal relationships and the judge of our souls.

In any case, the Court sees enough justification for certain *social* discriminations to distinguish "semisuspect" gender from the fully suspect classifications. In important ways, the Court has insisted on the equality of the sexes in social life. It has held, for example, that women cannot be excluded as trustees for their children, nor can they be given automatic preference in hearings to decide custody—rulings that reject the notion that all women are inferior in matters of finance and superior in matters of nurture. In 1979, moreover, it ruled that women, as well as men, are liable for alimony.[43] At the same time, the Court has accepted a limited number of traditional assumptions about the sexes and their roles. In 1981, it decided that draft registration may be limited to men. Including women, the Court

TABLE 14.1 Who Rules? (Percent of Men and Women in Public Office)

	1986	
	Men	Women
U.S. Senate	98	2
U.S. House of Representatives	95	5
State legislators	85	15
Statewide elective and appointed officials	86	14
County governing boards	92	8*
Mayors and municipal officials	86	14**
School boards	64	36**

Source: Center for the American Woman and Politics (Eagleton Institute of Politics, Rutgers University, New Brunswick, N.J. 08901), 1986.
*1984 figures.
**1985 figures.

observed, would cause great administrative difficulties for the military, given the fact that women are exempt from combat.[44] Even if we accept this argument, we should note that the Court did not challenge the idea that women may, legitimately, be excluded from combat. Perhaps because it accepted this exclusion, the Court had already agreed that civil service laws which give preference to veterans are constitutional, even though they disproportionately favor men.[45]

In *economic* life, as opposed to social relationships, the Burger Court was less tolerant of inequality. It did hold, in 1974, that the law may notice that widows have more economic difficulties than their male counterparts.[46] But it also ruled that the law may refuse to classify pregnancy as a "disability" for the purposes of disability insurance, and it decided that pregnancy may also be excluded from private health and accident benefits.[47]

In 1984, the Court opened two important doors for women. Many professional partnerships and civic clubs had claimed that, as private associations, they were permitted to discriminate on the basis of sex. The Court held, by contrast, that law firms and civic organizations like the Junior Chambers of Commerce are too much a part of the public sphere, and too essential to women's equality in economic life, to be allowed to practice discrimination.[48]

From Paternalism to Political Fragmentation Moreover, in economic life, the Burger Court seemed to reject the idea that a statistical difference between men and women is often a sufficient basis for distinctions between the sexes. Early in this century, the Oregon legislature, reasoning that prolonged labor was dangerous to the health and well-being of women, made it unlawful to employ women in most industries for more than ten hours a day. When the law came before the Supreme Court in the case of *Muller* v. *Oregon,* Louis Brandeis—then an attorney in private practice—submitted more than a hundred pages of data supporting the statistical generalizations about women on which the law was based, a form of legal argument that came to be called a "Brandeis brief." On the basis of this evidence (combined with a substantial dose of paternalism toward women), the Court sustained the ten-hour law.[49]

The contemporary Supreme Court reasons, by contrast, that it is not enough to treat *all* women on the basis of facts that are true only of *most* women. A law that makes no exceptions in distinguishing between men and women can be justified only if there *are* no exceptions. In relation to discrimination on the basis of sex, the Constitution is not satisfied by "assumptions about groups," the Court has declared; it demands a "thoughtful scrutiny of individuals."[50] Women usually live longer than men. Consequently, pension plans traditionally asked women to pay more into the plan; if payments were the same for both sexes, the annual pensions paid out to women would be smaller, on the assumption that payments would go on for a greater number of years. In 1983, the Burger Court categorically rejected that sort of discrimination, despite its strong basis in fact.[51] A state may be able to use statistical generalizations if it has no other realistic way of achieving an important purpose.[52] But if the issue is whether workers are strong enough to perform their jobs without endangering their health, a test of *strength* and *health*—by a physical examination, for example—is both practical and more to the point than a test of *gender.*[53]

Even if one sympathizes with these decisions of the Court, it is clear that its insistence that the sexes be treated as *individuals* rather than as members of groups edges in the direction of fragmentation and can lead to a politics of litigation and hearings. It encourages us to think in terms of private immunities rather than public equality. Feminists have reason to be troubled as well as encouraged, since much of their argument suggests that each woman is dependent on the condition of all women, and of the political society as a whole. Treatment that is equal in *form* does not by itself eliminate inequalities of *fact*. Law that is blind to differences between the sexes runs the same risk as law that is literally "color-blind": it may endanger affirmative action intended to bring about civic equality.[54]

Life-Styles and Handicaps

Such doubts, combined with a growing concern over social fragmentation, may have contributed to the Court's resistance to carrying the demand for equality any farther into social life.

In 1972, for example, it seemed that the Court was about to declare suspect any classification based on illegitimate birth. Historically, illegitimate children were denied civil equality in any number of ways, most obviously in being granted only second-class claims, at best, on their parents' estates. Courts traditionally respected the argument that such distinctions between legitimate and illegitimate offspring are a necessary support for the family. In *Weber* v. *Aetna Casualty*, however, Justice Powell spoke of the need for "stricter scrutiny" in this area of "sensitive and fundamental rights," and he referred to the idea of burdening children for their parents' misconduct as "illogical and unjust."[55] Powell's reasoning followed, in an important way, from the doctrine that race is a suspect category, since he was arguing that no person and no citizen can be stigmatized legally on the basis of his or her parentage or the circumstances of his or her birth.

Nevertheless, the Court backed away from this implication of the Weber case.[56] New worries about the stability and strength of the family added a certain weight to the old argument in favor of discrimination. Yet, although the courts hold back from declaring that illegitimacy is a suspect classification as a matter of law, in practice they continue to look very suspiciously at any discrimination involving illegitimate birth.[57]

Given the Burger Court's concern about social fragmentation and its own sharp tilt toward conservatism, it was not surprising that the Court refused to make sexual "life-style" into a civil right. The Court continued to uphold the right of communities to discharge teachers who engage in public homosexual activity, and it permitted a library to fire two employees who were living in "open adultery."[58] Nevertheless, mores are changing, and homosexuals have won a number of important victories in the Courts. For example, the New York Court of Appeals—the state's highest court—struck down laws prohibiting homosexual acts between consenting adults.[59] The Supreme Court, on the other hand, seems content to follow public opinion. In 1980, one poll indicated that most Americans were willing to let a homosexual speak in their communities or even to teach in a college or university. In both respects, the public was more tolerant of homosexuals than of atheists, racists, or communists.[60] In the same spirit, early in 1985, a

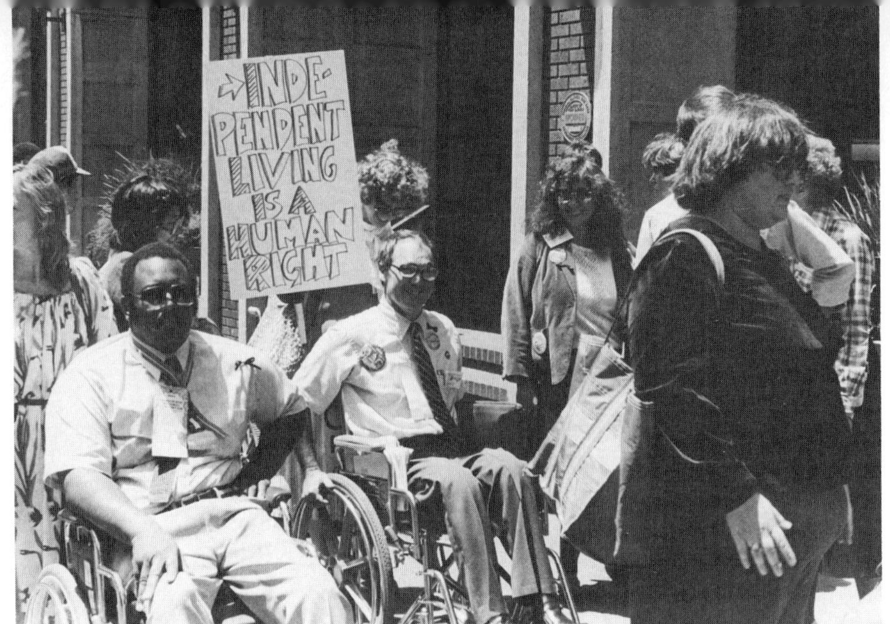

According to the Supreme Court, the handicapped, under federal law, have the right to no more than a minimally adequate education and a similarly limited access to public facilities. *(ISP/PSI)*

deadlocked Supreme Court (4–4, with Justice Powell not participating) upheld a lower court's decision striking down an Oklahoma law that permitted firing a teacher for "encouraging" or "advocating" homosexuality. The Court of Appeals upheld the right of states to discharge teachers for homosexual activity; it found, however, that the Oklahoma law violated a teacher's right to freedom of speech.[61] And, as we observed in Chapter 13, the Court refused, in 1986, to afford sexual relations between consenting adults the protection of the right to privacy. Barring a major change in the composition of the Court, it seems unlikely to go further.

After all, the Court's conservatism has been evident in a much less controversial area, the rights of the handicapped. In 1975, Congress passed the so-called "Bill of Rights for the Handicapped" (Public Law #94-142) that provided, among other things, for integrating handicapped children into the educational "mainstream" whenever possible. Special programs for handicapped children are costly, however, and with the decline of federal funding under Reagan, local communities, feeling the financial pinch, have been tempted to cut corners. The Supreme Court has been tolerant: as the Court sees it, the handicapped, under federal law, have the right to no more than a minimally adequate education and a similarly limited access to public facilities.[62] Many years ago, Judge Jerome Frank observed that "the test of the moral quality of a civilization is its treatment of the weak and powerless."[63] Judged by that standard, American law and policy in relation to the handicapped would probably receive a passing grade, but they are not yet entitled to any more.

Citizenship and Political Liberty

The Court has demonstrated little or no uncertainty, however, about the right of citizens to participate in political life. Almost immediately, for example, the doctrine of preferred position (see Chapter 13) led the Court to strike down the "white primary" by which black Americans were excluded from primary elections, most notably, Democratic primaries in Southern states. To attack the white primary, the Court had to enter and limit the sphere of private liberty.

Previously, the Court had held that states had no obligation to prevent racial discrimination by political parties acting as private associations.* The theory of preferred position, however, implies the positive right of citizens to participate in all phases of the electoral process, the choice of candidates as well as the choice between candidates. The Court, consequently, found that primaries are "integral parts" of a democratic system of elections, inherently public activities subject to the public standards of the Fifteenth Amendment.[64] In 1953, the Court ruled that the Jaybird Political Association, a political club, could not exclude racial minorities because the winners of its straw poll habitually won the local Democratic primary.[65] The Court, in other words, has ruled that citizens have a right to vote wherever the electoral choice is actually defined and made: political freedom outweighs any claims to private liberty.

The Voting Rights Acts The Court's concern for the right to vote has been paralleled and reinforced by the series of **Voting Rights Acts** that began, primarily, as attempts to protect black voters in the South. (These acts include laws passed in 1957, 1960, 1964, and the current law, originally passed in 1965, amended in 1970 and 1975 and extended in 1982.) This legislation involves an enormous extension of the role and presence of the federal government into areas of the electoral process traditionally left to the states or to private groups. In its current form, the Voting Rights Act (1) bans literacy tests and other discriminatory devices as requirements for voting; (2) requires states and localities that used discriminatory tests and had less than 50 percent turnout of the voting age population in 1964 to obtain approval from the attorney general or the federal courts for any change in voting laws (citizens may also file suit to have their localities brought under these "preclearance" rules); and (3) establishes criminal penalties for attempts to keep qualified persons from voting or for threatening civil rights workers assisting potential voters. These provisions involve major changes in American politics and law: nevertheless, the Supreme Court found that the federal government's duty to protect the right to vote gave it ample authority.[66]

The Voting Rights Act of 1965 was essential to the success of the Civil Rights Movement. *(Ann Meuer/Photo Researchers, Inc.)*

In 1966, moreover, the Supreme Court went beyond the Twenty-fourth Amendment to argue that the poll tax was illegitimate even in state elections. Since voting is a fundamental right, the Court reasoned, only a compelling interest could justify the tax, but "wealth or payment of a fee," far from being a compelling test of the voter's fitness, is "capricious and irrelevant" as a measure of civic virtue.[67]

"One Person, One Vote" The citizen's right to vote, moreover, is the right to an *equal* vote. But when legislative districts contain different numbers of people, the votes of citizens in more populous districts are proportionately "debased" or "diluted." If District A has 100,000 voters and District B has only 50,000, in District A it will take twice as many voters to elect a representative; in terms of political influence, a vote in District A is worth only half as much as a vote in District B. Consequently, the Supreme Court

**Grovey* v. *Townsend,* 295 U.S. 45 (1935); the state, however, could not require or authorize such a primary. *Nixon* v. *Condon,* 286 U.S. 73 (1932).

felt compelled, despite its reluctance to become involved in "political questions," to insist on legislative districts of relatively equal population, eventually applying the principle of "one person, one vote" to state legislative districts as well as to the House of Representatives.[68]*

Even if there is the same number of voters per representative, at-large elections or multimember districts can deny representation to groups that otherwise would be entitled to it. If one-third of the people in a city have low incomes and live in the same part of town, then, given reasonably fair districts, one-third of the members of the city council will have poorer citizens for their constituents. By contrast, if the members of council are elected at large, two-thirds of the constituents of *all* council members will be middle class or well-to-do, and there is a good chance that poorer citizens will go unrepresented. If we substitute blacks for the poor in this illustration, the result is even more probable, given the racism that still pervades American society.

The Supreme Court has argued, however, that multimember districts and at-large elections are permissible unless there is evidence that such systems were adopted with the *intent* or *purpose* of discriminating against a racial or political group.[69] Dissenting in the case of *Mobile* v. *Bolden* in 1980, Justice Thurgood Marshall argued that it is unnecessary to show an intent to deprive citizens of their "fundamental right to an equal vote." It is enough, Marshall maintained, to demonstrate that as a "forseeable effect" of an at-large system, a distinct racial or political group has been "effectively fenced out of the political process." So far, Marshall's reasoning has failed to persuade a majority of the Court.

Still, the Court's position does raise questions about the legitimacy of **gerrymandering,** the time-honored art by which legislatures draw district lines in a way calculated to give the largest number of seats to the majority party. Gerrymandering is undeniably intentional, and it does "dilute" the

*The Supreme Court will allow somewhat more variation in the population of state legislative districts than it will permit for districts in the House, provided that the differences derive from "legitimate considerations" of "rational state policy," such as the attempt to make district lines coincide with city and county boundaries. *Mahan* v. *Howell*, 410 U.S. 315 (1973); *Brown* v. *Thompson*, 103 S. Ct. 2690 (1983).

POLITICAL PERSPECTIVE

ORIGIN OF THE TERM "GERRYMANDER"

The term "gerrymander" originated in 1812 when the legislation of Massachusetts passed a law redistricting the state to give an advantage to the Democratic-Republicans led by Governor Elbridge Gerry. A political artist noticed that one of the new districts looked like a salamander. A member of the opposing Federalist party changed the title to "gerrymander," and the term came into use as a synonym for unfair districting of any kind.

Source: Based on *Collier's Encyclopedia*, Vol. II (New York: Macmillan Educational Company, 1981), p. 73.

strength of the minority party. Recently, a federal district court ruled that a plan adopted by the Republican-controlled Indiana legislature did violate the voting rights of Democrats as a "distinct political group." In 1986, the Supreme Court upheld Indiana's districting, but it indicated that there were limits beyond which it would not tolerate gerrymandering. The federal courts, in other words, have limited a practice as old as party politics in the interest of protecting a vote equal in effect as well as in form.*

Political Action Committees (PACs) The Supreme Court has gone beyond the right to vote to insist on other prerogatives of the citizen, including the right to seek and hold office. It has held, for example, that there is a right to serve on juries and, consequently, that jury lists may not discriminate on the basis of race, sex, or ethnicity.[70] For similar reasons, the Court has ruled that fees for filing as a candidate must not be so great as to be burdensome.[71]

No recent decision of the Supreme Court, however, has had a more profound effect on the shape of American politics than its ruling in *Buckley* v. *Valeo* in 1976.[72] The Federal Election Campaign Act of 1974 had provided that individual citizens could contribute (1) no more than $1000 in any year to any one candidate or political committee and (2) no more than a total of $25,000 to all candidates and committees combined. The Court

Davis v. *Bandemer*, 54 L.W. 4898 (1986).

"ACTUALLY, I THINK IT CAME BEFORE THE VIDEO GAME"

The Supreme Court's decisions have removed restrictions on the influence of money in political campaigns and have also increased the importance of political action committees (PACs). *(From* Herblock Through the Looking Glass *[W. W. Norton, 1984])*

upheld the first provision, but struck down the second. This means that individuals can contribute as much money as they wish, even on behalf of the same candidate, provided they make their contributions to separate, independent committees. The Court's decision greatly increased the number and importance of such political action committees (PACs) (see also Chapter 6). In 1984, the Republican party, restricted by law, spent $6.9 million on Ronald Reagan's campaign; the PACs spent $15.3 million. And in 1985, the Supreme Court upheld the right of each PAC to spend as much as it wants on behalf of a political candidate.[73] (For Democrats, with fewer wealthy donors, PACs matter much less, and the party relatively more). Certainly, the Court's decision defeated the objective of the Federal Election Campaign Act, which was to limit the power of wealth in American politics.

In *Buckley* v. *Valeo,* the Court argued that money is a form of political participation. In fact, in "today's mass society," money is effectively necessary to political communication. Money, the Court concluded, has become the virtual equivalent of speech.

Since *Buckley* v. *Valeo,* the Court has gone on to remove other limitations on the political power of money. Corporations, for example, had been prohibited from making political contributions in matters not "materially affecting" the corporation. The Supreme Court struck these regulations down, reasoning that speech by a corporation—a "legal person"—is no different from any other kind of speech.[74] In dissent, Justice Byron White argued that corporations are different from citizens because they are created for private, profit-making purposes. White went on to point out something the Court had neglected: that in the American republic, equal citizenship is itself a public purpose. Consequently, there is a public interest in preventing the "corporate domination of the political process." Democratic government, White maintained, has the right and the duty to look suspiciously at the public, political effects of private inequality.

The Court's majority has been unmoved by such arguments. As it often did, the Burger Court tipped the scales in the direction of private right, upholding the liberty of individuals to do as they please with their private resources even at considerable cost to the political equality of all citizens.

Civil Rights and Private Liberties

Civil rights and private liberties come into conflict in a much more basic way. Civil equality makes us equal in those things that have an important or essential relation to citizenship. We have the right to an equal vote; we are not expected to have the same tastes. We are equal "before the law"—in public matters, not in private life. The Fourteenth Amendment declares that no state may deny to any person the equal protection of the laws, but it does not define the sphere for which the state is responsible. This poses two distinct problems.

First, individualistic theories are concerned with our negative freedom from government intrusion (civil liberties), and in those terms the state denies equality only when it imposes laws or regulations that insist on inequality. If we are thinking of the positive right to the support of government (civil rights), we will consider that the state also denies equality when it tolerates inequality. In other words, is equal protection a claim on the state or a protection against it?

Second, individualistic teachings hold that government is intended to serve private liberties, and consequently, the state is limited to, and responsible for, only the narrow sphere of formal, public institutions. It has neither the duty nor the right to interfere with society. Defenders of public liberty, by contrast, are inclined to argue that public authority is responsible for ordering private life. In short, to what extent does our right to equal protection extend beyond formal public institutions into social and economic life?

The Supreme Court began by construing the Fourteenth Amendment narrowly, in terms of individualism and the protection of private rights. In one of its more generous opinions, the Court limited the amendment to "legal discriminations" that impose or imply inequality.[75] Moreover, in the *Civil Rights Cases* of 1883, the Court held that the amendment referred only to public institutions and not to the private, social, and economic spheres of life. Consequently, the Court held that Congress lacked the authority to forbid discrimination in hotels or other public accommodations.[76] The Court rejected the argument that since public accommodations are licensed by the state to be open to the public, any private rights are created by public authority for a public purpose.

In *Plessy* v. *Ferguson,* moreover, in addition to upholding "separate but equal" facilities, Justice Henry Brown declared that the Fourteenth Amendment was not intended to "enforce social, as distinct from political, equality," since this would have been contrary to the "nature of things."[77] Brown was, in fact, only articulating the doctrine of the framers: by nature, human beings are not equal but equally free. Political institutions can presume equality because they are unnatural contrivances designed to protect private inequalities. It would, however, be "contrary to nature" to impose unnatural public standards on the natural sphere of social and private right.

In his dissent, Justice Harlan proclaimed that the law "neither knows nor tolerates classes among citizens," and his language ("nor tolerates") implies that the law has a positive obligation to promote civic equality and that the state is accountable for what it does not do as well as for what it does. It is no surprise, then, that Justice Harlan spoke of "civil freedom," as opposed to Brown's reliance on individual liberties that precede political life.[78] Harlan's argument proclaims that law has the duty of ordering private life according to the demands of civil freedom. At the time, Harlan spoke only for himself. Over the years, his position has acquired increasing authority in the nation and on the Court.

In the late 1940s, the Court gave clear indications that it was moving toward a broader definition of "state action." It held, for example, that there was state action when state officials engaged in election fraud or when a sheriff had beaten a prisoner to death, even though, in both cases, state law forbade such conduct. The misuse of official power is "state action" because the state is responsible for preventing such abuse.[79] And in 1948, in *Shelley* v. *Kramer,* the Court held that **restrictive covenants**—agreements between property owners to sell their property only to whites—were not improper as private agreements but could not be enforced in state courts, a decision that made such covenants effectively valueless.[80] The idea that private conduct, enforced by state courts, is state action had far-reaching implications, since few private rights do not eventually rely on state law. The Court, in 1948, was not ready to go very far down that path. *Shelley* v. *Kramer,* however, was an unmistakable straw in the wind.

Desegregation and the Schools When the Supreme Court overturned *Plessy* v. *Ferguson,* striking down legally sanctioned segregation in the schools, Chief Justice Warren argued that schools could not be both "separate" and "equal" because separation produced "feelings of inferiority" incompatible with equal protection. But Justice Brown had conceded, in *Plessy,* that blacks were inclined to construe segregation as a mark of inferiority. He argued, however, that in formal terms segregation is not unequal, since it treats both races alike. The belief that segregation means inferiority, Brown observed, grew out of social inequality, which Brown regarded as beyond the reach of the Constitution. The state, in other words, was not accountable for feelings that grew out of private life; it could only be held responsible for what it did and said in the public sphere.

Warren argued, on the contrary, that given social inequality, a segregated system is in fact an unequal system. It is not enough to treat people according to the same rule. Whatever racial separation might mean in a racially equal society, in the United States, with our history of racism, segregation spelled inequality and indignity. The state, in other words, is responsible for the meaning of law that derives from the relationship between public institutions and private life. This does not require the states to produce economic and social equality. It does insist that government design laws and policies so that private inequalities do not taint or undermine the equality of citizens in public life. "Equal protection of the law," in other words, requires compensation for the inequalities and indignities of social and economic life.

As this argument implied, it was not enough to end segregation. An end to formal segregation did very little to unsettle the social patterns established by **Jim Crow**—laws and practices that discriminated against blacks—or to undo their impact on the feelings of children. Consequently, the Court began to demand Affirmative Action to integrate schools as opposed to merely desegregating them.[81] This led the Court to approve **busing**—transporting public school students from one district to another in order to integrate schools—as a means of overcoming the "vestiges of state-imposed segregation." As the Court reasoned, de facto segregation—segregation that results simply from social and economic factors—is beyond the reach of the law. Wherever legal segregation existed, however, the separation of the races is suspect and, given American history, any all-black school must be presumed to result from patterns established by legal segregation. All things being equal, the Court observed, neighborhood schools are probably the better policy, "but all things are not equal." The history of segregation requires policies like busing to break up the social patterns created by segregation.[82]

In most Northern states, of course, schools had not been formally segregated. Nevertheless, the Court argued, when school authorities intentionally designed policies to result in a "substantial measure" of segregation (that is, by drawing school districts so that almost all blacks would attend the same schools), the effect was the same as if formal segregation has existed. In such situations, busing may be required; remedial courses may also be demanded to make up for the uneven level of preparedness in basic skills of children bused in from poorer districts.[83]

The Burger Court had increasing doubts about the wisdom of busing. Nevertheless, when the Reagan administration, responding to antibusing sentiment, requested the Court to examine its earlier decisions, the Court refused to do so. And it struck down a Washington state ordinance that denied local school boards the option of using busing to overcome segregation.[84] However, the Burger Court held that the courts cannot integrate suburban school systems with those of a central city without some evidence of segregation in the suburban communities. Suburban towns, the Court observed, are separate political entities and must be treated separately in the absence of strong reasons to the contrary.[85] The Court is not blind to the fact that the growth of white suburbs results, to a considerable extent, from the desire to escape from racially mixed cities. It has maintained, however, that only where segregated effects in one community can be related to intentional segregation in another can the two be integrated by the courts.[86] Similarly, it ruled that once a locality achieves a racially neutral school system, free from the "vestiges" of official segregation, it cannot be required to reintegrate the schools if economic and social forces reestablish racial separation.[87]

The impact of these decisions is softened by the Court's ruling that federal courts may order the Department of Housing and Urban Development to build low-cost housing in suburbs to relieve racial segregation in the center city.[88] Moreover, the Burger Court approved when a federal district court, in response to the Supreme Court's decision blocking the integration of Detroit and its suburbs, issued an order requiring that more money be spent on inner-city education as a compensation for de facto segregation.[89] Up to this point, the Burger Court was concerned with asserting that social and economic inequality and de facto segregation are not violations of equal protection.

There are reasons to sympathize with the Court, and even more reason to doubt whether busing is an effective means of redressing inequality. The "vestiges" of official segregation, however, are more pervasive and persistent than the Burger Court seemed willing to admit. Racial separation sanctioned by law has, in vital ways, permeated American culture. (It does not strain the point to observe that slavery was a form of official separation.) Even the Burger Court realized that civic equality requires more than legal forms and that equal protection of the laws demands attention to the relation between private liberties and public rights.

Civil Rights and Social Equality

In response to the Civil Rights Movement, Congress passed the Civil Rights Act of 1964, aiming to create a greater measure of equality in economic and social life. For example, the act forbids discrimination in public accommodations, a provision the Supreme Court upheld as a legitimate exercise of

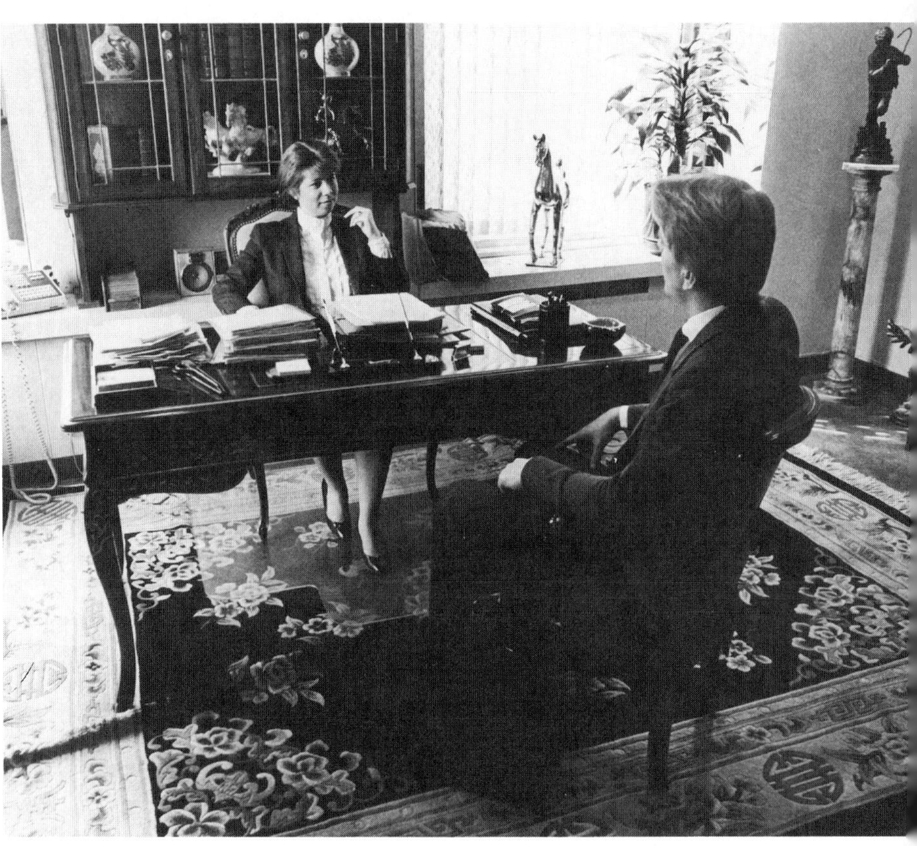

The Civil Rights Act of 1964 forbids discrimination in employment based on sex, race, religion, or ethnicity. *(Michael Kagan/Monkmeyer)*

the power to regulate interstate commerce, effectively overruling the *Civil Rights Cases.*[90]

The Civil Rights Act also forbids discrimination in employment on the basis of race, religion, sex, or ethnicity, a provision that now applies to all public employees and to all private businesses employing more than twenty-five persons. Employers, the Court has held, can make only those discriminations specifically related to job performance. A requirement of "experience," for example, discriminates against minorities and women—since past inequality deprived them of the chance to get experience—and is permissible only where experience is necessary to the job.[91]

A maximum-security prison for men may decline to hire women; a subway system may refuse to employ methadone addicts as drivers; Affirmative Action programs, compensating for the past, may give special advantages to minorities and women.[92] Nevertheless, an employer must be prepared to justify any case or pattern of discrimination.

The Civil Rights Act of 1968, moreover, outlaws discrimination in the sale and rental of housing. In relation to housing, in fact, the federal government does not need to derive its authority from the commerce power. Being a "free person," the Court observed, includes the right to "make and enforce contracts." The Thirteenth Amendment, then, gives Congress the authority to enforce equality in the making of contracts. Moreover, since the Thirteenth Amendment gives Congress the power to enforce the abolition of slavery without reference to states or state action (unlike the Fourteenth Amendment), Congress is free to regulate private conduct.[93] The implications of this decision point far beyond housing: they hint at a federal power to regulate almost all private transactions, at least in the interest of racial equality and possibly to forward the personal freedom of all citizens.

Such theoretical possibilities are very distant from current practices. Formal and open discrimination in housing, for example, has yielded to implicit and covert segregation. Zoning codes that effectively exclude blacks and low-income families are not unconstitutional without some demonstrable "intent" or "purpose" to discriminate.[94] Federal or state laws could compel changes in zoning, but such legislation—like other steps toward social equality—will have to wait for changes in public opinion beyond any that are now forseeable. At present, the current runs much more strongly in the direction of private rights and political fragmentation.

The New Property

Civil rights include our claim to participate, and to be treated with minimal decency, in social and economic life because such participation is a basic prerequisite of our membership in civil society. Necessarily, the shape and emphasis of these fundamental rights change with the kind of economy and society we have. In an agricultural society, participation implies access to land; in commercial and industrial society, it requires access to the market, to credit, and to employment. The law must respond to that sort of change.

The Supreme Court has held for a long time that we have a fundamental right to marry and establish families, a liberty that can be restricted only by due process of law.[95] Hoping to encourage stable families, Connecticut—like several other states—required a high fee to file for divorce. In 1971, the Supreme Court held this an unconstitutional restriction of the right to *end* a marriage, chiefly because it discriminated against the poor. Similarly, in 1978, the Court had to rule on a Wisconsin law which provided that anyone who had obligations to support a child could not marry without obtaining a court order. Here too, the Court found that the Wisconsin law unnecessarily infringed on the right to marry.[96] The contemporary Supreme Court, in other words, asserts that marriage, as that institution is understood in today's society, includes a right to *divorce* and *remarry.* The justices who proclaimed our right to marry back in 1923 almost certainly did not regard divorce and remarriage as routine matters, let alone as rights. Nevertheless, an important part of the right to marry is concerned with giving us access to a social institution, and to that extent, the right must be redefined to take account of changes in society itself.

There have been similar transformations in the meaning of the right to property. For most of us, "property" is likely to mean land, cars, personal possessions, and, above all else, our homes. Property, in this sense, refers to *things,* and that was the dominant usage in early America. We also speak of having a "right of property" in our bodies and to our labor, and that view was accepted by the framers, although they made a cruel exception in the case of slavery.

The meaning of property expanded, however, as America became a more and more commercial and industrial society. In the kind of society in which we live, the most important kinds of property are not tangible assets. They are contracts and commitments, reliable promises and stable understandings, obligations and entitlements. Common stocks, for example, are pieces of paper that give their owners *rights* in particular corporations. Accordingly, the courts came to speak of property as a "bundle of rights" including obligations and expectations on which people are entitled to rely.[97]

Until recently, however, the courts defined property as a strictly private right, limited to private possessions and relationships. Property rights were claims *on* private persons and *against* government (like the "freedom of contract" discussed in the preceding chapter). But the economic services and activities of government were "privileges" to which citizens did not have a right, and they certainly were not property.[98]

Increasingly, Americans have derived a good deal of their economic security from public policies like Social Security. Public policies, especially those that are long established, shape our expectations and plans about the future. They are commitments to us, promises explicit or implied, and it is not surprising that so many Americans regard a great many benefits from government as things to which they are entitled.

For example, in a 1981 poll an overwhelming majority of Americans (between 85 and 95 percent) asserted that they had various rights (see Table 14.2). Of course, relatively few of these "rights" are established in law or protected by the courts. The belief that we have such rights, however, constitutes a pressure on public institutions and may eventually transform the law. In any case, all of these "rights" indicate the public's conviction that Americans have a just claim on government and that they properly expect government to provide what is needed by controlling or regulating the private sphere.

Gradually, the Supreme Court has acknowledged that expectations of this sort, encouraged by laws and policies, can and do create a *new kind* of *property right* that entitles us to public support and that cannot be abridged without due process of law.[99]

TABLE 14.2 Rights to Which Americans Feel They Are Entitled

1. Protection against serious crimes
2. Literacy
3. Honest and reliable news reporting
4. Products certified to be safe
5. Adequate housing
6. Adequate public transportation
7. An improving standard of living
8. Legal protection against the misuse of confidential information
9. A retirement income sheltered against inflation
10. A job

Source: Based on *Public Opinion* (April/May 1981).

POLITICAL PERSPECTIVE

NEW CONDITIONS IMPOSE NEW REQUIREMENTS ON GOVERNMENT

The Declaration of Independence discusses the problem of government in terms of a contract. . . . Under such a contract, rulers were accorded power, and the people consented to that power on consideration that they be accorded certain rights. The task of statesmanship has always been the redefinition of these rights in terms of a changing and growing social order. New conditions impose new requirements upon government and those who conduct government.

Source: Franklin D. Roosevelt, Address to the Commonwealth Club, San Francisco, Calif., Sept. 23, 1932.

In 1970, for example, the Court ruled that welfare benefits cannot be cut off without a hearing.[100] A few years later, the Court decided that since state laws entitle students to public education, they cannot be suspended from school without a hearing.[101] In relation to public employment, this new doctrine has been especially striking.

Back in 1892, Justice Holmes, then a member of the Supreme Court of Massachusetts, in rejecting the appeal of a policeman dismissed for political reasons, remarked that there is a "constitutional right to talk politics" but "no constitutional right to be a policeman."[102] The contemporary Supreme Court, by contrast, has twice ruled against the "spoils system." In 1976, the Court held that a sheriff could not fire two non-civil service employees simply because of their political beliefs. Four years later, the Court ruled that even lower-level policymakers cannot be dismissed for political reasons unless it can be shown that their party affiliation has some important connection to the "effective performance" of their jobs. In effect, the Court was asserting that public employees, except at the very highest level, *do* have a right to their jobs and that they cannot be dismissed without some sort of due process.[103]

From time to time, the Burger Court upheld the authority of government and the discretion of public officials against the claims of the "new property," as it did in deciding that federal disability benefits may be terminated before a hearing.[104] Nevertheless, in law and in practical politics, the **new property** seems firmly entrenched as a civil right. This new property right entails problems for public policy.

Entitlements and Political Fragmentation

There has already been a major collision between an important public goal and the new rights of property. Systems that give preference to senior employees are one of the major gains won by labor in collective bargaining. Seniority gives the kind of job security that permits established workers to put down roots and encourages them to buy homes and start families. Seniority rights are also precious because older workers, ordinarily more highly paid than their juniors, find it harder to obtain comparable work if

In our society, the most important forms of property, like stocks and bonds, are rights rather than tangible assets. *(Jeffrey Apoian/Nawrocki Stock Photos)*

they are laid off. Younger workers, starting at the bottom, can look forward to the future; older workers lack such consolations. In short, it is no surprise that tenure and seniority are treasured as civil rights.

Until recently, however, racial bias went virtually unchecked in hiring and promotion, and covertly, it is still important. Senior employees are likely to be white. Giving them preference limits the opportunities available to racial minorities, continuing at least part of the old pattern that minorities are the last hired and the first fired. Nevertheless, the Court has come to accept seniority systems that were not adopted for a discriminatory purpose even if that is their effect.[105]

By contrast, local governments around the country have adopted Affirmative Action programs designed to increase the number of minority members employed in public service, and especially in those public services in which whites play a disproportionate role. This might have caused little problem if governments were simply *adding* new employees. It was a different story, however, when several cities, under pressure to reduce their budgets, laid off more senior white firefighters and retained more junior minority personnel. In the courts, firefighters' unions argued tenaciously in favor of seniority rights and the Reagan administration, hostile to Affirmative Action, supported their claims. Eventually, the Supreme Court ruled that since the Civil Rights Act of 1964 forbids discrimination on the basis of race, senior white workers cannot be deprived of their public entitlements without due process. Minority workers must show specific evidence of discrimination to justify violating a system of seniority established by public law or contract.[106] A major setback to public efforts to promote racial equality, the Court's decision was a decisive victory for the new right of property.

In one important respect, however, the Court treats such entitlements as second-class property, not quite the real thing. If "old" property is taken after due process, government at all levels must pay compensation. "New" property cannot be taken from us without a hearing, but if we are subsequently deprived of our benefits, the government owes us nothing. A person whose welfare benefits are cut off legitimately—because of a shift in policy, for example—has no right to anything, even if he or she had reason to expect those benefits to continue. Some legal theorists argue that people *are* entitled to compensation when their reasonable expectations are violated.[107] In this view, a family dropped from the welfare rolls should have a right to support during a reasonable period of transition. Similarly, a tenured teacher dismissed because of a fall in student enrollment, should be entitled to severance pay. In fact, a federal district court has held that tenants are entitled to compensation if they are displaced from their homes because government inspectors find these buildings in violation of the housing code.[108] Courts have been unwilling to go very far in this direction, fearing that the need to compensate existing beneficiaries for every shift of policy would restrict change by making it too costly, limiting the political process in unacceptable ways. In other words, there is a dangerous tendency toward fragmentation when public policy is made into a private right.

Private Associations and Public Rights

No private liberty is more deeply cherished than the right to choose one's own friends. The freedom of association has its own high constitutional status, and our ability to form close, exclusive bonds with one another is one of the personal foundations of citizenship. Private clubs and associations, consequently, are free to discriminate in their choice of members, public policy notwithstanding.

Nevertheless, this freedom only extends to genuine private associations in which there is at least some evidence of a real, personal relationship between members. A privately owned lake in Arkansas, for example, was made available for swimming and boating on a whites-only basis to 100,000 "members" who paid a 25-cent fee. Understandably, the Court ruled that this was a commercial operation, based on contract, and under the Civil Rights Act of 1866 must be open to blacks. In 1976, the Court held that health spas, even if nominally clubs, were really commercial "places of entertainment." Similarly, the Court has ruled that private schools operated as a business have forfeited any right to discriminate.[109]

Noncommercial schools—nonprofit religious schools, for example—are free to discriminate if they choose. The federal courts have held, however, that if a state makes such schools tax-exempt and certifies their graduates, this is a form of state action that makes discrimination impermissible, and the Supreme Court upheld these decisions by refusing to review them.[110]

It is not "state action," however, for a state to grant a liquor license to a discriminatory fraternal order (although a state can make a nondiscriminatory policy a condition for such a license). If such a fraternity allows guests on a fairly open basis, however, it risks being classified as a "public accommodation" and will be required to comply with civil rights laws.[111]

The Supreme Court also ruled that an association of the residents of a given area must make its benefits open to any resident of that area on a nondiscriminatory basis.[112] By defining membership in territorial, rather than personal terms, such associations make themselves fundamentally public and surrender any legitimate claim to be based on private bonds.

One Supreme Court justice, alarmed by the Court's decisions, felt obliged to protest on behalf of the right of individuals to be capricious in their "personal relationships," and other critics have worried lest the Court bar ethnic homes for the aged and similar organizations.* So far, these fears appear quite beside the point. In fact, the Court's decisions hold that a truly private association must be based on "personal relationships," a tie between more or less specific individuals.

Americans have a right to private associations that include their friends and incidentally exclude others. They do not have a right to organizations that exclude blacks or other minorities as a defining principle. Some evidence of a positive bond is necessary to take the taint off discrimination. A democratic political society can afford to give scope to many private rights, but it cannot afford to lose its suspicion of organizations and interests that threaten the equal dignity of citizens.

*See Justice Harlan's dissent in *Lombard* v. *Louisiana*, 323 U.S. 267 (1973); a similar view is expressed by Joseph Tussman, *The Supreme Court on Racial Discrimination* (New York: Oxford U. P., 1963), p. 5.

SUMMARY

Citizenship is the road to dignity and full participation within American democracy; citizenship cannot be taken away. The Fourteenth Amendment makes state citizenship derive from national citizenship, but the Supreme Court did not expand the list of rights protected by the federal judiciary all at once. Not until 1962 was the ban on cruel and unusual punishment extended to all states, and a few provisions of the Bill of Rights have still not been incorporated into due process.

In 1958, the Supreme Court declared citizenship the premise of all rights. All citizens are equal and enjoy equal protection of the laws. Most distinctions among citizens are suspect and must be justified by reference to a public goal, and today this rule applies to government, large industries, and social organizations. In the nineteenth century the Supreme Court had accepted "separate but equal" segregated public facilities, reasoning that this reflected underlying social conditions that were outside legal purview. Twentieth-century decisions by the Court overturned the separate but equal doctrine. In fact, the Court took the approach that not only would facilities be integrated, but that it could give its imprimatur to plans that discriminate in favor of nonwhites because of past discrimination.

Distinctions between citizens and aliens are also suspect, but economic distinctions are not questioned if they have a basis in a legitimate public purpose—differences in money are accidental, whereas differences in ethnicity or race touch on who we are as individual citizens. Vastly unequal economic political contributions are also tolerated despite their key role in influencing elections.

Gender is conspicuously absent from the list of "suspect" categories, although it is not directly relevant to good citizenship. Sex classifications have received more notice since the 1970s, but the courts have been reticent to delve into women's claims of equality, partially because such claims frequently extend into areas, like family relations, that traditionally have been viewed as part of the private sphere. Compounding this is declining agreement as to the proper roles within the family and other intimate relationships. This also explains the Court's reluctance to change statutes regarding homosexuality.

Economic distinctions based on sex have been more sympathetically received. However, the Court has rejected justification of sex-based inequality founded on statistical differences, unless there is no other way of achieving an important public goal. This reasoning suggests that citizens' equality of situation comes second to individuals' private immunities.

Citizens have the right to participate in all substantive aspects of political life, as outlined in the Federal Voting Rights Act and in decisions outlawing bars to participation, such as poll taxes. Citizens' votes should be of equal value, so the Court has ruled against gerrymandering of electoral districts. But the courts stop short of outlawing at-large elections, which can prevent minority representation.

The courts must also come to terms with changing social and economic patterns—the longtime right to marry and establish families had become by the early 1970s the right to marry, divorce, and remarry. Likewise, as America has become a more commercial society, the most important property rights are not tangible but intangible: stocks, and entitlements such as social security or seniority claims at work. The Supreme Court has gradually acknowledged that these *new kinds of property rights* should receive public support and cannot be abridged without due process of law.

The struggle between civil rights and private liberties, central to the history of Constitutional debate, surfaces today in the questions arising from the Fourteenth Amendment's equal protection of the law. Is equal protection a claim on the state or a protection against it? To what extent does our right to equal protection extend into our social and economic life? The Supreme Court will be grappling with these issues throughout the 1980s.

NOTES

1. G. K. Chesterton, *What I Saw in America* (New York: Dodd, 1922), pp. 16–17.
2. *Trop* v. *Dulles,* 356 U.S. 86 (1958).
3. *Rusk* v. *Cort,* 372 U.S. 144 (1963).
4. *Afroyim* v. *Rusk,* 387 U.S. 253 (1967).
5. *Barron* v. *Baltimore,* 7 Pet. 243 (1833).
6. 16 Wall 36 (1873).
7. *Hurtado* v. *California,* 110 U.S. 516 (1884); *C. B. & Q.* v. *Chicago,* 166 U.S. 226 (1897).
8. *Gitlow* v. *New York,* 268 U.S. 652 (1925); *Near* v. *Minnesota,* 283 U.S. 697 (1931).
9. *Powell* v. *Alabama,* 287 U.S. 45 (1932); *Hamilton* v. *Board of Regents,* 293 U.S. 245 (1934); *De Jonge* v. *Oregon,* 299 U.S. 353 (1937).
10. *Palko* v. *Connecticut,* 302 U.S. 319 (1937).
11. *Wolf* v. *Colorado,* 338 U.S. 25 (1949).
12. *Mapp* v. *Ohio,* 367 U.S. 643 (1961).
13. *Michigan* v. *DeFilippo,* 443 U.S. 31 (1979); *U.S.* v. *Leon,* 104 S. Ct. 3405 (1984).
14. *Nix* v. *Williams,* 104 S. Ct. 2501 (1984).
15. *Gideon* v. *Wainwright,* 392 U.S. 335 (1963); *Robinson* v. *California,* 370 U.S. 660 (1962); *Malloy* v. *Hogan,* 378 U.S. 1 (1964).
16. *Pointer* v. *Texas,* 380 U.S. 400 (1965); *Klopfer* v. *North Carolina,* 386 U.S. 213 (1967); *Duncan* v. *Louisiana,* 391 U.S. 145 (1968); *Benton* v. *Maryland,* 395 U.S. 784 (1969).
17. *Burton* v. *Sills,* 394 U.S. 812 (1969); *Lewis* v. *U.S.,* 445 U.S. 55 (1980); localities may ban the private possession of handguns, see *Quilici* v. *Morton Grove,* 464 U.S. 863 (1963).
18. *Furman* v. *Georgia,* 408 U.S. 238 (1972); *Gregg* v. *Georgia,* 428 U.S. 153 (1976); *Coker* v. *Georgia,* 433 U.S. 584 (1977).
19. *Beck* v. *Alabama,* 447 U.S. 625 (1980); *Eddings* v. *Oklahoma,* 455 U.S. 104 (1982); *Barefoot* v. *Estelle,* 77 L. Ed. 2d 1090 (1983).
20. *Solem* v. *Helm,* 463 U.S. 277 (1983).
21. *Tigner* v. *Texas,* 310 U.S. 141, 145 (1940). See also Ronald Dworkin, *Taking Rights Seriously* (Cambridge: Harvard U.P., 1973).
22. *Yick Wo* v. *Hopkins,* 118 U.S. 356 (1886); Richard B. Wilson, "The Merging Concepts of Liberty and Equality," *Washington and Lee Law Review,* vol. XII (1955), pp. 182–211.
23. 163 U.S. 537, 559 (1896).
24. *Brown* v. *Board of Education,* 347 U.S. 483 (1954); the Court began to undermine "separate but equal" in *Missouri ex. rel. Gaines* v. *Canada,* 305 U.S. 337 (1937).
25. *Dayton Board of Education* v. *Brinkman,* 443 U.S. 526 (1979).
26. *Regents* v. *Bakke,* 438 U.S. 265 (1978).

27. *United Steelworkers* v. *Weber,* 443 U.S. 193 (1979); *Fullilove* v. *Klutznick,* 448 U.S. 448 (1980).
28. *Martin* v. *Hunter's Lessee,* 1 Wh. 304 (1816).
29. *Graham* v. *Richardson,* 403 U.S. 365 (1971).
30. *Matthews* v. *Diaz,* 426 U.S. 67 (1976); *Hampton* v. *Mow Sun Wong,* 426 U.S. 88 (1976).
31. *Shapiro* v. *Thompson,* 394 U.S. 618 (1969).
32. *Bearden* v. *Georgia,* 461 U.S. 660 (1983).
33. *Harris* v. *McRae,* 448 U.S. 297 (1980).
34. *James* v. *Valtierra,* 402 U.S. 137 (1971); *Arlington Heights* v. *Metro Housing,* 429 U.S. 252 (1977).
35. *Lindsey* v. *Normet,* 405 U.S. 56 (1972); *San Antonio* v. *Rodrigues,* 411 U.S. 1 (1973).
36. Thomas Jefferson, *Notes on Virginia,* W. Peden, ed. (Chapel Hill: U. of North Carolina, 1955), pp. 146, 148.
37. *Frontiero* v. *Richardson,* 411 U.S. 677 (1973).
38. *Craig* v. *Boren,* 429 U.S. 190 (1976).
39. *Mississippi University for Women* v. *Hogan,* 458 U.S. 718 (1982).
40. *Taylor* v. *Louisiana,* 419 U.S. 522 (1975).
41. *Stanton* v. *Stanton,* 421 U.S. 7 (1975).
42. Catherine MacKinnon, *Sexual Harassment of Working Women: A Case of Sex Discrimination* (New Haven: Yale U. P., 1979).
43. *Orr* v. *Orr,* 440 U.S. 268 (1979).
44. *Rostker* v. *Goldberg,* 453 U.S. 57 (1981).
45. *Personnel Administrator* v. *Feeney,* 442 U.S. 256 (1979).
46. *Kahn* v. *Shevin,* 416 U.S. 351 (1974).
47. *Gedulig* v. *Aiello,* 417 U.S. 484 (1974); *General Electric* v. *Gilbert,* 429 U.S. 125 (1976).
48. *Hishon* v. *King and Spalding,* 464 U.S. 959 (1984), and *Roberts* v. *U.S. Jaycees,* 82 L. Ed. 2nd 462 (1984).
49. *Muller* v. *Oregon,* 208 U.S. 412 (1908).
50. *Manhart* v. *Dept. of Water and Power,* 435 U.S. 702 (1978).
51. *Arizona Governing Committee* v. *Norris,* 103 S. Ct. 3492 (1983).
52. *Vlandis* v. *Kline,* 412 U.S. 441, 452 (1973).
53. *Albemarle Paper Co.* v. *Moody,* 442 U.S. 405 (1975); *N.E.A.* v. *South Carolina,* 434 U.S. 1026 (1978).
54. In fact, the Burger Court ruled that "naked statistical arguments" do not prove an intent to discriminate on racial grounds, even if legislation affects the races in a strikingly unequal way. (*Jefferson* v. *Hackney,* 406 U.S. 535, 1972).
55. *Weber* v. *Aetna Casualty,* 406 U.S. 164 (1972).
56. *Mathews* v. *Lucas,* 427 U.S. 495 (1976).
57. *In Re Baby Girl,* 628 S.W. 2nd 261 (1982).
58. *Gaylord* v. *Tacoma School District,* 559 Pac. Rep. 1340 (1977); *Hollenbaugh* v. *Carnegie Library,* 439 U.S. 1052 (1978).
59. *The New York Times* (May 31, 1984), p. A19.
60. *Public Opinion* (Oct./Nov. 1980), p. 26.
61. *Board of Education* v. *National Gay Task Force,* 84 L. Ed. 2d 776 (1985); *Bowers* v. *Hardwick,* 54 L.W. 4919 (1986).
62. *Board of Education* v. *Rowley,* 102 S. Ct. 3034 (1982); *Community TV* v. *Gottfried,* 103 S. Ct. 885 (1983).
63. *U.S.* v. *Murphy,* 222 F.2nd 698, 706 (1955).
64. *U.S.* v. *Classic,* 313 U.S. 299 (1941); *Smith* v. *Allwright,* 321 U.S. 649 (1944).
65. *Terry* v. *Adams,* 345 U.S. 461 (1953).
66. *South Carolina* v. *Katzenback,* 383 U.S. 301 (1965).
67. *Harper* v. *Virginia State Board of Elections,* 383 U.S. 663 (1966)
68. *Baker* v. *Carr,* 369 U.S. 186 (1962); *Wesberry* v. *Sanders,* 376 U.S. 1 (1964); *Reynolds* v. *Simms,* 377 U.S. 533 (1964).
69. *Whitcomb* v. *Chavis,* 403 U.S. 124 (1971); *Mobile* v. *Bolden,* 446 U.S. 55 (1980). The Court did note the unequal effect of multimember and at-large systems, holding that there should be a preference for single-member districts whenever *courts* order a system of districting, but this preference does not bind legislatures. *Chapman* v. *Meier,* 420 U.S. 1 (1975).
70. *Carter* v. *Jury Commissioners* and *Duren* v. *Missouri,* 439 U.S. 357 (1979).
71. *Bullock* v. *Carter,* 405 U.S. 134 (1972).
72. *Buckley* v. *Valeo,* 424 U.S. 1 (1976).
73. *Federal Election Commission* v. *NCPAC,* 84 L. Ed. 2d 455 (1985).
74. *First National Bank of Boston* v. *Belotti,* 435 U.S. 765 (1978); in fact, the Court has gone on to hold that a utility may include political arguments along with its monthly bill. *Consolidated Edison* v. *Public Service Commission,* 447 U.S. 530 (1980).
75. *Strauder* v. *West Virginia,* 100 U.S. 303 (1880).
76. *Civil Rights Cases,* 109 U.S. 3 (1883).
77. *Plessy* v. *Ferguson,* 163 U.S. 537, 544 (1896).
78. Ibid., pp. 559, 562.
79. *U.S.* v. *Classic,* 313 U.S. 299 (1941); *Screws* v. *U.S.,* 325 U.S. 91 (1945).
80. *Shelley* v. *Kramer,* 334 U.S. 1 (1948).
81. *Green* v. *School Board,* 391 U.S. 430 (1968).
82. *Swann* v. *Charlotte-Mecklenburg Board of Education,* 402 U.S. 1 (1971).
83. *Keyes* v. *School District 1,* 413 U.S. 189 (1973); *McDonough* v. *Morgan,* 429 U.S. 1042 (1977).
84. *Metropolitan Board of Education* v. *Kelley,* 103 S. Ct. 834 (1983); *Washington* v. *Seattle School District,* 102 S. Ct. 3187 (1982).
85. *Milliken* v. *Bradley,* 418 U.S. 717 (1974).
86. *Evans* v. *Buchanan,* 423 U.S. 963 (1975).
87. *Pasadena Board of Education* v. *Spangler,* 423 U.S. 1335 (1976).
88. *Hills* v. *Gautreaux,* 425 U.S. 284 (1976).
89. *Milliken* v. *Bradley II,* 433 U.S. 267 (1977).
90. *Heart of Atlanta Motel* v. *U.S.,* 379 U.S. 241 (1964).
91. *Albemarle Paper Co.* v. *Moody,* 442 U.S. 405 (1979).
92. *Dothard* v. *Rawlinson,* 433 U.S. 321 (1977); *New York Transit Authority* v. *Beazer,* 440 U.S. 568 (1979); *United Steelworkers* v. *Weber,* 443 U.S. 193 (1979).
93. *Jones* v. *Alfred Mayer Co.,* 392 U.S. 409 (1968).
94. *Arlington Heights* v. *Metropolitan Housing Development Corp.,* 429 U.S. 252 (1977).
95. *Meyer* v. *Nebraska,* 262 U.S. 390 (1923).
96. *Boddie* v. *Connecticut,* 401 U.S. 371 (1971); *Zablocki* v. *Redhail,* 434 U.S. 374 (1978).
97. *Fidelity and Deposit Co.* v. *Arenz,* 290 U.S. 66 (1933); see also Judge David Bazelon's essay, "Facts and Fictions of U.S. Capitalism," *Reporter,* 21 (Sept. 1959), pp. 43–48.
98. *Packard* v. *Banton,* 264 U.S. 140, 145 (1924).
99. *Webb's Pharmacies* v. *Beckwith,* 449 U.S. 155 (1980); James Oakes "Property Rights in Constitutional Analysis Today," *Washington Law Review,* 56 (1981), pp. 583ff.
100. *Goldberg* v. *Kelly,* 397 U.S. 254 (1970).
101. *Goss* v. *Lopez,* 419 U.S. 565 (1975).

102. *McAuliffe* v. *New Bedford,* 115 Mass. 216, 219 (1892).
103. *Elrod* v. *Burns,* 427 U.S. 347 (1976); *Branti* v. *Finkel,* 445 U.S. 507 (1980).
104. *Matthews* v. *Eldridge,* 424 U.S. 319 (1976).
105. *California Brewers Association* v. *Bryant,* 444 U.S. 598 (1980); *American Tobacco Co.* v. *Patterson,* 456 U.S. 63 (1982).
106. *Firefighters* v. *Stotts,* 104 S. Ct. 2576 (1984).
107. Bruce Ackerman, *Private Property and the Constitution* (New Haven: Yale U.P., 1977), pp. 54–56.
108. *Devines* v. *Maier,* 665 F.2nd 138 (1981).
109. *Daniel* v. *Paul,* 395 U.S. 298 (1968); *Shape Spa* v. *Rousseve,* 425 U.S. 911 (1976); *Runyon* v. *McCrary,* 427 U.S. 160 (1976).
110. *Brown* v. *Pennsylvania,* 391 U.S. 921 (1968).
111. *Moose Lodge* v. *Irvis,* 407 U.S. 163 (1972); *B.P.O.E.* v. *Ingraham,* 412 U.S. 913 (1973); *Order of Moose* v. *The Human Rights Commission,* 409 U.S. 1052 (1972).
112. *Tillman* v. *Wheaton Haven Recreation Association,* 410 U.S. 431 (1973).

PART 5

Public Policy

We use the term "public policy" in many different connections in government and politics, but rarely do we stop to consider exactly what it means. We could say that a policy is the adoption and pursuit of a course of action by a public official or institution with some particular objective. In the United States, however, it is not always clear where public leaves off and private begins.

For example, it was the policy of the Carter administration in 1979 that the Chrysler Corporation—the nation's third-largest automobile maker—not go bankrupt. To this end, the president proposed to Congress that $3 billion in loans to the ailing company be guaranteed by the federal government. The loans, however, were not to be made by the federal government itself but by private banks, whose decision to make the loans also depended on wage and benefit agreements made between Chrysler and the United Auto Workers Union. Clearly, this is not a purely "public" policy but one involving bank policy and union policy as well.

We can see that there is no firm line demarcating the objectives, processes, and decisions made by public institutions (such as Congress and the White House) or officials (such as the president) from those of nongovernmental groups (unions, corporations, and banks). We may define public policy, then, as the end product of goals, decisions, and processes in which government is a major participant and so has an impact on the public at large. This distinguishes public policy from just any policy but, at the same time, indicates that more than just the institutions of government are involved.

We will begin the study of public policy by focusing on five main types of policy. Briefly summarized, these policy types are distributive, competitive regulatory, protective regulatory, redistributive, or strategic in nature. But keep in mind that these policy types are not mutually exclusive. There can be distributive elements in competitive regulatory policies and redistributive features in policies that are mainly protective regulatory. We use the categories as a convenience to identify the type that a policy most closely resembles.

Distributive Policies Payments, inducements, subsidies, or incentives for groups, industries, or individuals do things that are of general benefit and generate little political controversy. We call the policies behind such government actions "distributive policies." The most common distributive policies are such things as tax incentives that, for example, induce people to insulate their homes, install storm windows and doors, or to install solar hot-water systems. The general benefit here is conservation of fuel and, in economic hard times, stimulation of the economy.

Competitive Regulatory Policies Policies that usually involve giving certain providers of goods and services exclusive rights to render these goods and services are called "competitive regulatory policies." The government grants licenses to the provider and has the power to revoke them if the job is not done properly. One example of competitive regulatory policy is seen in the telephone industry. Until recently, telephone service in the United States was a "natural monopoly"; in the 1970s a series of court decisions laid the groundwork for the breakup of the American Telephone and Telegraph Company and the various operating companies that provided local phone service in most communities. The objective of these cases was to foster competition, especially in long-distance phone service. Thus competitive regulatory policy changed from tolerating a monopoly to eliminating it.

Protective Regulatory Policies When government acts to protect the public from harmful activities that might be undertaken by private businesses or individuals, the policies it enacts are called "protective regulatory policies." For example, regulations exist requiring that land being strip-mined for coal be restored to an acceptable condition; regulations limit the amount of pollutants that can be emitted by automobiles and factories; and regulations set the minimum number of miles per gallon a car gets in order to conserve gasoline.

Redistributive Policies Wealth is shifted from one group in society to another by redistributive policies. There are clear winners and losers in such policies, and efforts to redistribute wealth usually generate a good deal of controversy. In the energy area, the Windfall Profits Tax Act of 1980 is perhaps the best example. When Congress gave President Carter the authority to remove price controls from domestic crude oil, everyone knew that oil companies' profits would increase substantially. Accordingly, Congress passed the windfall tax to divert a percentage of those profits to be used for other energy-related needs. One of the recipients of windfall money was America's poor, who would receive about 25 percent of the money to defray the cost of heating their homes.

Strategic Policies Economic assistance to foreign countries or military assistance to their armed forces are examples of the strategic type of policy. In the energy area, the establishment of a Strategic Petroleum Reserve to set aside millions of barrels of oil as insurance against being cut off from our supplies of foreign oil would be classified as a strategic policy. Because of reasons that we will discuss in Chapter 17, the president tends to be the dominant force in this area rather than committees of Congress, bureaucrats, or interest groups.

In the chapters that follow, we will look at three general domains of policy—energy and the environment, economic policy in its broadest sense, and the foreign policy of the United States—and see how different policy types have prevailed.

In examining energy and the environment, we see an area in which distributive policies dominated, followed by a period in which regulatory policies multiplied.

In the second policy area—economic policy—we will see a broad array of policy types, ranging from the distributive subsidy policies of the nineteenth century to the economic regulatory actions by the Federal Reserve Board and the highly redistributive policies of the Great Depression.

Finally, in foreign policy, we see an area in which presidents have had the initiative and in which Congress has drawn the lines and warned the president not to step over them. In some ways, foreign policy is the least fragmented of the three policy areas we will discuss, but we also see that in the formulation of foreign policy—which takes place within the president's own branch of government—there is considerable fragmentation.

CHAPTER 15

Public Policy: Energy and the Environment

Dave Driver is a man with a major stake in an intelligent energy policy, even more than he realizes.

Dave is an executive for a power and light company in Ohio. He makes a good living—good enough to own two cars. The one he uses the most is the family station wagon—a full-sized Ford LTD that accommodates him, his wife Ellen, and their two children during the trips they take to their summer home in New York's Adirondack Mountains.

Dave's real automotive love, however, is the 1970 Buick Gran Sport 455 that's parked in his garage. He's owned it from the day it was new. It's not officially an antique, of course, but it's his pride and joy. He often tells his friends, "They don't make them like that any-more."

Being a utility company executive, Dave knows that the energy resources of this planet are limited. Twice, in the 1970s, he saw his company forced to switch from burning oil to burning coal to produce electricity. He also has some unhappy personal memories associated with those two energy crises: he remembers the days of getting up at 4 a.m. to beat the long lines at the Mobil station where he usually bought gasoline for his car. He remembers the energy crisis of 1979 with particular unhappiness. He and his family had to forego their visit to their summer home, and remained in Ohio.

Dave's been reading a good deal about energy in the local paper. One evening he reads that two of the three largest American automobile manufacturers—Ford and General Motors—have persuaded the Environmental Protection Agency of the federal government to lower the number of miles per gallon of gasoline that each company's cars are required to get. Congress passed a law in 1975, just after the first energy crisis, requiring that a manufacturer's whole line of cars average 27.5 miles per gallon. Ford and G.M. have managed to lobby EPA into reducing that to 26 miles per gallon.

Dave's glad, in a way, because that probably means that Ford will continue to make the big wagon he prefers. Although he feels that conservation measures such as the EPA mileage standards for cars have saved this country a good deal of oil, he wonders if a proposed big tax on oil imported into the United States wouldn't be a better way to conserve fuel. He feels that mileage standards can force automakers to abandon the manufacture of large cars. After all, Dave reasons, if I'm willing to spend my money on my own gas-guzzling car, shouldn't I be able to?

Dave also reads that sometime in the 1990s, the EPA will require refiners of gasoline to eliminate all lead from their fuels because lead in the human bloodstream can cause mental retardation in young children and kidney damage in adults. He's happy about that, but he knows that his pride and joy—the Buick Gran Sport with its 455-cubic-inch engine—can run only on leaded gas. So just about the time that his car becomes a genuine antique, it may also be unusable—confined to the garage for lack of proper fuel.

Then his eye settles on an article on an inside page about a study by the Environmental Defense Fund that links the discharge of sulfur dioxide from the smokestacks of power plants to "acid rain." As a power company executive, he knows all about sulfur dioxide and acid rain. He knows that power plants that burn coal to generate electricity emit sulfur dioxide into the atmosphere. He's heard charges that this sulfur dioxide changes chemically as it moves through the atmosphere—that it falls to the earth, sometimes hundreds of miles away, as highly acidic rain. Environmentalists charge that such acid rain kills all life in lakes and can even cause whole forests to die. He's watched the bass and sunfish disappear from his favorite fishing lake in the Adirondacks, and it concerns him. He knows that coal mined in the United States—much of it in his own state of Ohio—is our most abundant source of energy, but he suspects that this form of energy may come with a high environmental price tag.

In trying to find new sources of energy, the utility that Dave works for began construction of a plant to generate electricity with a nuclear reactor. The near disaster at Three Mile Island in 1979, however, caused a great deal of publicity about poor nuclear plant construction. And the concern that there is no entirely safe way to dispose of spent nuclear fuel rods caused Dave's company to cancel the project.

The energy concerns of our fictional friend Dave Driver are magnified for the purpose of making a point. Dave and his fellow Americans want to have their cake and eat it too. They want plentiful energy but don't like to conserve. They want a healthy environment but resent the cost of environmental controls that boost their utility bills. People in government are aware of this ambivalence on the part of citizens toward making adjustments in their lives to conserve energy and preserve the environment. One result of this awareness is that elected officials tend to write contradictory or fragmentary policies. This policy fragmentation is also promoted by the diverse sources of our energy.

To gain an understanding of how our energy and environmental policies evolved, we'll look first at the structure of energy use in the United States. By that we mean the kinds of fuels that we use and the effect that the use of these fuels has on our environment. We will then examine the political and economic forces that shaped the policies that contributed to the shortages we suffered in the 1970s. We will look at the particular role played by Congress where the diversity of energy sources—namely, oil, natural gas, nuclear, solar, and hydroelectric power—led to a highly fragmented approach to energy policy. We shall see how presidents, in response to shortages attempted to formulate comprehensive energy programs but succeeded only partially. The approach of all three presidents who served in the 1970s was to have the federal government intervene to adjust price and supply of oil and natural gas.

In the next section we will evaluate the interventionist approach, then compare it with the free-market approach used by President Reagan. We'll look at two energy programs: one that survived the new emphasis on market forces and another that did not. Finally, we'll ask the question: "Abundant Energy and a Safe Environment: Can We Have Both?"

A nuclear power plant in San Onofre, California. Even though it is a new source of energy, our reliance on nuclear power is considerable. *(Southern California Edison Co./API)*

The Structure of American Energy Use

Oil: Our Fuel of Preference and Necessity

Approximately 31 percent of the oil consumed in the United States is used to run cars, trucks, and buses. Half of this amount is consumed by cars alone. There is no ready substitute for oil. Coal, in its unprocessed form, is not a suitable fuel for transportation. Coal can be used to generate electricity to run electric locomotives, and alcohol distilled from farm products mixed with gasoline to produce gasohol can stretch gasoline supplies, but this is presently a minor factor. Basically, transportation is highly dependent on oil.

About 21 percent of oil use is devoted to heating homes, offices, factories, and public and private institutions, and for providing these facilities with hot water. Replacing oil as the fuel for these purposes is somewhat easier. Conversion to coal, natural gas, or some other often cheaper energy source is possible, but the installation of substitute boilers can be very costly. Price is a major factor in the conversion process itself.

The single largest consumer of oil is industry—36 percent of the oil is used in manufacturing processes. Here again, alternatives to oil are available, but the costs of conversion can be high.

Finally, 12 percent of the oil is used to generate electricity for homes, schools, stores, street lights, and indeed anything equipped with a cord and plug. Alternatives here are most numerous—coal, hydroelectric power, nuclear power, wood, or wind. The price of conversion and the cost of alternative fuels is again a problem, but other considerations emerge to cloud the picture. One dark cloud on the electric power horizon, but one that affects other sectors as well, is the environmental price that we must be willing to pay to eliminate the oil habit. If the oil we use is imported, there are economic and political prices to pay as well.

The Economic and Political Price Tag on Imported Oil The oil import bill for the United States between 1973 and 1984 came to $500 billion. Because we pay so much for this imported oil, we necessarily have less to spend on other things. We have to work more to buy the same amount of oil we used to get pre-1973 prices. What these increased prices do, quite simply, is to cause a direct loss in national income. There are indirect effects as well—much higher rates of inflation for virtually all goods and services, distortions of the international monetary system such as reducing the value of the dollar, and, because people have less to spend on other things, a reduced demand for the output of America's factories.[1]

One needs little imagination to figure out that the United States also becomes politically vulnerable to oil producers. Our foreign policy becomes hostage to the political objectives of the oil-producing nations. Since many of these countries are dictatorships or highly unstable regimes, the prospect of their using oil as political leverage against us is not a pleasant one. To maintain our sources of supply, we may be tempted to intervene militarily. We could find ourselves waging war to keep the oil flowing to our cars and factories.

Problems of Using Fossil Fuels

All fossil fuels except natural gas have a negative effect on the environment when burned. The combustion of coal or oil produces carbon dioxide, and the experts have warned that the continued use of these fuels could produce over the next 200 years serious changes in the earth's atmosphere. One prediction is that the huge floating ice packs at the North Pole may melt as the result of the warming of the atmosphere, which would raise ocean levels and cause flooding of coastal areas.[2]

Acid Rain It is not merely a far-off catastrophe that may be produced by the continued burning of fossil fuels. Already, about 50,000 lakes in northern New York State and Canada have had their fish populations destroyed because of **acid rain** which is produced when nitrogen oxide and sulfur dioxide escape into the atmosphere from industrial smokestacks. The fumes are carried along by wind currents, combine with water vapor molecules to produce nitric and sulfuric acid, and fall to the ground in the form of rain or snow many miles from the place where the stacks are located. The sulfur dioxide, which accounts for about 60 percent of the acids in the rain, is produced by the burning coal and oil in power plants, smelters, steel mills, and factories. Nitrogen oxide, about 35 percent of the acid, comes from automobile exhausts. In addition to the destruction and malformation of fish populations, acid rain can contaminate drinking water and destroy the fertility of soil.[3] The map in Figure 15.1 shows the extent of acid rainfall

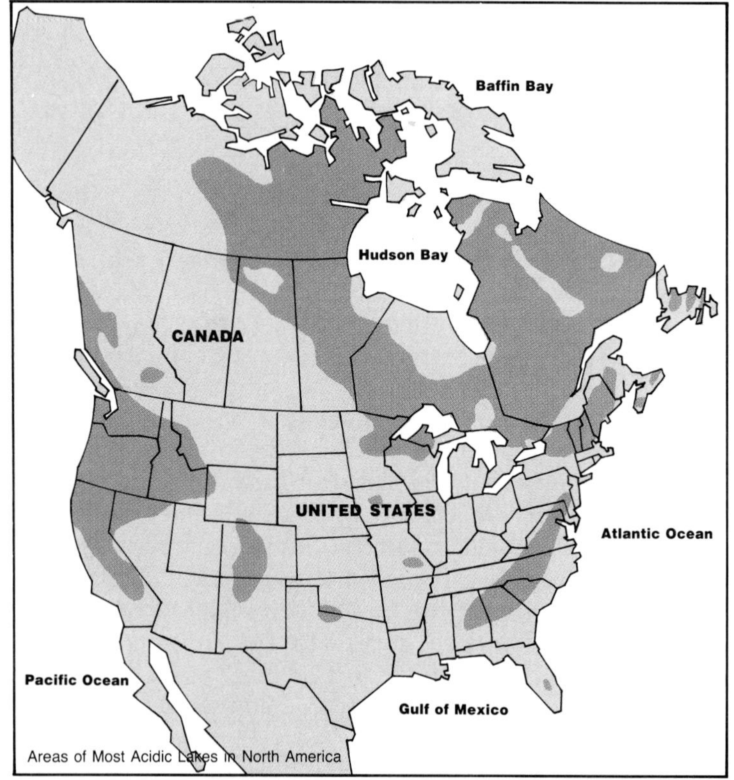

FIGURE 15.1
Areas with Most Acidic Lakes in North America
*(Drs. James Galloway and Ellis Cowling/*Journal of the Air Pollution Control Association, The New York Times *[Tuesday, November 6, 1979]. Copyright © 1979 by The New York Times Company. Reprinted by permission.)*

POLITICAL PERSPECTIVE

ACID RAIN AND THE ROLE OF COAL

Regional conflicts have erupted over efforts to control air pollution. In the case of acid rain, most of the sources of sulfur dioxide in the air over the Northeast are Midwestern power plants that burn high-sulfur coal. Midwestern waterways close to the plants are not as seriously affected as the lakes and rivers of the Northeast, which are hundreds of miles downwind. Low-sulfur coal is available to these power plants, but it is coal mined in places like Wyoming and is more expensive than the high-sulfur coal close at hand.

For the Western states, the acid rain problem has been traced to huge copper smelters in New Mexico and Arizona and even one across the border in Mexico. States of the Northeast want relief from acid rain by forcing Midwestern utilities to burn costlier Western coal or to install expensive stack scrubbers. Western states, like California and Oregon, want emissions controls on the copper smelters in the Southwest.

There are winners and losers if Congress decides to pass laws strictly controlling sulfur dioxide emissions from the Midwestern power plants or the Southwestern smelters. The big winners would be the states in the Northeast and West whose lakes and rivers would be spared acid rain. Western states with large deposits of low-sulfur coal would also benefit if a shift away from high-sulfur fuel was the chosen solution. Big losers would be in the Midwest. Power plants there would have to pay more for coal, raising their customers' fuel bills, and the coal industry in places like Ohio would lose business to states with low-sulfur coal. The depressed Southwestern copper industry would also lose if emissions controls were tightened. In the final count, a truly national acid rain policy might mean that through taxes we would all have to shoulder the economic burden of changing the way that Midwestern power plants and Southwestern smelters conduct their operations, even though we might not get any direct personal benefits in our own part of the country.

The conflict between national environment values and regional winners and losers could be seen during the effort by the House Energy and Commerce Committee in 1983–84 to write a bill to control acid rain. Most of the support for the Waxman-Sikorski Bill came from the Northeast and New England and very little from anywhere else besides California. In general, the Western states, whose representatives might have been more enthusiastic about the bill if it had relied less heavily on scrubbers and more on their own low-sulfur coal, showed little support for the bill.

---

in North America. A conversion of a large number of factories from scarce oil to plentiful coal would, if anything, cause the worsening of the problem.

The consequences of conversion to coal go beyond the borders of the United States. A Canadian government study has estimated that acid rain would kill the fish in 48,000 Canadian lakes over the next twenty years as a result of 25 million tons of sulfur dioxide from American factories and plants. Since sulfur dioxide will drift over national borders, the energy supply problem is more than merely a domestic concern; the environmental complications of escaping from our dependency on oil are, in fact, international.

The Alternatives to Oil and Their Shortcomings

Nuclear Power Other alternatives to imported oil present problems at least as great as or greater than conversion to coal. The near disaster that took place in March 1979 at the General Public Utilities plant at **Three Mile Island,** near Harrisburg, Pennsylvania, seemed to confirm what many op-

Demonstrations near a nuclear power plant in Pennsylvania, provoked in part by fears of another Three Mile Island disaster. *(© Tom Kelly/The Mercury)*

ponents of nuclear power had warned about: that serious deficiencies in nuclear reactor safety made a large-scale shift from oil to atomic power a very risky proposition. The fears provoked by Three Mile Island led many people to call for a total abandonment of nuclear power plants to generate electricity. Nevertheless, our reliance on nuclear power is considerable.

Nuclear electric generating capacity supplies the equivalent of 1 million barrels (or 40 million gallons) of oil per day. The electricity from nuclear power plants not only accounts for a significant proportion of our electricity, it also is substantially cheaper than electricity from oil-fired plants. Nuclear power costs about 1.7 cents per kilowatt hour as compared with 4.25 cents for power from oil-powered plants.[4]

Despite the sixfold increase in the price of uranium over the past six years and the huge costs of building nuclear power plants, electricity from nuclear reactors remains a bargain in many parts of the United States. Figure 15.2 shows that only in the Mountain states and parts of the South does coal have a clear-cut cost advantage. Nuclear-generated electricity is often a financial bargain, but the cost to humans and their environment can be great. One fact alone warns us about nuclear power: no satisfactory method of permanently disposing spent reactor fuel, which remains radioactive for hundreds of years, has been developed.

Hydroelectric Power There is, of course, hydroelectric power, which has no pollution problem per se, although it can have negative environmental consequences. Hydropower supplies about 3 percent of our energy needs: the equivalent amount of oil would be slightly more than 1 million barrels. It is a renewable energy source based on one of the cheapest commodities (water) and is highly efficient. The problem is that virtually every dammable stream and river in the United States has been dammed for power. Hydroelectric dams are restricted to areas of high rainfall, and many of these areas are remote from centers of population. We are approaching the limits of the potential of this source of electricity. By the year

2000, even if we double our capacity, hydroelectric power will probably account for no more than 1 to 2 percent of our energy needs. There are, of course, other sources with a much greater potential, but these have yet to be fully exploited. Solar power is one such source.

Solar Power Solar power comes in several forms. Even wood and plant matter can be included in the solar category, since trees and plants store the energy of the sun. More conventionally, however, we can consider it as: (1) the collection of sun rays to heat and cool buildings; (2) the generation of electric power from photovoltaic, or solar, cells made of thin wafers of silicon; (3) and the use of wind and tide to generate electricity.

The source of solar power (the sun) is abundant. It does not degrade the landscape, as does the mining of coal or the drilling for oil. Nor does it pollute rivers, streams, or the air. Unlike nuclear power, it threatens no great disasters and needs no pipelines to transport it, as does natural gas. Nevertheless, it does have its shortcomings. For one thing, some areas are much more favored by sunlight than others.

Wind power shares most of the advantages and disadvantages of sun power. Like sun power, the wind is nonpolluting, except for noise from the turbine, and does not disfigure the landscape, except insofar as the towers might be unsightly. But like the sun, the wind is more reliable in some places than in others.

Other Sources of Power Other potential or actual sources of clean, usable power to generate electricity are *tidal power* and *geothermal energy*, which is hot water trapped under the surface of the earth. Here, too, nature's gifts are not distributed equally. A tidal power plant makes sense in Maine but offers little to Indiana. Proven sources of geothermal power exist only in the eleven Western and Mountain states and hold out little promise to energy-poor New England.

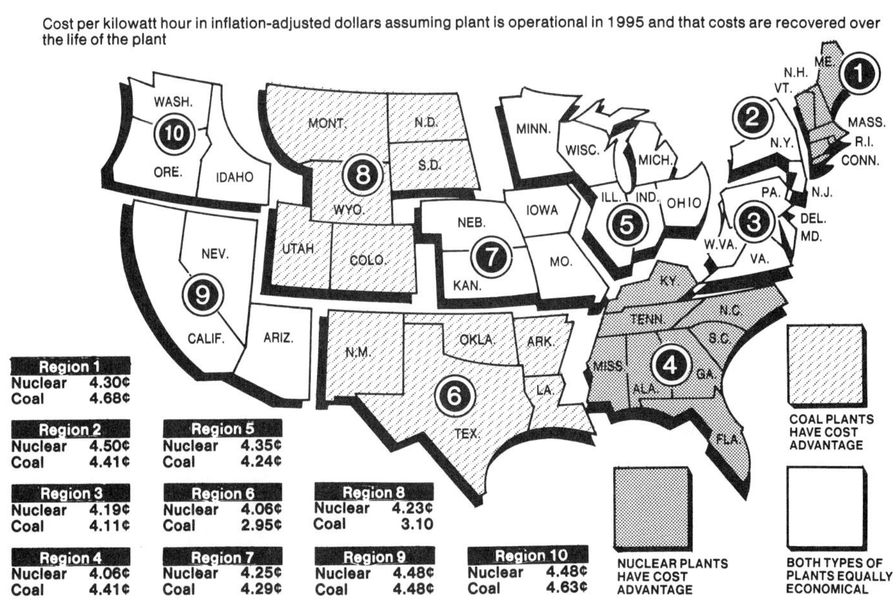

FIGURE 15.2
Nuclear versus Coal: The Costs of Electricity from New Power Plants
(Copyright © 1984 by The New York Times Company. Reprinted by permission.)

TABLE 15.1 Energy Sources for Generation of Electricity (as Percent of Total)

	Coal	Oil	Natural Gas	Nuclear	Hydro
1963	54%	6%	22%	0%	18%
1968	52	8	23	1	17
1973	46	17	18	4	15
1978	44	17	14	13	13
1983*	55	6	12	13	14
1985**	54	11	8	15	12
1990**	53	9	8	19	11

Source: Energy Information Administration.
Note: Percentage figures are rounded; other sources, including geothermal, constitute less than half of 1 percent.
*Estimate.
**Projections as of April 1983.

None of these sources of power that might be used to generate electricity, however, hold the answer for transportation, our second-largest consumer of oil. Our cars, trucks, buses, diesel locomotives, and ships are for the immediate future dependent on oil, much of it imported and all of it expensive.

But even for nontransportation uses, it is clear that such appealing sources of electricity as solar, wind, geothermal, or tidal power will not be very important factors in the immediate future. As Table 15.1 indicates, our single most important fuel for generating electricity in the year 1990 will be coal. Oil, hydro, and natural gas will all decline in importance as generator fuels; but nuclear power—somewhat ominously, given the waste disposal problem and the ever-present concern over reactor safety—will account for more electricity than it does today.

The Development of U.S. Energy Policy

Fragmentation of Public Policy

Complex policy matters can involve both governmental and nongovernmental groups (see box on page 517, "Acid Rain and the Role of Coal"). Therefore, it is not hard to imagine that a fragmentation of policy can occur or that contradictory policies can emerge. The fragmentation of public policy stems from four factors—two that are traceable directly to the form of government laid down in the Constitution, and two that have evolved over the years.

1. Separation of powers. The separation of powers and checks and balances built into the Constitution means that policymaking is the joint enterprise of executive, judicial, and legislative branches—not only on the federal level but in the states as well.
2. Federalism. Federalism produces a form of policymaking in which

federal, state, and local levels of government share policy responsibility. Although each may make policy that applies only to its own level of government, many national policies require the participation of state and local officials.
3. The scope of government. The scope of government has increased greatly. As government deals with more problems of greater complexity, the consequences of what government does (its policies) touch more peoples' lives.
4. Interest groups. Interest groups develop as people join together to influence policies of government. They attempt to influence not only the formation of policy but the manner in which policies are implemented, or carried out, by government.

Fragmentation of policy, then, is not very mysterious, since various types of policies are made at different levels of government by official groups wielding an assortment of powers under the influence of a multitude of interest groups that can bring their influence to bear at any number of stages. (We will see this recur throughout Chapters 16 and 17, as well as in this chapter.)

Public policy in the energy area lends itself to fragmentation not only because of the general factor we have just cited but also because of the natural divisions within the energy field—oil; coal; nuclear, geothermal, and synthetic fuels; hydroelectric power; wind; and biomass. Add this to the fact that the use of various types of power incurs certain environmental problems and you have a situation in which the formulation of a comprehensive national energy policy becomes exceedingly difficult. Indeed, as we shall see, there has not been, until the late 1970s, anything resembling a national energy policy.

Federal energy policy during that period had essentially four components:

1. Oil and natural gas price controls, all of which were designed to be phased out over time, and a windfall profits tax imposed on domestic oil when price controls were lifted.
2. Conservation programs such as automobile fuel-efficiency standards and programs aimed at reducing the amount of oil and gas in large industrial boilers.
3. Programs to encourage new technologies, such as synthetic fuels and solar energy.
4. Tax policies designed either to foster or discourage energy use and production.

Of these efforts to establish a comprehensive energy policy, one noted economist has asked:

> How can it be that Federal programs have on balance been so irrelevant in their impact on overall energy balances? These policies have arisen as the result of multiple objectives—attempting to prevent income redistribution, restrain inflation, accelerate substitution away from oil and gas, encourage drilling, or improve the environment. Because they are the product of different Presidents and competing Congressional committees, policies often end up contradictory.[5]

The Types of Energy Policy in Practice

At least part of the difficulty in producing a comprehensive energy policy has been the historical fact that different forms of energy came into common use in different periods. Water power and steam were the fuels of the early nineteenth century; coal came along in the latter part of that century as a major power source and persisted as the prime source of power until the 1920s when it was supplanted by oil and natural gas. Nuclear power did not become a reality until after World War II, and solar power has yet to reach its full potential. Because oil has been the main source of energy during the twentieth century, most of our discussion of energy policy will revolve around the development of oil policy.

The first governmental policies toward oil tended to be *distributive.* The U.S. Geological Survey helped oil companies identify promising locations where oil could be found, thus making their work easier and inducing them to drill for oil. The oil industry, in its infancy, soon came under the virtual monopoly of the Standard Oil Company, however. First the states and then the federal government moved to break up this giant company, and in 1906 the Justice Department brought suit under the Sherman Antitrust Act to dissolve the company for the purposes of bringing competition to the oil industry. In 1911, in the case of *Standard Oil Co.* v. *U.S.,* the court ordered the company to be broken up. This was an example of *competitive-regulatory* policy on the part of the federal government.

State Regulation and the Hot Oil Act After the *Standard Oil* case, the federal government tended to take a hands-off policy in regard to the oil industry. When oil surpluses in Texas and Oklahoma drove down the price

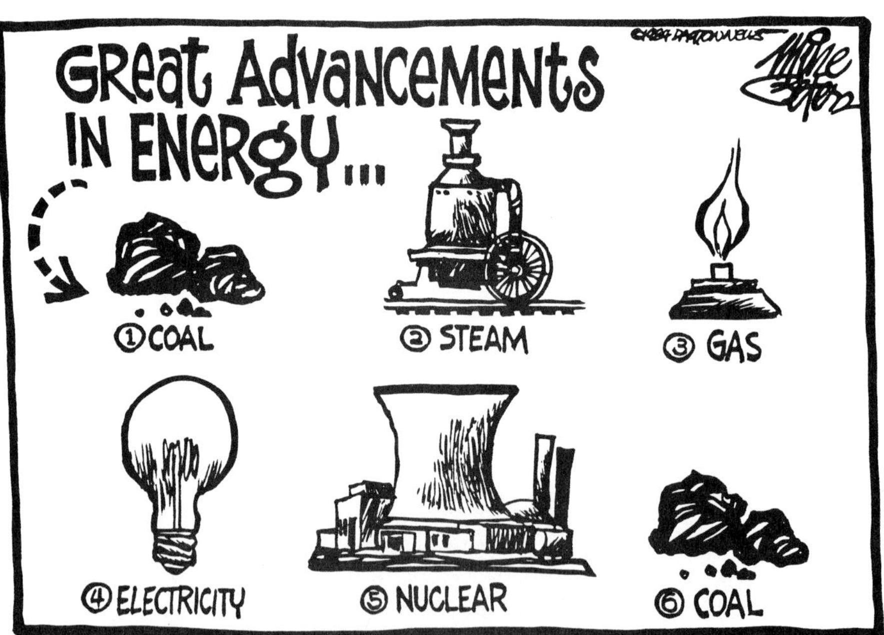

Reprinted by permission of United Features Syndicate, Inc.

Mass transit policy must take into account factors other than energy conservation, such as accessibility to the handicapped. *(Roger Archibald/ Woodfin Camp & Associates)*

of oil in the late 1920s, demands by companies that the federal government impose limits on the amount of oil that could be pumped were rejected by the Hoover administration.[6] Both states gave to state regulatory agencies (such as the oddly named Railroad Commission in Texas) power to limit oil production within their own boundaries. They quickly discovered, however, that operators were exceeding these quotas and selling their oil outside the state. States without quotas, moreover, could not be forced to restrain production by the states that did have them. What the Roosevelt New Deal gave the states and companies concerned with overproduction and low prices was a section in the National Industrial Recovery Act that was a mechanism for *self-regulation.* The role of the federal government was restricted to making it illegal to sell "hot oil" in interstate commerce—that is, oil pumped in excess of the quotas set by the states and oil companies. When, in 1935, the Supreme Court struck down the oil section of the NIRA as an unconstitutional delegation of its legislative power to such industry groups as those that were setting quotas,[7] Congress passed a separate Hot Oil Act to stop the sale of oil pumped in excess of state quotas.[8]

Tariffs Protecting U.S. Oil Producers A significant distributive policy was also established at roughly the same time—a tariff or import tax on all foreign oil brought into this country to protect U.S. oil producers from competition from cheaper foreign oil. This made foreign oil costlier but did not keep it out entirely.

The onset of war in Europe shifted the federal government's emphasis away from backstopping state efforts to limit production to maximizing production on behalf of the war effort. The fabulous new oil fields of the Persian Gulf became a major factor in U.S. war policy, and the basis for a long-term relationship between the United States and Saudi Arabia was laid by Roosevelt and King Ibn Saud. As far as postwar U.S. foreign policy regarding oil was concerned, the federal government was to encourage the development of overseas oil fields by U.S. companies. This meant a delicate balance between allowing enough oil into the country to supplement our own supplies but not so much as to threaten domestic producers.[9]

During the period in which little foreign oil was imported into the United States (less than 5 percent of U.S. production between 1932 and 1945), it was possible to maintain that delicate balance between imports and U.S. production. But beginning in 1947, imports of foreign oil edged ahead of U.S. oil going abroad, and this country became a net importer of oil for the first time. Major oil companies were having great success with fields in Venezuela and the Middle East. This cheaper foreign oil cut into the overseas markets for more expensive American oil, but significantly, this foreign oil also undersold the domestic oil in the United States, even with the tariff.[10]

THE OIL IMPORT QUOTA A split was developing within the oil industry with producers of domestic oil arrayed against the companies with interests in foreign wells. Domestic producers convinced Congress in 1958 to limit imports of foreign oil to 12 percent of U.S. production. The quota applied only to the Eastern states—the very region that benefited most strongly from access to cheaper foreign oil. The domestic oil producers packaged this quota, not as a distributive policy, which might have left them open to charges of greed, but as a strategic policy. Their arguments to Congress centered on the quota as a way of reducing U.S. dependency on oil carried over ocean routes, vulnerable to foreign intervention.

The quotas were finally lifted by President Nixon. He did this at the time of the 1973 oil crisis, brought about by the war between the Arabs and Israel in the Middle East.

The effectiveness of these quotas is a matter of debate. One school of thought holds that anything that keeps out foreign oil hastens the time when U.S. oil reserves run out.[11] It also argues that the quota discriminated against the Eastern states that might have had access to cheap oil for their petrochemical industries. In addition, the quota was said to be harmful to our oil-producing allies overseas. The other point of view is that the quotas would have been effective in relieving our dependency on foreign oil if only they had been applied rigorously. By the time the quotas were dropped, there had been so many exceptions granted that we were importing 30 percent of our oil needs. Defenders of the quota also feared that growing hostility between the United States and the Communist world made shipping oil across the seas a risky proposition.[12]

OPEC'S RESPONSE One outgrowth of the imposition of the quotas was the reaction of the foreign oil producers. They organized themselves into a group called OPEC—the Organization of Petroleum Exporting Countries. Scarcely noticed at first by the United States, OPEC became the driving force in boosting foreign oil prices throughout the 1970s.

In 1973, Arab members of OPEC placed an embargo on oil shipments to the United States because of American support of Israel in the "Yom Kippur War." Exceptions to the oil import quotas and price controls on heating oil and gasoline imposed by President Nixon in 1971 made us even more

An OPEC meeting in Geneva in 1981. *(Brucelle/Sygma)*

vulnerable to the oil embargo. The logic behind the original decision, in 1971, to impose price controls was to protect consumers from the first surge of OPEC price increases. In 1973, they were retained when OPEC quadrupled their price after the war.

Believing that controlled oil prices discouraged oil companies from exploring for new wells and consumers from conserving oil, President Ford proposed to Congress that the controls be ended immediately. Congress, under pressure from consumers who did not want their oil and gasoline bills to go through the roof, refused to end the controls. A compromise was worked out to continue the controls until 1979 and then give the president standby authority to lift controls. By the time that Ronald Reagan was inaugurated, these controls applied to roughly one-quarter of domestic oil. One of Reagan's first acts as president was to remove all controls on U.S.-produced oil.

Scarcity: The New Ground-Rule of Energy Politics

The simple abundance of oil at relatively low cost meant that government could pursue essentially distributive policies. Concessions to industry—such as oil import fees, quotas, and depletion allowances—might raise questions of fairness but were not seriously challenged so long as motorists had gasoline and home-heating fuel available at moderate cost. In a situation of abundant or expanding resources, the gains of one group do not necessarily mean losses for another. After the 1973 to 1974 oil embargo, however, it became clear that federal energy policy would have to confront the problem of managing scarcity.

Conrad/ © *The Los Angeles Times*, 1978; reprinted with permission.

The abundance that produced distributive policies in the energy area also meant that Congress had had a fairly easy time of it. When energy policies were little more than a series of subsidies for the oil, gas, and nuclear power industries, the ancient legislative practice of **logrolling** (supporting another member's favorite subsidy with the expectation that he or she would support yours) could be practiced with great ease. What emerged was not public policy in any coherent sense because of the very parochial manner in which members tended to interpret policy. As Morris Fiorina put it:

> Public policy emerges from the system almost as an afterthought . . . Congressmen know that the specific impact of broad national policies on their districts is difficult to see, that the effects are hidden, so to speak. They know too that individual congressmen are not held responsible for the collective outcome produced by 535 members of Congress. Thus, in order to attain reelection, congressmen focus on things that are both more recognizable in their impact and more credible indicators of the individual congressman's power—federal projects and individual favors for constituents. In order to purchase a steady flow of the latter, congressmen trade away less valuable currency—their views on public policy.[13]

Energy and the "Zero-Sum Game" As a consequence of the development of a legislative system that assumed that resources were unlimited, Congress found it exceedingly difficult to deal with problems of scarcity associated with a declining energy supply. Energy is a classic case of the **zero-sum game,** where one group's gain in supplies or resources is achieved at the expense of another group. For example, Ohio sees itself the loser when it is forced to buy expensive low-sulphur Wyoming coal rather than cheap high-sulphur Kentucky coal to cut down on the harmful emissions from its power plants. Or supplies of scarce gasoline allocated to California are seen as coming out of the tanks of New York motorists. Each member of Congress approaches these questions with the conviction that his or her state or district will not be the one to suffer.

When confronted with a comprehensive energy bill, such as the one submitted by President Carter to Congress in 1977 in the interest of establishing a truly national policy across all forms of energy, the general welfare runs up against the particular needs of members of Congress to protect their constituencies. The lament of House Speaker Thomas P. O'Neill summed it all up when, in 1975, President Ford sent a comprehensive energy bill to the 94th Congress: "It is extremely difficult to write an energy bill," O'Neill complained. "This, perhaps, has been the most parochial issue that could ever hit the floor."[14]

Congress and Energy Policy

In response to the 1973 Arab oil embargo, President Nixon asked Congress for comprehensive energy legislation. He received three things: a system to allocate fuel in the event of scarcity; a price control system; and authorization to build a pipeline across Alaska to bring down oil from the recently discovered North Slope fields.

Nixon's successor, Gerald Ford, proposed to Congress that the price controls instituted by Nixon in 1971 be scrapped and that import fees be placed on foreign oil brought into the country. By 1975 when these proposals were made, however, the ugly memories of the 1973 oil embargo were getting hazy in the minds of members of Congress. They also did not want to add further financial burdens on their constituents who were already reeling from OPEC's fourfold price increase.

By retaining price controls and even rolling back prices in some instances, Congress was telling the American people that they would subsidize the difference between the controlled price and the OPEC price that everyone else in the world had to pay. This was no incentive to conserve.

At the same time, however, Congress approved mandatory fuel-efficiency standards for American cars. The law forced Detroit to increase the average miles per gallon of their entire lines of cars from the current 14 to 28 miles per gallon by 1985. The car-makers, in effect, were told to build more small cars in response to scarce and costly fuel; consumers were being told that it was neither scarce nor costly. Detroit, then, found itself building small cars for people who could get government-subsidized gasoline to run large cars.

A more consistent policy might have been combining mileage-efficiency standards with the removal of price controls, but Congress sensed that Americans wanted to have it both ways—low fuel prices and large cars.

What Ford Got from Congress

Let us look at what Congress gave President Ford in terms of the various policy types. Of the five major titles of the 1975 Energy Policy and Conservation Act, the continuation of oil price controls and the rollback of domestic oil prices were principally distributive. Mandatory fuel economy standards to be monitored by the Department of Transportation were clearly regulatory. The federal testing and labeling program for appliances would probably fall into a special category of regulatory policies that has been called "self-regulation."[15] By setting goals for appliance manufacturers to meet in the energy efficiency of their products, the Congress was essentially allowing them to police their own industry's response to the energy crisis.

More obviously regulatory were provisions giving the Federal Energy Agency (FEA) power to compel utilities and factories to switch from burning oil and natural gas to coal and increasing the president's authority to require refineries to produce more of one petroleum than another (such as more fuel oil for winter months and more gasoline for spring and summer driving). In one action of potentially great significance, Congress authorized the creation of the **Strategic Petroleum Reserve.** This strategic policy, designed to create a buffer against the cutoff of foreign oil, provided for storing up to 1 billion gallons of oil in salt caverns in Louisiana.

Partisan differences played a major role in shaping the 1975 legislation. A Republican president had proposed an end to price controls and the imposition of a $2-a-barrel tax on imported oil. The Democratic Congress seemed persuaded at first that reducing American dependence on foreign oil was a desirable goal, but at least one technique for achieving that—letting oil prices rise to world levels by decontrol—was not popular. Democrats from the Northeast and Midwest, where winters are severe and commuting by car is a way of life, did not want their constituents to have to pay the increased prices that decontrol would bring.

What Carter Got from Congress

Toward a National Energy Policy When Jimmy Carter came to the White House in 1977, he lost little time in putting together his own comprehensive energy policy. In the manner of all presidents who present controversial programs, Carter invoked the overall good of the nation as opposed to the narrow and parochial outlooks of special interests. Sadly for him, he did not take into his confidence in drafting this **National Energy Plan**—a policy that would cover all forms of fuel—those most vulnerable to special interests, the members of Congress.

Despite this initial blunder and the failure of the White House to lobby effectively for the plan, it sailed through the House largely intact as the result of an ingenious tactic used by Speaker O'Neill. Acutely aware—considerably more so than the president—of the decentralization of the House and the tendency of subcommittee chairpersons to ensure that some part of a major bill falls into their jurisdiction and their tendency to break comprehensive measures into small pieces, O'Neill appointed a select committee dominated by members friendly to the Carter bill. In our discussion of the congressional leadership in Chapter 9, we discussed how much more influence the speaker of the House has had in that chamber than the majority leader has had in the Senate. The success of the Carter energy bill in 1977 is a good example of this. O'Neill stressed party unity in an institution in which votes along strict party lines are more common than in the Senate. He built up goodwill among recent members who had been elected in 1976 and were anxious to compile records on which they could run in 1978. He was also able to schedule committee hearings quite rigorously and to get the subcommittees to report their recommendations to the select committee quite promptly.[16]

In the Senate the strategy of combining the major portions of the National Energy Plan into a single bill failed. The Senate divided the plan into six bills: one to force industries and utilities to burn coal instead of natural gas and oil, one for matching grants for energy conservation in schools and hospitals, one for energy conservation tax incentives, one to deregulate the price of natural gas, another relating to electricity rates, and the last to provide energy tax incentives.[17]

What finally emerged from Congress in October 1978 was considerably less than what the president wanted. He got tax incentives for homeowners to insulate and tax penalties on buyers of gas-guzzling cars. Targets on energy efficiency in home appliances were replaced by mandatory standards of energy efficiency. Higher prices on natural gas, authority to force plants and utilities to burn coal instead of oil or gas, and the electricity rate reforms were also passed. What he did not get was a boost in the gasoline tax, a highly redistributive plan to rebate a tax on gas guzzlers to buyers of energy-efficient cars, taxes on crude oil, and taxes on the use of natural gas and oil by industries and utilities.

The unusual efforts by Speaker O'Neill in the House and the more business-as-usual attitude of the Senate produced a modestly significant but not dramatic change in the U.S. energy policy. The attitude of the Senate was perhaps a better reflection of public views of the energy situation. Throughout 1978 and even into 1979, fewer than 40 percent of the American people believed that energy was truly in short supply and that talk of crisis simply had the effect of preparing people for price increases by oil companies that had plenty of oil but were greedy for higher profits.

The Windfall Profits Tax This attitude prevailed even through the next great shock to befall the American public—the overthrow of the pro-American Shah of Iran in early 1979 and his replacement by anti-American government dominated by the Ayatollah Ruhollah Khomeini. The new Iranian government cut production of that country's oil, and by the late spring of 1979 Americans were once again lined up for gasoline. In the years between the Arab oil embargo and the overthrow of the Shah, the American people lived a fool's paradise of energy extravagance in the conviction that the first energy shock was a fluke not to be repeated. Congress, taking its cue from the voters, acted with complacency in its refusal to pass the toughest conservation and energy price decontrol measures.

President Carter responded to the reduction in Iranian oil supplies by using the standby authority that Congress had granted to President Ford in the Emergency Petroleum Allocation Act of 1973 to decontrol totally the price of oil over a two-year period. This decision precipitated an epic struggle in Congress—what to do with the **windfall profits** that the oil companies would gain by the removal of price ceilings on oil. Would these enormous additional sums paid by homeowners for oil and motorists for gasoline go to the oil companies or the government?

The president proposed other measures, as the Iranian situation intensified in its effects. He proposed gasoline rationing and allocation plans to distribute hardships as equitably as possible over the various regions of the country. A national plan for sharing scarcity proposed by a president whose concerns ran to all fifty states collided with a determination among the members of Congress to protect their constituents.

The gasoline rationing plan was defeated and it would be another year before a much less effective one was approved. At the time that the rationing plan was under debate in the House, Congressman Bill Hefner of North Carolina made the observation that "if worse comes to worse we could just give [gasoline] allocations to each of the 435 members and let them distribute it in an equitable way, and that would solve all of our problems.[18]

Part of the problem that the gasoline-rationing plan encountered in the House was that it became interwoven with an attempt to reform the committee structure of the House and to set up a House Energy Committee. The proposal to centralize jurisdiction over energy matters in a single committee posed a direct threat to the current fragmented arrangement in which responsibility for energy was dispersed among many committees and subcommittees. The effort failed for the reason that congressional power and energy share the same characteristic: there is not enough of it to go around. As Eric Uslaner put it:

> In contrast to the classical politics of distribution on policy areas such as housing, labor, business, agriculture, and public works, energy policy and Congressional power are both inherently conflictual because each is in very limited supply. . . .
>
> The reorganization effort constituted a direct attack on the distributive politics of a pluralist democracy in general and the Democratic party in Congress in particular, given the party's history of being all things to all people, which required few sacrifices from either clientele groups or the members themselves.[19]

The centerpiece of Carter's 1979 energy plan—the windfall profits tax—eventually did get through Congress, in large measure because the president made it a priority and had the strategy for the tax planned and run from the White House rather than through the recently created Department of Energy.

What Carter did points up William Keefe's observation that "the fragmentation of power within Congress, accompanied by indecision and particularism, impels the president to become deeply involved in the lawmaking process. Better than anyone else, the president can focus attention on national problems and help to break deadlocks that impede their resolution."[20]

SYNFUELS The Carter administration wanted the proceeds from the windfall profits tax to be applied to three purposes: energy aid for the poor to

The Alaskan pipeline was finally approved by Congress in 1974, despite strenuous objections by environmental groups. As a result of their concerns, however, the pipeline was elevated in some areas to allow free passage of wildlife from one place to another. *(Standard Oil of California/API)*

pay the increased costs of heating their homes; urban mass transit; and a ten-year program to develop synthetic fuels, or **synfuels,** from shale oil, coal, and tar sands. A quarter of the money was to go to pay the fuel bills of the poor. This was a redistributive proposal.

Such initiatives usually come from the White House, "and presidential participation in an active way is helpful and usually essential for those wanting to achieve redistribution—at least on behalf of the poorer segments of society."[21] Congress, by contrast, usually becomes involved in setting "limits on the original redistributive potential of the proposal, but some such potential often still remains."[22]

Carter won on windfall profits in 1980 but lost initially on gasoline rationing and on an Energy Mobilization Board that would have had the power to cut through environmental objections to energy development projects. This last proposal, naturally enough, was opposed by environmentalists, but they were joined in opposition by groups that felt that such a board would violate some very basic principles of federalism and ride roughshod over state and local laws designed to protect the environment. The country was also in an antibureaucratic mood, and the creation of another agency struck many people as wasteful.[23]

Fragmentation, Incrementalism, and Nondecision

We have seen that the process in Congress that led to the recent policies on energy has been subject to fragmentation. This fragmentation is the result of the historical practice of treating each energy source as a separate area with its own interest groups and bureaucratic allies in government, the emergence of environmental protection as an issue, and the practice of

Used primarily as a heating fuel, natural gas from gas fields in the United States has helped ease our dependence on foreign oil. *(Van Bucher/Photo Researchers, Inc.)*

Congress (most notably in the House) to keep jurisdiction fragmented and to resist the creation of a single committee to deal with energy legislation as a whole.

There is another characteristic of the policy process as it relates to Congress that also bears mention. This is the **incrementalism** that characterizes the process, so that "changes can only be achieved in small steps—each of which needs careful evaluation before another step can be taken.[24] Congressional fragmentation and policy incrementalism are mutually reinforcing: highly specialized committees dealing with highly technical aspects of a policy. In such a setting, the advantage is clearly in favor of those wanting to maintain the *status quo.*

Changes in energy policy have also been thwarted by the **politics of nondecision**—choking off changes before they can even be introduced or reported out of committee. The oil industry was successful for more than forty years in not allowing any changes in their 27.5 percent depletion allowance to get beyond the most preliminary discussion.[25] This could be done by the oil industry working to get "friendly" members appointed to key committees that dealt with oil and by providing those members with the resources to gain reelection.

The Implementation of Policy

The president having proposed a policy and Congress having acted on it, the question then presents itself: Whose job is it to carry out the policy? We discussed the bureaucracy's role in implementation in Chapter 11, but it is proper to observe here that once having made a policy, Congress must either turn the policy over to an existing bureaucracy to implement it or create a new one to perform that function of the policy process.

The way a law is actually implemented depends on the intention of Congress and the president, but perhaps equally as much on the nature of the bureaucratic agency responsible for it. As we saw in Chapter 11, bureaucrats operate "by the book" according to a set of standard operating procedures—steps that a bureaucracy typically follows in implementing policies. Generally, these procedures are established to limit the discretion that bureaucrats have in carrying out the work of the policymakers.[26] (The box on page 534 entitled "Confessions of an Energy Regulator" demonstrates the limitations on one bureaucrat in the system.)

The Correct Approach: Government Intervention or Market Forces?

Until Reagan took office in 1981, modern energy policy was a mixture of various policy types, most involving intervention by the federal or state governments. In energy production, supply, or pricing, government at some level was stepping in with distributive policies, such as those that encouraged domestic oil production; regulatory policies, such as that which limited Standard Oil's energy business; or redistributive policies, such as that which directed the windfall profits taxes to the poor. Mandatory conservation efforts such as these are interventionist, as are import quotas on foreign oil. Presidents Ford and Carter argued against federal price regulations on oil because they artificially held down the price Americans had to pay for oil products, while the rest of the world was having to pay what the oil-producing countries were charging. This discouraged both the search for new oil fields and deterred conservation.

When President Carter finally got Congress to end price controls, he was pursuing a **market approach.** He wanted the laws of supply and demand to set the price of oil. At the same time, however, he felt that letting the market set the price of energy was not a sufficient policy. He also favored, as we have seen, such mandatory conservation measures as the mileage standards for cars and the development of synthetic fuels.

The Reagan Approach: Commitment to Market Forces

The Reagan administration placed virtually its entire emphasis on letting market forces determine the price and supply of energy. Reagan dismissed conservation—a centerpiece of the Carter program—in a 1981 statement that, "conservation means we will all have to be too hot in the summer or too cold in the winter." In 1982 Reagan vetoed a bill that would have given him standby authority to allocate fuel supplies in a crisis. His feelings about the superiority of market forces, even in an emergency situation, led him to deny to himself the power to allocate.

There seems little doubt that much of the blame for making the energy crises worse than they should have been were the price controls on oil imposed in 1971 by President Nixon. These have now been removed and the forces of supply and demand have indeed worked in favor of moderate prices and plentiful supplies. But the role of simple price deregulation is not clear-cut.

A worldwide recession, brought on largely by soaring energy prices in 1979, cut oil consumption simply because so many factories were shut down. That does not, however, account for the relatively low prices and ample supplies nearly a decade later. It appears as if the free-market ap-

POLITICAL PERSPECTIVE

CONFESSIONS OF AN ENERGY REGULATOR

The limit on bureaucratic discretion can be seen in the energy field in the case of a young lawyer who worked for the Department of Energy's Office of Hearings and Appeals. His job was to hear appeals from gasoline station owners who felt that they had been allocated insufficient supplies of gasoline. Gasoline allocation was part of the authority given to the president by Congress in 1973 and gave station owners the right to receive additional supplies from the customary supplier during periods of shortage. It was pursuant to this authority that the young lawyer attempted to cope with the gasoline crisis in 1979.

> I recall one [gas station owner] who had expanded his station in Rancho Cucamonga, in freeway-happy Southern California, and he wanted more gasoline. He argued that the public interest would be served because "the community" was growing rapidly. I felt that the Los Angeles area was sprawling more than growing, and as a direct result of too much cheap gasoline. But neither my feelings nor his about "growth" mattered legally. The department granted special relief to the down and out, and the financial filings of the gentleman from Rancho Cucamonga showed he wasn't doing so badly. Relief denied.

The limits on discretion imposed by standard operating procedures are illustrated by another appeal that came to his office.

> Like most regulatory schemes designed for mass application, the Energy Department's rules often inflicted a dumb sort of cruelty on those who didn't fit the mold. I remember particularly a young man from Green Bay, Wis., who had lost the ability to speak when his brain was damaged in an automobile accident. Undaunted, he had bought a gasoline station and had found that pumping gas and servicing cars had been so therapeutic that he had begun to regain his speech. Could I please help him?
>
> He was in trouble because the gasoline allocation depended upon the amount sold during a previous "base period." But the regulations didn't allow for businesses that were just starting and therefore had unusually low base-period sales. The man from Green Bay was saved by a last-minute regulatory amendment that cured this problem. Telephoning him with that news is among the happiest memories of my life as a bureaucrat.

Source: Extracts from Thomas L. Jackson, "Confessions of an Energy Regulator," *Wall Street Journal* (Jan. 5, 1981).

proach did indeed have a powerful effect on how much oil we have available and how much we pay for it, but decontrol cannot receive all of the credit.

Without question, the mandatory mileage standards on cars that were imposed in 1975 have produced an almost total replacement of our national fleet of gas guzzlers with cars that are far easier on gas. Those who argue for a market-only approach might say that if we had repealed oil price controls in 1975, we could have achieved the same objective. It is difficult to dispute this argument, since we shall never know what effects decontrol in 1975 would be having today. What is beyond dispute, however, is that this interventionist regulatory policy of mandating minimum miles per gallon standards has produced a far more energy-efficient automobile population.

Given its preference for market forces, it is not surprising that the Reagan administration opposed the fuel-economy standards. When automobile makers were facing the 1985 deadline for achieving a fleet average of 27.5 miles per gallon, Ford and General Motors asked the National Highway Safety Traffic Administration that implements the economy standards to relax the standard to 26 miles per gallon. The other member of the automotive "Big Three," the Chrysler Corporation, did not join in the appeal because of its success across its entire line with fuel-efficient cars. Ultimately, the government granted the relaxation of the standards under the discretion given by Congress in the 1975 law.

Policy Survivors and Victims: Strategic Petroleum Reserve and Synfuels

One program of the 1970s that is still in place but not yet tested is the Strategic Petroleum Reserve. Unlike other interventionist approaches of the 1970s, this strategic policy was not targeted for elimination by the Reagan administration. Rather, that administration sought to slow down its efforts to achieve the 750-million-barrel goal of 1990. Arguing that about $2 billion could be saved each year by delaying the achievement of the 1990 goal, the Reagan administration in 1984–85 pointed to a worldwide surplus of oil as reason to hold the reserve at 466 barrels—a three months' supply. At this stage, the value of the Strategic Petroleum Reserve is purely psychological. To have even a three months' supply of oil for the country is likely to deter the kind of panic buying that characterized motorists in 1973 and 1979 when they feared the pumps would run dry.

The biggest casualty among the energy policies of the 1970s was synthetic fuels. This was a largely distributive program of loan guarantees to encourage new technology that was to produce 500,000 barrels of oil a day

Decontrolled domestic oil prices, mandatory mileage standards for cars, and falling OPEC prices led to a glut on the oil market in the mid-1980s. *(Anne Rippy/Don Klumpp Productions)*

from oil-bearing shale by 1987. The assumption behind the $88 billion loan program was that the price of oil would continue to rise to the point where costly synfuels would become competitive in cost. That did not occur. Indeed, when the OPEC oil price had fallen to $28 a barrel, the Synfuels Corporation chartered by the federal government was offering price guarantees for oil that cost $92 a barrel to produce.

Defenders of the synfuels program have made an essentially strategic argument that if we were cut off from oil from the Middle East, we would happily pay $92 a barrel rather than have no oil at all. That argument had little persuasive power, and some of the major oil companies that had looked favorably upon synfuels in the 1970s have abandoned their efforts to perfect a technology. In 1985, a plant at Beulah, North Dakota, that was converting coal to natural gas was closed down because it was uneconomic. The Beulah plant was producing gas from coal at $8.50 per thousand cubic feet, while conventional natural gas prices were around $2.50 per thousand cubic feet.

In political terms, fragmentation has returned to the energy policy area. Efforts by Presidents Carter and Ford to have energy treated as a comprehensive and unified policy have disappeared along with their administrations. This reversion to the practice of each energy source being dealt with only by its own little iron triangle was noted by Senator Bill Bradley of New Jersey. "It's returned to specialized interests," he said. "I don't see energy politics. I see coal politics. Or natural gas politics. The nuclear boys don't scratch the backs of the coal boys, and the coal boys don't scratch the backs of the oil boys. I don't see any coalition."[27] If it was difficult to fashion a comprehensive policy in the 1970s with the specter of shortages, it was impossible in the mid-1980s when the once-mighty OPEC was cutting prices in an effort to encourage buyers. The fall-off in demand had also humbled the domestic oil producers and led to calls for an oil-import fee to aid the U.S. oil industry.

Abundant Energy and a Safe Environment: Can We Have Both?

While the United States was coping with the problems of energy in the 1970s, there was a parallel struggle going on over the steps to take to preserve and improve the environment. These two areas were closely related because a number of the alternatives to oil were fuels that could create serious problems for the environment if widely used: coal, nuclear power, and, to a lesser extent, wood. Converting from foreign oil to any of these has the obvious benefit of freeing us from substantial amounts of insecure and expensive foreign oil, but all hold their own risks for human health. The objectives of an energy policy that aims for abundant and secure energy sometimes operates at cross-purposes with a national environmental policy whose objective is clean air and water and the preservation of our land and people. It may well be that we cannot pursue both objectives with equal determination. This means that policymakers must set priorities as to which is the most important objective. This priority setting is complicated by the fact that there are winners and losers, but who they are is not always clear.

Recalling our discussion of interest groups in Chapter 8, we made the point that there are public goods (or benefits) and private goods (or benefits) that emerge from public policy. The stockholder in a major oil company will receive private benefits from a public policy that encourages people to burn gasoline in their cars, but that same stockholder also benefits from the clean air that comes from a policy of reduced use of automobiles. A policy that encourages consumption will likely produce bigger profits for the oil company; the value of the stock will increase; and higher dividends will be paid. These are private goods, however, since they are shared only by those who are associated with the company. The benefit of clean air is a public good that everyone enjoys.

A public good such as clean air or clean water often tends to be taken for granted, and little public pressure is exerted to protect it except when some disaster strikes, such as the killing smog that hit Donora, Pennsylvania, in the 1950s or the oil well blowout in the Santa Barbara Channel in California in 1969. But even when such catastrophes occur, the indignation of the public tends to be short-lived. Public officials hoping to use the outrage of the public to pressure for environmental laws find that people have short memories. It is usually much different with private goods. Relatively few people receive dividend statements from oil companies or are the executives of energy companies who are reminded every quarter of the profit-and-loss status of a firm, with the result that pressure for favorable legislation on behalf of the company is more sustained.

Before 1969 this effect was evident in the fact that there was really very little national environmental legislation on the books. Public policy was heavily weighted in favor of energy development and consumption. For the first seventy years of the twentieth century, the use of cars was promoted without much thought being given to the environmental consequences of widespread air pollution problems brought about by automotive use on such a grand scale. The system of interstate highways was built with no concern at all about how this might have an impact on the environment. Nuclear power development also proceeded apace without, possibly, enough concern over reactor safety, and all kinds of mining expanded with the blessings of the Department of the Interior and not much attention to how it disfigured the landscape.[28]

What occurred in the late 1960s was nothing less than a revolution in public attitudes toward the environment. It was brought about by a number of events, including a redirection of the efforts of the antiwar movement toward environmental protection as the Vietnam conflict began to wind down; more attention by the media to the problems of the environment; and the development of environmentally oriented interest groups within the public. With new public awareness and support, members of Congress introduced legislation to safeguard the environment.

The **National Environmental Policy Act** became law in 1969. This landmark legislation set up the Environmental Protection Agency and the President's Council on Environmental Quality. It required all federal agencies to file environmental impact statements on any decision that they make that might have adverse effects on the environment.

The Clean Air Act of 1970 empowered the Environmental Protection Agency to set national air quality standards and required the individual states to file plans on how they were complying with these standards. The act also authorizes any person to sue a federal agency that is not enforcing the legislation.

It appeared for a brief time that the environmentalists' time had come and that the pendulum of public policy was swinging away from the encouragement of energy production at all costs toward a policy in which ecological concerns would be dominant.

The Arab oil embargo of 1973 changed that prospect. If the United States was to become independent of foreign energy sources, the new environmental controls on such activities as coal mining or oil drilling in wilderness areas might have to be relaxed. People spoke increasingly of trade-offs between energy and environment, or just how much environmental protection was consistent with adequate energy supplies.

Indecision over how much environmental protection was compatible with national energy needs was reflected in the federal bureaucracy with agencies such as the Department of Energy, which has the job of increasing national energy supplies, and the Environmental Protection Agency, whose task it is to protect the environment. Pro-energy and pro-environment bureaucracies had their own allies in Congress and in friendly interest groups, and each group competed with the other to shape public policy in the image that it favored.

The three administrations of the 1970s—Nixon, Ford, and Carter—attempted, with varying degrees of success, to balance off the energy and environmental needs of the country. At those times in which energy supplies seemed endangered, the environmental considerations received less emphasis. Even Jimmy Carter, who was seen by environmentalists as friendly to their cause, proposed the Energy Mobilization Board in his 1979 energy plan. This organization, which was rejected by Congress, would have been empowered to cut through local environmental regulations that threatened to block energy development.

Environmental Double Trouble: Acid Rain and Toxic Waste

The two most publicized environmental issues of the past ten years have been acid rain and toxic waste. Toxic waste is not necessarily related to energy production; it is more often the by-product of the petrochemical industries such as plastics, fertilizers, or insecticides.

The Reagan Administration and Acid Rain Until late in 1985, the Reagan administration took the position that the relationship between power plant and factory emissions and acid rain was unclear and that more study needed to be done. In September 1985, the president's special representative to a conference of New England governors asserted, "It seems to me that saying sulfates do not cause acid rain is the same as saying that smoking does not cause lung cancer."

But recognizing that a problem exists does not mean that a solution is at hand. Environmental groups had estimated the cost of removing the 10 to 12 million tons of sulfur that gets into the air annually at $5 billion to $6 billion. Budget cutbacks made an expenditure of that size very unlikely. The EPA, moreover, had not been very vigorous about enforcing existing

AUTH, by Tony Auth. Copyright 1985, Philadelphia Inquirer. Reprinted with permission of Universal Press Syndicate. All rights reserved.

emissions laws—a problem of implementation not money. More fundamentally, however, members of Congress defending the economic interests of their states is the most imposing barrier to action. (We saw this in our discussion of the Waxman-Sikorski bill.)

The Reagan Administration and Toxic Waste What was perhaps the most explosive environmental problem for the Reagan administration did not involve energy but rather the management of the "Superfund" toxic waste cleanup program. This program was created by Congress in 1980 with an initial budget of $1.6 billion, which was paid for by a special tax on the chemical industry. In 1982, charges of corruption were leveled against the Environmental Protection Agency, which administers the Superfund. EPA also administers such important environmental laws as: The Clean Air Act; The Clean Water Act; The Noise Control Act; and laws relating to hazardous wastes and toxic substances.

In the Interior Department and the Environmental Protection Agency, civil servants were replaced who opposed the Reagan strategy to cut back on regulations and ease the economic burdens that these regulations were felt to impose on industry. Often executives from the very industries subject to regulation were the replacements. One of these industry recruits, Rita Lavelle, a public relations officer for a California chemical company with a poor environmental record, was placed in charge of the Superfund. This is the other side of the "revolving door" effect described in Chapter 11, in which bureaucrats leave government to join the firms they have been regulating. This case, on the other hand, is an example of the efforts of industry to "capture" an agency that regulates it by having its personnel placed in that agency by a friendly administration.

What enabled the Reagan administration even to suggest that environmental regulation may have gone too far was a change in attitude in both Congress and the public in the early 1980s. This attitude was well summed up by the observation that, "as people found out what was involved in implementing the environmental legislation [placed] on the statute books [in the 1970s], the kinds of policy decisions that had to be made shifted from large-scale reform to fine tuning."[29]

The environmental movement had lost a good deal of its momentum by the early 1980s. In part, this was because so many of its major goals had been accomplished. But it was also because the public and Congress began to see environmental values not so much in absolute terms as in terms of the trade-offs we talked about. For example, how much should be sacrificed for costly pollution control devices that jeopardize the economic well-being of companies and end up costing the jobs of workers? Some environmental legislation was so sweeping or so exacting that it was difficult to enforce. This change in attitude permitted the Reagan administration to deemphasize strict environmental regulation. The deemphasis was not achieved by trying to get Congress to repeal major environmental legislation—there was still far too much support for those laws in Congress—but by asking Congress for less money to enforce environmental laws; by ordering EPA to cut back on regulatory rule making; and, as we have seen, by the transfer or replacement of bureaucrats too zealous in enforcing environmental laws.

Ultimately, every energy policy involves environmental questions, and the time has probably passed in which national policy will concentrate on one to the total exclusion of the other. Rather, the question will be, Which one will benefit in relative terms from the trade-offs that must be made? What this implies is a public policy debate that is far more contentious than was the case fifty years ago when supply and price of energy were the only items on the agenda. The American public is also ambivalent about what sacrifices, if any, it wants to make. Public officials note this ambivalence and back off from major policy shifts. The task of devising responsible and workable policies that pay due heed to both needs may well be one of the most crucial challenges facing the institutions of our government.

SUMMARY

The United States relies very heavily on imported oil even though a number of other energy sources are available to us. This is principally because oil alone is a suitable fuel for cars, trucks, and buses.

The energy crises of 1973 and 1979 that interrupted the flow of oil from overseas forced us to find substitutes for oil for those uses where substitution was possible. Since coal is the most plentiful fuel in the United States, a major effort was made to get power plants and factories to burn coal instead of oil. Enrivonmental problems began to develop in the form of acid rain, a by-product of coal burning. Other alternatives to oil had even grimmer environmental dangers associated with them—nuclear power generation in particular. There are less damaging ways to generate electricity such as hydroelectric power, wind power, and tidal and thermal power, but their role is small and diminishing. One promising source of power generation is the use of solar cells, but the cost is not competitive with oil.

American energy policy had always been fragmented because of the nature of the energy field. There were coal policies, oil policies, and natural gas policies. Only when we were faced with energy scarcity was there pressure for an energy policy that embraced all fuels. Presidents Nixon, Ford, and Carter were only partially successful in getting Congress to think in these comprehensive terms.

Most of the energy policies of the federal government before 1981 were of an interventionist nature in which distributive, regulatory, and redistributive types predominated. Some of these may have actually contributed to the severity of our energy crises of the 1970s. Others, such as the mileage standards for cars, seem to have encouraged conservation. With the advent of the Reagan administration in 1981, however, policies shifted toward allowing the laws of supply and demand to determine what we paid for energy products and how much would be available. Although the expiration of price controls on oil did stimulate production and discourage waste, there still seems to be a need for conservation measures and strategic policies such as the Strategic Petroleum Reserve.

Although our energy problems have given rise to some major environmental problems such as acid rain, there are other environmental problems that are not associated with energy production. The toxic waste problem is the most widespread. A lack of commitment to environmental protection was evident in the early years of the Reagan administration, but the abuses of the Superfund for toxic waste cleanup involved outright illegality.

Although no major environmental laws were repealed, the federal government's implementation of existing laws was sluggish and unenthusiastic. Environmental zeal on the part of the public also seemed to cool as people came to see both energy and environmental questions in terms of trade-offs and not absolute values. There has also been a turning back to the fragmented energy politics that preceded the energy crises of the 1970s due to an understandable lack of urgency that came from falling oil prices and plentiful oil.

NOTES

1. Robert Stobaugh and Daniel Yergin, eds., *Energy Future* (New York: Ballantine, 1980), p. 2.
2. "Use of Fossil Fuel Called Threat to World Climate," *The New York Times* (Jan. 15, 1980).
3. Bayard Webster, "Acid Rain: An Increasing Threat," *The New York Times* (Nov. 6, 1979).
4. Edwin McDowell, "After Three Mile Island," *The New York Times*, National Economic Survey (Jan. 6, 1980).
5. William Nordhaus, "Energy Policy: Mostly Sound and Fury," *The New York Times* (Nov. 30, 1980).
6. David Howard Davis, *Energy Politics*, 2nd ed. (New York: St. Martin's, 1978), p. 27.
7. *Panama Refining Co.* v. *Ryan*, 293 U.S. 388 (1935).
8. Davis, p. 59.
9. Gerald D. Nash, *United States Oil Policy, 1890–1964* (Pittsburgh: U. of Pittsburgh, 1968), p. 188.
10. Peter R. Odell, *Oil and World Power* (Baltimore: Penguin, 1974), p. 33.
11. John M. Blair, *The Control of Oil* (New York: Random House, 1978), p. 186.
12. William Tucker, "The Energy Crisis Is Over," *Harper's*, 263: 1578, p. 28.
13. Morris P. Fiorina, *Congress: Keystone of the Washington Establishment* (New Haven: Yale U.P., 1977), p. 73.
14. Editorial Research Reports, *Energy Policy* (Washington: Congressional Quarterly, 1979), p. 4-A.
15. Robert Salisbury and John P. Heinz, "A Theory of Policy Analysis and Some Preliminary Applications," in *Policy Analysis in Political Science*, Ira Sharkansky, ed. (Chicago: Markham, 1970), pp. 39–59.
16. Eric M. Uslaner, "The Congressional War on Energy: The Moral Equivalent of Leadership," paper delivered at the 1980 annual meeting of the Southern Political Science Association, Atlanta, Ga. (Nov. 6–8, 1980), p. 8.
17. Ibid.
18. *National Journal* (May 19, 1979), p. 834.
19. Uslaner, pp. 48–49.
20. William J. Keefe, *Congress and the American People* (Englewood Cliffs, N.J.: Prentice-Hall, 1980), p. 166.
21. Ripley and Franklin, p. 183.
22. Ibid.
23. Stobaugh and Yergin, p. 285.
24. Bruce Ian Oppenheimer, *Oil and the Congressional Process* (Lexington, Mass.: Heath, 1974), p. 91.
25. Ibid., pp. 95–96.
26. Francis E. Rourke, *Bureaucracy, Politics and Public Policy*, 2nd ed. (Boston: Little, Brown, 1976), pp. 28–29.
27. Stephen Gettinger, "The Energy Crisis May Be Over, But Some in Congress Worry the Nation is Still Unprepared," *Congressional Quarterly Weekly Report*, 43 (Jan. 1985), p. 80.
28. Walter A. Rosenbaum, *Energy, Politics, and Public Policy* (Washington: Congressional Quarterly, 1981), pp. 105–106.
29. Mary Etta Cook and Roger H. Davidson, "Deferral Politics: Congressional Decision Making on Environmental Issues in the 1980s," paper presented at the 1984 annual meeting of the American Political Science Association, Washington, D.C. (Aug. 30–Sept. 2, 1984), p. 33.

CHAPTER 16

Economic Policy

The year 1984 got off to a roaring start on the economic front. Democratic presidential candidates who disagreed on many things united in their condemnation of a federal deficit that threatened to exceed $200 billion, and laid the blame on President Reagan. The president's defense of his economic policies was based on a counterattack against the Democrats in Congress for their fondness for domestic spending. Some Democrats argued that it was the president's passion for military spending that had plunged the budget into red ink.

A few brave souls in the political world suggested that if the federal government was spending more than it was taking in, one cure, at least, was to raise taxes. (So sensitive is the matter of raising taxes in an election year that some officials could not bear to mention the word "taxes"—preferring instead the euphemism "revenue enhancers.") The president, especially, was steadfast in his opposition to tax increases. Even within his official family, however, there were words of dissent. Martin Feldstein, Chairperson of the Council of Economic Advisers, said on several public occasions that the deficit was such a serious problem that tax increases could not be ruled out.

Taxes were not the only big economic story of the presidential year. New Year's Day marked the official breakup of the Bell Telephone Company's virtual monopoly on phone service—an event that stemmed from an antitrust suit filed by the Justice Department (a good example of competitive regulatory policy).

The Justice Department, the Federal Trade Commission, and the Senate Judiciary Committee were also taking a hard look at the acquisition by Texaco of Getty Oil—a step that made Texaco the third largest energy company in America. Texaco, among the oil giants, was known to be the company with the slenderest reserves of petroleum and by acquiring Getty was picking up that company's reserves. Because the merger added so much oil to Texaco's reserves without the expense and trouble of exploring for it, some wags commented that the cheapest and easiest way to prospect for oil was on the floor of the New York Stock Exchange.

While all this was happening, Democrats in Congress were advocating the adoption of an **industrial policy.** Such a policy expands the involvement of the federal government in rescuing the nation's ailing factories, while encouraging the growth of high technology companies. It was this kind of governmental intervention that President Reagan was pointing to as the cause of most of our economic ills. Regarding the economic picture, you had little trouble telling the Democrats from the Republicans.

Even the Supreme Court involved itself in a controversy with enormous economic stakes when it ruled on January 17 that people were free to tape movies and other programs on their home video recorders—something that many people had been doing anyway. The movie industry immediately began to lobby Congress to impose a tax on every VCR and videotape sold in this country, with the proceeds going to the movie studios and actors. Members of Congress found themselves facing the uncomfortable possibility of having to levy taxes in an election year or alienate the powerful political action committees (see Chapter 6) of Hollywood and the television industry. This is not the type of situation members of Congress relish but one that the fragmentation of institutional power in some ways propagates.

In the previous chapter we discussed regulation and the involvement of federal regulatory agencies in rate-setting. It must be quite obvious to you by now, that practically everything the federal government does has an economic impact. Even the Supreme Court rulings on abortion, an apparently straightforward social issue, have far-reaching economic implications. These include welfare costs for children who might not have been born except for limitations on abortion, the size of the American work force in the next decade, how many workers will be paying into Social Security in 1998, and even who will man the counters at McDonald's if we run out of teenagers.

The long-awaited and controversial revision of our immigration laws is also entwined with economics. When it appeared, early in 1984, the speaker of the Democratic-controlled House and the Republican president had finally agreed on a bill, but the director of the Office of Management and Budget raised objections because of a provision in the bill that would have granted amnesty to all illegal aliens in the United States. This would have made them eligible for federal welfare programs. For an administration that had argued so strenuously for cuts in domestic social programs in order to reduce the $200 billion deficit, supporting amnesty with its costly implications would surely have been inconsistent.[1]

Even those acts of government that would seem to be purely symbolic become entangled in economics. When the Senate was about to vote on the creation of a national holiday to honor Dr. Martin Luther King, Jr., one of the opponents of the commemoration, Senator Jesse Helms (R-N.C.) argued that the day off for government workers and the closing of businesses would cost the economy between $4 billion and $12 billion. The bill's backers were forced to come up with their own figures and estimated the loss to be only $18 million.[2]

Fiscal and Monetary Policies

Any effort to wall off those aspects of government that are economic from those that are political is not very useful; but to say that economic gain or loss is at the root of every public policy is too simple. What we can say is that certain public policies are more directly economic than others and are acknowledged by virtually everyone to be appropriate exercises of governmental power—these are fiscal policy and monetary policy. **Fiscal policy** refers to the effect that the government's taxing, spending, and budgetary actions have on the economy. **Monetary policy** refers to government's role in the issuance of money and its control of the supply of money in circulation.

Schools of Thought: Keynesians vs. Classical Liberals

The Bureau of Engraving and Printing in Washington, D.C., where government monetary policy is carried out. Here sheets of dollars are counted and packed under a transparent plastic. *(Jean Pierre Laffont/Sygma)*

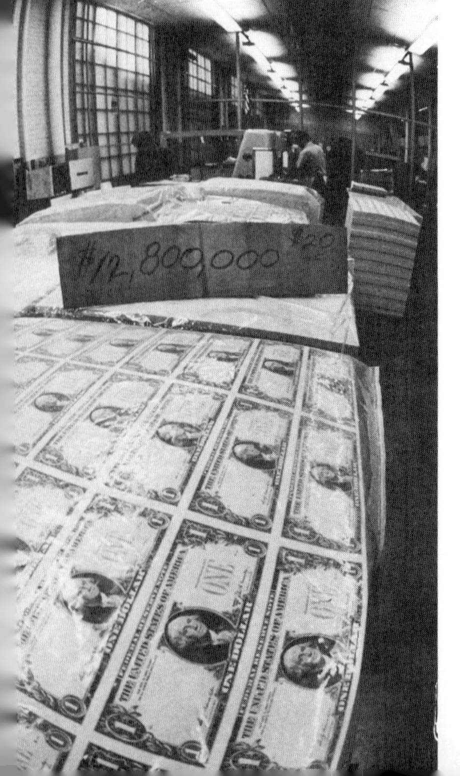

The most consistent antagonists over the proper role of government in fostering the economic well-being of the country for the past fifty years have been the Keynesians and the classical liberals. The **Keynesians,** the followers of the British economist Lord Keynes, favor the use of fiscal measures—taxing and spending—to promote economic growth and stability, and they are not afraid of government intervention in the economy. Franklin Roosevelt's New Deal recovery program was, to a great extent, based on the formulations of Lord Keynes, and it has been the school of economics embraced by most Democrats.

Republicans look to **classical liberals** for their economic advice. Some classical liberals—called **monetarists**—prefer to use the money supply as the fuel for the nation's economic engine. Other classical liberals called **supply-siders** believe in tax cuts to stimulate the economy. In general, all classical liberals prefer that government keep its hands off the economy as much as possible and reject the Keynesians' efforts to involve the government deeply in the workings of the economy. One way to ensure that the role of government is limited is to reduce the tax revenues that pay for government activities. Both monetarists and supply-siders favor low taxes because of the limitation they place on government activism.

Most American economists agree that the basic form of economic organization for the United States is **capitalism**—people freely acquiring or selling property or services in a context in which the **laws of supply and demand** are the principal influence on the transaction. In such an economic context, the market sets the value for things based on how scarce they are. If supplies of something are plentiful, demand will quickly be satisfied and the price will fall accordingly. Although there may be agreement on what American capitalism is, there is less agreement as to whether the simple operation of the laws of supply and demand (the **"market forces"** as they are often called) by themselves can generate enough economic well-being for all Americans.

If, left to its own devices, the interplay of supply and demand produces unhappy events such as **depressions** (when business activity declines so much that masses of people are thrown out of work), whose responsibility, if anyone's, is it to set things right? In particular, what role has government to play in helping the victims of market forces gone awry? If government steps in to help out the losers, does it change the basic nature of the capitalist system or does it improve it by making it more humane and less damaging to individuals? Once having intervened, does government then remain an eternal manipulator of the economic system by attempting to equalize the conditions of competition by siding with one group against another, and ultimately end up by allocating the resources of society?

But government has not just intervened to help losers—in fact, that kind of action is of recent vintage. For years, government has not only helped winners but helped to create winners. If government can give away vast tracts of land to encourage the building of railroads, is that "good" intervention? Is its use of public works projects to employ the jobless "bad" intervention? These questions—or variations on them—are questions that have been asked not only during the twentieth century, for the proper relationship between this society's institutions of government and the economy have been the subject of debate since the very beginning of the republic.

British economist John Maynard Keynes. *(AP/Wide World Photos)*

The Evolution of American Capitalism: Fiscal Policy in the Early Years

In order to understand fiscal policy during the early years of the republic, it is necessary to consider the prevailing attitudes of the time toward private property. The framers of the Constitution did not always share the same view of human nature or even of the proper role of government, but one point on which most of them agreed was that property was a good thing. Property, of course, means anything from land to cash, and they felt that if government did nothing else, it ought to refrain from taking away people's property. The taxes that Parliament imposed on the Americans without their consent was an effort by the British treasury to get its hands on the property of Americans. Americans did not dispute the need for taxes because they regarded them as the price to be paid for the protection of the British government. This protection enabled them to travel, trade, and otherwise conduct business. They did not want freedom from all government—they were not anarchists. They wanted, rather, a government strong enough to protect property, but not so strong as to be able to seize it at its own whim.

Property, from the perspective of the framers, gave people a stake in a political system and an incentive to preserve it. Not out of any lofty or patriotic motives would people strive to maintain the political system but because it could provide the peace and security within which they could pursue their personal goals. They believed that the strivings of all of these

POLITICAL PERSPECTIVE

A GUIDE TO THE LEADING APPROACHES TO THE AMERICAN ECONOMY

The Interventionists (Favor an activist government role in the economy.)

Keynesians. The Keynesians believe in the use primarily of *fiscal* policies to guide the operation of a capitalist economy. Though they emphasize the use of taxes, spending, and budgeting as their principal instruments, they also recognize the importance of credit, interest rates, and other monetary factors when market forces alone are not producing a healthy economy. But they believe that such monetary policies as restricting money and credit cause recessions.

The Free-Market Advocates (Classical liberals favor a limited role in the economy.)

Monetarists. For monetarists the principal involvement of government in the economy should be in its control of the money supply. They believe that the growth of the money supply should be adjusted enough to allow money and credit for economic growth but not enough to cause inflation. They reject the Keynesian notions of fostering prosperity by government spending in excess of revenues (deficits) to stimulate the economy.

Supply-Siders. Supply-side economists believe that tax laws favorable to business expansion will do more for the economy than either government spending (the preferred tool of the Keynesians) or money supply manipulations (the favorite of the monetarists). Corporations freed of heavy taxes will use the money that might have gone into the government coffers to invest in new plants and equipment and hire more workers, whose earnings will both stimulate the economy *and* provide tax revenues. This is classic "trickle-down" economics.

individuals, who asked nothing more from government than an environment safe for the pursuit of self-interest, would give us a fairly good approximation of the common good.

We must remember that, in 1789, there were few vast concentrations of wealth. The people who owned companies usually controlled what those companies did. Owners and employers generally knew each other by name. People with roughly the same endowments pursuing their self-interest was a process that Madison and others saw as appropriate and assumed that government would step in to referee only if rules were being broken. The framers had devised a system of government that would protect not only the rich from the poor but the poor from the rich, as well.

Property, they might also argue, was within the grasp of everyone, so that the most extreme form of political alienation—the kind that comes from being without property—would be unlikely to occur. Thus, Thomas Jefferson, who believed very strongly in a limited national government, could justify the huge expenditure of $15 million for the Louisiana Territory in terms of the number of small farms that could be carved out of this vast area and the millions of future Americans who would have a stake in the system.

THE LIMITED SCOPE OF EARLY GOVERNMENT Generally speaking, however, the economic role played by the federal government for the first eighty or so years was a limited, or at least an indirect one. As a consequence, both state and national governments "had a few debts and hastened to extinguish those promptly; and their current accounts frequently showed a surplus. Public penury reflected the unwillingness of citizens to allocate any significant part of their wealth to communal purposes."[3]

Projects such as road building and canal construction were undertaken, but the role of government in these undertakings was generally restricted to chartering the companies that would then sell the bonds for the project and do the actual building. The bonds were paid off from the tolls that were charged. The dominant policy type was distributive, though it usually did not involve great expenditures of public funds—such as encouraging the building of railroads by giving public lands to the railroad company as right-of-way for the tracks plus additional lands that they could use for other purposes or sell. Since such donations did not involve the expenditure of money raised through taxes, they were popular with the public.

The ability of a government to undertake new activities is related, principally, to two things: the desire on the part of the people for the government to take on projects and their willingness to tax themselves to support those activities of government. Where there is neither demand for government services nor the tax revenues to pay for those services, government tends to be small and inactive. When we discuss Reaganomics, we will see that President Reagan, who favored a limited role for the federal government outside the area of national defense, acted simultaneously in 1981 to get Congress to cut federal spending for nondefense programs by $40 billion, and at the same time, cut taxes by 25 percent.

Thomas Jefferson and, later, Andrew Jackson were mistrustful of government because they feared that it might favor one economic class over another and that the larger it became, the more benefits it could bestow on its favorite elements in the population. It was assumed by both men that those groups favored would be those with the time and the motive for influencing government—the moneyed groups. This attitude was reflected not only in taxing and spending policies of the new republic and early

Monroe and Livingston completing negotiations with Tallyrand for the Louisiana Territory, April 30, 1803. *(Library of Congress)*

nineteenth-century administrations but also in attitudes toward money and banking. If fiscal policy was based on a fear of a federal government taking sides in the economic struggle, large banking institutions seemed to confirm the public's worst fears that distant, impersonal forces sought to control their access to money and credit and their belief that the government should shun cooperation with these institutions or whittle them down to size if they become too powerful.

Banking and Monetary Policy in the Nineteenth Century

"Tight" or "Loose" Money When Andrew Jackson became president in 1829, the United States got the most democratic-minded government it had ever known. Privileges that had survived the Revolution were destroyed, and limitations on the political participation—of white male adults at least—were removed. But in economic policy, a fragmentation of interests resulted.

> The Jacksonians became spokesmen for the view that enterprise functioned best uninhibited by central controls of any sort—in currency, communications, manufacturing, and agriculture. Every assertion of common interest disguised a grab for private advantage; there was no *common wealth,* only an aggregation of private wealths, and therefore government served no transcendent unifying purpose, only the multifarious competing purposes of its individual citizens.[4]

One example of a government-granted privilege was the Bank of the United States—a nongovernmental institution designed to regulate the amount and quality of currency in circulation and to be the place where the federal government's money was placed on deposit. The first such bank—the First Bank of the United States—was chartered in 1791. When its federal charter expired in 1811, it was not replaced. From 1811 until 1816, when a Second Bank of the United States was chartered, the money supply was in the hands of state banks.

To understand the importance of central banks such as the Second Bank of the United States, you should remember that they served as a clearinghouse for bank notes that resembled today's paper money in appearance and were used for the same purpose. What these bank notes told those who used them was that they could be turned in at the bank that issued them for silver or gold coin equal to the amount printed on the face of the bank note. Today, we have a uniform currency, but then one could find in his or her pocket the bank notes of any number of banks. You were not always sure, however, that if you presented the note to the bank for payment in silver or gold, that they had enough coin in their vaults to pay you the face amount of the currency. Central banks were important in that they required those state banks to redeem their bank notes in precious metal and refused to accept those notes that were issued by banks that did not. Furthermore, with the federal government's money on deposit, a central bank would have a good deal to say about the amount and quality of money in circulation.

As we have seen, fiscal policy in the nineteenth century tended to sepa-

Bank of the United States in Philadelphia. From an engraving done in 1800. *(Library of Congress)*

rate those who feared the mischief of a tax-fattened government from those who saw government undertaking useful public projects. Monetary policy, by the same token, divided those who favored a regulatory approach to money and banking by some national or central authority from those who saw tight controls over the quality and quantity of currency in circulation as a technique for keeping money out of hands of small borrowers. These differences over economic policy helped to shape the political parties of the nineteenth century.

The Hard-Money–Soft-Money Controversy Others opposed the rechartering of the Second Bank for the very different—even contradictory reason—that they saw paper money of any kind as a fraud and insisted that the only money in circulation be silver or gold. Paradoxically, the opposition of those who saw the bank as imposing too much control on the money supply (soft-money people) and those who thought that only coin could be acceptable as money (hard-money people) combined to defeat the rechartering of the bank.

This hard-money–soft-money controversy raged throughout the rest of the nineteenth century. After the Civil War the soft-money–hard-money controversy saw those who favored a gold backing for all paper money—the "gold bugs"—arrayed against those who wanted paper currency banked by a mixture of gold and silver ("bimetallists"), silver ("silverites"), or just the full faith and credit of the U.S. government ("greenbackers"). The three groups opposed to a gold standard had one thing in common—they condemned a monetary system in which the supply of money in circulation was tied to the supply of a rare and expensive metal. If you could issue no more currency than there was gold in bank vaults to back it, you were not going to have much money in circulation.

This constriction of the money supply was particularly bothersome to the farmer of the West. Although his crop yields increased with the invention of farm machinery that allowed him to bring more land under cultivation, the supply of money—tied as it was to gold—grew little. Scarce dollars and plentiful wheat were a prescription for low farm prices. Many farmers believed that, except for the gold standard, they would enjoy unlimited prosperity. To be sure, a constricted money supply based on a reliance on gold did cause problems for some people in some places, but it was not the source of all economic woes. There were, by 1900, major discoveries of gold in Alaska and South Africa that helped to loosen up the flow of money. Banking and currency, however, were still largely unregulated by any central institution, and this lack of regulation often plunged the nation into financial depressions or **panics,** as they were known in earlier times.

Monetary and Fiscal Reform in the Twentieth Century

The Need for Monetary Reform

In the period before World War I there was a major effort at monetary reform that was partially a result of the Progressive movement (see Chapter 6) and partially a result of the Panic of 1907. In May 1908, Congress authorized the formation of a National Monetary Commission to inquire into changes that could be made in the monetary system. After extensive investigation of other countries in which central banks—such as the old Bank of the United States or the Bank of England—had been established, the commission recommended the establishment of the Federal Reserve Bank to give elasticity to the currency. Finally, in 1913, Congress passed the **Federal Reserve Act,** which divided power for regulating money and credit between a Federal Reserve Board in Washington (appointed by the president and confirmed by the Senate) and twelve regional federal reserve banks. Figure 16.1 shows the operation of the Federal Reserve system as it functions today.

In setting up the "Fed," as the Federal Reserve Board is now familiarly called, the United States went off the automatic **gold standard.** This meant that money in circulation was not tied rigidly to the supply of gold and that other forms of currency that did not necessarily have gold behind them could circulate. By the end of World War I, the Federal Reserve Board was the most powerful force in determining the quantity of money in circulation in the United States. It also had a profound effect on financial conditions throughout the world as this country's wealth and power increased.

Moving from a situation in which available currency was tied to the quantity of gold to a system in which the supply of currency was determined by bankers and economists did not necessarily ensure that panics would be averted. Indeed, monetarists of today blame the collapse of the American economy in the Great Depression of the 1930s on the Federal Reserve's decision to decrease the amount of money in circulation in order to curb stock market speculation.

The monetarists argue that at the very time when economic jitters were sending people to banks to clear out their accounts and get all their assets into currency, the Federal Reserve Board cut the banks off from that currency—thus creating a **liquidity,** or available money, crisis. Influential

FIGURE 16-1
The Federal Reserve System in Operation
(Reprinted from U.S. News & World Report (Apr. 26, 1984). Copyright 1984, U.S. News & World Report.)

monetarists such as Milton Friedman have made the case that the old automatic gold standard might not have headed off the Depression, but it would probably not have caused the liquidity crisis that made so many banks fail. In short, they argue, we would have been better off without a central bank that had the power to order an ill-advised contraction of currency.[5]

The establishment of the Federal Reserve Board did settle forever the old Jacksonian controversy over the wisdom of a central banking system for the regulation of monetary policy. Its establishment occurred at a time of great expansion of regulatory policies in the Progressive era.

The "Self-Righting" Mechanism

It was more or less accepted in the nineteenth and early twentieth centuries that economies went through normal cycles of boom and bust. It was also assumed, however, that busts—depressions, recessions, and panics—would never last long enough to bring on genuine national hardship because there was a basic **self-righting mechanism** in the economy. The Great Depression challenged this belief. The belief in the self-righting character of the economy was based on the relationship between savings and investment and wages and prices. We have spoken thus far about banks playing a role very unfamiliar to us—that is, issuing currency. But banks also did something that we all identify with the banks of today: they accepted deposits and made loans. In other words, they took in depositors' money, on which they paid interest, and lent out money to borrowers, on which they charged interest.

Ordinary people borrow money from banks to buy houses. We call these mortgage loans. More important for the overall economy, however, is when businesses borrow money. The more demand there is for loans, the higher interest rates the borrowers must pay and the depositors will receive. But if industry is not doing very well and business is in a slump—for whatever reason—the demand for loans decreases, and interest rates become a bargain. As the traditional wisdom has it, this is a green light for industries to come in and borrow the money that has been piling up in savings accounts during the period in which businesses were not expanding.[6]

During the Depression, a store owner accepts chickens and a crate of fresh eggs in return for an overcoat. *(Social Security Administration)*

Looked at in terms of wages and prices, the same self-righting mechanism was seen to operate. If people were unemployed, for example, wages would fall because there would be many people looking for work and willing to work for less just to get a job. Employers having to pay less for any given worker would, it was assumed, be willing to hire more of them. Because these workers would be receiving less money, they would be able to pay less for goods than they had when their wages were higher. This would mean, then, that prices would have to fall because the purchasing power of so many people had been lowered. When it refers to the ability of large numbers of people to buy things, economists use the term **aggregate demand** as a synonym for purchasing power.

In sum, in bad times lots of people are ready to buy goods at low prices and lots of businesses are eager to borrow money at low rates of interest from the savings accounts of those who saved rather than spent when prices were high. The problem in the Great Depression that began in 1929 was that the same people whose savings and purchasing power were required to set the economy right-side up again were the same people who were unemployed. The longer they were out of work, the more their savings were eaten up and their demands for anything but the essentials of life declined precipitously.

But why were the flaws in the conventional economic wisdom exposed only in 1929 and after the economy had indeed succeeded in righting itself after many previous economic busts? With the expansion of the lands in the West, the development of factories, railroads, and the infusion of massive immigration in the nineteenth century, the economy had achieved a kind of momentum that seemed to be almost self-sustaining. By the end of the 1920s, however, immigration had largely stopped, the frontier had been settled, and population growth slackened. With those sources of growth diminished, a good deal of the dynamic force went out of the economy.[7]

Nineteenth-Century Limited Government Concept vs. Twentieth-Century Economic Realities When the economic hardships that began in the fall of 1929 showed no signs of abating, as indicated by lengthening unemployment lines and businesses failing at an unprecedented rate, the limited government concepts of the nineteenth century ran headlong against the economic realities of the twentieth. The belief in limited government was still deeply implanted in many minds, and the idea that the federal government might intervene for the purpose of righting the economy was one that people had difficulty accepting.

Nevertheless, the idea of such intervention was not a novel one in 1929. Alexander Hamilton had argued for a positive role for government in the promotion of the Industrial Revolution in America; and the Whig party through most of the twenty-four years of its life between 1836 and 1860 had argued for a governmental role in what were known as "internal improvements"—highways, canals, and bridges. Jacksonians and Democrats at the time had argued in the Jeffersonian tradition that a government strong enough to promote industry was strong enough to take away the people's liberties. By the early twentieth century, however, thinkers such as Herbert Croly were saying that government intervention to promote economic growth or to aid victims of hard times did not necessarily carry with it any threat to liberty.

One possible instrument of federal involvement in the economy that the Hoover administration was very reluctant to use in the early stages of the Great Depression was welfare activity. Until the very end of his administration, Hoover resisted federal action to alleviate the misery of the depression. Such public assistance that was provided was strictly on a local basis.

The idea of statewide unemployment compensation or of a national system of Social Security would have struck most nineteenth-century Americans as visionary. It is not difficult to figure out why this was so. For one thing, the hard times had never lasted very long. For another, a strong prejudice existed against excessive involvement in the economy by all governments but especially by the federal government. Another reason was the belief that if things did not pick up, one could always move on to another place where conditions might be better. Or it was thought that people could fall back on family resources and savings to tide them over until conditions improved. As we have seen, however, the lengthening Depression caused people to use up the savings that not only served as their financial cushion but were also supposed to provide the pool of money on which industry would draw for expansion and the creation of jobs.

The Revolution in Fiscal Thinking

One result of the Depression was to focus attention more directly on fiscal matters. Until 1932, but even thereafter for a time, fiscal policy for most presidents could be summed up in the ideal of the **balanced budget,** the belief that what the government spends should be no greater than what it takes in in revenues. The idea of running a federal deficit struck most people as imprudent and reckless, despite the fact that the apostle of sound, well-established financial institutions, Alexander Hamilton, had written to Robert Morris in 1781 that "a national debt, if it is not excessive, will be to us a national blessing."

There are sound economic reasons for a government going into debt as there are sound reasons for individuals to do so. Few people today would think of waiting until they had all the cash in hand needed in order to buy a house. Normally, what people do is go into debt with an agreement called a *mortgage* which calls for the buyer to pay off the amount of the mortgage loan over a period of years, plus interest to the lender of the money. If we had to scrape all the money up out of our own savings at the time of purchase, there would be very little real estate activity and home building would come to a virtual halt.

Creating Purchasing Power: "Pump Priming" If you have a situation such as the one that existed in 1932, in which businesses had no incentive to borrow and expand because both the source of their borrowings and the potential buyers of their products had shrunk, the only way to break this vicious cycle would be to create purchasing power. The simplest way to do this is to put money in peoples' hands. In normal times jobs put money in peoples' hands. But if firms are not selling products because their customers are unemployed, they have no need for workers, and you have more jobless people.

What the Roosevelt administration did, instead, to enhance purchasing power was to provide work for the unemployed on public projects—soil and water conservation, forestry, and parks. Using the analogy of a pump that cannot operate because it needs to be primed by the liquid that it is supposed to lift, the federal government initiated **pump-priming** projects.

By priming the pump, more purchasing power would automatically be placed in consumers' hands. They would spend this money on products that would have to be made and sold by people, and this would create employment for the workers who made and sold products and profits for the firms for which they worked. If consumers were buying again, businesses would be inclined to invest money in new plants and equipment to meet this consumer demand. Through "make-work" programs, public works programs, and other devices to get money into the hands of consumers, the federal government broke the vicious cycle of underconsumption, underinvestment, and diminished savings. It also went into debt to do so, despite the promise of candidate Franklin D. Roosevelt in 1932 to balance the budget.

Although private investment and national income did pick up, pump priming did not cure the Depression. High levels of unemployment continued for the rest of the 1930s. One noted economist has argued that the

Although this view of how the economy works should not be taken too seriously, it does contain some insights into the political side of economic policy. *(TOLES, by Tom Toles. Copyright, 1982, Buffalo News. Reprinted with permission of Universal Press Syndicate. All rights reserved.)*

pump was not primed enough and that there should have been even more government spending. He points out that when wartime spending topped $100 billion, unemployment virtually disappeared. He admits, however, that such a level of spending would have been impossible in peacetime.[8]

Changes in Monetary Policy Roosevelt's first step as president was to order a bank holiday that closed all banks in order to stop the depletion of their money. Only those banks with sufficient liquidity were allowed to reopen after the holiday. The powers of the Federal Reserve to issue bank notes was expanded, and many banks that had not been members of the Federal Reserve system were brought into the system. The United States also totally abandoned the gold standard. The automatic gold standard had been scrapped in 1913 in favor of a flexible standard operating in conjunction with the Fed. From now on, however, the only hand on the money and credit tap would be the Fed's. Roosevelt specifically rejected the call for having the federal government take over all the banks, but regulations on what they did with the money of depositors was supervised more closely than ever.

Trade and the Tariff The additional element that makes the Great Depression the watershed of American economy was the revision in thinking about America's role in world trade and in the global economy.

Even more lengthy in its history than the monetary issue, the debate over free trade or protection is one as old as the republic. As a controversy of public policy, it was not really settled until the New Deal when free trade appeared to triumph. But every time we think that an issue of an earlier day has disappeared, it returns to life.

What does it mean to have a tariff or be in favor of free trade? Basically, a **tariff** is a tax on imports. A government imposes one either to raise revenues for the support of the government or to bring the cost of cheaper foreign goods into line with prices charged for locally made products. Sometimes a tariff on imports is so high that it puts imported products totally out of the reach of citizens and thus ensures that they buy only the local item. When the purpose of imposing a tariff is not to raise money but to make imported goods more expensive than equivalent domestic ones, we refer to the practice as **protectionism.** The opposite policy of imposing essentially no barriers to imports, we refer to as **free trade.**

The Democrats with their predominantly agrarian following in the South were fairly consistently a free-trade party; their conviction was that high American tariffs against foreign goods would bring forth retaliation against American agricultural exports. Republicans, and their forebears the Whigs, favored the use of tariffs in those days before a national income tax for the purpose of raising revenues that could be spent on roads, bridges, and canals—all projects that would contribute to the growth of industry and commerce. Later, the tariff protected manufactured goods. As a general rule, then, a Republican administration tended toward protectionism and a Democratic one toward free trade.

If the Depression years marked a major departure in attitudes toward fiscal and monetary policy, views on trade were profoundly affected as well. As the international economic situation began to deteriorate, many countries (the United States foremost among them) moved to seal off their local markets from the contagion of the Depression. In 1930, Congress passed the Smoot-Hawley Tariff that raised import duties well above the previous high rates of 1922. Foreign countries who owed us money could not sell their products in the United States and were forced to repudiate their debts. Worse, other nations retaliated in kind, affecting America's ability to sell abroad. U.S. exports, accordingly, declined from $5.2 billion in 1929 to $1.6 billion in 1933. Those whose jobs were tied to exports joined the ranks of the unemployed.

Taxes and Redistributive Policy Another of the long-term changes ushered in by the New Deal was a change in our attitude toward taxes and how tax laws can be used to make changes in the society we live in. We have not spent much time on taxes thus far because the tax that is most familiar to us, the federal income tax, has only been around since 1913 when the Sixteenth Amendment to the Constitution cleared the way for one.

Money for government expenditures most typically comes from taxes. By the time that Roosevelt hit upon the use of pump priming to restart the economy, a federal income tax had been in place for twenty years. With so many people out of work, however, it would have made little sense to increase income taxes to pay for these emergency projects. Such increases would have had the paradoxical effect of reducing purchasing power because the money that people might have spent on products would be diverted to paying their taxes.

A **tax** is a compulsory payment to the government to be spent for the general good. Indeed, in Article I of the Constitution, Congress is given the power to "lay and collect taxes . . ." but only for the purpose of paying the "debts and provid[ing] for the common defense and general welfare of the United States." The payment of taxes, then, is a very direct recognition on the part of citizens that they have a stake in common undertakings such as defense and the general welfare of the country. Fundamental to the concept of taxation is that no special or individual benefits necessarily result from being a taxpayer. No court would dream of upholding a citizen's claim that he or she should be allowed to escape that portion of city taxes devoted to the support of the police department because he or she has never had any call on such services and lives in the safest part of town. Taxes are, in a very real sense, the price we pay to live in an organized and civilized society. Taxes also play a major role in determining the scope of governmental activity. As we have seen, frugal tax-starved governments can do little ill;

POLITICAL PERSPECTIVE

WHAT WAS SO NEW ABOUT THE NEW DEAL?

You may be asking yourselves just about now, why changes in the economic system that took place almost sixty years ago help us understand economic policy today. The answer is that the basic elements of the economy and the interplay of economic forces are pretty much the same as they were in 1933. What was novel in the New Deal was the idea that the federal government, by its willingness to create purchasing power through its own expenditures, might restart a stalled economy and that the deficits that resulted might not only be tolerable but beneficial.

We associate this approach to economic policy with the name of John Maynard (later Lord) Keynes, and many people assume that the Roosevelt administration's decision to prime the economic pump was based on his theories. In fact, his *General Theory of Employment, Interest, and Money* did not come along until the New Deal was three years old and Keynes had had some opportunity to observe it. As in the case of Adam Smith's observance of the functioning of markets in North America before writing *Wealth of Nations,* the theory followed the practice.

What the New Deal acted on and what Keynes, in a sense, justified, was the notion that there was a public obligation to alleviate human suffering in the absence of the proper functioning of the economy. Private charity and voluntary action, though praiseworthy, were inadequate, given the enormity of the economic collapse. A nationwide calamity required a response by the federal government even at the cost of an unbalanced budget or the involvement of government in spheres of activity where it had never ventured before.

Old habits die hard in the economic realm, however. It cannot be stressed strongly enough that much of the innovation in the 1930s was only vaguely understood by the innovators, and they were often tempted to retreat to tried and true remedies. Roosevelt took the country entirely off the gold standard in 1933 even though its traditional force had been weakened by the creation of the Federal Reserve Board. It was really an old-fashioned soft-money remedy that had little effect on the Depression. In 1937, Roosevelt also decided to redeem his 1932 campaign pledge to balance the federal budget—an act that drove the country right back into Depression in 1938. There it languished until government spending for defense before the outbreak of World War II brought the economy back to health. This has led critics to argue that American leaders have resorted to war in order to fight economic slumps. In reality, any kind of large-scale federal spending, whether civilian or military, would most likely have stimulated the economy.

POLITICAL PERSPECTIVE

THE TAX REVOLUTION OF 1986

United States fiscal policy entered a new era when Congress adopted major tax reform in 1986. Proposals originated by Democratic Senator Bill Bradley and sponsored by President Reagan were enacted with strong bipartisan support, after passing a long row of hurdles in both houses.

The legislation reduces individual tax rates considerably. Six million low-income taxpayers are freed of any income tax costs, most people pay only 15% of their income to the federal government, and nobody pays more than 28%. (In the old law, tax rates went from 14% to 50%.) The law is intended to be "revenue-neutral," producing as much money for the government as came in under the previous system. More tax is paid by business corporations and less by individuals, while many special tax privileges are canceled.

Altogether, there will be a shift to corporations in the tax burden of $120 billion over five years. Individuals will lose such past privileges as paying lower taxes on money made in the stock market and deducting the interest paid to buy a new car from their federal tax bills.

The tax reform law marks a considerable change in the economic philosophy of both political parties. Republicans gave up many special tax breaks for corporations and high-income individuals, which had been defended as part of the "trickle-down" theory. Democrats reduced the "progressive" rate structure of the income tax, making it less significant as a means of redistributing money from the richer to the poorer. Both parties agreed on the principle of relieving the tax burden of the poorest groups.

As important as the legislation was economically, it was also something of a political miracle. Although its general principles had been discussed for five years, few observers expected it to pass when formally proposed by President Reagan in mid-1985. Even after a compromise had been worked out in committee, the bill was defeated on the House floor, and then revived. Senate consideration became mired in vote-swapping to protect particular tax benefits, until a deal was struck to eliminate most of these breaks in exchange for lowering all rates. The comprehensive nature of the tax reform is a notable exception to the usual pattern of fragmentation in policymaking. Why?

they can do little good either. When limited revenues combine with fear of deficits, one has a government that can do little but referee. But taxes do more than simply support the activities of government: depending on how they are set up, they can have a great deal of impact on how income is distributed in a society.

The type of tax best suited to achieve income redistribution is known as a **graduated tax**—one in which those with larger incomes pay a greater percentage of their income in taxes than those who make less. The graduation feature means that as you move up the income scale, a greater percentage of your income will be taken in taxes. These percentages are known as *tax rates,* and they can be adjusted to the point where a fair measure of income equality is achieved. The United States has never pursued such strongly redistributive policies, but a tax system can be an important device for fostering economic equality or for accomplishing quite the opposite: allowing the wealthy to hold onto more of their income in the hope that they will make investments or purchases that will benefit those lower down on the income ladder. The process at work here—sometimes called the **"trickle-down" theory**—maintains that the lightened tax burden on those most likely to invest or spend large amounts of money will do more for poorer people in the way of jobs than will the government programs paid for out of the taxes of the rich.

Post-World War II Economic Issues: Inflation, Deficits, and Oil Shocks

The Second World War for all of the devastation and misery visited on humanity served, once and for all, to pull the American economy out of the Depression. If Roosevelt had been reluctant about federal spending in rescuing the nation from the Depression, he felt no such restraint about spending to win the war. Taxes met part of the cost, but the long-term result was a fiscal deficit that rose from $3 billion in 1940 to a peak of $55 billion in 1943.[9] As we shall see, even this larger amount is but a fraction of our current federal deficit.

In the meantime, however, a new problem arose—that of **inflation.** When there is lots of money in peoples' pockets but an insufficient supply of things to buy, inflation occurs: too many dollars chase too few goods. Enforced savings and rationing during World War II and an industry that produced almost nothing but military goods meant that in 1945 people would spend any amount to get what they wanted.

This advertisement that ran in *Life* magazine in 1943 was typical of the message being given to consumers: wait until the war is over and you'll get everything you dreamed of. Ads like it helped to create an inflationary psychology among people with access to money but not products. *(Courtesy Life Picture Service.)*

Let's Hasten the Day
Let's all fight like demons today for that brave new world of tomorrow—a world that is swiftly and surely rising, like a new planet, from the blood, sweat and tears of all peoples as a shining tribute to Democratic Ideals.
Let the boys come home to a new America in which every one can live not only decently but well; in which, the luxuries of today will be the necessities of tomorrow. Modern Kitchens, for instance.
YPS designers and engineers are already planning new kitchen conveniences and new kitchen beauty for your present home or the new one you are planning.
★
There will be a YPS all-steel kitchen to fit your budget — and it will be worth waiting for!
BUY WAR BONDS and STAMPS TODAY
YPS KITCHENS TOMORROW
YOUNGSTOWN PRESSED STEEL DIVISION
MULLINS MANUFACTURING CORP.
WARREN, OHIO
It's OUR WAR let's fight it NOW!

From VJ Day to Vietnam

As had been the case in previous wars, there was enormous pent-up demand in 1941 to 1945 for goods that the wartime economy could not provide. Prewar Americans had received brief but dazzling glimpses of new products such as televisions, air conditioners, and cars with automatic transmissions. Unable to buy things during the war years, people saved. With victory, moreover, the 7 million service men and women who had served abroad came home to add to the clamor for goods, many of them with accumulated savings and mustering-out pay. But if they were coming home in search of civilian jobs, the defense projects that had employed so many would surely be closing down, and widespread unemployment might result as it had after World War I.

Unemployment turned out not to be the problem that inflation did.

> Sirloin steak went from fifty-five cents to one dollar a pound overnight; butter from eighty cents to a dollar; milk from sixteen cents a quart to twenty . . . The rent situation was even worse, with increases reported of from 15 to 1,000 percent.[10]

Whatever was happening to prices was probably inevitable and would have taken place immediately after any war. But the Truman administration was determined that widespread unemployment never again be a factor in American economic life, so long as the federal government had the ability to use its monetary tools and fiscal levers of taxation and spending. *The Employment Act of 1946,* which pledged a job to anyone who wanted one, stands as a statutory monument to the obligation of the federal government for economic growth and stability by maintaining income and employment. It was also a recognition, however, that during periods of full employment when demand is high and purchasing power strong that fiscal and monetary brakes need to be applied to stem inflation. The Act represented the triumph of the ideas of Lord Keynes: that the federal government had officially committed itself to level off the peaks and valleys of the business cycle.

President Truman signs the *Employment Act of 1946.* (AP/Wide World Photos)

The 1950s and early 1960s were a period of low unemployment and only moderate inflation. The Federal Reserve Board, independent as it was of direct control by the president, was never quite as generous with the money supply during this period as the White House might have wanted, but monetary constriction was nothing like that which had plagued the country in years past. The fragmentation of governmental power in dealing with the economy, a legacy of the era in which the Federal Reserve Board was created, was not a serious problem in a time of low inflation.

It was thirty years from the time that Roosevelt, with only the most imperfect understanding, used the power of government spending to get the nation from the clutches of the Depression to the day in 1962 when President Kennedy made the public statement that he was a Keynesian. The confession represented the acceptance not merely of a set of techniques for dealing with the economy but a new kind of role for the federal government. The federal government had taken off the striped shirt and whistle of the referee and donned the helmet and spikes of a player.

Johnson's "Guns and Butter" Strategy: The 1960s

It was the Vietnam War and the manner in which it was waged by the administrations of Presidents Lyndon B. Johnson and Richard M. Nixon more than any other single factor that unleashed the economic troubles of the late 1960s.

Against the advice of his economic advisors—most of them Keynesians—President Johnson pursued the economically unwise strategy of "guns and butter." What that means is waging a military conflict without economic sacrifice in the form of higher taxes, enforced savings in government bonds, or rationing of consumer goods—the sorts of actions taken during World War II. The government was pumping huge amounts of money into the economy in its effort to fight the war in Vietnam. By 1965, unemployment was at 4 percent of the labor force.

This small percentage of jobless, however, was not randomly distributed throughout the population but heavily concentrated in the ghetto communities of the large cities and in the chronically depressed areas of Appalachia. One can get a sense of the economic dilemma that faced policymakers, then, when one remembers that 1965 was the year of the first major escalation of the war in Vietnam and the first serious outbreaks of violence in the cities of America over the bleak economic prospects of black Americans.

But for all the misery of urban blacks and rural whites and blacks, their areas were referred to as "pockets" of poverty in an economy otherwise experiencing great prosperity. Massive defense spending, the federal money spent on the "war on poverty," and a tax cut that had been first proposed by President Kennedy when the economy needed stimulation all combined to set off a major surge in inflation. By 1969, the **Consumer Price Index,** the standard gauge for measuring inflation, was up by 5.4 percent, compared to an annual inflation increase of only 1 percent in the early 1960s.

If asked how to combat inflation, most economists will tell you that you must reduce *aggregate demand* (see page 552) and cause unemployment. Classical liberals with their belief in limited government have less trouble with this remedy for inflation than Keynesians with their commitment to full employment. There are three standard techniques used by government to reduce aggregate demand: (1) cut public spending, (2) cut private spending, or (3) raise taxes.

Since World War II, a substantial portion of public spending at the federal level, at least, has been on defense. It is always more difficult to cut defense spending than it is to cut spending for civilian services because no one wants to be accused of tampering with the nation's security.

As for cuts in private spending, this can be achieved through a monetary policy that reduces the money available for credit and investment. Interest rates rise because the price of borrowing scarce money is bid up by eager would-be borrowers, as we discussed earlier in the chapter. Taxes, of course, divert money from purchasing goods and services into the Treasury. Raising them is a very direct—and very politically unpopular way—to reduce aggregate demand. Taxes, however, are revenues for government and have the effect of reducing deficits.

Nixon in the Early 1970s: Wage and Price Controls

There is one additional approach to combating inflation, but it involves measures that many people find troubling—**wage and price controls.** John Kenneth Galbraith has argued very persuasively that the three standard approaches to combating inflation in the late 1960s and early 1970s simply did not work. He points out that the Nixon administration, on coming to office in 1969, used standard remedy number two—a tight-money policy to fight inflation and then watched in horror as, over the next two-and-a-half years, prices continued to rise and unemployment along with them. With an election year coming up in 1972, Nixon imposed wage-price controls in the summer of 1971. Not since World War II had there been actual regulation of what sellers could charge and what workers could receive.[11]

Yet, it has been maintained by Galbraith and others that not only did the period of wage and price controls succeed, but they should have been continued. These economists point to the paradox of a policy having proved itself effective being scrapped. Economic writer Leonard Silk called the controls "rigid and ineffective" and noted that inflation actually accelerated after they were removed.[12]

Inflationary Impact of the Energy Crisis: The Ford and Carter Years

The greatest surge in inflation occurred with the 1973 and 1979 disruptions in the flow of oil from the Middle East. The 1973 disruption brought about a fourfold increase in imported oil prices, and the 1979 shock caused the oil prices to double. Virtually everything made with oil, from fertilizer to football helmets, skyrocketed in price, and workers clamored for wage increases to compensate. What Nixon tried to fight with controls, his successor Gerald Ford tried to fight with persuasion and slogans. Ford went on television displaying a "WIN" button. "WIN" stood for "whip inflation now." A few Washington wise guys wore their WIN buttons upside down so that the letters came out "NIM"—"no immediate miracles." The paradoxical combination of high inflation and stagnating economic growth gave a new word to the economists' lexicon—**"stagflation."** Stagflation was the most persistent economic problem for the Carter administration.

The Era of Reaganomics: Supply-Side Economics and Deficit Financing

The economy was one of the two major issues in the election of 1980 that brought Ronald Reagan to the White House. The other—the state of the nation's defenses in the aftermath of the U.S. humiliation in Iran and the Soviet invasion of Afghanistan—had profound economic implications as well, because the promise of candidate Reagan to launch a massive buildup of America's military forces was often made in the same breath with his vow to cut taxes.

President Ford wearing a "WIN" button at a news conference in 1974. *(UPI/Bettmann Newsphotos)*

Supply-Side Economics

President Reagan's **supply-side economics** (see box on page 546) was not merely a gimmick to give the American people a tax cut. When it was combined with his promised defense buildup, it virtually required deep and radical cuts in domestic programs of all kinds. The president's principal targets were those domestic programs he liked the least: the many social programs of the New Deal and the Great Society that stood for an activist federal government.

Reagan's economic program was based on the argument that the best way to restore prosperity was to cut back drastically on federal government spending and to encourage private spending. One way to promote spending by private individuals and corporations is to cut their taxes. The spending will presumably stimulate the economy, create jobs, and generate considerable government revenues from the tax deductions in all those new pay envelopes.

The 1981 tax cuts were targeted in such a way as to direct the greatest savings to corporations and those in the highest income brackets. Its detractors pointed to the tax cut as a cruel use of the "trickle-down" theory; its supporters argued that the greatest cuts were going to those Americans most likely to spend the money from their cut on the goods and services needed to get the economy moving again. Behind the tax cut, however, lay the assumption that a federal government that is cut off from tax revenues

POLITICAL PERSPECTIVE

HOW BIG IS A BILLION?

With concern mounting over a budget deficit of almost $200 billion in 1985, people attempted to grasp the meaning of even a billion. Here are some efforts on the part of people in government to make these astronomical sums understandable.

> If Americans paid off the 1983 deficit at the rate of $1 million a day, the nation would require 535 years to break even for the last fiscal year alone. Put more graphically, if enough dollar bills to cover the 1983 deficit were laid end to end, we would circle the globe 756 times, or cover 39 round trips to the moon.

Source: *Representative Charles E. Grassley, Republican from Iowa.*

We read about the financial problems of Mexico, Brazil and some of the third world countries while we forget that the United States is in debt to the tune of $1.4 trillion. That is one thousand and four hundred billion dollars.

For most of us, these kinds of numbers are beyond comprehension. I do not know if I can put even a billion in perspective, but let me try.

A billion seconds ago, Harry Truman was President of the United States.

A billion minutes ago was just after the time of Christ.

A billion hours ago, many had not yet walked on the face of the earth.

And a billion dollars ago was late yesterday at the U.S. Treasury.

Source: *Donald E. Wilkinson, Governor, Farm Credit Administration.*

for almost everything but national defense will be a federal government unable to involve itself too deeply in social intervention and expensive welfare programs or burden too heavily private industry with regulations and controls on their activities.

If this sounds as if President Reagan simply wanted the federal government to return to the referee role it occupied before 1933, that is true in large measure. What is different, however, is that unlike those Jeffersonians and Jacksonians who feared the power of large government to encroach on the liberty of the people, or even unlike the Republican presidents of the last part of the nineteenth century who opposed using government as a counterweight to the power of industry, the Reagan administration incurred large federal deficits amounting to almost $200 billion. (See Figure 16-2.)

The Politics of the Deficit

Part of the problem in coming to grips with the deficit problem was that there was so little agreement about it and its implications. Keynesians who had once applauded deficits condemned them, while classical liberals who once regarded deficits as conclusive evidence of a bloated federal government defended them.

We have already seen how the inhibition against spending in excess of revenues was overcome in the 1930s, but one might ask how the federal government gets the money it needs when it spends more than it takes in. The answer, briefly, is that it borrows the money by selling Treasury notes

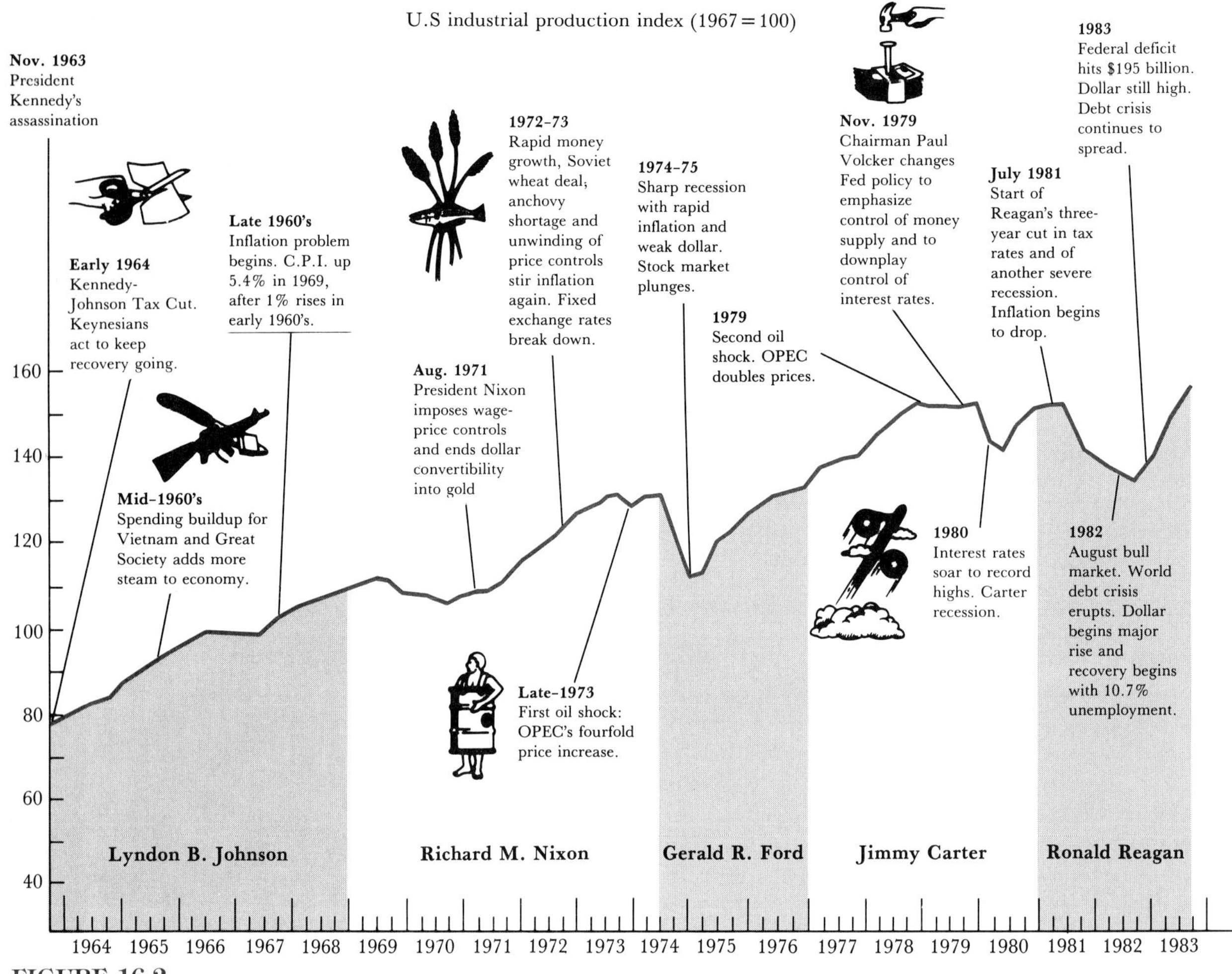
U.S industrial production index (1967 = 100)
Nov. 1963
President Kennedy's assassination
Early 1964
Kennedy-Johnson Tax Cut. Keynesians act to keep recovery going.
Late 1960's
Inflation problem begins. C.P.I. up 5.4% in 1969, after 1% rises in early 1960's.
Mid-1960's
Spending buildup for Vietnam and Great Society adds more steam to economy.
Aug. 1971
President Nixon imposes wage-price controls and ends dollar convertibility into gold
1972-73
Rapid money growth, Soviet wheat deal; anchovy shortage and unwinding of price controls stir inflation again. Fixed exchange rates break down.
Late-1973
First oil shock: OPEC's fourfold price increase.
1974-75
Sharp recession with rapid inflation and weak dollar. Stock market plunges.
1979
Second oil shock. OPEC doubles prices.
Nov. 1979
Chairman Paul Volcker changes Fed policy to emphasize control of money supply and to downplay control of interest rates.
1980
Interest rates soar to record highs. Carter recession.
July 1981
Start of Reagan's three-year cut in tax rates and of another severe recession. Inflation begins to drop.
1982
August bull market. World debt crisis erupts. Dollar begins major rise and recovery begins with 10.7% unemployment.
1983
Federal deficit hits $195 billion. Dollar still high. Debt crisis continues to spread.
160
140
120
100
80
60
40
Lyndon B. Johnson
Richard M. Nixon
Gerald R. Ford
Jimmy Carter
Ronald Reagan
1964 1965 1966 1967 1968 1969 1970 1971 1972 1973 1974 1975 1976 1977 1978 1979 1980 1981 1982 1983

FIGURE 16-2
Two Decades: The American Economic Experience
(Copyright © 1984 by the New York Times Company. Used by permission.)

or bonds to banks or individuals. We call this **deficit financing.** Not only must the principal amount of this borrowing be paid back but so must the interest as well. The money needed to pay off interest and principal comes from taxes. This may not trouble us at the time we do the borrowing, but when the bonds or securities mature—that is, when they are due to be paid off—the taxpayers will have to foot the bill for the face amount of the bond plus interest. As you can see, those people who are in a position to buy a Treasury Bill or a bond benefit when government borrows. Who loses? Generally, it is the taxpayer unless, of course, the taxpayer is also a bondholder. What we have, then, is a transfer of wealth from taxpayers to investors: the first group pays the interest; the second group receives it.

Deficits can also be interpreted in terms of what spending (over and above revenues) by the federal government is used for. Traditionally, political conservatives (see Chapter 6) opposed deficits on principle. But they began to look on them more kindly in the 1980s because so much of the deficit was the result of spending on the military—an activity conservatives approve of. They were also willing to accept the stimulation to the economy that came from military spending. This prompted some observers to ask whether long-time conservative Reagan was a Keynesian.

International Trade Deficits and the Dollar Problem

In an ironic way, the very strengths of the United States became sources of weakness for its economy in the 1980s. The greatest irony of all, perhaps, was that American industry had never suffered from war damage. The Germans and Japanese whose factories were devastated had to rebuild. This forced them to replace obsolete facilities with modern ones. As a result, their factories are more efficient than the U.S. plants, many of which have grown old and are less sophisticated technologically.

Another source of American pride was its well-paid labor force. Especially in the automobile and steel industries, self-satisfied workers in obsolete plants resulted in products of poor quality and high cost. It was not just the workers, however. American management that had once been looked to by the world for its daring and imagination was investing more in fat salaries for executives than in modernizing its plants and equipment. When the energy crises of the 1970s had Americans craving small cars, they found the Toyotas and Hondas not only fuel efficient but well built and inexpensive. In other areas of manufacturing from steel to shoes and from computers to farm equipment, foreign firms are not only surpassing their American counterparts in overseas markets but within the United States as well.

A further irony has compounded America's problem of competitiveness in trade. Because the United States is seen as an island of stability in a world of political turmoil, overseas investors nervous about the safety of their own currencies have stocked up on dollars rather than on pounds or marks, for example. This means that the dollar is "stronger" than other currencies—it takes more foreign currency to buy a dollar.

American tourists overseas love a strong dollar—their money goes farther in terms of how much of the local currency they can get when they exchange their money. For American industry, however, the strong dollar can be a disaster. If foreign factories are more modern and can produce something more efficiently and cheaper, and the strong U.S. dollar makes imported goods priced in foreign currencies less expensive, Americans will buy the imports. If the countries with which we trade also impose barriers to the sale of American-made products in their own markets, a **trade deficit** can result. A trade deficit is the gap between the value of the goods we sell

Political conservatives, who oppose government deficits on principle, have been willing to accept the stimulation of the economy that comes from military spending. *(Sygma)*

The Toyota pier for exports in Nagoya Harbor, Japan *(Jean-Pierre Laffont/ Sygma)*

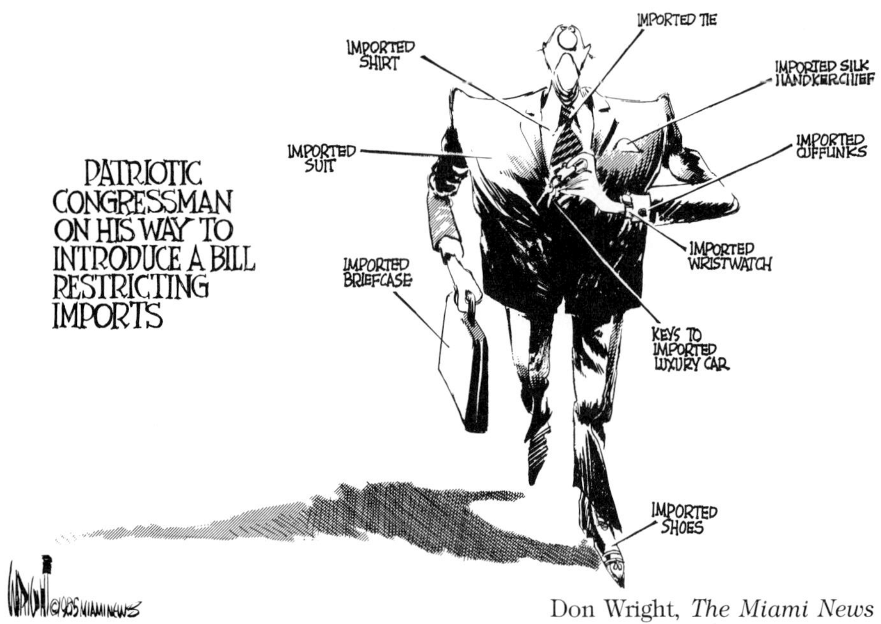

Don Wright, *The Miami News*

abroad and the value of the things we import. The trade deficit that the United States is currently suffering amounts to more than $100 billion.

As awesome as the dollar figures of the trade deficit are, they are really only the symbol of a loss of American competitiveness. What is more real for most people are closed factories, lost jobs, and ruined communities—especially those dependent on the old **smokestack industries** of steel and motor vehicles. But even American **high technology industries,** namely, producing computers, are finding themselves fighting off imports. And American farmers who once fed the world find that the strong dollar is forcing foreign buyers of farm products to get their food from countries whose price tags are not in dollars.

Political leaders have attempted to respond to the problem, but they cannot even agree on the cause. Some point to the deficit, which serves to attract foreign investors eager to lend us money and receive interest in dollars, thus strengthening our currency. Others point to protectionism by foreigners—notably the Japanese—who set up barriers to American-made products. Many strongly protectionist tariffs are outlawed by such international pacts as the **General Agreements on Tariffs and Trade (GATT),** in which the major trading nations are committed not to engage in the kind of protectionism that ruined the world economy in the 1930s and of which Smoot-Hawley was an example.

These **nontariff barriers** get around international trade agreements by imposing quality or safety standards on imports that are not applied to similar domestic-made goods.

Members of Congress—especially those who represent states and districts hard-hit by imports—introduced more than 300 protectionist bills in the mid-1980s. Many of these bills were introduced by Democrats whose party was, as we have seen, strongly committed to free trade. Opposition came from a Republican president whose party has been traditionally protectionist. Some of this turnaround in party positions on protectionism *versus* free trade is associated with the close ties between unions in industries hurt by trade and the Democrats. Other Democrats have favored an industrial policy to make U.S. industries more competitive. The Federal Reserve Board also drove down the value of the dollar in relationship to foreign currencies.

Fragmentation and the Economy

We find that in considering the question of the proper role of the federal government in the economy we must deal again with the question of fragmentation. Those concerned that government will grow too large and intrude on our liberties look upon fragmentation as a major safeguard. Government that is both limited in its scope and fragmented internally represents, for these people whom we have called classical liberals, government that is not likely to threaten our liberty or property. Economist Milton Friedman puts the case this way:

> . . . The scope of government must be limited. Its major function must be to protect our freedom both from the enemies outside our gates and from our fellow-citizens: to preserve law and order, to enforce private contracts, to foster competitive markets. . . .
>
> Government power must be dispersed. If government is to exercise power, better in the county than in the state, better in the state than in Washington. If I do not like what my local community does, be it in sewerage disposal, or zoning, or schools, I can move to another local community, and though few may take this step, the mere possibility acts as a check. If I do not like what my state does, I can move to another. . . .[13]

Friedman acknowledges the case made by those concerned about the institutions of American government lacking the authority to perform their tasks or the power to offset centers of great private power and wealth, but he concludes that individual freedom and the unhampered action of market forces are safer with decentralized and fragmented political authority.

Clearly, centralization of authority and adequacy of authority are not the same things. What is the issue is whether the institutions of American government have adequate authority at any level—local, state, or national—to assert the general good in the face of other sources of power who may not have the general good uppermost in their minds.

What, for example, should be the attitude of government toward the mergers and proposed mergers in the oil and steel industries that we spoke about at the beginning of this chapter? Mergers are not bad in and of themselves if they do not result in a significant decrease in competition within an industry, but they do raise the question of whether power in our society is falling into too few hands or whether the federal government is doing its job as referee.

The difficulties suffered by American industries from foreign competition also raises questions of the appropriate role for government in the economy. If an American industry loses its domestic market to a foreign competitor, what should the response of the federal government be?

Should workers who lose their jobs to foreign competition simply be written off or told to pick up stakes and move on? What effect does that have on families and communities? Should government become involved? Perhaps it should, but how? With protectionist measures that might put quality imports out of the reach of all consumers, or with programs to retrain workers for jobs in stronger industries?

To some extent, the *way* that government chooses to act is a political question. What is a far more basic philosophical question that goes directly to the theme of this book is: whether policies of any kind can be formulated and pursued with consistency by institutions that lack the necessary authority or are subject to fragmentation. This is not a liberal *versus* conservative dispute or one that pits Democrats against Republicans.

When *The New York Times* correspondent James Reston interviewed President Reagan's first director of the Office of Management and Budget, David Stockman, the refrain of this conservative was one that could be echoed by liberals. "I think," Stockman said,

> the executive branch has . . . an excess of machinery and a dispersion of authority. There is a notion that no questions are ever settled. If they appear to be settled one day then they're reopened, revisited, and revised the next day. Because of this excess of machinery, and . . . the lack of a firm chain of command toward the final level of authority, we tend to have the same kind of problem in executive branch policy that you have on Capitol Hill . . . [where] there has to be some semblance of a centralization of power and an orderly process for debating and deciding policy.[14]

Where Things Stand Now

The battle over how to pare down huge federal deficits is not simply a struggle over tactics, it is a contest between those who want to economize by shrinking the size of the federal government to proportions unknown in modern times and those who feel that citizens accustomed to a certain level of government services will consent to be taxed to pay for them. Even those who favor cutting the size of the federal government acknowledge that citizens do expect the kinds of services that the federal government has provided, but they insist that such services can be provided more efficiently by the private sector of the economy. They advocate **privatization**—that is, contracting with private firms to perform services or selling government agencies outright to private individuals. Such a solution was proposed for the Federal Housing Administration (FHA), which grants low-interest mortgages, and for the Bonneville Power Authority, which operates hydroelectric dams in the Northwest.

Without question some government services could be provided more cheaply and efficiently by private firms. The larger question is whether service is all that the federal government is about or whether the principles that guided an activity when performed by government would be the same that influenced a private firm. The public good that comes from providing home mortgages for low-income Americans may more than compensate for inefficiencies in the FHA. The same may or may not be true of a federally owned power company that provides power at much lower cost to some Americans, while others have to pay higher rates for power from a private firm.

When you hear these discussions on television news shows about proposals to cut several billion dollars here or suggestions that taxes may need to be raised, what lies behind that discussion is not necessarily bookkeeping but political philosophy.

What is most properly in the public sphere and what in the private sphere is a question that can never be answered with great precision. Although there seems little doubt that we will ever see an end to private property in this country, it is probably just as unlikely that we will see the federal government revert to the "hands-off" role it held in the years before the New Deal.

SUMMARY

The role played by the federal government in the American economy is a matter of considerable debate among economists even though there is overwhelming agreement on the desirability of capitalism and the market forces of supply and demand. *Keynesians* believe that the federal government ought to intervene by manipulating taxes and federal spending in bad economic times. *Classical liberals* generally oppose such fiscal stimulus. One group called *monetarists* believes that the key to a healthy economy is proper management of the money supply by the Federal Reserve. Another group known as *supply-siders* argues that tax cuts provide people with more money to spend and that stimulates business activity.

Until fifty years ago, the most prevalent view of the federal government's role in the economy was that people ought to be left alone to acquire and dispose of property. Jeffersonians and Jacksonians felt that government involvement in the economy was almost certain to be to the advantage of the wealthier people who had the time and motive for influencing government.

Jacksonian political philosophy was reflected in a monetary policy that favored "loose money"—the easiest possible availability of money—rather than a "tight-money" policy—money in circulation controlled by a central bank. Later in the nineteenth century, these differences in monetary policy took on another guise with those who favored "hard money" backed by gold arrayed against those favoring "soft money" backed by silver, a combination of gold and silver, or paper money known as "greenbacks." In general the Democrats were a soft-money party, whereas the Republicans favored a gold standard. Neither Democrats nor Republicans liked the idea of governmental intervention to alleviate the effects of the recurring "panics" or depressions. Both parties felt that there were normal ups and downs to the economy and that bad times never lasted very long.

The shabby banking practices that brought on the panic of 1907, however, convinced reformers that there was a need to impose some uniformity on the monetary system, and the *Federal Reserve System* was established. The Fed, as it came to be known, did not totally eliminate gold as the backing for U.S. currency, but it did make its effect on the money supply less automatic.

The greatest change in fiscal thinking came about as the result of the inability of the Hoover administration to deal with the Great Depression. Using fiscal measures, most notably federal spending, Franklin D. Roosevelt's New Deal overcame resistance to government intervention in the economy and put money in peoples' hands with "pump-priming" projects. The New Deal also resolved another old controversy that related to free trade versus protectionism by scrapping high tariffs. The free-trade policy worked well for the United States after World War II because many foreign countries with war damage to their factories could not compete with us.

The pent-up purchasing power of Americans who could not get their hands on consumer goods during the World War II years was unleashed when the war was won, and inflation resulted. As soon as consumer demand was satisfied, inflation died down. The unwise economic policies of the Johnson administration of trying to fight the Vietnam War and establish social programs to meet the needs of minority groups without raising taxes or demanding other sacrifices produced another surge of inflation.

The Nixon administration that followed Johnson attempted to stem inflation by controlling wages and prices, but this was abandoned. The inflation picture grew even worse when oil-producing countries raised their prices dramatically in the 1970s. A period of economic stagnation and inflation persisted into the early 1980s, but a combination of moderating energy prices and massive military spending by the Reagan administration, along with a sizable tax cut, ushered in a period of economic growth and lower inflation. Reagan's desire to shrink the size and role of government by cutting it off from taxes produced record deficits and declining American competitiveness, combined with a dollar that was worth too much in relationship to other currencies and, thus, produced a huge foreign trade deficit. This problem raised again the debate over the proper role for the federal government in assisting American industries to deal with foreign competition and the relationship between what is properly public and what is properly private in the economy.

NOTES

1. *The New York Times* (Jan. 19, 1984).
2. Robert Rothman, "Congress Clears King Holiday after Heated Debate," *Congressional Quarterly Weekly Report* (Oct. 4, 1973), p. 2175.
3. Oscar and Mary F. Handlin, *The Wealth of the American People* (New York: McGraw-Hill, 1975), p. 61.
4. Ibid., p. 73.
5. Milton Friedman, *Capitalism and Freedom* (Chicago: U. of Chicago, 1965), p. 48.
6. Robert L. Heilbroner, *The Worldly Philosophers,* 5th ed. (New York: Simon & Schuster, 1980), pp. 263–69.
7. Handlin and Handlin, p. 202.
8. Heilbroner, pp. 273–74.
9. Handlin and Handlin, p. 228.
10. Joseph C. Goulden, *The Best Years* (New York: Atheneum, 1976), p. 104.
11. John Kenneth Galbraith, *Economics and the Public Purpose* (New York: New American Library, 1973), p. 189.
12. Leonard Silk, "Recovering from Shocks," *The New York Times* (Jan. 8, 1984).
13. Friedman, p. 3.
14. James Reston, "Q & A: David A. Stockman, Discussing the Bugs in the Machinery," *The New York Times* (April 12, 1984).

CHAPTER 17

American Foreign Policy

The president of the United States summons the director of Central Intelligence and asks him to provide photographs of a battle raging in Africa. Knowing that the CIA has satellite reconnaissance, the director orders the deputy director to produce the photos the president wants. The deputy assures the CIA director that the pictures will be ready for presentation in three days, when the director is scheduled to meet with the president again. But seven days and two meetings later, the photos are still not available.

Frustrated in efforts to secure the photographs through the highly sophisticated satellite surveillance system, the CIA director charters a plane and pilot to fly over the battlefield and take photographs at a lower altitude. These pictures are not delivered either, however, because the plane crashes.

At about the same time, a U.S. Air Force officer, unaware of the president's and the CIA's needs, flies over the battlefield and takes an excellent set of pictures. Unfortunately, the existence of these unauthorized photos does not become known to the CIA director until months later. The CIA's satellite reconnaissance eventually does come through, but by this time the war is over and the photos show nothing but a jungle clearing.[1]

In times of deep international crisis, there is a strong impulse to rally to the president. Curiously, however, in the more ordinary course of diplomacy when war and peace do not hang in the balance, the person who can unleash apocalyptic forces of nuclear war cannot get a simple order carried out through a bureaucratic chain of command. The president, with the power to wage war even if he cannot formally declare it, finds it impossible in peacetime to get a routine request fulfilled. As Stanley Hoffman has noted,

> The American system of government, despite its recent and formidable concentration of authority around the presidency . . . is a system built on the open clash of arguments and interests between groups with a broad access to

The U.S. government's support of the deposed Shah of Iran during the Carter administration was probably a major provocation in Iran's holding of U.S. hostages in the American embassy in Teheran from November 1979 to January 1981. *(P. Ledru/Sygma)*

the machinery of government. The whole system of checks and balances that give Congress an independence that parliaments in cabinet regimes have lost . . . and the virtual autonomy of so many executive agencies make the problem of concerted action paramount.[2]

In addition to a domestic system that sometimes thwarts the formation and implementation of foreign policy, the international system in which the United States is but a single actor both challenges and constrains this country. Although Iran is by almost any measure a less powerful country than the United States, we suffered the indignity of being cut off from its oil supplies and of having our diplomats held hostage for fifteen months between November 1979 and January 1981. In a way, the United States is like a heavyweight boxer who can land powerful blows on an opponent of the same weight class but is repeatedly kicked in the shins by a multitude of flyweights, both domestic and foreign, who wander through the ring.

In examining the various influences on U.S. foreign policy, we will turn first to those that are external, but inasmuch as our emphasis in this book is on American government and politics, we will then turn to domestic sources of influence on foreign policy and devote more of our attention to them. We will examine the various institutions and groups within this country that shape our foreign policy and finally turn to the process by which foreign policy is made and carried out.

External Influences on U.S Foreign Policy

The United States emerged from World War II as the sole possessor of the greatest destructive force known to humankind—nuclear weapons. Alone among the major powers in the world it had suffered neither invasion nor significant damage from air attacks. Great Britain, though a victorious power, had been exhausted by the war, and its ability to maintain its vast worldwide empire was in question. The Soviet Union had suffered 20 million military and civilian deaths, and much of European Russia was in ruins. Although 300,000 Americans had been killed or wounded in the war, the Americans had suffered only one battle death for every seventy Soviet soldiers killed in action. The industrial base of the United States was not only intact but had grown considerably during the war to the point that by 1945 the United States accounted for half of the gross national product of the entire world.[3]

Bipolarity in the Western World

The end of the war had seen a division of Europe, for all practical purposes, into spheres of American and Soviet influence. Eastern Europe, through which the Red Army had moved as it pushed back the Nazi armies, was occupied by Soviet troops, and in the countries of Poland, Hungary, Czechoslovakia, Rumania, Bulgaria, and the Baltic nations, governments friendly to the Soviet Union were set up. Western Europe and half of Germany, which were liberated by the United States and its traditional allies, Great Britain and France, were organized along more or less democratic lines with competing political parties, free trade unions, and newspapers independent of the governments. In all of the states of Eastern Europe, the local communist parties were either in outright control or were clearly the dominant political forces.

The Truman Doctrine Outside the immediate area of Western Europe, notably in Greece and Turkey, the British had been a major influence before the war. In the aftermath of the war, with Britain nearing economic exhaustion, it found it could no longer maintain a presence in these areas. In February 1947 the British sent a diplomatic message to the United States stating that they lacked the ability to keep these two countries in the Western camp.

President Truman quickly pledged American aid and secured the cooperation of Congress to appropriate the necessary funds. In his message to Congress on the Greek-Turkish aid bill, Truman said, "I believe that it must be the policy of the United States to support free peoples who are resisting attempted subjugation by armed minorities or by outside pressures." This statement, part of a larger expression of intent, came to be known as the **Truman Doctrine,** a policy designed to enable American allies to resist communism. The general way in which it was phrased seemed to leave the door open for the United States to become involved anywhere in the world where noncommunist governments were threatened. In the words of a high State Department official at the time, George Kennan, "[The Truman Doctrine] implied that what we had decided to do in the case of Greece was something we would be prepared to do in the case of any other country, provided only that it was faced with the threat of 'subjugation by armed minorities or by outside pressures.'"[4]

The Truman Doctrine permitting U.S. intervention in postwar Europe was launched in 1947 to combat communism and stabilize Western Europe. *(Reprinted with permission of the Minneapolis Star and Tribune.)*

The Marshall Plan and NATO The economic weakness of the countries of Western Europe, coupled with the fear that strong communist parties in France and Italy might come to power, caused the United States to initiate the **Marshall Plan** in 1948. It provided $5.3 billion for European recovery and included help for Germany. The following year, the **North Atlantic Treaty Organization (NATO)** was established as the first peacetime alliance between the United States and other foreign powers; it tied the United States by treaty to most of the nations of Western Europe and to Canada. In the light of this country's charter membership in the United Nations, as well, the United States was shedding a long tradition of noninvolvement in long-term international commitments.

Some people argue that the United States broke with tradition in 1947 simply out of concern that the Soviet Union would move into the void in Europe left by the defeat of Nazi Germany in 1945. What enabled the United States partially to fill this vacuum was an economy that was not only undamaged by the war but actually strengthened. It was also the only country in the world with nuclear weapons. The challenger—the Soviet Union—claimed an influence in Europe based on a huge land army and a border in common with most of the countries of Eastern Europe. Smaller countries in the world tended to seek the protection of one or the other of these superpowers, creating a "bipolar power distribution." A gain by one superpower was seen by the other as its loss.

The Doctrine of Containment and the Cold War President Harry Truman and his advisers believed that the Soviet Union was bent on extending its power and influence, at the expense of the U.S. and its allies. By this analysis, then, it was necessary to "contain" the Soviet Union.

The **containment doctrine** that became the core of post-World War II U.S. foreign policy committed this country to oppose the efforts of the Soviet Union to expand its influence. By blocking Soviet expansion into new areas, the framers of the containment doctrine believed that Soviet frustration would combined with internal weaknesses in the USSR to produce more moderate behavior there. Another group of people, who have been labeled "revisionists," argue that containment was simply the continuation of a policy of hostility to communist governments that went back to the Bolshevik Revolution of 1917.

Whether American policy after World War II was designed to stem a totalitarian wave from the Soviet Union that was threatening to engulf unwilling victims, or whether it was just one more bit of evidence that the United States could not tolerate countries with opposing philosophies of government, the result was clear: the **Cold War,** a term coined by financial expert Bernard Baruch to describe a bipolar world divided between two hostile camps.

The Third World The period of strict bipolarity was remarkably brief. By the mid-1950s, the war-weakened British and French could no longer hold onto the vast colonial empires that they had assembled in the nineteenth century by conquests in Asia and Africa. Some of these colonies gained their independence by force and others by peaceful means, but few aligned themselves with either the United States or the USSR. They constituted a **Third World,** composed mostly of poor countries that wanted help from both superpowers and chose to avoid domination by either.

This desire to remain nonaligned did not prevent both the United States and the Soviet Union from seeing the weakness of the Third World as a power vacuum and a place to win new adherents. The United States offered economic assistance. The Soviet Union used itself as a model of a backward, agricultural country modernized under communism. It was fear that the countries of the Third World would become like the USSR—antagonistic toward the United States—that accounted for a good deal of American interest in the Third World.

The Korean War and Vietnam When the Soviet Union tested its first nuclear weapon in 1949 and later developed the missiles to carry such weapons, the ground rules of the Cold War began to change. Until this point, American leaders regarded the primary Soviet threat to be an attack on Western Europe, since Soviet planes did not have the range to strike directly at the United States. Now, there was a threat of a possible nuclear attack against the United States itself. This fear was intensified in 1957 when the Soviets launched a space satellite with a long-range missile capable of striking the United States.

Nevertheless, in the first twenty years of the Cold War, the United States committed massive numbers of Americans to combat twice. In neither case did they face Soviet troops directly. In the Korean War (1950–1953), American troops formed a major part of a United Nations force organized to repel an attack from communist North Korea on noncommunist South Korea. Later, American forces were involved for more than ten years in South Vietnam against local communist forces called the Vietcong and regular forces of communist North Vietnam. Both the Soviet Union and China aided the communist forces, but neither sent troops.

From Bipolarity to Bipolycentrism

We should not conclude from the fact that both the USSR and China aided the Vietnamese communists that all was harmony and cohesion in the communist world. A truly bipolar world lasted only about ten years. With the death of the Soviet leader Josef Stalin in 1953, a new leadership in the USSR began to modify his harsh dictatorship. Nikita S. Khrushchev, Stalin's successor, denounced the former leader in 1956 and suggested that "peaceful coexistence" with the United States was possible. He also declared that the Soviet path to socialism was not necessarily the only one. Khrushchev's views antagonized the leader of Communist China, Mao Tse-Tung, who regarded them as a retreat from the traditional communist desire for world revolution. Attempts to patch up the quarrel failed, and the two communist giants drifted apart.

The problem in the Western alliance was France, whose president Charles de Gaulle had come to power in 1958 with a pledge to restore his country's greatness. De Gaulle's image of his country did not fit very well with a NATO alliance in which the United States was clearly the leader. De Gaulle doubted that the Americans would retaliate against the Soviet Union if the Soviets invaded Western Europe, inasmuch as the United States no longer had a monopoly in nuclear weapons. The French reasoned that an American nuclear strike against the USSR in defense of Europe would lead

President Kennedy and Marshall Tito of Yugoslavia. Even though Yugoslavia is a communist country, it has nevertheless achieved a remarkable degree of independence from the Soviet Union. *(ISP/PSI)*

to a counterattack on the United States. De Gaulle believed that the United States would not run this risk. Accordingly, he demanded an independent nuclear strike force for France and went ahead with it despite American opposition. Later, he requested the removal of NATO headquarters from Paris and finally pulled French troops out of the NATO military command.

In some ways the Chinese grievances against the USSR and those of the French against the United States were similar: both were challenging the leadership of superpowers within their own alliances and both succeeded in staking out independent roles. Although both the Soviet Union and the United States continued to be the dominant military powers in the world, they began to lose their ability to command unswerving loyalty within their areas of influence. A communist government took hold in Cuba under Fidel Castro despite U.S. efforts to bring it down, while Yugoslavia, and later Rumania, achieved a remarkable degree of independence within the shadow of the Soviet Union.

The bipolar world was giving way to a **bipolycentric** world.[5] This meant that the two superpowers were still militarily dominant and continued to provide protection to the weaker countries allied with them but that these weaker countries were developing significant relations with members of the opposing alliance. The Soviet Union, accordingly, has developed important economic relations with West Germany (a NATO member) and sells natural gas to this alliance partner of the United States. The West Germans sell manufactured goods to the Soviets. Similarly, the bulk of Poland's output of canned hams goes to the United States for dollars, which communist Poland needs to buy materials from Western suppliers who will not accept Polish *zlotys* in payment.

The Problem of Nuclear Proliferation New centers of power emerged when countries acquired nuclear weapons. China, with her huge population, became, in a sense, another pole of power with the development of nuclear weapons. Yet her economic weakness prevents her from having the same kind of power that the United States and the USSR have. India, Israel, Egypt, and South Africa certainly can threaten their neighbors with nuclear weapons, but the more immediate threat they pose is in creating situations in which the United States and the USSR are tempted to intervene.

The problem of nuclear proliferation, or the spread of atomic weapons beyond the original two nuclear states, causes many people to yearn for the days when only two countries could precipitate a war. These people argue that nuclear weapons in only two hands is simply more stable and predictable than in many. They point out that both the United States and the Soviet Union have been able to pursue their rivalry while keeping the risks of nuclear war to a minimum. The combination of more nations with nuclear weapons and a decreasing ability of the superpowers to control lesser nations leads to a more unstable world situation.[6]

The old practice of forcing the nations of the developing world to choose sides between the great powers has given way to a greater tolerance of regimes that do not declare themselves wholly in favor of our own values. Even the Reagan administration, which moved strongly in the direction of helping states simply because they are friendly to us, considered socialist states such as Zimbabwe in south-central Africa worthy of assistance. In our own hemisphere, however, and in Western Europe, we still have a strong tendency to oppose the establishment of Marxist governments. Outside those areas within our sphere of influence, the trend has been toward greater flexibility.

Detente, a New Strategic Policy Our single most important relationship with any foreign state in recent years has been with the Soviet Union, if for no other reason than that we have the power to destroy each other. For the first twenty-five years after World War II this was not the case. For, although Soviet armies had the ability to overrun Western Europe, the United States was superior in intercontinental warfare. When the Soviets attempted to install medium- and intermediate-range ballistic missiles in Cuba in 1962, however, the United States nearly lost this advantage. The Soviets withdrew the missiles at American insistence because they realized that not doing so would mean having to engage in nuclear war with the United States or fight a conventional war thousands of miles from their nearest base.

"Détente."

This view of détente depicts some surprised American visitors at the May Day Parade in Moscow. It suggests that the value of détente may be to open the door for American culture in the Soviet Union. *(Drawing by Richter; © 1974, The New Yorker Magazine, Inc.)*

The United States, then, dealt with the Soviet Union from a position of strength, but ten years after the Cuban missile crisis that brought the United States and the USSR to the brink of war, the situation had changed. Two things accounted for this change. In combination they produced a period of ***détente,*** or relaxation of tensions, between the United States and the Soviet Union. The first was that the Soviet Union was catching up with the United States in strategic weapons. The second was that limits of containment had apparently been reached for the United States in Vietnam. We were simply war-weary and needed a breathing spell from a quarter-century of acting as the world's police.

The Soviet Union welcomed *détente* but for reasons different from those of the United States. So different were the reasons that one is now inclined to doubt that both countries shared a common definition of what the word meant. For the USSR, it was a recognition that they were now a global power in the same sense that the United States had been. *Détente* also meant increased trade with the United States, especially in high technology items that the Soviets craved. For Henry Kissinger, President Nixon's secretary of state and the architect of *détente,* it meant controlling competition between the superpowers and entering an era of greater cooperation. Kissinger hoped with *détente* to tie the Soviet Union to the United States with a "web of relationships"—trade agreements, cultural exchanges, and technical assistance. In effect, this was a new approach to a traditional American dilemma: how to "contain" the Soviet Union. Containment of the Soviet Union continues to be a keystone of American foreign policy. It has taken a variety of forms but has remained very much a constant element.

"Star Wars": Strategic Policy of the 1980s The *détente* of the Nixon-Kissinger era began to unravel when it appeared that the Soviets wanted superiority and not merely equality in weapons. The traditional superiority of the Soviet Union's ground forces in Europe was augmented by a new generation of medium-range missiles targeted on our allies. The Soviets also increased the number of intercontinental missiles that threaten the United States directly. These developments combined with the invasion of Afghanistan in 1979 made *détente* a dead issue.

The basis of President Reagan's military buildup after 1981 was to recapture military superiority. Huge amounts of money were spent on everything from upgrading military pay to new kinds of missiles to offset the Soviet advantage in medium- and intercontinental-range missiles.

Even more dramatic was Reagan's Strategic Defense Initiative (called **Star Wars** by its detractors). This would be a system of satellites and earth stations using lasers and particle beams to destroy attacking Soviet intercontinental missiles (see Figure 17.1). Although it is by no means certain that such a system is workable, the proposal created a flood of hostile comment from the Soviet Union. Others were also not so sure that "Star Wars" represented an advance. Some Americans thought it dangerous to militarize outer space. Because the system would be useless against the shorter-range Soviet missiles targeted on Western Europe, some Europeans pointed to "Star Wars" as another example of American neglect of NATO's security needs.

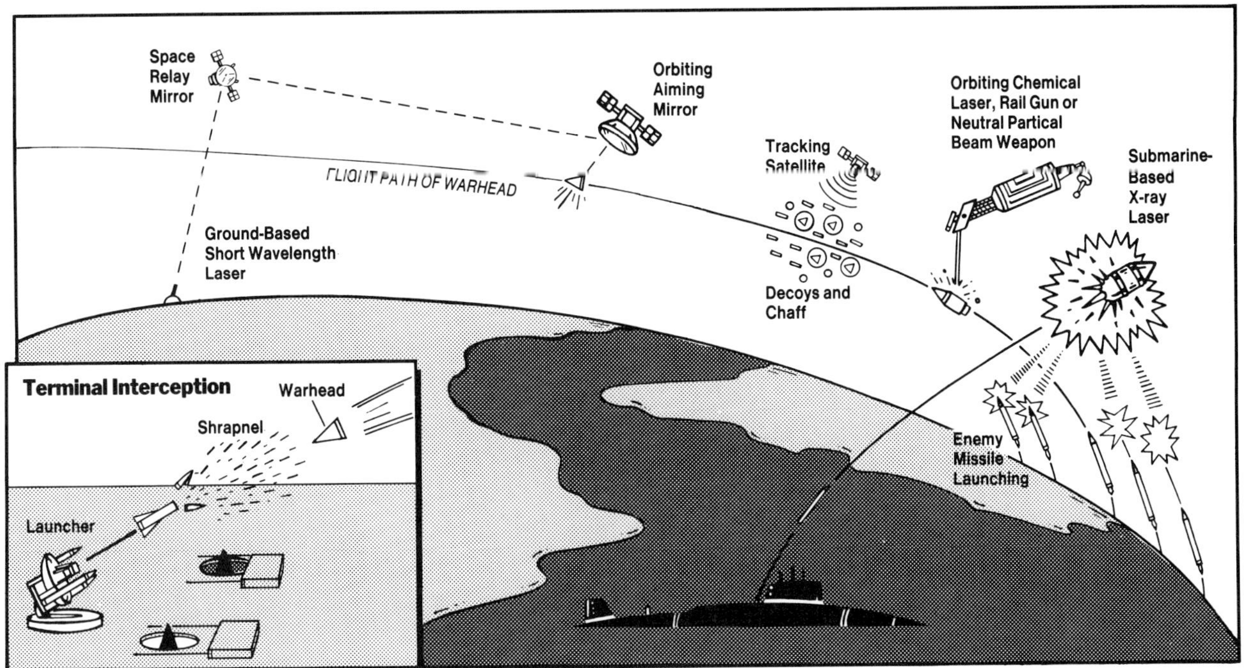

FIGURE 17-1
Proposed "Star Wars" Missile–Defense System
Still in an early stage of research, several possible elements of President Reagan's Strategic Defense Initiative are depicted here. *(Copyright © 1985 by the New York Times Company. Reprinted by permission.)*

THE WAY IT IS NOW In recent years, a clash between Western and Soviet forces in Europe has seemed fairly unlikely. As a result, the focus of American containment policy has shifted. Strategic concerns, of course, continue, and "Star Wars" is part of this ongoing quest for security, but the geographic focus of American policy is now on the Third World.

Despite the relatively smooth flow of oil from the region, American policymakers still look upon the Middle East with great concern. In the early 1980s, however, communist incursions into Latin America have caused even greater concern, especially because it places the Soviets so close to the borders of the United States. On the small Caribbean island of Grenada, American forces ousted a Cuban- and Soviet-backed government in 1983. And after his 1984 reelection, President Reagan tried to convince Congress to aid anticommunist rebels attempting to overthrow the Soviet-backed government of Nicaragua.

Although the tone of the U.S.-Soviet relations and its tactics have sometimes varied since World War II, the goals of both powers have changed very little. The Soviets still believe in the ultimate triumph of world socialism under Soviet guidance. It can be fostered by making the USSR greater in strength than the United States, through support of national liberation movements in the Third World, or even through *détente.* But this, after all, is not so different from the inevitability ascribed to our own objectives by our leaders. As President Reagan told the American Legion convention in 1983, "The American dream lives—not only in the hearts and minds of our countrymen but in the hearts and minds of millions of the world's people . . . "

Although both the United States and the Soviet Union want ultimately to shape the world in their own images, these are necessarily long-term goals.

Wasserman for *The Boston Globe*; © 1985 L.A. Times Syndicate. Reprinted by permission.

Both great powers face more immediate problems that require less grandiose approaches. In the United States, at least, there are influences that shape our foreign policy that may be only casually related to these ultimate objectives. In some cases, they seem to contradict them altogether. Under a Constitution in which power is vested in the people speaking through their elected representatives, in which there is a free and vocal press, and in which policy is filtered through large bureaucracies, achieving some grand design in foreign relations is not simple.

In the rest of the chapter, we will take a close look at the system of government in the United States through which foreign policy is generated and sometimes thwarted in its execution.

Domestic Influences on Foreign Policy

Foreign Policy Agencies of the Executive Branch

Because the Constitution vests in the executive branch of government the primary responsibility for the conduct of American diplomacy, let us first consider the role of the executive branch in the formulation of foreign policy.

The State Department The principal function of the secretary of state is to supervise the formulation of American foreign policy. In this function, of course, the secretary is merely acting as an agent of the president. Some presidents have given their chief diplomats great latitude in conducting foreign policy. Abraham Lincoln would be presented important papers by Secretary Seward, and his only response would be, "Where do I sign my name?" By contrast, President Kennedy wanted very much to be his own secretary of state and chose as the person to head the State Department a man who was unlikely to challenge him. Dean Rusk, according to one observer, seemed to see himself " . . . more as a personal adviser to the President than as representing any particular point of view, even the political. He seemed to view the Secretary not as the maker and advocate of policy, but, at the President's side, as a judge."[7]

Preferring to set foreign policy on his own. John Kennedy found the State Department suffocatingly bureaucratic—a "bowl of jelly." *(UPI)*

John F. Kennedy was the president who expressed most openly his frustration with a State Department whose Washington bureaucracy was 7,000 strong when he took the oath of office; there were more than 6,000 diplomats in foreign posts. The size of the department was a reflection of the activism of post-World War II American foreign policy. There were more countries in which we were represented, a multitude of economic assistance and foreign aid programs administered through the State Department, and a host of cultural and propaganda efforts that were run from the eight-floor structure that covered four square blocks in the Foggy Bottom section of Washington, D.C.

Although the foreign affairs bureaucracy developed quite naturally in response to the growing responsibilities and involvement of the United States in world affairs and, in theory at least, freed the top policymakers from a good deal of routine work, it also demanded more attention. Henry Kissinger described the problem in terms we became familiar with in Chapter 11:

> The purpose of bureaucracy is to devise a standard operating procedure which can cope effectively with most problems. A bureaucracy is efficient if the matters which it handles routinely are, in fact, the most frequent and if its procedures are relevant to their solution. If those criteria are met, the energies of the top leadership are freed to deal creatively with the unexpected occurrence or with the need for innovation. Bureaucracy becomes an obstacle when [what] it defines as routine does not address the most insignificant range of issues or when its prescribed mode of action proves irrelevant to the problem.
>
> When this occurs, the bureaucracy absorbs the energies of top executives in reconciling what is expected with what happens. . . . Serving the machine becomes a more absorbing occupation than defining its purpose.[8]

The Defense Department The State Department in the years after World War II lost its exclusive hold on American diplomacy and was forced to share the formulation of foreign policy with other departments. The most notable rival was the Department of Defense, established in 1947 out of the old Departments of War and Navy. The objective of the National Security Act, which established the department, familiarly known as DOD, was to centralize all of the uniformed services (Army, Navy, and Air Force) under a single Cabinet-level leader.

The reason for the Defense Department's challenge of the State Department for primacy in foreign affairs is not very mysterious. The end of World War II did not bring peace. The onset of the Cold War and the application of the doctrines of containment saw the permanent stationing of U.S. military forces in overseas bases. We contributed substantial forces as part of our commitment to NATO and sent abroad military missions and training groups to build up the military forces of those countries we saw as vulnerable to Soviet invasion or to subversion from internal communist movements.

There were so many U.S. military personnel located in American embassies overseas to advise the ambassador on military matters and to serve as liaison with foreign armed forces that by 1970, Defense Department personnel in U.S. diplomatic missions abroad outnumbered State Department people by 60 percent. The State Department had no control over the military personnel located in U.S. missions since they got their orders from the Defense Department's headquarters at the Pentagon building in Washington.

The Cold War was also fought in the shadows of an era that was characterized neither by total war nor total peace. There was espionage and counterespionage, subversion and countersubversion, on a continuous and permanent basis.

The Central Intelligence Agency The responsibility for waging this new type of conflict after World War II was given in 1947 to the Central Intelligence Agency (CIA). In most important overseas diplomatic posts there was a CIA station chief assisted by case officers who controlled numerous agents. The communications line from the CIA station to CIA headquarters also bypassed the ambassador's line to the State Department.

The USIA The need to deal with communist propaganda called forth our own propaganda agency—The United States Information Agency. This organization operated powerful radio stations such as Radio Free Europe

POLITICAL PERSPECTIVE

INTELLIGENCE COOKED TO ORDER

We would like to think that there is some objective truth or falsity in intelligence. In reality it is often tailored to the group that gathers it, as this example shows.

During the Vietnam War, a dispute developed between the CIA and the army over the size of the communist forces. The Defense Intelligence Agency (DIA), as if to prove that the army was doing its job, said that the number of regular communist troops had fallen to 110,000. A CIA analyst put the number at more like 500,000. At one meeting of CIA and DIA representatives, the military intelligence people were willing to concede that there were 270,000. Amazed at the military's reluctance to admit there were so many more enemy troops in the field, a CIA man asked his army counterpart why this was so. "You know," the officer replied, "our basic problem is that we've been told to keep the numbers under 300,000."

Source: Based on Thomas Powers, *The Man Who Kept the Secrets* (New York: Knopf, 1979), p. 188.

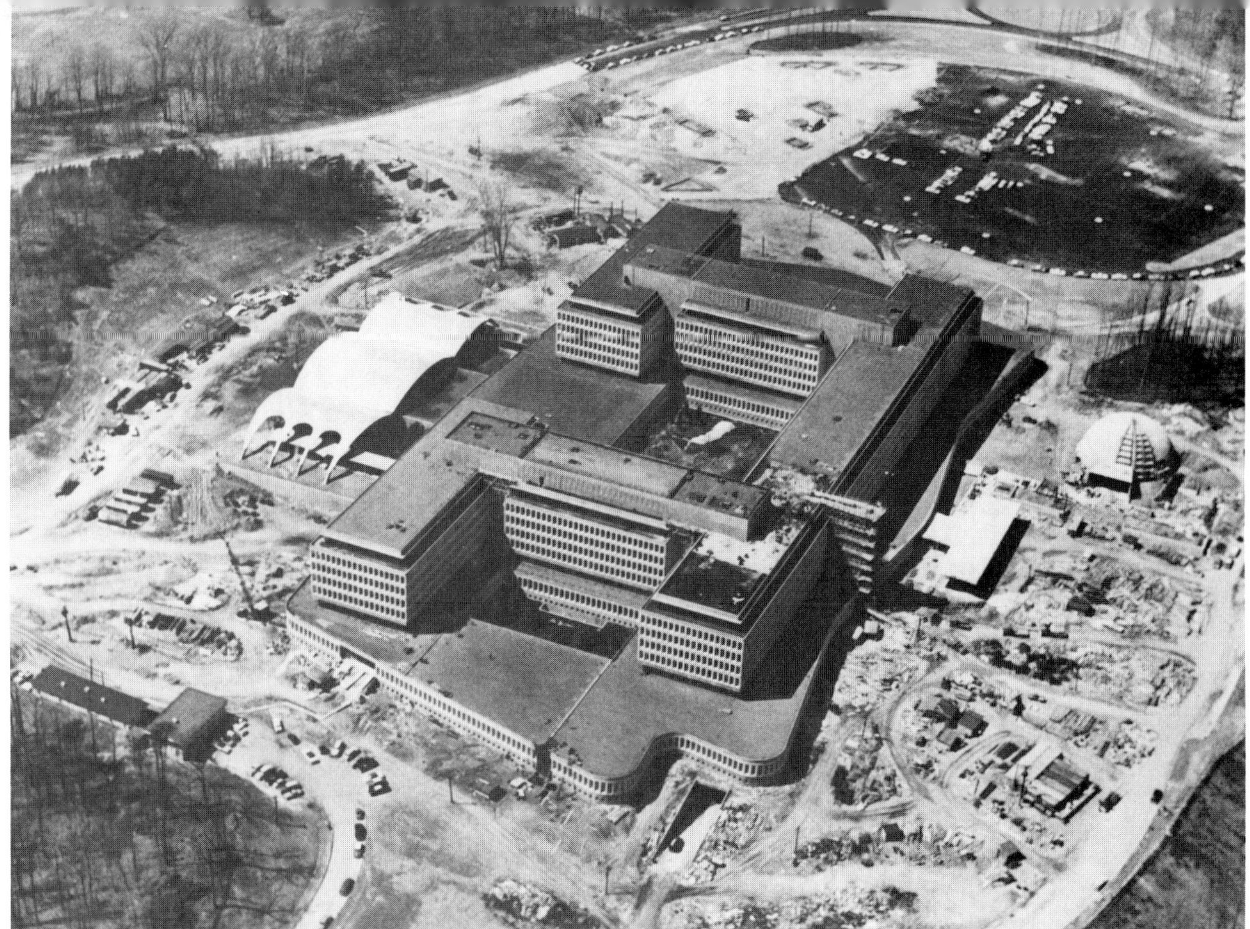

Although the number of employees is classified information, the CIA headquarters in Langley, Virginia, are massive in size. *(UPI)*

and Radio Liberty to broadcast to Eastern Europe and the Soviet Union. Cultural centers and libraries were set up in foreign capitals to inform local citizens about the United States by the overseas operating arm of the USIA over which the ambassador, and hence the State Department, had little day-to-day control.

Fragmentation of Responsibility The encroachments on the State Department's turf did not end there. There were agricultural attachés under the jurisdiction of the U.S. Department of Agriculture, labor attachés under the Labor Department, economic officers under the Treasury, and even the Social Security Administration had representation overseas to look after Americans who had retired abroad. The responsibility for formulating and carrying out American foreign policy, then, was subject to incredible fragmentation and resistance to change.

> Fragmented authority in this complex system tends to make government policies both inflexible and unstable. When delicate diplomacy is needed in the Middle East or in strategic arms talks with the Soviets, false starts and conflicting directives show the difficulty of obtaining agreement within separate American bureaucracies. Change is another casualty of the system, for with responsibilities so divided, it is the path of least resistance to stick with inherited policies and procedures.[9]

(The bureaucratic resistance to change can have chilling effects and spring surprises on even the president, as we can see in the box on page 584.)

POLITICAL PERSPECTIVE

OBSOLETE MISSILES PROVE A NASTY SURPRISE TO PRESIDENT KENNEDY

In October 1962 CIA overflights of Cuba revealed the presence of Soviet missiles in that island nation just off the Florida coast. President Kennedy demanded that the Soviets remove the missiles and was told by Soviet Premier Nikita S. Khrushchev that he would do so if U.S. missiles were removed from the territory of Turkey, a U.S. ally with a border with the Soviet Union.

Khrushchev's proposals for trade came as a surprise to Kennedy, who thought that the Turkish missile sites had been dismantled. He had told the State and Defense departments to remove them on at least three occasions prior to the crisis. For an assortment of reasons, neither State nor Defense had done so. As the president's brother Robert was to write of the incident later,

> The President believed he was President and that, his wishes having been made clear, they would be followed. He therefore dismissed the matter from his mind. Now he learned that the failure to follow up on this matter had permitted the same obsolete Turkish missiles to become hostages of the Soviet Union.
>
> He was angry. He obviously did not wish to order the withdrawal of the missiles from Turkey under threat from the Soviet Union. On the other hand, he did not want to involve the U.S. and mankind in a catastrophic war over missile sites in Turkey that were antiquated and useless.

The Turkish missiles were secretly withdrawn later as part of a deal that had the Soviets remove their missiles from Cuba, but the incident confirmed in Kennedy's mind his earlier description of the State Department as "a bowl of jelly."

Source: Based on Robert F. Kennedy, *Thirteen Days* (New York: Norton, 1969), p. 95.

In *Essence of Decision,*[10] Graham T. Allison makes the point that foreign policy bureaucrats do share an overall appreciation of the national security needs of the country and what constitutes the national interest but differ on how to meet these needs and interests. They tend to see their own organizations as being the instruments best suited to serve these needs and interests, and are inclined to advocate the point of view of the bureaucracy they represent. A foreign policy or the particular way a foreign policy is carried out, then, is the product of negotiations among bureaucracies and bureaucrats. An experienced foreign service officer admits that this is indeed the way things work in the foreign policy bureaucracies but argues that we should not accept this kind of fragmentation as a condition that is unchangeable.[11]

Given the increased scope and complexity of American foreign relations, it was inevitable that a bureaucracy of considerable size should develop. What was neither inevitable nor desirable was the incredible fragmentation of the foreign policy bureaucracy. The Department of State, traditionally the president's right hand in the field of foreign relations, is now just one finger of that hand. The expertise provided the president by this bureaucracy may be more than canceled out by the problems he or she has making it responsive to overall policies and maintaining the morale of the bureaucrats. Henry Kissinger once observed that many of the president's statements in the foreign policy area are directed less toward foreign government than they are to settling internal disputes within the foreign policy bureaucracy in Washington.[12]

The President and the National Security Council

The State Department became eclipsed by other agencies after World War II. Because of the new role of military, intelligence, and propaganda that had never before been a permanent feature of America's dealings with the world, the distinction between the purely political and the purely military became blurred. An important institutional response to this convergence of political and military considerations was the **National Security Council** which was established in 1947.

An early appraisal of the value of the National Security Council came from Harry Truman, who was president at the time the council was established. He wrote that it,

> . . . added a badly needed new facility to the government. This was now the place in the government where military, diplomatic, and resources problems could be studied and continually appraised. This new organization gave us a running balance and a perpetual inventory of where we stood and where we were going on all strategic questions affecting the national security.[13]

One obvious result of the establishment of the council was that the State Department's position would now have to be argued out with the other departments and agencies represented on the council. The current statutory membership of the National Security Council can be seen in Table 17.1. The function of the National Security Council is purely advisory. A "vote" in the NSC, as President Truman pointed out, "is merely a procedural step. It never decides policy. That can be done only with the President's approval to make it an official policy of the United States."[14]

Recent presidents have established a system by which the National Secu-

TABLE 17.1 The Membership of the National Security Council

The National Security Council:
- The president (chairperson)
- The vice-president
- The secretary of state
- The secretary of defense

There are two statutory advisers:
- The director of the CIA
- The chairperson of the Joint Chiefs of Staff

The president can also add to the membership; the following among others have been represented on the NSC:
- The secretary of the Treasury
- The director of the Office of Management and Budget
- The director of the Office of Defense Mobilization
- The attorney general
- The director of the United States Information Agency
- The director of the Agency for International Development

rity Council provides them with a list of options or choices on what policy should be adopted. This enables the president to choose from a small number of policies or, of course, to reject them all.

The National Security Adviser vs. the Secretary of State Despite his praise for the council, Truman used it sparingly. By contrast, his successor, Dwight D. Eisenhower, expanded the body beyond its original purpose by converting it into a kind of supercabinet and gave it responsibilities for seeing that policies were actually carried out. John F. Kennedy pledged to restore the State Department to its formerly preeminent role. He was greatly influenced by a report that stressed that "there can be no satisfactory substitute for a Secretary of State willing and able to exercise his leadership across the full range of national security matters. . . ."[15] The problem was that Dean Rusk was not such a secretary. However, the National Security Council as an institution did not fill the vacuum. Kennedy drew heavily on the services of the staff director of the council, the special assistant to the president for national security affairs. This man, McGeorge Bundy, was used more as a personal adviser, and his staff within the White House was expanded. This expansion of experts in the White House was not only at the expense of the State Department but at the expense of the other statutory members of the National Security Council as well. It set the stage for the growing influence of this single individual with the president, culminating in the appointment of the most powerful national security adviser of all, Henry Kissinger. Nixon gave Kissinger the green light to be his principal adviser in foreign affairs in 1969. This led to the almost total eclipse of the State Department as a source of policy advice to the president.

The desire of presidents to centralize foreign policymaking in the White House is certainly understandable. The president needs to have little to do with State Department bureaucrats who are left to tend to routine tasks. With a national security adviser who is not subject to Senate confirmation, the president can confer with an individual of his or her own choice and have those conversations cloaked in executive privilege. Even if called on to testify, the national security adviser need not divulge any of these conversations.

Nixon and Kissinger (right) with Mao Tse-tung and Chou En-lai (left). In 1969, Richard Nixon gave Henry Kissinger the green light to be his principal advisor on foreign affairs. *(UPI/Bettmann Newsphotos)*

Shultz's mixed record It is clear that there is now more to the formulation of foreign policy than simply political and military affairs. Although these two elements are still of primary importance, a panel of the National Academy of Public Administration concluded its report on the National Security Council by saying,

> We think it would be productive to place them within a larger frame of reference. Just as our society has become increasingly fragmented, so has the world. American influence has diminished, and we must now be partners as much as leaders and adversaries in world affairs. Economic, social, and cultural matters are assuming new importance on the international scene and must now be given attention equal to their importance.[16]

In terms of the relationship between the National Security Council and the Department of State, one of the most conspicuous achievements of George P. Shultz as secretary of state was his ability to make his office the preeminent instrument for the formulation of foreign policy. Part of his success was his ability to make an ally of National Security Adviser Robert C. McFarlane. One observer noted:

> A secretary of state–national security adviser alliance has been a rarity since the days when Kissinger held both jobs for 26 months in 1973–75. Now Shultz and McFarlane agree, "about 85 per cent of the time" . . . which contributes to Shultz's strength.[17]

Relations between the Secretary and the NSC turned bitter in November, 1986 over charges that Council staff were used by the President to arrange arms shipments to Iran despite a policy barring such shipments to nations supporting terrorism. Shultz claimed that the NSC had not kept him fully informed on the deal. The president defended the deal in terms of the strategic importance of Iran and as a way to free some U.S. hostages from Iranian-backed terrorists in Lebanon, but Shultz's effectiveness was damaged as was American credibility.

The Foreign Policy Role of Congress

One of the best descriptions of the relationship of Congress to the presidency in the area of foreign policy was provided by Representative Lee Hamilton of Indiana, a senior member of the House Foreign Affairs Committee:

> I think that the president is the chief policy maker. Congress reacts to the president's policies. Only on rare occasions does Congress initiate policy. We modify, we amend, we operate more on the margins. But I think we have an obligation, when we think the president is on the wrong course, to tell him where his policy has failed and how to correct it.[18]

Congress's Influence on the President Congress has several ways to influence the president. The Senate, whose foreign relations powers are greater than those of the House, can refuse to ratify a treaty or fail to confirm an ambassadorial or State Department nominee. The ultimate for-

POLITICAL PERSPECTIVE

CONGRESS'S RATIFICATION AND LEGISLATIVE POWERS BLOCK PRESIDENTS' FOREIGN POLICY POWERS

Because president Wilson failed to work cooperatively with Congress on the World War I peace terms, the Senate refused to ratify the Versailles Treaty and U.S. membership in the League of Nations.

Because he persisted in an undeclared war that had claimed 55,000 American lives, President Nixon was presented with the War Powers Resolution of 1973, which was passed over his veto. It set new limits on the ability of presidents to commit U.S. troops without congressional approval.

Because he attempted to send military aid to one of the factions in the three-sided Angolan Civil War of 1975, President Ford's hands were tied in that conflict by the passage of the Clark Amendment forbidding such aid.

Sometimes Congress does not even have to act formally when it draws a line in front of a president and tells him he may not cross it. Jimmy Carter knew that he did not have a chance of getting the SALT II arms limitation treaty ratified by the Senate in 1979, so he quietly withdrew it rather than risk certain defeat in a Senate hostile to the pact that Carter had made with the Soviet Union.

eign policy power enjoyed by Congress is that of declaring war. The **power of the purse**—the Constitutional power given to Congress to provide money for the operation of the federal government—can be used to good effect by both houses to deny a president resources he or she needs to carry a foreign policy into execution. On May 10, 1973, the House denied to President Nixon funds for the bombing of Cambodia. What was unusual about this vote was that American forces were fighting in Southeast Asia at the time. So unpopular had the war become that even Nixon's argument that Congress was denying our military forces the wherewithal to do their job made little impression, and the ban on money to bomb Cambodia passed by twenty-nine votes.

Less formal but no less persuasive are congressional hearings and investigations of aspects of foreign policy. Because of its preeminent congressional role in foreign policy, Senate hearings and investigations of the executive branch's conduct of foreign policy have been more significant than House investigations. Some of these investigations and hearings have been both important and useful. Among them were those held by the combined memberships of the Foreign Relations and Armed Services Committees into the dismissal of General Douglas MacArthur by President Harry Truman in 1951. These reaffirmed a president's right to dismiss a high-ranking military commander, even an immensely popular one. In more recent times, Senator Frank Church headed a committee that exposed numerous abuses by the Central Intelligence Agency.

Sometimes a committee of Congress can serve as the means for giving legitimacy to opponents of a president's policies. When Senator William Fulbright's Senate Foreign Relations Committee began, in 1968, to be dominated by opponents of the Vietnam War, it gave the antiwar movement a powerful ally within the government.

Individual members of Congress can also influence foreign policy. Senator Kenneth Keating of New York raised the possibility that there were Soviet missiles in Cuba well before the Kennedy administration had the hard evidence that they were there. Senator Barry Goldwater went into court to attempt to block the Carter administration from establishing full diplomatic relations with the government of mainland China at the expense of the rival Chinese government on Taiwan.

Limitations on Congress's Influence Inevitably, though, Congress loses out to the president so far as the conception and initiation of foreign policy are concerned. As we observed earlier, Congress simply does not have access to the volume and quality of information that is available to the president, and presidents can make it very difficult for Congress to get its hands on information the White House does not want it to have.

Another disadvantage the Congress suffers from in its attempts to shape foreign policy is the very obvious fragmentation of this policy area among large numbers of Congressional committees. For example, seventeen of twenty-two House committees have some jurisdiction over foreign policy. Given the varying compositions of the committees, the view of chairpersons and of the staffs, Congress does not often speak with a single voice, and power to influence policy is dispersed.

Often, when frustrated with its inability to influence the overall policy of a president, Congress resorts to "micromanagement"—it adds amendments to major pieces of foreign policy legislation. Examples are congressional amendments forbidding foreign aid money to be used to pay for abortions in poor countries, or making human rights activities a condition for a country's receiving aid. Congress can thus satisfy itself that it is keeping its hand in the formulation of foreign policy.

One of the reasons that conflicts emerge between the president and Congress is that when the president wants to frame a comprehensive foreign policy, members of Congress are more attuned to the voices of interest groups with narrower and more varied objectives. In the next section, we will see how various kinds of interest groups affect foreign policy through Congress, the executive branch (such as the departments of State and Treasury), and the media.

The Influence of Interest Groups

Although public opinion, in the most general sense, has only a limited impact on American foreign policy, interest groups drawn from the public can be influential. Their influence, however, is less on broad foreign policy than it is on very specific issues or on U.S. relations with individual foreign countries.

There are, in general, four types of interest groups that seek to influence U.S. foreign policy: ethnic and religious groups; defense and military groups; commercial groups and labor unions; and ideological groups. With the exception of the ideological ones, groups interested in foreign policy are concerned with one small part of the total foreign relations of this country.

Ethnic Groups In a society such as ours, composed of immigrants from scores of countries, strong ethnic attachments mean that many Americans favor the cause of their ancestral homelands. Greek-American organizations want Congress to deny arms to our NATO ally, Turkey, because of

LEGISLATIVE ALERT

"THE BRITISH ARE COMING"
"THE BRITISH ARE COMING"

®

FOR CAUCUS MEMBERS ONLY

Letterhead and envelope of the Irish National Caucus. Ethnic organizations, such as this non-violent group, lobby Congress energetically for their causes. In 1985, Caucus members were urged to pressure the Senate to turn down a proposed treaty of extradition between the U.S. and Britain that would allow the British to reclaim suspected terrorists from Northern Ireland who had taken refuge in the United States. *(Reprinted by permission.)*

historic injustices done to the Greeks by the Turks. Armenian-Americans dislike the Turks for similar reasons. For a president who wants to maintain the integrity of NATO but who still wants the votes from those two ethnic communities, the conflicts are great. For members of Congress, the pressures can be even more intense because in a single state or congressional district a nationality group can tip the balance in an election.

Many Irish-American groups protest the actions in Northern Ireland of our staunchest ally, Great Britain. Black Americans call for us to participate in sanctions against South Africa, even though that country supplies us with strategic minerals. Polish-Americans used their influence to get favored trade status for Poland, even though it is a communist country and a member of the Warsaw Pact. Yet with all this evidence of activity, there is little to suggest that ethnic, national, and religious groups have the ability to influence U.S. foreign policy outside a very narrow sphere.

Often one interest group's efforts will cancel out another's. When, for example, Senator Carl Levin (D-Mich.) introduced a resolution critical of Turkey in response to some of his Armenian-American constituents, the State Department lobbied vigorously against it, fearing that it would offend an ally. The lobbying was effective in delaying action on the resolution so that Congress adjourned without taking a vote. Even the interest groups that lobby on behalf of Israel, regarded as far and away the most effective, may not be of a single mind on policies affecting the Jewish state. Moreover, when presidents commit themselves strongly to a policy that an ethnic interest group opposes—such as the role of AWACS reconnaissance aircraft to Saudi Arabia that pro-Israel groups tried to block—they can usually win out.

It is not that easy for ethnic lobbies to capture even a segment of U.S. foreign policy. As one State Department official was quoted as saying, "We have managed to preserve relations with the Arab states when there are damned few Arabs in the United States."[19]

Defense and Military Groups It is a standard ritual of American politics for a president or presidential candidate to wear the distinctive blue overseas cap of the American Legion or the Veterans of Foreign Wars when addressing the conventions of those groups and to vow to build defenses second to none. Even George McGovern, who ran a peace campaign in 1972, did it.

Although very nationalistic and defense-minded, veterans' groups are by no means united on every aspect of foreign policy. Generation gaps exist between younger ex-servicemen and older, generally more conservative veterans. Nevertheless, despite their united opposition to the Panama Canal Treaty, it was ratified. The American Legion even gave qualified support to the first Strategic Arms Limitation Treaty and to the improvement of U.S. relations with the communist government of China. But foreign policy is not as high on the agenda of veterans' groups as are such things as pensions and benefits for former service personnel.

More central to the defense question in foreign policy is the role of what President Eisenhower referred to as **the military-industrial complex.** By this, Eisenhower meant the multibillion dollar defense industry that prospers financially when the nation increases its armaments to meet foreign threats. Can we then move from the premise that defense contractors have a vested financial interest in international tensions to the conclusion that they contribute to those tensions for self-serving reasons? There is certainly no respectable evidence to suggest this.

Members of Congress, moreover, can be very discriminating in what military supplies they want to buy. They may increase spending for cruise missiles and turn down the MX missile; they may willingly vote funds for Navy frigates but refuse to fund a new manned bomber. They may be more impressed by news stories showing poorly paid U.S. service personnel in Germany buying groceries with food stamps than by arguments from generals that military pay must be increased. There are, of course, voices on the other side—peace groups, church groups, environmental groups, and other citizens lobbies—that will speak out against greater defense spending. Such groups were quite successful in 1969 in restricting the deployment of the antiballistic missile (ABM) to only a few sites.

CORPORATIONS AND LABOR UNIONS Labor and management, who often find themselves on opposite sides of domestic issues, can often be found as allies on foreign policy questions. The American automobile industry and the United Auto Workers joined in efforts to limit the importation of Japanese cars, and the steel industry and the United Steel Workers Union joined forces on reducing the amount of foreign steel imported to the United States. Again, as in the case of the other types of interest groups, the impact of labor and business groups tends to be somewhat narrow and their successes not impressive.

More imposing has been the record of multinational corporations. The International Telephone and Telegraph Company (ITT) offered the CIA $1 million in 1970 to support the opponent of the Marxist candidate for president of Chile, Salvador Allende. The money was rejected, but the CIA did assist ITT in providing names of Chileans who could channel funds to Allende's opponent. This course of action had been specifically rejected by the State Department and the U.S. Ambassador in Chile.

Most cooperation between government and large multinationals does not, however, involve the overthrow of unfriendly governments. The United States has always seen the expansion of American business overseas as a useful way to spread American influence. American businesspeople are a useful source of information on foreign countries, and U.S. executives abroad often have closer relations with foreign heads of state than do our ambassadors.

IDEOLOGICAL GROUPS Groups of citizens motivated by some set of philosophical views have also attempted to shape American foreign policy with their support of or opposition to a range of issues. Peace groups such as The National Committee for a Sane Nuclear Policy (SANE) lobbied hard for President Carter's SALT treaties and a nuclear freeze. Conservative groups such as the American Security Council were arrayed on the other side. The American Conservative Union spent more than $1 million on a massive direct-mail campaign to defeat the Panama Canal Treaty when it was up for ratification in the Senate in 1978.

There was much activity among groups of this kind prior to American entry into World War II. Favoring American help for the British and Russians against the Nazis was The Committee to Defend America by Aiding the Allies, headed by Kansas editor William Allen White. On the side of keeping the United States out of the war was The America First Committee, one of whose organizers was Charles A. Lindbergh, the first man to fly the Atlantic alone. These groups tended to cancel each other out, however, and it was the pressure of events that resolved the question of American involvement.

The tendency of ideological groups, ethnic groups, patriotic groups, and business groups and unions to cancel each other out as shapers of foreign policy, except in very restricted areas of policy, is as true today as it was before World War II. This fragmentation clearly operates to the advantage of the president, who can often manipulate these groups or work around them and their congressional allies. The result contributes to his primacy in foreign policies.

Public Opinion and Foreign Policy

Theodore Sorensen, an aide to the late President Kennedy, wrote in 1963 that

> In domestic affairs, a presidential decision is usually the beginning of a public debate. In foreign affairs, the issues are frequently so complex, the facts to obscure, and the period for decision so short, that the American people have from the beginning—even more so in this century—delegated to the President more discretion in this vital area and they are usually willing to support any reasonable decision he makes.[20]

The opinions of the public at large are rarely expressed very strongly on particular matters of policy, even those of considerable importance. Few Americans understood, much less felt prompted to speak out on, the SALT arms limitation treaties with the USSR. A president might look to the public for guidance on, let us say, the role of NATO forces outside Western Europe and be greeted with a collective shrug of incomprehension that tells him, "Mr. President, we elected you to find solutions to those problems." Nevertheless, "public opinion shapes the context within which policymakers work. There is wide latitude for discretion in policymaking because in a representative democracy, the public mostly judges from results rather than insists on specific policies and actions."[21]

This means that the president has considerable room to maneuver when it comes to foreign policy. The president may even, within limits, defy or finesse the public. No president in modern times picked his way so adroitly along the limits of public opinion as did Franklin D. Roosevelt in years immediately before World War II. Roosevelt knew that ultimately the United States would have to enter the war on the side of Great Britain as it had done in World War I, but the mood of the public in 1940 was not ready for such a step. Besides, Congress had passed the Neutrality Act in 1935 that severely limited any military help the United States could give the British—even though, in the fall of 1940, they were facing almost certain invasion by the Nazis. Roosevelt was also facing an election in November of 1940, the first time an American president had sought a third term in office. He was afraid of getting too far ahead of public opinion, but by 1941 public opinion was swinging over to his position. Eventually, events convinced the public to support stronger measures.

Presidents, of course, are not merely passive instruments in the hands of public opinion. They attempt to guide it and mold it, to prepare the public to accept changes and to justify those changes after they occur. The public is usually generous in its support of presidents in the pursuit of foreign policy; there is even a forgiving quality to public opinion that is reflected in increased support for presidents after disastrous foreign adventures, such as the Bay of Pigs invasion and the failed attempt to rescue the American hostages from Iran. When the president and public do part company, however, over foreign policy or attempts to lead the public where they do not wish to go, he or she proceeds in that direction only at his or her own peril. If the president persists in this and is unable to persuade the people that success is likely, his or her downfall is assured.

The Mass Media and Foreign Policy

In examining the role of the media—newspapers, magazines, and television—on the formulation and conduct of American foreign policy, we really have to examine it from two perspectives: its effects on the public, and its effects on the policymakers. In the case of the public, a further distinction may be made between the mass public—the so-called "person in the street"—and what has been called the "elite," or the **attentive public.** This latter group, because of its affluence or education, pays a good deal more attention to developments overseas and even tends to seek out alternative interpretations from a variety of news sources and commentaries.

In first considering the influence of the media on the mass public's view of foreign policy, it is important to recognize that Americans have unsurpassed access to information. Virtually no person in this country is without a radio or TV, and every major community is served by a daily paper. Americans do watch news programs on TV and some are incredibly popular. The information, then, is at hand. So far as foreign news is concerned, however, the public tends to ignore it.

In screening out foreign policy news, the public is helped by the media's own preference for local news. Aside from such obvious exceptions among newspapers as *The New York Times* and *The Washington Post* and perhaps a half-dozen other major city daily papers, most dailies do not even have overseas correspondents. They rely on the wire services and the syndication services of the big New York, Washington, and Los Angeles papers and are free to run such of those stories as they choose. Studies show that foreign news accounts for only between 5 percent and 8 percent of total news.[22]

The Press as Agenda Setter Where the media does seem to be influential in shaping mass attitudes is in the role of "agenda setter"—that is, the media does not tell people what to think but what to think about. The mass media, and television most specifically, can arrest the attention of the public with dramatic news stories from Afghanistan or Nicaragua and probably convince people that something very important is going on in those places. But it usually does not give them any sense of what the U.S. government ought to be doing or even, necessarily, what the issues are.

When events abroad are so dramatic or the issues are so clear-cut—as, for example, in the cases of mass starvation in Ethiopia or the denial of political rights to blacks under the *apartheid* system in South Africa—media coverage can mobilize masses of people whose indignation may well change the policies of government. Press coverage of the Vietnam War contributed a great deal to public opposition to American involvement in that conflict. Although the press, except in such stirring instances as Vietnam, may not be able to mobilize public opinion in a particular direction and have the public, in turn, influence the policymakers, it may do so indirectly. There is a "two-step flow" process, which operates something like this: A minister in Wisconsin picks up a copy of *The New York Times* (a paper few members of his congregation read) and come across an editorial praising Israel for its help to the Christian faction in the Lebanese Civil War. He underlines a few choice quotations and includes them in his Sunday sermon. Since the minister is a respected figure, a member of the "attentive public," people take heed of what he says.

A television crew films U.S.-trained troops in El Salvador, for up-to-the-minute news coverage. *(UPI)*

POLITICAL PERSPECTIVE

CAN THE MEDIA INFLUENCE PUBLIC POLICY? YES AND NO.

Can the media with their vast access to the American people and their influence with public officials actually change the course of American foreign policy?

As with so many things in life, the answer is "yes" and "no." Let's take the "no" case first. It is known as the "Pentagon Papers" case and involved a study of how the Vietnam War began, which was commissioned by Secretary of State Robert S. McNamara in 1967 while the war was still raging. When the study was completed in 1971, it contained evidence that the U.S. government deliberately misled the American people in order to gain support for the war.

A man named Daniel Ellsberg who had written part of the secret study became so disillusioned with the deception of the government that he leaked parts of it to *The New York Times* in the hope that the American people, finding that they had been deceived, would demand that the United States get out of Vietnam.

The Nixon administration tried to block *The New York Times* from publishing the information leaked by Ellsberg, but this effort was ruled a violation of the First Amendment guarantees of a free press by the Supreme Court. Although the case was a civil liberties landmark, the publication itself did not end U.S. involvement in Vietnam as Ellsberg had hoped, and the war dragged on for another four years.

• • •

American foreign policy was clearly changed in the case of the hijacking of an American airliner by terrorists who forced the pilot to fly to Beirut, Lebanon, where the 39 American passengers were held for seventeen days. In the course of the incident, one American passenger was killed, and others were beaten and robbed by the terrorists.

It had been the stated policy of the United States not to negotiate with terrorists. The purpose of the no-negotiations policy was to discourage acts of terrorism by putting potential terrorists on notice that America officials would not even listen to their demands. This tough policy became more and more difficult to carry out as the TV networks made the American hostages nearly as familiar to the American public as members of their own families. We learned their names and faces and realized that the no-negotiation policy might result in the deaths of the hostages—so their release was negotiated.

Less extensive media coverage might have enabled the government to stick to its tough policy. From a humanitarian point of view the negotiations were successful when the hostages were released, but the policy lost virtually all of its credibility.

Thus, opinion on foreign policy may not be shaped directly but rather indirectly through these information brokers who, incidentally, often shape the information to fit their own views and prejudices.

For policymakers, the relationship with the media on foreign policy questions is a two-way street. Policymakers obviously want journalists to report news favorable to the agendas they have endorsed. The State Department news briefings are designed to get across to reporters the point of view of the State Department. Enterprising reporters, however, do not simply accept what the State Department's spokesperson announces, and these sessions often evolve into a spirited give-and-take with reporters trying to pry out more information and interpretation than the official wants to divulge. There is, then, an adversarial aspect to this relationship.

The Media and the Policymakers There is also a cooperative aspect to it. Stories are leaked through friendly reporters from "senior State Department officials" or "sources close to the president." These leaks of off-the-record statements or "backgrounders" may be used to get messages to foreign nations about steps about to be taken by the U.S. government or may be used by one agency of the foreign affairs bureaucracy to undercut the bureaucratic position of another agency. Such a war of leaks has characterized the relationships between the White House National Security Council staff and the State Department in recent years.

Conclusion

The question of what constitutes a "good" foreign policy is a difficult one to answer. One feature that all successful foreign policies seem to have in common is a central concept—a comprehensive vision of what our role in the world is to be and some clear idea of resources needed to reach that goal. In the absence of such a concept, we find ourselves reacting to day-to-day challenges with no overall plan. The public becomes mystified about our purpose in the world and can make no sense of any particular event. Foreign friends and rivals find U.S. actions unpredictable and full of unpleasant surprises. Not everyone will agree with a policy once it is formulated. Opponents will at least have the opportunity to dissent intelligently. Those who give it their support will know that it has some larger meaning and be reasonably sure that a given action is the product of a thoughtful and comprehensive view of the world and our place in it.

SUMMARY

Foreign policy is the president's game. The president is commander-in-chief of the armed forces and has the power to make treaties and appoint U.S ambassadors. Although denied the authority to declare war, the president often has the power of the people behind him or her to wage a war. In international crises the public has a tendency to rally behind the chief executive.

At the end of World War II, America shed its long tradition of isolationism and vied with the Soviet Union for the independent states that had emerged from the breakup of old colonial empires. The nonaligned countries were regarded as a power vacuum to be filled by either the United States or the USSR. Europe was divided into two camps. The distribution of power throughout the world was bipolar.

Eventually, weaker countries in an alliance with one superpower developed relations with members of the opposing alliance. New centers of power arose when countries like China acquired nuclear weapons. The distribution of power throughout the world became bipolycentric, and has remained so.

The first organization set up to aid the president in shaping foreign policy was the Department of State, which developed into a sizable bureaucracy as America's diplomatic ties grew increasingly complex. After World War II the State Department lost its exclusive hold on foreign affairs, most notably to the Department of Defense, established in 1947.

A rival emerged to the secretary of state in the form of the president's national security adviser, a post created in response to the convergence of military and political considerations after World War II. How well the secretary of state and national security adviser cooperate seems to be very much related to the nature of the individuals who occupy the jobs. Sometimes, secretaries of state are dominant; in other periods it is the national security adviser. There is also evidence that cooperation is possible when the national security adviser acknowledges the primacy of the secretary of state and does not try to duplicate the policymaking functions of the State Department.

Bureaucrats are called upon to implement the decisions of the top policymakers. Unfortunately, the fragmentation of responsibility among foreign policy bureaucracies makes the job a confusing one, with false starts and confusing directives often disrupting delicate diplomacy. Another function of bureaucrats is to provide information and intelligence to policymakers.

With a large number of its committees sharing foreign policy considerations and its lack of detailed information, the Congress is unable to initiate policy in this area. It does wield influence, however, in the form of the congressional power to declare war and the senatorial power to ratify treaties and confirm ambassadors.

Four types of special interests seek to be heard by those who shape foreign policy: ethnic and religious groups, defense and military groups, commercial outfits and labor unions, and ideological groups. The tendency of these forces, with their conflicting demands, generally to cancel one another out is one of the few examples of how fragmentation can work to the advantage of the president.

The relationship between public opinion and foreign policy is not a strong one. The public usually judges from the outcome of a policy, rather than insisting on specific actions. The media, with their emphasis on local news or at least on drama, do not usually contribute much to the shaping of foreign policy either.

In a world where no international code of conduct organizes diplomatic operations, it is difficult to avoid reacting to daily world events in an ad hoc way. To demystify the public and our foreign friends about our actions in the international sphere, we must maintain a comprehensive vision of our role in the world and have an idea of the resources needed to reach that goal.

NOTES

1. This account is taken from Stansfield Turner, *Secrecy and Democracy* (Boston: Houghton Mifflin, 1985), pp. 223–228.
2. Stanley Hoffmann, *Gulliver's Troubles* (New York: McGraw-Hill, 1968), p. 253.
3. Charles W. Kegley, Jr., and Eugene R. Wittkopf, *American Foreign Policy: Pattern and Process* (New York: St. Martin's, 1979), pp. 101–102.
4. George F. Kennan, *Memoirs, 1925–1950* (New York: Atlantic Monthly, 1967), p. 320.
5. See John Spanier, *Games Nations Play* (New York: Praeger, 1975).
6. Raymond Aron, "The Anarchical Order of Power," in *Conditions of World Order,* Stanley Hoffmann, ed. (New York: Simon & Schuster, 1970), pp. 37–38.
7. Roger Hilsman, *To Move a Nation* (Garden City, N.Y.: Doubleday, 1967), p. 59.
8. Henry A. Kissinger, *American Foreign Policy* (New York: Norton, 1969), p. 18.
9. John Franklin Campbell, *The Foreign Affairs Fudge Factory* (New York: Basic Books, 1971), p. 14.
10. Graham T. Allison, *Essence of Decision* (Boston: Little, Brown, 1971).
11. Campbell, p. 37.
12. Kissinger, p. 23.
13. Harry S. Truman, *Memoirs,* vol. 2 (Garden City, N.Y.: Doubleday, 1956), p. 59.
14. Ibid.
15. Hilsman, p. 22.
16. National Academy of Public Administration, *A Presidency for the 1980s* (Washington, 1981), p. 19.
17. Don Oberdorfer, "Shultz Firmly in Command," *The Washington Post* (Feb. 8, 1985).
18. Steven V. Roberts, "On the Foreign Policy Tightrope," *The New York Times* (Feb. 7, 1985).
19. Bernard C. Cohen, *The Public's Impact on Foreign Policy* (Boston: Little, Brown, 1973), p. 106.
20. Theodore C. Sorensen, *Decision Making in the White House* (New York: Columbia U. P., 1963), p. 48.
21. Daniel Yankelovitch and Larry Kagan, "Assertive America," *Foreign Affairs,* 59 (1981), p. 703.
22. Bernard C. Cohen, "Mass Communication and Foreign Policy," in *Domestic Sources of Foreign Policy,* James N. Rosenau, ed. (New York: Free Press, 1967), p. 196.

CHAPTER

18 The Future of American Democracy

Confidence in the future has sometimes seemed more American than apple pie. Even Americans who hated baseball and hot dogs believed in progress; the belief that tomorrow will be better is one of the traditional pillars of the American creed.[1] "Ideas of progression and of the indefinite perfectability of the human race belong to democratic ages," Tocqueville wrote. "Democratic nations care but little for what has been, but they are haunted by visions of what will be."[2]

In 1963, John F. Kennedy sounded this optimistic tone:

> I look forward to a great future for America, a future in which our country will match its military strength with moral restraint, its wealth with our wisdom, its power with our purposes. I look forward to an America which will not be afraid of grace and beauty, which will protect the beauty of our natural environment . . . [and] which will reward achievement in the arts as we reward achievement in business or statecraft. . . . I look forward to an America which commands respect throughout the world not only for its strength but for its civilization as well. And I look forward to a world which will be safe not only for democracy and diversity but also for personal distinction.[3]

In those days, Americans were assured about their country. Old political differences seemed to be giving way to the "politics of consensus," and most Americans thought their government was responsive, effective, and honest.[4]

In the twenty years since Kennedy's speech, however, Vietnam, Watergate, crime, political violence, and the deadly combination of inflation and limited economic growth created grave doubts about American government and the American future. Americans lost a good deal of their faith in the intentions and abilities of their government. In 1981, Henry Grunwald was moved to write:

> Our industry appears to have lost its productive magic, its daring, and sometimes even its competence. Our government is intrusive, inept—and expensive. Our democracy too often produces only mediocrity and deadlock.[5]

Some of this mood has changed during the Reagan years. Ronald Reagan has made effective use of presidential power; in many ways,

President John Kennedy's optimistic views regarding America's future were shared by most citizens at that time. *(UPI)*

the political deadlock has been broken, and although the economy is still troubled, inflation has declined. In 1984, even Walter Mondale credited Reagan with being a "good cheerleader," and in 1985, the Gallup poll found that Americans were recovering their optimism.[6]

Yet, Ronald Reagan has not significantly lessened American doubts about government and public life. In fact, many of Reagan's policies and more of his rhetoric are based on distrust of government, an urge to deregulate, to dismantle public bureaucracies and to "get government off the backs of the American people." Americans are bound to recognize the problems of the private sector: not since the Depression have there been so many farm mortgage foreclosures or so many bank failures, and never has the American economy run such massive deficits in the balance of trade. Americans are more favorable toward business than they have been in the past, but it seems likely that this is not because they trust the private sector more, but because they trust government less. A great many Americans appear to be retreating ever farther into private life, giving up on political solutions to our common problems.[7] This is unfortunate, because our efforts to deal with public problems by ourselves are so likely to make matters worse. (See Figure 18-1.)

At the same time, the disillusionments of the last two decades are also, as the term implies, a loss of illusions. Too many Americans for too many years believed that the future would take care of itself. Our past progress taught us to be complacent about political goals and about our duties as citizens. If Americans have lost that self-satisfied optimism, we will all be gainers. Our political life requires attention and concern.

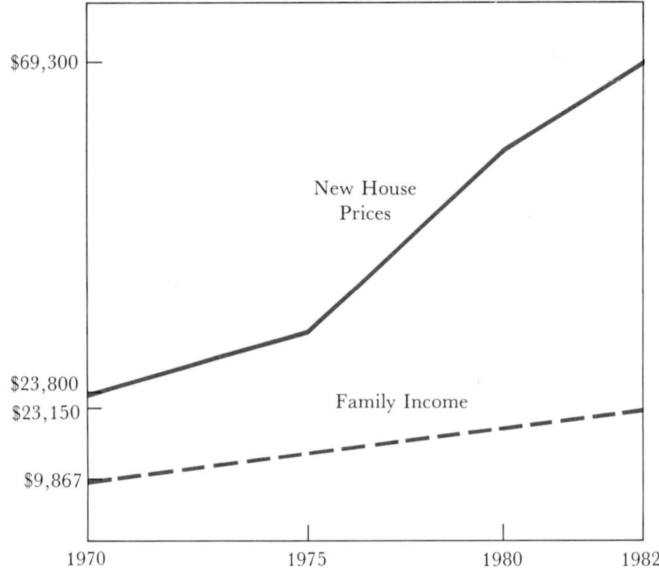

FIGURE 18-1
Recent Family Income and New House Prices
(U.S. Bureau of the Census)

The future is not likely to be friendly to American democracy. In this chapter, we will argue that the greatest challenges facing the United States are not "problems" that Americans can "solve," but conditions of modern life—continuing tests of our political institutions and our wisdom. This aspect of the future involves new political institutions and practices; but if we are lucky, they will be changes we help to shape rather than decisions imposed on us by events. In general, we argue that the best cure for the problems of American politics is more politics, and specifically, more democratic politics. The future of the United States calls for a government strong enough to direct change and a people strong enough to control government.

This position departs from the teaching of the framers. We will be looking for conscious direction rather than self-regulating mechanisms, and for a public organized in support of policies rather than fragmented into many factions or isolated individuals. American political life, in our view, needs something resembling a new foundation.

A New Constitution?

Does this mean that the United States needs a new Constitution? Critics of the framers have often thought it was time for a change; during the Progressive era in the early 1900s, for example, Walter Weyl referred to the Constitution as the "political wisdom of dead America."[8] Even those who agree with the framers, moreover, may wonder, as the Constitution approaches its two-hundredth year, if it is not outdated and unable to deal with the problems of a modern world.

In the early 1970s, Rexford G. Tugwell proposed that we scrap the Constitution in favor of a document based on unity rather than checks and balances. Tugwell urged that the House of Representatives be given greater powers and a longer term. Similarly, he suggested that the position of the House leadership (the speaker and the party leaders) be strengthened in order to pull the House together and focus its efforts. The Senate, Tugwell argued, should be limited to the right to delay legislation, like the British House of Lords, losing the power to block legislation. A stronger House of Representatives, Tugwell claimed, would make the United States less dependent on the president as a source of leadership and common purpose.

Tugwell went on to argue for a less powerful president, limited to one long nine-year term. Not being eligible for reelection and serving for so long a time, Tugwell reasoned, the president would be relatively free from the pressure of short-term public opinion and not so vulnerable to private interests. Reducing the president's powers would, Tugwell claimed, actually allow the president to pursue more coherent policies and longer-term goals.[9]

Whatever the merit of Tugwell's proposals, we think that any scheme for a new constitution is fundamentally mistaken. A constitution, as we have argued, is more than a set of mechanisms and legal forms. It is a complex relationship between the institutions and the culture of a people. Changing that relationship is tricky, particularly because the stability of basic political institutions is a major support for democratic government. Stable institutions are understandable; they tell us what to expect and how to act; they are a source of public security. In a world of rapid change, the value of familiar institutions and forms is especially important.

This is even more the case because our Constitution has proved so open through judicial interpretation and amendment. If constitutional change is needed, it is hard to make a case for radical, as opposed to incremental, change.

There is never a shortage of proposals to amend the Constitution. Some have argued for repealing the Twenty-second Amendment, which limits the president to two terms, pointing out that this restriction weakens the president during the second term. The possibility of a third term, rarely exercised, would give Congress more reason to listen. Similarly, it has been argued that presidents, like the governors of a great many states, should have an "item veto," enabling them to veto individual sections in the budget or other legislation. Congress could not then exert pressure on presidents to sign legislation they dislike by including it in some larger, necessary bill. (Opponents of the item veto argue that Congress is so weak in relation to the president that it needs whatever powers it can get.) All of these proposals, however, seem unlikely to succeed. There is no serious popular demand for any of them, and given the difficulty of amending the Constitution, that is probably fatal.

Four proposed amendments enjoy enough public support to be taken seriously. First, for many years there has been considerable sentiment for doing away with the Electoral College and replacing it with some more direct form of election. As we observed in Chapter 7, however, the Electoral College increases the political influence of large states and urban minorities, and it is supported by other groups who see the Electoral College strengthening federalism. The Electoral College is likely to remain with us, at least until it results again in the election of a president who receives fewer popular votes than his opponent.

Political considerations of a different sort seem likely to block any constitutional amendment limiting federal spending. President Reagan endorsed such an amendment in April 1982, and the idea appeals to a great many Americans.[10] It would be difficult, however, to draft an amendment that would prevent the ploy of "balancing" a budget by overestimating the amount of revenue coming in or underestimating the amount of expenditure going out. The Reagan administration did both, more or less consciously, when it presented its economic program in 1981. Moreover, if an amendment were effective in limiting spending or requiring a balanced budget, it would limit the ability of the government to respond to changing conditions and crises. A "balanced budget" amendment would, in other words, be a serious limitation on the ability of the government to cope with problems of national concern.

Finally, on opposite ends of the political spectrum, there are supporters of the Equal Rights Amendment (ERA) and of an amendment protecting

From *Herblock Through the Looking Glass* (W.W. Norton, 1984)

the Right to Life. The antiabortion forces of the Right-to-life movement, however, do not appear to be numerous enough to get their measure into the Constitution; although it has much broader support, the Equal Rights Amendment has been blocked by conservative groups, a defeat that is a serious setback for the women's movement.

The failure of ERA, however, also sheds light on the alternatives to the amending process. The Supreme Court could accomplish the same result as the amendment by making gender a "suspect category," forcing the states and the federal government to show a "compelling" interest when law or policy treats men and women differently. The failure of ERA will almost certainly lead feminists to concentrate their attention on electoral politics, specifically on efforts to elect a president who will appoint sympathetic judges to the federal courts. (Similarly, the best chance of antiabortion groups may lie in the appointment of judges who favor reversing the Supreme Court's recent rulings and returning the question to the states.)

Ordinarily, in fact, a change in the formal constitution reflects an attempt to legalize a change in the informal constitution of political life and culture. The Thirteenth Amendment did not end slavery; that result was achieved by the Civil War. Votes for women were won by the Suffrage movement, not the Nineteenth Amendment. Successful amendments merely make formal a political change that has already taken place. The renewal of America does not require a new constitution. It demands changes in the organization and content of political life, shaped to the future of the country and its people.

An Older, Less-White America

What will the United States be like in the future? For one thing, the American people will be older, and nonwhites will make up a larger percentage of the population. In 1980, the median age of Americans was thirty; in the year 2000, the Census Bureau estimates that it will be thirty-six. The number of Americans 65 and older is increasing twice as fast as the rest of the population.[11] Nonwhites are now approaching 20 percent of the population, nearly twice what they were at the end of World War II, and that increase seems likely to continue. Each of these changes involves its own political implications.

The aging of America means an increasing conflict between the interests of the old and those of the young. The battles over Social Security early in the Reagan administration tipped us off to the coming conflict. Cost-of-living increases built into Social Security have helped a great many old people out of poverty, but they are also costly. As the numbers of elderly Americans rise, the costs will rise too. A smaller number of young Americans will have to pay taxes to support a growing number of old people. Traditionally, the support of the elderly was like a pyramid: a relatively small number of the aged was supported by the broad base of the population. Increasingly, the pyramid seems to be standing on its head.[12]

In the interest of a balanced budget, the Reagan administration flirted with cutbacks in Social Security benefits. Politically, these proposals seem almost certain to fail. Pressure from interest groups representing the elderly will become more powerful because of the growing numbers of the old; so limiting Social Security is likely to grow more difficult with the years. The old, moreover, have ample reason to resist cutbacks: tampering with current benefits would push many old people into poverty, especially if they are women or members of racial minorities.

At the same time, no society can afford to ignore the interests and morale of the younger, more vigorous section of the public. This is especially true because young people today will have to do without many things Americans have come to consider their birthright, such as owning their own home.

As this suggests, the problems posed by an aging population go beyond Social Security. As the population ages, for example, there will be fewer people between eighteen and twenty-one, and the cost of recruiting soldiers on a voluntary basis will go up as the supply of young people declines because of our lower birthrate. The pressure to return to the draft will probably be irresistible.[13] Older Americans, moreover, are healthier than previously and want to hold on to their jobs; there is widespread pressure to raise or eliminate the mandatory age for retirement. In 1981, the Equal Opportunity Commission reported that complaints alleging age discrimination were growing faster than all others.[14] When jobs are scarce, this has the effect of excluding younger workers from jobs. Voters who are retired or approaching retirement are also more likely to see the impact of inflation on their pensions and savings as the key economic issue, especially since their jobs are often protected by seniority provisions. Younger workers, more likely to be laid off, have every reason to worry more about unemployment.

In the late 1960s, the "generation conflict" was a commonplace. The young rebels of that decade, however, felt certain that they could find work if they wished. They also knew that young Americans were numerous. They were part of the post-World War II "baby boom," and their numbers

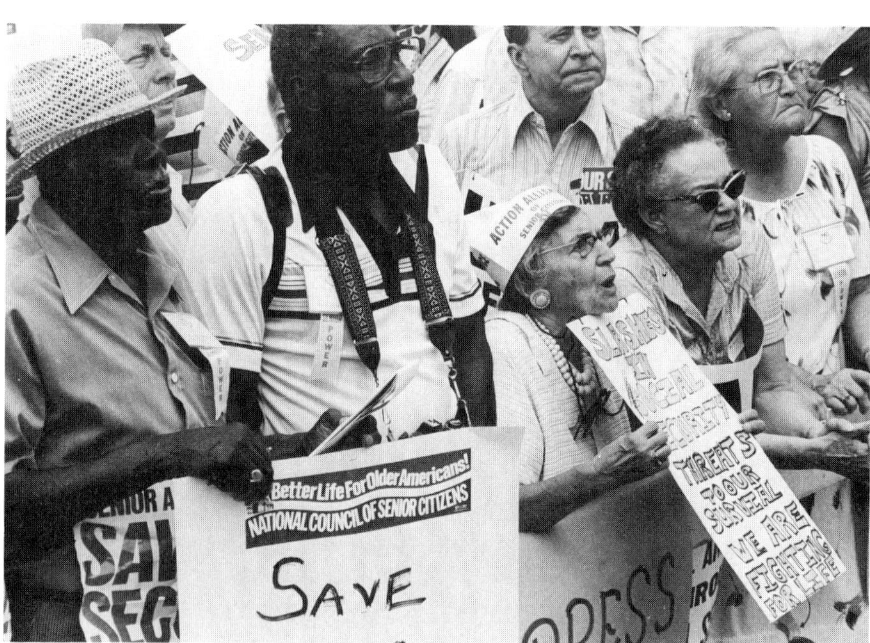

Growing numbers of the elderly means a more expensive Social Security system—but also more political clout to oppose any decreases in benefits. *(Martha Tabor/Working Images Photographs)*

gave them confidence. Younger Americans today lack these sources of confidence, but the cultural differences between young and old are still striking.[15] There may be more real bitterness in the emerging contest between young and old than there was in the struggles of the recent past.

The growth of the nonwhite population will pose similar problems. Racial minorities will have more votes and more political strength. At the same time, the increasing number of nonwhites is bound to create tensions because racism is still very much with us. More and more predominantly white schools and neighborhoods will feel pressure from black and Hispanic families, probably resulting in a continued flight by whites from the cities and the public schools.

Racial conflict may be moderated by the fact that blatant racism is no longer respectable. Nevertheless, economic inequality between the races is increasing, rather than declining, in some critical respects. In 1967, blacks were 3.75 times more likely to be poor than whites; in 1977, that figure had risen so that blacks were four times as likely to be poor. That small increase hides a starker reality. Black families with two parents had drawn closer to white families, but the position of black families headed by a single (usually female) parent deteriorated sharply, and the position of Hispanic women heading families was even worse.[16] In 1984, blacks earned only 64 percent of the median income of nonfarm households, but families composed of women with children, black or white, earned only 48 percent.[17] This "feminization of poverty," moreover, should not obscure the fact that poverty is much more likely for racial minorities, even with both parents present, than it is for whites. Minority youths suffer from unemployment much more than do whites of the same age and hence bear a disproportionate part of the burden of an aging, but working, population.

The needs and demands of the nonwhite poor, even when reinforced by increased strength at the polls, will run up against the widespread desire to tighten up and limit welfare and social programs generally. The strength of this mood may be overestimated or short-lived, but at present it has great force. The likelihood, for the immediate future, is that racial minorities will experience frustration, bitterness, betrayal, and an anger that is likely to increase the fears and resistance of white Americans.

Technological Change

The problems of age and race, however, seem trivial in comparison to the agonies of technological change. Whatever the benefits a new technology brings, it also disrupts the social and political relationships that were founded on the old technology. In modern America, as in advanced, industrial societies generally, technological change has become almost routine. Technological innovations may, in fact, sum up what modern life is all about.[18] Americans have learned that almost all social institutions are vulnerable.

Moreover, new technologies give human beings new power for good and evil alike. Every new technology tests human reason and goodwill and the capacity of governments to control the forces in their citizens' hands. More and more, we question whether humans with all their shortcomings can be trusted with their own inventions. Thermonuclear weapons and nuclear

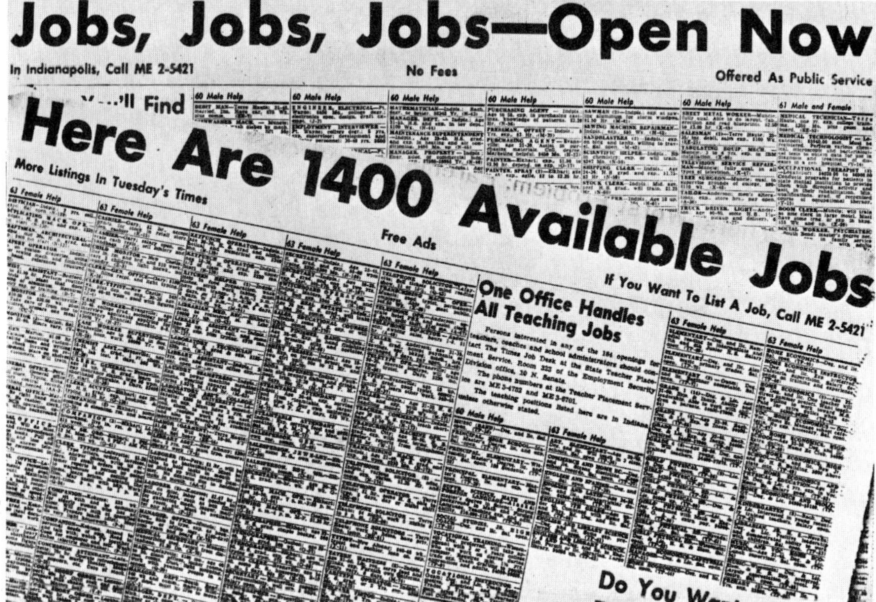

A job hunter with limited skills may fail to find work—even when the newspaper lists thousands of openings. *(UPI)*

reactors are the examples of technological challenges that come most readily to mind. Yet newer technologies may make those destructive powers seem almost crude.

Technology, moreover, has serious implications for employment and equality in the United States. America grew up as a frontier society in which land was abundant and labor scarce, and our culture still tends to take both conditions for granted.* A great many Americans presume that there are jobs available for anyone willing to work; in 1981, for example, President Reagan told a news conference that despite complaints about unemployment, he had found many pages of jobs advertised in *The Washington Post.* It was later pointed out that most of these were in the "high tech" fields that required sophisticated training. It has been hard for Americans to face the fact that changing technology and the market have created a class of individuals, numbering in the millions, who are almost permanently unemployed. And industrial robotics, so recently the stuff of science fiction, is a real force in American economic life. "For the first time since the industrial revolution," Robert Kuttner writes, "we seem to be entering a period when technology could wipe out more jobs than it creates."[19]

Computerization, moreover, has other implications for political life, since computers greatly increase the possibilities for central control in a large state or organization. Since no individual can watch or control more than a limited number of other people, rulers are really able to keep tabs on only a very limited circle of advisers and intimates. Computers, however, can do tasks it once took many layers of bureaucracy to perform, storing an enormous amount of information and making it available to rulers almost instantly. More important, computers—unlike bureaucrats—are relatively

*Despite seventy-five years of conservation, Americans are still cavalier about the land. About 3 million acres of farmland are lost every year to erosion or construction, making us radically dependent on technology to hold down food prices. Bob Tamarkin, "Growth Industry," *Forbes,* 127 (Mar. 2, 1981), p. 90; William Schmidt, "Plowing of Plains in the West Stirs Fears of New Dust Bowl," *The New York Times* (May 14, 1982), pp. 1ff.

neutral. They make it possible for central authorities to exert very close supervision and control over the dealings of the public at large. Much of what is called "decentralization" in government and business, for example, involves giving up the effort to control subordinates through rules and directives in favor of the more effective control exerted through computer surveillance.

Moreover, computers make it possible to record and recall more than any previous bureaucracy. The widespread use of credit cards means that the commercial transactions of billions of individuals become, potentially, subject to observation. The vision of an economy in which money is replaced by a credit card—not at all unrealistic, given present possibilities—also implies that all of an individual's economic life would be recorded and subject to scrutiny. As the Internal Revenue Service struggles with the growth of an "underground economy," where people demand payment in cash in order to avoid records of their transactions, it also attempts to have more and more payments reported on computer tape, since the second is an important check on the first. For similar reasons, the FBI has recommended developing a computerized file on persons suspected of white-collar crimes. Computers, to put it simply, greatly increase the government's capacity to plan and govern. They also increase the possibility that Big Brother—the totalitarian despot of George Orwell's *1984*—will really be watching us.[20]

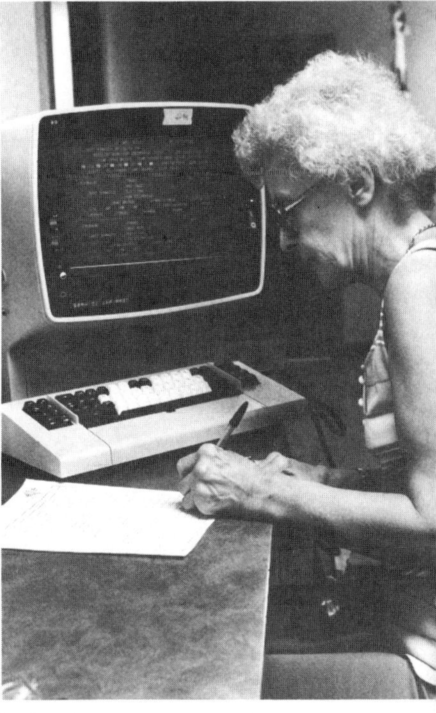

Individual privacy in a democracy is potentially threatened by the information-gathering capabilities of today's computers. *(USDA)*

Other technologies also increase the possibilities for central control: devices for eavesdropping, for example, have reached an altogether fantastic level of sophistication. In general, technology can be expected to continue to reduce the effective internal limits on what government is able to do. By lowering the physical barriers of tyranny, technology emphasizes the need for political protections. Technology implies that the security of democratic government must, more and more, be found in democratic politics and democratic citizens.

An Interdependent World

Technology is also helping to make it a much more interdependent world. The influence of foreign regimes and peoples on American life is something we can see and feel directly. Many American corporations are multinational, owning and operating business overseas. Similarly, a growing number of familiar American companies, like Standard Oil of Ohio or the A&P, are owned and controlled by non-American companies. Between 1980–1985, direct foreign investment in the United States increased 144 percent.[21] It becomes harder to separate domestic politics from foreign affairs, and they become more and more controlled by international processes and politics. Oil and OPEC are only one obvious example, and no one needs to be reminded of the threat and influence of thermonuclear weapons.[22]

The increasing importance of international politics seems to suggest that these long-term trends will continue: (1) the increasing importance of the federal government in the federal system, and (2) the ascendancy of the president and the bureaucracies that depend on him within the federal government.

International interdependence, however, also involves very important external limitations on the federal government and some important political limitations on the president. In the first place, governments find their ability to govern limited by what the international system permits. For example, foreign competition has captured great segments of the American market, causing serious problems for American business; Japanese automobiles and electronic equipment are obvious illustrations. Until recently, competition of that sort would probably have resulted in high protective tariffs to discourage imports that compete with American products. We were once relatively self-sufficient. Foreign trade was more or less marginal, and what mattered was the domestic market. Today, too many American corporations need access to materials and markets overseas. Since excluding the foreign competition would cause foreign governments to retaliate with tariffs of their own, we would lose at least as much as we would gain. Hence, the Reagan administration did not try to shut the Japanese out of the American automobile market. It attempted (successfully) to persuade them to reduce voluntarily their exports to us, hoping that Reagan's economic program would meanwhile improve our competitive position.[23] Our dependence on other nations means that the government, with greater frequency, will act like a mediator rather than a master.

State governments discovered long ago that nationwide corporations are difficult or impossible to control. National governments encounter some of the same difficulty with multinationals, although these problems are sometimes exaggerated.[24] The ability of the government to tax and regulate and the ability of unions to make demands are limited by the threat that corpo-

FIGURE 18-2
Total Employment in U.S. Manufacturing Industries
(Bureau of Labor Statistics)

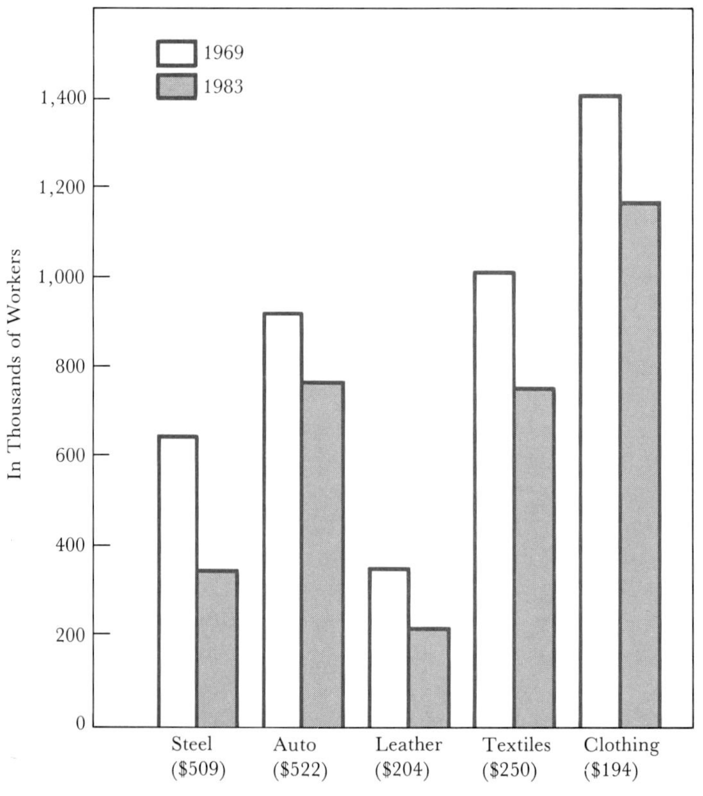

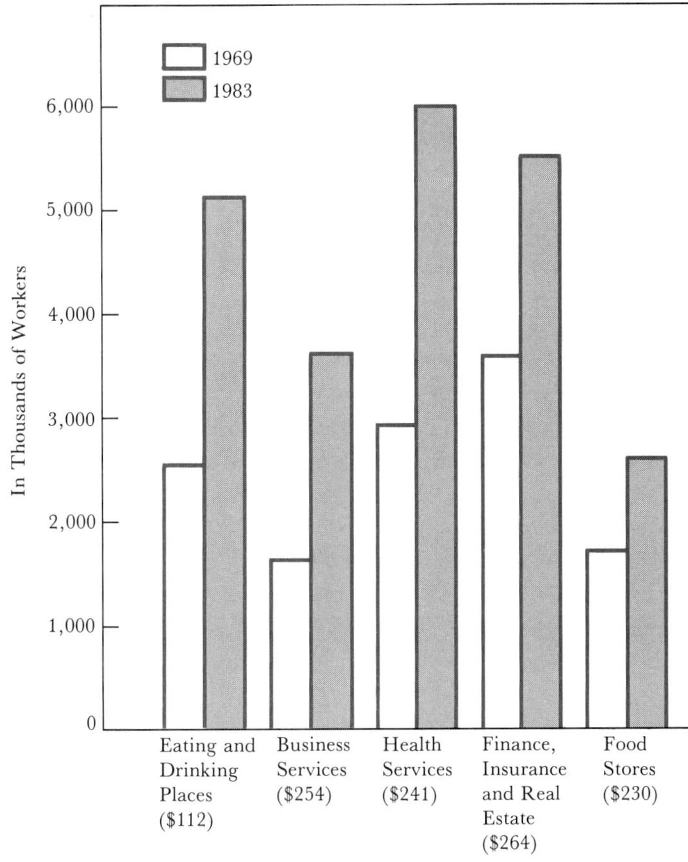

FIGURE 18-3
Total Employment in U.S. Service Industries
(Bureau of Labor Statistics)

rations will move their business to places where taxes are low and there are no unions. Moreover, a corporation with operations overseas must necessarily give part of its loyalty to the country in which it operates. The interests of a corporation like Chevron are so closely identified with those of Saudi Arabia that the corporation often acts as a virtual spokesperson for Saudi interests. Multinational corporations may contribute to our economic welfare or our political interests; they also tie us to regimes and policies we might otherwise avoid, and the international economy of which multinationals are a part increasingly limits American politics.[25]

For many economists, the new international economy makes the American market more competitive and gives American consumers access to products at the best possible prices. Others, however, see alarming political implications.

The American economy seems to be moving decisively away from manufacturing and into service industries—health care, financial services, restaurants, and the like. This change means an increase in jobs that pay very *high* wages, like those earned by engineers or computer programmers, and very *low* wages, like those earned by most food service workers or by computer assemblers. Jobs in the middle of the wage scale, the kind of jobs associated with unionized industrial labor, appear to be on the decline. This tendency toward wage polarization potentially involves "severe consequences for America's future as a middle class society."[26]

The decline of American industrial production is closely related to the increasing ability of technology and capital to move from one country to another. In this environment, industrial capital is attracted whenever low wages more than balance low productivity. For example, as one economist points out, "the world's most modern steel mill is currently in Nigeria; it pays workers $200 a month. Korean shipbuilding workers are only half as productive as Swedish workers, but they work at one-eighth the wages."[27]

More and more American industries and workers argue in favor of some sort of protection or "industrial policy." In this view, the advantage of newly industrializing countries and other foreign competitors is too often the result of authoritarian governments repressing free-trade unions in order to keep wages at rock-bottom levels or other forms of unfair competition. This sort of competition, the advocates of industrial policy assert, exerts a similar "union-busting" pressure in American economic and political life and is unhealthy for American democracy.

As all this suggests, the United States is becoming more vulnerable and less able to go it alone. Americans can be expected to find this frustrating or alarming, and the government must expect to be more exposed to criticism in its conduct of foreign policy. In the future, presidents may be less happy about their commanding role in foreign policy. In 1980, President Carter's appeals for unity in the face of the hostage crisis in Iran helped him defeat Senator Edward Kennedy for the Democratic nomination. On the other hand, Ronald Reagan made political capital out of the charge that Carter had allowed the United States to suffer "humiliations" in Iran and elsewhere. And as international politics grows more important in our political life, we cannot expect political disagreement to stop at the water's edge. What divides us at home will be likely to divide us abroad, and vice versa. For example, American policy on human rights includes the right to labor unions independent of government control. American support for human rights also opposes the labor conditions that prompt some American corporations to locate plants overseas. A tough human rights policy, conse-

Many seemingly "all-American" products are actually produced by multinational companies, which market these products worldwide. *(AP/Wide World Photos)*

quently, is the logical extension of support for trade unions at home, and the more important foreign competition is for American workers, the more important this will seem to them. Just as domestic concerns can be expected to enter more and more into foreign policy, our concerns about foreign policy will be increasingly likely to shape our domestic politics and will probably cause foreign policy debates to split along party lines.[28]

For many of the same reasons, the idea that an administration will pursue a single, coherent foreign policy is probably out of date. Presidents and secretaries of state will have dominant concerns and will establish themes and tones of policy. Nevertheless, as world politics penetrates our political life, every bureaucracy will make its own claims on, and want to conduct, foreign policy. The Department of State is already finding it difficult to keep track of, let alone control and coordinate, the politics of the separate bureaus. Fragmentation will noticeably afflict foreign affairs, and the president will be hard pressed to bring some order and direction into our dealings with the world.

Concentration of Power

The scale of political and economic life is growing larger, and even the federal government feels the strain. We have every reason, consequently, to suppose that corporations (and with them, other private organizations) will continue to grow larger and that economic power will be concentrated in relatively few hands.[29]

The arguments in favor of large-scale enterprise are familiar. Giant organizations can take advantage of the efficiency and economy that comes with size, especially because they can afford and can make full use of new technologies. Large organizations tend to have better information about broader markets and political conditions, and are more able to cope with a more integrated world. Finally, large organizations have better access to money; they know more potential lenders, and they look like better risks than smaller, newer companies with fewer resources and without a record of success. Consequently, large corporations and organizations are more likely to be able to borrow at relatively low rates of interest and can get, at more reasonable cost, the money needed to introduce new technologies or to expand into new markets.[30]

Some critics doubt these arguments in favor of big business. They claim that smaller companies often have less invested in existing technologies, and that their owners may be more willing to take risks and try new techniques because they have more to gain and less to lose. Because individuals matter more in small organizations, they are likely to be more identified with the small company and its business; if so, they will probably work with greater intensity, which balances many of the advantages of the large, highly specialized firm.[31]

But if there are economic arguments against the large organization, it is hard to argue with its political advantage. Giant organizations gain a measure of security because they can dominate or influence the market rather than be ruled by it. Size enables a corporation to escape or limit the pressure of competition. To a considerable extent, big corporations came into being and continue to be valued because they can span and organize the free market. Paradoxically, Robert Lekachman argues, since government planning offers the same protection, socialism could reduce the tendency for resources to be concentrated in a few hands and create a less centralized private sector.[32]

Be that as it may, American antitrust laws do restrict corporations from becoming monopolies through buying out their competitors, but those who believe in the superiority of big business say that antitrust laws should not be applied to corporations unless they use their dominant position to set unfair prices.[33] Since the antitrust laws limit companies in "vertical integration" (such as controlling all levels of the oil business from drilling and refining to retail sales), some companies have pursued "horizontal" mergers, acquiring companies in different lines of business. Sometimes, the two concerns are quite different; the International Telephone and Telegraph Company, for example, owns the Sheraton hotel chain and the Continental Baking Corporation. Sometimes, the two fields are related so closely that it is hard to tell "horizontal" from "vertical" mergers, as it was when du Pont, the largest chemical corporation, acquired the Continental Oil Corporation (Conoco). Economically, "horizontal" mergers often fail. Companies still pursue them in the hope that having eggs in many baskets will provide some protection against the swings of the market and in the certainty that mergers mean larger organizations with greater potential power.

The Reagan administration, moreover, has taken an extremely tolerant position in relation to corporate mergers, interpreting the antitrust laws very loosely. It permitted a wave of mergers in the oil industry (for example, Texaco and Chevron were allowed to acquire Getty and Gulf Oil, respectively). And, in a few months in 1985, three $5 billion mergers were announced—Allied Corporation merged with Signal, R. J. Reynolds bought Nabisco, and giant General Motors, which had previously acquired Electronic Data Systems for $2.5 billion, acquired Hughes Aircraft. We have every reason to expect this pattern to continue.

In any case, horizontal mergers and giant corporations generally have an important political consequence. They build ties among, and help to combine, very different interests and sectors of the economy. Whatever competition exists among the separate divisions of a corporation is controlled by their common structure and interests. Consequently, they reduce the number of separate groups and interests on which Madison and the framers relied. Scott and Hart speak, in fact, of a "national managerial system" made up of "a vast complex of interlocking management systems, sharing a common set of values, which control modern organizations and which provide order and stability in our national life," a "major departure from the way American society was supposed to be governed."[34] They may exaggerate a bit, at present. Nevertheless, the politics of corporate or organizational concentration is surely less competitive and less easily controlled than the pluralism Madison envisioned.[35]

One advantage of large corporations and organizations is precisely that they are better able to control government or to protect themselves against undesirable government regulation. This is a point to which we will return. For the moment, it is enough to observe that corporate organizations have enough political power to challenge governments at all levels. We can expect that power to grow with the size of corporations themselves and with the development of corporate political action committees (PACs), which apply that power directly to electoral politics.[36]

A New Federalism?

A larger economy and larger organizations mean a further decline in the position of the states and local governments. States and localities already approach corporations meekly, trying to persuade them to relocate or to stay where they are, bidding against one another with tax advantages and other benefits.[37] That pattern seems likely to go on, and the inability of states to regulate corporations and control economic life in general will continue to lead to demands for federal regulation and aid.

President Reagan proposed a "new federalism" that, he asserted, would strengthen local government and cut back federal bureaucracy by transferring the responsibility for various social programs from the federal government to the states and giving the states block grants of money that could be divided among these programs. Since, within broad guidelines, the states could spend this money as they chose, Reagan's proposals would add to the discretion and authority of state governments.

But the grants President Reagan suggested were much smaller than the amounts of money the states had previously received. If the states wished to keep programs and services at the same level, they would have to raise taxes under the "new federalism," a policy sure to be as unpopular at the state level as at the federal level and likely to weaken support for local government rather than strengthening it. The alternative would be cutbacks in service and less efficient and effective programs, which would displace a different group of voters. Since state and local governments would want a way out of this dilemma, state and local leaders would almost certainly rush to Washington, creating an intense and powerful lobby for more aid and assistance.[38] Reagan's program attempted to transfer the burden of certain responsibilities to the states without giving them the money to take on those burdens. President Reagan's tax plan, introduced in 1985, would make this even more likely. Since state and local taxes would no longer be deductible from federal income taxes under Reagan's plan, voters would probably be less willing to raise state taxes to pay for state programs.

The greatest problem of states and localities is the decline in loyalty to them among the citizens. Economic and social life do not respect state boundaries, and our culture is more and more national rather than local and regional. States and localities have only the weakest resources of loyalty and local patriotism. Any effort to check the decline of state and local governments must begin with that fact. States and localities are the victims of corporate concentration and political fragmentation, and before they can reassume any shaping role in American life, political loyalty to them would have to be built by changing those fundamental conditions. Obviously, states and localities cannot reconstruct themselves; any such policy would entail generous federal support and sympathetic and extensive federal regulation of economic and social life.

Social Disintegration

States and localities are only one instance of a more general rule. Given current conditions, we can expect to see a weakening of all those institutions and relationships from which Americans have gained a sense of identity and personal dignity. Since individuals feel unimportant compared to the great organizations and forces that shape mass society, a sense of identity is ever more important in preventing people from feeling that they do not matter; yet, it is harder and harder to achieve.

The smaller, more personal relationships and associations—town, family, church, and workplace—have all been shoved aside by the national market, and matters are growing worse with time.

Contemporary American life teaches us not to care about others too much or commit ourselves to them too deeply. Mobility and change, the two hallmarks of the market, mean that people and neighborhoods will come and go. Americans move very frequently; neighborhoods are less and less the sources of security and stability, and when we make friends, we are painfully aware of the terrible probability that we will be separated from those we come to care about. The effects of moving are most painful to those who are left behind—like the old in changing neighborhoods—because they feel helplessness as well as loss. It is not surprising that so many Americans vow never to be abandoned; they never really put down roots because of the pain of being uprooted. Our towns and cities seem, psychologically, to resemble the camps of nomads, relatively permanent but prepared to move along. The political consequences are obvious:

> The decision to devote one's time and energy to public things is foolhardy unless one is sure of staying in the same spot long enough to enjoy the fruits of those activities and to acquire confidence in the motives of the other citizens with whom one is working. Bargaining and haggling are activities which, under certain circumstances, can take place among strangers. Deliberation, sacrifice and conciliation can occur only among people who have had ample opportunity to get to know and trust one another.[39]

Americans, like all human beings, continue to need closeness and intimacy, especially in contrast to the massive scale and impersonality of so

Today as never before, Americans may find their ties to a community broken literally overnight by events such as the closing of a major industry's plant. Here, laid-off steelworkers sign up at the union hall for benefits. *(Martha Tabor/Working Images Photographs)*

The surge in divorce has left millions of children to be raised by just one parent. *(Jim Harrison/Stock Boston)*

much of economic and political life. They remarry, for example, almost as often as they divorce.[40] The pattern of instability, however, makes it harder for people to take personal risks and do the hard work that is required for strong bonds with another. Love can find a way, but it is hard pressed to do so against the feeling, born of painful experience, that nothing lasts. Our social life encourages relationships that are pleasant but superficial, and our private life seems to be becoming more private indeed.

This gloomy picture does not mean that there is no hope for the family or the other traditional sources of dignity and identity, or that there can be no new patterns to replace the old. The equality of the sexes within the family, for example, may strengthen the family as an institution. The tendency toward social fragmentation does mean, however, that today's social institutions probably cannot be saved. Reviving these social institutions will demand government policies that aim at the reconstruction of society as a whole.

This is a radically new pattern in America. The framers were either suspicious of social institutions or took them for granted. Increasingly, however, both liberals and conservatives have agreed that government has a responsibility for reconstructing society. President Reagan's support for prayer in the schools and his opposition to abortion are such efforts, as are President Carter's sympathy for affirmative action and for the Equal Rights Amendment.[41] It is interesting to note that both the defenders of the traditional institutions of society and those who favor more "liberated" patterns and values turn to government for help in achieving their goals. In the future, Americans are more likely to ask how government should regulate social and economic life, and for what ends, not whether it should do so. Social issues, at any rate, are certain to have a prominent place in the future agenda of American democracy.[42]

Government Planning

Without doubt, the federal government will shape the direction and character of American economic and social life, even by sidestepping the problem. Whether Americans are interested in strengthening social institutions, building a new federalism, limiting the power of corporations, or freeing them from restraint, sympathetic federal policies are an essential starting point. In this sense, all roads lead to Washington. But how much and what sort of government intervention and regulation can we expect in the future?

The Reagan administration committed itself to reducing the role of the federal government, but its designs for cutting federal regulation and bureaucracy were also *federal* policies. Willingly or unwillingly, the administration attempted to shape the economic and social life of America.

The Reagan administration believed, in the first place, that an increased reliance on market forces and the private sector would stimulate economic growth and breathe new life into our social institutions. In Reagan's view, federal welfare and social programs made local governments, private charities, and families less important as sources of social services. At the same time, the willingness of the federal government to pay the bills weakened the need for local governments and private individuals to act responsibly and to take care of their own. Reducing the federal government's role would put pressure on local and voluntary organizations, and on the family, to take up the slack. That, in turn, would make such groups more significant and would strengthen their claims on their members.

Many things could be said about the image of America on which this policy is based. It greatly overestimates, for example, the ability of local governments and institutions to cope with social problems. For present purposes, it is most important that the policy of relying on market forces is itself a system of regulation, designed to force Americans to take responsibility for the needy by making them choose between morally unacceptable alternatives.

One problem with this policy is also evident: it puts the heaviest burden on those public-spirited citizens who have consciences. In that sense, it amounts to an indirect tax on good citizens and a "free ride" for bad ones. Economically, the administration's program discourages moral feelings by making it costly for people to follow the dictates of the conscience while the market forces tell them to put economic goals first.

Market competition requires economic growth and expansion as the conditions for survival. The administration turned to the market forces because it favored economic growth as the chief goal of policy. But Reagan's enthusiasm for economic growth left a number of questions unanswered. What kind of growth do we want? And whom do we expect to pay for it?

For example, low gasoline prices in the postwar years were critical in making America a more suburban society, dependent on the automobile and on foreign oil producers. At best, the market allows such decisions about the future to be made by producers and consumers acting on the basis of private motives—the desire to sell oil or automobiles, on one hand, and the demand for cheap fuel, on the other. Public goods like a clean environment and a consistent foreign policy were effectively subordinated to private interests. Also, since the market is dominated by the great corporations, this amounts to allowing a relatively small number of private organizations to determine the shape of America's future.[43]

President Reagan's desire to increase such delegation of public authority to the private sector would, if carried into effect, produce political consequences that can be predicted. In the first place, it would further social disintegration because, as we have observed, the market values profit above benefits like social stability and loyalty to family. It rewards self-seeking individuals with few ties to others. Second, the market places little value on work as a source of human dignity. The market aims at material output, not at full employment. Since our goal, in the theory of the market, is material well-being, "the act of labor itself is regarded as nothing more than an unfortunate necessity to which we must submit in order to obtain (the) end."[44] In fact, welfare policies that rely on payments to the poor rather than on efforts to increase employment reflect the ideology of the market. They focus on material output, not human input—a policy that has human, social, and political costs even if it increases national wealth.

Finally, market forces demand a rapid, accelerating rate of growth. They demand more and more resources and expand into new areas until, finally, they encounter a rate of diminishing returns and diminishing material resources.[45] This is especially true today as more and more people around the world compete for resources, raising the cost of growth. (The United States feels this competition with particular intensity: in 1970, America, with 5 percent of the world's people, used 27 percent of the world's raw materials. This imbalance makes us, necessarily, the target of competition and political pressure.)[46] This revolution in demand for resources and capital, here and abroad, helps fuel inflation: it makes us borrow rather than save at a time when ever more massive investment is needed to generate growth. In 1950, the average corporation had $43 of operating income to cover every dollar of interest payments; in 1982, this has declined[47] to about $4. As the costs of growth increase, the rate of growth can be expected to slow down. That, in turn, lessens our ability to help the poor without taking money away from the well-to-do. If the size of the economic pie does not grow, it means that when I help myself to a larger slice, there is less for someone else. Since the market needs capital for growth, this could only mean harder

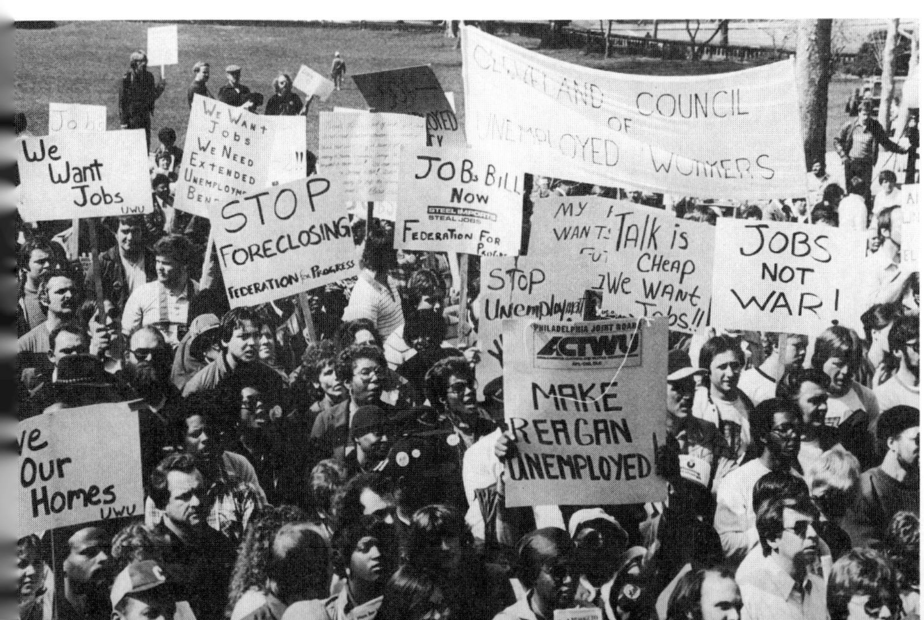

As the costs of economic growth increase, the rate of growth can be expected to slow down. This can only mean harder times for working- and middle-class Americans. *(Martha Tabor/Working Images Photographs)*

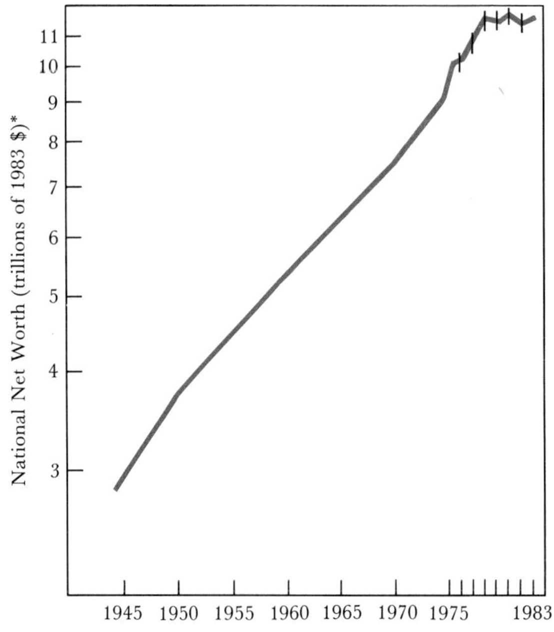

FIGURE 18-4
National Net Worth, 1945–1983
(Forbes, Jan. 28, 1985)

times for working and middle-class Americans, who are less able to compete for capital than large corporations.[48]

This could change, of course, with a period of rapid and sustained growth, which has been the Reagan administration's continuing hope. Our best evidence, however, makes this seem unlikely. In fact, our "national worth"—the net value of everything Americans and their government own—has been essentially stagnant since 1978 (see Figure 18.4).[49] Americans may be consuming more, but they are also borrowing more. The federal debt is growing faster than the gross national product (see Figure 18.5),

FIGURE 18-5
Federal Debt Up, GNP Down
(OMB)

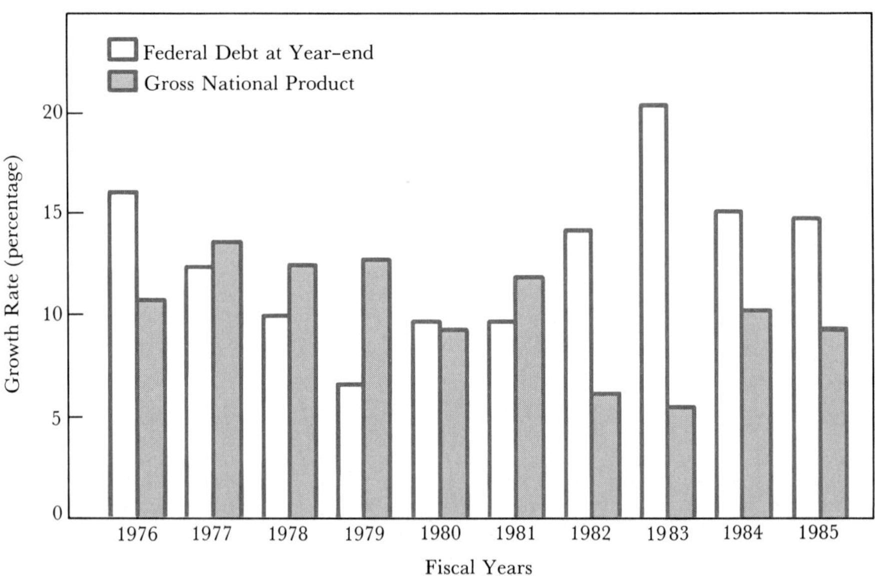

and outstanding debts—public and private—rose about $800 billion in 1984, around two and a half times the increase in the GNP. "The American people," writes conservative columnist Ashby Bladen, "are now spending a great deal more than they are earning by producing, and they are borrowing to make up the difference."[50]

The political and social costs all but rule out reliance on market forces. Economic and technical change challenges and shatters the foundations of social and political life, and people expect the federal government to cope with these problems. Even Americans who detest "welfare," and who believe the government is wasteful and taxes us too much, show an "irreversible commitment to basic government welfare programs." Government involvement in economic and social life is "as natural to them as getting up in the morning."[51] Increasing government intervention and planning, consequently, is virtually a certainty.

Planning and Power

The great aim of public planning, as all of this implies, is to make private power accountable to the people, making economic and social life compatible with democracy.[52] Government regulation, however, may not be the way to achieve it.

The United States Constitution, according to the framers' design, fragments power and protects private rights. Even when the government has legal authority to override private interests, public majorities are usually temporary coalitions, rarely able to exert any lasting control over American life. As a result, it is difficult for government to command any sizable section of the business community. As Charles Lindblom observes, government regulation normally seeks to encourage businesses to do the right thing by promising them greater rewards. A conservative political scientist like Samuel P. Huntington finds common ground with a liberal like Walter Dean Burnham on an important point: America, since the New Deal of the 1930s, has expanded the role and responsibility of government without expanding its authority. The individualism of American culture and institutions makes it difficult for government to rule. Liberalism, the doctrine of the framers, "stacks the deck against the public sector in its domestic role."[53]

This weakness of the government's position is emphasized by the fact that the popular approval of every administration rises and falls with the prosperity of business in general and with changes in opinion in the business and financial communities. The government is not tied to any particular corporation or interest. Nevertheless, if it is impossible to rule by the market, it is equally impossible to oppose it.

In fact, public policy is likely to reflect the needs of the private sector. This is especially true, since powerful corporations and private organizations are less concerned with their ability to protect themselves against government than they are with their ability to use government for their own purposes. John Kenneth Galbraith calls this "socialism by and for nonsocialists." The Carter administration rescued the Chrysler Corporation by a package of federal loan guarantees because the social and economic consequences of letting Chrysler fail—especially the loss of jobs—would have been politically unacceptable. Its size and importance allowed Chrysler to invoke the government to save the company from its own mistakes. In the same way, the Reagan administration rushed to save the Continental Illinois Bank in 1984 because the failure of the bank, the largest in Chicago and the ninth largest in the United States, would have had serious repercussions for the banking system as a whole. Reagan allowed smaller banks to fail, however, just as he vetoed a bill to help hard-pressed farmers in 1985. In principle, Reagan favors leaving the private sector to the discipline of the market; in practice, the president applies this rule only to small- and middle-sized firms. As Galbraith writes, "if you are in trouble and big enough, you will be rescued and recapitalized in one way or another by the government."[54]

Government planning, moreover, has often encouraged concentration and organized cooperation between interests because government officials find it easier to control and coordinate a small number of larger companies than a large number of small ones. Computerization and greater ease of control may reduce this tendency. It will still be true that companies will find it expensive and annoying to comply with government regulations. Regulations, as we saw in Chapter 10, can squeeze out firms that are small or financially weak.* For example, security clearances and procedures make it very costly to engage in defense contracting. As a result, the number of defense contractors is shrinking to a handful of relatively powerful companies.[55]

Could a socialist regime do a better job of controlling private power? In theory, socialism promises to transform private power into public power by assuming public control of the means of production. In practice, however, socialist governments fall into two categories. In the Soviet Union and similar states, socialism has meant bureaucratic tyranny, rule by the "new class" of party members and technical experts. In the USSR this has resulted in considerable inequality.[56] In Western industrial societies, socialism has remained democratic, but the policies of socialist parties are less distinctly "socialistic" than they are similar to those policies already followed by the Democratic party in the United States.[57]

The problem of power, in other words, is not solved by changing the system of ownership. Large-scale organizations create power centers beyond the control of ordinary citizens, and it makes matters worse if all organizations are brought under the control of a single state bureaucracy. Economist Robert Heilbroner argues that the problems of the future are really the problems of industrial societies, and whether they are capitalist or socialist is less important than the fact that they are industrial.[58]

For America, government planning seems unlikely to attempt to eliminate the private sector (as socialism would do) and not apt to regulate directly by telling Americans what to do (as traditional bureaucracy does). Rather, government intervention will manipulate and try to use the private sector for public purposes, regulating the market rather than allowing the market to regulate society. Instead of drawing up detailed codes to control

*Chrysler, for example, claimed a right to government aid because it had found it far more difficult to comply with government regulations than its major competitors. *The Wall Street Journal* (Sept. 27, 1979), p. 22.

pollution, the government may tax polluters to give them a reason to control pollution themselves. Similarly, if we want to promote social stability, the government could make it more expensive for us to move by repealing the deduction for moving expenses. President Reagan's 1985 plan for tax reform, for example, favored companies in high technology fields, penalized heavy industry, and gave advantages to the South and West at the expense of the Northeast and Midwest. This form of regulation is less complicated than bureaucracy, and people resent it less since the force it applies is subtler and less visible. It also has the advantage of reducing bureaucratic power and preserving some independence for the private sector.[59]

The limitations of this form of regulation are also clear. It shares some of the problems of the market on which it relies. This "managed market" approach appeals to, and really promotes, selfishness and indifference to the good of communities, the public, and families except when it forces people to pay when they behave in undesirable ways.[60] Even if managing the market succeeded in curbing private power and directing it to the public good, it would produce a democratic *system* but not democratic *citizens*. The political society would be democratic in form but private in content.

That result is strikingly similar to the framers' design but with an important difference. The framers hoped that their system would be virtually self-regulating; managed market theory requires management and rule. Making public use of private motives presumes that the planners (1) know the public and its purposes, and (2) can impose stiff enough penalties in the form of taxes and other costs to make individuals act in ways to promote the public good. Both premises take for granted public support and some version of civic spirit. Market managers tend to ignore citizenship and political organization, but they depend heavily on both.

Public Purposes: Liberty and Equality

Americans want both liberty and equality, and any political program must appeal to both values to stand a chance of success. Nevertheless, choices are necessary in a world of limited resources and possibilities. American politics will continue to depend on where we place our priorities, and the competing claims of liberty and equality will continue to be the first principle of the republic.

For the immediate future, the case for individual liberty seems likely to be best expressed by the diverse movement called **"neoconservatism,"** which provided important intellectual support for Ronald Reagan.* Neoconservatism is a part of the age of technology, with its large-scale organization and government planning; the "rugged individualism" of old-style conservatism is declining along with the autonomous, small town middle class with which it was always associated. Neoconservatives often praise the market or the private sector and condemn the federal bureaucracy. Their teaching, nevertheless, is an argument for government intervention on behalf of individual liberty. "We are unable," Michael Novak writes, "to go back to individualism alone, for our task is public and social."[61]

*Many people ordinarily called neoconservative object to the label; nevertheless, it does refer to a core of common beliefs and persuasions.

Neoconservatives believe that a good education (and an end to discrimination in the market-place) will be enough to ensure the advancement of minorities. (*Tom Kelly*/The Mercury)

It is the job of the government, neoconservatives maintain, to eliminate racial or sexual discrimination and to give the individual a decent education. Once government has removed the barriers to equal opportunity, however, it should allow and encourage individuals to get ahead on the basis of work and ability. Accepting Madison's precept that the "first object of government" is to protect "the diversity in the faculties of men," neoconservatives insist on scope for the talented and ambitious, and they incline toward the principle of "meritocracy," that the ablest ought to rise to the top in both public and private life.[62]

The government has gone too far, neoconservatives claim, in promoting an "equality of result." Affirmative Action programs that give women and racial minorities an edge in hiring and promotion amount to special privilege, "reverse discrimination" against whites and males. The argument that Affirmative Action attempts to compensate minorities and women for discrimination in the past seems, to neoconservatives, even more dangerous than the policy of Affirmative Action. Trying to undo the unfairness of the past will lead the government to seek to control compensation for early childhood education and to manage political culture to remove inequalities in speech and manners. Such a policy threatens the autonomy of private life and entails a federal bureaucracy with alarming powers, which neoconservatives dread.

Moreover, neoconservatives suspect any loosening of the connection between achievement, moral conduct, and personal responsibility, on one hand, and material rewards, on the other. Given the fact of social fragmentation, the foundations of virtue and morality are weak. The hope of success and the fear of failure are necessary to discipline a private, self-seeking public; neoconservatives admire the framers and their appeal to the mechanisms of competition as a substitute for self-restraint.[63] Neoconservatives do not imagine, however, that such substitutes are enough. It is necessary to adopt a "new philosophy of *laissez faire*" that seeks to limit the actions of the state by public policies aimed at creating "new contexts of association and moral cohesion" that will allow social institutions to revive and prosper.[64]

Morality and social institutions are not, for neoconservatives, ends in themselves. They are means to the end of individual liberty. In a democracy, individuals will be allowed to enjoy inequalities of wealth and power only because competition and equal opportunity are principles supported by the people. The majority, however, cannot be winners in the competition. All Americans want to make it to the top, but most know that they will have to settle for less. If most people support equality of opportunity, it is not because that policy benefits them or advances their interests. It can only be because they feel an obligation to play by the rules even when they no longer hope to win, "to fulfill his or her part," Paul Johson writes, "in the Divine Contract."[65] Individual liberty, in other words, requires moral restraint, for the majority at any rate. Radical individualism and libertarianism are dangerous. The political foundation of individual liberty, neoconservatives contend, is not private interest but a vision of freedom as a public good.[66]

On the other side of the political debate, liberals and the democratic left emphasize equality rather than individual liberty. Just as neoconservatives are not old-line individualists, most contemporary **egalitarians** are not in love with the state, but they do worry about the impact on public life of America's inequalities of wealth and power.

Egalitarians argue that it is foolish to speak as though America were approaching an "equality of result." There has been virtually no decline in economic inequality in the United States in the last forty years. By almost every measure, inequality in the United States is greater than in other industrial countries.[67] About 5 percent of the American people control 50 percent of the national wealth; one-fifth of Americans control three-quarters of the wealth.[68] In one decisive respect, egalitarians observe, the United States is growing even less equal: the numbers of rich and poor are increasing, but there are relatively fewer Americans in the middle.[69]

Egalitarians go on to argue that inequality undermines the moral foundations of democracy and of civic responsibility. Poor Americans who are chronically unemployed, for example, are only too likely to feel worthless, since American society is telling them they have nothing to contribute. Further, egalitarians observe, people who are convinced that they are powerless, who believe that what they do or do not do makes little or no difference, have small reason to act responsibly or to practice self-restraint.[70]

Consequently, contemporary egalitarians are likely to criticize the "war on poverty" for concentrating on reducing poverty rather than lessening inequality, and for emphasizing federal payments to the poor rather than full employment. The federal government, they argue, must pursue a variety of policies, public programs and incentives to the private sector, in order to guarantee every American a decent job. Full employment, in this view, rivals economic growth as a goal of national economic policy.[71]

Although egalitarians think a great deal remains to be done, they concede that the American political system has made impressive advances toward equal rights. At the same time, they insist that, in practice, politics depends more and more on money and organizational power. Private inequalities, translated into unequal political power, make equal rights into a kind of fiction. In the egalitarian view, this sort of political inequality encourages the belief that the law is not something we make through our representatives, but something "they"—the wealthy and powerful—control through the charade of democratic elections. Inequality, egalitarians argue, contributes to political disillusionment and a lessened sense of political obligation.[72]

Most contemporary egalitarians agree that America needs to strengthen morality and civic spirit, fostering civility and a willingness to sacrifice for the common good. They argue, however, that such restraint and sacrifice can only develop if people feel that the burden is justly shared. Hard-pressed middle- and working-class taxpayers, hearing about the tax shelters and evasions of the well-to-do and the great corporations, can only be expected to feel a feebler sense of obligation to the law. The basis of the egalitarian case is the contention that the very idea of a common good requires that each citizen share justly in the duties and rewards of political life. This does not require us to be equal in all things; it does demand that each citizen be treated as an equal, with something approaching equal dignity.[73]

Dignity, however, is very scarce in mass society. Americans in increasing numbers feel helpless and unimportant, especially since the implicit ideal of the great organizations is to reduce individuals to interchangeable and disposable parts. There seems less and less connection between the sphere in which individuals matter and the mass organizations that shape so much of our national life.[74]

Neoconservatives on the right and egalitarians on the left agree, in general, on the need for institutions and organizations that can bridge that gap. Such "mediating structures" must be "people-sized"—small enough to allow the individual to feel significant but strong enough to be effective. Conservatives are sometimes tempted to believe that all would be well if the government would "cease and desist" from damaging mediating structures, and they stress the healthy side of contemporary families and localities. Liberals and people on the democratic left are more inclined to see families and communities as strained or shattered by a dynamic economy and by technological change, needing the active support of government against such forces. In this view, there is every need for federal policies designed to defend, encourage, or construct the kind of families and local publics suited to provide for the political education of citizens.[75] Despite their differences, in other words, both neoconservatives and egalitarians are concerned to restore or rebuild the private foundations of personal dignity and public life.[76]

This is as it should be. American democracy faces a future that is radically challenging, full of threat and promise. The political landscape will be unfamiliar and many of our old landmarks will no longer serve. Laws and institutions will protect us less, and will require our support more. Constitutional government will be more dependent on human virtues. It will demand more public attention to training in citizenship and in statecraft and to developing the means by which public feelings and opinions can be translated into effective ideals of justice and the common good. Political institutions are the bloodstream of citizenship, and now, more than ever, citizens are the heart of American democracy.

NOTES

1. Robin Williams, *American Society* (New York: Knopf, 1951), p. 406.
2. Alexis de Tocqueville, *Democracy in America,* vol. 2 (New York: Schocken, 1961), p. 88.
3. Address at Amherst College, Oct. 26, 1963.
4. Robert E. Lane, "The Politics of Consensus in an Age of Affluence," *American Political Science Review,* 59 (1965), pp. 874–75.
5. Henry Grunwald, "American Renewal," *Fortune,* 103 (Mar. 9, 1981), p. 71.
6. *The Chicago Sun-Times* (June 2, 1985), p. 47.
7. William G. Scott and David K. Hart, *Organizational America* (Boston: Houghton, 1979), pp. 14–15; see also Sidney Verba and Norman Nie, *Participation in America: Political Democracy and Social Equality* (New York: Harper, 1972), pp. 229–47.
8. Walter Weyl, *The New Democracy* (New York: Macmillan, 1912), p. 13.
9. Rexford G. Tugwell, *The Emerging Constitution* (New York: Harpers Magazine, 1974); for a similar view, see Charles M. Hardin, *Presidential Power and Accountability* (Chicago: U. of Chicago, 1974).
10. For example, see Aaron B. Wildavsky, *How to Limit Government Spending* (Berkeley: U. of California, 1980).
11. *The New York Times* (June 3, 1984), p. 29.
12. James Duffy, *Domestic Affairs* (New York: Simon & Schuster, 1978), p. 68.
13. James Fallows, *National Defense* (New York: Random House, 1981), p. 138.
14. *Congressional Quarterly Weekly Report* (Nov. 28, 1981), p. 2333.
15. Ronald Inglehart, "The Silent Revolution in Europe: Intergenerational Change in Post-Industrial Societies," *American Political Science Review,* 65 (1971) pp. 991–1017.
16. National Council on Employment Opportunity, *Critical Choices for the 80s* (Washington: GPO, 1980), pp. 17–19.
17. *The New York Times* (Sept. 27, 1984), p. B10.

18. John Kenneth Galbraith, *Economics and the Public Purpose* (Boston: Houghton Mifflin, 1973), pp. 146–54; Alvin Toffler, *Future Shock* (New York: Bantam, 1969); Robert Heilbroner, *Business Civilization in Decline* (New York: Norton, 1976), pp. 56–58.
19. Robert Kuttner, "Jobs," *Dissent,* 31 (Winter 1984), p. 32; on robotics, see John Holusha, "Robots that 'See' and 'Feel,'" *The New York Times* (June 6, 1985), p. D2. The number of industrial robots is growing at a rate of 30 percent per year; see *Harper's,* 270 (April 1985), p. 11.
20. David Burnham, *The Rise of the Computer State* (New York: Random House, 1983); the FBI's recommendation is reported in *The New York Times* (Oct. 25, 1984), p. 1.
21. *Harper's,* 270 (April 1985), p. 11.
22. Lester Brown, *World Without Borders* (New York: Vintage, 1972); Peter Brown and Henry Shue, eds., *Boundaries: National Autonomy and Its Limits* (Totowa, N.J.: Rowman & Littlefield, 1981).
23. On some of these issues, see William Bowen, "How to Regain our Competitive Edge," *Fortune,* 103 (Mar. 9, 1981), pp. 74ff.
24. Heilbroner, pp. 93–94.
25. Galbraith, pp. 164–75.
26. Kuttner, p. 32.
27. Ibid., p. 31.
28. For one example, see Norman Podhoretz, "The Neo-Conservative Anguish over Reagan's Foreign Policy," *The New York Times Magazine* (May 2, 1982), pp. 30ff.
29. John Blair, *Economic Concentration* (New York: Harcourt, 1972); Peter Drucker warns us to expect a world with only eight automobile companies, "Why Some Mergers Work and Many More Don't," *Forbes,* 129 (Jan. 18, 1982), p. 34.
30. Galbraith, *Economics;* Neil Jacoby, *Corporate Power and Social Responsibility* (New York: Macmillan, 1973).
31. Drucker, "Why Some Mergers Work. . . ."
32. Robert Lekachman, "The Promise of Democratic Socialism," in *Democracy and Mediating Structures,* Michael Novak, ed. (Washington: American Enterprise Institute, 1980), p. 40; on the origin of great corporations, see George Wheeler, *Pierpont Morgan and Friends: The Anatomy of a Myth* (Englewood Cliffs, N.J.: Prentice-Hall, 1973).
33. Richard Posner, *Antitrust Law: An Economic Perspective* (Chicago: U. of Chicago, 1976).
34. Scott and Hart, p. 5.
35. Robert A. Dahl, "Pluralism Revisited," *Comparative Politics,* 10 (1978), pp. 191–203.
36. David Vogel, "The Corporation as Government: Challenges and Dilemmas," *Polity,* 8 (1975), pp. 5–37.
37. Lekachman, p. 38.
38. Samuel Beer, "Political Overload and Federalism," *Polity,* 10 (1977), pp. 5–17; Arthur Blaustein, "Moral Responsibility and National Character," *Society,* 19 (May/June 1982), pp. 26–27.
39. Marc K. Landy and Henry Plotkin, "The Limits of the Market Metaphor," *Society,* 19 (May/June 1982), p. 14.
40. Brigitte Berger, "The Family as a Mediating Structure," in Novak, ed., *Democracy,* p. 145.
41. Duffy, pp. 266–69.
42. Seymour Martin Lipset, "Whatever Happened to the Proletariat?" *Encounter,* 56 (June 1981), p. 24.
43. William Connolly, "The Politics of Reindustrialization," *Democracy,* 1 (1981), pp. 9–21; Michael Reagan, *The Managed Economy* (New York: Oxford U. P., 1963).
44. Heilbroner, p. 115.
45. Ibid., p. 102; Robert Theobald, *The Challenge of Abundance* (New York: New American Library, 1962).
46. Nicholas Wade, "Raw Materials: U.S. Grows More Vulnerable to Third World Cartels," *Science,* 183 (1974), p. 186.
47. William Baldwin, "Do You Sincerely Want to End Inflation?," *Forbes,* 129 (Mar. 29, 1982), p. 99.
48. Lester Thurow, *The Zero-Sum Society* (New York: Basic Books, 1980); Heilbroner, p. 110.
49. William Baldwin, "A Nation of Spendthrifts," *Forbes,* 135 (Jan. 28, 1985), pp. 33–34.
50. Ashby Bladen, "Volcker and the Tiger's Tail," *Forbes,* 135 (Mar. 25, 1985) p. 281.
51. Seymour Martin Lipset and Earl Raab, "The Message of Proposition Thirteen," *Commentary,* 66 (Sept. 1978), p. 44; see also Michael Best and William Connolly, *The Politicized Economy* (Lexington: Heath, 1976), pp. 27–28.
52. Robert Dahl, "On Removing Certain Impediments to Democracy in the United States," *Political Science Quarterly,* 92 (1977), pp. 1–20; see also Mark Nadel, *Corporations and Political Accountability* (Lexington, Mass.: Heath, 1976).
53. Charles Lindblom, *Politics and Markets* (New York: Basic Books, 1977), pp. 173, 179–80; Samuel P. Huntington, "Paradigms of American Politics," *Political Science Quarterly,* 89 (1974), pp. 1–26; Walter Dean Burnham, "American Politics in the 1980s," *Dissent* (Spring 1980), p. 155.
54. John Kenneth Galbraith, "Taking the Sting Out of Capitalism," *The New York Times* (May 26, 1985), pp. F1ff.
55. Fallows, p. 68.
56. B. Bruce-Biggs, ed., *The New Class* (New Brunswick, N.J.: Transaction, 1979).
57. Michael Harrington, *Socialism* (New York: Saturday Review Press, 1972), p. 251.
58. Heilbroner, p. 58.
59. Charles Schultze, *The Public Use of Private Interest* (Washington, D.C.: Brookings, 1977).
60. Landy and Plotkin, "The Limits of the Market Metaphor."
61. Novak, p. 196.
62. Ibid., p. 197. See also Irving Kristol, *Two Cheers for Capitalism* (New York: Basic, 1978); Robert Nisbet, *The Twilight of Authority* (New York: Oxford U.P., 1975), pp. 198–199.
63. Irving Kristol, *On the Democratic Idea in America* (New York: Harper, 1972); Nisbet, *Twilight of Authority,* pp. 203–210; Aaron Wildavsky, "Government and the People," *Commentary,* 61 (Aug. 1973), pp. 25–32.
64. Nisbet, *Community and Power,* pp. 23, 73; *Twilight of Authority,* p. 74.
65. Novak, p. 56.
66. Novak, p. 197.
67. Sidney Verba and Gary Orren, *Equality in America* (Cambridge: Harvard U.P., 1985), pp. 9–10; Michael Harrington, "The New Gradgrinds," *Dissent* (Spring 1984), p. 173.
68. Herbert Gans, *More Equality* (New York: Pantheon, 1973).
69. Verba and Orren, pp. 248, 323.
70. David Miller, "Democracy and Social Justice," *British Journal of Political Science,* 8 (1978), pp. 1–19.

71. Robert Kuttner, *The Economic Illusion* (Boston: Houghton, 1984); Michael Harrington, "The Welfare State and its Conservative Critics," *Dissent* (Fall 1973), pp. 435–454.
72. Robert Dahl, "The Moscow Discourse: Fundamental Rights in a Democratic Order," *Government and Opposition,* 15 (1980), pp. 3–30.
73. Michael Walzer, *Radical Principles* (New York: Basic, 1980), pp. 291–299.
74. Scott and Hart, pp. 65–68.
75. Jane J. Mansbridge, *Beyond Adversary Democracy* (New York: Basic, 1980).
76. David Price, "Community, 'Mediating Structures' and Public Policy," *Soundings,* 62 (1979), pp. 385–386; Peter Berger and Richard J. Neuhaus, *To Empower People* (Washington, D.C.: American Enterprise Institute, 1977).

The Declaration of Independence

Preamble

When, in the course of human events, it becomes necessary for one people to dissolve the political bands which have connected them with another, and to assume, among the powers of the earth, the separate and equal station to which the laws of nature and of nature's God entitle them, a decent respect to the opinions of mankind requires that they should declare the causes which impel them to the separation.

New Principles of Government

We hold these truths to be self-evident; that all men are created equal, that they are endowed by their Creator with certain unalienable rights, that among these are life, liberty, and the pursuit of happiness.

That, to secure these rights, governments are instituted among men, deriving their just powers from the consent of the governed;

That whenever any form of government becomes destructive of these ends, it is the right of the people to alter or to abolish it, and to institute new government, laying its foundation on such principles, and organizing its powers in such form, as to them shall seem most likely to effect their safety and happiness. Prudence, indeed, will dictate that governments long established should not be changed for light and transient causes; and accordingly all experience hath shown that mankind are more disposed to suffer while evils are sufferable, than to right themselves by abolishing the forms to which they are accustomed. But when a long train of abuses and usurpations, pursuing invariably the same object, evinces a design to reduce them under absolute despotism, it is their right, it is their duty, to throw off such government, and to provide new guards for their future security.

Reasons for Separation

Such has been the patient sufferance of these colonies; and such is now the necessity which constrains them to alter their former systems of government. The history of the present king of Great Britain is a history of repeated injuries and usurpations, all having in direct object the establishment of an absolute tyranny over these states. To prove this, let facts be submitted to a candid world.

He has refused his assent to laws the most wholesome and necessary for the public good.

He has forbidden his governors to pass laws of immediate and pressing importance unless suspended in their operation till his assent should be obtained; and when so suspended, he has utterly neglected to attend to them.

He has refused to pass other laws for the accommodation of large districts of people, unless those people would relinquish the right of representation in the legislature, a right inestimable to them, and formidable to tyrants only.

He has called together legislative bodies at places unusual, uncomfortable, and distant from the depository of their public records, for the sole purpose of fatiguing them into compliance with his measures.

He has dissolved representative houses repeatedly, for opposing, with manly firmness, his invasions on the rights of the people.

He has refused, for a long time after such dissolutions, to cause others to be elected; whereby the legislative powers, incapable of annihilation, have returned to the people at large for their exercise; the state remaining, in the mean time, exposed to all the dangers of invasion from without and convulsions within.

He has endeavored to prevent the population of these states; for that purpose obstructing the laws of naturalization of foreigners, refusing to pass others to encourage their migration hither, and raising the conditions of new appropriations of lands.

He has obstructed the administration of justice, by refusing his assent to laws for establishing judiciary powers.

He has made judges dependent on his will alone for the tenure of their offices, and the amount and payment of their salaries.

He has erected a multitude of new offices, and sent hither swarms of officers to harass our people and eat out their substance.

He has kept among us, in times of peace, standing armies, without the consent of our legislature.

He has affected to render the military independent of, and superior to, the civil power.

He has combined with others to subject us to a jurisdiction foreign to our constitution and unacknowledged by our laws, giving his assent to their acts of pretended legislation:

For quartering large bodies of armed troops among us;

For protecting them, by a mock trial, from punishment for any murders which they should commit on the inhabitants of these states;

For cutting off our trade with all parts of the world;

For imposing taxes on us without our consent;

For depriving us, in many cases, of the benefits of trial by jury;

For transporting us beyond seas, to be tried for pretended offenses;

For abolishing the free system of English laws in a neighboring province, establishing therein an arbitrary government, and enlarging its boundaries, so as to render it at once an example and fit instrument for introducing the same absolute rule into these colonies;

For taking away our charters, abolishing our most valuable laws, and altering, fundamentally, the forms of our governments;

For suspending our own legislatures, and declaring themselves invested with power to legislate for us in all cases whatsoever.

He has abdicated government here, by declaring us out of his protection and waging war against us.

He has plundered our seas, ravaged our coasts, burned our towns, and destroyed the lives of our people.

He is at this time transporting large armies of foreign mercenaries to complete the works of death, desolation, and tyranny already begun with circumstances of cruelty and perfidy scarcely paralleled in the most barbarous ages and totally unworthy the head of a civilized nation.

He has constrained our fellow-citizens, taken captive on the high seas, to bear arms against their country, to become the executioners of their friends and brethren, or to fall themselves by their hands.

He has excited domestic insurrections among us, and has endeavored to bring on the inhabitants of our frontiers the merciless Indian savages, whose known rule of warfare is an undistinguished destruction of all ages, sexes, and conditions.

In every stage of these oppressions we have petitioned for redress in the most humble terms; our repeated petitions have been answered only by repeated injury. A prince whose character is thus marked by every act which may define a tyrant is unfit to be the ruler of a free people.

Nor have we been wanting in attention to our British brethren. We have warned them, from time to time, of attempts by their legislature to extend an unwarrantable jurisdiction over us. We have reminded them of the circumstances of our emigration and settlement here. We have appealed to their native justice and magnanimity; and we have conjured them by the ties of our common kindred, to disavow these usurpations, which would inevitably interrupt our connections and correspondence. They, too, have been deaf to the voice of justice and of consanguinity. We must, therefore, acquiesce in the necessity which denounces our separation, and hold them, as we hold the rest of mankind, enemies in war, in peace, friends.

We, therefore, the representatives of the United States of America, in General Congress assembled, appealing to the Supreme Judge of the world for the rectitude of our intentions, do, in the name and by authority of the good people of these colonies, solemnly publish and declare, that these united colonies are, and of right ought to be, free and independent states; that they are absolved from all allegiance to the British crown, and that all political connection between them and the state of Great Britain is, and ought to be, totally dissolved; and that, as free and independent states, they have full power to levy war, conclude peace, contract alliances, establish commerce, and do all other acts and things which independent states may of a right do. And, for the support of this declaration, with a firm reliance on the protection of Divine Providence, we mutually pledge to each other our lives, our fortunes, and our sacred honor.

The Constitution of the United States of America*

We the people of the United States, in Order to form a more perfect Union, establish Justice, insure domestic Tranquility, provide for the common defence, promote the general Welfare, and secure the Blessings of Liberty to ourselves and our Posterity, do ordain and establish this Constitution for the United States of America.

Article I

SECTION 1. All legislative Powers herein granted shall be vested in a Congress of the United States, which shall consist of a Senate and House of Representatives.

SECTION 2. The House of Representatives shall be composed of Members chosen every second Year by the People of the several States, and the Electors in each State shall have the Qualifications requisite for Electors of the most numerous Branch of the State Legislature.

No Person shall be a Representative who shall not have attained to the Age of twenty-five Years, and been seven Years a Citizen of the United States, and who shall not, when elected, be an Inhabitant of that state in which he shall be chosen.

[Representatives and direct Taxes shall be apportioned among the several States which may be included within this Union, according to their respective Numbers, which shall be determined by adding to the whole Number of free Persons, including those bound to Service for a Term of Years, and excluding Indians not taxed, three-fifths of all other Persons.]† The actual Enumeration shall be made within three Years after the first Meeting of the Congress of the United States, and within every subsequent Term of ten Years, in such Manner as they shall by Law direct. The Number of Representatives shall not exceed one for every thirty Thousand, but each State shall have at Least one Representative; and until such enumeration shall be made, the State of New Hampshire shall be entitled to choose three, Massachusetts eight, Rhode Island and Providence Plantations one, Connecticut five, New York six, New Jersey four, Pennsylvania eight, Delaware one, Maryland six, Virginia ten, North Carolina five, South Carolina five, and Georgia three.

When vacancies happen in the Representation from any State, the Executive Authority thereof shall issue Writs of Election to fill such Vacancies.

The House of Representatives shall choose their Speaker and other Officers; and shall have the sole Power of Impeachment.

SECTION 3. The Senate of the United States shall be composed of two Senators from each State, [chosen by the Legislature thereof,]‡ for six Years; and each Senator shall have one Vote.

Immediately after they shall be assembled in Consequence of the first Election, they shall be divided as equally as may be into three Classes. The Seats of the Senators of the first Class shall be vacated at the Expiration of the second Year, of the second Class at the Expiration of the fourth Year, and of the third Class at the Expiration of the sixth Year, so that one-third may be chosen every second Year; [and if Vacancies happen by Resignation, or otherwise, during the Recess of the Legislature of any State, the Executive thereof may make temporary Appointments until the next Meeting of the Legislature, which shall then fill such Vacancies].§

No Person shall be a Senator who shall not have attained to the Age of thirty Years, and been nine Years a

*The Constitution and all amendments are shown in their original form. Parts that have been amended or superseded are bracketed and explained in the footnotes.

†Modified by the Fourteenth and Sixteenth Amendments.

‡Superseded by the Seventeenth Amendment.

§Modified by the Seventeenth Amendment.

Citizen of the United States, and who shall not, when elected, be an Inhabitant of that State in which he shall be chosen.

The Vice President of the United States shall be President of the Senate, but shall have no vote, unless they be equally divided.

The Senate shall choose their other Officers, and also a President pro tempore, in the absence of the Vice President, or when he shall exercise the Office of the President of the United States.

The Senate shall have the sole Power to try all Impeachments. When sitting for that purpose, they shall be on Oath or Affirmation. When the President of the United States is tried, the Chief Justice shall preside: And no person shall be convicted without the Concurrence of two thirds of the Members present.

Judgment in Cases of Impeachment shall not extend further than to removal from Office, and disqualification to hold and enjoy any Office of honor, Trust, or Profit under the United States: but the Party convicted shall nevertheless be liable and subject to Indictment, Trial, Judgment, and Punishment, according to Law.

SECTION 4. The Times, Places, and Manner of holding Elections for Senators and Representatives, shall be prescribed in each state by the Legislature thereof; but the Congress may at any time by Law make or alter such Regulations, except as to the Places of Choosing Senators.

The Congress shall assemble at least once in every Year, and such Meeting shall [be on the first Monday in December],* unless they shall by Law appoint a different Day.

SECTION 5. Each House shall be the Judge of the Elections, Returns, and Qualifications of its own Members, and a Majority of each shall constitute a Quorum to do Business; but a smaller number may adjourn from day to day, and may be authorized to compel the Attendance of absent Members, in such Manner, and under such Penalties, as each House may provide.

Each House may determine the Rules of its Proceedings, punish its Members for disorderly Behavior, and, with the Concurrence of two-thirds, expel a Member.

Each House shall keep a Journal of its Proceedings, and from time to time publish the same, excepting such Parts as may in their Judgment require Secrecy; and the Yeas and Nays of the Members of either House on any question shall, at the Desire of one-fifth of those Present, be entered on the Journal.

Neither House, during the Session of Congress, shall, without the Consent of the other, adjourn for more than three days, nor to any other Place than that in which the two Houses shall be sitting.

SECTION 6. The Senators and Representatives shall receive a Compensation for their Services, to be ascertained by Law, and paid out of the Treasury of the United States. They shall in all Cases, except Treason, Felony, and Breach of the Peace, be privileged from Arrest during their Attendance at the Session of their respective Houses, and in going to and returning from the same; and for any Speech or Debate in either House, they shall not be questioned in any other Place.

No Senator or Representative shall, during the Time for which he was elected, be appointed to any civil Office under the Authority of the United States, which shall have been created, or the Emoluments whereof shall have been increased, during such time; and no Person holding any Office under the United States shall be a Member of either House during his continuance in Office.

SECTION 7. All Bills for raising Revenue shall originate in the House of Representatives; but the Senate may propose or concur with Amendments as on other bills.

Every Bill which shall have passed the House of Representatives and the Senate, shall, before it become a Law, be presented to the President of the United States; if he approve he shall sign it, but if not he shall return it, with his Objections, to that House in which it shall have originated, who shall enter the Objections at large on their Journal, and proceed to reconsider it. If after such Reconsideration two thirds of that House shall agree to pass the bill, it shall be sent, together with the objections, to the other House, by which it shall likewise be reconsidered, and if approved by two thirds of that House, it shall become a Law. But in all such Cases the Votes of both Houses shall be determined by Yeas and Nays, and the Names of the Persons voting for and against the Bill shall be entered on the Journal of each House respectively. If any Bill shall not be returned by the President within ten Days (Sundays excepted) after it shall have been presented to him, the Same shall be a Law, in like Manner as if he had signed it, unless the Congress by their Adjournment prevent its Return, in which Case it shall not be a Law.

Every Order, Resolution, or Vote to which the Concurrence of the Senate and House of Representatives may be necessary (except on a question of Adjournment) shall be presented to the President of the United States; and before the Same shall take Effect, shall be approved by him, or being disapproved by him, shall be repassed by two-thirds of the Senate and House of Representatives, according to the Rules and Limitations prescribed in the Case of a Bill.

SECTION 8. The Congress shall have Power to lay and col-

*Superseded by the Twentieth Amendment.

lect Taxes, Duties, Imposts, and Excises, to pay the Debts and provide for the common Defense and general Welfare of the United States; but all Duties, Imposts, and Excises shall be uniform throughout the United States;

To borrow money on the credit of the United States;

To regulate Commerce with foreign Nations, and among the several States, and with the Indian Tribes;

To establish an uniform Rule of Naturalization, and uniform Laws on the subject of Bankruptcies throughout the United States;

To coin Money, regulate the Value thereof, and of foreign Coin, and fix the Standard of Weights and Measures;

To provide for the Punishment of counterfeiting the Securities and current Coin of the United States;

To establish Post Offices and post Roads;

To promote the Progress of Science and useful Arts, by securing for limited Times to Authors and Inventors the exclusive Right to their respective Writings and Discoveries;

To constitute Tribunals inferior to the Supreme Court;

To define and punish Piracies and Felonies committed on the high Seas, and Offenses against the Laws of Nations;

To declare War, grant Letters of Marque and Reprisal, and make Rules concerning Captures on Land and Water;

To raise and support Armies, but no Appropriation of Money to that Use shall be for a longer Term than two Years;

To provide and maintain a Navy;

To make Rules for the Government and Regulation of the land and naval forces;

To provide for calling forth the Militia to execute the Laws of the Union, suppress Insurrections and repel Invasions;

To provide for organizing, arming, and disciplining the Militia, and for governing such Part of them as may be employed in the Service of the United States, reserving to the States respectively, the Appointment of the Officers, and the Authority of training the Militia according to the discipline prescribed by Congress;

To exercise exclusive Legislation in all Cases whatsoever, over such District (not exceeding ten Miles square) as may, by Cession of particular States, and the acceptance of Congress, become the Seat of the Government of the United States, and to exercise like Authority over all Places purchased by the Consent of the Legislature of the State in which the Same shall be, for the Erection of Forts, Magazines, Arsenals, dock-Yards, and other needful Buildings;—And

To make all Laws which shall be necessary and proper for carrying into Execution the foregoing Powers, and all other Powers vested by this Constitution in the Government of the United States, or in any Department or Officer thereof.

SECTION 9. The Migration or Importation of such Persons as any of the States now existing shall think proper to admit shall not be prohibited by the Congress prior to the Year one thousand eight hundred and eight, but a tax or duty may be imposed on such Importation, not exceeding ten dollars for each Person.

The privilege of the Writ of *Habeas Corpus* shall not be suspended, unless when in Cases of Rebellion or Invasion the public Safety may require it.

No Bill of Attainder or ex post facto Law shall be passed.

[No capitation, or other direct, Tax shall be laid unless in Proportion to the Census or Enumeration herein before directed to be taken.]*

No Tax or Duty shall be laid on Articles exported from any State.

No Preference shall be given by any Regulation of Commerce or Revenue to the Ports of one State over those of another: nor shall Vessels bound to, or from, one State, be obliged to enter, clear, or pay Duties in another.

No Money shall be drawn from the Treasury, but in Consequence of Appropriations made by Law; and a regular Statement and Account of the Receipts and Expenditures of all public Money shall be published from time to time.

No Title of Nobility shall be granted by the United States: And no Person holding any Office of Profit or Trust under them, shall, without the Consent of the Congress, accept of any present, Emolument, Office, or Title, of any kind whatever, from any King, Prince, or foreign State.

SECTION 10. No State shall enter into any Treaty, Alliance, or Confederation; grant Letters of Marque and Reprisal; coin Money; emit Bills of Credit; make any Thing but gold and silver Coin a Tender in Payment of Debts; pass any Bill of Attainder, ex post facto Law, or Law impairing the Obligation of Contracts, or grant any Title of Nobility.

No State shall, without the Consent of the Congress, lay any Imposts or Duties on Imports or Exports, except what may be absolutely necessary for executing its inspection Laws: and the net Produce of all Duties and Imposts, laid by any State on Imports or Exports, shall be for the Use of the Treasury of the United States; and all such Laws shall be subject to the Revision and Control of the Congress.

No State shall, without the Consent of Congress, lay any duty of Tonnage, keep Troops, or Ships of War in time of Peace, enter into any Agreement or Compact with another State, or with a foreign Power, or engage in War, unless actually invaded, or in such imminent Danger as will not admit of delay.

*Modified by the Sixteenth Amendment.

Article II

SECTION 1. The executive Power shall be vested in a President of the United States of America. He shall hold his Office during the Term of four years, and, together with the Vice President, chosen for the same Term, be elected, as follows:

Each State shall appoint, in such Manner as the Legislature thereof may direct, a Number of Electors, equal to the whole Number of Senators and Representatives to which the State may be entitled in the Congress: but no Senator or Representative, or Person holding an Office of Trust or Profit under the United States, shall be appointed an Elector.

[The Electors shall meet in their respective States, and vote by Ballot for two persons, of whom one at least shall not be an Inhabitant of the same State with themselves. And they shall make a List of all the Persons voted for, and of the Number of Votes for each; which List they shall sign and certify, and transmit sealed to the Seat of the Government of the United States, directed to the President of the Senate. The President of the Senate shall, in the Presence of the Senate and House of Representatives, open all the Certificates, and the Votes shall then be counted. The Person having the greatest Number of Votes shall be the President, if such Number be a Majority of the whole Number of Electors appointed; and if there be more than one who have such Majority, and have an equal Number of Votes, then the House of Representatives shall immediately choose by Ballot one of them for President; and if no Person have a Majority, then from the five highest on the List the said House shall in like Manner choose the President. But in choosing the President, the Votes shall be taken by States, the Representation from each State having one Vote; a quorum for this Purpose shall consist of a Member or Members from two-thirds of the States, and a Majority of all the States shall be necessary to a Choice. In every Case, after the Choice of the President, the Person having the greatest Number of Votes of the Electors shall be the Vice President. But if there should remain two or more who have equal votes, the Senate shall choose from them by Ballot the Vice President.]*

The Congress may determine the Time of choosing the Electors, and the Day on which they shall give their Votes; which Day shall be the same throughout the United States.

No person except a natural-born Citizen, or a Citizen of the United States, at the time of the Adoption of this Constitution, shall be eligible to the Office of President; neither shall any Person be eligible to that Office who shall not have attained to the Age of thirty-five years, and been fourteen Years a Resident within the United States.

[In Case of the Removal of the President from Office, or of his Death, Resignation, or Inability to discharge the Powers and Duties of the said Office, the same shall devolve on the Vice President, and the Congress may by Law provide for the Case of Removal, Death, Resignation, or Inability, both of the President and Vice President, declaring what Officer shall then act as President, and such Officer shall act accordingly, until the disability be removed, or a President shall be elected.]†

The President shall, at stated Times, receive for his Services a Compensation, which shall neither be increased nor diminished during the Period for which he shall have been elected, and he shall not receive within that Period any other Emolument from the United States, or any of them.

Before he enter on the execution of his Office, he shall take the following Oath or Affirmation:—"I do solemnly swear (or affirm) that I will faithfully execute the Office of President of the United States, and will, to the best of my Ability, preserve, protect, and defend the Constitution of the United States."

SECTION 2. The President shall be Commander in Chief of the Army and Navy of the United States, and of the Militia of the several States, when called into the actual Service of the United States; he may require the Opinion, in writing, of the principal Officer in each of the executive Departments, upon any subject relating to the Duties of their respective Offices, and he shall have Power to Grant Reprieves and Pardons for Offenses against the United States, except in Cases of Impeachment.

He shall have Power, by and with the Advice and Consent of the Senate, to make Treaties, provided two thirds of the Senators present concur; and he shall nominate, and by and with the Advice and Consent of the Senate, shall appoint Ambassadors, other public Ministers and Consuls, Judges of the Supreme Court, and all other Officers of the United States, whose Appointments are not herein otherwise provided for, and which shall be established by Law: but the Congress may by Law vest the Appointment of such inferior Officers, as they think proper, in the President alone, in the Courts of Law, or in the Heads of Departments.

The President shall have Power to fill up all Vacancies that may happen during the Recess of the Senate, by granting Commissions which shall expire at the End of their next Session.

SECTION 3. He shall from time to time give to the Congress Information of the State of the Union, and recommend to their Consideration such Measures as he shall judge neces-

*Superseded by the Twelfth Amendment.

†Modified by the Twenty-fifth Amendment.

sary and expedient; he may, on extraordinary occasions, convene both Houses, or either of them, and in Case of Disagreement between them, with respect to the Time of Adjournment, he may adjourn them to such Time as he shall think proper; he shall receive Ambassadors and other public Ministers; he shall take Care that the Laws be faithfully executed, and shall Commission all the Officers of the United States.

SECTION 4. The President, Vice President, and all civil Officers of the United States, shall be removed from Office on Impeachment for, and Conviction of, Treason, Bribery, or other high Crimes and Misdemeanors.

Article III

SECTION 1. The judicial Power of the United States, shall be vested in one Supreme Court, and in such inferior Courts as the Congress may from time to time ordain and establish. The Judges, both of the Supreme and inferior Courts, shall hold their Offices during good Behavior, and shall, at stated Times, receive for their Services, a Compensation, which shall not be diminished during their Continuance in Office.

SECTION 2. The judicial Power shall extend to all Cases, in Law and Equity, arising under this Constitution, the Laws of the United States, and treaties made, or which shall be made, under their Authority;—to all Cases affecting ambassadors, other public ministers and consuls;—to all cases of admiralty and maritime Jurisdiction;—to Controversies to which the United States shall be a Party;—to Controversies between two or more States;—[between a State and Citizens of another State;]*—between Citizens of different States,—between Citizens of the same State claiming Lands under Grants of different States, and between a State, or the Citizens thereof, and foreign States, Citizens, or Subjects.

In all Cases affecting Ambassadors, other public Ministers and Consuls, and those in which a State shall be Party, the Supreme Court shall have original Jurisdiction. In all the other Cases before mentioned, the Supreme Court shall have appellate Jurisdiction, both as to Law and Fact, with such Exceptions, and under such Regulations as the Congress shall make.

The trial of all Crimes, except in Cases of Impeachment, shall be by Jury; and such Trial shall be held in the State where the said Crimes shall have been committed; but when not committed within any State, the Trial shall be at such Place or Places as the Congress may by Law have directed.

*Modified by the Eleventh Amendment.

SECTION 3. Treason against the United States, shall consist only in levying War against them, or in adhering to their Enemies, giving them Aid and Comfort. No Person shall be convicted of Treason unless on the Testimony of two Witnesses to the same overt Act, or on Confession in open Court.

The Congress shall have power to declare the Punishment of Treason, but no Attainder of Treason shall work Corruption of Blood, or Forfeiture except during the Life of the Person attainted.

Article IV

SECTION 1. Full Faith and Credit shall be given in each State to the public Acts, Records, and judicial Proceedings of every other State. And the Congress may by general Laws prescribe the Manner in which such Acts, Records, and Proceedings shall be proved, and the Effect thereof.

SECTION 2. The Citizens of each State shall be entitled to all Privileges and Immunities of Citizens in the several States.

A Person charged in any State with Treason, Felony, or other Crime, who shall flee from Justice, and be found in another State, shall on demand of the executive Authority of the State from which he fled, be delivered up, to be removed to the State having Jurisdiction of the crime.

[No Person held to Service or Labor in one State, under the Laws thereof, escaping into another, shall, in Consequence of any Law or Regulation therein, be discharged from such Service or Labor, but shall be delivered up on Claim of the Party to whom such Service or Labor may be due.]†

SECTION 3. New States may be admitted by the Congress into this Union; but no new State shall be formed or erected within the Jurisdiction of any other State; nor any State be formed by the Junction of two or more States, or parts of States, without the Consent of the Legislatures of the States concerned as well as of the Congress.

The Congress shall have Power to dispose of and make all needful Rules and Regulations respecting the Territory or other Property belonging to the United States; and nothing in this Constitution shall be so construed as to Prejudice any Claims of the United States, or of any particular State.

SECTION 4. The United States shall guarantee to every State in this Union a Republican Form of Government, and shall protect each of them against Invasion; and on Application of the Legislature, or of the Executive (when

†Superseded by the Thirteenth Amendment.

the Legislature cannot be convened) against domestic Violence.

Article V

The Congress, whenever two-thirds of both Houses shall deem it necessary, shall propose Amendments to this Constitution, or, on the Application of the Legislatures of two-thirds of the several States, shall call a Convention for proposing Amendments, which, in either Case, shall be valid to all Intents and Purposes, as part of this Constitution, when ratified by the Legislatures of three-fourths of the several States, or by Conventions in three-fourths thereof, as the one or the other Mode of Ratification may be proposed by the Congress; Provided that no Amendment which may be made prior to the Year One thousand eight hundred and eight shall in any Manner affect the first and fourth Clauses in the Ninth Section of the first Article; and that no State, without its Consent, shall be deprived of its equal Suffrage in the State.

Article VI

All Debts contracted and Engagements entered into, before the Adoption of this Constitution, shall be as valid against the United States under this Constitution, as under the Confederation.

This Constitution, and the Laws of the United States which shall be made in Pursuance thereof; and all Treaties made, or which shall be made, under the Authority of the United States, shall be the supreme Law of the Land; and the Judges in every State shall be bound thereby, any Thing in the Constitution or Laws of any State to the Contrary notwithstanding.

The Senators and Representatives before mentioned, and the Members of the several State Legislatures, and all executive and judicial Officers, both of the United States and of the several States, shall be bound by Oath or Affirmation to support this Constitution; but no religious Test shall ever be required as a qualification to any Office or public Trust under the United States.

Article VII

The Ratification of the Conventions of nine States shall be sufficient for the Establishment of this Constitution between the States so ratifying the same.

Done in Convention by the Unanimous Consent of the States present the Seventeenth Day of September in the Year of our Lord one thousand seven hundred and Eighty seven, and of the Independence of the United States of America the Twelfth. In Witness whereof We have hereunto subscribed our Names.

Articles in Addition to, and Amendment of, the Constitution of the United States of America, Proposed by Congress, and Ratified by the Legislatures of the Several States, Pursuant to the Fifth Article of the Original Constitution.

Amendment I*

Congress shall make no law respecting an establishment of religion, or prohibiting the free exercise thereof; or abridging the freedom of speech, or of the press; or the right of the people peaceably to assemble, and to petition the Government for a redress of grievances.

Amendment II

A well regulated Militia, being necessary to the security of a free State, the right of the people to keep and bear Arms shall not be infringed.

Amendment III

No Soldier shall, in time of peace, be quartered in any house, without the consent of the Owner, nor in time of war, but in a manner to be prescribed by law.

Amendment IV

The right of the people to be secure in their persons, houses, papers, and effects, against unreasonable searches and seizures, shall not be violated, and no Warrants shall issue, but upon probable cause, supported by Oath or affirmation, and particularly describing the place to be searched, and the persons or things to be seized.

Amendment V

No person shall be held to answer for a capital or otherwise infamous crime, unless on a presentment or indictment of a Grand Jury, except in cases arising in the land or naval forces, or in the Militia, when in actual service in time of War or public danger; nor shall any person be subject for the same offense to be twice put in jeopardy of life or limb; nor shall be compelled in any criminal case to be a witness against himself, nor be deprived of life, liberty, or property, without due process of law; nor shall private property be taken for public use, without just compensation.

*The first ten amendments were passed by Congress on September 25, 1789. They were ratified by three-fourths of the states on December 15, 1791.

Amendment VI

In all criminal prosecutions, the accused shall enjoy the right to a speedy and public trial, by an impartial jury of the State and district wherein the crime shall have been committed, which district shall have been previously ascertained by law, and to be informed of the nature and cause of the accusation; to be confronted with the witnesses against him; to have compulsory process for obtaining witnesses in his favor, and to have the Assistance of Counsel for his defense.

Amendment VII

In suits at common law, where the value in controversy shall exceed twenty dollars, the right of trial by jury shall be preserved, and no fact tried by a jury, shall be otherwise reexamined in any Court of the United States, than according to the rules of the common law.

Amendment VIII

Excessive bail shall not be required, nor excessive fines imposed, nor cruel and unusual punishments inflicted.

Amendment IX

The enumeration in the Constitution, of certain rights, shall not be construed to deny or disparage others retained by the people.

Amendment X

The powers not delegated to the United States by the Constitution, nor prohibited by it to the States, are reserved to the States respectively, or to the people.

Amendment XI (1795)*

The Judicial power of the United States shall not be construed to extend to any suit in law or equity, commenced or prosecuted against one of the United States by Citizens of another State, or by Citizens or Subjects of any Foreign State.

Amendment XII (1804)

The Electors shall meet in their respective States and vote by ballot for President and Vice President, one of whom, at least, shall not be an inhabitant of the same State with themselves; they shall name in their ballots the person voted for as President, and in distinct ballots the person voted for as Vice President, and they shall make distinct lists of all persons voted for as President, and of all persons voted for as Vice President, and of the number of votes for each, which lists they shall sign and certify, and transmit sealed to the seat of the government of the United States, directed to the President of the Senate;—The President of the Senate shall, in the presence of the Senate and House of Representatives, open all the certificates and the votes shall then be counted;—The person having the greatest number of votes for President, shall be the President, if such number be a majority of the whole number of Electors appointed; and if no person have such majority, then from the persons having the highest numbers not exceeding three on the list of those voted for as President, the House of Representatives shall choose immediately, by ballot, the President. But in choosing the President, the votes shall be taken by states, the representation from each state having one vote; a quorum for this purpose shall consist of a member or members from two thirds of the states, and a majority of all the states shall be necessary to a choice. [And if the House of Representatives shall not choose a President whenever the right of choice shall devolve upon them, before the fourth day of March next following, then the Vice President shall act as President, as in the case of the death or other constitutional disability of the President.]†—The person having the greatest number of votes as Vice President, shall be the Vice President, if such number be a majority of the whole number of Electors appointed, and if no person have a majority, then from the two highest numbers on the list, the Senate shall choose the Vice President; a quorum for the purpose shall consist of two-thirds of the whole number of Senators, and a majority of the whole number shall be necessary to a choice. But no person constitutionally ineligible to the office of President shall be eligible to that of Vice President of the United States.

Amendment XIII (1865)

Section 1. Neither slavery nor involuntary servitude, except as a punishment for crime whereof the party shall have been duly convicted, shall exist within the United States, or any place subject to their jurisdiction.

Section 2. Congress shall have power to enforce this article by appropriate legislation.

Amendment XIV (1868)

Section 1. All persons born or naturalized in the United

*Date of ratification.

†Superseded by the Twentieth Amendment.

States, and subject to the jurisdiction thereof, are citizens of the United States and of the State wherein they reside. No State shall make or enforce any law which shall abridge the privileges or immunities of citizens of the United States; nor shall any State deprive any person of life; liberty, or property, without due process of law; nor deny to any person within its jurisdiction the equal protection of the laws.

SECTION 2. Representatives shall be apportioned among the several States according to their respective numbers, counting the whole number of persons in each State, excluding Indians not taxed. But when the right to vote at any election for the choice of electors for President and Vice President of the United States, Representatives in Congress, the Executive and Judicial officers of a State, or the members of the Legislature thereof, is denied to any of the male inhabitants of such State, being twenty-one years of age, and citizens of the United States, or in any way abridged, except for participation in rebellion, or other crime, the basis of representation therein shall be reduced in the proportion which the number of such male citizens shall bear to the whole number of male citizens twenty-one years of age in such State.

SECTION 3. No person shall be a Senator or Representative in Congress, or elector of President and Vice President, or hold any office, civil or military, under the United States, or under any State, who, have previously taken an oath, as a member of Congress, or as an officer of the United States, or as a member of any State legislature, or as an executive or judicial officer of any State, to support the Constitution of the United States, shall have engaged in insurrection or rebellion against the same, or given aid or comfort to the enemies thereof. But Congress may by a vote of two-thirds of each House, remove such disability.

SECTION 4. The validity of the public debt of the United States, authorized by law, including debts incurred for payment of pensions and bounties for services in suppressing insurrection or rebellion, shall not be questioned. But neither the United States nor any State shall assume or pay any debt or obligation incurred in aid of insurrection or rebellion against the United States, or any claim for the loss or emancipation of any slave; but all such debts, obligations, and claims shall be held illegal and void.

SECTION 5. The Congress shall have the power to enforce, by appropriate legislation, the provisions of this article.

Amendment XV (1870)

SECTION 1. The right of citizens of the United States to vote shall not be denied or abridged by the United States or by any State on account of race, color, or previous condition of servitude—

SECTION 2. The Congress shall have power to enforce this article by appropriate legislation.

Amendment XVI (1913)

The Congress shall have power to lay and collect taxes on incomes, from whatever source derived, without apportionment among the several States, and without regard to any census or enumeration.

Amendment XVII (1913)

The Senate of the United States shall be composed of two Senators from each State, elected by the people thereof, for six years; and each Senator shall have one vote. The electors in each State shall have the qualifications requisite for electors of the most numerous branch of the State legislatures.

When vacancies happen in the representation of any State in the Senate, the executive authority of such State shall issue writs of election to fill such vacancies: *Provided,* That the legislature of any State may empower the executive thereof to make temporary appointments until the people fill the vacancies by election as the legislature may direct.

This amendment shall not be so construed as to affect the election or term of any Senator chosen before it becomes valid as part of the Constitution.

Amendment XVIII (1919)*

SECTION 1. After one year from the ratification of this article the manufacture, sale, or transportation of intoxicating liquors within, the importation thereof into, or the exportation thereof from the United States and all territory subject to the jurisdiction thereof for beverage purposes is hereby prohibited.

SECTION 2. The Congress and the several States shall have concurrent power to enforce this article by appropriate legislation.

SECTION 3. This article shall be inoperative unless it shall have been ratified as an amendment to the Constitution by the legislatures of the several States, as provided in the Constitution, within seven years from the date of the submission hereof to the States by the Congress.

Amendment XIX (1920)

The right of citizens of the United States to vote shall not be denied or abridged by the United States or by any State on account of sex.

Congress shall have power to enforce this article by appropriate legislation.

*Repealed by the Twenty-first Amendment.

Amendment XX (1933)

Section 1. The terms of the President and Vice President shall end at noon on the 20th day of January, and the terms of Senators and Representatives at noon on the 3d day of January, of the years in which such terms would have ended if this article had not been ratified; and the terms of their successors shall then begin.

Section 2. The Congress shall assemble at least once in every year, and such meeting shall begin at noon on the 3d day of January, unless they shall by law appoint a different day.

Section 3. If, at the time fixed for the beginning of the term of the President, the President elect shall have died, the Vice President elect shall become President. If a President shall not have been chosen before the time fixed for the beginning of his term, or if the President elect shall have failed to qualify, then the Vice President elect shall act as President until a President shall have qualified; and the Congress may by law provide for the case wherein neither a President elect nor a Vice President elect shall have qualified, declaring who shall then act as President, or the manner in which one who is to act shall be selected, and such person shall act accordingly until a President or Vice President shall have qualified.

Section 4. The Congress may by law provide for the case of the death of any of the persons from whom the House of Representatives may choose a President whenever the right of choice shall have devolved upon them, and for the case of the death of any of the persons from whom the Senate may choose a Vice President whenever the right of choice shall have devolved upon them.

Section 5. Sections 1 and 2 shall take effect on the 15th day of October following the ratification of this article.

Section 6. This article shall be inoperative unless it shall have been ratified as an amendment to the Constitution by the legislatures of three-fourths of the several States within seven years from the date of its submission.

Amendment XXI (1933)

Section 1. The eighteenth article of amendment to the Constitution of the United States is hereby repealed.

Section 2. The transportation or importation into any State, Territory, or possession of the United States for delivery or use therein of intoxicating liquors, in violation of the laws thereof, is hereby prohibited.

Section 3. This article shall be inoperative unless it shall have been ratified as an amendment to the Constitution by conventions in the several States, as provided in the Constitution, within seven years from the date of the submission hereof to the States by the Congress.

Amendment XXII (1951)

No person shall be elected to the office of the President more than twice, and no person who has held the office of President, or acted as President, for more than two years of a term to which some other person was elected President shall be elected to the office of the President more than once.

But this Article shall not apply to any person holding the office of President when this Article was proposed by the Congress, and shall not prevent any person who may be holding the office of President, or acting as President, during the term within which this Article becomes operative from holding the office of President or acting as President during the remainder of such term.

Amendment XXIII (1961)

Section 1. The District constituting the seat of Government of the United States shall appoint in such manner as the Congress may direct:

A number of electors of President and Vice President equal to the whole number of Senators and Representatives in Congress to which the District would be entitled if it were a State, but in no event more than the least populous State; they shall be in addition to those appointed by the States, but they shall be considered, for the purposes of the election of President and Vice President, to be electors appointed by the State; and they shall meet in the District and perform such duties as provided by the twelfth article of amendment.

Section 2. The Congress shall have power to enforce this article by appropriate legislation.

Amendment XXIV (1964)

Section 1. The right of citizens of the United States to vote in any primary or other election for President or Vice President, for electors for President or Vice President, or for Senator or Representative in Congress, shall not be denied or abridged by the United States or any State by reason of failure to pay any poll tax or other tax.

Section 2. The Congress shall have power to enforce this article by appropriate legislation.

Amendment XXV (1967)

Section 1. In case of the removal of the President from

office or of his death or resignation, the Vice President shall become President.

SECTION 2. Whenever there is a vacancy in the office of the Vice President, the President shall nominate a Vice President who shall take office upon confirmation by a majority vote of both Houses of Congress.

SECTION 3. Whenever the President transmits to the President pro tempore of the Senate and the Speaker of the House of Representatives his written declaration that he is unable to discharge the powers and duties of his office, and until he transmits to them a written declaration to the contrary, such powers and duties shall be discharged by the Vice President as Acting President.

SECTION 4. Whenever the Vice President and a majority of either the principal officers of the executive department or of such other body as Congress may by law provide, transmit to the President pro tempore of the Senate and the Speaker of the House of Representatives their written declaration that the President is unable to discharge the powers and duties of his office, the Vice President shall immediately assume the powers and duties of the office as Acting President.

Thereafter, when the President transmits to the President pro tempore of the Senate and the Speaker of the House of Representatives his written declaration that no inability exists, he shall resume the powers and duties of his office unless the Vice President and a majority of either the principal officers of the executive department or of such other body as Congress may by law provide, transmit within four days to the President pro tempore of the Senate and the Speaker of the House of Representatives their written declaration that the President is unable to discharge the powers and duties of his office. Thereupon Congress shall decide the issue, assembling within forty-eight hours for that purpose if not in session. If the Congress, within twenty-one days after receipt of the latter written declaration, or, if Congress is not in session, within twenty-one days after Congress is required to assemble, determines by two-thirds vote of both Houses that the President is unable to discharge the powers and duties of his office, the Vice-President shall continue to discharge the same as Acting President; otherwise, the President shall resume the powers and duties of his office.

Amendment XXVI (1971)

SECTION 1. The right of citizens of the United States, who are eighteen years of age or older, to vote shall not be denied or abridged by the United States or by any State on account of age.

SECTION 2. The Congress shall have power to enforce this article by appropriate legislation.

Glossary

acid rain An acidic rain (or snow) produced when nitrogen oxide and sulfur dioxide escape from industrial smokestacks and combine with water vapor molecules many miles from the stacks; acid rain contaminates drinking water, harms fish populations, and destroys soil fertility.
Affirmative Action programs An attempt to compensate racial and other minorities, such as women, for the inequalities they suffered in the past by encouraging employers, schools, and other institutions to make a special effort to include and accommodate them.
aggregate demand An economic term meaning "purchasing power" when it applies to the ability of large numbers of people to buy things.
attentive public The section of the public that, because of its affluence or education, pays more attention to developments overseas than the rest of the public and even tends to seek out alternative interpretations from a variety of news sources and commentaries.

balanced budget A situation in which the government or any group or individual spends no more than what it receives in revenue.
bipolycentric The concept of a world in which two militarily dominant superpowers provide protection to the weaker countries allied to them, but with the weaker countries developing significant relationships with members of the opposing alliance.
block grant A federal grant providing funds for a broad policy area and for which the state or city is allowed to decide specifically how to spend the money.
bullet vote A solitary vote in Congress on an issue that causes an unhappy group to launch a campaign against the member of Congress who cast the vote.
bureaucracy A large, hierarchical organization made up of career personnel whose functions and activities are governed by internal rules and whose work is evaluated by an internal standard of performance rather than by an outside market or judge.
bureaucratese The language of bureaucrats; specifically, language filled with jargon.
busing The practice of transporting public school students from one district to another in order to integrate schools.

Cabinet The president's "official family" in the executive branch, whose members provide the president with policy advice and carry out his or her policies.
calendars Categories to which all bills that are reported out of committee are assigned. Assigning bills to calendars that specify when the bill will be voted on is a practice more common in the House than in the Senate.
capitalism An economic system in which people freely acquire or sell property or services in such a context that the laws of supply and demand are the principal influences on the transaction.
case and controversy rule A rule stating that the Supreme Court cannot in general take the initiative in raising a public question but instead must wait for a case to arise.
categorical formula grant A federal grant for a designated project in which funds are divided among the states according to a formula and are usually matched by the states.
checks and balances A system designed to keep the power of the constitution in check through a division of power between the executive, legislative, and judicial branches.
citizen A member of a nation or a state who participates in voting.
civil liberties Areas of life in which citizens are protected against interference by government.
civil rights Those areas in which citizens are entitled to government's active support.

Civil Rights Movement The series of actions during the 1950s and 1960s intended to end policies and practices of racial segregation.
civil service A system of hiring government employees on the basis or merit or qualifications rather than political loyalty.
class action A type of lawsuit in which an adversary speaks not only for his or her own interests but for all similar persons.
class action suit A suit in which a person who has been injured is permitted to sue on behalf of all similarly injured persons.
classical liberals A school of economic thought that maintains that the government should have a limited role in the economy; included among the classical liberals are the monetarists and the supply-siders, both of whom favor low taxes because of the limitations this places on government activism. *See also* Keynesians.
clientelism A too great dependency of Cabinet members on the approval and support of interest groups or clients and insufficient loyalty to the programs of the president.
closed primary A primary election in which participation is limited to people who declare themselves members of a political party.
closed rules Highly restrictive rules set by the House Rules Committee that severely limit amendments on a bill before it is reported out of a committee. *See also* open rules.
cloture petition A means of halting a Senate filibuster, in which supporters of a bill obtain a petition—signed by three-fifths of the members—that imposes a one-hour time limit on each Senator's discussion of a bill.
coattails When candidates hope to be carried along to victory by association with a popular individual who is either in office or on the party ticket.
Cold War The confrontation of idealogies as well as the economic and military rivalry that existed between Communist and Western countries following World War II.
concurrent jurisdiction A situation in which both federal and state courts share the authority to hear a case, such as for bank robbery or embezzlement.
concurring opinion A situation in which a Supreme Court judge accepts the decision of the majority but departs from its reasons.
conference committee A committee composed of senators and House members convened to formulate a bill acceptable in all particulars to both houses of Congress.
conscientious objection The privilege of refusing to take part in military service, granted by the public to pacifists.
conservatism A political idealogy that advocates reducing government spending and the role of government, slowing the pace of change, and bringing about a more traditional morality in regard to religion, sexual relations, and personal conduct. *See also* liberalism.
constitution Usually a written document containing the basic ruling principles of a society.
constitutional courts Courts established under the Constitution and Federal Judiciary Act of 1789, which include 93 Federal District Courts, 11 Circuit Courts of Appeal, and the Supreme Court; the judges serve until they die, resign, or are impeached, and they are not allowed to give advisory opinions or administer statutes. *See also* legislative courts.
constraint The underlying structure in the public's belief system; a well-organized system of beliefs in which issue positions are logically related to each other is characterized by high constraint.
Consumer Price Index The standard gauge for measuring inflation.
containment doctrine A policy of blocking Soviet expansion in new areas that became the core of post-World War II American foreign policy; it was based on the belief that the Soviet Union was intent on extending its power and influence throughout the world at the expense of the United States and its allies.
cooperative Federalism A model of federalism that encourages cooperation between state and national governments.
cosponsors Members of Congress who formally announce support of a particular bill.
cost-benefit analysis A calculation that balances the benefits that come from a regulation against the costs of implementing it.
cruel and unusual punishment A provision of the Eighth Amendment that forbids punishment too severe for the crime (for example, a person's citizenship cannot be taken away for the crime of draft evasion).

deficit financing A situation in which the government borrows money by selling Treasury notes or bonds to banks or individuals; both the principal and the interest from this borrowed money are later recouped through taxes.
delegation of legislative power Congress's allotment of some of its powers to the executive branch bureaucracy.
democracy Literally, "rule by the people"; a government in which the people hold the ruling power, either directly or through elected representation.
depression An economic situation in which very slow business activity creates mass unemployment.
détente A relaxation of tensions between the United States and the Soviet Union that occurred in 1972; by creating a "web of relationships" (cultural exchanges, trade agreements, etc.), *détente* created improved cooperation and controlled military competition between the two nations.
diffusion of conflict Distributing political disputes into

smaller areas, usually defining an issue as a matter for state, not national, decision in order to reduce its emotional impact.

diplomatic recognition The president's power to establish or break diplomatic relations on his or her own.

direction The way the people line up on an issue.

direct primaries An election in which candidates are nominated through mass elections rather than by party organizations.

discharge petition A rejection of a committee's decision not to report out a bill, made by the bill's sponsors in an attempt to rescue the bill.

dissenting opinions Opinions of Supreme Court justices not in agreement with the majority opinion of the Court.

distribution The form and degree of public agreement on an issue, which includes both consensus and conflict; when opinion is concentrated toward the middle, this is called "normal distribution."

division of powers The separation of powers between the national and state/local governments. *See also* federalism.

doctrine of executive privilege The right of the president to refuse to provide Congress with information the president wants withheld.

dual citizenship The idea that Americans are citizens of both the United States and of their respective state, equally.

due process of law The principle, guaranteed by the Fourteenth Amendment, that no person shall be deprived of life, liberty, or property without lawful procedure. *See also* substantive due process.

economic regulation Government intervention in the free operation of markets and the laws of supply and demand.

egalitarians Those who support a political idealogy that favors equality above individual liberty; egalitarians believe that the government must pursue a variety of policies—incentives to the private sector as well as public programs—in order to achieve "equality of result." *See also* neoconservatives.

Electoral College In a national election, the group of people selected by the voters in each state to cast the official vote for president.

electoral mandate The relationship between the public and governmental policies in which the public takes an outright stand on an issue and chooses representatives who have pledged themselves to the same position.

elitism (elitist theory) A theory that holds that political decisions are made by a small and united group, usually big business. *See also* pluralistic theory.

eminent domain The public's right to take property for public purposes, which is an inherent right granted to the government by the Constitution.

Equal Employment Opportunity Commission A regulatory commission created in 1972 by Congress to see that states and localities did not practice job discrimination on the basis or race, religion, sex, or national origin.

equal protection of the laws The clause in the Fourteenth Amendment that says states must protect every person equally under the law.

Equal Rights Amendment A constitutional amendment proposed in the 1970s that prohibits discrimination on the basis of sex.

equal time provision The most direct regulation of political coverage imposed by the FCC, which requires stations who give or sell time to one election candidate to provide the same opportunity for all candidate opponents.

executive agreement An agreement between heads of state having the force of law, which the president resorts to when Senate ratification seems unlikely.

fairness doctrine The obligation for broadcasters to present divergent points of view when they present a program, or to provide time for reply to station editorials, in order to ensure that political diversity is maintained.

Federalism The division of power between the states and the national government.

Federal Reserve Act An act of monetary reform passed by Congress in 1913 that divided power for regulating money and credit between a Federal Reserve Board in Washington and twelve regional Federal Reserve Banks.

filibuster Attempts to block the other business of the Senate, whereby a senator or group of senators monopolizes the floor with lengthy speeches.

fiscal policy A plan or course of action that requires government taxing, spending, and other budgetary efforts to manage the economy. *See also* monetary policy.

fragmentation A division in the loyalties of citizens, limiting their commitment to any one group or association; also a situation when the human and material resources in a country are scattered and devoted to differing, conflicting, or incompatible goals.

freedom of contract An individual's right to enter into and negotiate all contracts related to one's calling, and not to be violated by government except in cases of public necessity; part of the assumption that government exists to protect private rights.

freedom of the press Based on the Constitution's First Amendment, this right enables newspapers to be free from any prepublication censorship of material, with radio and television subject to only limited censorship. This freedom allows the press to maintain a posture separate from the government and other groups.

free trade A practice of imposing no tariffs on imported goods.

gender gap Voting differences between men and women.

General Agreements on Tariffs and Trade (GATT) An international pact in which major trading nations are committed not to engage in protectionism.
generation gap A situation in which different age groups have different opinions due to the individual experiences of each age group.
gerrymandering The drawing of district lines by members of the legislature that is calculated to give the largest number of seats to the majority party and dilute the strength of the minority party; loosely, any kind of unfair districting.
gold standard A means of regulating a country's monetary system in which all the supply of money in circulation is tied to the country's supply of gold.
graduated tax The type of tax best suited to achieve income redistribution, in which citizens with large incomes pay a greater percentage of their incomes in taxes than those with smaller incomes.
Gramm-Rudman Act A law passed by Congress in 1985 stipulating that if the president and Congress do not enact the cuts necessary to eliminate the deficit, funds already appropriated may be withheld.
grandfather clauses Laws that were used to disqualify blacks from voting by limiting the right to vote to voters, almost all of them white, whose ancestors had been able to vote.
grass-roots lobbying Lobbying by interest groups through public relations, electioneering, or mass demonstration.

heckler's veto The idea that an otherwise legal meeting cannot be broken up simply because the speaker's words incite anger or hostility in the audience; although a citizen is not permitted to incite overtly an audience to riot or overthrow the government, he or she has the right to advocate these ideas if done in a theoretical way.
high technology industries Industries made up of electronics and light manufacturing.
House Majority leader The House's chief strategist and spokesperson, who also controls the legislative schedule.
House member A member of the "lower house" of Congress, the House of Representatives, in which states are represented proportionate to their population.
hurry-up spending A bureaucratic agency's desire to spend its yearly budget by September 30 so as to show the need to receive a larger budget the following year.

industrial policy An economic policy that expands the federal government's role in the economy by rescuing ailing industries while also encouraging the growth of high-technology companies.
inflation An economic situation that occurs when there is plenty of money in people's pockets but an insufficient supply of things to buy; this situation results in dramatically rising prices.
initiative One of three ways in which the Progressive movement demanded greater power for public opinion; initiative allowed citizens to introduce legislation and constitutional revisions.
intensity The amount of feeling that one attaches to an issue.
interest groups Organizations that seek to influence public decisions through lobbying and similar activities.
intergovernmental relations A model of relationships between local, state, and national governments that stresses variety and complexity in their interactions.
iron triangle The three-sided combination of Congress, bureaucrats, and interest groups who together have the ability to stop the president from pursuing a policy they see as unfavorable. *See also* subgovernments.
issue public Those concerned with a particular issue.

Jim Crow (Jim Crowism) Laws and practices that discriminated against blacks.
Joint Committee A committee composed of members of both the Senate and the House in equal numbers, set up usually on a temporary basis to examine a particular problem.
joint resolution A formal statement by Congress that has the force of law if approved by both houses and is signed by the president; generally used when a single item or issue, such as an emergency appropriations bill, is raised, or for proposing amendments to the Constitution.
judicial activism The belief that the elected branches of government are not necessarily suited to reflect the values and the opinions of their constituents, but that the Supreme Court is and must take an active part in promoting the rights and views of the public.
judicial discretion The Supreme Court's right to decide which cases it will hear.
judicial review The right of the Supreme Court to rule a law unconstitutional.
judicial self-restraint The doctrine that the Supreme Court is an essentially undemocratic institution and should not mistake its views for public values.

Keynesians A school of economic thought that favors the use of fiscal (taxing and spending) measures to promote economic growth and stability; though the use of taxes, spending, and budgeting are important in helping the economy, Keynesians also use credit, interest rates, and other monetary factors when market forces alone are not producing a healthy economy. *See also* classical liberals.

lame duck An elected official who has not been or cannot be reelected but who continues to hold political office for the duration of his or her term; such officials may have less success in getting their policies instated because it is known that they will not be around to implement them.
latent opinion Beliefs that exist but are not active, and that often become active when an event brings the issue to people's attention.
laws of supply and demand The economic theory that prices of goods or services will rise or fall according to the demands of the marketplace.
legislative courts Courts inferior to constitutional courts, in which judges do not have life tenure and are allowed to give advisory opinions and to administer statutes.
liberalism A political idealogy that advocates spending money and increasing government activity on behalf of programs aiding various groups, supporting action to promote change, and a tolerant morality in regard to religion, sexual relations, and personal conduct. *See also* conservatism.
limited government A government that does not exceed the literal commandments of the Constitution—defense, tax collection, coining money, delivering mail, taking the census, and meting out justice—and does not have need for large bureaucracies. *See also* positive government.
liquidity Available money in circulation; a liquidity crisis results when the Federal Reserve Board decreases the amount of money in circulation at the same time that people try to put their assets into currency.
literacy tests Tests that were once used by some states to determine if voters could read or write; the purpose of the tests was to disqualify blacks, many of whom were uneducated, from voting.
litigant A party to a suit.
lobbyists People representing special interest groups who present their case and provide information to government agencies.
logrolling The practice of supporting a fellow senator or representative's favorite subsidy with the expectation that he or she will in turn support your own.

machine A political party organization that recruits its workers by providing material incentives such as patronage or public jobs.
majority Fifty percent plus 1; the amount of votes needed for a candidate to win an election or a policy or for a law to be passed. *See also* plurality.
market approach An approach to price setting that revolves around the laws of supply and demand, rather than around government intervention, and that leads to an end of price controls.
market forces Another term for the laws of supply and demand.
markup The process of altering and amending a bill after it has been through a hearing; usually performed by a subcommittee.
Marshall Plan A plan initiated by the United States in 1948 in response to the economic weakness of Western European countries and fear of potentially powerful Communist parties in France and Italy; the plan provided funds for European recovery and included aid for Germany.
mechanistic theory of constitutionalism A rational order in which laws and institutions channel human impulses toward desired ends in a self-regulating manner.
media events Actions staged by politicians and groups to get the attention of television and newspapers.
military-industrial complex A phrase coined by President Dwight D. Eisenhower that refers to the multibillion-dollar defense industry, which prospers financially when the nation increases its armaments to meet foreign demands.
Miranda Doctrine The 1964 law that gives any suspect in custody the right to be advised of his or her rights including the right to be silent, to have an attorney, and to be told that any statements made can be held against him or her.
monetarists A subgroup of the classical-liberal school of economic thought, who believe that the government's principal involvement in the economy should be in its control of the money supply; this should be adjusted enough to allow money and credit for economic growth but not enough to cause inflation.
monetary policy A plan or course of action that requires control of credit and the supply of money in circulation in order to manage the economy. *See also* fiscal policy.

National Energy Plan A comprehensive energy policy drafted by President Jimmy Carter in 1977 which was only partially successful because of Congress' desire to protect the needs of its constituents.
National Environmental Policy Act A law enacted in 1969 that established the landmark Environmental Protection Agency and the President's Council on Environmental Energy; the act required all federal agencies to file environmental impact statements on any decision that might have adverse effects on the environment.
National Security Council An executive office of the president created in 1947 to advise the president on foreign and military matters; permanent members include the president, the secretary of state, and the secretary of defense.
NATO (North Atlantic Treaty Organization) A pact established in 1949 that tied the United States to most of the nations of Western Europe and Canada; the formation of NATO was central to ending an American tradition of noninvolvement in long-term international commitments.

neoconservatives Those who support a political idealogy that favors individual liberty above equality; neoconservatives often condemn the federal bureaucracy but believe in government intervention to protect the private sector and "equality of opportunity." *See also* egalitarians.
New Deal An economic and social reform policy, based on the works of John Maynard Keynes, that was instigated by President Franklin Delano Roosevelt in 1933 to alleviate the effects of the Great Depression; the government, even at the expense of a balanced budget, engaged in large-scale spending in order to create purchasing power for the American people.
New Deal Coalition A coalition formed in the 1930s who followed Franklin Roosevelt's legislative program and made the Democrats the majority party; it was comprised of urban residents, the working class, ethnic minorities, and Southerners.
New Federalism An early proposal of President Ronald Reagan to curb the size of the federal government and return functions to the states, leaving the states to decide at the end of four years whether or not they wanted to continue these programs.
New Jersey Plan A proposal at the Constitutional Convention that the Articles of Confederation, with a single-house legislature and no executive or judiciary, be kept and that power remain in the hands of the states; apportionment in the legislature was to be based on equal representation by state, regardless of population. *See also* Virginia Plan.
new property An expanded meaning or property that includes such intangible things as contracts and commitments, reliable promises, stable understandings, the right to marry and establish families, and the right to our bodies and our labor; these rights now receive public support and cannot be abridged without due process of law.
nominations The political parties' selection of candidates to run in the general election.
nontariff barriers A means of getting around normal trade agreements by imposing quality or safety standards on imports that are not applied to similar domestic goods.
NOW (National Organization for Women) An interest group formed in the 1960s to promote equality for women.

open primary A primary election in which the voter decides in the voting booth whether to participate as a Republican or as a Democrat.
open rules Liberal debate and amendment limitations made by the House Rules Committee on a bill before the bill is reported out of committee. *See also* closed rules.
organic theory of constitutionalism A theory that a constitution is not "created" but discovered through an examination of the past and the underlying principles found in the actual institutions, habits, and practices of a political society.
oversight The process by which Congress checks up on how laws are executed by the executive branch.

PAC (political action committee) A form of political financing designed to get around laws curtailing individual contributions; in this form of financing, political groups collect individual donations and then give sizable contributions to the candidates they prefer.
panic A sudden and pervasive fear of the collapse of the financial system resulting in unreasoned attempts to sell property for cash, withdraw money from banks, and so on; this fear can precipitate or precede a depression.
parliamentarian A congressional employee who decides which committee in either house a bill should be sent to.
partisanship Loyalty to a political party.
party dealignment A decrease in voters' attachment to their political parties.
party identification People's long-standing loyalty to their political party, as measured in public opinion polls.
party platform Programs adopted by political parties at their national conventions that later serve as the basis for the winning party's governmental policy.
patronage the practice of distributing public jobs or privileges for reasons of politics rather than merit.
Pentagon Papers Internal documents of the Defense Department that described the increasing involvement of the United States in Vietnam in the 1960s.
plural elitism A combination of two theories of politics: pluralism and elitism.
pluralistic theory A theory that politics is seen as a relatively open contest between interest groups. *See also* elitism.
plurality A system of vote counting that allows a candidate to win by getting the most votes, even if he or she obtains less than 50 percent of the vote. *See also* majority.
pocket veto The veto that occurs through inaction when Congress passes a bill with fewer than 10 days left in the legislative session and the president fails to sign the bill.
point-counterpoint journalism A type of journalism aimed at presenting conflict most simply and dramatically, in which all issues are seen as having two—and only two—sides.
police power An inherent right of government, granted by the Constitution, to pass laws for the health, good order, and general welfare of the political society as a whole.
policy of incrementalism An example of congressional fragmentation in which changes can only be achieved in small steps, each needing careful evaluation before another step can be taken.
political culture The character and beliefs of a people regarding government and political life.

political party A group that tries to elect public officials under its label.
political socialization The way in which people learn about politics, especially through such long-term influences as family, religion, the schools, and the mass media.
politics of nondecision A way of defeating proposed policy changes by choking off changes before they can even be introduced or reported out of committee.
"pork" Federal projects for home districts which members of Congress procure in order to maintain their popularity in office; such projects typically involve construction that creates jobs in the state or district.
positive government A government that actively intervenes to protect, regulate, set standards, and otherwise smooth out the conditions of the citizens' lives. *See also* limited government.
power of the purse The constitutional power given to Congress to provide money for the operation of the federal government; Congress may use this power to deny funds to the president if it disagrees with the president's policy.
precedent Using past legal cases to interpret current and future ones.
preferred position The theory that certain rights are more important to a free political society than are others; freedom of thought and speech, for example, are considered essential to a free political society and therefore enjoy preferred position over the right of property, which is dependent on, not essential to, a free society.
preferments Those areas in which presidents have discretion in deciding where money is spent.
presidential succession The process through which a successor is chosen when a president dies, becomes too ill to serve, or is removed through impeachment or resignation.
president pro tem A congressional member who presides in the place of the vice-president as president of the Senate when the vice-president is absent.
principle of aggregation The Supreme Court's effort to settle a case by a common rule.
prior restraint Censorship or restrictions on publication *before* material has been published (as opposed to restraints and penalties, like those on libel, which operate after the fact).
private liberty The right of Americans to do as they please in large areas of life; based on the framers' idea of humans as private beings endowed with natural rights, and government as created to secure and enhance those rights.
privatization Contracting with private firms to perform services, or the outright selling of government agencies to private individuals, in an effort to cut the size of the federal government and provide services more cheaply and efficiently.
privileges and immunities clause A section of the Fourteenth Amendment that forbids the states to abridge the rights of citizens granted by the federal government.
project grant A federal grant for a specified purpose whose funding is allocated by federal administrators.
proportional representation System of voting for state and national legislatures in which candidates are chosen not as individuals but in proportion to the votes won by their parties.
protectionism A system of imposing tariffs to ensure that imported goods are more expensive than equivalent domestic ones so that citizens buy only domestic goods.
public The people as a whole, as opposed to being divided into different segments.
public liberty The citizen's right to share in a free political life; the concept that genuine individuality can unfold only in a political society that fosters our individual talents and qualities.
pump priming The government's means of enhancing purchasing power during the Depression by providing work on public projects for the unemployed.
pure democracy Democracy in which citizens participate directly in making laws or in holding public office. *See also* representative democracy.

random (or probability) sampling Choosing a sample of people's opinions in an effort to estimate the views of the entire public; choosing is done in such a way that theoretically everyone in the country has an equal chance of being contacted.
realigning election An election that changes the basic character or relative strength of a political party, either through the previous minority party becoming dominant or through a fundamental change in the majority party's voting coalition.
recall One of three ways in which the Progressive movement sought to increase the power of public opinion; recall allows citizens to remove elected officials from office before the end of their normal term.
recess appointment A temporary appointment made by the president while Congress is not in session.
recommit a bill A device for delaying or sidetracking a bill by sending the bill back to the original committee after it has been debated on the floor.
recorded vote A rule accompanying most important bills or amendments that requires that all congressional votes be recorded.
referendum One of three ways in which the Progressive movement sought to increase the power of public opinion; referendum allows citizens to have a direct vote on legislation and constitutional revisions.
regulatory federalism Federal legal and administrative regulation of the states, often tied to grants.

representative democracy Democracy in which citizens participate in making laws and ruling through elected representatives. *See also* pure democracy.
restrictive covenants Agreements made between property owners to sell their property only to whites.
revenue-sharing grant A federal grant that gives national tax revenues back to the states or localities to use in whatever programs they wish.
"revolving door" process A process whereby regulated industries strongly influence the choice of personnel in regulatory commissions, and later hire them once they leave government service.

salience The amount of concern or relevance that the public attaches to an issue; the less salience an issue has, the more readily the public can be persuaded to change its opinion.
saturation effect A phenomenon in which people cannot absorb any more messages because they have been overexposed to the media.
scope of conflict The number of people and groups involved in a political dispute.
segmented Divided into separate groups, for example, American citizens divided over certain political issues.
Select Committee One of four types of congressional committees set up to investigate or study a particular problem and make a recommendation; such a committee is usually disbanded at the end of the two-year Congress in which it is created. Also called "special committee."
self-righting mechanism The belief held in the nineteenth and early twentieth centuries that because of the inherent ability of the economy to "right" itself, recessions, panics, and other economic busts would never last long enough to bring on genuine national hardship.
senator A member of the "upper house" of Congress, the Senate, in which every state has at least two representatives.
senatorial courtesy The Senate's refusal to grant a judge or other official a post in a state if the person is "personally obnoxious" to a senator from that state who is also a member of the president's political party.
seniority The system of electing a congressional committee chairperson that gives the position to the member of the majority party longest on the committee.
separation of powers The division of the federal government into legislative, executive, and judicial systems that nevertheless allows them to overlap.
setting the agenda In representative government, the process of identifying certain problems as matters that demand and deserve political attention.
smokestack industries Industries made up mainly of factories that produce heavy industrial goods such as steel or automobiles.
socialization of conflict Bringing more people into a political dispute—usually escalating it from the state to the national level—often changing the outcome.
speaker of the House The true presiding officer and chief strategist of the House of Representatives.
Special Committee *See* Select Committee.
spoils system The practice of giving out public jobs or contracts to those who are politically loyal, rather than on the basis of merit.
sponsor A member of Congress who introduces a particular bill.
stability The degree of change in public opinion as shown over time.
stagflation An economic situation marked by a combination of high inflation and stagnating economic growth.
standard operating procedures Rules that lay out the precise way to perform a task.
Standing Committee A permanent congressional committee that reports out bills for each of the houses to vote on.
standing to sue A rule stating that in order to bring suit, someone must have a personal interest in the outcome greater than the interest of the public at large.
"Star Wars" President Ronald Reagan's proposed Strategic Defense Initiative, a system of satellites and earth stations that would use lasers and particle beams to destroy attacking Soviet intercontinental missiles.
state delegation All of the members of either congressional house who come from one state.
Strategic Petroleum Reserve A reserve supply of up to one billion gallons of oil authorized by Congress in 1975 and meant to create a buffer against the cutoff of foreign oil.
subcommittee Subgroups of large standing committees, select committees, or joint committees.
subgovernments A system in which decisions on policy are made in effect through a triangular relationship of the relevant interest group, administrative agency, and congressional subcommittee. *See also* iron triangle.
substantive due process The principle that not only must the procedure be examined but also the purpose behind an action to deprive an individual of life, liberty, or property.
sunset laws State laws requiring periodic examination of programs.
sunshine laws State laws requiring government meetings to be open to the public.
supply side economics The economic school of thought endorsed by supply-siders. *See also* supply-siders.
supply-siders A subgroup of the classical-liberal school of economic thought, who believe tax laws that favor business expansion will be more beneficial to the economy than either government spending (favored by the Keynesians) or money supply manipulations (favored by the

monetarists); thus, corporations freed of heavy taxes will invest in new plants and equipment and hire more workers whose earning, in turn, will stimulate the economy and provide more tax revenues.

suspect category A classification of people—usually based on racial, ethnic, or alien background—that is "suspect" if used for purposes of discrimination without a strong "public purpose."

synfuels Synthetic fuels developed from shale oil, coal, and tar sands.

tariff A tax imposed on imports to raise revenues for the government or to bring the cost of cheaper foreign goods into line with the prices of locally made products.

tax A compulsory payment to the government that is spent on such things as defense and the general welfare of the country.

theory of sovereignty The argument that a political society must have a supreme will somewhere.

Third World A group of countries, once colonies under British or French rule, that gained their independence in the 1950s and have remained nonaligned with either superpower.

Three Mile Island The site of an American nuclear reactor, near Hershey, Pennsylvania, where a nuclear accident took place in 1979 that provoked many people to call for the total abandonment of nuclear power plants in generating electricity.

Tonkin Gulf Resolution The resolution secured from Congress by President Lyndon B. Johnson in 1964 after an attack on U.S. warships by the North Vietnamese. The resolution authorized use of whatever force was necessary to repel attacks on U.S. forces in Vietnam. This was in lieu of an outright declaration of war.

trade deficit The gap between the value of the goods that are sold abroad and the value of the things that are imported.

trickle-down theory A theory of taxation promoting the idea that if the wealthy are allowed to hold on to more of their income, they will invest or spend large amounts of money that will do more for poorer people in the way of jobs than will the government programs paid for out of the taxes of the rich.

Truman Doctrine A statement made by President Harry S Truman in 1947 that pledged aid to keep Greece and Turkey in the Western camp; implied in the doctrine was support for other noncommunist countries threatened by communism.

turnout Voter participation in an election.

unanimous consent agreement The Senate's method for getting quick floor action on a bill, which requires the assent of all senators; usually involving noncontroversial bills.

unreasonable searches and seizures The Fourth Amendment clause that limits search and seizure in any place where a person has a "legitimate expectation of privacy."

videomalaise The negative impact that the media, especially television, has on public confidence in government institutions and leaders.

Virginia Plan A proposal introduced at the Constitutional Convention that the national government derive its power directly from the people rather than from the states, and that membership apportionment in both the Senate and the House be according to population; it also proposed executive and judiciary branches, besides the legislative. *See also* New Jersey Plan.

vote of confidence A vote to determine whether the existing government will remain in office.

Voting Rights Acts A series of acts brought about in the 1950s, 1960s, and 1970s that was designed to protect the voting rights of blacks in the South and that extended the role and presence of the federal government into areas of the electoral process traditionally left to private groups.

wage and price controls A means of combating inflation that enforces regulation of what sellers can charge for their products and what workers can receive for their labor.

war power The national government's constitutional right to raise armies, conduct diplomacy, and engage in war.

War Powers Act An act that limits the president's ability to deploy U.S. troops beyond a period of ninety days, unless Congress gives express approval.

welfare state capitalism An economic system in which most business is run privately, with government providing aid for such groups as the elderly and the unemployed.

whip Assistant to the House Majority Leader.

windfall profits Specifically, the unexpected profits that resulted from the lifting of price ceilings on oil in 1979; the question was whether the profits from decontrol should go to the government in the form of a tax, or to the oil companies themselves; more generally, unexpected profits.

writ of habeas corpus A law preventing long detention before trial.

zero-sum game A situation in which one group's gain in supplies or resources is achieved at the expense of another group's resources.

Author Index

Subject Index